THE LEGAL PROTECTION O

The Legal Protection of Human Rights: Sceptical Essays

Edited by
TOM CAMPBELL,
K. D. EWING,
and
ADAM TOMKINS

OXFORD
UNIVERSITY PRESS

OXFORD
UNIVERSITY PRESS

Great Clarendon Street, Oxford OX2 6DP

Oxford University Press is a department of the University of Oxford.
It furthers the University's objective of excellence in research, scholarship,
and education by publishing worldwide in

Oxford New York

Auckland Cape Town Dar es Salaam Hong Kong Karachi
Kuala Lumpur Madrid Melbourne Mexico City Nairobi
New Delhi Shanghai Taipei Toronto

With offices in

Argentina Austria Brazil Chile Czech Republic France Greece
Guatemala Hungary Italy Japan Poland Portugal Singapore
South Korea Switzerland Thailand Turkey Ukraine Vietnam

Oxford is a registered trade mark of Oxford University Press
in the UK and in certain other countries

Published in the United States
by Oxford University Press Inc., New York

British Library Cataloguing in Publication Data
Data available

Library of Congress Cataloging in Publication Data
Data available

Typeset by Newgen
Printed in Great Britain
on acid-free paper by
CPI Antony Rowe
Chippenham, Wiltshire

ISBN 978–0–19–960607–8 (hbk)
ISBN 978–0–19–960608–5 (pbk)

1 3 5 7 9 10 8 6 4 2

Acknowledgements

The evolution of *The Legal Protection of Human Rights* involved a small workshop; those who took part share a range of critical viewpoints on the UK Human Rights Act 1998 and similar enactments in other jurisdictions, but nevertheless maintain that there is a need for more effective human rights regimes with a more political and democratic focus.

At the workshop, which took place at King's College London on 20 and 21 March 2009, 19 of the 24 contributors to this volume presented papers which were discussed in the light of the intention to publish a coherent collection of sceptical but constructive essays after ten years' experience of the UK Human Rights Act.

Following the workshop, the editors have worked with the contributors to produce a book of essays that takes forward the debate about Bills of Rights and judicial review generally in the current climate, and plots different strands of response by those who have expressed scepticism in the past.

The editors would like to acknowledge and thank the School of Law, King's College London, the Centre for Applied Philosophy and Public Ethics (CAPPE), Charles Sturt University, and the Australian Research Council, for providing administrative and financial support for the workshop.

The editors would also like to thank Alex Flach, John Louth, and all at OUP for their interest in and support for this project. Warm thanks are also due to Nicholas Barry, Simone Gubler, and Hayley Hooper who all made valuable contributions to this project.

TC
KDE
AT
26 July 2010

Contents

List of Contributors   ix
Table of Cases   xi
Table of Treaties and Legislation   xix

1. Introduction   1
   Tom Campbell, K. D. Ewing, and Adam Tomkins

PART I FAILURES OF JURIDIFICATION

2. Parliament, Human Rights, and Counter-Terrorism   13
   Adam Tomkins

3. Governing Like Judges?   40
   Janet L. Hiebert

4. Human Rights at the Interface of State and
   Sub-state: The Case of Scotland   66
   Chris Himsworth

5. Inter-institutional 'Rights Dialogue' under the New Zealand
   Bill of Rights Act   87
   Andrew Geddis

6. Statutory Bills of Rights: You Read Words In, You Read
   Words Out, You Take Parliament's Clear Intention and
   You Shake it All About—Doin' the Sankey Hanky Panky   108
   James Allan

7. Constitutionalism, the Rule of Law, and the Cold War   127
   Joan Mahoney

8. The Cold War, Civil Liberties, and the House of Lords   148
   K. D. Ewing

9. Lessons from the Past? Northern Ireland, Terrorism
   Now and Then, and the Human Rights Act   177
   Aileen McColgan

10. Constitutional Law Meets Comparative Politics: Socio-economic
    Rights and Political Realities   207
    Ran Hirschl and Evan Rosevear

11. Business Rights as Human Rights   229
    Danny Nicol

12. Constitutionalizing Labour Rights in Europe   244
    Judy Fudge

13. Freedom, Security, and Justice in the European Court of Justice:
    The Ambiguous Nature of Judicial Review   268
    Sionaidh Douglas-Scott

PART II POLITICIZING HUMAN RIGHTS

14. The Political Institutions of Rights-Protection   297
    Mark Tushnet

15. Reclaiming the Political Protection of Rights: A Defence of
    Australian Party Politics   312
    Joo-Cheong Tham

16. Messages from the Front Line: Parliamentarians' Perspectives
    on Rights Protection   329
    Carolyn Evans and Simon Evans

17. Human Rights and the Global South   347
    Gavin W. Anderson

18. Judicial Constitutional Review as a Last Resort   365
    Kaarlo Tuori

19. Judges without a Court—Judicial Preview in Sweden   392
    Thomas Bull

20. Rights and the Citation of Foreign Law   410
    Jeremy Waldron

21. Amateur Operatics: The Realization of Parliamentary
    Protection of Civil Liberties   428
    Jonathan Morgan

22. Parliamentary Review with a Democratic Charter of Rights   453
    Tom Campbell

23. Beyond the Human Rights Act   472
    Conor Gearty

Index   487

List of Contributors

James Allan
Garrick Professor of Law, University of Queensland

Gavin W. Anderson
Senior Lecturer in Law, University of Glasgow

Thomas Bull
Professor of Constitutional Law, Uppsala University

Tom Campbell
Professorial Fellow, Centre for Applied Philosophy and Public Ethics (CAPPE), Charles Sturt University, and Visiting Professor, King's College London School of Law

Sionaidh Douglas-Scott
Professor of European Law and Human Rights, University of Oxford

K. D. Ewing
Professor of Public Law, King's College London

Carolyn Evans
Professor of Law, University of Melbourne

Simon Evans
Professor of Law, University of Melbourne

Judy Fudge
Lansdowne Chair of Law, University of Victoria, Victoria

Conor Gearty
Professor of Human Rights Law, London School of Economics

Andrew Geddis
Associate Professor of Law, University of Otago

Janet L. Hiebert
Professor, Political Studies, Queen's University, Canada

Chris Himsworth
Professor of Administrative Law, University of Edinburgh

Ran Hirschl
Professor of Political Science and Law, Canada Research Chair in Constitutionalism, Democracy and Development, University of Toronto

Aileen McColgan
Professor of Human Rights Law, King's College London

Joan Mahoney
Professor Emeritus, Wayne State University

Jonathan Morgan
Fellow and Tutor in Law, St Catherine's College, University of Oxford

Danny Nicol
Professor of Public Law, University of Westminster, London

Evan Rosevear
Joint PhD/JD candidate, Department of Political Science and Faculty of Law, University of Toronto

Joo-Cheong Tham
Senior Lecturer in Law, University of Melbourne

Adam Tomkins
John Millar Professor of Public Law, University of Glasgow

Kaarlo Tuori
Professor of Jurisprudence, University of Helsinki

Mark Tushnet
William Nelson Cromwell Professor of Law, Harvard University

Jeremy Waldron
University Professor, New York University School of Law, and Chichele Professor of Social and Political Theory, University of Oxford

Table of Cases

Australia

Byrnes v The Queen (1999) 199 CLR 1 345
Evans v NSW (2008) 250 ALR 33 345
Ex parte H v McKay (1907) 2 CAR 1 328
Plaintiff S157/2002 v Commonwealth (2003) 211 CLR 474 340
R v Hughes (2000) 202 CLR 535 345
SI by his next friend CC v KS by his next friend IS (2005) 195 FLR 151 111
Watson v Lee (1979) 144 CLR 374 345

Canada

Auton (Guardian ad litem of) v British Columbia (AG) [2004] 3 SCR 657 212
British Columbia (Attorney General) v Christie [2007] 1 SCR 873 212
Chaoulli v Quebec (AG) [2005] 1 SCR 791 212
Edwards v Attorney-General for Canada [1930] AC 124 . . . . 113, 114
Gosselin v Quebec (AG) [2002] 4 SCR 429 212
Health Services and Support-Facilities Subsector Bargaining Assn v British
    Columbia [2007] 2 SCR 391 . . . . .212, 213
Newfoundland (Treasury Board) v NAPE [2004] 3 SCR 381 212
R v Daviault [1994] 3 SCR 63 57
R v Oakes [1986] 1 SCR 103 45
R v O'Connor [1995] 4 SCR 411 57
R v Prosper [1994] 3 SCR 236 212
RJR-Macdonald Inc. v Canada (Attorney General) [1995] 3 SCR 199 229
Schacter v Canada [1992] 2 SCR 679 45
Singh v Minister of Employment and Immigration [1985] 1 SCR 177 45
Vriend v Alberta [1998] 1 SCR 493 115

Council of Europe and European Union

A and others v United Kingdom [2009] UKHL 28, [2009] 3 WLR 74 . . . . 18, 38, 204, 480
Advocaaten voor de Wereld v Leden van de Ministerraad
    (Case C-303/05) [2007] ECR I-3633 . . . . .278, 280, 289
Albany International BV v Stichting Bedrijfspensioenfonds
    Textielindustrie [1999] ECR I-5751 255
Alpine Investments BV v Minister van Financiën (Case C-384/93) [1995] ECR I-1141 235
Amministrazione delle Finanze dello Stato v Simmenthal SpA (Case 106/77)
    [1978] ECR 629 233
Angonese v Cassa di Riparmio di Bozano SpA (Case C-281/98) [2000] ECR I-4139 235
Behrami and Behrami v France [2007] 45 EHRR SE10 287
Brannigan and McBride v United Kingdom (1993) 17 EHRR 539 . . . . 195, 479
Brecknell v UK (2008) 46 EHRR 42 202
Brind and McLaughlin v United Kingdom 77-A DR 42 (1994), E Com HR 201
Brogan v United Kingdom (1988) 11 EHRR 117 . . . . 195, 479
Centrafarm v Sterling Drug (Case 15/74) [1974] ECR 1147; [1974] 2 CMLR 480 238
Centro Europa 7 (Case C-380/05) [2008] ECR I-349 269
Commission of the European Communities v Grand Duchy of Luxembourg
    (Case C-319/06) [2008] ECR I-04323 236

Costa v ENEL (Case 4/64) [1964] ECR 585 . . . . .233, 286
Danilenkov and Others v Russia, App. No. 67336/01, 30 July 2009 . . . . .245, 262
Demir and Baykara v Turkey, App. No. 34503/97, 12 November 2008 . . . . 245, 260, 261, 264
Enerji Yapi-Yol Sen v Turkey, App. No. 68959/01, 21 April 2009. . . . . .245, 261
Enforcement of a European Arrest Warrant, Re [2006] 1 CMLR 36 278
Finucane v UK (2003) 37 EHRR 29 202
Gebhard v Consiglio dell'Ordine degli Avvocati e Procuratori di Milano
    (Case C-55/94) [1995] ECR I-4165 235
Gillan & Quinton v United Kingdom, App. No. 4158/05, 12 Jan 2010 205
Gottfried Heinrich (Case C-345/06) 10 March 2009 . . . . 273, 274
Höfner and Elser v Macrotron GmbH (Case C-41/90) [1991] ECR I-1979,
    [1993] 4 CMLR 306 239
Hüseyin Gözütok and Klaus Brügge (Cases C-187/01 and C-385/01) [2003] ECR I-5689 279
Internationale Handelsgesellschaft (Case 11/70) [1970] ECR 01125 . . . . .268, 288
International Transport Workers' Federation v Viking Line ABP
    (Case C-438/05) [2007] ECR I-10779; [2008] 1 CMLR 51 . . . . .3, 235, 236, 237,
                                              245, 253, 254, 255, 256, 257, 258,
                                              259, 260, 263, 267, 289, 290, 292
Ireland v UK (1980) 2 EHRR 25 186
James v United Kingdom (1986) 8 EHRR 123 480
Job Centre coop. arl. (Case C-55/96) [1997] ECR I-7119 239
Jordan v UK (2003) 37 EHRR 2 201
Kadi v Council & Commission (Case T-315/01) [2005] ECR II-3649 286
Kadi & Al Barakaat Int'l Found. v Council & Commission
    (Cases C-402 & 415/05P) [2008] ECR I-6351 . . . . 15, 285, 286, 287, 288, 289
Kaya and Seyhan v Turkey, App. No. 30946/04, 15 September 2009. . . . . .245, 262
Kelly v UK App. No. 30054/96 [2001] Inquest Law Review 125 201
Laval un Partneri Ltd v Svenska Byggnadsarbetareförbundet (Case C-341/05)
    [2007] ECR I-11767; [2008] 2 CMLR 9 . . . . 3, 235, 236, 237, 245, 253, 254,
                                              255, 256, 257, 259, 260, 263,
                                              267, 289, 290, 292
Lithgow and others v United Kingdom, App. nos 9006/80, 9262/81,
    9263/81, 9265/81, 9266/81, 9313/81, 9405/81, 8 July 1986. 242
Marleasing SA v La Comercial Internacional de Alimentacion SA [1991] 1 ECR 4135. 431
Mary Carpenter v Secretary of State for the Home Department (Case C-60/00)
    [2002] ECR 1–6279 . . . . .289, 290
McCann v United Kingdom (1995) 21 EHRR 97 . . . . .201, 479
McCartney v UK, App. No. 34575/04, 3 June 2007 202
McKerr v UK (2002) 34 EHRR 553 . . . . .201, 202, 204
McShane (2002) 35 EHRR 23. 201
Mr and Mrs F v Belgium (Case 7/75) [1975] 6 ECR 679 277
Observer and Guardian v United Kingdom (1991) 14 EHRR 153 479
Omar Mohammed Othman v Council and Commission [2008] ECR 1-0000 287
Omega Speilhallen-und Automate naufstellungs-GmbH v Oberbürgermeisterin
    des Bundesstadt Bonn (Case C-36/02) [2004] ECR I-9609. . . . . 237, 289, 290
Otto-Preminger Institut v Austria (1994) 19 ENRR 34, E Com HR 236
Parliament v Council (Case 540/03) [2006] ECR I-5769. 284
Parliament v Council and Commission
    (Case C-317/04 and C-318/04) [2006] ECR I-4721 283
Procureur du Roi v Paul Corbeau (Case C-320/91P) [1993] ECR I-2533 . . . . .239, 240
Pupino (Case C-105 /03) [2005] ECR I-5285 . . . . .288, 289
Reavey v UK, App. No. 346040/04, 3 June 2007. 202

Rewe-Zentrale AG v Bundesmonopolverwaltung für Branntwein
    (Case 120/78) [1979] ECR 649 ....235, 238
Rüffert v Land Niedersachsen (Case C-346/06) [2008] 2 CMLR 39 236
S and Marper v United Kingdom, App. No. 30562/04 [2008] ECHR 1581
    (4 December 2008) 477
Saime Özcan v Turkey, App. No. 22943/04, 12 September 2009. ....245, 262
Schmidberger, Internationale Transporte und Planzuge v Austria
    (Case C-112/00) [2003] ECR I-5659............................236, 264, 289, 290
Selmouni v France (1999) 29 EHRR 403...186
Shanagan v UK, App. No 37715/97, 4 May 2001..............................201, 202
Soering v United Kingdom (1989) 11 EHRR 439 423
Sunday Times v United Kingdom (No 2) (1991) 14 EHRR 229.......................479
Syndicat National de la police belge v Belgium, 27 October 1975, Series A No 19 258
Van Binsbergen v Bestuur van de Bedrijfsvereniging voor de Metaalnijverheid
    (Case 33/74) [1974] ECR 1299 235
Van Gend en Loos (Case 26/26) [1963] ECR 1 ....233, 286
VgT Verein gegen Tierfabriken v Switzerland (2001) 34 EHRR 159 ....439, 473
Wilson & The National Union of Journalists (and Others) v the United Kingdom,
    App. Nos 30668/96, 30671/96 and 30678/96 of 2 July 2002 258
Wingrove v United Kingdom (1996) 24 EHRR 1 479
Yusuf & Al Barakaat International Foundation v Council of the EU & EC
    Commission (Case T-306/01) [2005] ECR II-3533.............................286

Denmark
Tvind case (U 1999 841H)...213

Finland
KHO 2003:24 367
KHO 2004:21 367
KHO 2006:77 367
KHO 2002:91 367
KKO 2004:26 381
KKO 2005:82 367
KKO 2005:132 367
KKO 2006:20 367

France
Daoudi v France 3 December 2009 480
Irrastorza Dorronsoro (No 238/2003), judgment of 16 May 2003, Cour d'Appel de Pau.......279

Germany
Lüth, BVerfGE 7, 15 January 1958..385

Hungary
Austerity Package Decisions ('Bokros cases') 225

India
Olga Tellis v Bombay Municipal Corporation, AIR 1986 SC 180 213
Unni Krishnan, JP v State of Andhra Pradesh, AIR 1993 SC 2178......................213

Israel
CA 6821/93 United Mizrahi Bank v Migdal Coop. Village [1995] IsrSC 49(4) 195........226, 27

HCJ 1074/93 Attorney-General v Nat'l Labour Court [1995] IsrSC 49(2) 485 226
HCJ 1554/95 Amutat Shokharey Gilat v Sar Ha-Khinukh, Ha-Tarbut V'Ha-Sport
  Shocharei GILAT Assoc. v Minister of Educ., Culture and
  Sport [1996] IsrSC 50(3) 2. 226

New Zealand
Belcher v Chief Executive of the Department of Corrections [2007] NZSC 54 103
Boscawen v Attorney-General (No 2) [2008] NZAR 468 97
Boscawen v Attorney-General [2009] NZCA 12 . . . . 96, 97, 103
Brooker v Police [2007] 3 NZLR 91. 89
Choudry v Attorney-General [1999] 2 NZLR 582 102
Choudry v Attorney-General (No 2) [1999] 3 NZLR 399 102
Commissioner of Inland Revenue v West-Walker [1954] NZLR 191 102
Cropp v Judicial Committee [2008] 3 NZLR 774 89
Drew v Attorney-General [2002] 1 NZLR 58 102
Lange v Atkinson [1997] 2 NZLR 22 89
Lange v Atkinson [1998] 3 NZLR 424 89
Mangawaro Enterprises Ltd v Attorney-General [1994] 2 NZLR 451 96
Martin v District Court at Tauranga [1995] 2 NZLR 419 89
Ministry of Transport v Noort; Police v Curran [1992] 3 NZLR 260. . . . . 47, 89, 103
Moonen v Film & Literature Board of Review [2000] 1 NZLR 9. . . . . .93, 103
Newspaper Publishers' Association of New Zealand v Family Court [1999]
  2 NZLR 344 102
Ngati Apa Ki Te Waipounamu Trust v R [2000] 2 NZLR 659. 102
Police v Beggs [1999] 3 NZLR 615. 102
Police v Hopkinson [2004] 3 NZLR 704. 421
Quilter v Attorney-General [1998] 1 NZLR 523 . . . . 47, 103
R v Hansen [2007] 3 NZLR 1 . . . . 47, 93, 101, 102,
                                                                      103, 104
R v Laugalis [1993] 10 CRNZ 563. 102
R v Phillips [1991] 3 NZLR 175. . . . . 47, 103
R v Pora [2001] 2 NZLR 37 . . . . 89, 102
R v Poumako [2000] 2 NZLR 695. . . . . 89, 102, 103
R v Shaheed [2002] 2 NZLR 377. 89
Simpson v Attorney-General [Baigent's Case] [1994] 3 NZLR 667 . . . . 89, 102, 110
Tangiora v Wellington District Legal Services Commission [2000] 1 NZLR 17 105
Taunoa v Attorney-General [2008] 1 NZLR 429. . . . . 89, 412
Te Runanga o Wharekauri Rehohu Inc v Attorney-General [1993] 2 NZLR 301. 95
Tuckers Wool Processors v Harrison [1999] 1 ERNZ 894, 917 (CA) 89
Williams v R [2009] NZSC 41. 89
Zaoui v Attorney-General [2004] 2 NZLR 339 103

Sweden
RÅ 1998 ref 42. 395

South Africa
Government of RSA v Grootboom 2001 (1) SA 46 (CC) 217, 218
Mazibuko v Johannesburg [2009] ZACC 28 218
Minister of Health v Treatment Action Campaign 2002 (5) SA 721 (CC) 217, 218
Nokotyana v Ekurhuleni Metropolitan Municipality [2009] ZACC 33 218
President of the Republic v Hugo (1997) (6) BCLR 708. . . . . 413, 421
Soobramoney v Minister of Health (KwaZulu-Natal) 1998 (1) SA 765 (CC) 217

United Kingdom and Ireland

A v Home Secretary [2004] QB 335. 272
A v Secretary of State for the Home Department [2004] UKHL 56;
    [2005] 2 AC 68 . . . . 4, 13, 14, 19, 26, 46, 121,
                                                         122, 204, 433, 436
A v Secretary of State for the Home Department (No 2) [2006] 2 AC 221 204
Adler v George [1964] 2 QB 7 167
Attorney General's Reference No 2 of 2001 [2004] 2 AC 72 . . . . .73, 74
Al Megrahi v HM Advocate 2002 JC 99 75
Al Rawi and others v The Security Service and others [2009] EWHC 2959 14
Allen v Flood [1898] AC 1 449
Attorney General v BBC [1981] AC 303 482
Austin v Commissioner of Police of the Metropolis [2009] 1 AC 564 .205
Bellinger v Bellinger [2003] 2 AC 467 432
Birdi v Secretary of State for Home Affairs (1975) 119 Solicitors Journal 322 483
Brown v Stott 2000 SCCR 314 74
Bugdaycay v Secretary of State for the Home Department [1987] AC 514 483
Burden and Burden v United Kingdom, 29 April 2008 . . . . 436, 437, 476, 477, 484
Cameron v HM Advocate 1991 JC 251 75
Chandler v DPP [1964] AC 763 . . . . 149, 159, 173, 174, 175, 176, 230, 232
Cheney v Conn [1968] 1 All ER 779 173
Christie v Leachinsky [1947] AC 573 197
Countryside Alliance and others v Attorney General [2007] UKHL 52 .108
Dennis v Ministry of Defence [2003] EWHC 793 (QB), [2003] Env LR 34 482
Devlin v Armstrong [1971] NI 13 179
Doherty and Ors v Birmingham City Council [2008] UKHL 57 108
Douglas v Hello! Ltd [2001] QB 967 . . . . .474, 482
Ex parte Lynch [1980] NI 126 . . . . .195, 197
Fitzpatrick v Sterling Housing Association [2001] AC 27 . . . . 112, 118, 122, 124, 126, 431
Gillick v West Norfolk and Wisbech Area Health Authority [1986] AC 112 434
Gouriet v Union of Post Office Workers [1978] AC 435 434
H M Advocate v Burns 2000 SCCR 884 74
Holland v H M Advocate 2005 SC (PC) 3 75
Jackson v Attorney-General [2006] 1 AC 262 108
Jordan v Burgoyne [1963] 2 QB 744 174
Jordan v Lord Chancellor [2007] 2 AC 226 202
L v Birmingham City Council [2008] 1 AC 95 . . . . .77, 85
Liversidge v Anderson [1942] AC 206 . . . . .13, 197
Lord Alton of Liverpool v Secretary of State for the Home Department (POAC,
    30 November 2007; upheld on appeal at [2008] EWCA Civ 443;
    [2008] 1 WLR 2341) 14, 26
Lowdens v Keaveney [1903] IR 82 171
Macnaughton v Macnaughton's Trustees 1953 SC 387 435
Martin v HMA [2010] UKSC 10; 2010 SLT 412 79
McCartan Turkington Breen v Times Newspapers [2001] 2 AC 277 473
McCaughey v Chief Constable of PSNI [2007] 2 AC 226 204
McE v Prison Service for NI and Anor [2009] 1 AC 908 195
McEldowney v Forde [1971] 1 AC 632 . . . . .179, 197
McElduff, In re [1972] NI 1 . . . . .194, 197
McIntosh, Petitioner 2000 SCCR 1017 74
McKearney (1974) NIJB 198
McKee v Chief Constable for Northern Ireland [1984] 1 WLR 1358 195

McKerr, Re [2004] 1 WLR 807 202
McKerr v Armagh Coroner [1990] 1 WLR 649 202
Metrobus v Unite the Union [2009] EWCA Civ 829 264
Miller v H M Advocate 2003 SC (PC) 1 74
Montgomery v HMA 2001 SC (PC) 1 74
Moore v Shillington and Ministry of Defence [1980] NILR 126 198
Napier v Scottish Ministers 2005 1 SC 307 76
National Westminster Bank v Spectrum Plus [2005] UKHL 41 108
O'Hara v Chief Constable of the RUC [1997] AC 286 195
Oxfordshire County Council v Oxford City Council [2006] UKHL 25 435
P and Ors, Re (Northern Ireland) [2008] UKHL 38 108
Papworth v Coventry [1967] 2 All ER 41 . . . . 152, 173
R (Al Jedda) v Secretary of State for Defence [2007] UKHL 58; [2008] 1 AC 332 . . . . 15, 287
R (Al Sweady) v Secretary of State for Defence [2009] EWHC 1687 . . . . .205, 206
R (Amin) v Secretary of State for the Home Department [2004] 1 AC 653 202
R (Anderson) v Secretary of State for the Home Department [2003] 1 AC 837 430
R (Animal Defenders International) v Secretary of State for Culture
    Media and Sport [2008] UKHL 15; [2008] 2 WLR 781 . . . . 439, 473
R (Bancoult) v Secretary of State for Foreign and Commonwealth
    Affairs [2008] UKHL 61; [2009] 1 AC 453 . . . . 15, 165
R (Bhajan Singh) v Secretary of State for Home Affairs [1975] 3 WLR 225 482
R (BM) v Secretary of State for Foreign and Commonwealth Affairs (No 1)
    [2008] EWHC 2048 (Admin); [2009] 1 WLR 2579 . . . . .14, 26
R (BM) v Secretary of State for Foreign and Commonwealth Affairs (No 4)
    [2009] EWHC 152 (Admin); [2009] 1 WLR 2653 . . . . .14, 26
R (BM) v Secretary of State for Foreign and Commonwealth Affairs (No 5) [2009]
    EWHC 2549 . . . . .14, 26
R (Corner House) v Director of the Serious Fraud Office [2008] UKHL 60;
    [2009] 1 AC 756 15
R (Daly) v Secretary of State for the Home Department [2001] UKHL 26;
    [2001] 2 AC 532 483
R (Factortame) v Secretary of State for Transport (No 2) [1991] 1 AC 603 483
R (Gentle) v Prime Minister [2008] UKHL 20, [2008] 1 AC 1356 15
R (Gillan) v Metropolitan Police Commissioner [2006] UKHL 12;
    [2006] 2 AC 307 . . . . 14, 205
R (Hurst) v London Northern District Coroner [2007] 2 AC 189 202
R (Jackson) v Attorney General [2006] 1 AC 262 . . . . .69, 483–4
R (Laporte) v Chief Constable of Gloucestershire [2006] UKHL 55 482
R (Limbuela) v Secretary of State for the Home Department [2005]
    UKHL 66; [2006] 1 AC 396 481
R (McQuillan) v Secretary of State for the Home Department [1995] 4 All ER 400 483
R (Middleton) v West Somerset Coroner [2004] UKHL 10, [2004] 2 AC 182 . . . . .202, 481
R (O'Hanlon) v Governor of Belfast Prison 197
R (Phansopkar) v Secretary of State for Home Affairs; R (Begum) v Secretary of
    State for Home Affairs [1975] 3 All ER 497 482
R (Rusbridger) v Attorney-General [2003] UKHL 38; [2004] AC 357 435
R (Sacker) v West Yorkshire Coroner [2004] 1 WLR 796 202
R (Secretary of State for the Home Department) v BC and BB [2009] EWHC 2927 14
R (Secretary of State for the Home Department) v Bullivant [2008] EWHC 337 (Admin) 14
R (Simms) v Secretary of State for the Home Department [2000] 2 AC 115 483
R v A (No 2) [2002] 1 AC 45 433
R v Attorney General for Northern Ireland, ex P Devine [1992] 1 WLR 262 202
R v Clark (No 2) [1964] 2 QB 315 151
R v Culbert (1982) NIJB (CA) 198

R v G; R v J [2009] UKHL 13 29
R v H and C [2004] UKHL 3; [2004] 2 AC 134 33
R v Halliday, ex parte Zadig [1917] AC 260 13
R v Hetherington (1975) NI 160 198
R v H M Advocate 2003 SC (PC) 21 . . . . .73, 74
R v Home Secretary, ex p Pierson [1998] AC 539 102
R v Horncastle [2009] UKSC 14; [2010] 2 WLR 47 477
R v Lambert [2002] 2 AC 545 . . . . .47, 101
R v McCormick (1977) NI 105 198
R v Milne (1978) NI 110 198
R v O'Halloran 1979 2 NIJB (CA) 198
R v Offen [2001] 1 WLR 253 481
R v Robinson, Montgomery and Brannigan (1984), unreported 201
R v Secretary of State for the Home Department, ex p Brind [1991] 1 AC 696 201
R v Secretary of State for the Home Department, ex p Ramda [2002] EWHC 1278 279
R v Secretary of State, ex parte Daly [2001] 3 All ER 433 98
R v Secretary of State for Home Affairs, ex p Hosenball [1977] 1 WLR 766 13
R v Secretary of State for the Home Department, ex p Cheblak [1991] 1 WLR 890 13
R v Shayler [2003] 1 AC 247 35
R v Tohill (1977) NI 105 198
R v Z (AG for Northern Ireland's Reference) [2005] 2 WLR 1286 197
RB (Algeria) v Secretary of State for the Home Department [2009] UKHL 10;
    [2009] 2 WLR 512 15
Reynolds v Times Newspapers Ltd [2001] 2 AC 127 473
Ruddle v Secretary of State for Scotland 1999 GWD 29–1395 85
S (Minors) (Care Order: Implementation of Care Plan), In Re [2002] 2 AC 291 432
Salomon v Commissioners of Customs and Excise [1967] 2 QB 116 482
Secretary of State for the Home Department v E [2008] 1 AC 499 204
Secretary of State for the Home Department v MB [2007] UKHL 46 108
Secretary of State for the Home Department v AF [2009] UKHL 28;
    [2009] 3 WLR 74 . . . . .15, 38, 39
Secretary of State for the Home Department v JJ [2007] UKHL 45;
    [2008] 1 AC 385 . . . . .14, 24, 34, 35, 39, 204
Secretary of State for the Home Department v MB [2007] UKHL 46;
    [2008] 1 AC 440 . . . . .14, 24, 34, 35, 36,
                                                                                               37, 38, 39, 204
Secretary of State for the Home Department v Rehman [2001]
    UKHL 47; [2003] 1 AC 153 13
Secretary of State for Work and Pensions v M [2006] UKHL 11 .108
Sheldrake v Director of Public Prosecutions [2004] UKHL 43 108
Sinclair v H M Advocate 2005 SC(PC)28 75
Somerville v Scottish Ministers 2008 SC (HL) 45 . . . . .68, 75, 76, 85
Spiers v Ruddy 2008 SLT 39 74
SSHD v AR [2009] All ER (D) 125 (Jan) 204
SSHD v AU [2009] All ER (D) 93 (Mar) 204
Starrs v Ruxton 2000 JC 208 . . . . .66, 73, 74
Waddington v Miah [1974] 1 WLR 683 482
Wilson v Jaymarke Estates Ltd 2007 SC (HL) 135 71
YL v Birmingham City Council and Others [2007] UKHL 27 46
Zamora, The [1916] 2 AC 77 161

United States of America

Abrams v United States, 250 US 616, 630 (1919) 308
Atkins v Virginia, 536 US 304 (2002) 411

Foster v Florida, 123 S Ct 470, 472 (2002) 413
Joint Anti-Fascist Refugee Committee v McGrath, 341 US 123 (1951) 144, 146
Korematsu v United States (1944) 323 US 214 (1944) 311, 446
Lochner v New York, 198 US 45 (1905) 227, 243, 310, 371
Marbury v Madison, 5 US 137 (1803) 371
Medellin v Texas 552 US 491 (2008) 287
Planned Parenthood of Southeastern Pennsylvania et al v Casey, Governor of
    Pennsylvania, 505 US 833 (1991) 419
Plessy v Ferguson (1896) 163 US 537 (1896) 311, 446
Roe v Wade (1973) 410 US 113 (1973) 444, 447
Roper v Simmons, 543 US 551 (2005) 410, 411, 412, 414, 415,
                                                                                    419, 420, 421, 422
United States v Carolene Products Co, 304 US 144, 152–53 n 4 (1938) 307

World Trade Organisation
United States—Import Prohibition on Certain Shrimp and Shrimp Products,
    WTO Case Nos 58 (and 61) WT/DS58/AB/R 238

Table of Treaties and Legislation

Australia

Commonwealth of Australia
    Constitution Act 411
Charter of Human Rights and
    Responsibilities Act 2006
    (Victorian Acts, No 43) 40, 87, 111,
                                    315, 316, 333
    s 28 119
    s 32(1) 111
Dangerous Prisoners (Sexual Offenders)
    Act 2003 (Qld) 345
Fair Work Act 2009 (Cth) 312, 314, 315,
                                319, 320, 324, 417,
                                422, 423, 429
    s 3(c) 315
    s 3(f) 315
Human Rights Act 2004
    (ACT Laws 2004–5) 40, 87, 111
Law Enforcement Legislation
    Amendment (Public Safety)
    Act 2005 (NSW) 345
Workplace Relations Act 1996 (Cth) 312
    s 326 315
    s 348(2) 314
    s 349 314
Workplace Relations Amendment
    (Transition to Forward with
    Fairness) Act 2008 (Cth)
    Sch 1 315
    Sch 7A 315
Workplace Relations Amendment
    (Work Choices) Act 2005 (Cth) 314

Belgium

Belgian Law implementing the
    European Arrest Warrant
    Art.5(4) 280

Canada

Canada Health Act 1984 211
Canadian Bill of Rights
    Act 1960 . . . . 45, 87, 90, 126
Canadian Charter of Rights and
    Freedoms 1982 . . . . 40, 45, 48, 50,
                52, 55, 56, 57, 58, 61, 62, 89, 90,
                97, 106, 110, 113, 115, 117, 121,
                            127, 209, 212, 213, 221, 315,
                            418, 432, 436, 463
    s 1 . . . . .209, 425
    s 7 . . . . .212, 213
    s 24 47
    s 33 . . . . .52, 56, 106, 117, 209,
                            381, 432, 463
    s 33(1) 380
    s 33(3)–(4) 380
Constitution of Canada 47, 432
    s 52 47
Department of Justice Act 48
    s 4.1 48

Denmark

Constitution of Denmark 213

Europe

Charter of Fundamental Rights of the
    European Union 241, 246, 249,
                            251, 252, 255
                            261, 268, 269, 276,
                            278, 284, 285, 366
    Art 16 241
    Art 28 . . . . .252, 255
    Art 36 241
    Art 47 284
    Art 52(3) 263
    Protocol 252
Community Charter of the Fundamental
    Social Rights of Workers 255
Convention of 26 July 1995, based on
    Article K.3 of the Treaty on
    European Union, on the
    establishment of a European
    Police Office 270, 271
    Arts 2–3 271
Convention Implementing the
    Schengen Agreement
    of 14 June 1985 270
EC Treaty 240, 253, 255, 263,
                            273, 283, 286
    Art 6(2) 263
    Art 43 259
    Art 49 . . . . 254, 255, 256, 257, 260
    Art 56 . . . . 254, 255, 256, 257, 260

Art 234 445
European Convention for the Protection of
   Human Rights and
   Fundamental Freedoms. 2, 20,
       35, 36, 40, 47, 52, 66, 74, 83, 84, 80,
       97, 121, 127, 186, 198, 209, 230, 245,
       263, 264, 268, 276, 278, 281, 293,
       365, 367, 370, 404, 417, 428, 429,
       430, 433, 434, 436, 437, 438, 439,
       440, 442, 443, 444, 447, 449, 452,
       466, 467, 469, 470, 473, 476, 477,
       478, 480, 481, 482, 483, 484
   Art 2 . . . . 201, 202, 206
   Art 3 . . . . 76, 186, 105, 206, 418
   Art 5 . . . . 13, 15, 20, 35, 46, 204,
                             205, 272, 287, 479
   Art 5(1) 388
   Art 6 . . . . 14, 33, 37, 73, 396
   Art 8 . . . . 33, 284, 285
   Art 8(1) 390
   Art 8(2) 390
   Art 10 . . . . 264, 435, 439
   Art 11 . . . . 245, 260, 261, 262, 264
   Art 11(1) 262
   Art 13 . . . . .74, 405, 436, 437, 476,
                             477, 478, 484
   Art 14 262
   Art 15 . . . . 13, 195
   Art 34 242
   Protocol 1, Art 1 242
   Protocol 1, Art 2 485
   Protocol 14 477
European Social Charter 2, 246, 255,
                             260, 262
Single European Act 1987 251
Treaty of Amsterdam. 269
Treaty Establishing the
   European Community 245, 247,
                             250, 268
   Art 49 . . . . 255, 256, 257, 260
   Art 56 . . . . 254, 255, 256, 257, 260
   Art 145(f). 255
Treaty on European Union 236, 252,
                             267, 288, 292
   Art 2 293
   Art 6 . . . . 268, 269, 291
   Art 6(1) 276
   Art 6(2) 268, 276
   Art 7 293
   Art 34 273
   Art 35 273
   Art 39 273
   Art 48 234

Treaty on the Functioning of
   the European Union 230, 236
   Title V 272, 276
   Art 49 . . . . .236, 237
   Art 56 . . . . .236, 237
   Art 67(1) 276
   Art 106 . . . . .239, 240
   Art 114. 241
   Art 267 234
   Art 276 276
   Art 345 230
   Art 352 241
Treaty of Lisbon 2009 . . . . .251, 258, 263,
                             267, 268, 269, 272, 276
Treaty of Prüm. .274

Finland

Constitution of Finland 2000 . . . . . .370, 377,
                             379, 380, 381, 382,
                             384, 385, 387
   Art 7(1) 388
   Art 22 . . . . .384, 387
   Art 106 . . . . .381, 382, 385,
                             387, 391
   Art 124 . . . . .384, 385

India

Constitution of India. 213
   s 21 213
   s 21A 213

International Treaties

Geneva Conventions 173, 186
ILO Convention 87: Freedom of Association
   and Protection of the Right to
   Organise Convention 255, 262, 315
ILO Convention 98: Right to
   Organise and Collective
   Bargaining Convention. 261, 315
   Art 4 315
ILO Declaration on Fundamental
   Principles and Rights at Work,
   June 1998 315
International Covenant on Civil and
   Political Rights 105, 333, 417,
                             418, 425
   Art 14(1) 425
   Art 21 425
   Art 22(2) 425
International Covenant on Economic,
   Social and Cultural Rights 222, 334
North American Free Trade
   Agreement. 3, 229, 247

Israel

Basic Law: Human Dignity and
  Liberty 1992 . . . . 221, 226, 227
  Art. 3 226
Basic Law: Freedom of
  Occupation 1994 . . . . 221, 226

New Zealand

Electoral Finance Act 2007 103
Guardianship Act 1968 102
  s 23 102
New Zealand Bill of Rights
  Act 1990 . . . . 40, 87–107, 111,
                    221, 411–12, 417, 418
  s 3 120
  s 3(a) 92
  s 4 . . . . 91, 97, 103, 106
  s 5 . . . . 92, 96, 97, 425
  s 6 . . . . 97, 101, 102, 103, 111, 112
  s 7 . . . . .48, 55, 89, 90,
                        95, 96, 97, 98, 99,
                        100, 105, 106, 119
  s 21 102
Official Information Act 1982 94
  s 9(1)(f) 94
  s 9(1)(g) 94
Prostitution Reform Act 2003 106
  s 13(2) 106
Trespass Act 1980 102
  s 3(1) 102

Poland

Constitution of Poland 277–8

South Africa

Bill of Rights/Constitution 217, 218, 418
  s 26 218
  s 36 425

Sweden

Constitution 391
Freedom of Press Act 395, 406, 407
Instrument of Government 392, 394
  Ch 1 s 2 403
  Ch 7 s 2 393
  Ch 7 ss 3 and 5 .396
  Ch 8 400
  Ch 8 s 18 . . . . 392, 398, 399, 400
  Ch 11 s 14 . . . . 392, 399, 405
  Ch 12 . . . . .396, 400
  Ch 12 s 2 396
  Ch 12 s 3 396
  Ch 12 s 5 396

Law SFS 2007:978 406
Openness and Secrecy Act 2009 . . . .395, 406

United Kingdom and Ireland

Act of 1301 150
Anti-terrorism, Crime and
  Security Act 2001 . . . . 18, 19, 21,
                        433, 438
  Pt 2 31
  s 21 19
  s 23 13
  s 122 19
Bill of Rights of 1689 418
Civil Authority (Special Powers)
  Act 1922 . . . . 183, 193, 194
Civil Contingencies Act 2004 18
Claim of Right 1689 83
Communications Act 2003 439
Constitutional Reform Act 2005 . . . . 71, 124,
                        449
  s 38 449
  s 41 71
  s 137 449
Convention Rights Proceedings (Amendment)
  (Scotland) Act 2009 . . . . 77, 85
Coroners' Act 1959 204
Coroners and Justice Act 2009 24
  s 5(2) 481
Counter-terrorism Act 2008 . . . . . .18, 19, 20,
                        21, 22, 28, 31,
                        33, 34, 38
  s 22 31
  s 23 31
  s 24 31
  s 26 31
  s 63 31
  s 69 31
  s 74 31
  ss 78–81 34
  s 82 28
Criminal Justice Act 2003 25
Criminal Justice and Public Order
  Act 1994 200
Criminal Procedure and Investigations
  Act 1996 33
Defence of the Realm (Amendment)
  Act 1915 16
Defence of the Realm (No 2) Act 1914 16
Defence of the Realm Act 1914 16
Defence of the Realm Consolidation
  Act 1915 16
Detention of Terrorists (Northern
  Ireland) Order 1972 . . . . 193, 194

Emergency Powers (Defence)
    Act 1939 16
    s 1(2) 16
Government of Wales Act 1998 481
Health and Social Care
    Act 2008 .... 77, 79, 81
    s 145 .... 77, 81, 85
Human Rights Act 1998 ..... 1, 5, 8, 35, 36,
        40, 46, 47, 50, 51, 52, 62, 66, 67, 69,
        73, 74, 75, 76, 77, 78, 79, 81, 82, 83,
        85, 86, 87, 101, 108, 110, 111, 116,
        117, 118, 122, 123, 124, 125, 126, 177,
        178, 202, 204, 209, 229, 230, 233, 234,
        330, 369, 417, 418, 428, 429, 430, 432,
        433, 434, 436, 437, 440, 442, 443,
        446, 449, 451, 453, 459, 463, 464,
        466, 467, 470, 472, 473, 474, 475, 476,
        477, 478, 480, 481, 482, 483, 484, 486
    s 1(1) 437
    s 2 478
    s 3 .... 8, 36, 108, 112, 115, 118, 120,
            122, 125, 429–34, 436, 438,
            442, 444, 445, 446, 478
    s 3(1) 111, 112, 482
    s 3(2) 484
    s 4 .... 36, 117, 118, 119, 234, 429,
            430, 432–9, 442, 444,
            446, 476, 477, 478
    s 4(2) 116, 434
    s 4(6) 434
    s 6 .... 442, 481, 483
    s 6(2) 442, 484
    s 6(3)(a) 482
    ss 6–8 .... 442, 447
    s 10 .... 434, 436, 442
    s 10(1)(b) 442
    s 12 474
    s 19 .... 48, 119, 438, 439, 442
    s 19(1)(a) 119
    Sch.1 .... 472, 478
Hunting Act 2004 484
Inquiries Act 2005 .... 203, 206
Mental Health (Public Safety and
    Appeals (Scotland)) Act 1999 85
Metropolitan Police Act 1839 152,
                        169, 173
    s 59 152
Military Land Act 1842 168
Northern Ireland (Emergency Powers)
    Act 1978 .... 195, 196
    s 11(3) 195
Northern Ireland (Emergency Provisions)
    Act 1973 .... 194, 195
    s 10 195

    s 11 196
Northern Ireland Act 1998 481
Official Secrets Act 1889 159
    s 1 159
    s 1(1) 159
Official Secrets Act 1911 ...... 156, 158, 159,
                162, 163, 164, 169, 171
    s 1 .... 156, 158, 167
    s 1(1) 167
Official Secrets Act 1920 .... 159, 167
    s 3 167
    s 8(2) 167
Official Secrets Act 1989 35
Parliament Acts 1911–49 484
Police and Criminal Evidence Act 1984 25
    ss 41–44 25
Prevention of Crimes Act 1871 160
Prevention of Terrorism (Additional
    Powers) Act 1996 21
Prevention of Terrorism Act 1974 ...... 21, 25
Prevention of Terrorism Act 1984 197
Prevention of Terrorism Act 2005 ..... 18, 19,
                20, 21, 35, 36, 37
Prevention of Terrorism (Temporary
    Provisions) Act 1974 .... 17, 194
Public Order Act 1936 152
Regulation of Investigatory Powers
    Act 2000 195
    s 17 .... 28, 29, 33, 34
    s 18 28
Rent Act 1977 431
Scotland Act 1998 .... 5, 66, 67, 69, 73,
            75, 76, 77, 80, 81, 85, 86, 481
    s 30(2) 77
    s 57(2) 74, 75
    s 126(1) 78
    Sch 4 .... 77, 78, 79
    Sch 5 81
    Sch 5, Pt II, S L2 81
Scottish Commission for Human
    Rights Act 2006 81
Serious Organised Crime and Police
    Act 2005 18
Sexual Offences Act 2003 433
    s 75 433
Social Work (Scotland)
    Act 1968 .... 77, 78
Special Immigration Appeals
    Commission Act 1997 37
Terrorism Act 2000 .... 18, 25, 272
    s 11 29
    s 11(1) 197
    s 15 29
    ss 44–47 14

s 56 29
s 57 29
Terrorism Act 2006 . . . .   18, 19, 20, 21, 22, 24
s 1 . . . . .21, 30
s 5 30
s 6 30
Treason Felony Act 1848 435
s 3 435
Tribunals and Inquiries Act 1971. 203
Tribunals and Inquiries Act 1992. 203

United Nations
Universal Declaration of Human
     Rights 80, 103, 186, 222,
                          333, 454, 455

Art 5 186
UN Charter. 287

United States of America
American Bill of Rights 110, 126, 127,
                          128, 147, 418
Constitution of the United
     States of America. 127, 128, 306,
                          411, 417
     Art 6 306
     Fourth Amendment. 128
     Eighth Amendment. 411, 416, 418
Freedom of Information Act 284
Privacy Act. 284

1

Introduction

Tom Campbell, K. D. Ewing, and Adam Tomkins

Although human rights are protected by a battery of international treaties and domestic laws, disquiet continues as to the efficacy, the political outcomes, the unanticipated side effects, and general legitimacy of the enhanced judicial powers that are such a feature of statutory bills and charters of rights such as the UK Human Rights Act 1998.

In the United Kingdom much of that disquiet has been fuelled by what some see as the weak response of the British courts at the highest level to the protection of human rights in an age of heightened security concern in the so-called 'war on terror'. It has been fuelled further by the apparent paradox of a Human Rights Act being introduced by a government which then proceeded to go a long way to dismantle the very rights and freedoms which the Human Rights Act was designed to protect. Little wonder that people are sceptical. In the period since the enactment of the Human Rights Act, police powers of arrest and search have been extended; the surveillance powers of local authorities and other public bodies have been expanded (and may be exercised without the inconvenience of a judicial warrant), and the use of CCTV has grown as has the DNA database, now said to be the largest in the world. At the same time there has been a growing militarization of the police, the indefinite detention of terrorist suspects without having been convicted of any offence, the use of house arrest in the form of control orders, and credible allegations of British complicity in the use of torture.

Although not all human rights commentators are critical of the courts, the 'juridification' of human rights has nevertheless evoked a variety of human rights scepticisms, which may be divided into two broad categories: ideological and institutional. Ideological scepticism ranges from rejection of the very idea of human rights to doubts about the politically biased content of much human rights law. Institutional scepticism, on the other hand, focuses more on the mechanisms that are associated with contemporary human rights law, particularly those that diminish the role of parliaments and extend the political role of courts, which are considered to be both illegitimate and ineffective. These two varieties of scepticism are most evident in Part I of the book, 'Failures of Juridification'. The limited capacity of the courts has led a number of human rights scholars to consider alternative forms of human rights protection, with a focus on the institutional mechanisms that may help to restrain human rights violations in the first place. This involves more fully recognizing the role of political parties and addressing questions about whether human rights activists have a role to play at this level, as well as more fully understanding the power of legislatures and their capacities to better protect human rights standards. This more constructive theme comes to the fore in Part II of the book, 'Politicizing Human Rights'.

I. Ideological Scepticism

Ideological critiques of the very idea of human rights can be traced back to the writings of the young Karl Marx, who, in a critique of the late eighteenth-century French and American revolutionary texts, poured scorn on the idea of the so-called rights of man. Marx distinguished between the rights of the citizen (political rights designed to promote participation in the life of the community), and the rights of man (the rights of man separated from other men and from the community in which they live). The latter—including the rights of property—are seen by Marx as an instrument for subordinating the former and for limiting the power of the community and the rights of political participation. This is done to serve the ends of 'egoistic man', said to be 'an individual withdrawn into himself, his private interest and his private desires'. In other words, the so-called rights of man are about limiting the right of men and women to govern themselves, by subordinating the interests of all of the people to the interests of a few of the people.

But ideological sceptics have different kinds of concerns with the human rights movement. Partly it is a scepticism about the very idea of human rights, seen as an instrument for reinforcing economic power rather than distributing it. This is a concern sometimes reinforced by a belief that the human rights movement appears to be heavily impregnated by the soft liberal centre. Although human rights treaties cover both civil and political rights (with a commitment to personal liberty) *and* social and economic rights (embracing a commitment to equality), the exclusive focus is so often on the former rather than the latter, which are sometimes barely acknowledged and are usually treated as second-class human rights citizens. So while civil and political rights may be enforced under the European Convention on Human Rights (ECHR) by way of a *complaint* to a *court* (such as the European Court of Human Rights) for *adjudication*, at least in the case of the United Kingdom, social and economic rights are *supervised* under the European Social Charter by a process of regular government *reports* to the Social Rights *Committee* of the Council of Europe. Some countries allow complaints to be made to the Committee, but it has limited authority.

Different concerns about the ideological bias of human rights and human rights instruments are to be found in a number of essays in Part I. Danny Nicol takes a typically direct approach to the ideological failures of human rights acts by addressing the content of the rights that are commonly classified as 'human rights' in human rights law. Nicol's analysis suggests that there is no compelling basis on which business rights can be disentangled from classic political human rights. For instance, while free trade and competition may not be overtly labelled as human rights, they turn out to have the same fundamental status. Nicol examines how the supra-nationality of the EU Treaties, the WTO Agreements and the North American Free Trade Agreement establish a supra-national constitution entrenching free trade in the private sector and increasingly in the public sector as well. In support, he cites private sector dominance in service industries, the exclusion of social rights, and nationalization, thus making neo-liberalism a human right, entrenching a particular view of 'what is owed to each of us as human'.

Nicol's concerns are reinforced by Ran Hirschl and Evan Rosevear, who demonstrate the lack of correlation between variations in court-based human rights protection for social welfare rights and the reality of welfare provisions in different countries. In an extensive survey of the impact of a number of social, political, and legal variables, they find that a paradigm model of weak-form protection of rights (in Canada) has 'failed to yield effective constitutional protection of social welfare rights' and that, despite the considerable academic attention given to those cases in which the South African Constitutional Court considered the scope and nature of the protection afforded to a number of social and economic rights in the Constitution, the actual 'reality of social and economic rights in South Africa is, alas, quite appalling'. This not only challenges the substance of most human rights instruments, but also presents as a deep scepticism a direct challenge to those who would argue that many of the ideological biases of human rights instruments could be addressed by following the much-vaunted South African example of including social and economic rights along with civil and political rights.

An analysis raising similar questions in a different context is provided by Judy Fudge with respect to the extent to which the market rules of neo-liberalism have become embedded in the European Union, as a result of a series of now well-known cases, referred to as *Viking* and *Laval*. This judicial activism has elevated the rights of business above the rights of labour in the EU legal order, and is now challenged by the very different jurisprudence of the European Court of Human Rights. This conflict raises the intriguing question of whether in the long run economic or social rights will prevail, and if so on what terms. A milder but similar critique pervades Sionaidh Douglas-Scott's account of the imbalance between freedom and security in the European Court of Justice. The European Union, she argues, has been quick to adopt more coercive and potentially rights-violating measures such as the European Arrest Warrant, and the extremely broad EU definition of terrorism. Judicial review by the European Court of Justice has achieved little.

Finally, a radically different form of ideological scepticism and concern is at the heart of the deep analysis by Gavin Anderson in Part II. Although Anderson is also concerned with questions of human rights and political power, here the concern is with the power of the developed economies of the North. In order to address these concerns, Anderson argues for the need to develop an alternative epistemology of human rights associated with the phenomenon of 'globalization from below'. This relates to the emergence of transnational networks of social movements, such as NGOs and umbrella groupings such as the World Social Forum, which call into question the Western neo-liberal paradigm and its version of human rights. He sees signs of a transformed rights discourse, rooted in the politics of the global South, which rejects the human rights used in the justification of colonialism and the dominance of international corporations. Rather, its emphasis is on public health over property rights and on the differences rather than the universal features of human cultures. An example is the globalization of Western economic and social rights which privilege developed countries in international markets.

II. Institutional Scepticism

Institutional scepticism focuses on the *means* adopted to protect human rights. Institutional sceptics are particularly concerned with the role of human rights instruments in domestic law, especially those relating to judicial review. While this brand of scepticism may accept some commitment to human rights, it questions the legitimacy and/or the effectiveness of courts in upholding these human rights. So far as legitimacy is concerned, some scholars point to the contradiction of judicial protection of human rights if this means that unelected, unaccountable, and irremovable judges are to second-guess decisions made by elected and representative politicians with an electoral mandate. While this brand of scepticism does not diminish the importance of human rights, it would challenge the autonomy of the discipline and the attempt to insulate it through the legal process from political control. Sceptics of this hue may argue for greater parliamentary controls over the executive, and may also argue for a more holistic vision of human rights which embraces both civil and political rights along with social and economic rights.

Some of these different strands are unravelled in a number of the essays that follow. These essays also address the attempt by some lawyers to meet the sceptics head on by contending that judges are not involved in an undemocratic grab for power in human rights adjudication, but are engaged in a dialogue with the other branches of government. The limitations of this 'dialogue model' are addressed from a number of angles. The details are complex but overall the picture is clear enough: 'dialogue' is not the name of the game. The metaphor of dialogue fails to capture the dynamics of a process that is more a mixture, in different proportions, of unpredicted consequences, little or no reasoned interaction between the branches of government, routine judicial inaction, and, where courts do intervene, a de facto transfer of political power which weakens the role of parliaments in holding executives to account. Thus, in the UK, court decisions, and such declarations of incompatibility as have been made, have yet to prove challenging to government and have been routinely accepted by the executive without taking up the debate, and, in the process, used to curtail the opportunities to openly debate the alternatives in Parliament.

From his analysis of the passage of anti-terror legislation in the United Kingdom, Adam Tomkins argues that even the high-point of judicial interventionism in the case of *Belmarsh* has proved to be largely ineffectual with respect to the oppressiveness of the regimes adopted to deal with terrorist suspects. Janet Hiebert's institutional scepticism is directed to the extent to which bills of rights can be crafted so as to avoid the damaging consequences of strong judicial review in which courts can actually invalidate legislation. Her research on how bills of rights affect bur-eaucratic and political behaviour when developing and evaluating legislation in Canada, New Zealand, and the United Kingdom, shows that even 'weak' bills of rights, which are limited to interpretive and declaratory forms of judicial review, lead to cautious executives who refrain from bringing forward legislation that might be considered inconsistent with judicial decisions. In this way they may be said to be 'governing like judges', producing case-law-proof legislation which dis-torts the moral and political judgments of the issues at stake.

Chris Himsworth, dealing with the continuing peculiarities of the human rights regime in Scotland, where the Human Rights Act 1998 and the Scotland Act 1998 interact in an unpredictable and tortuously complex manner, explains the different and very limited character and contribution of 'dialogue' in such devolved conditions, where parliamentarians as well as the public are bemused by legal and political goings on around the controversial place of human rights in a devolved jurisdiction. The conclusion of his intricate and engrossing story is 'that the situation which has prevailed for the first decade of devolution is ill-suited to the judicial protection of human rights'. Commenting that 'those disposed to be sceptical about such judicial involvement will have had many of their worst fears confirmed', Himsworth concludes that 'in the case of devolution, there is little prospect of dialogue'.

Andrew Geddis highlights a different way in which the dialogue model fails to capture political reality, this time in New Zealand. Geddis goes beyond Hiebert's finding that New Zealand is much less given than Canada and the United Kingdom to lapsing into governing like judges, arguing that the New Zealand Parliament gives little or no attention even to ministerial statements that proposed legislation is not compatible with human rights legislation and seems perfectly relaxed about passing government legislation that the Attorney-General deems incompatible with the Bill of Rights. Taking another avenue of dialogue scepticism, James Allan points out that where there have been actual changes to legislation by the courts, this has been achieved through the process of human rights 'interpretation' whereby the courts can effectively rewrite the legislation to make it, in their opinion, human rights compatible, without taking part in any sort of dialogue with the government or the Parliament. Several of these essays endorse the contention of Mark Tushnet that weak forms of human rights judicial review are unstable and move towards either strong, US-style, versions of judicial review, in effect permitting judicial invalida-tion of legislation, or submission to parliamentary legislative sovereignty.

III. Scepticism, Human Rights, and Political Institutions

As already indicated, a third theme of this book is to address underlying scepticism by assessing the potential for other means of human rights protection, which take us beyond the failings of juridification. Foremost in this respect is the attention paid to enhancing the powers and quality of political and parliamentary scrutiny of legislative and executive actions. Parliamentary scrutiny in the context of human rights has long been open to the same criticism that is alleged against pre-legislative process, namely that it degenerates into second-guessing what might be judicial reactions to the legislation once enacted. However, in considering the parliamentary debates regarding anti-terror legislation, Tomkins charts the emergence of a more persistent, challenging, and informed input from the United Kingdom's parliamentary Joint Committee on Human Rights, which has led to a more rigorous and evidence-based parliamentary debate than used to be the case with respect to this type of legislation, the potential of which is taken up in Part II by Tom Campbell and Jonathan Morgan.

This analysis is considerably widened in Mark Tushnet's overview in Part II of the key determinants of a politics that is directed at rights, in which he identifies a number of variables, including the nature of the political system and the role of parties and others. The motif of political parties is taken up by Joo-Cheong Tham, who agrees that there are problems where parties operate like cartels and internally centralize power, but argues against the common belief that parties are 'unprincipled' and uninvolved in debate and dialogue to the point where they cannot be a significant player in protecting human rights. Political parties are often morally disqualified because of their collectivist outlook, their concern with bargaining, and their focus on mobilization. However, Tham shows that political parties are necessary intermediaries between interest groups and the formulation of comprehensive policies. Parties can be agents of and forums for political deliberation and activism, activities that may enhance human rights, and influence and structure political opinion.

Moving from party to Parliament, but also addressing themes identified by Tushnet, Carolyn Evans and Simon Evans report on their research relating to the Australian Commonwealth Parliament, examining the argument that the new statutory bills of rights encourage parliaments to play a more significant role in the protection of rights. They identify a number of constraints on the capacity of parliamentarians to undertake serious rights-based scrutiny of legislation, particularly lack of time, resources and expertise, the impact of party discipline in small legislatures, and the dominance of the executive. Making practical suggestions to combat these problems, including the use of electronic technologies to gain more direct public input into policy-making and developing a more team-based approach, they argue that empowering elected politicians is a crucial ingredient in promoting the political protection of human rights. A major issue here, however, is the lack of formal power vested in the Australian Parliament to block legislation specifically on human rights grounds.

Looking elsewhere for leads to combat institutional scepticism, this latter point is addressed by Scandinavian experience where there has traditionally been a focus on human rights protection by strong legislatures rather than by courts. Part II thus contains two highly informative chapters which reflect on the Scandinavian experience of pre-legislative review. Kaarlo Tuori presents a moderately critical analysis of what he calls external constitutional review of legislation in Finland by the abstract ex ante review exercised by the Constitutional Law Committee of Parliament, a quasi-judicial body composed of Members of Parliament and advised by constitutional experts whose opinions tend to be adopted by the Committee and are respected by the courts, but does not have to be followed by the Parliament. He then describes the impact of the ex post concrete constitutional review of legislation introduced in 2000 by Parliament, whereby the courts can now bypass the legislation it considers 'in evident conflict with the Constitution'. It remains the case, however, that the primary duty of the courts is to interpret legislation consistently with constitutional provisions.

Tuori presents this as a hybrid model which has retained a strong parliamentary involvement, although he accepts that there is a certain juridification of legislative politics involved through the Constitutional Law Committee of Parliament. Thomas Bull describes the Swedish system of preview of legislation in order to ensure that constitutional and human rights are respected. It consists of four main components: (1) the system of legislative committees in preparing legislation, (2) wide access to public documents and the right to publish those, (3) the Law Council (consisting of judges), and (4) the Constitutional Committee of the Parliament. Bull argues that together these four components of the preview system make it hard, though not impossible, to legislate in a way that infringes rights. The government is in no way obliged to follow the Law Council, but not doing so gives rise to a political debate and may alert courts that the legislation passed might not be constitutionally sound (in a review situation). Tuori and Bull each provide a fascinating insight into how things can be done differently in political cultures and legal systems beyond the common law and its traditions.

This idea of a more intense political response to the protection of human rights is considered from a more philosophical standpoint by Tom Campbell, who explores the concept of a political conception of human rights according to which the enumerated rights serve as a basis for enacting specific legislation and guiding legislative review. The proposed human rights regime is one in which a statutory bill of rights is used institutionally, not to service judicial review, but to provide the terms of reference for a variety of political mechanisms for agendizing, prioritizing, and developing a polity's human rights commitments within the mainstream democratic process. Campbell addresses the tricky problem of how to arrive at a conception of human rights that is not tied to judge-made human rights law, drawing on recent debates as to the functions of the UK parliamentary Joint Committee on Human Rights. This involves identifying key human rights values together with those political and social institutions and practices essential for their effective realization.

IV. Scepticism, Human Rights, and the Courts

Lawyers being lawyers, not all of a sceptical disposition are prepared to write off the courts just yet. Several essays consider ways by which judicial performance might be improved, or make a calculation about particular legal forms as being preferred to other legal forms. Linking with earlier themes, Jonathan Morgan's essay presents the parliamentary Joint Committee on Human Rights as part of the culture of compliance in which legislatures try to predict and pre-empt adverse judicial decisions. He proposes repealing section 4 and amending section 3 to make it clear that interpretation cannot include distorting the meaning of statutory language. The JCHR could then operate more politically. More radically, he also suggests that there should be provision for courts to adjourn particular cases of apparent injustices arising from legislation and refer them to a new body, the 'High Court of Parliament', which would combine investigative and judicial methods to determine the matter and, if necessary, introduce an amendment to the offending legislation.

Writing from the different context of the United States and a controversy in that jurisdiction, a specific proposal to increase the acceptability of human rights constitutional review, without endorsing the process as a whole, is taken up in the essay by Jeremy Waldron, who urges that courts involved in judicial review of legislation on human rights grounds should cite foreign law. He argues that, whatever we may think of the legitimacy of such powers, where they exist, it is preferable that courts should be able to draw on the experience of comparable decisions in other jurisdictions. This enables courts to learn from the deliberations that have taken place elsewhere. It also generates more informed public debate on rights. Further, the citation of foreign cases and statutes contributes to the harmonization of human rights law. However, improving the quality of human rights decision-making and promoting the global consistency of human rights law should not be confused with the propriety of the judicial review in question.

Finally on this theme, Conor Gearty, in a survey of current UK political party human rights policies, looks beyond the Human Rights Act to the prospect of its amendment or abolition, although concerns in some quarters that the Conservatives might have repealed the HRA are assuaged by the fact that it must now govern with a Coalition partner strongly committed to the HRA. Pinpointing the potential conflict with the Strasbourg courts which would follow from an independently human rights-minded government, unconstrained by judicial interpretations of legislation under section 3 and unmoved by multiplying declarations of incompatibility, Gearty reflects on how this might affect UK relations with the Council of Europe and the EU. Domestically, he notes how difficult it would be to unscramble the practices deriving from the HRA. He dangles the prospect of a constitutional crises arising from courts bent on implementing common law constitutionalism. In this fluid and unpredictable situation, the way forward, for a social democrat, he suggests, is to stick with the HRA.

Some may see these latter contributions as a pragmatic response to the difficult situation of progressive human rights democrats, with there currently being majority support for court-centred human rights provisions. Is the ideological imbalance of existing bills and charters of rights a basis for advocating the extension of such instruments to include social and economic rights, or should the process of judicial review based on judicial interpretation of abstract moral rights be wound back? Given the political difficulty of going back on charter-like judicial review once it has become routinized in a judicial system, is it better to recommend improvements to that mechanism, by 'educating' judiciaries and encouraging the use of a broader range of legal sources, such as legal precedents drawn from more progressive jurisdictions all over the world? Or is it better to argue for updated procedural changes that serve to regenerate the moral consciousness and popular accountability of elected politicians and enhance the opportunities of minorities and civil society leadership to wield more power and generate more public support?

V. Conclusion

Scepticism and recovery are thus the themes underlying this book, to which we may add that none of the concerns addressed here is new. The violation of human rights by governments, the failings of the courts, and the lack of adequate response from legislatures have been preoccupations of generations of activists and scholars. We are reminded of this in three chapters in Part I which place the foregoing material in a historical context, and which illustrate the divergent histories of civil rights protection under different human rights regimes, the lessons of which include the foolishness of relying on judicial review for robust human rights protection. Each in its own way calls into question reliance on court-centred mechanisms for determining the scope and practical implications of human rights. Joan Mahoney explores the interaction of constitutionalism, the rule of law, and politics in the context of civil liberties in Britain and the United States during the Cold War. She concludes that having a Bill of Rights failed to contain anti-Communism in the United States during the Cold War period, while politics achieved in Britain what human rights constitutionalism failed to achieve in the United States.

Building on this, Keith Ewing provides further historical data on the fate of civil liberties during the Cold War, this time in relation to the heavy-handed way in which the UK government, police, and courts dealt with the Campaign for Nuclear Disarmament. Aileen McColgan brings this theme up to date in a dramatic account of civil rights violations in Northern Ireland, with which she illustrates the continuing inability of judges to make a significant impact on civil rights outcomes. The better protection of civil liberties was secured in Northern Ireland despite rather than because of laws, lawyers, and judges. These three historical chapters reveal the strength of politics as a tool of human rights/civil liberties and as the most effective weapon for seeking to contain the power of the state. As Ewing points out, the general election is the most effective of all restraints on a government that loses sight of its duty to protect liberty and its responsibility to protect all of its citizens.

The lessons of the past are thus important for reinforcing the view that the protection of human rights ultimately depends on the capacities of political institutions, such as parliaments, political parties, the trade union movement, and interest groups. In these circumstances it is appropriate to turn to working out alternative, more democratic, human rights mechanisms for the protection of the basic interests of citizens and employees in a neo-liberal world. Precisely how this democratic revitalization might materialize is far from clear, but it is evident that something will depend on the future reputation and effectiveness of human rights, seen, perhaps, less as a moral foundation qualitatively different from all others, and more as a value framework within which policy issues should be debated and decided. Despite their different emphases, the essays in this book support to some degree the desire to break the perceived link between promoting human rights and extending the juristocratic practice of human rights-based judicial review. Human rights juristocracy feeds the unfortunate assumption that if human rights are at issue then we have a matter that should be de-politicized and therefore de-democratized to the point where we look to courts rather than parliaments to solve our major political problems.

At this stage the strategies for recovering human rights from its close association with the sometimes ineffectual and generally undemocratic mechanisms of the courts are far from self-evident, as the essays in this book amply illustrate. We have probably now got to the stage of moving beyond a polarized debate in which human rights enthusiasts castigate human rights sceptics for being naive about real world twenty-first-century democracy, while human rights sceptics attribute even greater naivety to those who see courts as democratic substitutes. The contribution of the progressive human rights scepticism explored in this volume embraces the view that a democratic human rights renaissance must include a crucial role for courts in the implementation of democratically endorsed legislation. It may be alarmist to predict grim futures giving rise to repressive regimes, environmental disintegration, and increasingly military-style security, but it is nonetheless prudent to consider how the idea and practice of democracy can have its ethical potential revitalized as these challenges unfold.

PART I

FAILURES OF JURIDIFICATION

2

Parliament, Human Rights, and Counter-Terrorism

Adam Tomkins

I. The National Security Constitution and Judicial Review

It is well established that, in the twentieth century, British courts were routinely weak in judicially reviewing the legality and reasonableness of government actions alleged to have been taken in the interests of national security. Even those who support the idea of robust judicial review in this area—and who believe it possible to achieve—concede as much, David Dyzenhaus, for example, describing the judicial record as being 'at worst dismal, at best ambiguous'.[1] The courts notoriously failed to enforce the rule of law in a whole series of war-time and peace-time decisions[2] concerning such issues as internment and deportation, ranging from *R v Halliday*[3] in 1917, through *Liversidge v Anderson*[4] in 1942, to *Hosenball*,[5] *Cheblak*,[6] and even *Rehman*,[7] as late as 2001.

It is because of this consistent record of failure that their Lordships' decision in the *Belmarsh* case[8] was so surprising and resulted in such a remarkable outpouring of praise—not to say relief—in the pages of the law reviews and elsewhere. This was the case in which an 8:1 majority of the House of Lords declared that a scheme of indefinite detention without trial for suspected international terrorists[9] was incompatible, *inter alia*, with the Convention right to liberty under Article 5 ECHR. The government's purported derogation from Article 5 was held to be unlawful as the scheme of incarceration was not 'strictly required' within the meaning of Article 15 ECHR (which governs the legality

---

[1] D. Dyzenhaus, *The Constitution of Law: Legality in a Time of Emergency* (Cambridge: Cambridge University Press, 2006), 17.

[2] For a summary, see C. Turpin and A. Tomkins, *British Government and the Constitution*, 6th edn (Cambridge: Cambridge University Press, 2007), 756–62.

[3] *R v Halliday, ex p Zadig* [1917] AC 260.

[4] *Liversidge v Anderson* [1942] AC 206.

[5] *R v Secretary of State for Home Affairs, ex p Hosenball* [1977] 1 WLR 766.

[6] *R v Secretary of State for the Home Department, ex p Cheblak* [1991] 1 WLR 890.

[7] *Secretary of State for the Home Department v Rehman* [2001] UKHL 47, [2003] 1 AC 153.

[8] *A v Secretary of State for the Home Department* [2004] UKHL 56, [2005] 2 AC 68.

[9] See Anti-terrorism, Crime and Security Act 2001, s 23.

of derogations), even though, it should not be forgotten, eight of their Lordships ruled that there was a 'public emergency threatening the life of the nation'.[10] David Feldman claimed that this case amounted to 'perhaps the most powerful judicial defence of liberty' since the 1770s and that it 'will long remain a benchmark in public law'.[11] Arden LJ was equally fulsome in her admiration for the judgment, describing it as 'a landmark decision' that should be seen as 'a powerful statement by the highest court in the land of what it means to live in a society where the executive is subject to the rule of law'.[12] As such, it was 'a beacon of light', she claimed.[13]

Six years on and these claims already ring hollow. Even if the House of Lords' record since *Belmarsh* is not quite 'dismal', 'ambiguous' would be too generous a label to describe their Lordships' commitment to the rule of law and to the protection of individual liberty in the face of government claims as to what is necessary in the interests of national (or, increasingly, international) security.[14] *Belmarsh*, far from establishing itself as a new 'benchmark', now looks more like a one-off. To summarize, consider the following:

- *R (Gillan) v Metropolitan Police Commissioner* [2006] UKHL 12, [2006] 2 AC 307 (ruling that the 'extraordinary' and 'sweeping' stop and search powers contained in the Terrorism Act 2000, ss 44–7, may lawfully be used to stop peaceful protesters with no connection to terrorism);

- *Secretary of State for the Home Department v JJ* [2007] UKHL 45, [2008] 1 AC 385 (the House of Lords, by a 3:2 majority, ruling that particular control orders were improperly made but, unanimously, upholding the legality of the control order regime);

- *Secretary of State for the Home Department v MB* [2007] UKHL 46, [2008] 1 AC 440 (the House of Lords declining to take a strong line on the (in)compatibility of the use of special advocates with Article 6 ECHR; the House of Lords was subsequently required to change its line on this matter as a result of the European Court of Human Rights making it clear that it took a different view; several of their Lordships were clearly extremely reluctant to do this: see *Secretary of State for the Home Department v AF* [2009] UKHL 28, [2009] 3 WLR 74);[15]

---

[10] The European Court of Human Rights subsequently endorsed these rulings: see *A and others v United Kingdom* (2009) 49 EHRR 29.

[11] D. Feldman, 'Proportionality and Discrimination in Anti-Terrorist Legislation' [2005] *Cambridge Law Journal* 271, 273.

[12] M. Arden, 'Human Rights in the Age of Terrorism' (2005) 121 *Law Quarterly Review* 604, 622.

[13] Ibid 625.

[14] The record of the lower courts since *Belmarsh* is better, but, even here, remains mixed: see A. Tomkins, 'National Security, and the Role of the Court: A Changed Landscape?' (2010) 126 *Law Quarterly Review* 543. In the lower courts there have been some remarkable triumphs for liberty in the face of Government claims as to what is necessary in the interests of national security but, equally, there continue to be disturbing decisions made at every level.

[15] We return to this case below.

- *R (Al Jedda) v Secretary of State for Defence* [2007] UKHL 58, [2008] 1 AC 332 (ruling that UN Security Council Resolutions authorized British military detention in Iraq and severely restricted the relevance of Article 5 ECHR to that detention: a stark contrast to the significantly more robust approach to UN Security Council resolutions subsequently adopted by the European Court of Justice in Joined Cases C-402/05 P and C-415/05 P, *Kadi v Council*, [2008] 3 CMLR 41);

- *R (Gentle) v Prime Minister* [2008] UKHL 20, [2008] 1 AC 1356 (ruling that the law is incapable of requiring an inquiry to be held into the legality of the Iraq War);

- *R (Corner House) v Director of the Serious Fraud Office* [2008] UKHL 60, [2009] 1 AC 756 (House of Lords unanimously overturning a remarkably strongly worded judgment of the Divisional Court, their Lordships ruling that there had been no illegality in the SFO abandoning its criminal investigation into British Aerospace's 'Al Yamamah' arms deal with Saudi Arabia; the Divisional Court had ruled that the political involvement in the SFO's decision was an 'outrageous' violation of the rule of law);

- *R (Bancoult) v Secretary of State for Foreign and Commonwealth Affairs* [2008] UKHL 61, [2009] 1 AC 453 (ruling that the right of abode in the British Indian Ocean Territory (the Chagos Islands) may lawfully be denied to the Chagossians in the interests of defence and international security and, moreover, that this result may lawfully be achieved by prerogative Order in Council with no parliamentary oversight);

- *RB (Algeria) v Secretary of State for the Home Department* [2009] UKHL 10, [2009] 2 WLR 512 (ruling, *inter alia*, that the Home Secretary may lawfully deport Abu Qatada to Jordan, where he has been convicted in his absence of terrorist offences, these convictions, it is claimed, having been secured on the basis of evidence obtained by torture).

II. The National Security Constitution and Parliamentary Scrutiny—the Twentieth Century

What is perhaps less widely remarked upon, at least by lawyers, is Parliament's record in scrutinizing government claims of what policies, actions, and decisions are necessary in the interests of national security. When the parliamentary record is examined, we find that in the twentieth century, while it was a little better than the judicial record, it was not exactly impressive. Parliament did not fail as consistently or as spectacularly as did the judges, but its successes were modest and, oftentimes, marginal. Three examples can be taken to illustrate this, dating from 1914, 1939, and 1974.

When the Home Secretary Sir Reginald McKenna introduced into Parliament the measure which became the Defence of the Realm Act 1914, he offered, from 'half a sheet of notes', only the sketchiest argument. As Charles Townshend puts it, the legislation was 'more or less made up as the Government went along'.[16] The entire Commons debate on the measure was so short that it was reprinted in full in the *Michigan Law Review*—as a footnote![17] In the House of Lords there was no debate at all.[18] The Defence of the Realm Act 1914 was swiftly followed by further enactments, including the Defence of the Realm (No 2) Act 1914, the Defence of the Realm Consolidation Act 1914 and the Defence of the Realm (Amendment) Act 1915.[19] This last measure, brought forward in part because of parliamentary disquiet expressed during the passage of the Consolidation Act, restored some of the rights to trial by jury (rather than by courts martial) which the government had sought to repress. Thus, Parliament was not completely docile in 1914–15. Even in the context of the beginning of the First World War, Parliament and, in particular, the House of Lords, was able to insist on the government making some concessions. Ewing and Gearty's verdict on the parliamentary record in this period is cautious, however: these concessions were 'important', but they 'ought not to be exaggerated', they suggest. 'Notwithstanding the[se] triumphs... the war-time experience is generally one of parliamentary neglect and ineffectiveness...'.[20]

The position had improved a bit by the time of the Second World War. Unlike in 1914, the government in the late 1930s considered that the power to intern was so severe that it should be expressly authorized by Act of Parliament.[21] As Simpson records, 'This made it unlikely that Parliament would pass the bill in peacetime, except in conditions of crisis'.[22] In the event, the relevant legislation—the Emergency Powers (Defence) Act 1939—was passed in August 1939 'with little trouble'.[23] However, the publication of the Regulations (made under the Act) containing the detailed executive powers the government proposed for itself 'triggered a serious revolt in the Commons'.[24] Led by Dingle Foot (Liberal MP for Dundee) and supported by Stafford Cripps and others, opposition in the Commons was so strong that the government withdrew the Regulations rather

[16] C. Townshend, *Making the Peace: Public Order and Public Security in Modern Britain* (Oxford: Oxford University Press, 1993), 113. See also K. D. Ewing and C. A. Gearty, *The Struggle for Civil Liberties* (Oxford: Oxford University Press, 2000), 400.

[17] H. M. Bowman, 'Martial Law and the English Constitution' (1916) 15 *Michigan Law Review* 96.

[18] Townshend, above n 16, 57.

[19] See Ewing and Gearty, above n 16, 43–51.

[20] Ibid 50. Brian Simpson is of the same view: in the First World War, he writes, 'the executive became the legislature, and Parliament declined into a relatively unimportant sounding board for public opinion' (see A. W. B. Simpson, *In the Highest Degree Odious: Detention without Trial in Wartime Britain* (Oxford: Clarendon Press, 1992), 6–7).

[21] In the First World War, internment was authorized by Regulation 14B, one of the Defence of the Realm Regulations, made under the Defence of the Realm Act. That Act did not specifically confer on the Crown the power to intern. In the Second World War, the Emergency Powers (Defence) Act 1939, s 1(2) expressly conferred on the Crown the power to make regulations providing for internment. The relevant regulation during World War Two was Regulation 18B of the Defence (General) Regulations. The authoritative account is Simpson, ibid.

[22] Ibid 46.

[23] Ibid 49.

[24] Ibid 58.

than risk a division.[25] All-party consultations led to the Regulations being revised. Restrictions on freedom of expression were dropped and procedural safeguards were added to the power to intern, such that detainees would have a right to be informed of the grounds for their detention. Additionally, the Home Secretary would have to report regularly to Parliament on the use of the internment power.[26] In their revised form, the Regulations were presented once more to Parliament and were successfully brought into force. While it is impressive that the House of Commons was active even in the heat and panic of late 1939 in seeking to ensure that civil liberties were not overlooked in the rush to confer emergency powers on the executive, Simpson's verdict as to what Parliament actually achieved is depressing. The revisions, he claims, 'made no practical difference';[27] Foot, Cripps, and their supporters 'achieved virtually nothing'.[28] Their amendments had the effect of removing criticism without making serious inroads into the reach of the executive's powers. The government fought off the parliamentary critics on a whole range of issues, including any right to counsel, any explicit power of judicial review, anything in the nature of a fair trial for internees, and any right to a full statement of reasons, etc.[29] That said, however, and as Simpson concedes, it may well be that the extent of parliamentary disquiet over the executive's emergency powers significantly restricted the extent to which these powers were actually used, at least in the first stages of the war.

Our third twentieth-century example finds Parliament, once again, at its least effective. When Roy Jenkins (as Home Secretary) introduced into Parliament the measure that became the Prevention of Terrorism (Temporary Provisions) Act 1974[30] he described the measure as 'draconian' and 'unprecedented in peace time'[31] and considered that no one would wish the 'exceptional powers' it contained to remain in force 'a moment longer than necessary'.[32] Yet, the bill was rushed through the Commons in 42 hours without there even being a division at second reading because, according to Gearty, 'no Member was willing to act as teller for the noes'.[33] Even though the Act provided for its own expiry after six months, when it came in May 1975 to renewing the legislation by affirmative resolution in the Commons only 171 MPs bothered to turn up for the debate, the renewal being voted for by 161 MPs, a mere 10 voting against.[34]

[25] Ibid 61.
[26] Ibid 67.
[27] Ibid.
[28] Ibid 69.
[29] Ibid.
[30] For a fascinating account, see D. Bonner, 'Responding to Crisis: Legislating Against Terrorism' (2006) 122 *Law Quarterly Review* 602.
[31] HC Debs, vol 882, cols 35–6 (25 Nov 1974).
[32] HC Debs, vol 882, col 642 (28 Nov 1974).
[33] C. Gearty, 'Political Violence and Civil Liberties', in C. McCrudden and G. Chambers (eds), *Individual Rights and the Law in Britain* (Oxford: Clarendon Press, 1994), 164.
[34] Gearty, ibid 164–5.

III. Parliamentary Scrutiny and National Security Now

The primary question addressed in this chapter is: what is the contemporary position with regard to parliamentary scrutiny of government policy on questions of national security? Is it as depressing now as these episodes suggest it was in the twentieth century, or has it improved? If it has improved, is that improvement likely to be fleeting, or can a plausible case be made for it being more securely established?

There is a very great deal of evidence and documentation that could be examined in order to address these questions. In the years following '9/11', the UK Parliament has enacted four major statutes in the field of counter-terrorism alone, as well as numerous others touching on additional aspects of national and international security and public order (not least the Civil Contingencies Act 2004 and the Serious Organised Crime and Police Act 2005). Concerning counter-terrorism, the statutes are the Anti-terrorism, Crime and Security Act 2001, the Prevention of Terrorism Act 2005, the Terrorism Act 2006, and the Counter-terrorism Act 2008. These four, it should not be forgotten, sit on top of the pre-existing Terrorism Act 2000, itself a fearsome and extensive code of criminal offences and police powers, described in 2005 by the European Commissioner for Human Rights as being 'amongst the toughest and most comprehensive anti-terror legislation in Europe'.[35]

Even a cursory reading of the parliamentary record shows that, in the passage of these Acts, the government has not found it straightforward to proceed always as it would have wished. For sure, the government's bills have been enacted. But, in the process, all have been subject to serious and often probing scrutiny in Parliament, and all have been passed only subject to amendments. While, as we shall see, parliamentarians have not been successful in insisting on all the amendments they would have liked, at the same time, the government has been required to make a series of concessions and in some instances even to abandon core aspects of its preferred policies.

Later in this essay I shall take as a detailed case-study parliamentary consideration of the Counter-Terrorism Act 2008, focusing in particular on the extensive work undertaken in connection with this measure by the Joint Committee on Human Rights (JCHR). As we shall see, that committee produced no fewer than six full reports on the policies that led to, or were contained in, the Counter-Terrorism Bill. These reports, and the oral and written evidence obtained and published in their support, are important in their own right. But, additionally, the ways in which they shaped and added value to debates in both Houses only augment their significance. Before we come to the 2008 Act, however, it is worth pausing to highlight some of the notable features of parliamentary engagement in the passage of the Acts of 2001, 2005, and 2006.

---

[35] Cited by the ECtHR in *A and others v United Kingdom* (2009) 49 EHRR 29, para 104.

The Anti-terrorism, Crime and Security Act 2001 was presented as emergency legislation—the 'emergency' being the threat to national and international security manifested by the events of '9/11'. The bill, all 125 clauses and eight schedules of it, was allotted only 16 hours of the House of Commons' time, although the measure took nine days to pass its various stages in the House of Lords.[36] Yet, despite this, Parliament's select committees managed to produce no fewer than five reports on aspects of the bill as it was being debated in Parliament. The Joint Committee on Human Rights published two reports on the bill,[37] and the House of Commons Home Affairs Committee,[38] the House of Commons Defence Committee,[39] and the House of Lords Select Committee on Delegated Powers and Regulatory Reform[40] each published one. Evidence obtained in support of these reports (particularly in connection with the JCHR's second report on the bill) and recommendations contained within them strengthened Parliament's ability to force concessions from the government, at least one of which turned out to be crucial. Among the concessions, the scope of the Secretary of State's power to certify an individual as a 'suspected international terrorist' was confined to cases where the Secretary of State *reasonably* believed the person's presence in the United Kingdom to be a risk to national security.[41] Additionally, Parliament ensured that the most controversial aspects of the bill—the Secretary of State's powers to order a suspected international terrorist to be detained indefinitely without charge—were subject to a series of reviews.[42] Among these, section 122 of the Act provided that the Act as a whole be reviewed within two years by a committee of Privy Counsellors appointed for the purpose. This review turned out to be damning in its criticism,[43] criticism on which the appellate committee of the House of Lords extensively relied when it came judicially to review the legality of the extraordinary detention powers in the *Belmarsh* case.[44]

Janet Hiebert has reviewed Parliament's consideration of the 2001 bill and, in particular, the roles played by the JCHR in this process, in the following terms:

The JCHR's review of…the Anti-terrorism, Crime and Security Bill, one of its first undertakings, helped establish its position and reputation as an important component in the HRA project of facilitating a rights culture within [Parliament]….[Despite the legislative timetable, the committee showed considerable] determination to arm

---

[36] A. Tomkins, 'Legislating against Terror: the Anti-terrorism, Crime and Security Act 2001' [2002] *Public Law* 205.
[37] The JCHR's first report on the Bill was HL (2001–2) 37; HC (2001–2) 372. Its second report on the Bill was HL (2001–2) 51; HC (2001–2) 420.
[38] HC (2001–2) 351.
[39] HC (2001–2) 382.
[40] HL (2001–2) 45.
[41] Anti-terrorism, Crime and Security Act 2001, s 21. As the Bill was originally drafted, there had been no requirement for the Secretary of State's belief to be reasonable. See Tomkins, above n 36, 211.
[42] See Tomkins, ibid 218–19.
[43] *Report of the Privy Counsellor Review Committee*, HC (2003–4) 100.
[44] See Turpin and Tomkins, above n 2, 769.

Parliament with sufficient information to deliberate on whether the Bill was justified from a rights perspective.[45]

To this end, as Hiebert reports, the JCHR questioned the Home Secretary two days after the bill was introduced and published its first report on the bill two days later. The JCHR's achievement was threefold, in Hiebert's view. First, it brought to Parliament's attention critical facts which otherwise would not have been highlighted—facts such as that the United Kingdom was the only state in the Council of Europe to consider that the events of '9/11' required it to derogate from the terms of the European Convention on Human Rights.[46] Secondly, it supplied a narrative of the key human rights issues, identifying what they were and offering critical arguments about what it saw as unnecessary or overly intrusive interferences with rights. Thirdly, and as we have already seen, it helped Parliament to gain important concessions from the government.[47]

When we come to examine Parliament's scrutiny of the measures contained in the Counter-Terrorism Act 2008 and, especially, the roles played by the JCHR with regard to that legislation, we shall see many of these points being amplified and further illustrated. Before we come to that, however, a brief word first about the 2005 and 2006 Acts. Here our focus shifts from the committee corridor to the floor of the House of Commons. What is remarkable about the passage of both these Acts is the government's inability to persuade significant numbers of MPs to vote in support of the measures they contained. At the second reading of the Prevention of Terrorism Bill in early 2005, the government's majority was halved, with 32 Labour MPs joining the Opposition parties in voting against the measure. The result would have been worse for the government but for the fact that even at this early stage in the passage of the bill the Home Secretary had been required to make a series of concessions, diluting certain of his powers with regard to the making of control orders. At the committee stage, the government's majority was at one point cut to 14 (the second lowest since the Labour government had come to power in 1997), with 62 Labour MPs voting against the government on the issue of requiring judicial rather than ministerial authorization for control orders restrictive of the right to liberty (so-called non-derogating control orders). Again, the government was required to make concessions in order to allow the bill to proceed.[48] The passage of the Terrorism Act 2006 was even more dramatic, as it witnessed the first legislative defeat suffered by the Blair government on the floor

[45] J. Hiebert, 'Parliament and the Human Rights Act: Can the JCHR Help Facilitate a Culture of Rights?' (2006) 4 *International Journal of Constitutional Law* 1, 28.

[46] The provisions with regard to indefinite detention without trial required a derogation from Article 5 ECHR, the right to liberty and security of the person.

[47] Dominic McGoldrick has endorsed this positive appraisal of the JCHR's work: his view is that 'it has operated in a non-partisan manner and the standard of its analysis has been very high': see D. McGoldrick, 'Terrorism and Human Rights Paradigms: The United Kingdom after 11 September 2001', in A. Bianchi and A. Keller (eds), *Counter-terrorism: Democracy's Challenge* (Oxford: Hart Publishing, 2008), 119.

[48] This account relies on Philip Cowley's online database of parliamentary rebellions under New Labour: see http://www.revolts.co.uk/. See further P. Cowley, *The Rebels: How Blair Mislaid his Majority* (London: Politico's, 2005).

of the House of Commons, with 49 Labour MPs voting, against the government line, for pre-charge detention in connection with a terrorist offence to be capped at 28 days (instead of 42 days as the government would have preferred—or, indeed, instead of 90 days as the government had initially proposed). The government would have suffered a further defeat but for concessions it made to the drafting of the offence under what became section 1 of the Terrorism Act 2006, the offence of 'encouragement of terrorism'.

IV. Case-Study: the Counter-Terrorism Act 2008

One significant difference between the Terrorism Act 2006 and the Counter-Terrorism Act 2008, on the one hand, and the Anti-terrorism, Crime and Security Act 2001 and the Prevention of Terrorism Act 2005, on the other, is that the 2006 and 2008 Acts were not introduced as emergency measures. Whereas the 2001 and 2005 legislation was rushed through Parliament, the bill that became the 2006 Act spent five months in Parliament and the bill that became the 2008 Act spent ten months in Parliament. This marks an important change. The most recent counter-terrorism legislation has not been urged upon Parliament by a panicked government seeking immediately and in the heat of the moment to respond to the latest atrocity. This had been the pattern long before the Anti-terrorism, Crime and Security Act was introduced in the wake of '9/11'.[49] There is no guarantee, of course, that the government will not revert to this pattern once again in the future but, for the time being, the current approach is as set out by the Home Secretary (John Reid) in a statement to Parliament made in the last weeks of the Blair government in June 2007. The Secretary of State explained that it was the government's 'intention, wherever possible, to proceed to build national consensus on national security' and that it would seek 'cross-party and cross-Parliament support' for the measures it proposed to introduce. To this end, he promised 'extensive consultation before any legislation is introduced'.[50] It is to the government's credit that it did not waver from this path in the wake of the terrorist attack on Glasgow airport in 2007.

In his statement to Parliament, the Secretary of State announced that he intended later in the year to introduce fresh legislation concerning a variety of aspects of counter-terrorism policy. He signalled that one aspect under active consideration within government was the 28-day limit on pre-charge detention enacted under the Terrorism Act 2006. It will be recalled that the government had wanted this limit set at 42 days. Mr Reid indicated that the government would once again seek to have the limit extended. The Joint Committee on Human Rights (JCHR) immediately embarked on an inquiry into this and other related matters, publishing a lengthy report at the end of July 2007. This would turn out to be the first of a series of six reports the JCHR would publish on the government's policies that led

[49] Previous examples include the Prevention of Terrorism (Additional Powers) Act 1996 and, of course, the Prevention of Terrorism Act 1974 itself.
[50] HC Debs, vol 461, col 421, 7 June 2007.

to, and were contained in, the Counter-Terrorism Act 2008. It is on these reports, and on the parliamentary debates they fed into, that we will focus in this section of this essay—they provide the core of our case-study of parliamentary scrutiny of government actions, policies, and decisions in this area.

Before we come to this, however, two final preliminary observations need to be made. The JCHR was not the only parliamentary committee to conduct inquiries into and to draw up reports on the Counter-Terrorism Act 2008. The House of Lords Select Committee on the Constitution published a report on the implications of the Act for relations between ministers, Parliament, and the judiciary, an area of constitutional practice that is of ongoing importance, in the view of that committee.[51] The Home Affairs Committee of the House of Commons published a detailed report (along with considerable accompanying evidence) that focused mainly on the '42 days' issue of pre-charge detention.[52] And the Justice Committee of the House of Commons published a short report on a measure, contained in the bill but withdrawn from it before it was enacted, concerning coroner's inquests.[53] Our primary focus here on the work of the JCHR is not intended to underplay the significance of other committees' work in this area. It should certainly not be thought that the JCHR is the only parliamentary committee to be seriously engaged in the scrutiny of counter-terrorism and national security policy.[54] Secondly, it should also be pointed out that the JCHR's work in the area of counter-terrorism was not limited in 2007–8 to scrutiny of the policies that led to and that were contained in the 2008 Act. On the contrary, the JCHR is a remarkably energetic committee, which undertakes a formidable workload, and not only in this area. At the same time as it produced its six reports on the Counter-Terrorism Bill, it also published a (deeply critical) report on the annual renewal of the control orders legislation[55] and another (similarly critical) on the annual renewal of the 28 days limit to pre-charge detention as enacted under the Terrorism Act 2006.[56] Space precludes a detailed discussion of these reports here but a full appreciation of the JCHR's work in the field of counter-terrorism would include consideration of these reports as well as an assessment of the reports on which we can now focus.

The six reports are as follows. For ease of reference we will refer to them as 'JCHR 1', 'JCHR 2', 'JCHR 3', and so on. The first three reports included the publication of extensive written and oral evidence.

- 'JCHR 1': 19th report of 2006–7, *28 Days, Intercept and Post-charge Questioning*, HL 157, HC 396, 30 July 2007;

[51] HL (2007–8) 167. See the committee's main report on this issue at HL (2006–7) 151. After this chapter was drafted, I was appointed legal adviser to the House of Lords Constitution Committee. This chapter is written in a purely personal capacity and is not to be taken as representing the view of any member, committee, or officer of the House of Lords.

[52] HC (2007–8) 43.

[53] HC (2007–8) 405.

[54] In November 2008, for example, the Home Affairs Committee of the House of Commons announced a major new inquiry into 'Project CONTEST—The Government's Counter-Terrorism Strategy'.

[55] HL (2007–8) 57; HC (2007–8) 356.

[56] HL (2007–8) 132; HC (2007–8) 825.

- 'JCHR 2': 2nd report of 2007–8, *42 Days*, HL 23, HC 156, 14 December 2007;
- 'JCHR 3': 9th report of 2007–8, *Counter-Terrorism Bill*, HL 50, HC 199, 7 February 2008;
- 'JCHR 4': 20th report of 2007–8, *Counter-Terrorism Bill*, HL 108, HC 554, 14 May 2008 (see also government response: JCHR 24th report of 2007–8, HL 127, HC 756, 26 June 2008);
- 'JCHR 5': 21st report of 2007–8, *42 Days and Public Emergencies*, HL 116, HC 635, 5 June 2008 (see also government response: JCHR 24th report of 2007–8, HL 127, HC 756, 26 June 2008);
- 'JCHR 6': 30th report of 2007–8, *Counter-Terrorism Bill*, HL 172, HC 1077, 8 October 2008.

Examination of these reports reveals that the JCHR had seven main areas of concern with regard to the implications for human rights of the government's proposals. These can be summarized as follows:

- that the government had not established the necessity of increasing the maximum length of pre-charge detention for terrorist offences from 28 days to 42 days and, further, that there was a good deal of evidence that such a move was not necessary;
- that the rule of law preventing the use in criminal trials of evidence derived from the interception of communications should be relaxed;
- that the government's proposals to allow post-charge questioning in terrorist cases should be welcomed, but that the proposals needed to be supplemented with various procedural safeguards;
- that the apparent lowering of the threshold test for charging an offence (from 'realistic prospect of conviction' to 'reasonable suspicion that the suspect has committed the offence') should be welcomed but should be placed on a statutory footing;
- that various aspects of the control orders regime were deeply unsatisfactory and should be amended as a matter of urgency;
- that bail should be made available in some terrorist offences;
- that the inclusion, late in the development of the bill, of a new provision empowering the Secretary of State to certify that a coroner's inquest should, in the interests of national security, be held without a jury, was unwarranted, was contrary to the government's stated approach of proceeding only after consultation, and should be dropped.

We will examine these in detail below but, before doing so, it may be worth summarizing the outcome. With regard to the first (moving from 28 to 42 days), the government lost, when its proposal was so comprehensively defeated in the House of Lords that the government abandoned its proposal. On intercept evidence, the Home Secretary announced in his June 2007 statement that he would commission a review of this matter on Privy Council terms. While the review (the *Chilcot Review*[57]) was published in early 2008, its recommendations, broadly in support of the JCHR's view that the current ban on the use of intercept as evidence should be relaxed, were not implemented in the 2008 legislation, much to the JCHR's disappointment. On post-charge questioning, the government's proposals were enacted. Some, but not all, of the safeguards proposed by the JCHR were enacted. On the lowering of the threshold test for charging in terrorist offences, the JCHR was unsuccessful in insisting that this be placed on a statutory footing. On reforming the control orders regime, the JCHR lost. As we shall see, one of the principal arguments used against the JCHR by the government was that in *JJ* and *MB* the House of Lords had not found the legislative scheme to be incompatible with Convention rights, on either substantive or procedural grounds.[58] This is a fascinating example of the government using a weak judicial decision to legitimate illiberal policy and effectively to close down parliamentary debate. We return to this issue below. The JCHR's proposals regarding the (non-)availability of bail for terrorist offences were not implemented. Finally, the controversial provisions regarding coroner's inquests were dropped from the bill. They were subsequently re-introduced in the Coroners and Justice Bill, but were again withdrawn from that measure before it was passed and do not appear in the Coroners and Justice Act 2009.

In terms crudely of *outcomes*, then, the JCHR was only partly successful. But, as Janet Hiebert has argued, this should not be our only measure of the achievements of parliamentary scrutiny. It is the *influence* which the JCHR may have, and its ability to *raise awareness* of issues concerning human rights, that we should additionally focus on. If the JCHR makes ministers or officials 'more sensitive to the need to evaluate their own proposals and to justify their assumptions in terms of rights',[59] it will have achieved some measure of success. Likewise, if its reports 'reflect and stimulate rights-based interventions by others', its work will have been worthwhile.[60] What we are assessing when we examine the work of a committee such as the JCHR is the extent to which it helps to foster and facilitate informed parliamentary scrutiny, so that when Parliament legislates in a manner that affects human rights it does so as fully as possible in the *knowledge* that this is what it is doing.

(a) Pre-charge detention: 42 days

The JCHR was clear throughout its reports that any further extension of pre-charge detention beyond the 28 days permitted under the Terrorism Act 2006 could be justified only if the government showed that it was strictly necessary.[61] It should not be forgotten that the 28-day limit is already exceptional. The normal limit on pre-charge detention in English criminal law is 24 hours, which may be extended on the authority of a superintendent to 36 hours and on the authority of a magistrate

[57] Cm 7324.
[58] See above, text at n 15.
[59] Hiebert, above n 45, 27.
[60] Ibid.
[61] See eg JCHR 1, para 52.

to 96 hours.[62] The latter limit, in the words of Bradley and Ewing, is for 'extreme cases' only.[63] Under the Prevention of Terrorism Act 1974 pre-charge detention in connection with a terrorist offence could be extended to five days. Under the Terrorism Act 2000 this was increased to seven days. Under the Criminal Justice Act 2003 the limit was further extended to fourteen days. And, as we have seen, this was doubled to 28 days in 2006. Thus, we moved from the government being content in 2000 with a maximum of seven days' pre-charge detention for terrorist offences to the government in 2006 urging a limit of 90 days, more than *twelve times* the maximum length allowed for under the Terrorism Act as it was enacted in 2000! In this context perhaps it is not surprising that the JCHR insisted that a further increase could be justified only if it could be shown to be strictly necessary.

The first task the JCHR set itself, therefore, was to discover and examine the evidence. To this end the JCHR obtained a detailed breakdown from the police of the use that had been made since 2006 of the 28-day limit and it asked the Commissioner of the Metropolitan Police for his views. He replied to the committee that 'There is currently no direct evidence to support an increase in detention without charge beyond 28 days...'.[64] This statement, and the fact that it was not contradicted by Home Office ministers when they gave evidence to the committee, led the JCHR to conclude that the extension from 28 to 42 days was not justified, as it had not been shown to be necessary.[65] This was the JCHR's conclusion in July 2007, expressed in a report which, as we saw above, was in large part designed to respond to the policy announcements of John Reid as Home Secretary in the final days in the Blair government.

Six months later, with Gordon Brown as Prime Minister and Jacqui Smith as Home Secretary, the Home Office published a further document confirming its plan to introduce in the forthcoming Counter-Terrorism Bill provisions to extend the maximum length of pre-charge detention to 42 days.[66] The change of personnel in government clearly did not mean that there would be any change in policy, at least not in this area. At this point both the JCHR and the House of Commons Home Affairs Committee launched further inquiries into the policy and published further reports. Evidence obtained by these committees established that the Metropolitan Police Commissioner was not alone in his view that the necessity of the increase to 42 days had not been made out. The Director of Public Prosecutions (DPP), when pressed by the Home Affairs Committee, conceded that he was satisfied with the 28-day limit and was not asking for an increase.[67] Likewise, Lord Goldsmith, who had until June 2007 been the Attorney General, stated that during his period of office he had seen no evidence that 28 days was insufficient.[68] Evidence to the JCHR from the Crown Prosecution Service (CPS)

[62] Police and Criminal Evidence Act 1984, ss 41–4.
[63] A. W. Bradley and K. D. Ewing, *Constitutional and Administrative Law*, 14th edn (London: Longman, 2007), 491.
[64] JCHR 1, para 47.
[65] JCHR 1, para 52.
[66] Home Office, *Pre-Charge Detention of Terrorist Suspects* (Dec 2007).
[67] HC (2007–8) 43, para 33.
[68] Ibid, para 34.

was in identical terms. The Head of the Counter-Terrorism Division at the CPS told the JCHR 'quite robustly' that she had never found the current 28-day limit on pre-charge detention too restrictive: 'we think the 28 days has been sufficient in each case that we have had. We have not seen any evidence that we have needed beyond 28 days.'[69] The JCHR rightly described this evidence as 'devastating to the Government's case for an extension'.[70]

This was so, the JCHR insisted, notwithstanding the fact that the government had subtly changed the nature of its argument. By December 2007 the government was not claiming that *experience* proved an extension to 42 days necessary. It was instead insisting that the terrorist threat was so great—and was *increasing*—such that a precautionary or prudential approach required that the limit be raised from 28 to 42 days.[71] Neither the JCHR nor the Home Affairs Committee were fooled, however. The Home Affairs Committee quoted Lord Goldsmith's apparent dismissal of the government's new approach. The former Attorney General stated that the question is 'Is it necessary to do this?', not 'Might it be helpful to do this?'. The civil liberties context of this area of policy-making required this approach, he suggested.[72] As we have seen, the JCHR strongly agreed with this and, throughout its reports, insisted that the only test was one of strict necessity.

Furthermore, in a forensic analysis, the JCHR showed that the government's claim that the terrorist threat was increasing was neither consistently nor convincingly made out, casting further doubt on the appropriateness of the government's use of the precautionary principle.[73] This is a remarkable achievement and serves significantly to distinguish the work of the JCHR from most of the case law in this area. Courts are generally very strongly inclined to defer to the government's assessment of the level of threat. Such is reconfirmed, for example, by the judgments both of the House of Lords and of the European Court of Human Rights in the *Belmarsh* case.[74] Both courts, the ECtHR unanimously, held that the United Kingdom government had acted lawfully and appropriately in deciding that there was a 'public emergency threatening the life of the nation'. This, despite the fact that the evidence in support of this view, as Lord Hoffmann made clear in his lone dissent, is absurdly thin. The JCHR, to its enormous credit, is not so blithe. Neither is it at all deferential on this point. Its sole concern is with the evidence. And the evidence, much of it obtained by the JCHR itself, either in oral hearings or in correspondence, did not support the view that the threat had increased or was increasing.[75] When the Director General of the Security Service gave a lecture

[69] JCHR 2, para 41.

[70] Ibid, para 43. The Home Affairs Committee agreed, stating that 'Neither the police nor the Government have made a convincing case for the need to extend the 28-day limit': HC (2007–8) 43, para 70.

[71] See JCHR 2, paras 10 ff.

[72] See HC (2007–8) 43, para 40.

[73] JCHR 2, paras 24–33.

[74] This said, a number of counter-examples are beginning to emerge, at least in the lower courts: see Tomkins, above at n 14.

[75] See JCHR 2, para 27, citing ministerial evidence as well as evidence from the police.

in which he suggested that the threat was increasing, the JCHR wrote to him, inviting him to give evidence to the committee. He declined to do so. Instead of the JCHR caving in and meekly accepting the government's (and MI5's) assertions, the JCHR publicized the fact that what MI5 was saying in public was not supported by the evidence and repeated its complaint that there remain too few opportunities for parliamentary scrutiny of the government's and the security service's assessment of the level of threat. In a conclusion containing not a hint of deference, the JCHR robustly stated that 'We have not seen any evidence to suggest that the level of threat from terrorism has increased...'.[76] Thus is the refrain of the JCHR repeated: if the government wishes to increase the maximum length of pre-charge detention for terrorist suspects, it must publicly demonstrate the evidence which shows this to be necessary; and this is so irrespective of whether the government's case is based on past experience or future fears. If the threat is such that 42 days' detention is needed, this must be explained and the explanations tested. Mere assertion will not suffice.

Another strength of parliamentary scrutiny that is not generally shared by judicial review is that Parliament has the in-built ability repeatedly to return to the same subject (whereas courts are dependent on litigants bringing cases before them). The JCHR, again to its considerable credit, made the most of this opportunity and repeated its forthright approach to and recommendations concerning 42 days throughout the period that the measure remained before Parliament.[77] In this way the JCHR was able to keep the matter alive, making it impossible for the government to do as if the problem had somehow gone away. This is the nature of parliamentary politics—those able to wage a war of attrition are liable to be more effective than those who hunt headlines by scoring dramatic but one-off victories. And effective the JCHR certainly turned out to be on this issue. Its reports were heavily relied upon in debates on the bill in both Houses. In the Commons the government won the key division but with a massively reduced majority.[78] In the Lords the government lost so overwhelmingly that, instead of fighting on, the government simply gave up and abandoned its 42-days policy entirely.[79]

We have dealt with the JCHR's principal concern with regard to the maximum length of pre-charge detention. But the (lack of an) evidence base for the need to increase this to 42 days was not the committee's sole concern. It was additionally concerned with the safeguards, both judicial and parliamentary, that attend the use of extended detention in practice. The JCHR was particularly concerned at the way in which judicial oversight had been limited. As the committee explained:

On an application by the police for extended detention, the court must ask two questions: first, are there reasonable grounds for believing that further detention is necessary

---

[76] JCHR 2, para 33.
[77] See eg JCHR 3, para 10; JCHR 4, para 8; JCHR 5, paras 2, 9, and 45; and JCHR 6, paras 23, 24, and 86.
[78] HC Debs, vol 477, cols 312–422 (11 June 2008). The vote in the Commons was 315 to 306, a government majority of nine. Thirty-six Labour MPs voted against the government.
[79] HL Debs, vol 704, cols 491–544 (13 Oct 2008). The vote in the Lords was 309 to 118 against the government.

to preserve relevant evidence; and, second, is the investigation being conducted diligently and expeditiously. Neither of these questions goes to the substantive question of whether there is material giving reasonable grounds to believe that the suspect has committed a terrorism related offence. There is no onus on the police to satisfy the court of the basic premise of the suspect's detention.[80]

As the JCHR noted, the inadequacy of this process was underscored by the fact that three suspects arrested in August 2006 in connection with an alleged airline bomb plot were judicially authorized to be detained for up to 28 days yet were eventually released without charge at the very end of that period.[81] For these reasons the JCHR recommended that 'there should be a full adversarial hearing before a judge when deciding whether further pre-charge detention is necessary'.[82] No such amendment was made by the Counter-Terrorism Act, as all the provisions concerning pre-charge detention were withdrawn from the bill following the government's defeat on the 42-days issue in the House of Lords.[83]

(b) Intercept evidence and criminal procedure

While the interception of communications is very widely employed in the United Kingdom as a means of acquiring intelligence, statute currently prohibits its use as evidence in criminal trials. Section 17 of the Regulation of Investigatory Powers Act 2000 (RIPA) provides that

> no evidence shall be adduced, question asked, assertion or disclosure made ... for the purposes of or in connection with any legal proceedings which (in any manner)—(a) discloses ... any of the contents of an intercepted communication ...

Momentum has been building for some time behind the idea that this ban on the use of intercept as evidence is 'one of the principal obstacles to bringing more successful prosecutions of people suspected of involvement with terrorism'.[84] Exceptions are made for proceedings before certain tribunals, including the Special Immigration Appeals Commission (SIAC) and the Proscribed Organisations Appeal Commission (POAC), so the rule is not absolute.[85] Nor does the rule apply to evidence deriving from the interception of communications by foreign agencies in countries other than the UK. The reason for the rule is not that there is in principle any objection to the use of intercept as evidence. It is, rather, that allowing intercept to be used as evidence entails risks to national security and to the operational effectiveness of interception as an intelligence tool, and also entails potentially significant resource implications for the security and secret intelligence services.[86]

---

[80] JCHR 1, para 60.
[81] Ibid.
[82] Ibid, para 59. See further JCHR 2, paras 64–100, especially the detailed recommendations at para 89.
[83] With one (very) minor exception: see Counter-Terrorism Act 2008, s 82.
[84] JCHR 1, para 107.
[85] Regulation of Investigatory Powers Act 2000, s 18.
[86] *Chilcot Review* (Cm 7324, 2008), para 5.

In 2006 both the JCHR and the Home Affairs Committee of the House of Commons recommended that the rule should be relaxed.[87] Both committees repeated this recommendation the following year, in both cases in strongly worded terms. The JCHR, having secured evidence from the Director of Public Prosecutions and from the Attorney General that relaxing the rule would be 'very beneficial' (as the Attorney General put it), described this evidence as putting the matter

beyond doubt:... the ability to use intercept as evidence would be of enormous benefit in bringing prosecutions against terrorists in circumstances where prosecutions cannot currently be brought,... the current prohibition is the single biggest obstacle to bringing more prosecutions for terrorism.[88]

The Home Affairs Committee stated that it considered it 'ridiculous that our prosecutors are denied the use of a type of evidence that has been proved helpful in many other jurisdictions'.[89] In November 2006 the former law lord, Lord Lloyd, introduced as a private member's bill the Interception of Communications (Admissibility of Evidence) Bill. The Bill, if enacted, would have relaxed the rule in RIPA s 17. Expressly relying on the DPP's evidence to the JCHR Lord Lloyd argued that the case for the law to be changed was 'overwhelming'.[90] In April 2007 the House of Lords, on an amendment moved by Lord Lloyd, amended the Serious Crime Bill to allow for the admissibility of intercept evidence in cases involving serious crime. The amendment was subsequently reversed in the Commons. Beyond Parliament, campaign groups such as JUSTICE, Democratic Audit and Liberty have each argued that the ban should be lifted or relaxed.[91]

Why all this disquiet? The government has repeatedly stated that its preferred method of tackling terrorism is through the criminal courts.[92] Terrorism is, of course, a criminal offence.[93] Mere membership of a proscribed (terrorist) organization is an offence punishable by up to ten years' imprisonment.[94] Fund-raising for terrorist causes is a criminal offence.[95] Possessing an article for 'a purpose connected with' terrorism is a criminal offence punishable by up to ten years' imprisonment.[96] Engaging in 'any conduct in preparation' for committing or assisting

---

[87] JCHR: HL (2005–6) 240; HC (2005–6) 1576. Home Affairs Committee: HC (2005–6) 910.

[88] JCHR 1, para 126.

[89] HC (2007–8) 43, para 86.

[90] See JCHR 1, para 122. Lord Lloyd first recommended that the rule be reconsidered as early as 1996, in his *Inquiry into Legislation against Terrorism* (Cm 3420, 1996).

[91] See JUSTICE, *Intercept Evidence: Lifting the Ban* (2006); Democratic Audit, *Evidence for Change: Lifting the Ban on Intercept Evidence in Court* (2007); Liberty, *Memorandum of Evidence to JCHR* (2007)—published at JCHR 1, Ev 86. See further, JUSTICE, *Secret Evidence* (2009).

[92] This view is widely shared, including by the DPP and the Head of the Metropolitan Police Counter-Terrorism Command: see JCHR 1, paras 11–12.

[93] The Terrorism Act 2000, s 56 provides that 'A person commits an offence if he directs, at any level, the activities of an organisation which is concerned in the commission of acts of terrorism'. Persons convicted of this offence may be imprisoned for life.

[94] Terrorism Act 2000, s 11.

[95] Ibid, s 15.

[96] Ibid, s 57. On the scope of this offence and of the burdens of proof associated with it, see *R v G; R v J* [2009] UKHL 13.

another to commit a terrorist act is a criminal offence punishable by life imprisonment.[97] Training terrorists is a criminal offence.[98] Even 'encouragement of terrorism' is now a criminal offence, punishable by up to seven years' imprisonment.[99]
It is to be noted that not very much needs to happen before these offences are
committed. Relying on the criminal law does *not* mean that the state has to wait
for a terrorist atrocity to kill and maim before it can act. Of course the state will
endeavour to disrupt as much terrorist activity as possible before it occurs. Such is
the principal task, in this area, of the security and secret intelligence services. And
such is the principal reason for intercept—it is used as a means whereby the security and secret intelligence services can disrupt terrorist activity. But the two means
at the state's disposal—disruption on the one hand and securing criminal convictions on the other—are not mutually exclusive, particularly given the nature of the
criminal offences which Parliament has legislated for in this area. Nor should it be
overlooked that these various 'preparatory' offences are *serious* criminal offences,
punishable by very long terms of imprisonment.

   Yet, as we have seen, contemporary counter-terrorist strategy in the United
Kingdom has sought to rely not only on the criminal law, but also on a range of
extraordinary executive powers, most notably indefinite detention without trial,
control orders, and extended pre-charge detention. And, whenever such powers
are introduced by the government, the reason for their introduction is always the
same: namely, that we cannot rely on the criminal law alone, not least because of
the difficulty of securing convictions.[100] And why is it so difficult to secure convictions? Not least because of the prohibition on using intercept as evidence!

   To relax this prohibition is not the only means available to make it easier to rely
on the criminal justice system in cases of terrorism (and thereby to lessen the need
for extraordinary measures, such as control orders and the like). As such, arguments about intercept as evidence need to be seen alongside debates concerning
other reforms to criminal justice. Two such are particularly pertinent here: allowing post-charge questioning and lowering the threshold for charging in terrorist
cases. Both of these were welcomed by the JCHR. As to the former, it stated that
'human rights law presents no obstacle in principle to the relaxation of the current
restriction on post-charge questioning'.[101] The committee was anxious, however,
that any new power of post-charge questioning be accompanied by adequate procedural safeguards. Accordingly, it recommended the following: that post-charge
questioning be authorized judicially; that the purpose of post-charge questioning
be confined to questioning about new evidence; that the total period of post-charge
questioning be limited to no more than five days in aggregate; that the accused's
lawyer always be present during post-charge questioning; and that there should

----

   [97] Terrorism Act 2006, s 5.
   [98] Ibid, s 6.
   [99] Ibid, s 1.
   [100] As the JCHR reported (JCHR 1, para 116), with regard to indefinite detention without trial,
to control orders and to increased pre-charge detention, 'in each case the government has repeated its
preference for criminal prosecution, but has cited evidential difficulties as one of the main justifications for its exceptional measures'.
   [101] JCHR 3, para 24.

be no further questioning once a trial has actually commenced.[102] Some, but not all, of these safeguards were written into the Counter-Terrorism Act. Others may follow in the code of practice on post-charge questioning that is to be issued by the Secretary of State.[103] Thus, the requirement for judicial authorization has been written into the statute,[104] as have limits as to the duration of post-charge questioning.[105] On the lowering of the threshold for charging in terrorist cases (from 'realistic prospect of conviction' to 'reasonable suspicion that the suspect has committed an offence') the JCHR was equally positive. Its concern was that instead of leaving this to largely unregulated prosecutorial discretion, it should be placed on a statutory footing.[106] The JCHR was unsuccessful in this regard.

Allowing post-charge questioning and permitting the threshold for charging to be lowered in terrorist cases are important measures but it remained the case that the JCHR saw them as additional to and not as substitutes for the core issue of relaxing the ban on the use of intercept as evidence in criminal trials. As we saw above, the government announced in June 2007 that the prohibition on the use of intercept as evidence would be reviewed by a small cross-party group of Privy Counsellors. This move was welcomed by the JCHR, who noted the 'growing frustration at the lack of progress on this issue in the face of steadily mounting evidence' that it required urgent reconsideration.[107] The Privy Counsellors, chaired by Sir John Chilcot, reported in January 2008.[108] Their report concluded that the ban on intercept as evidence should be substantially relaxed, albeit that certain procedural safeguards would need to be legislated for so as to minimize the risks to national security and to the operational effectiveness of intercept as intelligence. The Counter-Terrorism Bill was introduced in the House of Commons that same month. Despite the bill's ten-month progress through Parliament, the opportunity was not taken to amend the legislation so as to implement the changes to the law that Chilcot advocated. The JCHR recorded that it was 'extremely disappointed'[109] about this failure but, in its subsequent reports it did not return to the issue, focusing not on the bill's omissions, but on what was included in it. The Counter-Terrorism Act 2008 is not wholly silent on the use of intercept as evidence. It enacts two modest exceptions to the rule (which run additionally to those which already existed[110]): namely, that intercept evidence may be used in 'financial restrictions proceedings'[111] and in public inquiries.[112] But these are small exceptions to the

---

[102] Ibid, para 37. See also JCHR 4, paras 57–66.
[103] Counter-Terrorism Act 2008, s 26.
[104] Ibid, ss 22 (England and Wales), 23 (Scotland), and 24 (Northern Ireland).
[105] Ibid. The Act imposes a 48-hour limit but this can be judicially renewed.
[106] See JCHR 3, paras 74–84 and JCHR 4, paras 37–49.
[107] JCHR 1, para 107.
[108] Cm 7324.
[109] JCHR 3, para 87.
[110] See above n 85.
[111] Counter-Terrorism Act 2008, s 69. Financial restrictions proceedings are concerned with freezing orders and such matters: see Counter-Terrorism Act 2008, s 63 and Anti-terrorism, Crime and Security Act 2001, part 2.
[112] Counter-Terrorism Act 2008, s 74.

general prohibition, which remains the norm, rather than a revision of the rule as a whole.

Before we move on it is worth pausing to consider the findings and recommendations of the *Chilcot Review* in a little more detail, not least because it puts into question some of the claims made by the JCHR and others. The *Chilcot Review* was the seventh report on this matter to ministers in the past thirteen years, although it was the first to be produced by people independent of government.[113] Despite the JCHR's (and others') frustration about the lack of apparent progress on this issue, the *Chilcot Review* found that this was not the product of 'rigid, unthinking resistance to change' but was due to the failure, thus far, despite a variety of 'serious, creative efforts', to find a workable solution.[114] Part of the reason why this has proved so difficult is that intercept has become unusually important in the United Kingdom as an intelligence tool, not only in terrorist cases, but in serious crime generally. *Chilcot* reported that 'very few major criminal investigations do not involve interception'.[115] According to the Serious Organised Crime Agency (SOCA), interception is 'the single most powerful tool for responding to serious and organised crime'.[116] *Chilcot* described interception as 'a critical component of the UK's strategic intelligence capability', insisting that 'this capability is essential for national security and so must be retained and protected' and that 'any scheme for the use of intercept in evidence in criminal cases must respect this strategic imperative'.[117] *Chilcot* accepted that there was an inescapable risk that, if intercept was disclosed as evidence in court, 'a wide range of targets [may] . . . change their behaviour in ways that would make them more difficult to investigate in the future'.[118] This was further explained as follows:

> The existence of an official capability to intercept telephone conversations is not a secret. However, beyond that basic fact there has never been confirmation of what communications can be intercepted (and how) and what not (and why not). It is often suggested that criminals 'know' what the government's capabilities are. In reality, they do not know; they often presume based on partial information . . . and rumour. Some of their presumptions are right, others wrong. Many intelligence and law enforcement targets take pains to avoid interception . . . At present they cannot know which of their efforts are successful and which not. The damage from disclosure of capabilities in criminal cases would not be limited to law enforcement. Targets that threaten national security (including terrorists . . . and spies) have access to the same communications as criminals, and would quickly draw their own conclusions from revelations in the courts.[119]

For these and other reasons, *Chilcot* recommended that the following principles should govern any relaxation of the rule prohibiting the use of intercept as evidence: that the intercepting agency should decide whether a prosecution involving

---

[113] *Chilcot Review*, para 11.
[114] Ibid, para 12.
[115] Ibid, para 32.
[116] Ibid.
[117] Ibid, para 46.
[118] Ibid, para 65.
[119] Ibid, paras 66–8.

their intercepted material should proceed; that intercepted evidence originating from the intelligence agencies should not be disclosed beyond cleared judges, prosecutors and special (defence) advocates, except in a form agreed by the originator; and that such material should not be disclosed without the consent of the Secretary of State.[120]

As long as these principles were maintained, however, *Chilcot* concluded that a legal regime for the managed use of intercept as evidence, which was compliant with Convention rights, 'could be devised'.[121] Taking into account the experience of twelve other European or common law jurisdictions with more permissive regimes than under RIPA s 17, *Chilcot* examined three alternative models, recommending the further development of what it called 'PII Plus'. This model would run along the following lines: all intercepted material would be potentially admissible as evidence; agencies could decide whether or not to conduct interception to evidential standards; if they chose to do so, they would record and retain all the product; they would be required to transcribe any sections required by the prosecution and to keep minimal records of the rest.[122] Once charges had been laid, all potentially exculpatory evidence would be reviewed and, if it met the threshold for disclosure,[123] it would be disclosed subject to Public Interest Immunity (PII). Closed hearings, at which the defendant's interest would be represented by a Special Advocate, would be used to address any defence challenges to admissibility. PII would be enhanced and placed on a statutory footing, replacing the current common law. There would be a statutory bar on judges ordering the disclosure of sensitive material: instead the judge would have to stop the trial if he concluded that a fair trial was impossible.[124]

It can readily be seen that changing the law along these lines is a considerable undertaking. While the JCHR's view, that it was disappointing that the opportunity was not taken in the passage of the Counter-Terrorism Act 2008 to amend the law, is understandable, especially given the mounting frustration shared with numerous campaigners that progress on the issue had been stalled for some time, it should equally be noted that the *Chilcot Review* was far from urging the government to take immediate legislative action. On the contrary, the core of its recommendation was that its preferred 'PII Plus' required further development, and also that key stakeholders (not least those in the telecommunications industry) required considerable persuasion that allowing intercept as evidence would not compromise

---

[120] Ibid, para 91 (see also para 208). Further principles addressed the resource implications for the law enforcement, security, and secret intelligence agencies. These are potentially considerable, especially if large quantities of material are required to be kept and/or transcribed. For these reasons, *Chilcot* recommended various limitations as to what would be required to be kept and transcribed.

[121] Ibid, para 206. Two Convention rights are engaged: the right of the accused to a fair trial (Art 6 ECHR) and the right to privacy (Art 8 ECHR). The latter is of course engaged by every interception of communications, whether that interception is for reasons of intelligence, investigation, or prosecution.

[122] If they chose not to do so, but to conduct interception only for intelligence purposes, different standards of retention and recording would be required.

[123] See the Criminal Procedure and Investigations Act 1996. See further the decision of the House of Lords in *R v H and C* [2004] UKHL 3, [2004] 2 AC 134.

[124] *Chilcot Review*, paras 191–3.

their interests or the safety of their employees (who could potentially be called as witnesses for the Crown in trials of extremely dangerous and violent individuals). In short, the message of the *Chilcot Review* was that more work needs to be done. Proceed, yes, but proceed with caution.[125]

A final point to note about the *Chilcot Review* is perhaps its most surprising finding. *Chilcot* found that, despite all the agitation for reform of this area of law, it would actually be likely to make very little difference in terrorist cases. While a relaxing of the rule in RIPA s 17 may enable modestly greater numbers of successful prosecutions for non-terrorist serious crimes, there is apparently very little evidence that it would facilitate greater numbers of convictions for terrorist offences. In particular, it would seemingly make *no* difference in cases currently dealt with by control orders. *Chilcot* was shown a review of nine current or former control order cases, conducted for the Home Office by independent senior counsel. 'It concluded that the ability to use intercepted material in evidence would not have enabled a criminal prosecution to be brought in any of the cases studied.'[126] In four cases this was because there was no intercepted material capable of meeting evidential standards. In the remaining five it was because the costs to national security in disclosing the material as evidence would outweigh any potential gains offered by prosecution.

This is surely an astonishing conclusion, which can only raise serious questions about the strength of the evidence against which control orders have been obtained. It is to control orders that we can now turn.

(c) Reform of control orders

The Counter-Terrorism Act 2008 contains a small number of minor amendments to the control order regime.[127] In this respect it is a 'tidying-up' exercise.[128] The JCHR argued with passion and force that the opportunity should be taken in the 2008 Act to reform control orders more fundamentally. The government was entirely successful in its efforts to resist the changes urged by the JCHR. Of critical importance for our purposes was the use the government repeatedly made of the judgments of the House of Lords in the *JJ* and *MB* cases. One of the main reasons why the government so easily brushed the JCHR's criticisms aside—detailed and informed as they were—was because they went considerably further in their aim

---

[125] The Prime Minister accepted the findings of the *Chilcot Review* and established an Advisory Group of Privy Counsellors to take the matter forward. In December 2009 (nearly two years after the publication of the *Chilcot Review*), the Home Secretary announced in the House of Commons that this group, having developed and tested the model preferred by *Chilcot*, had found it to be operationally viable, but not 'legally viable, in that it would not ensure...fairness at court' (because it would be inconsistent with rulings of the European Court of Human Rights). The Secretary of State stated that 'these findings are disappointing' and reported that the group would continue to work in an attempt to develop an alternative solution. See HC Debs, vol 502, col 31WS (10 Dec 2009).

[126] *Chilcot Review*, para 58.

[127] The amendments, contained in the Counter-Terrorism Act 2008, ss 78–81, concern the following: a new police power to enter and search premises for the purpose of determining whether a controlled person has absconded; a clarification slightly narrowing the meaning of 'involvement in terrorist-related activity'; a provision allowing a controlled person more time to make representations; and a provision extending a controlled person's right to apply for anonymity.

[128] JCHR 3, para 40.

of protecting liberty than their Lordships had ruled was required as a matter of law. The government was able comprehensively to resist parliamentary attempts to reform the control orders regime simply by proclaiming that 'as a result of the House of Lords' judgments in October 2007, the control orders legislation is fully compliant with the European Convention on Human Rights'.[129] Thus, this aspect of our story is a compelling instance of what was probably my principal reason for being sceptical about the Human Rights Act: namely, that the government would use the weak or illiberal rulings of the courts effectively to shut down parliamentary, political, or popular debate about the ways in which government policy fails sufficiently to protect individual freedoms and civil liberties. Judicial decisions under the Human Rights Act, I feared, would be used by the government to legitimate its illiberal policies. *JJ* and *MB* are not the only instances of this. I have argued elsewhere that the *Shayler* judgment effectively prevented Parliament from re-visiting the vast extent to which the Official Secrets Act 1989 interferes with freedom of expression.[130] But *JJ* and *MB* are probably the clearest examples of this so far, because, thanks to the JCHR, it is clear what Parliament *could* have achieved had the courts been as eager to protect liberty under the Human Rights Act as the JCHR is.

Naturally, this did not go unnoticed by the JCHR and the committee's reports are replete with clearly angry remarks about how unhelpful and, indeed, misguided, their Lordships were in these cases. This applies both to the substantive issues considered in *JJ* and to the procedural matters in *MB*. Lord Brown's suggestion in *JJ* that a 16-hour curfew would not generally breach Article 5 ECHR was strongly criticized, not least because (as the politicians on the JCHR would have foreseen even if the naïve Lord Brown did not) it led directly to the government *increasing* the length of the curfews imposed in four control orders from 12 to 16 hours (out of every 24).[131] The JCHR argued that the Prevention of Terrorism Act 2005 should be amended to make it clear that a non-derogating control order could impose no curfew of more than 12 hours. This was one of many JCHR recommendations on control orders that the government swept aside on the basis that the law lords had not required such an amendment. It was not just the length of the curfew that the JCHR was concerned about: it was the way in which the House of Lords singled this issue out as being of prime importance. In the JCHR's view the court should have had regard not only to the length of the curfew, but also to 'the nature, effects and manner of implementation' of the totality of the restrictions imposed by the control order. That is to say, when considering the compatibility of any particular control order with Article 5 ECHR, the court should consider 'the cumulative effect of the obligations' and not the length of curfew alone.[132]

---

[129] JCHR 4, para 68.

[130] *R v Shayler* [2003] 1 AC 247; see A. Tomkins, *Our Republican Constitution* (Oxford: Hart, 2005), 30–1.

[131] JCHR 4, paras 82–9.

[132] Ibid, paras 84–5. This is how the Administrative Court now deals with the matter when it reviews the necessity of a control order: see the case law on control orders considered in Tomkins, above n 14.

The JCHR was even more critical of their Lordships' judgment in *MB*. In this case a majority of the House of Lords ruled that the question of whether legal proceedings in cases where a control order is challenged are fair is one that should be determined on a case-by-case basis in the light of s 3 of the Human Rights Act (that is to say, in the light of the rule that the relevant statutory framework must if possible be read and given effect in a way that makes it compatible with Convention rights). The JCHR argued that their Lordships should instead have employed s 4 of the Human Rights Act—the declaration of incompatibility. This was for the following, constitutionally significant, reasons:

> we are surprised at the Lords' interpretation of the scope of their power under s. 3 of the Human Rights Act to read words into a statute to avoid an incompatibility with a Convention right. In 2005, in the Prevention of Terrorism Act, Parliament grappled with how to strike the right balance between the right to a fair hearing and keeping sensitive information secret. It decided (against our advice) to strike that balance by placing a duty on courts in control order proceedings to receive and act on material even the gist of which is not disclosed to the controlled person. It used mandatory language to make that clear. To weaken Parliament's clear mandatory language by 'reading in' the words 'except where to do so would be incompatible with the right of the controlled person to a fair trial' does, as Lord Bingham observed, 'very clearly fly in the face of Parliament's intention' [*MB* at para 44]. The scheme of the Human Rights Act deliberately gives Parliament a central role in deciding how best to protect the rights protected in the ECHR... In our view it would have been more consistent with the scheme of the Human Rights Act for the House of Lords to have given a declaration of incompatibility, requiring Parliament to think again about the balance it struck in the control order legislation... [133]

Despite the fact that the House of Lords in *MB* did not require Parliament to think again, the JCHR was adamant that Parliament should do precisely that. Both the overall experience of the control orders regime and, critically, new evidence obtained by the JCHR in 2007 (on which more below) conclusively showed, in the JCHR's view, that fundamental reforms were urgently needed. Needless to say, the government abruptly dismissed the committee's careful and detailed work on this score, too, insisting that as the House of Lords had not required Parliament to revisit the procedural fairness of control order hearings, Parliament should leave well alone.[134]

The JCHR sought a series of reforms to due process and, in particular, to the roles of special advocates. The use of special advocates is designed to square the circle between the right to a fair trial and the need to protect public safety, a need which may frequently require sensitive information to remain undisclosed. Special advocates are appointed from a list maintained by the Law Officers to make arguments on behalf of parties who are not privy to 'closed material'. Special advocates are cleared to see closed material but, once they have done so, they are permitted no further contact either with the parties on behalf of whom they appear or with their

[133] JCHR 3, paras 46–7.
[134] JCHR 4, para 91.

lawyers. This means that special advocates cannot take instructions from their 'clients' about how to respond to information contained in closed material.[135] Special advocates are used in the United Kingdom in a variety of legal proceedings.[136] What follows here relates only to their use in proceedings concerned with control orders. In March 2007 the JCHR took oral evidence from four barristers who had acted as special advocates.[137] These barristers detailed a number of serious reservations they had about the fairness of the system. The JCHR reported that it found their evidence 'disquieting' in the way it portrayed a system which is 'very far removed from what we would consider to be anything like a fair procedure'.[138] The committee stated that it was 'left in no doubt' that the system fails to afford a 'substantial measure of procedural fairness'—the test for compatibility with Article 6 ECHR.[139]

The first main reason for the committee coming to this conclusion was that, as the system then operated, there were many control order cases in which *very* little material was disclosed to the controlee. Indeed, there were cases where *all* the relevant material was closed.[140] Where a controlee was given some material, he had no means of knowing whether it represented 1 per cent or 99 per cent of the case against him.[141] The problems this caused in practice were (and still are) compounded by the JCHR's second concern: namely, the inability of a special advocate to communicate with a controlee once he has seen the closed material. The JCHR made a series of detailed recommendations that the Prevention of Terrorism Act 2005 should be amended, as follows:[142]

(1)   the Act should make express reference to the right to a fair hearing (ie this should be clear on the face of the statute rather than 'read in' as the House of Lords ruled in *MB*);

(2)   the Act should confer on the Secretary of State a duty to give as full an explanation as possible of her reasons for the making of a control order;

(3)   the Act should confer on the Secretary of State a duty in all cases to provide the controlee with at least a summary of the material against the controlee;

(4)   special advocates should be empowered to apply *ex parte* to a High Court judge for permission to ask questions of the controlee after the special advocate has seen the closed material;

(5)   the standard of proof in control order hearings should be raised;

---

[135] This system was introduced in the United Kingdom by the Special Immigration Appeals Commission Act 1997. For an overview, see J. Ip, 'The Rise and Spread of the Special Advocate', [2008] *Public Law* 717.

[136] Including hearings before SIAC and POAC, as well as others. For a comprehensive overview, see JUSTICE, *Secret Evidence* (2009).

[137] Published at JCHR 1, Ev 10–21.

[138] JCHR 1, para 192.

[139] Ibid.

[140] Ibid, para 195.

[141] Ibid.

[142] Set out in detail at JCHR 3, paras 55–73 and JCHR 4, paras 70–1.

(6) it should become a formal pre-condition of the making of a control order that the Secretary of State be satisfied that there is no reasonable prospect of a successful prosecution for a terrorist offence;

(7) a statutory duty should be imposed on the Secretary of State to keep actively under review the possibility of prosecuting a controlee for a terrorist offence; and

(8) decisions about whether to prosecute controlees should be made more transparent by imposing a statutory duty to give reasons.

The question of the procedural fairness of control order hearings was revisited by the House of Lords after the Counter-Terrorism Act 2008 was passed: *Secretary of State for the Home Department v AF*.[143] Their Lordships' opinions in *MB* had been interpreted and applied in a number of different ways by judges in the Administrative Court.[144] *MB* was found to be unclear and confusing in a number of respects, and a clarification was required. A few days before *AF* was argued in the House, the European Court of Human Rights handed down its judgment in *A v UK* (*Belmarsh* in Strasbourg).[145] That judgment included an important ruling on procedural fairness and, in particular, on the degree of disclosure required by the state in proceedings involving special advocates and closed material. The European Court ruled that even where full disclosure was not possible by reason of national security, sufficient disclosure nonetheless had to occur such as to enable the individual 'effectively to challenge the allegations against him'.[146] The House of Lords unanimously (but in several instances clearly very reluctantly) applied this ruling to hearings concerning control orders. Lord Phillips ruled as follows: 'the controlee must be given sufficient information about the allegations against him to enable him to give effective instructions in relation to those allegations'.[147] The House found that this test had not been satisfied in AF's case and remitted the case to the Administrative Court. That court has subsequently found the test not to have been satisfied in a number of control order cases. In each instance the Secretary of State has been required to choose whether to disclose more information, in order to satisfy the requirements of procedural fairness, or to discharge the control order. In a number of cases the Secretary of State has decided that it is impossible to disclose the requisite degree of information without jeopardizing national security and has, very reluctantly, been forced to discharge a controlee.

The result of this case law is that the position is no longer quite as bad as it was when the JCHR made its recommendations outlined above. While the regime of control orders survives, at least for the time being, there is no doubt that it has become more difficult for the government lawfully to impose a control order than it was before the decisions in *A v UK* and *AF*. However, the regime does survive and, moreover, it does so in a manner in which only two of the JCHR's eight

[143] [2009] UKHL 28, [2009] 3 WLR 74.
[144] The differences are summarized in the opinion of Lord Phillips: ibid, paras 23 ff.
[145] See above n 10.
[146] Ibid, para 218.
[147] Above n 143, at para 59.

recommendations have been put into practice.[148] The decision of the House of Lords in *AF* means that the JCHR's second and third recommendations (above) have become legal requirements. Its remaining recommendations, on the other hand, have not been implemented by the government; and nor have they been required by the courts. It remains the case that the JCHR might well have been more successful in persuading Parliament that control orders proceedings required to be amended had the House of Lords not ruled as it did in *JJ* and *MB*. That story alone is sufficient to justify the conclusion that even in an area as difficult and unpromising as national security and counter-terrorism, the evidence of recent years in the United Kingdom, at least, is that parliamentary committees such as the JCHR are more committed guardians of our human rights than are the appeal courts.

---

[148] In February 2010, after taking further evidence from a number of special advocates, the JCHR reported that, even after the progress made in *AF*, the system of closed material and special advocates was still 'not capable of answering...procedural justice...': see HL (2009–10) 64, HC (2009–10) 395, para 90.

3

Governing Like Judges?[*]

Janet L. Hiebert

Since 1960 Canada,[1] New Zealand,[2] the United Kingdom,[3] and two Australian jurisdictions (ACT[4] and Victoria[5]) have given judges new authority to review legislation from a rights perspective in a way previously not countenanced in Westminster-based parliamentary systems. Although judicial remedial powers lack the capacity to declare inconsistent legislation invalid (in all jurisdictions but Canada), hopes nevertheless abound that these bills of rights will impose substantive checks on legislation that restricts rights unjustifiably. Protection is expected to occur both directly, through judicial interpretative powers to render legislation consistent with rights (Canadian courts also have the power to declare invalid legislation inconsistent with the Charter of Rights and Freedoms), as well as indirectly, through political pressure to reflect upon judicial norms when passing legislation or to introduce remedies in the face of a judicial ruling that rights are violated.

Those supporting parliamentary bills of rights tend to fall within one of two camps. One is occupied by those who are sceptical about the virtues of an American-style bill of rights that has evolved so as to give courts the final say when interpreting rights or pronouncing on remedies, but yet are optimistic that parliamentary bills of rights will tread an alternate, previously unrealized path. For these sceptics-come-optimists, this idealized path is one in which legislative decisions are justified in terms of their implications for rights, but in a manner not dominated by courts. The hope rests heavily on the structure of the bill of rights. By creating obligations for ministers to acknowledge whether and how legislative initiatives implicate rights, implementing parliamentary oversight on compatibility,

[*] I would like to acknowledge Alec Stone Sweet, whose book *Governing with Judges* inspired this title. I would also like to acknowledge the helpful comments from Andrew Geddis, Jim Kelly, Mark Tushnet, Emmett Macfarlane, Adam Tomkins, and Christine Rothmayr. Finally, I would like to acknowledge financial assistance in the form of a grant from the Social Science and Humanities Research Council of Canada.

[1] In 1960, Canada adopted a statutory bill of rights that applied to the federal government only. In 1982, it adopted the Canadian Charter of Rights and Freedoms, a constitutional bill of rights that applied to all levels of government.

[2] In 1990, New Zealand adopted the New Zealand Bill of Rights Act, a statutory bill of rights.

[3] In 1998, the United Kingdom introduced the Human Rights Act, which incorporated the European Convention of Human Rights into domestic law. The HRA came into effect in 2000.

[4] In 2004, the Australian Capital Territory adopted the Human Rights Act.

[5] In 2006, Victoria enacted the Charter of Human Rights and Responsibilities Act.

and treating judicial review as the penultimate rather than final say on whether rights have been implicated unduly, legislative outcomes are expected to reflect more principled political judgment about rights, and in a manner that does not assume judicial exclusivity or judicial domination. Stated differently, the optimistic expectation is that these new bills of rights will ratchet up the quality of decision-making by providing a different context (consistency with rights) along with introducing a new incentive (the prospect of judicial review) for public and political officials to take rights seriously in the calculations and deliberations over what constitutes good public policy decisions.

The second camp is occupied by those who are far more confident in the primacy of judicial judgment on how rights should guide or constrain state actions. The hope is not simply that judges will now look over the shoulders of politicians in the sense of reviewing legislation that has already been passed. It is both more ambitious and profound: that rights will be protected by preventing possible infringements from occurring, as contrasted with relying on after-the-fact judicial remedies for rights violations that have already happened. This preference for proactive rights contemplation takes a particular form. It has less to do with the idea that politicians will engage in philosophical debates about whether and how rights should guide or constrain legislative decisions than with the idea that legislative initiatives will be evaluated for their consistency with relevant case law. The hope, in other words, is that politicians will legislate as if judges were in the actual policy corridors at the time legislation is being developed, in the sense of anticipating and emulating judicial interpretations of rights and norms of proportionality when designing and evaluating legislation. Such intentions are not expressed quite so starkly, and instead are couched in the language of dialogue.[6] But underlying many claims about the principal benefit of a bill of rights is the expectation that judicial norms will (and should) be used both to evaluate legislative decisions already passed, as well as internalized as the standards against which all future legislative initiatives and their means are assessed.

Critics and sceptics are troubled by the substantive and normative implications of these accounts of how a bill of rights will (or should) function, and lament the movement towards a more juridical form of constitutionalism,[7] which they say will distort policy objectives,[8] transform complex moral and political conflicts into

---

[6] Supporters of bills of rights in the United Kingdom and Canada make frequent reference to dialogue, suggesting that these bills of rights will or should function in a way that allows those developing and evaluating legislation to reflect upon whether these proposed actions are consistent with judicial interpretations of rights. The Canadian version of dialogue is far more court-centric than its British or Australian counterparts. See P. W. Hogg and A. A. Bushell, 'The Charter Dialogue between Courts and Legislatures (Or Perhaps the Charter of Rights Isn't Such A Bad Thing After All)', (1997) 35 *Osgoode Hall Law Journal* 75; K. Roach, *The Supreme Court on Trial: Judicial Activism or Democratic Dialogue* (Toronto: Irwin Law, 2001); F. Klug, *Values for a Godless Age: The Story of the United Kingdom's New Bill of Rights* (London: Penguin, 2000), 179–91.

[7] For a range of sceptical perspectives, see T. Campbell, K. D. Ewing, and A. Tomkins, *Sceptical Essays on Human Rights* (Oxford: Oxford University Press, 2001).

[8] M. Tushnet, 'Policy Distortion and Democratic Debilitation: Comparative Illumination of the Countermajoritarian Difficulty', (1995) 94 *Michigan Law Review* 245; J. L. Hiebert, *Charter Conflicts: What is Parliament's Role?* (Montreal: McGill-Queen's University, 2002), ch 3.

technical disagreements about compliance with judicial norms,[9] and undermine democratic ideals of representative government.[10]

This chapter examines how bills of rights are influencing bureaucratic and legislative judgment in Canada, New Zealand, and the United Kingdom. The research was conducted as part of a larger project with James Kelly to discern how recently adopted bills of rights have changed the way legislation is conceived and evaluated, altered bureaucratic and political assumptions, and influenced legislative outcomes. The research comprised more than 150 interviews conducted between 1997 and 2009 with public and political officials who have responsibility to develop and evaluate legislative initiatives and who provide advice on questions of rights-based compatibility in Canada,[11] New Zealand, the United Kingdom, and Australia.[12]

The chapter makes four arguments. First, the degree to which a bill of rights alters or constrains legislation in Westminster-based parliamentary systems is influenced significantly by whether governments perceive there are substantial political and legal consequences for failing to comply with rights. These costs are most substantial in Canada, but are also significant in the United Kingdom, while far weaker in New Zealand. Secondly, sceptics understate the influence bills of rights exert on the Canadian and UK political systems because they focus primarily on judicial decisions that either alter or invalidate legislation that has already been passed or generate pressure for amendments to redress judicial concerns. Bills of rights have created new concerns for governments about the stability or

---

[9] T. Campbell, 'Incorporation through Interpretation', in Campbell et al, above n 7.

[10] J. Allan, 'Bills of Rights and Judicial Power—A Liberal's Quandary' (1996) 16 *Oxford Journal of Legal Studies* 337.

[11] Earlier Canadian interviews (between 1997 and 2003) were conducted for separate research projects and led to publications by J. B. Kelly, 'Bureaucratic Activism and the Charter of Rights and Freedoms: The Department of Justice and its Entry into the Centre of Government' (1999) 42 *Canadian Public Administration* 476 and *Governing with the Charter: Legislative and Judicial Activism and Framers' Intent* (Vancouver: UBC Press, 2005); J. L. Hiebert, above n 8. Subsequent interviews were conducted in the UK (2004, 2005, 2006, 2009); New Zealand (2006–7); Canada (2007), and Australia (Canberra and Melbourne 2006, 2008, and 2009). Interviews with public officials were all conducted on the basis of anonymity. From herein: interviews.

[12] Questions include: what kind of training was introduced to understand how the bill of rights relates to the department or agency's responsibilities? Was this training adequate? How has the bill of rights altered the process or considerations for assessing legislative proposals? How is the bill of rights interpreted at the departmental or agency level? Are those evaluating policy knowledgeable about the bill of rights? Do policy officials participate in judgment about compatibility? Who determines whether proposed legislation is compatible? Do lawyers dominate determinations of compatibility? Are determinations of compatibility a task that only lawyers can or should perform? How relevant is case law when determining the meaning and scope of rights? How difficult is it to determine whether a legislative initiative is consistent with case law? Does departmental guidance on compatibility change as case law changes? Is there resistance to advice about compatibility? How is resistance expressed? Would the policy process be improved if more departmental officials (non-lawyers in particular) saw their role as requiring assessments about compatibility? How much discretion is there for departments and ministers to proceed with an initiative that is inconsistent with case law? Do ministers resist advice about compatibility? Do ministers place pressure on legal advisers to alter their advice on compatibility so as to permit a positive report? Does political criticism of the bill of rights affect policy evaluation or assessments of compatibility? Will ministers claim that a bill is compatible in the face of contrary legal advice? Will a minister proceed to cabinet and sponsor a bill that would require a report of incompatibility? Do departments/ministers shop around for more favourable legal advice on compatibility?

longer-term viability of legislation and, in response, case law is being integrated in policy processes to gauge the level of risk associated with proposed legislation and to derive principles or rules to reduce that risk. Consequently, as many supporters of these bills of rights had hoped, judicial influence is being felt across a broad range of governments' legislative agendas in Canada and the United Kingdom. Thirdly, the early evolution of these bills of rights confirms Mark Tushnet's prediction that weak-form bills of rights will be unstable, and that instability occurs at both ends of the continuum, distinguishing weak from strong-form systems.[13] Fourth, optimists have misplaced confidence that parliamentary bills of rights will augment parliament's capacity to hold the government to account for legislation that implicates rights adversely. The very idea that these bills of rights would increase parliament's capacity in this way reflects a basic paradox; parliamentary bills of rights are simultaneously defended because parliament is considered too weak to force government to ensure that legislation is consistent with rights, and yet are celebrated because of the hope that parliament will play a strong rights-protecting role. But these bills of rights have not augmented parliament's powers. The remainder of the chapter addresses these arguments.

I. The degree to which a bill of rights alters or constrains legislation in Westminster-based parliamentary systems is influenced significantly by whether governments perceive there are substantial political and legal consequences for failing to comply with rights

Although a bill of rights can have significant consequences for a political system, its mere introduction does not determine the societal or institutional effects that follow. Nor does the introduction of rights-based judicial review dictate whether or how courts will influence legislation. Scholars have examined the question of why political leaders have been willing to surrender power to courts to constrain or even reverse legislation,[14] but relatively little attention has been paid to what impact a bill of rights has on the legislative process. What work has been done identifies several variables necessary for judicial decisions to influence legislation at the time it is being developed. One is suggested by Mark Tushnet: clarity in how judges articulate constitutional norms.[15] Alec Stone Sweet suggests several other variables, at least in the context of European parliaments. Judicial decisions

---

[13] Tushnet discusses the possibility of blended systems, with strong-form review occurring with respect to some constitutional issues, and weak-form review for others. M. Tushnet, *Weak Courts, Strong Rights: Judicial Review and Social Welfare Rights in Comparative Constitutional Law* (Princeton: Princeton University Press, 2008), 36.

[14] See eg T. Ginsburg and R. A. Kagan (eds), *Institutions and Public Law: Comparative Approaches* (New York: Peter Lang Publishing, 2005); R. Hirschl, *Towards Juristocracy: The Origins and Consequences of the New Constitutionalism* (Harvard: Harvard University, 2004).

[15] M. Tushnet, 'Policy Distortion and Democratic Debilitation: Comparative Illumination of the Countermajoritarian Difficulty', (1995) 94 *Michigan Law Review* 245, 261.

influence legislative decisions where (i) potential litigators believe that initiating constitutional law review is beneficial, leading to a steady case load for the court; and (ii) litigators believe that constitutional court decisions provide authoritative and therefore precedential value.[16] When these conditions occur, legislators express their policy differences in the vocabulary of constitutional judges, in that debates about the merits of policy take the form of debates about constitutional compliance. Thus, as Stone Sweet argues, 'governing with judges means governing like judges'.[17] A third variable is political concern of risk: the threat of judicial sanction, which compels legislatures to anticipate how the courts will rule, or exercise what has been referred to as auto-limitation; self-restraint by government and its parliamentary majority in anticipation of an annulment by the constitutional court.[18] A fourth variable Stone Sweet identifies, but which distinguishes European from Westminster systems, is the potential use of abstract judicial review as political strategy. Parliamentarians (usually from opposition parties) take advantage of the practice of abstract review by constitutional courts, which represents a popular and relatively cost-free way for opposition politicians to pursue their own policy objectives by pursuing judicial review that could bind the legislative majority, without the possibility for appeal.[19]

This chapter focuses on the third variable that Stone Sweet discusses, political concerns of risk, and argues that Westminster governments exercise political judgment about the political and legal costs associated with passing risky or cautious legislation (risky in terms of a realistic chance of being declared unconstitutional or incompatible, and cautious in terms of the restricted scope of the objective or the means used to achieve it in an effort to minimize the likelihood of judicial censure). But unlike European governments, Westminster governments have considerable autonomy from parliamentary pressure when determining whether and how to incorporate judicial norms into the policy process, and their judgment about whether to pursue risky or compliant legislation is only weakly influenced by parliament. Where costs are significant, bureaucratic and governmental actors have a strong incentive to protect legislation from the risk of being declared unconstitutional, incompatible, or altered through judicial interpretation, and will incorporate case law into the legislative process in order to lower the risk of judicial censure. Two factors affect the perception of costs: the willingness of courts to interpret rights and remedies broadly; and the extent to which prior judicial rulings have compelled significant legislative changes (either through rulings that directly alter or invalidate legislation or from a treaty obligation that elevates judicial rulings to the status where they cannot easily be

---

[16] A. Stone Sweet, *Governing With Judges: Constitutional Politics in Europe* (Oxford: Oxford University Press 2000), 202.

[17] Ibid 204.

[18] Ibid 75–9. Stone Sweet uses this term, which he attributes to the earlier work of Favoreu and which was also used by Christine Landfried. See Louis Favoreau, 'Décentralisation et Constitution' (1982) 98 *Revue du Droit Public* 1259–95; Christine Landfried, *Bundesverfassungsgericht und Gesetzgeber* (Baden-Baden: Nomos, 1984); and Christine Landfried, 'Judicial Policymaking in Germany. The Federal Constitutional Court' (1992) 15 *West European Politics* 50–67.

[19] Stone Sweet, above n 16, 74–5.

ignored). These costs will be amplified if political legitimacy for determining the scope of rights and how they should guide or constrain legislation resides with courts rather than parliament, but will be diminished if legitimacy resides with parliament.

Costs associated with failing to comply with judicial rulings are highest and exert the most substantial influence on legislation in Canada, but are also significant in the United Kingdom, while far weaker in New Zealand. As will be argued below, where costs are high for passing legislation that is subject to judicial censure, government will take advantage of the hegemony over the legislative process afforded to them by the workings of a Westminster parliamentary system, to insulate legislation from unwelcome policy and fiscal consequences that could accompany a negative judicial ruling. Conversely, if costs are low, government is far more reticent about constraining legislative choices because they may be inconsistent with relevant case law or rights-based claims.

(a) Canada

The incentive to incorporate case law in the legislative process as a form of risk aversion is most substantial in Canada, where the Charter gives the judiciary remedial powers that allow for the invalidation of inconsistent legislation. This was not the case under the statutory 1960 Canadian Bill of Rights, where the limited remedial power combined with a narrow judicial interpretation of rights to convey to government the message it need not worry that judicial review would constrain legislation unduly. However, within a decade of the Charter's adoption in 1982, complacency about the impact of judicial review gave way to growing anxiety about whether legislation would be challenged and, if so, whether it could be successfully defended. This shift can be attributed to several factors: a clear indication of judicial willingness under the Charter to interpret rights and remedies broadly;[20] the popularity of the Charter as contrasted with the relatively ineffective and uncelebrated status of the 1960 Bill of Rights; and the growing realization that losing Charter cases could have serious policy and fiscal consequences.[21]

---

[20] Examples of legislation declared invalid for violating rights include the criminalization of abortion without exemptions necessitated by concerns for a woman's health, procedures for evaluating refugee determination that denied an oral appeal, the ban on prisoners' voting in elections, regulations on tobacco advertising, election rules that ban the publication of polling results or require political parties to nominate a certain number of candidates during elections to be recognized as registered parties, and legislation that denied social benefits and relationship recognition for same-sex partners.

[21] A series of early decisions such as *Singh v Minister of Employment and Immigration* (which set aside Canada's refugee determination process, necessitating very costly changes); *Schacter v Canada* (in which the Court indicated it was prepared to 'read in' new meaning to legislation as a remedy for a rights violation) and *R v Oakes* (establishing what appear to be difficult criteria for justifying legislative restrictions on rights) reinforced a growing awareness within government and the bureaucracy that the Charter could be interpreted in a manner that could derail legislative priorities.

(b) United Kingdom

Assessing the incentive for political compliance with protected rights is complicated by the dual layers of judicial review (domestic and the European Court of
Human Rights (ECtHR)).

The HRA is a statutory rather than constitutional bill of rights and authorizes
more limited judicial powers than in Canada. Judges are obliged to interpret legislation 'so far as possible so as to be compatible with Convention rights' and where
such interpretations are not possible, the HRA empowers a superior court to make
a 'declaration of incompatibility' if primary legislation cannot be interpreted in a
manner that is consistent with Convention rights. UK judges cannot invalidate
inconsistent legislation, as can judges in Canada. The judicial approach taken
has been relatively meek in terms of constraining legislation. A good example is
review of the government's anti-terrorist measures. The House of Lords ruling
in the *Belmarsh* case (that indefinite detention without trial for suspected international terrorists was incompatible with liberty under Article 5 of the ECHR)[22]
put pressure on the government to revise its anti-terrorist regime. The government responded with a range of alternative coercive measures that provoked considerable debate about their consistency with rights (control orders authorizing
sustained periods of house arrest and other significant restrictions on liberty).[23]
The House of Lords subsequently upheld the rationale of the government's control order regime.[24] Another important example of how a narrow interpretation of
rights has reduced the impact of the HRA is on what constitutes a public authority
for purposes of HRA compliance. In 2007, the Law Lords ruled that a private care
home providing accommodation to elderly residents under contract with a local
authority was not itself exercising 'functions of a public nature' for the purposes of
the Human Rights Act 1998.[25] This ruling has serious implications for rights, particularly in light of the government's heavy reliance on contracting out the delivery
of many programmes and services.[26]

At first blush, it might be tempting to assume that the statutory rather than
constitutional status of the HRA, limited judicial powers that lack the capacity to
declare inconsistent legislation invalid, and a restrained judicial approach to interpreting the HRA would minimize bureaucratic and political concerns associated
with passing incompatible legislation, and thus reduce the incentive to incorporate

---

[22] *A v Secretary of State for the Home Department* [2004] UKHL 56, [2005] 2 AC 68.
[23] The JCHR, amongst others, has been extremely critical of claims of compatibility. See also
K. D. Ewing and J. C. Tham, 'The Continuing Futility of the Human Rights Act' [2008] *Public
Law* 668.
[24] For analysis and criticism of these decisions, see Ewing and Tham, ibid.
[25] *YL v Birmingham City Council and Others* [2007] UKHL 27.
[26] As the JCHR reported, 'the protection of human rights is dependent not on the type of power
being exercised, nor on its capacity to interfere with human rights, but on the relatively arbitrary
criterion of the body's administrative links with institutions of State.' JCHR, Session 2006–7,
Ninth Report, para 18. See also the following reports of the JCHR: Sixth Report of Session 2002–3,
Seventh Report, Session 2003–4, Nineteenth Report of Session 2004–5, Thirty-Second Report
of Session 2005–6, Ninth Report, Session 2006–7, 18th Report of Session 2006–7, and Second
Report, Session 2008–9.

case law in the legislative process so as to protect legislation from a potential negative judgment. But this assumption does not consider the consequences of appeals to the ECtHR, which interprets the scope of treaty obligations that government is expected to respect. Although the HRA lacks any obvious equivalent to the Canadian constitutional supremacy provision in s 52 or the broad judicial remedy power of s 24 of the Charter, the treaty character of the European Convention of Human Rights creates a similar presumptive expectation of compliance with judicial review as occurs in Canada.[27] Thus, as is the case in Canada, this expectation of compliance with judicial rulings discourages government from pursuing legislation that is patently inconsistent with relevant precedents or, at the very least, forces it to make difficult political calculations as to whether it is willing to incur the risks associated with passing legislation that will likely be subject to a negative judicial ruling.

(c) New Zealand

New Zealand judges have the weakest powers of all three jurisdictions. Judges are instructed that wherever an enactment can be given a meaning that is consistent with the rights and freedoms contained in the bill of rights, this 'meaning shall be preferred to any other meaning'. Judges are not formally empowered to rule that other enactments have been impliedly repealed or revoked or to decline to apply any provision considered to be inconsistent with any provision in the Bill of Rights. New Zealand also lacks a constitutional structure to encourage compliance with judicial rulings. But while legislation is not as vulnerable to judicially imposed or inspired changes as in Canada or the United Kingdom, it is not entirely immune. Like each of the other countries, legislation can and has been changed from 'rights friendly' interpretations of legislation[28] that alter the scope or effects of legislation. Yet this happens infrequently. The judiciary has been reluctant to read down or alter the scope or effects of legislation to remedy a conflict between a right and legislative intent.[29] When the judiciary has been willing to use its interpretive powers to make legislation compatible with rights, it has usually confined interpretations to those plausible in light of the statutory language used to express its legislative goals.[30] Thus, the scope of the judicial power, judicial approach taken, and the lack of a political norm of compliance

---

[27] Interviews.

[28] A. Geddis and B. Fenton, ' "Which is to be Master?"—Rights Friendly Statutory Interpretation in New Zealand and the United Kingdom' 25 (2008) *Arizona Journal of International and Comparative Law* 733.

[29] A good example is in *R v Hansen*, [2007] 3 NZLR 1. In this case, despite the court's finding that a reverse onus provision was an unreasonable limit on the right of an accused to be presumed innocent, the court did not interpret the law so as to eliminate this reverse onus effect. This contrasts with the House of Lords' willingness to alter legislative intent to remedy a reverse onus provision in UK Law in *R v Lambert* [2002] 2 AC 545 (HL). For discussion, see Geddis and Fenton, above at n 28, 749–54.

[30] *R v Phillips* [1991] 3 NZLR 175 (CA); *Police v Curran* [1992] 3 NZLR 260 (CA); *Quilter v Attorney-General*, [1998] 1 NZLR 523 (CA), as referred to by Geddis (chapter in this book).

with judicial rights rulings minimize the costs of passing inconsistent legislation and make it relatively easy for government and parliament to operate as if rights impose minimal constraints on their decisions.

II. Sceptics underestimate the extent or breadth of judicial influence on legislation

This argument flows from the preceding one. Concerns that a negative judicial ruling could have substantial policy and fiscal consequences, and high expectations of compliance with judicial rulings, have led to significant changes to the criteria and processes for evaluating proposed legislation in Canada and United Kingdom. The implications of these changes are undervalued by a majority of scholars who focus on court decisions that alter legislation already passed.

Most scholars who focus on court rulings can provide only partial insights into how judicial review influences legislation. Notwithstanding the pressure that a judicial ruling of unconstitutionality or incompatibility exerts on governments to revise or abandon an earlier legislative decision, the more substantial way judicial decisions influence legislation is actually indirect. This influence arises from incentives to incorporate judicial norms in the complex interplay of bureaucratic and political ruminations on the policy proposals that eventually emerge as legislative bills requiring parliament's approval. Why this emphasis is so significant is that only a fraction of legislation is ever litigated, only a small portion of which rules against the government. But reliance on case law alters the norms of policy-making and has the potential to influence a broad range of government's legislative agenda.

Despite varying costs associated with a negative judicial ruling, all three jurisdictions have altered legislative processes in order to pay significantly more attention to whether proposed legislation is consistent with case law. Two incentives drive this focus on compatibility. The first is to fulfil a statutory requirement all these jurisdictions impose on the Minister of Justice (Canada), Attorney General (New Zealand), or relevant cabinet minister (United Kingdom) to report to parliament on whether legislation is compatible with their respective bill of rights.[31] In all three countries, this reporting requirement precipitates bureaucratic evaluations of proposed legislation, which are conducted by the government's legal advisers, to

---

[31] In Canada, s 4.1 of the Department of Justice Act requires the Minister of Justice in Canada (who also serves as Attorney General) to alert parliament where bills are inconsistent with the Charter. Section 7 of the New Zealand Bill of Rights Act requires that the Attorney General advise parliament when bills are not consistent with its provisions. The reporting obligation differs in the United Kingdom. Section 19 of the HRA requires the sponsoring minister of a bill of report either that it is compatible with Convention rights or that he or she is unable to make a report of compatibility. The United Kingdom reporting requirement also differs in its recognition that reports on the compatibility status of bills must be made to both houses of parliament (Canada requires a report only to the House of Commons while New Zealand is a unicameral system). What this means in the UK is that when a bill passes from one house to the other, a second statement will be required, and which must take into account earlier amendments made. The respective statements will be made by whichever minister has been given responsibility in the particular house.

allow the relevant minister to make his or her determination about compatibility. Although not technically required by their respective bills of rights, consistency with case law is interpreted as the essential condition for claiming compatibility.[32] Thus, the more broadly rights are interpreted, the greater likelihood that legislative activities will be found to conflict with rights. This is particularly significant in Canada and the United Kingdom, which have strong presumptions against making reports that acknowledge an inability to claim compatibility. The refusal (Canada) or reluctance (United Kingdom) to introduce legislation that is so patently inconsistent with case law as to require this acknowledgment triggers pre-introduction changes to reduce the necessity for the relevant minister to acknowledge that the measure is not compatible with rights (although this judgment does entail considerable discretion, as will be discussed later). New Zealand Attorneys General are far less reticent about acknowledging inconsistency and therefore advice that a bill may not be consistent with case law does not lead to the same degree of pre-legislative changes as occurs in Canada or the United Kingdom.

The second and more powerful incentive to incorporate judicial norms into the policy process is to insulate legislation from unintended changes that could result from judicial rulings. This incentive is far more significant for Canada and the United Kingdom than in New Zealand because of their considerably stronger concerns about the costs or consequences of litigation. Regardless of which political party is in power, governments are concerned about the costs of defending legislation and by the practical and political consequences of having their legislative priorities derailed by judicial review. Governments are also loath to be put in the position of expending additional political resources that would be required to mobilize policy communities and political allies to revisit a legislative goal should it be declared unconstitutional, incompatible, or altered through judicial interpretation. Bureaucratic and ministerial processes have changed for developing and approving legislative initiatives, by adopting frameworks and procedures to assess the level of risk that litigation will occur and to reduce the likelihood of litigation or at least litigation that they would likely lose. This focus on risk aversion has led to a significant increase in the role and influence of government lawyers, whose professional background looks to case law to provide the benchmark for determinations of compatibility, and who also provide advice about how to reduce the risk of litigation or the possibility of a negative judicial ruling.

(a) Canada

Apprehension about losing Charter cases has led to substantial changes in the bureaucratic and governmental processes for evaluating legislation. Proactive efforts to insulate legislation have taken two forms. One is a requirement introduced in

---

[32] This point is contested. See D. Feldman, 'Institutional Roles and Meanings of "Compatibility"', in H. Fenwick, G. Phillipson, and R. Masterson (eds), *Judicial Reasoning under the UK Human Rights Act* (Cambridge: Cambridge University Press, 2007), 99.

1991 that Charter issues be anticipated and litigation risks identified as part of the process for securing approval before an initiative can go to Cabinet for consideration. Thus, the Memorandum to Cabinet was changed to include Charter analysis in terms of 'an assessment of the risk of successful challenge in the courts, the impact of an adverse decision, and possible litigation costs'.[33] A second way this objective of protecting legislation from Charter vulnerability has been implemented is by seeking legal advice about how to lower the risk of litigation and invalidation earlier in the policy process. Pre-legislative review focuses heavily on whether legislative initiatives are likely to satisfy judicial interpretations of proportionality, and has regularly involved government lawyers in the role of advising relevant departments to seek alternative means to accomplish a legislative goal in a manner that is likely to satisfy courts.[34]

The Canadian government's legal advice is centralized in the Department of Justice. The Department established a Human Rights Law Section in 1982 to bring existing legislation into conformity with the newly adopted Charter. As the Charter has evolved, the Department of Justice's role has been transformed from providing merely 'a technical review of legislation to a substantive role in the development of new policy',[35] so much so that other departments now regularly rely on its advice in the course of developing legislation.[36] Many provincial governments, particularly in the larger provinces, have adopted procedures that similarly give emphasis to the identification of possible Charter problems,[37] but at least two former Attorneys General have questioned the desirability of a case-law-driven risk-averse approach.[38]

(b) United Kingdom

The adoption of the HRA did not initiate pre-legislative assessments of legislation in terms of public law norms. The impetus came from the UK's treaty obligation

[33] M. Dawson, 'The Impact of the Charter on the Public Policy Process and the Department of Justice', in P. Monahan and M. Finkelstein (eds), *The Impact of the Charter on the Public Policy Process* (North York: York University Centre for Public Law and Public Policy, 1993), 53.

[34] Interviews.

[35] J. B. Kelly, 'Bureaucratic Activism and the Charter of Rights and Freedoms: The Department of Justice and its Entry into the Centre of Government' (1999) 42 *Canadian Public Administration* 95.

[36] Ibid 495–6. Also see Kelly's assessment in *Governing with the Charter*, above at n 11, 232–4.

[37] Ibid 214.

[38] A. Petter, 'Legalise This: The *Chartering* of Canadian Politics', in J. B. Kelly and C. P. Manfredi (eds), *Contested Constitutionalism: Reflection on the Canadian Charter of Rights and Freedoms* (Vancouver: UBC Press, 2009), 34–49. Another former British Columbia Attorney General, Geoffrey Plant, said of this process: 'Charter compliance in the legislative process is inherently reactive, rather than proactive, as it requires government to approach policy-making from the perspective of risk analysis rather than from the perspective of broader social and economic priorities or the balancing of differing societal interests. In other words, although the question "Is this legislation Charter-compliant?" often leads to a different answer than the question "Is this legislation good public policy?", the former question often takes precedence in public policy analysis. As a result, risk management becomes the driver of the analysis.' G. Plant, 'Governing in the Shadow of the Charter', unpublished paper (Calgary: Canadian Bar Association Meeting, 1 June 2007).

to respect European Court of Human Rights jurisprudence. But while the Foreign Office used to play a prominent role in policy advice with respect to judicial review, this advice has become far more decentralized under the HRA, as public servants within and across departments have been subject to human rights training.[39] Those interviewed suggest the advice given is both more robust and systematic than before the HRA came into effect and attribute changes to the HRA's requirement that ministers report on the compatibility status of all government bills, which is claimed to have sharpened the focus, regularity, and rigour of rights-based vetting.[40]

Ultimately, the decision about whether to proceed with bills that incur high levels of risk involves political judgment; individual ministers decide how much risk to take. But even if a minister decides to pursue a legislative initiative with a high risk of being declared incompatible, he or she must ultimately secure approval from the Legislation Committee, a committee of cabinet. This requires a memorandum outlining the rights that are engaged, the legal advisers' proportionality assessment, and the reasons for concluding that a bill is compatible, if this is being claimed. The Attorney General sits on the Legislation Committee and can decide to seek or offer other advice in terms of compatibility. Once this Committee gives its approval, a statement for parliament is finalized, declaring whether or not a minister can claim compatibility, and the bill is introduced to parliament.[41]

(c) New Zealand

Like Canada and the United Kingdom, New Zealand has also changed its legislative process to require compatibility assessments of all legislative initiatives before proceeding to cabinet. Compatibility is interpreted by government lawyers in the Ministry of Justice and Crown Law as consistency with case law, both domestic and international. Government departments are expected to adhere to guidelines, published by the Legislation Advisory Committee, which include a chapter on how to identify and address human rights issues.[42] But the primary impetus for this focus on compatibility is to allow the Attorney General to meet his or her reporting obligation on compatibility rather than to insulate legislation from the consequences of a negative judicial ruling. Of the three jurisdictions, New Zealand's political process is the least constrained by expectations that legislation should be consistent with judicial interpretations of rights or legal advice about compatibility. Attorneys General from different political parties have expressed reservations about the prudence of being constrained by legal perspectives on compatibility.[43] Some go so far as to suggest that introducing legislation that would require an

---

[39] Interviews.
[40] Interviews.
[41] Interviews.
[42] Legislation Advisory Committee, 'Guidelines on Process and Content of Legislation', <http://www.justice.govt.nz/lac/pubs/2001/legislative_guide_2000/chapter_4.html> (checked 30 Apr 2009).
[43] Interviews.

acknowledgment of inconsistency can be viewed as a badge of honour, depending on the issue(s) involved.[44]

III. The evolution of these bills of rights confirms Tushnet's prediction that weak-form bills of rights are unstable

Some defenders of recently introduced bills of rights have strong expectations that a prudently constructed bill of rights is capable of changing bureaucratic, governmental, and parliamentary behaviour to bring about more principled judgment about rights. For example, when the United Kingdom's Human Rights Act was debated, then Home Secretary Jack Straw argued that incorporating the European Convention of Human Rights into domestic law would help create 'a culture of rights and responsibilities in the UK' by changing habits of mind, intellectual reflexes, and professional sensibilities of public and political authorities.[45] But this assumption that a bill of rights will alter political behaviour begs the following questions. What influence does judicial review have on political behaviour? Is robust judicial review an essential condition for government to take seriously the idea that rights constrain legislative decisions? Is parliament willing and able to force government to justify decisions from a rights perspective or amend problematic bills?

A different way of framing the above questions is the following: do parliamentary bills of rights confirm or challenge Mark Tushnet's thesis about the instability of this parliamentary or weak-court model? Tushnet characterizes parliamentary bills of rights as a weak-court model, which he distinguishes from strong-form judicial review where judicial interpretations of the bill of rights are final and unrevisable through ordinary legislative means.[46] In weak-court systems, judicial review is penultimate rather than final,[47] does not encompass the power to declare legislation invalid (Canada is an exception), and bills of rights allow parliaments to either ignore rulings the legislation is inconsistent with rights or set aside the effects through ordinary legislation.[48] Tushnet's thesis of the instability of this model is premised on the expectation that weak-court systems will mimic strong-form systems of judicial review, where courts dominate judgment about the legitimacy of legislation from a rights perspective or, alternatively, will revert back to parliamentary supremacy, where Westminster-based governments encounter weak pressures to change or justify decisions that implicate rights adversely.

---

[44] Interviews.

[45] J. Straw, 'Building a Human Rights Culture', Address to Civil Service College Seminar, 19 Dec 1999. <http://www.nationalarchives.gov.uk/ERORecords/HO/415/1/hract/cscspe.htm> (checked 22 Apr 2008).

[46] Tushnet, above at n 13, 18–42.

[47] Canada is an exception here because judicial review represents the authoritative interpretation of the Canadian Charter of Rights and Freedoms. For this reason, I quibble with the characterization of Canada as a weak-form system. See J. L. Hiebert, 'Parliamentary Bills of Rights: An Alternative Model?' (2006) 69 *Modern Law Review* 7, 10–12.

[48] In Canada this requires use of the notwithstanding clause of s 33 of the Charter.

The early evolution of these bills of rights confirms Tushnet's prediction of instability. These systems operate at both ends of the continuum distinguishing weak from strong-form systems. As argued earlier, pre-legislative processes have changed significantly to incorporate case law as a critical criterion when evaluating legislation. This has not only led to a strong form of judicial influence on Canadian and United Kingdom legislation (although far less so in New Zealand), but to a degree that likely surpasses what occurs in strong-form systems such as the United States. This statement might seem odd, particularly to those who regard the United States as a highly litigious, judicially influenced polity.

The explanation for why such strong judicial influence on legislation occurs in these weak-form systems is the juxtaposition of a bill of rights (particularly one with high costs for failure to comply) with a Westminster system. Westminster systems allow government to dominate the legislative agenda, particularly if it has a majority, which under a single member plurality electoral system in the United Kingdom and Canada is most often the case (although Canadian federal elections have recently produced minority governments and the 2010 United Kingdom election necessitated the establishment of a coalition government). Moreover, legislation does not usually arise in parliament but instead is introduced by the executive at an advanced stage of development after extensive pre-legislative evaluation, where it is then subject to debate by highly disciplined and cohesive political parties. Governments in Canada and the United Kingdom are able to take advantage of their hegemony in the legislative process to insulate legislation from unwelcome policy and fiscal consequences that could accompany a negative judicial ruling, by utilizing case law in the pre-legislative evaluation process to anticipate and avoid possible judicial objections. This is not an occasional or ad hoc occurrence but, increasingly, has become a regular and systematic part of how legislation is developed. Once legislation reaches parliament, the government generally encounters weak resistance to the influence case law has had on the shape or scope of legislative bills.

In contrast, the US Congress plays a substantially larger legislative role than Westminster parliaments. But it is a legislative role that does not pay particularly close attention to whether proposed legislation is consistent with rights or case law. Scholars have recently begun to assess to what extent, and in what ways, constitutional norms affect how Congress behaves.[49] Parallel surveys conducted over a twenty-year interval reveal that a majority of congressional respondents believe Congress 'should form its own considered judgment' on constitutional questions.[50] But this perception does not appear to have radically skewed how Congress operates. Constitutional considerations 'occasionally affect' congressional behaviour, particularly if the constitutional implications of an issue are particularly germane to a committee, address issues of importance to a particular member, or can be used by political opponents to bolster other arguments against a legislative initiative. But for the most part, constitutional issues are not

[49] See eg N. Devins and K. E. Whittington (eds), *Congress and the Constitution* (Durham, NC: Duke University Press, 2005).

[50] B. G. Peabody, 'Congressional Attitudes toward Constitutional Interpretation', in Devins and Whittington, ibid 39–63.

treated as priority concerns for Congress where decision-making is dominated by political and policy considerations.[51] Moreover, the US congressional system lacks an institutional requirement to report on compatibility when proposed legislation is before Congress, which means there is not the same incentive to conduct pre-legislative evaluations in this way (or amend proposed legislation to avoid a negative report). But even if this requirement existed, the separation of powers ensures Congress has far greater institutional capacity to amend or derail proposed legislation, thus making it difficult to ensure that legislation is consistent with case law.

In short, judicial influence in Canada and the United Kingdom is often indirect, yet its effects can be extensive and systematic, with the potential to influence a broad range of the legislation parliament passes. In contrast, judicial influence in the United States is blunt—but relatively infrequent; confined primarily to those specific circumstances that are litigated successfully, in which remedies might have the result of invalidating a law. Thus, it seems ironic that despite the fact that the United States is the epitome of what Tushnet characterizes as a strong court system, there is a greater possibility for the systematic reliance on case law when developing and defining legislation in supposedly weak-form systems such as Canada and the United Kingdom.

But parliamentary bills of rights also operate at the weak end of Tushnet's continuum. Thus, although Canadian and UK governments regularly exploit their domination over the legislative process to incorporate judicial norms into policy processes to manage risk, these same political systems occasionally retreat from the idea that rights or prior judicial decisions legitimately constrain legislation. The longer-term incentive to ensure the stability of legislation can and has taken a backseat to more immediate political calculations, such as: does the benefit of adopting measures that restrict rights but garner strong political and popular support outweigh the longer-term interest of protecting legislation from a possible negative judicial decision? How will this decision play out politically and electorally? For example, will losing a case be beneficial politically, by allowing government to claim that it was forced to adopt controversial measures? Or will support for apparent 'rights violation' harm the government's reputation? Other considerations reflect the strength of lobbying efforts in support of the legislative initiative in question and philosophical differences about what constitutes the public interest (often involving contested views about what comprises an appropriate balance between security and liberty) and what constitutes the appropriate division of labour between courts and parliament for resolving particular contested issues. Examples of these calculations leading to risky legislation include the UK's counter-terrorist measures after 2001,[52] Canada's revised rules of evidence in

---

[51] M. Pickerill, *Constitutional Deliberation in Congress: The Impact of Judicial Review in a Separated System* (Durham, NC: Duke University Press, 2004), 133–45.
[52] A. Tomkins, 'Parliament, Human Rights, and Counter-Terrorism' (Chapter 2 in this book); Ewing and Tham, above at n 23.

sexual assault trials,[53] and New Zealand's retrospective increase in the penalty for murder involving home invasions.[54]

The willingness of governments to both incorporate and reject judicial norms when developing legislation raises several questions relating to why this instability occurs. Is legal advice vulnerable to political manipulation? How much discretion does the Attorney General or relevant minister have to ignore advice about compatibility? And can parliament prevent government from pursuing legislation that might restrict rights or force it to amend contested bills?

Although ministers or the Attorney General occasionally reject the primacy of case law when advocating that legislative initiative be put forth as a bill for parliament's consideration, they are not anxious to admit that proposed legislation is incompatible with rights. This is hardly surprising. Governments have no interest in raising obstacles to passing legislation, which might occur if required to acknowledge an inability to claim compatibility. This is not as serious an obstacle in New Zealand, where the risks of negative judicial rulings are lower. But in Canada and United Kingdom, in situations of knowingly pursuing risky legislation, ministers do their best to interpret the advice they receive from their legal advisers in a way that allows a claim of compatibility to be made. The advice from the government's legal advisers is not binding and necessitates judgment about whether to proceed with legislation that has been identified as having a high degree of risk of being found incompatible with protected rights. These judgments are subject to varying degrees of political pressure, influenced by whether responsibility for providing legal advice resides with the sponsoring minister or Attorney General, as well as the political relationship between the Attorney General and cabinet.

In Canada, political responsibility for judgment on compatibility resides with the Minister of Justice, who also serves as Attorney General and is a minister of the Crown and member of cabinet.[55] Although a former deputy-minister of justice has suggested that the Attorney General would likely resign if his or her opinion on Charter compatibility was not acted upon by cabinet,[56] this position is difficult to substantiate. Moreover, it is not obviously the case that the Attorney General's view of the law can be separated from the broader partisan and philosophical character of party-political judgment about the nature and scope of rights, and how they implicate legislative objectives of cabinet (of which, the Attorney General is a key member). In the United Kingdom, individual ministers have responsibility for reaching judgment on compatibility but the ultimate government authority on these matters is the Attorney General, who is a member of the ministry but, by convention, is independent of cabinet. But the United Kingdom has recently encountered serious controversy and debate about the role

[53] Roach, above n 6; Hiebert, above at n 8.
[54] C. Archer, 'Section 7 of the Bill of Rights Act' [2004] *New Zealand Law Journal* 320.
[55] For a good discussion on some of the limitations of insufficient independence of the office of the Attorney General from cabinet, see K. Roach, 'Not Just the Government's Lawyer: The Attorney General as Defender of the Rule of Law' (2006) 31 *Queen's Law Journal* 598.
[56] Interviews.

and independence of the Attorney General.[57] In New Zealand, the Attorney General has responsibility for legal advice about compatibility and is a member of cabinet but, by convention, is not bound by cabinet solidarity on questions of the law. Like Canada, it is difficult to imagine that the Attorney General's judgment about compatibility is completely independent of the broader partisan and philosophical viewpoints of those from his or her party who form government, about how rights relate to or appropriately guide consideration of the government's policy agenda.

Quite apart from whether or to what extent the Attorney General is independent from the policy views of government, other factors explain why these judgment calls about compatibility are subject to broad discretion: (i) it is often difficult to predict the implications of earlier cases for new issues; (ii) political and ideological differences between political parties lead to different views about how protected rights implicate the role of the state, or what responsibility government has to pursue perceived social problems or address substantive inequality in power or resources; and (iii) political considerations for the resources required to mobilize policy communities and political allies to revisit an impugned legislative objective, or whether the immediate political gains of passing legislation exceed the anticipated costs if legislation is subsequently declared unconstitutional or incompatible with rights.

(a) Canada

Canadian governments have strong incentives to avoid introducing legislation that is obviously inconsistent with the Supreme Court's interpretation of the Charter. As discussed above, this has encouraged the incorporation of judicial norms in the policy process to assess and amend proposed legislation as a form of risk management. These incentives comprise the extreme popularity of the Charter, the legitimacy problems associated with the notwithstanding clause (which can be used to pre-empt or set aside temporarily judicial review of most sections of the Charter),[58] public confidence in judicial rather than political interpretations of the Charter,[59] and concerns about political reprisals and judicial consequences that would accompany the obligatory incompatibility report to Parliament should a legislative bill be introduced that is patently inconsistent with the Charter.

[57] See eg: House of Commons, Constitutional Affairs Committee, 'Constitutional Role of the Attorney General', Fifth Report of Session 2006–7, HC 306; 'The Governance of Britain: A Consultation on the Role of the Attorney General', 2007, CM 7192; Ministry of Justice, 'The Governance of Britain—Analysis of Consultations', Mar 2008, CM 7342–iii; House of Lords Select Committee on the Constitution, 7th Report of Session 2007–8, 'Reform of the Office of Attorney General', HL Paper 93.
[58] Section 33 of the Charter, the notwithstanding clause, allows provincial or federal legislatures to pre-empt judicial review or set aside the effects of a judicial ruling for most sections of the Charter on a temporary but renewable basis.
[59] Nik Nanos, 'The Charter Values Don't Equal Canadian Values: Strong Support for Same-Sex and Property Rights' (2007) 28 *Policy Options* 50.

Yet these political constraints have not prevented government from introducing legislation with a high degree of risk.[60] They have done so without reporting to parliament that proposed legislation conflicts with the Charter or invoking the notwithstanding clause.[61] A recent interview with a senior Canadian Department of Justice legal adviser suggests a pattern by the current Conservative government of ignoring legal advice on compatibility, particularly on questions of whether a new law and order political agenda is consistent with the Charter, and a willingness to claim that the proposed act is consistent with the Charter and 'let the judiciary fix it later'.[62]

Governments have also exploited the Supreme Court's loose jurisprudence on the general limitation clause of s 1 to engage in proactive interpretations of what constitutes a reasonable limit, by gambling that they can convince the court that the measure is reasonable and justified[63] or at least, to buy time before the constitutional question is resolved by the Supreme Court. Canadian governments anticipate and occasionally prepare their case in advance, by building into the legislative record evidence to support their argument should litigation occur. This can also include drafting techniques, such as legislative preambles.[64] Yet, however risky the government's initial legislative strategy, legislation is generally revised if the Supreme Court rules against the government,[65] because of a strong culture of legal

---

[60] See for example a range of legislation that addresses rules of evidence for sexual assault trials that conflict with relevant case law, as discussed by Hiebert, n 8, ch 5.

[61] The explanation for why no government is prepared to acknowledge to parliament that proposed legislation is inconsistent with the Charter has three parts. First, are the political consequences of the judiciary's power under the Charter to grant remedies when legislation constitutes an unreasonable restriction of a protected right, which include declaring legislation invalid or altering the scope or intent of legislation to redress the perceived Charter problem. Thus, if the Minister of Justice were to report to parliament that legislation violates rights in a manner that is not consistent with a 'free and democratic society' (the standard for determining Charter consistency once a prima-facie rights violation has been established), such legislation would be highly susceptible to litigation and judicial invalidation. Second, is the emergence of a political culture in cabinet decision-making that forbids the introduction of any bill that would require the Minister of Justice to report an inconsistency to parliament. Third, is that the political criterion for determining that a report to parliament *is not necessary* is sufficiently broad—whether the Minister of Justice concludes that a credible Charter justification exists—that it permits a broad range of the policy goals, even those that are highly risky. Hiebert, n 8, 12–13.

[62] Kirk Makin, 'Canadian Crime and American Punishment', *The Globe and Mail*, 28 Nov 28 2009, F1, 7, citing an anonymous 'well-connected Justice Department insider'.

[63] This was the approach taken by a Liberal government on two occasions when it strongly disagreed with judicial decisions that (i) introduced a new common law rule that evidence of extreme intoxication is relevant to the defence of sexual assault (*R v Daviault*), and (ii) allowed judges to order counsellors or others working at sexual assault centres to provide confidential records of alleged victims of sexual assault, for lawyers' use when defending their clients (*R v O'Connor*). In both cases, the government introduced legislation that clearly contradicted the relevant majority ruling. But instead of acknowledging incompatibility, or invoking the notwithstanding clause, the government advanced its view about why the legislation was consistent with the Charter during parliamentary debate, within the legislation itself (in a preamble), and in arguments in litigation that occurred in one instance. Had the Court rejected this alternative Charter interpretation, the government would likely have perceived its options as to either abandon the legislative goal or invoke the notwithstanding clause (of which the former is more likely). Hiebert, n 8, 91–117.

[64] For examples see Hiebert, n 8, 94–5, 105–6, 112–13.

[65] See Peter W. Hogg, Allison A. Bushell-Thornton, and Wade K. Wright, 'Charter Dialogue Revisited—Or Much Ado about Metaphors' (2007) 45 *Osgoode Hall Law Journal* 1.

compliance with high court rulings and extreme political reticence to enact the notwithstanding clause (which allows legislatures to set aside the effects of a negative judicial ruling for most sections of the Charter on a temporary but renewable basis).

(b) United Kingdom

In the United Kingdom, most of those interviewed indicated it is unlikely that cabinet (or more specifically, the Legislative Policy Committee) would regularly approve of a bill that required a 19(b) report (indicating compatibility cannot be claimed). On only one occasion has the United Kingdom reported an inability to claim compatibility for a government bill (political communications bill that banned political advertising), which the government defended as important for democracy and indicated that it would 'mount a robust defence' if the legislation were legally challenged.[66] But the government also suggested that should it lose the case it would have to 'reconsider' its position and amend the legislation to comply with any judgment of the European Court of Human Rights, because the government takes it 'international obligations extremely seriously'.[67]

The presumption against introducing a bill requiring a s 19(b) report necessitates ongoing discussions between policy officials and legal advisers on how to ensure legislation is compatible with Convention rights. Asked if they are ever pressured by ministers to alter their judgment on compatibility so as to allow a positive claim to be made against their judgment, government lawyers insisted this does not happen and that even if it did, they would not compromise their professional judgment. Having said this, some of those interviewed indicated that where a range of opinion exists, legal advice is often framed in a way that would permit a minister to claim that a bill is compatible.[68] Although no one admitted to having been pressured to change legal advice so as to claim compatibility, there is evidence that the Labour government was willing to claim compatibility despite receiving contrary legal advice.[69] Although the context did not pertain to compatibility for s 19 purposes (the issue was the legality of the Iraq war), the incident nevertheless raises serious questions as to whether pressure was placed on the Attorney General to abandon his independent legal judgment to support the government's position.[70]

---

[66] Tessa Jowell (3 Dec 2002), HC Debs, vol 395, col 787.

[67] Ibid, col 789.

[68] Interviews.

[69] The example is the government's claim about the legality of the Iraq war, despite consistent legal advice from its own advisers (and the initial judgment of the Attorney General) that it was not lawful to use force against Iraq without a second Security Council resolution to revive earlier authorization. <http://news.bbc.co.uk/1/hi/uk_politics/4377605.stm>; <http://www.globalpolicy.org/security/issues/iraq/attack/law/2005/0324wilmshurst.htm> (checked 8 Apr 2009).

[70] 'Was the Attorney General leant on to change his mind?', (24 Mar 2005) *The Independent*, <http://www.independent.co.uk/news/uk/politics/was-the-attorney-general-leant-on-to-change-his-mind-529761.html> (checked 8 Apr 2009); 'Revealed: Attorney General Changed his Advice on Legality of Iraq War' (29 Feb 2004) *The Independent*, <http://www.independent.co.uk/news/

The criterion for a negative report on compatibility is whether the chances are greater than not that courts will rule legislation incompatible. This has resulted in ministerial reports claiming compatibility, even in situations that legal advisers identify a high degree of risk. This is most likely to occur where the case law is not settled, or has not addressed critical issues raised by a legislative initiative. Legal advisers also acknowledge that as questions of compatibility often turn on assessments of proportionality, these assessments leave open considerable room for disagreement about whether the legislative means proposed are overly restrictive.[71] Moreover, although the government might not be willing to defy Strasbourg, the knowledge that this second level of judicial review would delay any necessary remedial response almost certainly influences political decisions about whether to pursue risky legislation. Although the UK government might introduce risky legislation, there has not been the conscious practice that occurs occasionally in Canada, of anticipating the legal defence of legislation at the time it is being developed or proceeding through parliament, such as preparing evidence or using drafting techniques to explain or attempt to justify risky legislation.[72]

(c) New Zealand

Governments across the New Zealand ideological spectrum seem willing to introduce legislation that requires a statement of incompatibility, including Labour-led and National governments. At the time of writing, more than 40 reports of inconsistency have been made, of which 25 involved government bills.[73] The restricted judicial role to grant remedies for rights violations goes a long way towards explaining the inconsistency between a legalized policy-vetting process at the bureaucratic level, and a reluctance to be constrained by the implications of ensuring compatibility (as legally interpreted) at the governmental and parliamentary levels. Moreover, parliamentary debates on bills that had reports of inconsistency reveal little sustained criticism of government for proceeding with inconsistent legislation, at least in terms of the rights dimension,[74] reinforcing the perception that the political cost of non-compliance is relatively low.

New Zealand governments appear most willing to resolve serious compatibility problems before submitting draft legislation to the House if the policy objective is particularly important to the government, rather than being part an agreement

---

uk/politics/revealed-attorney-general-changed-his-advice-on-legality-of-iraq-war-571613.html> (checked 8 Apr 2009).

[71] Interviews.

[72] Interviews.

[73] For discussion of many of these, see A. Geddis, 'Inter-institutional "Rights Dialogue" under the New Zealand Bill of Rights Act' (Chapter 5 in this book); G. Huscroft, 'The Attorney-General's Reporting Duty', in P. Rishworth, G. Huscroft, S. Optican, and R. Mahoney (eds), *The New Zealand Bill of Rights* (Melbourne: Oxford University Press, 2003); J. L. Hiebert, 'Rights-Vetting in New Zealand and Canada: Similar Idea, Different Outcomes' (2005) 1 *New Zealand Journal of Public and International Law* 63.

[74] Hiebert, ibid.

with a minority or coalition partner.[75] Since New Zealand's electoral system (Mixed Member Proportional representation) (MMP) denies the governing party the capacity to form a majority and requires agreements with one or more party to pass any particular bill, the government may not have the same level of commitment to all bills that are introduced, particularly if the measure was included to satisfy a coalition partner.[76] An example of this was the Electoral Amendment Bill 2001, in which Labour agreed to a measure supported by NZ First (to ban opinion polling prior to elections). The ban was the subject of an s 7 inconsistency report, and was eventually dropped from the bill after the Select Committee recommended not proceeding further with the measure.[77]

IV. Optimists have misplaced confidence that parliamentary bills of rights will augment parliament's capacity to hold the government to account for legislation that implicates rights adversely

Optimists who expect parliamentary bills of rights will regularly alter political judgment are insufficiently attentive to the serious paradox in how parliament's rights-protecting role is conceived. On the one hand, parliament's weakness is said to be an important reason why a bill of rights is necessary. But on the other hand, parliament is being portrayed as playing an important role in protecting rights, by pressuring government to justify or amend bills where rights are undermined. Yet apart from this reporting requirement, no substantive reforms have been passed to alter the balance of power between parliament and the executive.

There is little evidence that any of these bills of rights have altered the balance of power between government and parliament so as to enable parliament to marshal sufficient power to force government to justify or modify decisions that implicate rights adversely. Moreover, although all three jurisdictions have statutory requirements to report on the compatibility of legislative bills with rights, the idea that government should justify decisions in terms of consistency with a bill of rights represents a significant shift in the assumptions and behaviour of how a modern Westminster system operates. Westminster parliaments have a highly disciplined and adversarial political party system that orients the resolution of complex issues to two viewpoints—in favour or opposed. This framework is not conducive to principled debate on questions of rights justification.

Government dominates parliament, and regardless of which political party forms government, it will resist challenges to its abilities to control the legislative agenda. Once a government has decided on a course of action, has consulted with the various stakeholders, attempted to redress objections, addressed internal

---

[75] Interviews.
[76] 'Peters Pushing Polling Ban' (13 Mar 2001) *TVNZ* <http://tvnz.co.nz/content/32627> (checked 8 Apr 2009).
[77] Electoral Amendment Bill (No 2) 2000, no 110-2 (Select Committee report) 11.

disagreements, and has publicized its commitment in the form of a legislative bill, it is generally loath to reopen the issue, commit additional resources to defend actions that can reopen internal conflicts, or dedicate more time for debate in an often crowded parliamentary calendar. Not only do governments fear that concessions will be interpreted as a sign of weakness, but rights claims have more symbolic force than more partisan-based objections. To criticize legislation on ideological or policy grounds suggests disagreement with ideas. This is widely expected and is explained by ideological and policy differences between political parties. But to criticize legislation on rights grounds is potentially far more potent; it comes dangerously close to saying the legislation is morally suspect. In short, governments will have strong incentives to resist rights-based arguments being marshalled in a way that introduce new obstacles its policy agenda, particularly given the peremptory assumptions associated with rights.

Research in all three jurisdictions suggests that legal costs are more persuasive than parliamentary criticism when encouraging government to take rights seriously when guiding or constraining decisions. Unless parliamentary pressure is sufficient to threaten defeat of a bill, governments have generally been unwilling to amend bills. But if this is the situation, there is a significant irony here with respect to the idealism associated with the claim that weak-form bills of rights will promote intra-institutional dialogue and will strengthen parliament's rights-protecting role. Higher legal costs encourage government reliance on case law. But this way of ensuring compatibility does not treat parliament as a relevant venue for justifying legislation.

(a) Canada

Concerns about the costs of defending legislation and the practical and political consequences of having legislative priorities derailed by judicial review have both encouraged government to rely heavily on legal risk assessments when approving legislative bills and also to downplay any possible Charter problem. From the government's perspective, parliament is simply not relevant to the exercise of explaining, justifying, or contributing to Charter judgment. This willingness to invoke judicial criteria as the context for evaluating legislative proposals has contributed to a political culture that increasingly questions the capacity or legitimacy of political actors to exercise independent judgment where rights are implicated, particularly where this judgment differs from judicial perspectives. Partisan critics and others dismiss as illegitimate policy positions that are inconsistent with judicial interpretations of the Charter.

Parliament provides little check on whether governments are consistent with the Charter. The Canadian parliamentary system is characterized by intense partisanship, extremely disciplined parties that rarely tolerate dissent from the leader's position (particularly from government), and weak committees. Moreover, with rare exceptions, the House of Commons reinforces this sense that judgment about compatibility is largely a legal exercise, as opposition parties rarely question government's implicit claims of compatibility (implicit because no report of incompatibility is ever made)[78] even in situations of minority government. Exceptions occur when extremely high profile and contested issues are debated and where a clear and apparent difference exists between the government's position and jurisprudence. A good example of this exception to parliament's otherwise deferential position on questions of rights compatibility occurred when a minority Conservative government tried to restore Canada's historic definition of marriage as recognizing opposite sex couples exclusively, by claiming that the Charter permits denying same-sex couples the opportunity to marry if civil union is instituted as a legal alternative.[79] The proposed action generated considerable debate focusing on competing claims about the meaning and scope of equality rights. When robust parliamentary Charter debate occurs, the venue is usually in the Senate. But the Canadian Senate has serious legitimacy problems arising from the appointed and partisan nature of appointments and only infrequently is willing to defeat legislation (on Charter or other grounds).

(b) United Kingdom

The United Kingdom has a far more effective parliamentary committee system than in Canada, particularly in terms of evaluating whether bills implicate rights. Moreover, the United Kingdom has a dedicated committee for evaluating matters pertaining to rights: the Joint Committee on Human Rights. The JCHR is extremely impressive by all measures of what can be expected from a parliamentary scrutiny committee. It is independent of government, conducts rigorous and principled reviews of bills that are generally devoid of overt partisanship, reports in a timely fashion in that a bill is still being debated in at least one house of parliament, and is persistent in asking hard questions and following-up in terms of governmental responses.[80] Adam Tomkins emphasizes one other important contribution the JCHR makes in terms of provoking and promoting parliamentary debate: an emphatic assistance on evidence-based policy decisions by government, particularly where rights appear to be implicated aversely. If the government refuses to reveal evidence to support its claim, the JCHR is willing to conduct hearings and call upon experts to obtain relevant and necessary advice. A good example was in assessing the government's claim that it was necessary to increase the pre-charge detention period for terrorist suspects to 42 days.[81] Moreover, the JCHR operates within a large enough parliament to ensure it can draw from a sufficiently

---

[78] Interviews indicate that members rarely avail themselves of legal advice related to the Charter.

[79] In December 2006, a motion calling on the government to introduce legislation to restore the traditional definition of marriage was defeated by a vote of 175–123.

[80] J. L. Hiebert, 'Parliament and the Human Rights Act: Can the JCHR Help Facilitate a Culture of Rights?' (2006) 4 *International Journal of Constitutional Law* 1. On the issue of persistence, Adam Tomkins makes the important observation that this perseverance, keeping an issue on the agenda through updated and thematic reports, is the way to win in politics by not letting an issue die or being dependent on an accident of litigation. Tomkins, 'Parliament, Human Rights and Counter-Terrorism' (Chapter 2 in this book).

[81] Ibid, Tomkins.

large body of parliamentarians who view their role as such, and allows for more independent-minded members.

Yet the existence of a specialized parliamentary committee, even one that performs its role robustly, does not alter substantially the fact that parliament remains weak relative to the executive and, as a general matter, is not able to regularly compel government to amend bills or explain its assumptions for why legislation is compatible in the face of serious contestation. Although the JCHR has had some success pressuring government to provide more complete explanations for claims of compatibility, and in securing some amendments to bills (particularly the anti-terrorist measures), it has not been particularly effective at getting the government to revisit claims of compatibility for which it contests. Those public officials interviewed indicated that a negative report by the JCHR does not generally result in the government changing its decision about whether to proceed with a bill. Although departments anticipate the JCHR's review, and where possible make adjustments to avoid a negative report, their primary focus is on whether proposed legislation satisfies the government's legal advisers' assessment of compatibility in the complex pre-legislative review process that can include review by the Attorney General. Thus, the government is unlikely to change its mind on the basis of a single but contrary parliamentary committee report.[82] This view was reiterated in 2006 by then Minister of State for Constitutional Affairs, who made the frank admission that a negative JCHR report is not likely to persuade the government to consider amendments.[83]

The government generally considers amendments to redress rights-based concerns only when it fears losing a vote, which is more likely to occur in the House of Lords.[84] The JCHR reports are often referred to in parliament (more often in the House of Lords than in the Commons). But it is difficult to conclude that its reports regularly alter or influence parliamentary voting behaviour.

(c) New Zealand

New Zealand parliamentary committees have more influence than in Canada, which almost certainly has more to do with the electoral system—MMP—than with a political rights culture. Bills are rarely evaluated in parliament in terms of their consistency with rights.[85] In a sense this is ironic, because New Zealand does not suffer the same obstacle that all of the other parliamentary systems incur: information crucial for assessing the government's claims about compatibility. This information is readily available in New Zealand because the government publishes its legal advice on compatibility on the web.

---

[82] Interviews.
[83] JCHR, Session 2005–6, 'Oral Evidence and Memoranda Given by Harriet Harman, Minister of State, Department of Constitutional Affairs' (16 Jan 2006) HL 143/HC 830–i.
[84] Interviews.
[85] J. L. Hiebert, 'Rights-Vetting in New Zealand and Canada: Similar Idea, Different Outcomes' (2005) 1 *New Zealand Journal of Public and International Law* 63.

V. Conclusions

Research on how parliamentary bills of rights are evolving suggests that sceptics understate the extent of judicial influence on a polity because they do not give sufficient consideration to the extensive reliance on case law in pre-legislative processes of developing legislation. Thus, the breadth of judicial influence far exceeds how court rulings impact on those specific legislative decisions that are litigated. It also suggests that optimists who think that bills of rights will alter political behaviour overestimate the relationship between constitutional design and political power, at least in terms of encouraging a greater parliamentary role. Robust judicial review, along with remedial powers that can compel government to revisit and revise impugned legislation, appear essential for governments to take seriously the idea that rights should guide or constrain their legislative agenda, particularly when these considerations conflict with their ideological position, sense of the public interest, and strategic considerations about what will pay off politically and electorally. If rights conflict with policy objectives to which governments are seriously committed, governments are unlikely to change their position unless they anticipate serious costs from failing to abide by rights principles. Although these costs could come from political sanctions, in the sense of a strong cultural commitment to rights that would penalize governments at the ballot box, they are more likely to come from courts. And if they come from courts, then it is to courts that governments look to justify decisions, not to parliaments. But if judicial review is essential for altering government behaviour, it is also somewhat damning, at least to the extent of developing a bill of rights that is not court-centric. Governments seem to be more willing to anticipate judicial objections as the way to protect legislation from incompatibility, than to participate in normative and public debate about the meaning or scope of rights.

These two conclusions beg the following question. Is it possible to imagine a parliamentary-centred bill of rights where the meaning of rights is not equated with or derivative of case law? Perhaps if a bill of rights were equated with a normative statement of values, a code of political and philosophical conduct, a political community could get away from the idea that judges are uniquely qualified to interpret these, or the myth that law provides better or more principled answers. Alternatively, parliamentary rules could be reformed to give parliament authority to block legislation on rights grounds, so as to force governments to explain and justify their decisions (perhaps something along the lines of what Tom Campbell has suggested in calling for a Rights Council).[86] But procedural changes alone would not alter significantly the balance of power between parliaments and executives, so that governments are compelled to justify or amend decisions involving rights. Other changes that would more likely affect the power relationship between

---

[86] T. Campbell, 'Human Rights Strategies: An Australian Alternative', in T. Campbell, J. Goldsworthy, and A. Stone (eds), *Protecting Rights without a Bill of Rights* (Aldershot: Ashgate Publishing, 2006), 319.

government and parliament include electoral reform, to prevent government domination of parliament, a large enough parliament (to ensure sufficient numbers of members who view their role as parliamentarians, rather than through the lens of their party-political aspirations), and/or effective bicameralism, to provide more independence from the governing party. But just as there is no guarantee that the design of a bill of rights will produce intended changes to political behaviour, there is no way to predict how these kinds of large-scale institutional reforms will affect governmental or parliamentary behaviour.

4

Human Rights at the Interface of State and Sub-state: The Case of Scotland

Chris Himsworth

I. Introduction

From the launch of devolved government in Scotland in 1999, it was apparent that the superimposition of the rights regime of the Human Rights Act 1998 (HRA) would bring a number of special consequences. The discipline of compliance with the European Convention on Human Rights (ECHR) was to be imposed, asymmetrically, on the Scottish Parliament and the Scottish Executive well ahead of the general HRA start date of 2 October 2000 and, a few years into the operation of devolved government, it had become noticeable that the intended interaction of the HRA and the Scotland Act 1998 was not working as smoothly as predicted. Whilst 'human rights' were not, in terms, retained as reserved matters by the Westminster Parliament, the protection of the HRA itself from modification by the Scottish Parliament was bound to detract from its general devolved freedom. Furthermore, in the implementation of the clichéd 'law of unintended consequences', it was apparent that the application by the courts of the twin codes of the two Acts was producing some curious effects.

I argued, at that time, that similarities could be drawn between the process of superimposing a system of human rights protection on Canadian federalism and on devolution in the United Kingdom.[1] In the case of Scotland, the HRA was placed beyond the reach of the Scottish Parliament and Acts of the Scottish Parliament are 'subordinate legislation' for the purposes of the Act. Although the HRA and the Scotland Act were intended to operate in parallel, their interaction had already produced some intrusive results, especially noticeable in their early (and, it seemed, unexpected) impact on the criminal justice system. There had, most prominently, been the case of *Starrs v Ruxton*[2] which had led to the abrupt abolition of the office of temporary sheriff.

Now, a few years further on and rather over a decade after the beginning of devolved government itself, it may be valuable to revisit these issues and to reassess

---

[1] See C. Himsworth, 'Rights versus Devolution', in T. Campbell, K. D. Ewing, and A. Tomkins, (eds), *Sceptical Essays on Human Rights* (Oxford: Oxford University Press, 2001), 145–62.
[2] 2000 JC 208.

the relationship between human rights and devolution. That review is the subject matter of the next sections of this essay and there are two linked themes. The major concern is to adopt a devolution-related perspective[3] on the pursuit by both the previous UK Labour government and the new Conservative/Liberal-Democrat coalition government of a UK or British Bill of Rights to supplement or replace the HRA regime. It will be argued that a number of obstacles lie in the way of this project if it adopts the path of judicially enforceable additional rights (and responsibilities). Some of those obstacles arise from the constitutional and, in particular, the political circumstances of the general devolution settlement. These will be considered in Section II. In addition, however, the Bill of Rights debate has to take account (in Section III) of the record of the further difficulties encountered in the implementation of the HRA in parallel with the implementation of the Scotland Act. Some of these have related to legislative intervention, although the main focus will be on judicial decision-making, in some cases prompting legislative responses. These developments will be an important contribution to the UK Bill of Rights debate if it is indeed taken forward. But, to an extent, they have a free-standing significance. Even if the Bill of Rights project dies a death or takes a path with few new consequences for judicial enforcement, the record of the interaction of the HRA and the Scotland Act is likely to endure. And the conclusions to be drawn from it are that the introduction of judicially enforceable rights under the Acts of 1998 has indeed brought with it some pronounced special effects for Scotland; that many of these effects have had an unexpected and somewhat arbitrary character; that these provide the basis for a continued scepticism as to the contribution and value of 'centrally imposed' rights regimes; and that the prospects for the 'rescue' of rights under devolutionary conditions are limited. In particular, it has to be very strongly doubted whether a route to rescue by the construction of a theory of 'dialogue' between courts and parliaments—whatever may be the more general attractions (if any) of that notion[4]—can be seriously deployed in the context of devolution. The interaction of the two Parliaments, the two governments and the two legal systems and systems of courts complicates and confuses any prospect of dialogue and the opportunity for the systematic and intelligent exchange of views between the parties never arises. The possibility of creating a new legitimacy for the institutions and procedures as a whole is undermined.

Perhaps things could have been otherwise. Perhaps a cleverer and potentially more legitimate basis for the relationship between the HRA and the Scotland Act could have been established. Perhaps this could yet be achieved. For the time being, however, it seems more realistic to conclude that the mechanisms required to 'devolve rights' contribute directly to their failure to achieve legitimacy. Things could, of course, have worked out differently in their detail. It is indeed an aspect of the intermeshing of the rules that an unpredictability of outcomes is generated.

---

[3] As will be explained, this is primarily, for present purposes, a Scotland-related perspective, although a wider view, including, in particular, the complex position of Northern Ireland, would be necessary to paint the full picture.

[4] See n 88 below.

In the landmark case of *Somerville*[5] to be discussed below, it was a very fragile majority in the House of Lords which overturned a unanimous First Division in the Court of Session to produce the problematic consequences of the case for governments and Parliaments. The case might quite easily have gone the other way to quite different effect. The interweaving of the rules creates an autonomous and unpredictable contribution of its own. The courts have an input. Governments and Parliaments have an input. But there is no basis here for a principled engagement between rights and policy which might, under more favourable circumstances, produce a sustainable legitimacy for judicially enforceable human rights regimes.

In this essay no attempt will be made to extrapolate from the specific instance of devolved Scottish government within the United Kingdom and to attempt more general conclusions applicable to the interaction of rights regimes and sub-state governance under other conditions in other parts of the world, although it may be suspected that some similarities would be observable.

In any event the Scottish circumstance may be a valuable case study in the examination of that process sometimes said to characterize the overall human rights project—that general rights of global application and relying for their enforcement primarily on the institutions and procedures of international law cascade down with increasing specificity through regional and national institutions and are eventually to be found at the sub-state level. There may be many other reasons to be sceptical about the benefits of such a vision, but one must, if the Scottish case is in any way typical, be aware of the problems inherent in its realization through parliaments and courts.

The orientation of this essay has two consequences. One is that the emphasis on the interaction of political and legal systems means that there is little systematic consideration of the judicial consideration of specific Convention rights in a Scottish context. Such studies are available elsewhere.[6] Another acknowledgement which has to be made is that the discussion necessarily takes on what is perhaps a forbiddingly technical character at some points. Regrettably, however, devils are, as is often the case, in the detail.

II. A British/UK Bill of Rights[7]

The former Labour government's proposal for a new Bill of Rights was a project at the centre of the Brown package of constitutional reforms and it was, it seemed, at the centre of the wider 'Britishness' project. And one might have thought that the Britishness theme was one which would, from the start, have rung some

---

[5] *Somerville v Scottish Ministers* 2008 SC (HL) 45.

[6] See, in particular, R. Reed and J. Murdoch, *A Guide to Human Rights Law in Scotland*, 2nd edn (Edinburgh: Tottel Publishing, 2008).

[7] To an extent, the material which follows draws on the text of a lecture given at the Institute of Advanced Legal Studies (University of London) on 8 December 2008 and subsequently published in revised form as 'Greater than the Sum of its Parts: The Growing Impact of Devolution on the Processes of Constitutional Reform in the United Kingdom', (2009) 77 *Amicus Curiae* 2.

devolution-sensitive bells in Whitehall. But there had, in fact, been no discussion of devolution-related aspects of human rights in the reform Green Paper of July 2007.[8] There was, however, some treatment of the impact of devolution on any new UK Bill of Rights in the report of the Joint Committee on Human Rights which was published in August 2008.[9]

I shall return to the Joint Committee report, the UK government's response to it,[10] and to the Green Paper of March 2009[11]—but it may be helpful first to make two digressions. It is necessary to place the UK Bill of Rights debate in context in two respects. In the first place we should take account of the general constitutional and political conditions created by the devolution settlement and the impact of these conditions on the prospects for other constitutional reform in the human rights and other sectors. Secondly (in Section III below), we need to consider the effect of some of the court decisions made so far at the intersection of the HRA and the Scotland Act.

Taking, first, the constitutional point, the proposition is that the particular conditions of devolution in Scotland—accentuated by, but not wholly dependent upon, the results of the Scottish Parliament elections of 2007 which produced a minority SNP government—are having a limiting, if not at times a paralysing, effect on the general constitutional debate at the UK level. It is the particular mix of constitutional, legal, and political conditions which creates the difficulty. It does, of course, remain the case that, in a formal sense, the UK Parliament remains supreme.[12] There may still be some lingering truth in the claim that power devolved is power retained. But for most practical purposes we have to acknowledge that devolution has delivered a new constitutional environment which places constraints (which may or may not be a good thing) on the central government and Parliament. This may seem obvious but it is not, I think, fully appreciated. There are a number of factors.

There are, first, the powers formally devolved. Coupled with the obligations which flow from the Sewel convention,[13] these effectively leave many areas of constitutional activity beyond the reach of the UK government and Parliament acting alone. They also create the tricky areas where the boundaries of reserved and devolved power are less than clear, where, for instance, reserved immigration powers overlap with devolved areas of social provision. And the example highlighted in the former UK government's submission to the Calman Commission,[14] where

---

[8] *The Governance of Britain*, Cm 7170, July 2007.

[9] *A Bill of Rights for the UK?* (2007–8) HL 165, HC 150, vol I, ch 3. My own two-line submission to the Committee had raised questions about the viability of the project, given the probable need for a 'Sewel Motion' and the consent of the Scottish Parliament. In the light of developments since, my comment would have to become more nuanced.

[10] *A Bill of Rights for the UK? Government Response to the Committee's 29th Report of Session 2007–08* (2008–9) HL15, HC 145.

[11] See n 71 below.

[12] Subject to the qualifications expressed by their Lordships in the *R(Jackson) v Attorney General* [2006] 1 AC 262.

[13] The understanding that the Westminster Parliament will not legislate on devolved matters despite its formal power to do so, without the consent of the Scottish Parliament.

[14] See n 18 below.

reserved powers of energy (including nuclear) provision overlap with devolved powers of land use and development control.

Then, secondly, there is a close connection between the powers constitutionally devolved and the resulting *politics* of devolution. In the first place, there is no rowing back. There are too many beneficiaries of devolution—right across the political party spectrum—to contemplate a substantial redistribution of powers back to the centre. Just as important, however, for present purposes, is the emerging consensus that (a) the devolutionary status quo is not sustainable in the longer term, but equally that (b) there is a lack of agreement as to what might be done. The unsustainability derives from particular manifestations of the asymmetry of the devolution settlement across the United Kingdom in the shape of problems of, first, political representation—especially in the shape of the West Lothian Question; and secondly, resentments, on all sides, of the current model for the distribution of financial resources under the Barnett formula.[15] Thirdly, there are resentments in England about not just extra funding in Scotland but also its benefits in terms of free personal care for the elderly, free university education, and free medical prescriptions to come. Finally, in a situation exaggerated but not invented by the election of the new SNP government in 2007, there are insufficient means for the formal anticipation and resolution of potential disputes between governments.

On the one side of the debate about ways forward, the solution is seen in terms of weakening of the Union in the direction of independence—but with increasingly sophisticated versions of what independence within Europe and in association with neighbouring states might mean. On the other side, those whose constitutional policy futures assume the continuity of the Union have lost sight of a credible vision of a future Union.[16] Hence the paralysis. There is no consensus as to what even the minimum requirements of Union are; in particular, what *shared* rights of citizens across the United Kingdom there ought to be. The result is that constitutional and legal reform at the UK level has to take its place, along with other proposed reforms in this highly contested zone. Symptomatic of the contest has been the turf war between the SNP government's National Conversation about Scotland's constitutional future and, on the other hand, the Calman Commission on Scottish Devolution, established by resolution of the Scottish Parliament and with the support of the UK government of the time.

The relationship between the two visions of the future can be expected to be in flux for some time. It may be that the SNP goal of a referendum will be undermined by a combination of the political fallout from the current financial crisis and their minority status in the Parliament, although the Scottish government has renewed its commitment to the project as a major element in its legislative

---

[15] These have been well documented in the reports of the Calman Commission (below), the (Holtham) Independent Commission on Funding and Finance for Wales, and the ad hoc House of Lords Committee on Barnett—(2008–9) HL 139.

[16] See C. Jeffery, 'The Scottish Parliament, Constitutional Change and the UK's Haphazard Union', in C. Jeffery and J. Mitchell (eds), *The Scottish Parliament 1999–2009: The First Decade* (Edinburgh: Luath Press, 2009).

programme for 2009–10.[17] Meanwhile the Calman Commission has issued its reports[18] and perhaps the principal significance of the reports lies in their robust defence of devolution so far and the beginning of an exploration of the basis on which the future of the Union may be best analysed and the detailed reallocation of powers adjusted. The new UK coalition government has made commitments to implement some at least of the Calman proposals, but it is extremely unlikely that this will produce the early resolution of these fundamental differences.

Although human rights reform may be a particular casualty of the broader constitutional impasse, it is not alone and it is useful to recall at this point the not unrelated issue of the recent establishment of the UK Supreme Court and the continuing debate in Scotland about what should be the future of final appeals in the Scottish legal system. We should remember the unhappy launch of the constitutional project in the aftermath of the Lord Chancellor (abolition of) announcement in June 2003. Suddenly, so suddenly, we gather, that even existing Law Lords were caught unawares, in an associated reform, the Appellate Committee was to be replaced by a new UK Supreme Court. Inevitably great sensitivities were raised and doubts expressed and, as the Constitutional Reform Bill proceeded, one result was that the clause protective of the separateness of the UK jurisdictions was incorporated.[19] It was certainly not the right climate for the serious consideration of whether, for instance, there might be greater uniformity of appellate jurisdictions across the UK. The apparent oddity in the supreme court of a state in its having a shared *civil* jurisdiction but an asymmetry in *criminal* appeals was retained. Perhaps this is, in any event, the right way forward, but alternatives were un-discussable and only those criminal matters which are raised as 'devolution matters' now reach the Supreme Court following the absorption of the former jurisdiction of the Judicial Committee of the Privy Council (JCPC). Similarly the rules on access to the court remain on an asymmetric basis, which leaves Scotland with access as of right once the case is certified—a situation which gave rise to some embarrassment because of the risk of abuse in the *Jaymarke* case.[20]

What was quite apparent at the time of the debates on the Constitutional Reform Act was that there were, within Scotland and in ways that did not simply divide political nationalists and unionists, quite different perceptions of what purposes a UK Supreme Court might serve—broadly a division between those who have seen the House of Lords and now the Supreme Court as providing a service to the Scottish legal system and those who see it as having an explicit UK-wide responsibility to resolve the biggest legal questions in the state as a whole.

Perhaps of more continuing significance in a devolutionary context is that, ever since the Scotland Act was passed, there has been speculation[21] about whether the

---

[17] SPOR, 2 Sept 2009, cols 19201–10.

[18] Following an interim report in December 2008, the Commission's final report was published as *Serving Scotland Better: Scotland and the United Kingdom in the 21st Century* in June 2009.

[19] Constitutional Reform Act 2005, s 41.

[20] *Wilson v Jaymarke Estates Ltd* 2007 SC (HL) 135.

[21] See eg discussion by Robert Reed QC (now Lord Reed) in J. Beatson, *Constitutional Reform in the United Kingdom: Practice and Principles* (Oxford: Hart Publishing, 1998), 30.

Scottish Parliament could itself competently abolish appeals from Scotland to the House of Lords. Then, in 2004, in the course of a debate on the Sewel motion on the Constitutional Reform Bill, it was reconfirmed that it was the policy of the SNP to repatriate Scottish appeals and to abolish appeals to the House of Lords or UK Supreme Court[22] and the issue was given a more concrete form when, in 2006, a bill—a Member's bill promoted by Adam Ingram MSP[23]—was introduced which would have abolished House of Lords appeals but, at the same time, establish a new Civil Appeals Committee in Scotland.

However, that Bill quickly ran into difficulties. The Presiding Officer of the Parliament issued his statement on legislative competence and declared several provisions of the Bill to be beyond competence on the grounds of encroachment on the reserved matter of the Constitution and incompatibility with Convention rights.[24] There has been criticism of the lack of any requirement in the Scotland Act that the content of the legal advice to the Presiding Officer be published,[25] but, in any event, in this case, the consequence of the statement was that the Parliament took advantage of procedures available under its standing orders to prevent further progress on the Bill. The indignant opposition of Adam Ingram—including attempts on his part to call in aid supportive views known to have been expressed by tutors in the Law School at the University of Edinburgh—was overridden by the then coalition government's parliamentary majority.

Since May 2007, of course, that is a position which has changed. Adam Ingram is now a minister in the SNP Scottish government. That government does not have an overall majority in the Parliament, but it might well be that support from other parties would be forthcoming. The UK Supreme Court is now launched and another Civil Appeals Bill may be some way away, but there may yet be, from the devolved government of Scotland, a counter project in the making and it might well be a counter project which would attract support, not just from other political parties, but also from others who simply have a less centrist view of what top courts are supposed to do. A first step in this direction was the appointment by the Scottish government in December 2008 of Professor Neil Walker of Edinburgh University to conduct a review of final appellate jurisdiction in the Scottish legal system. Professor Walker's report was published in January 2010[26] and he offered six different models for the future of Scotland's top court arrangements, with a preference for the creation of a new quasi-federal UK Supreme Court which would leave all Scottish cases addressing distinct questions of Scots law for final resolution in the indigenous Scottish courts.

[22] See SPOR, 29 Jan 2004, cols 5301–6 (Nicola Sturgeon MSP). A commitment to abolish appeals to the Lords had been contained in the SNP manifesto prior to the 1999 Scottish Parliament elections.
[23] He had earlier lodged a proposal for such a bill in 2003 but it fell in November 2004.
[24] C. Himsworth, 'Presiding Officer Statements on the Competence of Bills' (2007) 11 *Edinburgh Law Review* 397.
[25] See I. Jamieson in his written submission to the Calman Commission (n 18 above).
[26] *Final Appellate Jurisdiction in the Scottish Legal System* (2010).

III. The Human Rights Act and the Scotland Act

Turning now to Scotland's experience of (post-1998) human rights law developments so far, it has been a difficult journey—in ways which would not have been
predicted in 1998 when it seemed to be assumed that the Human Rights Act
regime had been quite carefully enmeshed with that of the Scotland Act to produce an integrated code. I would pick out five aspects.

1. In the first place, as already mentioned, the subjection of the Scottish Parliament
and Executive to human rights limitations from their start-up in 1999 (and thus well
in advance of the general HRA commencement date of 2 October 2000) brought
the unexpected exposure of the Scottish criminal courts to human rights challenges,
resulting from the involvement of the Lord Advocate—a member of the Scottish
Executive—as prosecutor and with the particularly intrusive decision in *Starrs v
Ruxton*[27] that temporary sheriffs were unacceptable and had to be abolished.

2. A second high-profile consequence of an unexpected interaction between the
HRA and the Scotland Act was the divergence which emerged between the JCPC
in the case of *R v HMA*[28] and the Appellate Committee of the House of Lords in
AG's Reference No 2 of 2001[29] on the question of the impact of Convention rights
on prosecutorial delay in criminal trials. The principal issue was what should be the
consequence of undue delays challenged in the course of criminal proceedings and
held to be a breach of the rights of the accused person under Article 6. It was clear
that, in the case of a successful challenge brought after the conclusion of the proceedings, this could result in a range of remedial consequences. A complete annulment of the guilty verdict (and, of course, of any punishment imposed) *might* be a
necessary outcome. On the other hand, in the case of a lesser breach, a reduction in
sentence might be appropriate. It was this range of final possibilities which raised
the nice question of what should be the response at the mid-proceedings stage.
Should a reviewing court necessarily put a stop to the proceedings on the grounds
that no prosecution already found to be in breach of the Convention could be
permitted to continue? Or should the trial be permitted to continue, pending consideration of the consequences of the breach at its conclusion? Or, as a middle way,
should the trial be stopped, if the view is taken that a fair hearing is no longer possible but, otherwise, permitted to continue? At the time the two cases were decided,
there was no clear guidance on the issue from the Strasbourg court.

What was so interesting from an inter-jurisdictional point of view is that the
Privy Council in the Scottish case of *R* took the view (by a 3–2 majority) that trials
should automatically be stopped. In the English case, a nine-judge House of Lords
(with only Lord Hope of Craighead dissenting) concluded in favour of the middle

---

[27] 2000 JC 208.
[28] *R v HMA* 2003 SC (PC) 21.
[29] *AG's Reference No 2 of 2001* [2004] 2 AC 72.

way. A number of different arguments were deployed.[30] There was substantial reference to comparative material from other jurisdictions. What was primarily determinative, however, for the three Scottish judges in *R* was that section 57(2) of the Scotland Act dictates categorically that a member of the Scottish Executive cannot do any act which is incompatible with a Convention right. In the case of the Lord Advocate, this served to prevent his proceeding with a prosecution once a Convention contravention had been established. It might be arguable that the UK Parliament had thereby gone down an unfortunate track. In the meantime, however, it was not within the power of the courts to defy the clear words of the statute.

Subsequently, the Strasbourg Court did adopt a view on the issue and, in *Spiers v Ruddy*,[31] the opportunity was taken for a unanimous JCPC (including both Lord Hope and Lord Rodger) to conclude in favour of the view initially taken in *AG's Reference No 2 of 2001*. The reliance placed by Strasbourg on the remedial demands of Art 13 of the Convention removed the basis for the majority position in *R*. Even section 57(2) of the Scotland Act could not be used as a basis for the automatic stopping of a prosecution once a contravention by delay had been detected.

3. The issues raised in *Starrs v Ruxton* and *R v HMA* along with many other cases illustrate a bigger general point about the Scotland Act's capacity to remould the application of the EHCR in a Scottish context. The reliance on section 57(2) of the Act and the obligations it imposes on the Lord Advocate as a member of the Scottish Executive ensured, almost certainly unwittingly, a very much greater intrusion into criminal trials than could have been anticipated. These consequences were not inevitable and indeed different views have been taken in the High Court of Justiciary and the JCPC of the extent to which the proceedings of the criminal courts may be tainted by the participation of the Lord Advocate as a prosecutor.[32] Not only may the apparent unpredictability and unexpectedness of these consequences be the subject of criticism, but so also, in particular, may be their procedural effects. Once identified as flowing from the acts of the Lord Advocate, these human rights challenges are defined as 'devolution issues' and may, therefore, be taken on appeal to the JCPC (now the Supreme Court), rather than being finally resolved, as are all other criminal appeals, by the High Court in Edinburgh. It is this issue which has provided judicial criticism from two different quarters. The first was in Lord Bonomy's report on the Scottish criminal justice system.[33] Lord Bonomy was unable to see what principled reason there could be for the devolution issue procedures to apply to the acts of the Lord Advocate as prosecutor. Perhaps the point was to ensure the immediate application of human rights standards in criminal trials prior to the full implementation of the HRA.

---

[30] For fuller treatment, see C. Himsworth, 'Jurisdictional Divergences over the Reasonable Time Guarantee in Criminal Trials' (2004) 8 *Edinburgh Law Review* 255.

[31] 2008 SLT 39.

[32] See eg *Montgomery v HMA* 2001 SC (PC) 1; *Brown v Stott* 2000 SCCR 314; *McIntosh, Petitioner* 2000 SCCR 1017; *HMA v Burns* 2000 SCCR 884; *Miller v HMA* 2003 SC (PC) 1. For discussion see Reed and Murdoch, above n 6.

[33] 'Improving Practice: The Reform of the High Court of Justiciary' (2002).

But, if so, that time had passed and substantial delays were now being caused. The Scottish government should urge the UK Parliament to amend the Scotland Act.[34] The second intervention was in the evidence submitted by 'the judiciary in the Court of Session' to the Calman Commission.[35] As they said, '[i]t is far from clear that the framers of the Scotland Act 1998 envisaged that devolution issues would be raised in prosecutions to anything like the extent to which they have'.[36] They complained that this had led to an unacceptable divergence between the outcomes of cases which had been somewhat arbitrarily divided for final decision between the High Court and the JCPC[37] and also to much delay in those criminal trials which required the JCPC's involvement. The proposal of the judges was that the solution lay in the amendment of the Scotland Act either to exempt the Lord Advocate from section 57(2) or to remove the Lord Advocate's prosecutorial function. A (controversial) further possibility might be to send all criminal appeals to the JCPC/UK Supreme Court. The Calman Commission's response was that the issue raised questions which went beyond their own remit and declined to make a recommendation.[38]

4. Another occasion for a sharp divergence—this time between the Inner House of the Court of Session and the House of Lords—came in the *Somerville* case,[39] where a particularly strong difference of opinion arose over whether the 12-- month time ban on proceedings under the HRA should also apply to proceedings brought as a devolution issue against the Scottish Executive under the Scotland Act. And the result has been, through the decision of the House of Lords in the case, that it does not. The case brought conflicting interpretations of the two Acts too complex to explore fully here but which, put crudely, forced a choice between the logic of similarity of treatment under the two human rights codes—which had attracted the Inner House to a 12-month rule common to both—and, on the other hand, the logic of treating the human rights challenge as one of several which might be brought as competence issues under the Scotland Act where, quite plainly, no general 12-month rule applied—the view which, on its interpretation of that Act, attracted a majority in the House of Lords.[40]

Somerville was notable on three counts. In the first place, it revealed a quite extraordinary bitterness in the rejection by the two Scottish Law Lords of the conclusions reached by the First Division. They delivered lectures on the need to avoid speculation as to what Parliament might have intended to achieve when it passed the HRA and the Scotland Act and instead to focus on 'the words used by the

---

[34] Ibid, ch 17.

[35] 2008. See the Commission's website.

[36] Ibid, para 13.

[37] Their particular illustration was by reference to cases involving the emergence of fresh evidence. See *Cameron v HMA* 1991 JC 251; *Al Megrahi v HMA* 2002 JC 99; *Holland v HMA* 2005 SC (PC) 3; and *Sinclair v HMA* 2005 SC (PC) 28.

[38] *Serving Scotland Better* (2009), para 5.37. But see the Commission's view on the consequences of the *Somerville* case at n 46 below.

[39] *Somerville v Scottish Ministers* 2008 SC (HL) 45.

[40] For discussion see C. Himsworth, 'Conflicting Interpretations of a Relationship: Damages for Human Rights Breaches' (2008) 12 *Edinburgh Law Review* 321.

statutes, to which careful attention must be paid in order to discover the intention of Parliament'; a 'careful and accurate reading' was important; and the Division had failed to address the 'precise wording'.[41] The Division had avoided the analysis without which it was 'impossible to determine the meaning and purpose of the provision'.[42] But, as Lord Walker of Gestingthorpe put it, these views were opposed by Lord Scott of Foscote and Lord Mance who had concluded to contrary effect and had regarded their own conclusion as 'tolerably clear'.[43] He himself had found the point much more difficult but, in a short speech, expressed himself eventually persuaded by the Scottish judges.

The second significant feature of *Somerville* was that the issues of law decided[44] were so decided, at least as far as the speeches in the case reveal, without regard to the policy (and political) issues also at stake. *Somerville* itself concerned a number of decisions by prison authorities to segregate prisoners in a matter alleged to be in contravention of their Convention rights. It was well-known, however, at the time that, riding on *Somerville* litigation, was also the fate of scores of other cases which depended on whether the First Division's view on the 12-month rule was upheld or not. These were the so-called 'slopping-out' cases brought to seek damages for treatment by the Scottish Prison Service which had been held to be contrary to Art 3 of the ECHR in *Napier v Scottish Ministers*.[45] If the 12-month rule were to be sustained in *Somerville*, these cases would fall. If the House of Lords were to decide as they eventually did, they would be injected with new life. The actual consequences of *Somerville* will be mentioned below, but what is significant from the point of view of the reasoning in the decision itself is that such potential consequences were at no stage considered. And perhaps, it may be argued, they were quite properly ignored. In the normal process of statutory interpretation, they might be regarded as quite irrelevant to the process of divining the intention of the UK Parliament when it constructed the relationship between the HRA and the Scotland Act. There is, on the other hand, some room for the view that, in constitutional litigation where substantial human rights issues are at stake, the role of the courts is 'rescued' from the illegitimacy it may otherwise suffer only if such consequentialist arguments are taken into account. The impact of the decision in hand on the fate of many others may not, of course, necessarily determine what is the correct answer, but it should not, on this view, be wholly irrelevant to the decision.

The third consequence of *Somerville* and the one which established its high political profile was the way in which the 'slopping-out' cases were subsequently handled. The decision prompted an indignant complaint by the Scottish government that it should not be left to carry the financial can represented by the damages potentially awardable against it for cases already launched and yet to be launched. Why should the lottery of a majority House of Lords decision place the Scottish

---

[41] 2009 SC (HL) 45 at paras 11, 24, and 30, per Lord Hope.
[42] Ibid, para 120, Lord Rodger.
[43] Ibid, para 163.
[44] In addition to the resolution of the 12-month rule point, several other unrelated points of law were also at issue.
[45] 2005 1 SC 307.

government in a notably worse position than the UK government, which could claim the benefit of the HRA 12-month rule? Such discrimination was unintended and unfair. Something should be done. The law should be changed.

For a long time, however, those arguments fell on stony ground in London.[46] Suddenly, however, in March 2009, the Scottish Cabinet Secretary for Justice, Kenny MacAskill MSP, announced to the Scottish Parliament that agreement had been reached.[47] Of the £67 million set aside to pay to prisoners in respect of slopping-out claims, some £50 million could now be 'put to better uses'. The legal anomaly could be removed. Following meetings between the First Minister and the Lord Advocate, on the one side, and Lord Chancellor and the Advocate General for Scotland, on the other, a solution had been agreed. The Scottish Parliament would be asked to amend the HRA in such a way as to impose a 12-month time bar on proceedings launched after an early prescribed date. In order to enable that to happen, however, the competence of the Scottish Parliament would be expanded, to overcome the restrictions imposed by Schedule 4 to the Scotland Act, by an Order in Council under section 30(2) of the Act. And, in due course, the Order[48] and the Convention Rights Proceedings (Amendment) (Scotland) Act 2009 were enacted.[49]

5. There has been another quite separate human rights development with a devolutionary aspect to it. No Scottish court has had the opportunity to engage with the question of what constitutes a 'public authority'—a 'person certain of whose functions are functions of a public nature'—for the purposes of section 6(3) of the HRA. But, in the light of *L v Birmingham City Council*,[50] the opportunity was taken in section 145 of the (Westminster) Health and Social Care Act 2008 to amend not only the England and Wales statute but also the Social Work (Scotland) Act 1968 to ensure that private providers become subject to the HRA. Whether or not this ad hoc style of approach to the resolution of the issue is appropriate is an interesting question. Perhaps, in order to achieve a new across-the-board under- standing of what should constitute a public authority or public function, there should have been a more direct amendment of the HRA itself. That broader ques- tion will not, however, be pursued here. What instead is of interest is the much nar- rower point that, although other sections of the Health and Social Care Bill were the subject of a legislative consent motion in the Scottish Parliament, the clause

[46] It may be noted that the Secretary of State for Scotland sought guidance on what should be done from the Calman Commission. The Commission advised that the 12-month time limit should be extended to cases brought under the Scotland Act. See 'Serving Scotland Better: Scotland and the United Kingdom in the 21st Century' (2009), para 5.36.

[47] SPOR 11 March 2009, cols 15604–13.

[48] The Scotland Act 1998 (Modification of Schedule 4) Order 2009, SI 2009/1380. For debates on the Order, see HL Debs, 19 May 2009, cols 1360–66; HC First Delegated Legislation Committee, 11 May 2009; Scottish Parliament Justice Committee, 5 May 2009, cols 1736–41.

[49] Clauses to achieve a similar result for Northern Ireland and for Wales were included in the Constitutional Reform and Governance Bill before the Westminster Parliament prior to the dissol- ution of 2010, but were not retained in the Act as passed. It seems probable that the case of *Cadder v HMA* (on police powers of interrogation in the absence of a solicitor) currently before the UK Supreme Court may be another to produce the need for emergency legislation in the Scottish Parliament.

[50] [2008] 1 AC 95.

which became section 145 was not. This is not a merely technical matter. It might have been thought that the absence of a 'Sewel motion' would have come about simply because the clause was a late amendment to the bill. This was not, however, the case. The reason was that both the UK and Scottish governments considered that the change made to the Social Work (Scotland) Act 1968 would not have been within the competence of the Scottish Parliament. The route to this view is by way of treating the amendments of the 1968 Act as a 'modification' of the Human Rights Act 1998.[51] This might, at first sight, seem counter-intuitive, but the origins of this interpretation can be explained. Its consequences extend well beyond the merely technical. 'Modify' is defined by section 126(1) of the Scotland Act, where it is stated that it 'includes amend or repeal' and a nice question arises as to whether this formula embraces the amendment of a second Act of Parliament in such a way as to 'modify' the Human Rights Act. Clearly this depends on whether 'includes' can be interpreted to embrace, in addition to 'repeal' and 'amend', such an amendment—admittedly with consequences for the application of the Human Rights Act. A sub-question is whether, in this context, 'amend *or* repeal' casts the net more or less widely than 'amend *and* repeal'. At all events, the two governments concluded that a broad interpretation of this sort was justified and it is understood that, in doing so, they were relying on the interpretation offered by a minister in the House of Lords at committee stage on the Human Rights Bill. There, Baroness Ramsay of Cartvale said that the term 'modify' had been used deliberately:

...so that, in the case of enactments, the various restrictions on the competence of the Scottish Parliament to modify aspects of the law apply to any change to the effect of an enactment, for example, by a gloss placed on its interpretation by another enactment, not just those modifications which involve textual amendments. It is therefore felt that narrowing these provisions to apply only to textual amendments—which is the effect that we believe the use of the word 'amendment' and not 'modify' would produce—would subvert their purpose. I do not know whether that provides the noble and learned Lord with an adequate reply, but that is why the word 'modify' is used. We believe that it is preferable to the word 'amend' or 'amendment'.[52]

It seems at least questionable whether the use of the language of modification, in combination with that of repeal or amendment, successfully achieves the broad interpretation sought by the noble Baroness. Plainly the amendment of the Social Work (Scotland) Act and the other legislation has affected the reach of the HRA. But whether the HRA itself has thereby been 'modified' is more doubtful. If, however, a basis for the broad ministerial interpretation has been achieved, the consequences for the interpretation of the remaining competences of the Scottish Parliament in relation to human rights require to be carefully considered. No harm is done, from a Westminster perspective, if exclusive control is retained over these wider aspects of the application of the HRA. From the point of view of Holyrood, however, the concession by the Scottish government that there was no need for a

[51] Such modification by the Scottish Parliament is forbidden by Sched 4 to the Scotland Act 1998.
[52] HL Debs, 21 July 1998, col 830.

legislative consent motion in respect of the 2008 Act may have the effect of narrowing the presumed competence of the Scottish Parliament if a proposed new bill were interpreted as 'modifying' the HRA.[53] There is a return to this question below.

IV. Back to the UK Bill of Rights

I mention these developments mainly to remind us that the quest for compliance with Convention rights has brought some quite difficult consequences—many of them wholly unforeseen—for the working of the human rights settlement so far. To talk now of whether and, if so, how to superimpose a new form of UK or British Bill of Rights revives these questions of compatibility between the human rights and devolution regimes. Some of these questions are narrow and technical. Some of them are broader questions about the legislative competence of the Scottish Parliament.

Let me try to illustrate the difficulties which arise by reference to the Joint Committee report I have already mentioned.[54] The Committee came to Edinburgh and took evidence from the Scottish government's Cabinet Secretary for Justice, Mr Kenny McAskill MSP, and representatives of the Law Society of Scotland.[55] The Committee also took evidence on Northern Ireland,[56] where arguably the problems involved in talking about a new and explicitly British or UK Bill of Rights which could disrupt the delicate understandings underpinning the Belfast Agreement of 1998 might loom much larger than anything thrown up by Scotland. I have two principal comments on the Committee's response to their encounters with evidence from Scotland and Northern Ireland. The first is to note the Committee's correct insistence on the need for communication between the UK government and the devolved administrations. Kenny MacAskill had been asked about the extent to which the Scottish government had been involved in discussions on a Bill of Rights. He said: 'Not really a great deal at all and I think the fact that devolution is not mentioned is perhaps an indicator of that.'[57] The UK Justice Secretary had accepted in evidence that the UK government had, he said, 'to ensure that what we say does not collide with the devolution settlement and, if there is a question of that, it has the consent of the devolved administrations'. The Committee agreed. 'A UK Bill of Rights must be based on a detailed dialogue between central government and the devolved administrations. We note that this dialogue does not yet seem to have begun.'[58] And later the Committee repeated the need for 'early engagement' with the devolved administrations.[59] This was, in

---

[53] For an important recent case on Sched 4 to the Scotland Act, the first in the Supreme Court, see *Martin v HMA* [2010] UKSC 10, 2010 SLT 412.

[54] See n 9 above.

[55] Vol II, 59–77.

[56] Vol II, 23–30.

[57] Vol I, para 103.

[58] Paras 103–4 (footnotes omitted)

[59] Para 110.

part, in response to the UK Justice Secretary's view that there were 'tricky' drafting questions rather than matters of *principle* arising from the devolution settlement.

A second comment on the Committee's report, however, is to doubt whether it is simply drafting questions which are involved. The Committee's own broad conclusion on the dimensions of the devolution-related problems was as follows:

The devolution settlement creates certain difficulties for a UK Bill of Rights, but we do not accept that it creates an insuperable obstacle to such a Bill. Ever since the Universal Declaration of Human Rights, human rights norms have gradually become embedded at global, regional and national level. Provided the hierarchy between these levels is clear, there is a positive virtue in the broadly defined rights in the international standards being fleshed out into more concrete norms and standards at the regional, national and sub-national level. Each Bill of Rights, from the global through the regional to the national and sub-national levels, becomes more specific and detailed in its provisions, and is free to be more generous but must not fall below the minimum floor of the higher level of protection. It is common for federated states, such as Canada, the US and Germany, to have both federal Bills of Rights and state-level Bills of Rights, and for any questions about the hierarchical relationship between these different levels of rights protection to be resolved by the federation's Constitutional Court.

'In our view', the Committee continued, 'the devolution settlement creates fewer difficulties than face federated states in this respect, because constitutional matters, including human rights, are not devolved matters'.[60] 'Nevertheless', they said, 'devolution raises complex issues, particularly if a UK Bill of Rights concerned devolved matters'.

Professor Carol Harlow had argued:

Human rights are not, of course, a devolved issue, a division of functions that perhaps remains largely uncontroversial so long as the matter is governed by the Convention and our shared heritage in that respect. Were this to change and more particularly if a proposed new text were to penetrate deeply into economic and social rights, devolved areas would be involved.... Whether further regionalisation is desirable and what the relationship of regional texts could be with the ECHR and Strasbourg courts are very difficult and delicate questions.[61]

And the Committee itself went on to say that they had received some helpful evidence from the Law Society of Scotland about the difficulties of a UK Bill of Rights in a Scottish context. Some well-known civil rights south of the border, such as the right to trial by jury, were not, they conceded, part of Scotland's constitutional heritage. In addition, an amendment to the Scotland Act 1998 would be required to ensure that provisions of a UK Bill of Rights relating to devolved matters could not be repealed or derogated from by the Scottish Parliament.[62]

In response, it has to be agreed that problems would arise if newly defined 'rights' promulgated at a UK level began to impinge on those areas of social policy currently devolved to the Scottish Parliament—whether or not they are in areas where

[60] Para 107.
[61] Para 108.
[62] Para 109.

Scotland's 'constitutional heritage' has been different from that of other parts of the United Kingdom. There would, at the very least, be the problem of protecting them from future modification or derogation by the Scottish Parliament. But there are other preliminary problems. The first is the conclusion by both Professor Harlow and the Committee that human rights are not devolved matters. And the main difficulty here is that, in terms of the Scotland Act, that conclusion is simply not technically correct. For a matter to be 'not devolved', it must be reserved and there is no indication in Schedule 5 to the Act that this is the case. Certain 'constitutional' matters *are* reserved, but these are contained in a closed list which does not refer to human rights. There *is* a reservation of equality/non-discrimination rights,[63] but this does not extend to human rights in general. When the Scottish Commission for Human Rights was created by the Scottish Parliament,[64] no one would have challenged the competence of the Scottish Parliament to legislate to create the Commission itself or presumably on human rights in general. It is true that the HRA joins other statutes (mainly large parts of the Scotland Act itself) which cannot, by virtue of Schedule 4 to the Act, be modified by the Scottish Parliament, but it has to be at least questionable whether a bill in the UK Parliament designed to repeal or amend or replace the HRA could avoid the requirement of a legislative consent (Sewel) motion in the Scottish Parliament because of the bill's encroachment on devolved matters—both in respect of its touching on human rights at all and, if this were the case, its extension into other aspects of devolved legislative competence such as criminal justice or education or housing policy. But it is at this point that the discussion earlier about the avoidance of a legislative consent motion in respect of section 145 of the Health and Social Care Act 2008 becomes relevant. If the provisions of any new bill were deemed to 'modify' the HRA in the broad sense relied on for the 2008 Act, then, it seems, the formal consent of the Scottish Parliament might not be required.

But this is not simply a technical matter of getting a legislative consent motion approved (or not) by the Scottish Parliament. Of course, that is, in any event, a matter of mere convention rather than law. But this is where the line in the Joint Committee's report about an amendment to the Scotland Act being required and the optimistic reference to the devolution settlement's creating 'fewer difficulties than face federated states' becomes problematic. *Of course*, in a formal sense, the sovereignty of the UK Parliament could in theory be asserted in a way that would not be the case in a federation, but to say this is to ignore the constitutional realities of the United Kingdom to which I have referred. We have to bear in mind that in Mr MacAskill's evidence to the Joint Committee, he spoke not only of a lack of communication between governments, but also of his own general antipathy to the project. In answer to the straight question of whether a UK Bill of Rights was needed, his one-word answer was a simple 'no'.[65]

---

[63] Sched 5, Pt II, S L2. In the reservation elsewhere of such issues as immigration and terrorism, other competences with human rights consequences are also reserved.

[64] Scottish Commission for Human Rights Act 2006.

[65] Vol II, 59.

In the Labour government's response to the Committee's report,[66] they repeated their commitment to engage with the devolved administrations[67] and agreed with the Committee's observations both on the need to address the differences between the United Kingdom's three legal jurisdictions and also on the lower level of difficulties to be encountered than in federated states.[68] We should also take account, however, of another view expressed by the Committee and the UK government response in a section of the report dealing not with devolution itself but with the more general question of inter-institutional relationships. It has sharp consequences for the devolution/human rights nexus. The Committee had said in their report:

We are not in favour of a Bill of Rights which confers a power on the courts to strike down legislation. We consider this to be fundamentally at odds with this country's tradition of parliamentary democracy. In our view the innovative and widely admired parliamentary model of human rights protection contained in the HRA is the appropriate model of rights protection for our democracy. Within that model, we consider that there is scope to enhance Parliament's role further, at the same time as strengthening the protection provided for human rights, as discussed below.[69]

In response, the then UK government said:

The Government welcomes the Committee's recognition that the Parliamentary model of rights protection contained in the Human Rights Act is 'innovative and widely admired' and is appropriate in our system of Parliamentary democracy. The Government would not wish to depart from the model whereby Parliament retains the final say as to the protection of rights and freedoms under either the Human Rights Act or any future Bill of Rights. The Government welcomes the discussion as to the possible variations within that model in the context of any future Bill of Rights.[70]

What is, of course, so interesting from a Scottish perspective about these expressions of opinion is that they, perhaps unconsciously, rub salt into the wound of the differential treatment of the UK and Scottish Parliaments under the HRA regime. Not for the *Scottish* Parliament is the sensitive avoidance of a Bill of Rights which 'confers a power on the courts to strike down legislation'. There has been no problem treating the *Scottish* Parliament in a way which is 'fundamentally at odds with this country's tradition of parliamentary democracy'. There has apparently been (and would be) no problem in departing, in respect of the *Scottish* Parliament, 'from the model whereby Parliament retains the final say as to the protection of rights and freedoms under either the Human Rights Act or any future Bill of Rights'.

The Ministry of Justice published their Green Paper in March 2009. Under the rubric of 'seeking stability in times of uncertainty', *Rights and Responsibilities: Developing our Constitutional Framework*[71] surveyed world practice (and UK

---

[66] See n 10 above.
[67] Para 18.
[68] Paras 19, 20.
[69] Vol 1, para 218.
[70] (2008–9) HL 15, HC 145, para 44.
[71] *Rights and Responsibilities: Developing our Constitutional Framework*, Cm 7577, 2009.

practice, including, for Scotland, the historic instances of the Declaration of Arbroath of 1320 and the Claim of Right of 1689) before moving on to the case for combining the guarantee of rights with a parallel reconfirmation of citizen responsibilities. Central to the proposals, however, was the consideration, in chapter 4 of the Green Paper, of the legal effect and enforceability of any future Bill of Rights and Responsibilities. There was 'an opportunity to look again at assumptions about how best to ensure that rights and responsibilities are respected and understood. The possible range of approaches to a Bill of Rights and Responsibilities represents a continuum'.[72] A full discussion of the range of approaches is not needed here. Three broad categories were identified: a declaration of rights and responsibilities, general interpretative provisions, and specific provisions enforceable in the courts. Whilst no final conclusions were reached, there was a clear statement that the Labour government '[did] not consider that a generally applicable model of directly legally enforceable rights or responsibilities would be the most appropriate for a future Bill of Rights and Responsibilities'.[73] At the same time, there was a recommitment to the HRA of which the government remained proud and it would neither resile from the Act nor repeal it.[74] There was also a renewed commitment to the incorporation of the ECHR and to continued membership of the European Union.[75]

As to devolution, the Green Paper displayed a new sensitivity. Some paragraphs[76] were devoted to a description of the position in Scotland, Wales, and, most prominently, Northern Ireland and they concluded with the statement:

Consideration of a Bill of Rights and Responsibilities for the UK—whatever form it might take—will clearly need to involve Parliament, the devolved legislatures, and the devolved executive bodies as well as the Human Rights Commissions which operate in the different parts of the UK. Each has its own history, conventions and identity and has different responsibilities and obligations in relation to fundamental rights, how they are safeguarded, and how they are respected in the delivery of key public services. In order to generate the degree of consensus appropriate for a Bill of Rights and Responsibilities, each will have an important contribution to make about the way rights and responsibilities should be expressed. This will require further careful consideration.[77]

It has also to be acknowledged that, at many points, the Green Paper contained specific references to the different parts of the United Kingdom and especially to points at which the law was different. There was, for instance, reference to the different provision made in Scotland in relation to criminal justice,[78] although not specifically on trial by jury, equality rights,[79] good administration and

---

[72] Ibid, paras 4.1–4.2.
[73] Para 4.25.
[74] Para 4.30.
[75] Para 4.31.
[76] Paras 4.32–4.42.
[77] Para 4.42.
[78] Paras 3.20, 3.24.
[79] Para 3.34.

ombudsmen,[80] healthcare,[81] children,[82] and the environment.[83] On the other hand, the renewed commitments in the Green Paper to parliamentary sovereignty admitted no consideration of the different impact of that doctrine on the devolved legislatures. It was stated that parliamentary sovereignty 'resided at the heart of our constitutional arrangements'.[84] And also, in the context of 'decision-making and resource allocation':

One of the key questions in relation to the constitutional expression of rights is the extent to which the courts should make decisions which have a direct effect on resource alloca-tion. Different jurisdictions have arrived at different answers depending on their constitu-tions and their history and social and economic conditions. For the United Kingdom, it is the Government's clear view that Parliamentary sovereignty must remain as the corner-stone of the UK constitution.

Ministers are democratically accountable to Parliament for the prioritisation of social needs, and for the way in which resources are targeted towards meeting them. The process of adjudication of individual claims cannot take account of broader public policy argu-ments in a way which ensures such accountability. Nor do the judiciary have any demo-cratic mandate to take such decisions. The Government is satisfied that there is no case for extending the UK courts' jurisdiction over such areas.[85]

Whilst, in the more general discussion of devolution, it was noted that it is outside the competence of the devolved legislatures to pass laws which are incompatible with Convention rights,[86] there was no discussion of the wholly different role for the courts (whether in relation to resource allocation or otherwise) that this pro-duces. However, the principal devolution-related aspect of the Green Paper was its evident preference for a Bill of Rights and Responsibilities which was not directly judicially enforceable.

V. Conclusions

Since the general election of May 2010, the new governing coalition of the Conservatives and the Liberal Democrats has said, in *The Coalition: Our Programme for Government,* that it 'will establish a Commission to investigate the creation of a British Bill of Rights that incorporates and builds on all our obligations under the European Convention on Human Rights, ensures that these rights continue to be enshrined in British law, and protects and extends British liberties'. The proposals for change which have been tabled during 2009–10, whether the Labour Bill of Rights and Responsibilities or the new coalition's British Bill of Rights, raise two different groups of difficulties when viewed from a devolved Scottish perspective.

---

[80] Para 3.45.
[81] Paras 3.64, 3.65.
[82] Para 3.69.
[83] Para 3.80.
[84] Foreword, para xv.
[85] Para 4.27.
[86] Paras 4.34, 4.36.

In the first place, it is quite evident that, in the constitutional and political conditions which obtain north of the border, there are considerable obstacles in the way of undertaking any high level constitutional reform which makes any assumptions at all about the future of the Union and the form it may take in the coming years. If there is no shared understanding about the United Kingdom, there can be no basis for a shared understanding about common rights and responsibilities. The Calman Commission may have done its best to recreate the vision of a Union with its own proposals for reform in the light of that vision. But that initiative has been met immediately by the SNP's launch of a Referendum Bill. The SNP may not be in government for ever, but, even with a different political leadership in Edinburgh, it is difficult to imagine that there will be a majority at Holyrood in the near future which will be anxious to collaborate in grand constitutional reform at the UK level. If there are future reforms, they will have to be integrated with or superimposed on current institutions and procedures for human rights protection. If there are no reforms, the current position will endure.

And the second conclusion to be drawn from the survey undertaken in this essay is that the situation which has prevailed for the first decade of devolution has been profoundly ill-suited to the judicial protection of rights. Those predisposed to be sceptical about such judicial involvement will have had many of their worst fears confirmed. Perhaps there has been a certain amount of bad luck in the working out of the Scottish example of cascading rights protection down from state to sub-state. But perhaps too it should have been predictable that, because of the UK's patchwork of legal systems, the superimposition upon that of an asymmetric model of devolution, the use (for Scotland) of the two principal 'constitutional statutes'—the HRA and the Scotland Act, and the subjection of those statutes to old-fashioned, tightly reasoned, plain-meaning statutory interpretation, there might be problems.

There will, of course, be many who will rejoice that courts and lawyers in general stick to their last; that the forms and limits of adjudication[87] are adhered to; and that the ordinances of judicial restraint are duly observed. Human rights sceptics, in particular, are naturally critical of the results that the greater liberation of judges to adopt a more policy-orientated stance might bring. This includes hostility to any notion of dialogue between courts and parliaments.[88] But, in the case of devolution, there is little prospect of dialogue. Too much confusion of courts, statutes, and parliaments.[89]

---

[87] See L. Fuller, 'The Forms and Limits of Adjudication' (1978) 92 *Harvard Law Review* 353.

[88] For a flavour of the debate, see T. R. Hickman, 'Constitutional Dialogue, Constitutional Theories and the Human Rights Act 1998' [2005] *Public Law* 306; and K. D. Ewing and H. C. Tham, 'The Continuing Futility of the Human Rights Act' [2008] *Public Law* 668, at 691.

[89] Although there has been some to-ing and fro-ing of a sort. The Mental Health (Public Safety and Appeals (Scotland) Act 1999 was a response to *Ruddle v Secretary of State for Scotland* 1999 GWD 29-1395. Section 145 of the Health and Social Care Act 2008 (with its devolutionary spin-off) was a response to *L v Birmingham City Council* [2008] 1 AC 95. At the time it was proposed, there were threats of legal challenge to the Convention Rights Proceedings (Amendment) (Scotland) Act 2009, which was itself a response to *Somerville v Scottish Ministers* 2008 SC (HL) 45.

In the meantime, however, the courts have left us with their interpretation of 'devolution issues', with its unexpected consequences for temporary sheriffs and then for its wider impact on criminal business distributed between the High Court of Justiciary and (now) the Supreme Court; their bitter interpretative disagreements about the effect of delay in criminal trials; and their even more highly contested views on the 12-month time bar where fundamental fissures between the logic of the HRA and of the Scotland Act were exposed. We also have the debate over what the Scotland Act means by 'modify' and the future possibility of judicial interventions there too if the Scottish Parliament were ever suspected of legislating in such a way as to 'modify' the HRA.

Even without the immediate prospect of a new UK Bill of Rights, life at the interface between the HRA and the Scotland Act, at the point where in the United Kingdom rights are cascaded down from state to sub-state, has been deeply uncomfortable.

5

Inter-institutional 'Rights Dialogue' under the New Zealand Bill of Rights Act

Andrew Geddis

Despite the fact that the New Zealand Bill of Rights Act 1990 (NZBORA) was modelled on the Canadian Bill of Rights Act 1960, it nevertheless commonly is viewed as the progenitor of the 'parliamentary bills of rights',[1] subsequently adopted in the United Kingdom[2] and various Australian states.[3] The basic features of these 'Commonwealth models',[4] also described as 'hybrid bills of rights',[5] can be stated succinctly. The NZBORA (along with its British and Australian cousins) authorizes full, rights-based judicial review of the acts and omissions of public actors, except where those actors are operating pursuant to a power or duty specifically legislated for by Parliament. In such latter cases, the judiciary is restricted to searching for a 'rights friendly' interpretation of the statutory language,[6] to ensure (where it 'can' or it is 'possible' to do so) that Parliament's enactment does not authorize an unjustifiable limit on some individual right. However, absent any available rights-friendly interpretation of the relevant statutory language—in a situation where the judiciary simply *cannot* read a statute in a manner consistent with the relevant rights instrument—the judiciary is required to apply the enactment irrespective of its consequences for individual rights. In the United Kingdom and Australian states, the courts can then issue a formal declaration—in effect, an explicit and direct message to the legislature—that it considers the enactment is incompatible with the relevant rights instrument, with it then being for Parliament to decide if and how to respond. The NZBORA does not provide for an express

---

[1] J. Hiebert, 'Parliamentary Bills of Rights: An Alternative Model?' (2006) 69 *Modern Law Review* 7.

[2] Human Rights Act 1998 (c 42).

[3] Human Rights Act 2004 (ACT Laws 2004–5); Charter of Human Rights and Responsibilities Act 2006 (Victorian Acts, No 43).

[4] S. Gardbaum, 'The New Commonwealth Model of Constitutionalism' (2001) 49 *American Journal of Comparative Law* 707.

484. [5] J. Goldsworthy, 'Homogenising Constitutions' (2003) 23 *Oxford Journal of Legal Studies* 484,

[6] A. Geddis and B. Fenton, '"Which is to be Master?"—Rights-Friendly Statutory Interpretation in New Zealand and the United Kingdom' (2008) 25 *Arizona Journal of International and Comparative Law* 733.

power to issue such declarations; whether New Zealand's courts nonetheless may do so is an as-yet unanswered question considered later in this chapter.

The proponents of this approach to protecting individual rights claim that it successfully synthesizes the comparative advantages of judicial and legislative viewpoints. Certainly, such claims are made for the NZBORA. Philip Joseph sees the adoption of the NZBORA as reinforcing the 'collaborative enterprise' of the legislative and judicial arms of government, bolstering the 'complex, reciprocal linkages'[7] between them as they seek to 'vouchsafe liberties and freedoms in a representative democracy'.[8] This invocation of a collaborative enterprise repackages the concept of an inter-branch 'dialogue' on individual rights issues currently enjoying some popularity in constitutional theory circles.[9] Petra Butler argues that this dialogue concept is particularly relevant in respect of a parliamentary bill of rights such as the NZBORA, precisely because such instruments give both the courts and the legislature considerable freedom within their respective spheres.[10] Drawing on the institutional strengths of each branch then helps to create and sustain a general 'culture of justification', which ensures the reasons for a public actor limiting a right are carefully considered and explained.[11]

Other commentators on the NZBORA express less positive sentiments. Perhaps the most trenchant critique has come from James Allan, who over a number of articles damns the NZBORA for simply transferring social decision-making power into the unaccountable hands of the judiciary.[12] A similar claim is made by John Smillie, who recommends; 'Parliament should repeal the New Zealand Bill of Rights Act 1990 and take care not to fall into the trap again of attempting to regulate behaviour by enacting vague open-ended standards that leave judges with virtually unconfined discretion at the point of application'.[13] Certainly, it is true that the judiciary has employed the NZBORA to expand its oversight of the executive arm of government (and other actors exercising 'public' powers or functions). For example, it has used the NZBORA to substantially rework the law governing

---

[7] P. Joseph, 'Parliament, the Courts and the Collaborative Enterprise' (2004) 15 *King's College Law Journal* 321, 336.

[8] P. Joseph, 'Parliament, the Courts and the Collaborative Enterprise' (2004) 15 *King's College Law Journal* 321, 345. See also S. Elias, 'Sovereignty in the 21st Century: Another Spin on the Merry-Go-Round' (2003) *Public Law Review* 148.

[9] The seminal article for this school of thought is P. Hogg and A. Bushell, 'The Charter Dialogue between Courts and Legislatures (Or Perhaps the Charter of Rights isn't Such A Bad Thing After All)' (1997) 35 *Osgoode Hall Law Journal* 75. For a discussion of its application in the New Zealand context, see S. Jackson, 'Designing Human Rights Legislation: "Dialogue", the Commonwealth Model and the Roles of Parliaments and Courts' (2007) 13 *Auckland University Law Review* 89.

[10] P. Butler, 'Human Rights and Parliamentary Sovereignty in New Zealand' (2004) 35 *Victoria University Wellington Law Review* 341.

[11] A. Butler and P. Butler, *The New Zealand Bill of Rights Act: A Commentary* (Wellington: LexisNexis New Zealand, 2005), para 6.6.25.

[12] J. Allan, 'The Rise of Judicial Activism in New Zealand' (1997) 4 *Agenda* 465; J. Allan, 'Turning Clark Kent into Superman: The New Zealand Bill of Rights Act 1990', (2000) 9 *Otago Law Review* 613; J. Allan, 'Take Heed Australia—A Statutory Bill of Rights and its Inflationary Effects' (2001) 6 *Deakin Law Review* 322; J Allan, 'Portia, Bassanio or Dick the Butcher? Constraining Judges in the Twenty-First Century' (2006) 17 *King's College Law Journal* 1.

[13] J. Smillie, 'Who wants Juristocracy?' (2006) 11 *Otago Law Review* 183, 191.

criminal procedure matters,[14] the collection of evidence,[15] and the rights of the accused.[16] Areas as diverse as the policing of protest activities,[17] the workplace drug testing of employees,[18] and the law of defamation[19] also changed substantially under the NZBORA's influence. Furthermore, the judiciary has extended its remedial powers under the NZBORA by taking upon itself the power to grant stays of criminal proceedings,[20] as well as monetary damages,[21] where considered necessary to compensate for a rights breach.

However, this chapter is not concerned with the NZBORA's impact on New Zealand's law as a whole, but rather examines the narrower question of how it has affected the relationship between New Zealand's Parliament and the courts. The decision in 1990 to downgrade the NZBORA from a higher law document modelled on the Canadian Charter of Rights and Freedoms, 1982 to a weaker, 'parliamentary' bill of rights left final lawmaking authority in Parliament's hands.[22] Nevertheless, the principal architect of the NZBORA, Sir Geoffrey Palmer, still envisioned that the new legislation would exert considerable influence over Parliament's use of its legislative power. Discussing the NZBORA, section 7 requirement that the Attorney-General notify the House of Representatives of any inconsistency between proposed legislation and the NZBORA, he stated:

Public opinion is usually in support of the basic principles stated in the Bill of Rights Act. The fact that a proposed measure is contrary to one of the principles is likely to cause opposition to it for that reason alone. Governments will not want to be seen to be abridging peoples' rights. They will be loath to introduce legislation doing so without good reason and substantial public backing. Thus there is distinct political value in the provision requiring the Attorney-General's certificate. It sounds a warning bell.[23]

In an early commentary on the NZBORA's influence over the legislative process, Grant Huscroft concurred that the NZBORA was intended to restrain Parliament's lawmaking practice:

The assumption was that the Attorney-General's report would dissuade the House from passing legislation inconsistent with the Bill of Rights. More than this, s.7 might prevent bills inconsistent with the Bill of Rights from reaching the House in the first place, if the government were keen to avoid the Attorney-General's report. Even if it did not have this

[14] *R v Poumako* [2000] 2 NZLR 695 (CA); *R v Pora* [2001] 2 NZLR 37 (CA).
[15] *R v Shaheed* [2002] 2 NZLR 377 (CA).
[16] *Ministry of Transport v Noort; Police v Curran* [1992] 3 NZLR 260 (CA).
[17] *Brooker v Police* [2007] 3 NZLR 91 (SCNZ).
[18] *Tuckers Wool Processors v Harrison* [1999] 1 ERNZ 894, 917 (CA); *Cropp v Judicial Committee* [2008] 3 NZLR 774 (SCNZ).
[19] *Lange v Atkinson* [1997] NZLR 22 (HC); *Lange v Atkinson* [1998] 3 NZLR 424 (CA).
[20] *Martin v District Court at Tauranga* [1995] 2 NZLR 419 (CA); *Williams v R* [2009] NZSC 41.
[21] *Simpson v Attorney-General [Baigent's Case]* [1994] 3 NZLR 667 (CA); *Taunoa v Attorney-General* [2008] 1 NZLR 429 (SCNZ).
[22] For an account of this move, see P. Rishworth, 'The Birth and Rebirth of the Bill of Rights', in P. Rishworth and G. Huscroft (eds), *Rights and Freedoms: The New Zealand Bill of Rights 1990 and the Human Rights Act 1993* (Wellington: Brookers, 1995), 1 at 13–25.
[23] G. Palmer, *New Zealand's Constitution in Crisis: Reforming our Political System* (Dunedin: John McIndoe, 1992), 59. See also his comments to the House during the Third Reading debate; 50 *NZPD* 3760 (21 August 1990).

prophylactic effect, s.7 might at least ensure the Bill of Rights would be given consideration during the policy development process.[24]

Huscroft then suggested that even though 'rejection of the Attorney-General's advice is the right of the House, in the long run it should not occur very often'; while '[t]he decision to *ignore* a report from the Attorney-General is even less likely to occur, but more serious if it does'.[25]

Such predictions about the NZBORA's restraining influence on legislative practice assumed that governmental actors, up to and including the Attorney-General, will be motivated to carefully scrutinize legislative proposals for NZBORA inconsistencies and weed out measures that fail this test. Parliamentarians, concerned to avoid a public backlash against perceived 'rights unfriendly' lawmakers, will think long and hard before agreeing to enact any surviving bill that the Attorney-General flags as NZBORA inconsistent. Consequently, it would be a relatively infrequent event for a bill attracting a section 7 notice to be introduced into the House, with the passage of any such bills into law being even rarer.[26] This expectation then fits with the claims of both bills of rights proponents and critics. For proponents, it sets up an inter-institutional, cross-government incentive to identify and uphold individual rights that may help to counteract the majoritarian pressures that otherwise govern parliamentary lawmaking practices. For critics, the fact that parliamentarians might in practice be cowed into accepting the Attorney-General's *diktat* on the rights-consistency of some legislative proposal is yet another way in which even parliamentary bills of rights can take power away from elected representatives, handing it instead to those judicial actors who ultimately determine what rights 'mean'.

My argument in this chapter is that both interpretations have missed the mark, because their basic premise is false. Rather than New Zealand's governmental actors and parliamentarians feeling compelled to abide by the judiciary's interpretation of what individual rights require, as critics of the NZBORA fear, they repeatedly have proven willing to introduce and pass legislation implementing their own understanding of those rights. However, the attention paid to the judiciary's views on NZBORA issues by both government when designing legislation and parliamentarians when considering it has been less than the NZBORA's boosters might wish. So instead of fostering a genuine inter-institutional dialogue on rights issues, or acting as a Trojan horse that enables judges to penetrate the ramparts of parliamentary sovereignty, I will argue that the NZBORA really has not done much

---

[24] G. Huscroft, 'The Attorney-General, the Bill of Rights, and the Public Interest', in Rishworth and Huscroft, above n 22, at 137.

[25] Ibid at 146.

[26] I am speculating here, but it may be that such predictions reflected experience under first the Canadian Bill of Rights 1960, then the Canadian Charter of Rights and Freedoms 1982. Even though both these instruments impose a similar reporting function to the NZBORA, s 7 on Canada's Attorney-General, only one report was issued in 22 years under the former statute, while no report has ever been issued under the latter. See P. Joseph, 'The New Zealand Bill of Rights Experience', in P. Alston (ed), *Promoting Human Rights through Bills of Rights* (Oxford: Oxford University Press, 1999), 283, 313; G. Huscroft, 'Reconciling Duty and Discretion: The Attorney General in the Charter Era' (2009) 34 *Queens Law Journal* 769.

at all to change how New Zealand's legislative branch functions. Instead, I think that New Zealand's legislative experience under the NZBORA partly vindicates a hypothesis put forward by Mark Tushnet;[27] namely, that parliamentary bills of rights authorizing weak-form judicial review of legislation may develop over time in the direction of strong-form review, or else revert to parliamentary sovereignty *simpliciter*. While the United Kingdom may provide an example of the former tendency (given the judiciary's preparedness to aggressively 'interpret' away rights inconsistencies in legislation and Parliament's almost universal practice of amending legislation that cannot be so interpreted),[28] New Zealand provides an example of the latter.

That, anyway, will be the thrust of the argument put forward here. In order to substantiate it, I first look at the various features in the NZBORA designed to interweave legislative and judicial perspectives on rights. This examination involves both *ex ante* measures intended to ensure Parliament does not legislate inadvertently or accidentally in a manner that is inconsistent with the NZBORA, and *ex post* measures that allow the judiciary to ameliorate the effects of any NZBORA inconsistent legislative provisions. I will suggest that both these approaches exert such a weak influence over Parliament's lawmaking practices that the NZBORA essentially is irrelevant. The chapter then concludes with some suggestions for why this state of affairs has developed in the New Zealand context, and considers a range of suggested reforms to increase the NZBORA's relevance to the legislative process.

I. How the NZBORA Structures the Relationship of Parliament and the Courts

Before looking at how the NZBORA configures the relationship of Parliament and the courts, it is worth re-emphasizing that this rights instrument does not purport to limit Parliament's formal, sovereign authority to make whatever law it chooses. Section 4 explicitly states that a court cannot declare invalid or refuse to apply any competing statutory provision 'by reason only that the provision is inconsistent with any provision of this Bill of Rights'. And while the NZBORA

---

[27] M. Tushnet, *Weak Courts, Strong Rights: Judicial Review and Social Welfare Rights in Comparative Constitutional Law* (Princeton: Princeton University Press, 2008), 43–76; M. Tushnet, 'Weak-Form Judicial Review: Its Implications for Legislatures' (2004) 2 *New Zealand Journal of Public and International Law* 7, 17–23; M. Tushnet, 'New Forms of Judicial Review and the Persistence of Rights-and Democracy-Based Worries' (2003) 38 *Wake Forest Law Review* 813, 824 (noting that weak-form judicial review 'may well be transformed in either direction—reducing [its] scope so that weak-form systems are actually systems of parliamentary supremacy (and thereby reproducing the worry about inadequate protection of liberal rights), or expanding [its] scope so that weak-form systems are actually strong-form systems (and thereby reproducing the worry about interfering with democratic self-governance)'). See also J. Hiebert, 'New Constitutional Ideas: Can New Parliamentary Models Resist Judicial Dominance When Interpreting Rights?' (2004) 82 *Texas Law Review* 1963.

[28] Geddis and Fenton, n 6 above, at 754–60; 766-770. See also the chapter in this volume by James Allan.

does apply by virtue of section 3(a) to 'acts done' by the legislative branch of government, Claudia Geiringer convincingly argues that this section encompasses
only Parliament's internal procedures and processes, not the substantive content
of legislation considered and enacted by that body.[29] Consequently, not only does
the NZBORA itself expressly prohibit the judiciary from enforcing its provisions
by striking down inconsistent legislation, as a matter of constitutional theory the
provisions of the NZBORA impose no more than a politico-moral, not legal, constraint on Parliament's power to make law.[30]

The content of this politico-moral constraint is that New Zealand's Parliament
should not legislate in a manner that limits one of the fundamental rights and
freedoms guaranteed in the NZBORA, unless satisfied that the limit meets the
section 5 test of being 'demonstrably justified in a free and democratic society'.
A number of mechanisms designed to institutionalize and actualize this politico-
moral constraint then apply. Three of these operate *ex ante*, in an effort to ensure
that Parliament will only enact limits it is satisfied are NZBORA consistent (ie that
it considers demonstrably justified as per section 5). Two operate *ex post*, giving the
courts some role in assessing and responding to parliamentary enactments that
give rise to NZBORA concerns. However, despite this apparently neat division
of labour between the branches of government, there actually is a considerable
bleed between them. When those involved in creating legislation are considering
whether any proposed limit on a NZBORA right is demonstrably justified, they
should have reference to previous judicial decisions discussing what that 'right' and
the 'demonstrably justified limits' on it mean. Equally, when the courts are called
on to interpret and apply legislation in light of the NZBORA, they should be conscious of where final responsibility for creating the law lies within the New Zealand
constitutional framework. Dialogue proponents value this interplay between the
two branches as leading to the best (or most reasonable, or most defensible) understanding of what individual rights guarantees require, while rights-sceptics fear it
will result in the judicial view coming to dominate over that of the legislature. In
the discussion below, I seek to raise a third possibility: the impact of the NZBORA
on Parliament's behaviour is so minimal in nature as to be almost irrelevant.

(a) NZBORA scrutiny of legislation during its development

The first means by which NZBORA considerations may influence legislative outcomes actually occurs before a matter enters the parliamentary realm, during the
process of a bill's development within the executive branch. Most law enacted by
New Zealand's Parliament originates as a government bill. Although minority government has become something of the norm under New Zealand's Mixed-Member
Proportional (MMP) electoral system, Standing Orders continue to give the government's legislative programme precedence on the House of Representatives'

[29] C. Geiringer, 'The Dead Hand of the Bill of Rights?' (2007) 11 *Otago Law Review* 389.
[30] Ibid at 390.

timetable.[31] The result is that, except for a limited amount of time set aside to deal with members and local bills, the bulk of Parliament's lawmaking activity revolves around debating, deliberating, and voting on the government's legislative proposals. Therefore, the NZBORA's influence on the development of legislation within government departments has enormous potential consequences for the parliamentary consideration of rights matters. In particular, if government departments habitually display a hyper-cautious approach toward potential NZBORA inconsistencies when developing legislative proposals, then Parliament will never get to see and evaluate a number of possible policy measures.

Various mechanisms exist to ensure government departments consider and flag NZBORA issues when developing legislation; a process termed 'NZBORA vetting'. Before introduction into the House, all government Bills require a sign-off from Cabinet. Cabinet's guidelines require that:

Cabinet papers accompanying a draft bill/regulations should include a statement about any inconsistencies with the rights and freedoms contained in the New Zealand Bill of Rights Act 1990 and the Human Rights Act 1993. Specifically, the statement must state the nature of the potential inconsistencies identified, or state that there are none, and note the steps taken to address the issue, or include information on any justifications for the bill/regulations infringing a right or freedom.[32]

When creating legislative proposals for submission to Cabinet, government departments are expected to follow the guidelines developed by the Legislation Advisory Committee.[33] This 'best-practice' manual includes a chapter on how to identify and address human rights issues, which in essence summarizes what the New Zealand courts have said on the matter.[34] Legal advisors in government departments also may seek advice from the specialist NZBORA unit in the Ministry of Justice. Again, as this is legal advice proffered by lawyers, it takes the form of predicting what a court would say on the matter if ever called upon to adjudicate it. What this means is that consideration of whether a policy proposal is NZBORA consistent—is 'demonstrably justified in a free and democratic society'—mainly revolves around a legalistic assessment of the judiciary's likely view of the matter.[35]

---

[31] Standing Orders of the House of Representatives (2008), SO 60–73. Furthermore, all governments negotiate support for urgency motions as part of their post-election agreements with other parties; see R. Malone, *Rebalancing the Constitution: The Challenge of Government Law-Making under MMP* (Wellington: Institute of Policy Studies, 2008), 61–84.

[32] See <http://www.cabguide.cabinetoffice.govt.nz/procedures/legislation/checking-human-rights-issues>.

[33] Cabinet Office, *Cabinet Manual* (Wellington: Cabinet Office, 2008), [7.60]. However, this expectation is not always realized. The founder and current chair of the LAC, Sir Geoffrey Palmer, has described its role in the legislative process as 'benign, but peripheral'. G. Palmer, 'Improving the Quality of Legislation—the Legislation Advisory Committee, the Legislation Design Committee and What Lies Beyond?', (2007) 15 *Waikato Law Review* 12, 16.

[34] See <http://www.justice.govt.nz/lac/pubs/2001/legislative_guide_2000/chapter_4.html>. The current LAC Guidelines simply replicate the approach adopted by the Court of Appeal in *Moonen v Film and Literature Board of Review* [2000] 2 NZLR 9 (CA); these are in the process of being updated to reflect the Supreme Court's decision in *Hansen v R* [2007] 3 NZLR 1 (SC).

[35] For why this must be so, see P. Rishworth, 'The Inevitability of Judicial Review under Interpretive Bills of Rights: Canada's Legacy to New Zealand and Commonwealth Constitutionalism', in G. Huscroft and I. Brodie (eds), *Constitutionalism in the Charter Era* (Toronto: LexisNexis Canada, 2004), 233.

Both Janet Hiebert[36] and Grant Huscroft[37] have expressed concern that this dependency on legal advice during the NZBORA vetting process could lead to a back-door triumph of the judiciary's view on rights. If the legal advice—primarily based on prior judicial decisions—is that a rights-limiting measure likely fails the section 5 justificatory test, and for that reason the measure is dropped from the government's legislative programme, then the judiciary is (in effect) dictating what measures Parliament will get to consider and vote on. However, it is difficult to gauge how reasonable such fears are, as it is impossible to measure just how much of an impact the NZBORA vetting process actually has on the creation of the government's legislative proposals. The development of bills within the executive branch takes place inside something of a black box. It is very difficult to obtain draft bills or official advice under the Official Information Act 1982.[38] I also know of no quantitative academic research into the issue in New Zealand.[39] Consequently, only a couple of generalized observations are appropriate here.

First, there is no doubt that the government will decide against bringing some legislative proposals before Parliament after receiving advice that they are NZBORA inconsistent. This outcome may occur because the government accepts that the apparent NZBORA inconsistency means the measure would be a bad one to make into law, or fears the political costs of being seen to propose 'rights breach-ing' law, or some mix of the two motives. It also is true that the identification of an apparent NZBORA inconsistency predominantly will reflect legal advice that a court would, if it ever were to look at the rights-limiting measure, conclude it can-not be demonstrably justified in a free and democratic society. However, it is not possible to quantify with any certainty the number of such measures that disappear from the government's legislative programme for this reason (ie whether this is a frequent occurrence, or a relatively rare one). Nor is it possible to know what would have happened to a given measure if the NZBORA did not exist (ie whether the proposal would have been dropped or changed in any case, because of the existence of general 'rule of law' or individual rights concerns irrespective of any NZBORA analysis). Therefore, it is entirely possible that the entire vetting process of legisla-tion has produced nothing more than what Mark Tushnet calls 'noise around zero'; that is 'essentially random changes, sometimes good and sometimes bad, to what the political system [otherwise would have produced]'.[40]

---

[36] J. Hiebert, 'Parliamentary Bills of Rights: An Alternative Model?' (2006) 69 *Modern Law Review* 7, 26. See also her chapter in this volume.

[37] G. Huscroft, 'Is the Defeat of Health Warnings a Victory for Human Rights? The Attorney-General and Pre-legislative Scrutiny for Consistency with the New Zealand Bill of Rights' (2003) 14 *Public Law Review* 109.

[38] See Official Information Act 1982, s 9(1)(f) and (g).

[39] G. Palmer and M. Palmer, *Bridled Power: New Zealand's Constitution and Government*, 4th edn (Oxford: Oxford University Press, 2004), 326 do express the opinion that 'it is already clear that the requirement to test legislative proposals against a clear set of principles has a beneficial effect in protecting the values embodied in the Bill of Rights Act.' However, they provide no evidence to substantiate that assertion.

[40] M. Tushnet, *Taking the Constitution Away from the Courts* (Princeton: Princeton University Press, 2000), 153.

Secondly, even accepting that the NZBORA vetting process might well result in the abandonment or amendment of *some* legislative proposals, the fact a measure apparently is NZBORA inconsistent does not raise an *absolute* barrier to government including it in a bill. As a matter of formal constitutional theory, the NZBORA does not prevent a minister from introducing apparently inconsistent legislative proposals into the House of Representatives.[41] Furthermore, as a matter of practice, successive governments have been quite prepared to push forward with legislative proposals after being told these contain apparently NZBORA-inconsistent measures (as is discussed further in the next section). As such, the best description for the purpose of the NZBORA vetting process during the development of legislation is 'no surprises/minimize problems'. A government wishes to know all the potential implications of including a measure in its legislative agenda, including the possibility it might attract criticism for proposing apparently NZBORA-inconsistent law. If it is possible to avoid the risk of such criticism while still achieving the desired policy end, then obviously this will be the government's preferred outcome. However, if the NZBORA inconsistency cannot be avoided, and the government believes the policy measure important enough (or politically popular enough) to warrant attracting a measure of criticism, it remains completely free in both theory and practice to bring it before Parliament. Scrutiny of the NZBORA implications of the proposal then passes into the hands of the legislative branch, with section 7 mandating a procedure designed to facilitate that scrutiny.

(b) The Attorney-General's reporting duty

Section 7 of the NZBORA places a duty on the Attorney-General to report to Parliament on any bill that, in the Attorney-General's opinion, contains measures that appear to be inconsistent with the NZBORA's guaranteed rights and freedoms. This reporting duty takes the form of a notice attached to the bill when first introduced into the House of Representatives;[42] setting out the Attorney-General's reasons for believing an inconsistency exists. In practice, these reasons largely reproduce the advice given to the Attorney-General by legally trained officials in the Ministry of Justice (or, where a bill is introduced by the Minister of Justice, the Crown Law Office).[43] Furthermore, the Attorney-General's practice is

---

[41] See C. Geiringer, 'The Dead Hand of the Bill of Rights?' (2007) 11 *Otago Law Review* 389. Any such interpretation of the NZBORA would make redundant the s 7 reporting duty (discussed in the following section). Furthermore, even if the NZBORA *was* interpreted as preventing a minister from introducing apparently inconsistent legislation into the House of Representatives, the courts could not enforce this bar due to the 'established principle of non-interference by the Courts in parliamentary proceedings'. *Te Runanga o Wharekauri Rehohu Inc v Attorney-General* [1993] 2 NZLR 301, 307–8 (CA).

[42] See Standing Order 266.

[43] G. Huscroft, 'The Attorney-General's Reporting Duty', in P. Rishworth, G. Huscroft, S. Optican, and R. Mahoney, *The New Zealand Bill of Rights Act* (Oxford: Oxford University Press, 2003), 215. But see also the comments of the current Attorney-General, Chris Finlayson: 'I don't take the view that I'm some kind of automaton and just sign off on what is given to me. I will examine the matter carefully.' P. Gower, 'Finlayson "Just Doing My Duty" on Crime Bills' (4 Mar 2009) *New Zealand Herald*.

only to issue a section 7 report when this advice is that the bill *is* inconsistent with the NZBORA; that is, it contains a limit on a substantive right that cannot be justified in terms of section 5. Where the advice is that the limit can be so justified, a section 7 report will not be issued. However, since 2003 the government voluntarily has made the advice provided to the Attorney-General on each bill available on the Ministry of Justice website.[44]

The section 7 reporting process is the main mechanism by which Parliament is empowered to consider NZBORA issues when legislating. Andrew and Petra Butler explain its purpose this way; 'in those instances where the promoter of a Bill proceeds with a version that is inconsistent with the NZBORA, Parliament is informed of that fact and is able to squarely address issues of NZBORA-inconsistency to the extent that it regards that inconsistency as a matter of public concern'.[45] Janet Hiebert considers that section 7 embodies the 'idea of political rights-vetting',[46] by which she means 'the establishment of new responsibilities and procedures for public and political officials to assess policy initiatives and legislative Bills in terms of their consistency with protected rights'.[47] Of course, the value of a section 7 report heavily depends upon the quality and accuracy of the advice provided to the Attorney-General. Differing opinions on this matter have been expressed: Caroline Archer has argued that the Attorney-General generally is too slow to report NZBORA inconsistencies;[48] while Grant Huscroft believes there has been significant over-reportage.[49] This disagreement perhaps reflects a more basic division on the proper purpose of section 7: should it be a red flag raised whenever *any* possibly NZBORA-inconsistent matter comes before the House; or should it be a backstop warning mechanism utilized only when there is *no* possible justification for the measure?

There also has been some debate as to whether the courts could oversee the Attorney-General's exercise of his statutory duty under standard principles of judicial review. After all, given that a section 7 report is predicated on legal advice that (in effect) guesses what judges might think of the NZBORA consistency of proposed legislation, should not a court be able to examine the content of that advice and pass judgment on whether the Attorney-General has properly carried out his functions under the NZBORA? As superficially attractive as this argument may appear, however, the courts have firmly rejected it on two separate occasions.[50] Most recently, in *Boscowan v Attorney-General* the Court of Appeal upheld the striking out of an application to judicially review the Attorney-General's failure to attach a section 7 report to the Electoral Finance Bill 2007. It did so on the

[44] See <http://www.justice.govt.nz/bill-of-rights/index.html> (last visited 1 Aug 2009).

[45] Butler and Butler, above n 11, para 8.4.1.

[46] J. Hiebert, 'Rights-Vetting in New Zealand and Canada: Similar Idea, Different Outcomes' (2005) 3 *New Zealand Journal of Public and International Law* 63, 68.

[47] Ibid 64.

[48] C. Archer, 'Section 7 of the Bill of Rights Act' [2004] *New Zealand Law Journal* 320.

[49] G. Huscroft, 'The Attorney-General's Reporting Duty', in Rishworth et al., above n 43, 215.

[50] *Mangawaro Enterprises Ltd v Attorney-General* [1994] 2 NZLR 451 (HC); *Boscawen v Attorney-General* [2009] NZCA 12.

grounds of comity between the legislative and judicial branches,[51] concluding that to engage in a review of the Attorney-General's decision would:

[P]lace the Court at the heart of a political debate actually being carried on in the House. It would effectively force a confrontation between the Attorney-General and the Courts, on a topic in which Parliament has entrusted the required assessment to the Attorney-General, not to the Courts. If the Court took a different view from that of the Attorney-General, it is hard to see how it could require the Attorney-General to make a report to Parliament which the Attorney-General considered to be incorrect.... A declaration that the Attorney-General should recommend that the Bill be reintroduced would be an even greater interference with the political and legislative processes of the House. In short, a review of the s 7 duty in this manner would be the antithesis of the comity principle.[52]

The Court of Appeal thus affirmed the view of Clifford J in the High Court as to the basic division of labour envisaged by the NZBORA.

The roles accorded to Parliament and the Courts by [the NZBORA] seem reasonably clear. The NZBORA provides for scrutiny specifically by Parliament via s 7, and scrutiny by the Courts through ss 4, 5 and 6. In terms of comity and common sense..., the Court would in my view therefore be unwise to exercise a power of review of s 7 actions.[53]

The next section will discuss how Parliament scrutinizes legislative proposals from a NZBORA perspective. Before turning to this matter, however, the frequency of section 7 reports needs to be considered as context. Since 1990, the Attorney-General has issued a total of forty-seven section 7 reports.[54] Of these, twenty-two related to government bills, with the remaining twenty-five relating to members or local bills. The greater number of section 7 reports issued for the latter two types of bills has occurred despite far fewer of these actually being introduced into the House. This disproportionality reflects the fact that those preparing members and local bills cannot call on the assistance of either government officials or parliamentary drafters. Consequently, the process of identifying and resolving potential NZBORA inconsistencies in the course of policy development and legislative drafting that occurs with government bills does not apply to them. That said, twenty-two section 7 reports for government bills is a not inconsiderable number,[55] and is evidence that governments are prepared to advance legislative proposals even after being told these apparently are NZBORA inconsistent. It also is relevant that seventeen of these section 7 reports apply to Bills introduced since 2000, indicating that even after more than a decade of experience with the NZBORA, governments still are prepared to bring apparently NZBORA-inconsistent legislation before the House. This seems true of

---

[51] *Boscawen v Attorney-General* [2009] NZCA 12, [42].
[52] Ibid at [36].
[53] *Boscawen v Attorney-General (No 2)* [2008] NZAR 468, [49] (HC).
[54] All the figures cited in this chapter are current as of 1 Aug 2009.
[55] Especially when put alongside Canada (where no government bill has been introduced into the House with an Attorney-General's notice that it may be inconsistent with the Canadian Charter of Rights and Freedoms 1982) and the United Kingdom (where only one government bill has been introduced with a ministerial notice that it may be incompatible with the European Convention on Human Rights).

parties on both the left and right of the New Zealand political spectrum: the Labour-led government introduced fourteen bills with section 7 reports attached between 1999–2008; while the new National Government's legislative programme attracted three section 7 reports in just its first six months in office.

(c) Parliamentary scrutiny of NZBORA issues

The fact that the Attorney-General has attached a section 7 report to a bill has no formal implications for that proposed legislation's status. No special parliamentary procedures apply to a bill that has received a section 7 report. It does not go, for instance, to a special select committee for greater scrutiny,[56] nor does it require a super-majority vote in order to proceed. Instead, the consequences of a section 7 report depend entirely on the importance that the members of Parliament attach to it during the normal legislative process. The consensus amongst academic commentators is that parliamentarians do not necessarily think such notices are a matter of any particular concern. Janet Hiebert suggests that; 'despite the frequency of section 7 reports, they have seldom led to amendments to redress the perceived inconsistencies'.[57] Tessa Bromwich concurs: 'On occasion, Parliament has lived up to [the ideal of squarely confronting the rights implications of proposed legislation], but too often it has ignored the human rights issues raised by the Attorney-General.'[58] These rather generalized comments indicate that there is no universal response—certainly, no universal *negative* response—on the part of parliamentarians to the Attorney-General's flagging of a NZBORA inconsistency. Rather, if I may be forgiven for paraphrasing Lord Steyn,[59] context is everything when legislating under the shadow of the NZBORA.

That is to say, the parliamentarians' perception of the importance of a section 7 report on any given legislative proposal depends on a number of factors.[60] Foremost is whether the proposed legislation is a government bill, or a local or members bill. A section 7 report attached to a government bill almost always has negligible impact, as the government already has committed substantial policy resources and political capital by introducing it into the House, so has a vested interest in pushing it through to enactment. Of the twenty-two government bills to receive section 7 reports, eighteen have become law without any change to the apparently NZBORA-inconsistent measure.[61] Two of the remaining bills currently are before parliamentary select committees. Therefore, only two government bills receiving section 7 reports have been amended to remove the reported NZBORA

---

[56] As was suggested by the Justice and Law Reform Committee, 'Final Report on a White Paper: A Bill of Rights for New Zealand' (1987–90) 27 *Australian Journal of Human Rights* I.8c.

[57] .Hiebert, above note 46, 88.

[58] T. Bromwich, 'Parliamentary rights-vetting under the NZBORA' [2009] *New Zealand Law Journal* 192.

[59] *R v Secretary of State, ex parte Daly* [2001] 3 All ER 433, [28].

[60] Bromwich, above n 58, 189.

[61] Indeed, the most recent government bill to receive an s 7 notice, the Parole (Extended Supervision Orders) Amendment Bill 2009, was introduced, debated under urgency, and passed by the House in a single day!

inconsistency.[62] By contrast, nineteen of the twenty-five local and members bills receiving section 7 reports either were defeated on the floor of the House, or were passed only after the apparently NZBORA-inconsistent measure was amended. Only five such bills were enacted with the apparently NZBORA-inconsistent measure intact, while one currently remains before the House.

However, some caution is required before attributing a direct causal relationship between the fate of these latter legislative proposals and the existence of a section 7 report. Most members or local bills fail to make it through the legislative process, irrespective of whether they raise any NZBORA issues. In particular, if the governing party chooses not to give its support to a members or local bill, there almost certainly will not be a majority of votes for it on the floor of the House. Furthermore, as noted above, the sponsors of such bills cannot call upon the resources of public servants or parliamentary drafters when creating their legislative proposals. This lack of policy advice means the bill often enters the House in a hopelessly confused state. Consequently, the presence of a section 7 report may correlate to wider problems in the bill's conception and execution, which would cause it to be rejected in any case. Thus, the relevant conclusion is that a government bill attracting a section 7 report almost always will become law in its original form (as is the case for most government bills), while most members or local bills attracting a section 7 report will be rejected or amended by Parliament (as is the case for most members or local bills).

Of course, a section 7 report is not the only way in which parliamentarians come to consider NZBORA issues when legislating. Concerned individuals or groups may raise a bill's NZBORA implications through public submissions during its select committee stage. The publication since 2003 of the NZBORA advice provided to the Attorney-General helps facilitate such submissions, as it makes transparent the basis for his or her decision to not attach a section 7 report. Because this advice involves judgment calls on issues generating reasonable disagreement, submitters may take a quite different view of those issues. Such submissions on a bill's NZBORA implications, on occasion, result in the select committee recommending amendments to its provisions, even though the Attorney-General believed the original measures generated no apparent NZBORA inconsistency.[63] However, it is important not to overstate the NZBORA's influence during this scrutiny process. For one thing, select committees frequently recommend amendments to bills in response to a wide variety of arguments raised during select

---

[62] Children, Young Persons and their Families Bill 1993 (provisions requiring the mandatory reporting of suspected child abuse dropped from the bill); Electoral Amendment Bill 2001 (provisions banning the publication of opinion polls in the month preceding an election dropped from the bill). Note, however, that this latter measure only was included in the government bill due to a deal struck with one of its support parties. The government agreed only to support this measure as far as select committee, with no guarantee of its support thereafter.

[63] The *Report of the Foreign Affairs, Defence and Trade Committee on the Climate Change Response Bill 2002* (212-2) (2002) provides an example of this phenomenon, where provisions authorizing officials to enter land for the purpose of searching it were amended by the select committee after numerous submissions that this power was inconsistent with the NZBORA's guarantee against unreasonable search and seizure. The bill had not attracted an s 7 report from the Attorney-General.

committee hearings. Submissions on a bill's NZBORA implications may thus be no different to any other policy argument. That is to say, the relevant metric is not whether a particular select committee cites the NZBORA when recommending amendments to a bill, but rather whether the existence of the NZBORA makes that select committee *more likely to* recommend amendments than otherwise. Parliamentarians' interest in and concern for individual rights did not begin in 1990, so the NZBORA only really is relevant to the legislative process if it leads parliamentarians to adopt a different approach than they would without it. There is no real evidence that this is the case; certainly, there is none that a mere allegation that a bill is inconsistent with the NZBORA will spur members of Parliament to change its provisions.

I admit that this overview of the NZBORA's impact on Parliament's legislative behaviour is somewhat anecdotal and impressionistic. Nevertheless, I think that it contains enough substance to warrant a couple of conclusions. For one thing, there is little to support a hypothesis that the NZBORA has led parliamentarians to fall under the spell of judicial interpretations of rights. Parliament has instead repeatedly proven willing to enact legislative measures after being told they appear to be inconsistent with the NZBORA. This outcome is particularly pronounced where the bill at issue contains policy formulated and presented by the government.[64] Second, while parliamentarians clearly are prepared to enact legislation embodying their own interpretations of individual rights, this process does not really represent the sort of 'dialogue' many NZBORA proponents desire. For one thing, Parliament has differed from the Attorney-General's view on the apparent NZBORA inconsistency of a bill over half the time.[65] With regard to government bills, it has differed from the Attorney-General's view 90 per cent of the time.[66] These raw numbers inevitably call into question any expectation that the NZBORA will operate as a significant check on Parliament's legislative behaviour,[67] in that the fear of appearing to be 'anti-rights' will dissuade MPs from routinely deciding to enact laws that they have been told unjustifiably limit individual rights.[68]

---

[64] Indeed, Paul Rishworth speculates that 'there is now a question whether a s 7 report is truly criticism [of the relevant Bill]; in matters of criminal procedure and the like, it may be coming to be a badge of honour.' P. Rishworth, 'Human Rights—Section 7 and the Attorney-General's Reporting Duty' [2005] *New Zealand Law Review* 87, 103.

[65] As of 1 August 2009, 44 bills receiving s 7 notices had been enacted or voted down. Of these, 23 were enacted without any change to the apparently NZBORA-inconsistent provision.

[66] As of 1 August 2009, 20 government Bills receiving s 7 notices had been enacted. Of these, 18 were enacted without any change to the apparently NZBORA-inconsistent provision.

[67] See above, nn 23–5 and accompanying text.

[68] Certainly, Parliament's practice in this regard has disappointed some academic commentators; see M. Taggart, 'Tugging on Superman's Cape: Lessons from Experience with the New Zealand Bill of Rights Act 1990' [1998] *Public Law* 266, 272 ('On the negative side is the undignified sight—as has occurred in New Zealand—of the House disregarding or rejecting the view of the Attorney-General on consistency'); P. Joseph, *Constitutional and Administrative Law in New Zealand*, 3rd edn (Oxford: Oxford University Press, 2007), 1174 ('The reporting procedure was intended to have a salutary effect on government legislation.... However, the reporting function has not had the deterrent effect that was hoped.').

(d) 'Rights friendly' statutory interpretation by the judiciary

Once Parliament has made its decision on individual rights during the legislative process, the matter then passes over into the adjudicative context. That
is to say, Parliament's general conclusions on individual rights—as embodied
in the text of its enactment—inevitably experiences judicial interpretation
and application in the process of hearing and deciding individual cases. The
NZBORA itself recognizes this fact, with section 6 specifically instructing
the courts: 'Wherever an enactment can be given a meaning that is consistent
with the rights and freedoms contained in this Bill of Rights, that meaning
shall be preferred to any other meaning.' This interpretative command creates
further potential for dialogue (or conflict) between the legislative and judicial
branches. When seeking and adopting 'rights friendly' readings of statutes, the
courts may endeavour to avoid what they consider to be NZBORA-inconsistent
outcomes in the particular circumstances of the individual case, despite what
appears to be Parliament's general intention as expressed through its enactment.
That, anyway, is the hope of dialogue proponents, as well as the fear of rights
sceptics.[69]

However, the issue of rights friendly-interpretation in New Zealand perhaps
is less pressing following the Supreme Court's decision in *R v Hansen*.[70] In this
case, four of the five-strong bench concluded that a statutory provision deeming
a person in possession of a set amount of cannabis to possess that drug for the
purpose of supply,[71] then requiring the accused to 'prove' the contrary, was an
unreasonable limit on the accused's NZBORA right to be presumed innocent.
Even so, none of the judges felt able to give the provision a meaning that would
avoid this NZBORA-inconsistent outcome. This judicial refusal to depart from
Parliament's apparent intention that the accused must bear the legal burden of
disproving an intention to supply came despite the fact that the House of Lords
had used the equivalent interpretative provision in the Human Rights Act 1998
to read down the same reverse onus provision in UK law.[72] The New Zealand
Supreme Court considered, and then expressly rejected, the UK judiciary's view
that the search for rights-friendly interpretations 'mandate[s] a judicial override
of Parliament, if Parliament's meaning is inconsistent with a right or freedom'.[73]
As Justice Tipping diplomatically stated: 'whether [such an approach] is appropriate in England is not for me to say, but I am satisfied that it is not appropriate
in New Zealand'.[74]

In light of the *Hansen* decision, Claudia Geiringer points out that there is
no real difference between the judiciary's interpretative approach under the

[69] I discuss this issue in greater depth in Geddis and Fenton, above n 6.
[70] *R v Hansen* [2007] 3 NZLR 1.
[71] The offence of possession with intent to supply carries a significantly greater sentencing tariff
than does simple possession.
[72] *R v Lambert* [2002] 2 AC 545 (H.L.).
[73] *R v Hansen* [2007] 3 NZLR 1, [158] (per Tipping J). See also ibid, [256] (per McGrath J).
[74] *R v Hansen* [2007] 3 NZLR 1, [158].

NZBORA, section 6, and that already practised under the common-law 'principle of legality':[75]

New Zealand judges, by contrast with some United Kingdom judges, have not understood section 6 of the Bill of Rights Act as inviting a new and distinctive approach to statutory interpretation. Rather, they have treated section 6 as a legislative manifestation of the established common law principle that legislation is, where possible, to be interpreted consistently with fundamental rights recognized by the common law. The *Hansen* decision is consistent with that general orientation.[76]

This is not to say that the courts have completely ignored the section 6 interpretative mandate. For example, it has been used to limit the application of general statutory language in a rights-consistent manner.[77] Similarly, the Court of Appeal in *Drew v Attorney-General* used section 6 to interpret a statute's general regulation-making power so that any NZBORA-inconsistent regulations will be deemed *ultra vires*.[78] To realize the NZBORA, section 21 guarantees against 'unreasonable' searches and seizures, narrow interpretations of the statutory powers[79] (and related immunities[80]) of the police and other state actors have been adopted. Several members of the Court of Appeal also concluded (albeit in obiter comments) that section 6 justified adopting a quite inventive understanding of the relationship between various legislative amendments to avoid the application of retrospective criminal penalties in two particular cases.[81]

However, even in cases where the courts have invoked section 6 to justify a particular rights-friendly reading of an enactment, they are quick to stress that the adopted meaning always must be plausible in light of the particular language

---

[75] This term is used in *R v Home Secretary, ex p Pierson* [1998] AC 539, 587–9 (HL) (per Lord Steyn) and in *Ngati Apa Ki Te Waipounamu Trust v R* [2000] 2 NZLR 659, 675 (CA) (per Elias CJ). See also *Commissioner of Inland Revenue v West-Walker* [1954] NZLR 191, 212 (CA):

> Where the Legislature uses plain unequivocal language capable of only one meaning, it must be taken to mean what it has plainly expressed whatever may be the consequences. But, unless the language produces a conviction that it was the intention of the Legislature to effect what would constitute a most serious interference with the liberty of the subject and to perpetuate what can fairly be regarded as an injustice, one should be slow to attribute such an intention to the Legislature.

[76] C. Geiringer, 'The Principle of Legality and the Bill of Rights Act: A Critical Examination of *R v Hansen*' (2008) 6 *New Zealand Journal of Public and International Law* 59, 73.

[77] *Newspaper Publishers Association of New Zealand v Family Court* [1999] 2 NZLR 344, 350–1 (HC) (interpreting the Guardianship Act 1968, s 23); *Police v Beggs* [1999] 3 NZLR 615 (HC) (interpreting the Trespass Act 1980, s 3(1)).

[78] [2002] 1 NZLR 58 (CA).

[79] *R v Laugalis* [1993] 10 CRNZ 563 (CA); *Choudry v Attorney-General* [1999] 2 NZLR 582 (CA); *Choudry v Attorney-General (no 2)* [1999] 3 NZLR 399 (CA).

[80] *Simpson v Attorney-General [Baigent's Case]* [1994] 3 NZLR 667 (CA).

[81] *R v Poumako* [2000] 2 NZLR 695 (CA); *R v Pora* [2001] 2 NZLR 37 (CA). These cases arguably mark the high-water mark of judicial use of the section 6 mandate. As context, it should be noted that both involved a statutory provision introduced in the final stages of the House's consideration of legislation, which received no detailed or extended debate before enactment. As such, Elias CJ characterized Parliament as having 'misfired' on this occasion, thereby permitting more assertive interpretative techniques than would be permissible in the case of 'proper' legislation; *R v Pora* [2001] 2 NZLR 37, [49]. See also P. Joseph, 'When Parliament "Misfires": Retrospective Criminal Penalties' (2001) 4 *New Zealand Law Review* 451.

Parliament has used to express its policy goals.[82] As the *Hansen* judgment now firmly establishes, the courts may use section 6 to shade or colour general words used in a statute, but they cannot impose outcomes beyond what those words 'reasonably' require.[83] The plain text of Parliament's enactments, in the final analysis, remains the law, irrespective of its NZBORA implications. Consequently, Parliament can be reasonably certain that the judiciary will respect and put into practice its decision (as expressed through the words chosen for its enactment) on what policies and rules are consistent with the NZBORA.

(e) Declarations of inconsistency

The final way in which judicial and legislative views on individual rights may interact is through a court issuing a formal declaration that Parliament has legislated inconsistently with the NZBORA. I note at the outset that such declarations remain theoretical in New Zealand. The NZBORA confers no express power to issue such a remedy. Moreover, while various courts have intimated that a declaration of inconsistency *might* be available in an 'appropriate case',[84] to date they have found various procedural ways of avoiding having to decide the issue. Most recently, the Court of Appeal struck out an action seeking to have the Electoral Finance Act 2007 declared inconsistent with the NZBORA, on the grounds that the courts do not have the power to make such declarations 'in the abstract'.[85] Nevertheless, the court did not rule out the possibility that a declaration might be available 'where there is a dispute between the parties'.[86] Consequently, whether formal declarations of inconsistency are a part of the judiciary's remedial toolbox under the NZBORA, along with when such declarations are available, very much remain open questions.[87]

While this unsettled conclusion is somewhat unsatisfying, there are three reasons to think that the issue might not actually matter that much. First, any declaration would have no impact on the formal status of the inconsistent enactment, as this would remain valid and binding law by virtue of the NZBORA, section 4. Therefore, the only consequence of the declaration would be to put pressure on Parliament to rectify the inconsistency. As the above discussion shows, however, Parliament repeatedly has proven willing to legislate in the face of the

---

[82] *R v Phillips* [1991] 3 NZLR 175 (CA); *Ministry of Transport v Noort; Police v Curran* [1992] 3 NZLR 260 (CA); *Quilter v Attorney-General*, [1998] 1 NZLR 523 (CA).

[83] *R v Hansen* [2007] 3 NZLR 1, [25]; [95]; [97]; [165]; [256]; [288]. See also J. McGrath, 'Purpose, *Hansard*, Rights and Language', in R. Bigwood (ed), *The Statute: Making and Meaning* (Wellington: LexisNexis New Zealand, 2004), 234.

[84] *Quilter v Attorney-General* [1998] 1 NZLR 523, 554 (CA); *Moonen v Film & Literature Board of Review* [2000] 1 NZLR 9, 17 (CA); *R v Poumako* [2000] 2 NZLR 695, 716–17 (CA); *Zaoui v Attorney-General* [2004] 2 NZLR 339 (HC); *Belcher v Chief Executive of the Department of Corrections* [2007] NZSC 54.

[85] *Boscawen v Attorney-General* [2009] NZCA 12, [55].

[86] Ibid at [56].

[87] C. Geiringer, 'An Update on Implied Declarations of Inconsistency under the New Zealand Bill of Rights Act', (Wellington: Paper presented at 'Celebrating 60 years of the Universal Declaration of Human Rights', 9 and 10 Dec 2008).

Attorney-General's advice on NZBORA consistency; it is debatable whether the judiciary's declared opinion would have any greater effect. Finally, the judiciary *already* can espouse its views on the NZBORA consistency of some statutory provision in the course of searching for rights-friendly interpretations. As Justice McGrath points out in his judgment in the *Hansen* case:

[A] New Zealand court must never shirk its responsibility to indicate, in any case where it concludes that the measure being considered is inconsistent with protected rights, that it has inquired into the possibility of there being an available rights consistent interpretation, that none could be found, and that it has been necessary for the court to revert to s[ection] 4 of the Bill of Rights Act and uphold the ordinary meaning of the other statute...Articulating that reasoning serves the important function of bringing to the attention of the executive branch of government that the court is of the view that there is a measure on the statute book which infringes protected rights and freedoms, which the court has decided is not a justified limitation. It is then for the other branches of government to consider how to respond to the court's finding. While they are under no obligation to change the law and remedy the inconsistency, it is a reasonable constitutional expectation that there will be a reappraisal of the objectives of the particular measure, and of the means by which they were implemented in the legislation, in light of the finding of inconsistency with these fundamental rights and freedoms concerning which there is general consensus in New Zealand society and there are international obligations to affirm.[88]

I struggle to see what adding a formal declaration of inconsistency at the end of this interpretative process would achieve, aside from perhaps generating a greater measure of publicity around the issue. Whether that outcome would even occur— whether New Zealand's media would notice and highlight a judicial declaration of inconsistency—is a further moot point.

II. Conclusion: How to make Parliament more rights responsive?

My basic thesis in this chapter is that irrespective of the NZBORA's impact on other aspects of New Zealand's legal system, this rights instrument has not significantly changed either how Parliament makes law, or what laws Parliament makes. This outcome was not the expected one at the time of the NZBORA's introduction. It was not envisaged that successive governments would be prepared to bring apparently NZBORA-inconsistent measures before the House, or that parliamentarians repeatedly would vote such measures into law. Nor is this outcome bound to occur with a parliamentary bill of rights instrument. As Janet Hiebert's chapter in this volume makes clear, the NZBORA's impact on the legislative process has been much less observable than that of the equivalent rights instruments in Canada and the United Kingdom.

Therefore, one question that might be asked is why has New Zealand's legislative process remained comparatively unaffected by the NZBORA's enactment. A large part of the answer lies in New Zealand's strong, ongoing constitutional

---

[88] *R v Hansen* [2007] 3 NZLR 1, [253]–[254].

attachment to the theory of pure parliamentary sovereignty. The idea that anything, even judicial views on what individual rights require of society, should get in the way of an elected Parliament's lawmaking role simply does not get much traction in this nation's thinking about how its constitution ought to work. In turn, New Zealand's fundamental constitutional faith in Parliament as sovereign lawmaker reveals something about its national culture. Matthew Palmer attributes it to a mixture of authoritarianism, egalitarianism, and pragmatism in the Kiwi psyche.[89] These 'characteristics of our constitutional culture' pose significant obstacles for any move to limit parliamentary action because of judicial interpretations of abstract individual rights claims.

To this we might add the absence of any real super-national check on legislative practice. New Zealand is not subject to a body like the European Court of Human Rights that effectively can embarrass the government into acting in a 'rights consistent' manner. It is true that New Zealand citizens are able to lodge an 'individual communication' with the UN's Human Rights Committee (HRC), alleging that some legislative measure infringes on his or her rights under the International Covenant on Civil and Political Rights (ICCPR). If the HRC finds that the legislation does infringe on the complainant's ICCPR rights, it may express its 'final view' to the New Zealand government. However, the only sanction the government faces for failing to follow this recommendation is naming and shaming in subsequent HRC reports.[90] Consequently, the force of any recommendation is contingent upon the extent to which a nation's government wishes to avoid the domestic embarrassment of being tarred as 'anti-rights' or to escape international opprobrium for failing to live up to generally agreed moral norms. In practice, these costs have not always been substantial enough to persuade even a good global citizen, such as New Zealand, to accept and comply with the expressed views of this international human rights body.

Finally, a large proportion of the apparently NZBORA-inconsistent legislation that Parliament has enacted relates to groups possessing only marginal political influence: drug users; gang members; 'boy racers'; prisoners on parole; paedophiles; etc. A government can expect to pay a minimal political cost by appearing to limit the rights of these groups. Indeed, it may even attract greater voter support for doing so.[91] This fact might then generate a rather uncomfortable conclusion. The NZBORA appears to be at its weakest when it comes to protecting those most likely to be overlooked in the legislative process, while the situations in which it may actually have some effect are those relating to matters that the majority have

---

[89] M. Palmer, 'New Zealand's Constitutional Culture' (2007) 22 *New Zealand Universities Law Review* 565, 582–6.

[90] See *Tangiora v Wellington District Legal Services Commission* [2000] 1 NZLR 17, 21; E. Evatt, 'The Impact of International Human Rights on Domestic Law', in G. Huscroft and P. Rishworth (eds), *Litigating Rights: Perspectives from Domestic and International Law* (Wellington: LexisNexis New Zealand, 2001), 300–1.

[91] See eg Rishworth, above n 64, 104 (expressing the concern that 'there is now a question whether a section 7 notice is truly criticism; in matters of criminal procedure and the like, it may be coming to be a badge of honour').

an active interest in. If so, then the NZBORA would appear to have little utility, at least in so far as it relates to New Zealand's legislative process.

If this analysis is in any way correct, is there anything that can be done to improve the attention that Parliament pays to NZBORA issues when legislating? A number of reform proposals have been floated in recent years, mostly based on the example of other nations' rights instruments. Some of these proposals focus on changing the text of the NZBORA itself. For example, at the more adventurous end of the spectrum is the suggestion that New Zealand replace section 4 of the NZBORA with the equivalent of the section 33 'notwithstanding' override in the Canadian Charter of Rights and Freedoms, 1982.[92] A less far-reaching proposal is to amend section 7 to require the Attorney-General to provide a report on the NZBORA consistency of *every* bill that comes before the House, not just on those considered to be inconsistent.[93] Changing the NZBORA to give the courts an express power to issue declarations of inconsistency and requiring the government to table a formal response to such declarations in Parliament also has been suggested.[94] Other reform ideas focus on changing the internal workings of Parliament. The creation of a standing committee of the House of Representatives with responsibility for considering NZBORA matters has been mooted,[95] modelled on the United Kingdom's Joint Committee on Human Rights.[96] Additionally, it has been suggested that a member in charge of any bill that receives a section 7 notice should be required to table a response that explains why the member considers the rights breach to be justified.[97] Because these latter two proposals involve matters of pure parliamentary procedure, they would only require changes to the Standing Orders of the House of Representatives, rather than statutory amendment.

However, rather than approaching parliamentary scrutiny of individual rights as a discrete problem, it might be more valuable to view it as one part of a wider reform agenda for New Zealand's legislature. Jeremy Waldron recently has criticized strongly the general process by which New Zealand's Parliament makes law.[98] He claims it too often does so in an overly hasty and ill-considered fashion, under the unhealthy domination of executive government. 'New Zealand', Waldron worries, 'has stripped safeguard after safeguard away from its legislative process—leaving it with virtually none of the safeguards that most working

[92] A. Butler, 'Strengthening the Bill of Rights' (2000) 31 *Victoria University of Wellington Law Review* 129, 141–4. Doing so would mean the courts could declare NZBORA-inconsistent legislation invalid, unless Parliament specifically states that the legislation is to apply 'notwithstanding' that inconsistency. New Zealand's Parliament already has been prepared to take this step: the Prostitution Reform Act 2003, s 13(2) specifically empowers local councils to make bylaws that are inconsistent with the NZBORA.
[93] New Zealand Law Society Human Rights Committee, *Submission to the 96th Session of the Human Rights Committee: Shadow Report to New Zealand's Fifth Periodic Report Under the ICCPR* (22 May, 2009), 3–4.
[94] Ibid 4.
[95] Butler and Butler, above n 11, para 8.14.5.
[96] Adam Tompkins discusses the operations of this Committee in his chapter in this volume.
[97] Bromwich, above n 58, 192.
[98] J. Waldron, *Parliamentary Recklessness: Why We Need to Legislate More Carefully* (Auckland: Maxim Institute, 2008).

democracies take for granted.'[99] This winnowing away of parliamentary procedure 'is defended on grounds of efficiency, value-for-money, and the procedural niceties that are pushed aside are derided as unimportant formalities, costly and dispensable in that quest for legislative efficiency'.[100] Certainly, there is evidence that the New Zealand Parliament makes much greater use of urgency motions to speed legislation through the House than is the case with other common law jurisdictions.[101] Given this background legislative culture, it will be difficult to generate a greater concern for NZBORA issues, where such concerns threaten to slow or derail the legislative express. So perhaps rather than just seeking ways to make New Zealand's Parliament pay closer attention to the issue of individual rights when making law, it is first necessary to find ways to make New Zealand's Parliament pay closer attention to making law, full stop.

[99] Ibid at 18.
[100] Ibid at 27.
[101] See House of Lords Select Committee on the Constitution, *Fast-Track Legislation: Constitutional Implications and Safeguards, Volume I: Report* (London: The Stationary Office, 7 July 2009), Appendix 6.

6

Statutory Bills of Rights: You Read Words In, You Read Words Out, You Take Parliament's Clear Intention and You Shake it All About—Doin' the Sankey Hanky Panky

James Allan

> It is now generally accepted that the application of s. 3 [the reading down pro-
> vision in the United Kingdom's *Human Rights Act*] does not depend upon the
> presence of ambiguity in the legislation being interpreted. Even if, construed
> according to the ordinary principles of interpretation, the meaning admits of
> no doubt, s. 3 may none the less require the court to...depart from the inten-
> tion of the Parliament which enacted the legislation...It is also apt to require
> a court to read in words which change the meaning of the enacted legislation,
> so as to make it convention-compliant, [meaning bill of rights compliant].[1]
>
> The Human Rights Act 1998 (incorporating the European Convention on
> Human Rights – the United Kingdom's bill of rights] created a new legal order.[2]
>
> The majority opinions...in [*Ghaidan*] do not lend themselves easily to a
> brief summary. But they leave no room for doubt...[that] the interpretative
> obligation under section 3 is a very strong and far reaching one, and may
> require the court to depart from the legislative intention of Parliament.[3]

The Human Rights Act makes me angry. I am angry that this statutory bill of rights
has increased the decision-making power at the point-of-application of unelected
judges, of committees of ex-lawyers (as Jeremy Waldron enjoys describing them).

---

[1] *Ghaidan v Godin-Mendoza* [2004] 3 All ER 411; 2 AC 557 at paras [29], [30], and [32] per Lord
Nicholls. (Hereinafter this case will be referred to as '*Ghaidan*'). All the other Lordships, even Lord
Millett in dissent, broadly agreed on the question of this new interpretive approach. See my 'Portia,
Bassanio or Dick the Butcher? Constraining Judges in the Twenty-First Century' (2006) 17 *King's
College Law Journal* 1. *Ghaidan's* interpretive approach has been affirmed in *National Westminster
Bank v Spectrum Plus* [2005] UKHL 41; *Secretary of State for Work and Pensions v M* [2006] UKHL
11; *Countryside Alliance and others v Attorney General* [2007] UKHL 52 and *P & Ors, Re (Northern
Ireland)* [2008] UKHL 38, *inter alia*. That said, there have been moments of uncertainty. See eg Lord
Bingham in *Secretary of State for the Home Department v MB* [2007] UKHL 46 at para [44] and Lord
Hope in *Doherty & Ors v Birmingham City Council* [2008] UKHL 57.
[2] *Jackson v Attorney-General* [2006] 1 AC 262 at para [102] per Lord Steyn.
[3] *Sheldrake v Director of Public Prosecutions* [2004] UKHL 43, per Lord Bingham at para [28].

I believe that none of the new powers this statutory bill of rights has afforded the judiciary is legitimate in the sense that the decisions involved are somehow ones over which ex-lawyers have special or greater than average expertise or in the sense that judges deliver noticeably better outcomes than elected legislators or even in the emasculated or enfeebled sense that judges provide some sort of desirable, aristocratic Upper House-type checking and balancing review (by themselves, or as a complement to the one already in existence). None of that stands up to scrutiny, in my view. And so it angers me that these judges, these ex-lawyers, have more say in fundamental social line-drawing exercises of the sort bill of rights litigation inevitably demands than I do. Or my sister and friends do. Or that plumbers, secretaries, teachers, tennis players, even journalists and bond traders do.

This sort of response, I know, surprises many people in the Human Rights Act or bill of rights establishment. They know themselves to be well-intentioned—as no doubt the vast preponderance of them are—and so it surprises, even shocks, many of them that anger and moral indignation could be the response to their aiming to 'protect people's rights' by means of a bill of rights, and even more so when it is a statutory bill of rights.

Put differently, moral indignation is not the exclusive preserve of one side of this debate—of those who, by championing a bill of rights, feel themselves to be on the right side of upholding rights and of how to resolve rights disagreements (and probably of history too).

Of course the merits and demerits of 'strong form' or entrenched and constitutionalized bills of rights have been debated at length.[4] I do not intend to re-enter that debate here, other than to repeat my view that US-style striking down of primary legislation powers in the hands of unelected judges cannot be justified on superior moral expertise grounds, on ersatz Upper House grounds, on achieving better consequentialist outcomes grounds, and plainly not on its being a more legitimate decision-making process grounds.

A good many bill of rights supporters will disagree with that view. But a good many will not. These latter ones will agree that constitutionalized bills of rights hand too much power to unelected judges. They will say that what is needed is a 'weak form' or statutory bill of rights that preserves parliamentary sovereignty. Indeed they will be most careful to frame the debate in those terms, as being about a statutory bill of rights where the elected legislature retains last-word sovereignty.

Ten years ago, in an essay in the *Sceptical Essays on Human Rights* book,[5] I took a gloomy (or, in the words of one of the editors in the introduction,

[4] See, as a small sample, M. Tushnet, *Taking the Constitution Away from the Courts* (Princeton: Princeton University Press, 1999); J. Waldron, *Law and Disagreement* (Oxford: Oxford University Press, 1999); J. Waldron, 'The Core of the Case Against Judicial Review' (2006) 115 *Yale Law Journal* 1346; R. Dworkin, *Taking Rights Seriously* (Harvard: Harvard University Press, 1978); S. Freeman, 'Constitutional Democracy and the Legitimacy of Judicial Review' (1990–1) 9 *Law and Philosophy* 329; C. Eisgruber, 'Constitutional Self-Government and Judicial Review: A Reply to Five Critics' (2002) 37 *University of San Francisco Law Review* 115; and J. Allan, 'Bills of Rights and Judicial Power—A Liberal's Quandary' (1996) 16 *Oxford Journal of Legal Studies* 337.
[5] Edited by T. Campbell, K.D. Ewing, and A. Tomkins (Oxford: Oxford University Press, 2000).

'uncompromising'[6]) view of the then soon to come into force Human Rights Act. Today, with the benefit of hindsight, I would say that the effects of this statutory bill of rights here in the United Kingdom have been worse than I gloomily predicted. More specifically, this statutory bill of rights—for virtually all practical purposes—has not offered 'weak form' review at all, but rather something indistinguishable in its effects from 'strong form' review. The enticing prospect of being able to have your cake and eat it too has been shown to have been a mirage. If you opt to delegate to judges the power to tell all the rest of us what our fundamental human rights are in any and all specific cases or issues (the elected Parliament simply having incorporated a list of vague, amorphous, and highly indeterminate moral abstractions to which, in such disagreement-finessing terms, virtually everyone can agree), they will not be gainsaid by the elected legislature. At least they will not be gainsaid when it is a statutory bill of rights like Britain's.[7]

In other words, the hoped-for middle ground desired by some bill of rights proponents is elusive. The Human Rights Act has not left us with parliamentary sovereignty in any substantive sense—*not* when judges can use the reading down provision to rewrite legislation they (and they alone by majority vote amongst themselves) happen to think infringes the enumerated rights and *not* when every single Declaration of Incompatibility, without exception, is met by the capitulation of the elected branches.

The Human Rights Act, no less than the US Bill of Rights or the Canadian Charter of Rights, has created a situation in which the judges' view of what the rights-respecting outcome is magically transmogrifies into the correct view. What *they say* our rights are, in effect, gets equated to what our rights actually are, as though these are not highly contentious issues over which committees of ex-lawyers have no pipeline to God, no special expertise, and no obvious grounds for being deferred to.

The rest of this chapter will be an attempt to defend my anger and moral indignation as a wholly justified response to the enactment of the Human Rights Act. That will involve making the case that this statutory bill of rights empowers the point-of-application judiciary to a much greater extent than proponents of these instruments acknowledge or pretend. In other words, if you object to an entrenched, constitutionalized bill of rights, there is little or no basis for not objecting to statutory versions too. Or so I will argue.

That argument will come in four sections. The first of these will be the longest. Here I will consider the reading down provision and the interpretation of it thus far adopted by their Lordships, the gist of which I set out at the start of this chapter. Next, in Section B, I will look at other ways in which statutory bills of rights, in substance, empower judges at the expense of the elected legislature. In Secion C I will briefly digress, confronting head-on two possible rejoinders from supporters of

---

[6] Ibid 10.
[7] We can argue about New Zealand's. Cf Andrew Geddis's chapter in this book. But even if the reading down provision has been less virulent in New Zealand, the statutory bill of rights there has inflated judicial power. And *Baigent's Case* [1994] 3 NZLR 667 is, implicitly, one where the relevant statute was aggressively read down because of the bill of rights.

statutory bills of rights. Finally, I will leave the Human Rights Act and turn briefly to the related topic of judicial appointments, where again of late the interests of those committed to majoritarian decision-making premised on counting everyone as equal have lost out to the push for a more powerful, more insulated judiciary.

I. The Reading Down or *Sankey Hanky Panky* Provision

The main tool for increasing the power of the judiciary under a statutory bill of rights is the reading down provision. No provision has more potential to transmogrify the powers available under statutory versions into something approaching those under constitutionalized versions. Indeed (and here is what proponents downplay in the time when they are pushing for the enactment of a statutory bill of rights), if judges take such reading down provisions to be Spike Lee-like licences 'to do the right thing', then these provisions leave open the possibility of affording judges scope to do what the disinterested observer would characterize as an out-and-out rewriting or redrafting of other statutes.

Consider the reading down provision in the *Human Rights Act 1998* which reads to start:

So far *as it is possible to do so*, primary legislation and subordinate legislation *must be read* and given effect in a way which is compatible with Convention rights.[8]

The danger with these sort of reading down provisions—these directions to give the words of other statutes a meaning that you, the point-of-application interpreter, happen to think is more moral and more in keeping with your own sense of the demands of fundamental human rights—is that just about any statutory language (however clear in wording and intent) might possibly be given some other meaning or reading.

Here is how I framed the danger, the scope for abuse, of these provisions in an earlier article:

Put differently, reading down provisions such as these throw open the possibility of 'Alice in Wonderland' judicial interpretations; they confer an 'interpretation on steroids' power on the unelected judges. So although there is no power to invalidate or strike down legislation, the judges can potentially accomplish just as much by rewriting it, by saying that seen through the prism (that is, their own prism) of human rights, 'near black' means 'near white' or 'interim order becomes a final order' means 'interim order does *not* become a final order'.[9] They can make bill of rights sceptics half long for the honesty

---

[8] Human Rights Act 1998, c 42, s 3(1), emphasis added. The reading down provision in the New Zealand Bill of Rights Act 1990 reads: 'Whenever an enactment *can be given a meaning* that is consistent with the rights and freedoms contained in this Bill of Rights, that meaning *shall be preferred* to any other meanings' (s 6, emphasis added). And the reading down provision in the Australian State of Victoria's Charter of Rights reads: 'So far as it is possible to do so consistently with their purpose, all statutory provisions *must be interpreted* in a way that is compatible with human rights' (s 32(1), emphasis added).

[9] See *SI by his next friend CC v KS by his next friend IS* (2005) 195 FLR 151, at 154 (Higgins CJ of the Australian Capital Territory using a similar provision in the ACT Human Rights Act 2004).

of judges (under constitutionalised bills of rights) who strike down legislation rather than gut it of the meaning everyone knows it was intended to have (rule of law values notwithstanding).[10]

Whether that characterization is alarmist or not, indeed how different the judicial approach to interpreting other statutes will be, is a question of fact. In the United Kingdom we have to look to see how the top judges in the House of Lords—judges who a decade or two ago were widely considered to be the most interpretively conservative judges in the Anglo-American common law world—have used the section 3 reading down provision to alter their former approach to interpretation.

And so let us return to the *Ghaidan* case. What is remarkable in that case is not what the judges did, but what they were prepared openly and explicitly to admit they believed they could now do with the section 3 reading down provision in place.[11] When interpreting all other statutes they could 'depart from the intention of…Parliament'.[12] They could do so when 'the meaning admits of no doubt'.[13] They could 'read in words which change the meaning of the enacted legislation'.[14] They could assert that '[t]he word "possible" in s. 3(1) is used in a different and much stronger sense'.[15] They could imply that anything short of outright 'judicial vandalism' is now within their purview at the point-of-application.[16] They could even use this new interpretive power to overrule one of their own House of Lords authorities—a case on the meaning of exactly the same statutory provision, an authority under four years old, and one that had held the meaning of that same statute to be clear.[17]

I could go on. I could note again that this *Ghaidan* approach to using the reading down provision is no outlier and continues to be affirmed[18] and that the top judges now see themselves operating under 'a new legal order'[19]—one in which their views on a host of political and moral line-drawing exercises are significantly more influential than before. I could explore the rule of law implications of this new

---

[10] J. Allan, 'The Victorian *Charter of Human Rights and Responsibilities: Exegesis and Criticism*', (2006) 30 *Melbourne University Law Review* 906, at 909–10.

[11] I take it to be uncontentious that judges very occasionally will lie; they will do the thing they think is right and proper despite believing the settled law prevents it and yet structure their judgment so as to pretend their preferred outcome was mandated by that settled law. In other words, they will indulge in hypocrisy—the compliment that vice pays to virtue. See A. Scalia, 'Romancing the Constitution: Interpretation as Invention', in G. Huscroft and I. Brodie (eds.), *Constitutionalism in the Charter Era* (Toronto: LexisNexis, 2004), at 337. Such lying, in my view, will sometimes be justified, though extremely rarely so in a democracy. Put differently, a theory of how best to interpret is distinct from a theory of when judicial disobedience to law is warranted or justified.

[12] *Ghaidan*, para [30], per Lord Nicholls. And could do so despite a total lack of ambiguity. Para [29]. For a similar New Zealand example of the relevant statute being blatantly read down, though without the judges explicitly referring to the s 6 reading down provision of the New Zealand Bill of Rights Act, see *Baigent's Case* (op cit, n 7 above).

[13] *Ghaidan*, para [29], per Lord Nicholls.

[14] *Ghaidan*, para [32], per Lord Nicholls.

[15] *Ghaidan* AC 573, per Lord Steyn.

[16] *Ghaidan*, paras [111]–[112] per Lord Rodger.

[17] *Fitzpatrick v Sterling Housing Association* [2001] AC 27.

[18] See above n 1.

[19] See above n 2.

Ghaidan approach to interpretation—how citizens' knowledge of what any statute means becomes wholly and inextricably linked to judges' views of the scope, range, content, and reasonable limits on human rights, all of which are contentious and debatable and give rise to reasonable disagreement amongst smart, well-informed and even nice people. Put bluntly, this new *Ghaidan* approach to interpretation, whatever other sins it might have, most assuredly magnifies uncertainty from the citizen's vantage-point and hence lessens the ability of all non-judges to know what the law demands of them and to be able to shape their conduct and expectations accordingly. I could even look at the historical evidence to determine the extent to which those enacting this statutory bill of rights, and British voters more generally, were made aware of the possibility or probability of this revolutionary ('new legal order'[20]) approach to statutory interpretation that in fact followed in the wake of its passage.

Instead, I want to consider more carefully what sort of understanding of the act of interpretation allows authors' intentions to be ignored, words to be read in, and the otherwise unassailable plain meaning to be gainsaid. Is this really interpretation at all, or just a form of after-the-fact, *ex post facto* creation or construction of deemed meaning at the point-of-application, one that will prevail until latter-day judges reconsider the issue and change their minds? That is the question I want to probe.

And what strikes me about this question is the extent to which it mimics issues raised in constitutional interpretation, and more particularly the interpretation of constitutionalized bills of rights (as opposed to, say, heads of powers disputes). When it comes to normal statutory interpretation, talk of 'purpose' and of some sort of 'purposive approach' to arrive at meaning is not severed from (at least not wholly severed from) the intentions of those who enacted the statute. Purpose and intention overlap, though perhaps not to the same exact extent for different proponents of a 'purposive approach'. But the basic point is that purpose is not some unmoored, changeable-through-time concept that disregards completely the issue of the enactors' intentions.

When it comes to constitutional interpretation, however, that same claim is for many interpreters of an entrenched bill of rights simply untrue. They refer to their preferred approach to interpretation in terms of a metaphor, that of a 'living document' or 'living tree'. The latter of these was made famous by Lord Sankey in what in Canada is known as the *Persons'* case.[21] And, truth be told, constitutional interpretation in Canada today involves regular use of reference to the Charter of Rights' 'purpose'—but a purpose that is completely and assiduously severed from any link to the actual intentions of any and all real life people who had any role at all in the drafting, framing, adopting, or ratifying of the Charter of Rights, or indeed from what was the public meaning at the time of adoption. In other words, reference to 'purpose' in Canada is reference to a judicial

---

[20] See above n 2.
[21] *Edwards v Attorney-General for Canada* [1930] AC 124 (PC).

construct at the point-of-application,[22] one that can grow and alter and change in accord with the judges' shifting perceptions over time (by a majority vote amongst themselves) of what is best or necessary or in keeping with society's or civilization's shifting moral standards (though, of course, for all other non-judges in Canada, the meaning of the constitution is locked-in, absent a successful use of the amending formula). Put bluntly, talk of 'purpose' under Canadian-style 'living tree' constitutional bill of rights interpretation has no connection at all to what is normally meant by 'purpose' in day-to-day or in normal statutory interpretation. It amounts to little more than a pleasant-sounding mask for judicial construction at the point-of-application, or if you prefer, for judges to update what the amorphous rights-based constitutional provisions do and do not allow in specific instances.

The preceding two paragraphs require me to add a qualification and two comments. The qualification is this: although I have followed orthodoxy in attributing the 'living tree' label to Lord Sankey, not least because he himself uses that label, his judgment in the *Persons'* case actually reads much like one grounded in an originalist interpretive approach.[23] As for the two comments, in a comparison between (a) 'living tree' constitutional interpretive approaches and (b) approaches adopting a version of originalism (say, original intentions or original public meaning[24]), the latter is far more compatible with retaining as much majoritarian democratic input as possible, given the existence of a constitutionalized bill of rights. Indeed, I have argued this point at length.[25] Secondly, although originalism is alive and breathing in the United States, progressivist or 'living document' or 'living tree' type approaches to constitutional bill of rights interpretation are more in use and more widespread. In Canada, meanwhile, they are the only game in town.

I have called this 'living tree' category the Sankey Hanky Panky approach in the title to this chapter. And, as should be clear by now, I mean that to be taken in a disparaging way. For anyone attached to majoritarian democratic decision-making, the 'living tree' approach to interpretation—by allowing judges the power to update and refashion what is and is not legislatively permissible based on what those same judges happen to think is not in keeping with what *they, the judges, take* the rights-articulated moral abstractions in the entrenched bill of rights to require—is not obviously at the heart of the notion of self-government.

---

[22] For example, the 'purpose' of the equality provision in the Canadian Charter of Rights used to be linked to human dignity but it is not any longer. See, too, Bradley Miller's 'Beguiled by Metaphors: The "Living Tree" and Originalist Constitutional Interpretation in Canada' (2009) 22 *Canadian Journal of Law and Jurisprudence* 331.

[23] See Bradley Miller, 'The Persons' Case: Canada's Silver Bullet Against Originalism' (on file with the author).

[24] The American literature on originalism is extensive and flourishing. See eg K. Whittington, 'The New Originalism' (2004) 2 *Georgetown Journal of Law & Public Policy* 599 and the various references therein to other originalists. See too R. Kay, 'Adherence to Original Intentions in Constitutional Adjudication: Three Objections and Responses' (1988) 82 *Northwestern University Law Review* 226.

[25] See J. Allan, 'The Curious Concept of the "Living Tree" (or Non-Locked-In) Constitution', in G. Huscroft and B. Miller (eds), *The Challenge of Originalism: Essays in Constitutional Theory* (New York: Cambridge University Press, forthcoming) and on file with the author.

Neither, in my view, is the Sankey two-step able to be defended as some least-bad interpretive option going, from that same democratic vantage-point.[26] In fact, it is probably the worst. And nothing requires or demands that the judges opt for it.[27]

That said, I do not intend here to argue any further for those claims about 'living tree' constitutional bill of rights interpretation. I will simply ask that they be accepted or assumed. And that done, let us return to the section 3 reading down provision in the United Kingdom's statutory bill of rights.

Notice, immediately, how great the similarity is between the *Ghaidan* and Sankey Hanky Panky approaches. The former allows judges (up to some unspecified point on the spectrum denominated as 'judicial vandalism') to redraft and rewrite legislation by reading words in, ignoring clear intentions, trumping the otherwise plain meaning, and not requiring the least ambiguity before doing so. Once engaged in that redrafting or refashioning task, the legislation under consideration is not in any real sense being interpreted. It is being rewritten. The most that can be said is that the section 3 reading down provision has itself been interpreted, and it has been interpreted as granting judges a licence to rewrite (short of some indeterminate point termed 'vandalism') all other legislation. Hence the reading down provision—or to be rather more accurate, the House of Lords judges' contingent interpretation of that provision, which is in no way mandated by the provision itself—becomes the basis for a wholly new activity that really is no longer aptly described as interpretation at all, at least where interpretation is thought to have some connection to the task of discovering the speaker's intended meaning, or even the meaning readers would usually associate (at the time of enactment) with the words used.

And that strikes me as highly reminiscent of the sense in which 'purpose' is claimed by Canadian courts to lie at the heart of constitutional *Charter of Rights* interpretation. It is a postmodern sense, amounting, as I said, to little more than a pleasant-sounding mask for judicial construction at the point-of-application.

Understanding the section 3 reading down provision as a one-off licence to give up the task of interpretation for some quite different undertaking—let us call it the Sankey Hanky Panky tree-shaping job—is an extremely unattractive understanding for anyone who is a majoritarian democrat. It helps to inflate the job of judges under a statutory bill of rights into something much closer to what they would be doing under an entrenched, constitutionalized bill of rights, albeit something less honest.[28] In any substantive sense, this understanding of the section 3 reading down provision undermines parliamentary sovereignty. Only in an incredibly formalistic and legalistic sense can a jurisdiction with judges openly and explicitly

---

[26] See ibid.
[27] See J. Allan, 'The Travails of Justice Waldron', in G. Huscroft (ed.), *Expounding the Constitution* (Cambridge: Cambridge University Press, 2008), 161–83.
[28] Of course even in Canada judges sometimes choose not to strike down legislation, but instead to read things in (see, say, *Vriend v Alberta* [1998] 1 SCR 493)—the pretence being that this is less invasive than striking the legislation down.

engaged in this sort of Sankey Hanky Panky be said to retain parliamentary sovereignty.

Worse, as gloomy as I was ten years ago about the likely effects of the then looming Human Rights Act, it never crossed my mind that things would be this bad; that this statutory bill of rights would be said by the judges to license them to this degree to rewrite all other legislation (short of vandalism) that *they* happened to think fell short of *their* view of what the indeterminate rights standards required. I never would have guessed, in other words, that the top judges would have increased their own moral and political line-drawing power to the extent they did by saying what they did in *Ghaidan*, and then affirming it and affirming it and affirming it again.

Whether, if this outcome had been made plain beforehand, voters or parliamentarians would have supported the Human Rights Act I leave to the reader to ponder. I simply say that it makes me angry.

II. Other Ways Statutory Bills of Rights Empower Judges

If the above discussed reading down provision were the only means by which the Human Rights Act increased the power of the unelected judges at the expense of the elected branches of government, that would be bad enough. Indeed, in my view it would be more than sufficient grounds for seeking repeal of the Human Rights Act. However, it is not the only means—just the most egregious.

Let me in this second section of the chapter detail two other means by which the United Kingdom's statutory bill of rights increases the decision-making powers of the point-of-application judges. I will be relatively brief.

The more potent of these two is the Declaration of Incompatibility power. Section 4(2) of the Human Rights Act reads: 'If the court is satisfied that the [under consideration statutory] provision is incompatible with a Convention right, it may make a declaration of that incompatibility'.

Now notice carefully that wording—*if the court is satisfied that the provision is incompatible.* And notice what that wording implies, namely that the judges' decisions about rights are to be treated as somehow the correct or right or indisputable and certainly the authoritative ones. The implication, then—an incorrect and inaccurate one in my view—is that when the judges issue one of these Declarations of Incompatibility, the elected Parliament's legislation is at that point definitely and without doubt at odds with some individual's enumerated human rights and so if the legislation stands, rights *will be* infringed. As I put it in an earlier article, these Declarations of Incompatibility:

… can convey the impression that the unelected judges have some authoritative, definitive (and to me, mysterious) ability to know and to declare precisely where to draw all the highly contestable and disputed lines (including knowing just what amounts to a reasonable limit and what does not). So if the judges say that statutory provision X breaches rights, then the wording of the declaration section implies (wrongly, but for some persuasively all the same) that *their view* is incontestably correct.[29]

The point is that this section 4 Declaration of Incompatibility provision is worded in a way that is both factually incorrect as regards what is often in dispute and that makes it extremely difficult for the elected Parliament to stand up to, and gainsay, the unelected judges.[30]

Take the second point first. It is a remarkable and relevant fact that since the enactment of the Human Rights Act, the United Kingdom Parliament has never once stood up to the judges when a Declaration of Incompatibility has been issued—not one single time ever![31] There have been some 24 such declarations and '[i]n *every case* where remedial action had not been taken before the [judicial] declaration was made, the government responded by repealing, amending or committing to repeal or amend, the relevant provision'.[32]

One is tempted to remark that parliamentary sovereignty should be made of sterner stuff.

One reason for this reticence, in my view, is that the declaration power is structured implicitly to hand power to judges to declare what are and are not our fundamental rights in the whole cross-section of line-drawing calls that bills of rights ask judges to make (including what limits on them are and are not reasonable), and then Parliament is left with the power to say 'We're going to take your rights away'. That sort of parliamentary response may, *in extremis*, be a usable power. I do

---

[29] See n 10 above, 914. For an excellent discussion of the related issue of dialogue theory, and in particular its shortcomings, see G. Huscroft, 'Rationalizing Judicial Power: The Mischief of Dialogue Theory', in J. B. Kelly and C. P. Manfredi (eds), *Contested Constitutionalism* (Vancouver: University of British Columbia Press, 2009).

[30] This issue about the biased wording of Declarations of Incompatibility repeats a similar point made about Canada's s 33 notwithstanding clause. See eg J. Goldsworthy, 'Judicial Review, Legislative Override, and Democracy', in T. Campbell, J. Goldsworthy, and A. Stone (eds), *Protecting Human Rights: Instruments and Institutions* (Oxford: Oxford University Press, 2003); G. Huscroft, 'Rights, Bills of Rights, and the Role of Courts and Legislatures', in G. Huscroft and P. Rishworth (eds), *Litigating Rights* (Oxford: Hart, 2002); and J. Waldron, ('Some Models of Dialogue between Judges and Legislators', in Huscroft and Brodie, above n 11, who makes a similar point. Indeed, Waldron goes on to assert that, as an empirical matter, 'one could never get a Canadian enthusiast for the Charter to accept a "notwithstanding" clause that involved an honest acknowledgment that rights might be disputable or...that a...legislature might have a view of rights that was, though controversial, no less reasonable than the view arrived at by the judiciary' (ibid 38–9). On both points see James Allan, 'The Travails of Justice Waldron' in G. Huscroft (ed), *Expounding the Constitution: Essays in Constitutional Theory* (New York: Cambridge University Press, 2008).

[31] See F. Klug and K. Starmer, 'Standing Back from the *Human Rights Act*: How Effective Is It Five Years On?' [2005] *Public Law* 715, 721, and 'Monitoring the Government's Response to Human Rights Judgments: Annual Report 2008', A Report by a Standing Committee of the House of Lords and House of Commons. Note, for what it is worth, that in both instances the lack of any legislative gainsaying of the judiciary is presumed to be a good thing.

[32] Klug and Starmer, above n 31, 721. The Joint Committee on Human Rights (above n 31), at para 109 says: 'The Ministry of Justice reports that between the Human Rights Act coming into force on 2 October 2000 and 23 May 2007 a total of 24 declarations of incompatibility have been made by domestic courts under the Human Rights Act'. In none of these instances has Parliament gainsaid the judges.

not know. What is clear is that we still await Parliament's first ever exercise of that power some decade after the bill of rights' enactment.

Think of it this way. Suppose there were a marriage and in that marriage decision-making was divided up in the following manner. The wife, and only the wife, gets to write down what the couple will do: who is allowed in their home; what their daughter can wear to school; whom their son can marry; everything. She writes it down, not the husband.

The husband, however, is given a *Ghaidan*-like power of interpretation. He can read all of his wife's directives in accord with *his view* of what is in keeping with everyone else's fundamental rights. And so we might well expect that husband to treat the section 3 'is it possible?' test as one that can surprisingly often be answered in the affirmative. 'Yes it is possible', thinks this sort of husband, 'for me to read a whole host of my wife's provisions and directives (however lacking in ambiguity and however clear her intentions) in a new, different manner than before *Ghaidan*, in a way I happen to think is a better, more rights-respecting way'.

But that is not all. For those leftover cases where the husband constrains himself and feels he has reached the point of vandalism and so in this case he cannot take his wife's directives and read words in, ignore her clear intentions, and override meaning of hers that admits of no doubt, he can nevertheless declare that his wife is taking away people's fundamental rights. His wife is then left with the option of prevailing by saying 'yes, I will override my husband and breach your rights'.

Those who sell the Human Rights Act as being a 'weak form' of judicial review and as retaining parliamentary sovereignty in some real sense, want you to believe that the wife has the last word in this hypothetical marriage and that being forced into the position of saying 'I will breach people's rights' is somehow a live option for the wife. Put differently, statutory bill of rights proponents need, at a bare minimum, to convince you that the wife is in the preferable position in this marriage, not the husband (not to mention giving you some grounds for thinking husbands have better rights intuitions than wives).

And this takes us back to the first point I made about section 4 Declarations of Incompatibility above, that the wording is factually incorrect as regards what is often in dispute between the judiciary and the legislature. In many, many instances the elected legislature and the unelected judiciary (or, rather, a majority of the former and a majority of the latter) simply disagree over a highly contestable decision about how best to respect rights and about what limits on them are reasonable. This is Jeremy Waldron's oft-repeated point. And so it is grossly misleading in terms of a characterization of what is in fact happening and in dispute to portray the legislature (and indeed to force them to portray themselves) as wanting to take people's rights away. They are, in fact, disagreeing about the scope, reach, and limits of rights in a way that happens every day, all the time, amongst smart, well-informed, reasonable people. Moreover, absent some implicit assumption that committees of ex-lawyers have better moral antennae than elected legislators, there is no reason for preferring judges' moral and political rights-related views just because they are judges.[33]

Accordingly, it is at least plausible to think that this mischaracterization that lies at the heart of the section 4 Declaration of Incompatibility power—the suggestion that our unelected judges are infallible determiners of what is and is not compatible with human rights—has contributed to the obvious reality that Parliament thus far has never once second-guessed or gainsaid the judges.

There remains for me to mention one further way that statutory bills of rights inflate the role and power of judges, though in this instance I think it is fair to say that this effect was in all likelihood an unintended one. I refer to Statements of Compatibility. This provision (s 19 in the Human Rights Act[34]) relates to the oft-proclaimed goal of making the elected legislature think more about rights before enacting laws. And this was to be done by making the minister in charge of a bill, before the Second Reading, 'make a statement to the effect that in his view the provisions of the Bill are compatible with the Convention rights'.[35]

As I said, the intended consequence of such Statements of Compatibility is to make parliamentarians think more about rights-related aspects of bills. For that to happen, though, these determinations that bills are, or are not, compatible with the enumerated rights need to be made on the basis of the elected parliamentarians' own considered views about rights.

Yet this pre-supposes that such:

...a requirement on elected officials will not collapse into a legalistic determination of whether *the judges* (not the elected legislators or elected members of the executive, but the unelected judges) are likely to think that the Bill is consistent or inconsistent with the statutory bill of rights. If this requirement on the Minister does indeed collapse into some form of in-house government lawyers sifting through past judgments, and overseas judgments, to guess what unelected judges might think, then describing that as something that will improve self-government is downright audacious.

And the facts so far point precisely in this direction of these compatibility statements collapsing into a lawyer and judge-driven exercise wholly outside anything that might improve elected self-government.[36]

---

[33] An ancillary, but related, point has to do with a government's ability to ignore a Declaration of Incompatibility, to portray such lack of action as not having to do with violating rights—or judge-declared rights. My view on this hypothetical issue is that it would be exceedingly difficult for any government to succeed in such an attempt, given that the judges' view of what is rights-respecting has been made the default one and that newspapers and interest groups will assuredly rely on it. And given Jeremy Waldron's empirical claims about a fair, non-question-begging override never in fact coming into existence (see above n 30), he presumably would share my scepticism on this related empirical question.

[34] And s 7 in New Zealand and s 28 in the State of Victoria, Australia.

[35] Section 19(1)(a), Human Rights Act.

[36] J. Allan, 'Meagher's Mischaracterisations of Majoritarianism: A Reply' (2009) 20 *King's Law Journal* 115, 122. Janet Hiebert and Grant Huscroft both make this claim, that pre-legislative scrutiny is based on guesswork as to what a court would hold. See J. Hiebert, 'New Constitutional Ideas: Can New Parliamentary Models Resist Judicial Dominance when Interpreting Rights?', (2004) 82 *Texas Law Review* 1963; 'Parliament and the Human Rights Act: Can the JCHR Help Facilitate a Culture of Rights?' (2006) 4 *International Journal of Constitutional Law* 1 and G. Huscroft, 'Is the

In other words, these Statements of Compatibility have collapsed into a wholly legalized account of how some right or other *has been treated* in various domestic and overseas courts, or how they are *likely to be treated* by the top judges. And once that happens, whether intended or not, yet more weight will be put on what the unelected judiciary thinks about rights. Their power, albeit indirectly and preemptively this time, will be increased yet again because of the enactment of the statutory bill of rights.

III. Two Brief Digressions

There are two rejoinders that defenders of statutory bills of rights might be tempted to make at this point. In fact, few such bill of rights proponents resist these temptations. One of these rejoinders is theoretical; the other is eminently practical. The former involves shifting the focus away from after-enactment outcomes and forcing it onto the process that led to the statutory bill of rights becoming law.

Of course many proponents of statutory bills of rights claim that, once in place, such instruments will leave majoritarian decision-making largely untrammelled. They claim that parliamentary sovereignty will continue. My arguments thus far have been directed at convincing you that such a line of defence is unconvincing—because of the scope that reading down provisions such as the Human Rights Act, section 3 afford to judges, because of the way judges' decisions about rights are explicitly and implicitly treated as somehow the correct or right or indisputable (and certainly the authoritative) ones, because the accumulated evidence thus far is that elected politicians always cave into (or defer to) judges' declarations of incompatibility, and because the statements by ministers pertaining to whether a bill being introduced is rights-respecting have collapsed into lawyer-driven prognostications of what judges happen, or are likely, to think.

In the face of such arguments directed at the *effects* of a statutory bill of rights—at how so-called weak-form judicial review collapses into strong-form review, taking parliamentary sovereignty with it in all but the most formalistic and, yes, lawyerly senses—one theoretical rejoinder is to look instead at the *process* by which a statutory bill of rights became law. If that pre-enactment process appears to have complied with some defensible version of majoritarianism, of 'letting the numbers count', then this rejoinder suggests that the post-enactment grievances are significantly enervated, perhaps even wholly negated, especially as a similar process can be used to repeal the statutory bill of rights at any time.

I have argued at length why that rejoinder fails, or rather why it fails for those majoritarian democrats who support rights on an instrumental or consequentialist

Defeat of Health Warnings a Victory for Human Rights? The Attorney-General and Pre-legislative Scrutiny for Consistency with the New Zealand Bill of Rights', (2003) 14 *Public Law Review* 109; 'Reconciling Duty and Discretion: The Attorney General in the Charter Era' (2009) 34 *Queen's Law Journal* 773.

basis.[37] It is not just because of the trite point that from the fact that a democratic majority might vote henceforth to live under a dictatorship or aristocracy it in no way follows that the legitimacy and desirability of the process used to make *that initial decision* (distinguishing process from outcome here) entails or makes it likely that the new decision-making process will also be a legitimate or desirable one. Not even the fact that the majority could at some future point pull back from aristocracy or dictatorship will do that, will make more palatable the decision-making process now being used until that unspecified day arrives.

It is not just that, as I said. This rejoinder also fails because those, like me, who base their majoritarianism on a consequentialist foundation can look at the effects of a statutory bill of rights and point to:

> ...all the bad consequences that will flow from abdicating these decisions to the unelected judiciary—the voter apathy, the growing cynicism about politics, the temptation for politicians to take irresponsible positions (think of flag-burning in the US) knowing the judges are standing behind them to overrule them, the focus on how judges are chosen, the even more elevated position in society that lawyers (and for that matter legal academics) will win, all the various lost republican virtues associated with an involved citizenry, the plausible claim that on many issues there is wisdom in numbers, and more.[38]

And those consequences are overwhelmingly independent of whether the statutory bill of rights was adopted after a referendum, or after a general election in which it features centrally, or on a party-political basis, or without any referendum or election at all bearing on the question, but simply by passage through the legislature without prior signalling to the electorate.[39]

If that is the theoretical rejoinder likely to tempt (albeit unwarrantedly) defenders of statutory bills of rights, the other one involves looking at the effects of a bill of rights, but only one specific, narrow category of effects. I refer to those effects related to anti-terrorism legislation. The rejoinder this time involves claiming that our newly empowered, bill of rights-wielding judges will ensure any such legislation is more rights-respecting than it otherwise would be. And the main exhibit in the United Kingdom for such arguments is the case of *A v Secretary of State for the Home Department*.[40]

This sort of assertion or rejoinder clearly subsumes many areas of contention, both empirical and value-based. To weigh such a rejoinder requires far more, say, than some simplistic noting that in Australia (without a national bill of rights) suspected terrorists can be held for a maximum of seven days before being charged, whereas in the United Kingdom (with a statutory bill of rights, and indeed the incorporated European Convention on Human Rights) the maximum is 28 days—four times longer. But it also requires more than some simplistic assumption that

---

[37] See Allan, above n 36. The rejoinder may have force when directed at those who oppose bills of rights on a non-consequentialist, Waldronian, strong right to participate or right-of-rights basis, as I explain from p 124 of that article.

[38] Ibid 126–7 (internal footnotes omitted).

[39] I would say the last of these is a plausible description of what happened in Canada with the Charter of Rights there.

[40] [2004] UKHL 56; [2005] 2 AC 68 (hereinafter 'the *A* case').

the *A* case was in reality a victory for human rights, just because the top judges deciding the case presented it in those terms. In fact, the *A* case has been stridently criticized from both ends of the political spectrum. Professor John Finnis describes the judges in the case as being 'led away ... by argumentation which seems partly erroneous and partly *per incuriam*'.[41] Meanwhile Professor David Campbell is even more biting, arguing 'that the alchemy by which an act of mercy and generosity by a national government can be treated as a case of discrimination in the pejorative sense, incurring judicial criticism which makes it difficult for that government to perform its basic functions, is unacceptable to all other than those engaged in the promulgation of the HRA jurisprudence'.[42]

I will limit myself, for present purposes, to asserting that it is far from obvious to me that the United Kingdom's bill of rights-empowered judges have improved matters—from a rights-respecting outcomes perspective, let me be clear—when it comes to the government's legislative response to terrorism. Those suggesting the top judges have been a positive force here certainly do not have a clear-cut case, or even one that commands widespread support amongst smart, well-informed, nice people (and probably not as much support as might be expected even amongst lawyers and legal academics).

So in my opinion this second rejoinder, as with the first one, fails. Neither can salvage the case proponents of a statutory bill of rights attempt to make.

IV. Gloomier and Gloomier

You might think that my Cassandra-like attack on statutory bills of rights leaves no room for further pessimism (assuming you come to the issue as a supporter of parliamentary sovereignty and majoritarian 'letting the numbers count' democratic decision-making, even as regards issues raising rights concerns). Ten years ago I was gloomy; today I am gloomier still. And I am also angry at the way this statutory enactment has surreptitiously positioned the unelected British judges in a decision-making role that approximates that of judges in Canada and the United States—or does so to the extent you think, like me, that when judges interpret section 3 in a *Ghaidan*-like way, and when the elected legislature never (not once) gainsays or second-guesses Declarations of Incompatibility, and when the determination of what is rights-compatible defaults wholly into some 'what will the judges think' guessing game, that at that point there is not any major difference of substance between the UK state of affairs and one where judges openly do strike down legislation (save that the former is less honest and transparent, perhaps).

As it happens, however, there is room for even more pessimism. This further pessimism or gloominess comes not from considering the Human Rights Act

[41] J. Finnis, 'Nationality, Alienage and Constitutional Principle' (2007) 123 *Law Quarterly Review* 417, at 418.
[42] D. Campbell, 'The Threat of Terror and the Plausibility of Positivism' [2009] *Public Law* 501.

itself, but from turning our attention to the related issue of how judges are chosen or selected.

One of the typical responses one hears from defenders and supporters of bills of rights (be they constitutionalized or statutory) is that the unelected judiciary in fact has a modicum of democratic legitimacy given that it is appointed by the Executive. This sort of claim has more force in the United States than anywhere else. When it comes to their top federal judges, and especially their Supreme Court judges, the appointments process is openly political. The Executive nominates someone, but that candidate has to be approved by a legislative committee,[43] and then by a vote of the Upper House. Nominees are vigorously questioned by elected legislators. Some nominees are rejected. The party of the President who does the appointing does not always control the Upper House, and so there is often no guarantee that a nominee will be approved.

All of this goes some way (nowhere near far enough, in my view, but some way) towards buttressing the type of argument that claims that unelected judges operating a bill of rights will never veer too far from the political mainstream.[44] The court may get slightly ahead of, or lag slightly behind, majoritarian sentiment, but it will ultimately fall into line because new appointees will be vetted to ensure that it does. Or so goes this type of argument.

Notice that this sort of openly political looking appointments process requires that the jurisdiction using it have real bicameralism, with an elected Upper House not always under the control of the political party making the nomination. Of the main, wealthy, Western common law countries only Australia meets that test. Canada and the United Kingdom do not have elected Upper Houses. New Zealand does not have an Upper House of any sort at all.

Absent an American-style appointments process (and, indeed, absent even the possibility of its adoption), Westminster systems could traditionally claim that unelected judges were nevertheless appointed by the elected Prime Minister and Cabinet. True, there was no legislative vetting of the choice made by the Executive. But it was still the case that the unelected judge was being selected by the elected official.

This traditional Westminster system of appointments was preferable to the American system, in my opinion, provided no bill of rights was in existence that handed extra moral and political line-drawing powers to the judges. For one thing, when it is clear judges will defer to a sovereign Parliament on contentious moral and political issues—even those articulated in the language of rights—then it is also comparatively easier to select judges on technical legal expertise grounds, with a fair degree of insouciance about the fact the nominee does not share the political and moral views of the appointer. However, once a bill of rights is enacted, or adopted, that comparative insouciance disappears. The values of the appointee matter, not just his or her technical merit as a lawyer. At that point—because of

---

[43] That is, the Senate Judiciary Committee.
[44] See eg M. Tushnet, 'Judicial Review of Legislation', in P. Cane and M. Tushnet (eds), *Oxford Handbook of Legal Studies* (Oxford: Oxford University Press, 2003), 164 and R. Posner, 'Introduction', *Frontiers of Legal Theory* (Harvard: Harvard University Press, 2001), 14–27.

the bill of rights—I think the American appointments system is preferable to the traditional Westminster one.[45]

But here is the rub. Some half-dozen years or so after we were given the Human Rights Act, we were also given a new judicial appointments process. This new process is characterized by its proponents as 'significantly limiting the role of the executive'[46] and as 'making selections "solely on merit"'.[47] It leaves the elected branches of government almost completely neutered in so far as appointing the unelected judges who will be operating this *Ghaidan*-fuelled bill of rights is concerned. A Judicial Appointments Commission (JAC) now picks the judge, with the Lord Chancellor having only a highly constrained power to reject the JAC's choice on the basis the person 'is not suitable for the office',[48] or to ask the JAC to reconsider due to a lack of evidence that 'the person is suitable'.[49] And the Lord Chancellor has to give reasons in writing for doing this. If either of these steps is taken by the Lord Chancellor, the same one cannot be taken a second time by the Lord Chancellor when the JAC resubmits a name. And at the next stage the Lord Chancellor 'must accept the person selected by the JAC'.[50]

This new appointments process may be many things, but what it assuredly is not is one that allows supporters of the statutory bill of rights to claim the newly empowered judges have a modicum of democratic legitimacy (in the way such a claim is open to Americans or those in jurisdictions with the traditional Westminster process). Quite simply, under this new system there is virtually no democratic input whatsoever into the appointment of judges. Indeed, for those who prefer a strong aristocratic element in their jurisdiction's governing arrangements, this combination of the Human Rights Act and the JAC satisfies that preference remarkably well—at least if judges get to count as today's aristocracy.

The JAC has 15 members, including five judges, two lawyers, and a tribunal member. This body will select the judges for England and Wales, with similar commissions for Scotland and for Northern Ireland. Judges for the soon-to-be created United Kingdom Supreme Court will be selected by a separate, new commission with the country's two most senior existing judges on it, plus members taken from the commissions for Scotland, Northern Ireland, and England and Wales.

In a book chapter I wrote three years ago, I argued that appointments processes like these are highly suspect, indeed undesirable, and especially so in a world where unelected judges have become very powerful indeed (not least due

---

[45] I have made just these arguments, and those in the next few paragraphs, in 'Appointing Judges in New Zealand: If It Were Done When 'tis Done, then 'twere Well It Were Done Openly and Directly', in P. Russell and K. Malleson (eds), *Appointing Judges in an Age of Judicial Power* (Toronto: University of Toronto Press, 2006), 125–61.

[46] *The Governance of Britain: Judicial Appointments*, Report of the Lord Chancellor and Secretary of State for Justice, Oct 2007, ch 3, p 22. The legislation bringing in these changes was the Constitutional Reform Act 2005 (c 4).

[47] Ibid 23.

[48] Ibid.

[49] Ibid.

[50] Ibid 24.

to the proliferation of bills of rights). One drawback, and this despite the way such processes are sold as 'transparent' and 'independent', is the near total lack of any democratic input into who ends up on the bench. Such an absence can only be thought desirable if one thinks, or assumes, that the unelected judges do not have the upper hand over—do not generally prevail in any rights-articulated disagreements with—the elected Parliament. I have argued earlier in this chapter that such an assumption is difficult to maintain in the face of what I will describe as 'the facts'.

Related to this almost total lack of democratic input into the appointment of judges, however, is the not unrelated concern of self-selection or memes. Judges and lawyers have a big role on these new commissions. They make up just a shade under half of the members of these commissions, but even at that level it is hard to believe lay members will overrule judicial and lawyer members—ever, in any circumstances in which the judges feel at all strongly. And that means, as I put it a few years ago in a book chapter about New Zealand, that the danger:

…is not simply one of the potential mediocrity of indirectly appointed nominees. The danger is greater than that; it is of a lack of heterogeneity among those ultimately chosen as judges, that we might end up with an insulated, self-selecting lawyerly caste—mediocre or otherwise—whose views on abortion, euthanasia, and other contentious issues are noticeably at odds with the general voting public's. Nor is this a far-fetched worry, as a moment's comparison of the general views of most—not all, but most—New Zealand lawyers (and legal academics) as opposed to the public at large on, say, homosexual rights and sentencing, reveals.

Relatedly, an indirect appointments process can make it difficult, perhaps very difficult, for a political party that has been out of power for some time, but has now won an election, to appoint a judge from among those lawyers who hold minority views (for lawyers that is, they may quite possibly be majority views among the public at large). Those on any Appointments Board may fall victim to the temptation to feel most comfortable with lawyers who share broadly similar world-views. Indeed, the notion of merit itself may come to be viewed through this prism of a candidate's general, small 'p' political views—on the proper role and influence of the jurisdiction's Bill of Rights, for example.[51]

This risk of self-selection and the perpetuation of an insulated, lawyerly caste does not seem an insubstantial one to me. Taking all the politics out of appointments is not at all a self-evidently good thing. Once a bill of rights is in place it is, to the contrary, a bad thing. Indeed, for those of us worried about the increasing power of unelected judges—of the legalization of politics and of the settling by judges of rights-based disagreements in society—this sort of judicial appointments process makes things worse, not better.

It gives added grounds for pessimism and gloominess about the long-term effects of the Human Rights Act.

---

[51] Allan, above n 45, 110. Notice, too, that a certain orthodoxy as regards the best interpretive approach to take to, say, the bill of rights or to s 3 can develop. And shifting that orthodoxy by the explicit appointment of outlier candidates is now also foreclosed to the elected government.

V. Concluding Remarks

The United Kingdom is the textbook example of how weak-form judicial review under a statutory bill of rights can collapse, and has collapsed, into something functionally indistinguishable from strong-form judicial review under an entrenched, constitutionalized bill of rights. If you think the latter is objectionable on democratic, count-everyone-as-equal grounds, then it seems to me you have very little room indeed to distinguish the former or to take a different position as regards this statutory bill of rights. If US-style and Canadian-style bills of rights make you angry and morally indignant, then so should the Human Rights Act.

The first decade of operation of this statutory bill of rights has been even worse for the majoritarian democrat than anticipated. Opting to hand over to a self-selected, insulated lawyerly caste the deciding of society's highly debatable and contested rights-based issues—with *Ghaidan* looming over them and the elected legislature yet to gainsay or second-guess them even once—seems to offer little basis for the majoritarian democrat to feel optimistic about the future.

7

Constitutionalism, the Rule of Law, and the Cold War

Joan Mahoney

The goal of constitutionalism is, or should be, to enshrine the rule of law: to protect individuals, specifically members of political minorities, from the power of political majorities. And, when it works, it does just that. Unfortunately, there are times when constitutionalism breaks down, when all the written rules in the world fail to protect the politically weak, and, conversely, the rule of law may be observed even without a written constitution. During the early Cold War period, the American Bill of Rights did little for those accused of being Communists or, to use the expression of the day, fellow travellers, while in Britain, without a written constitution, the rule of law was generally observed. By the 1960s, a change in the political climate and some significant Supreme Court decisions expanded civil liberties in the United States. On the other hand, despite an increase in constitutionalism in Britain, as a result of the European Convention on Human Rights and its enforceability through the European Court, there was an increase in government secrecy and disregard for the rule of law. By using illustrations from the Cold War period in both Britain and the United States, as part of a longer work in progress on the history of civil liberties in Britain during the Cold War, we hope to show the interaction of constitutionalism, politics, and the rule of law.

Constitutionalism means the adoption of a set of principles, usually, although not necessarily written, that may prescribe the form and structure of government but certainly includes a framework for the protection of the rights of all citizens, in particular those in the minority. The American Constitution, with the addition of the Bill of Rights (and, in addition, the post-Civil War Amendments that expanded coverage to the freed slaves), is a prime example, but there are numerous others, especially in recent years. Some, like the Canadian Charter of Rights and Freedoms of 1982, apply to one country only, while others, like the European Convention on Human Rights, are multi-national.

The rule of law refers not to written principles but to actual practice. At a minimum, the rule of law requires the observance of what Americans call due process and what the British call natural rights—notice, the opportunity to be heard, and decisions made by a neutral fact-finder before any significant deprivation of property or liberty. In addition, the rule of law might also include protections for privacy of one's home and person as provided by the Fourth Amendment in the United States.

Constitutions, of course, include human rights documents, but, in addition, they may also outline the structure of the government. Many, if not most, law schools in the United States teach two different constitutional law courses, one on individual rights and one on structure. While most students—and, perhaps, professors—prefer the former, the latter is equally important. Indeed, it is the structure of the American government, as well as the failure of the judiciary to enforce individual rights, that accounts for what happened during the Cold War, and, in fact, the extraordinary increase in executive power during the recent Bush administration.

It is fairly well known that during what is known as the McCarthy period, the United States failed to observe the rule of law, despite the written Constitution and the Bill of Rights. Two alleged spies were executed, the leaders of the Communist Party were sent to jail based on their positions with the Party, and others went to jail for refusing to answer questions before Congressional investigating committees. Members of the Communist Party were denied passports, and any number of people lost their jobs in the government, with universities, unions, or in the entertainment industry.

It is less well known that there was no comparable red scare in Britain at the time.[1] There were no laws passed to make the Communist Party illegal, and, in fact, two Communists were elected to Parliament in 1945. A number of the Americans who were blacklisted in the United States emigrated to Britain and continued their careers in acting, writing, and directing. Communists continued to be active in the trade unions, and although there were a few instances of university professors who were fired, allegedly because of their politics, there was no wholesale purge of the academy.

The one area in which there were actions by the British government that could be compared to those in the United States were in the introduction of processes to determine whether members of the civil service posed a security threat and to remove any who were deemed to do so. It would be fruitful, therefore, to compare the way these processes were introduced and applied to see the interaction of constitutionalism, politics, and the rule of law in Britain and the United States.

The triggering factor leading to the British attempt to screen civil servants in sensitive positions was the Gouzenko defection in Canada in 1945. That led to the arrest and conviction of Dr Alan Nunn May, who spied for the Soviet Union while working on a joint American-British-Canadian atomic project.[2] A committee was put together, headed by Sir Edward Bridges of the civil service and Sir Percy Sillitoe of MI5, although the actual work was primarily done by A. J. D. Winnifrith and Graham Mitchell.[3] The purpose of the committee was to develop a security procedure for the civil service.

[1] 'Civil Liberties in Britain During the Cold War: The Role of the Central Government' (1989) 33 *American Journal of Legal History* 53.
[2] P. Hennessy and G. Brownfeld, 'Britain's Cold War Security Purge' (1982) 25 *Historical Journal* 966.
[3] Ibid.

Although the committee's work did not lead to a public announcement until 1948, Hennessy and Brownfeld cite private information for the proposition that transfers to less sensitive posts were already taking place in the two years between Gouzenko's debriefing and Attlee's speech setting up the purge procedures.[4] According to Jonathan Schneer, six Communist civil servants lost their jobs the spring before Attlee's speech in Parliament.[5] In late 1947, some months prior to the announcement, Attlee responded to a minute from the Secretary of Defence, 'I agree. We cannot afford to take risks here, and the general public will support us. Fellow travellers may protest, but we should face up to this. Action should be taken in regard to Fascists as well as Communists, although the former are feeble.'[6]

On 15 March 1948, Attlee announced the new security procedures in Parliament, as follows:

The Government have, therefore, reached the conclusion that the only prudent course to adopt is to ensure that no one who is known to be a member of the Communist Party, or to be associated with it in such a way as to raise legitimate doubts about his or her reliability, is employed in connection with work, the nature of which is vital to the security of the State.[7]

He added that the same rule would govern those who were known to be actively associated with Fascist organisations, and that as far as possible alternative work would be provided for those whose reliability was suspect.

There was an immediate reaction to the announcement, including the question from John Platts-Mills, 'In view of the Prime Minister's beginning of a purge of Communists, is there any reason why he should not go on to Jews and Socialists?', to which Attlee replied, 'Yes, every reason, because Jews and Socialists have a loyalty to this country. That is not so with many Communists, and some fellow travellers.'[8] Other questions dealt with the procedure that would be provided, about which the Prime Minister was vague but reassuring, and the possibility of extending the purge to the BBC, which the Prime Minister said was their responsibility, not the responsibility of the State. He concluded with the statement that the purge would be restricted to 'very narrow limits where security matters were of importance'.[9]

Three days later, a motion was tabled in the House by Harold Davies, on behalf of himself and forty-two other members, regretting the Prime Minister's statement on the ground that it constituted a departure from the principles of democracy and civil liberty and arguing that adequate safeguards had been provided in the past by the Official Secrets Act and other measures.[10] A debate on the question was scheduled for the following week.

---

[4] Ibid 967.
[5] J. Schneer, *Labour's Conscience: The Labour Left, 1945–51* (Boston: Unwin, 1988), 136.
[6] PRO, CAB 21/2278, 'Prime Minister's Minutes' (21 Dec 1947).
[7] 448 *Hansard* 1704.
[8] Ibid 1705.
[9] Ibid 1706.
[10] Ibid (18 Mar 1947), 2305.

At the 25 March meeting of the Cabinet, just prior to the discussion in Parliament, Attlee informed the Cabinet of the procedure to be followed, drawing their attention to the following:

(1) Civil servants hold office at the pleasure of the Crown and are not able to claim the protection of the courts if they are dismissed because their 'conduct or ability fell below the standard required'.

(2) Where there was serious doubt about a person's reliability, that person should be suspended until enquiries were complete.

(3) While persons who had been members of the Communist Party during the war or earlier might have changed their views, they should not be presumed to be reliable. 'Full enquiries should be made in such cases' although 'no stigma should attach to a person merely because he had been the subject of enquiries'.

(4) The final decision to dismiss or transfer would rest with the Minister in charge of the department. He proposed to appoint an advisory board, composed of three retired civil servants, to assist the Minister. The civil servant would be entitled to make written representations to the advisory body and, if he wished, to appear personally, but he would not be permitted to be represented by either counsel or a member of his union, although he could ask the advisory body to see witnesses who could testify as to his character. 'He would be given sufficient particulars of the information against him to enable him to bring rebutting evidence, but it would be impracticable to disclose to him the sources from which the information had been obtained.'

(5) The government would need to resist any suggestion that the report of the advisory body should be made public.

(6) The majority of cases would be dealt with by transfer and few civil servants would be dismissed. Those that were should be given the option of resigning, although in either case, whether they resigned or were dismissed, they would lose their pension rights.

He added that the armed forces were taking similar measures.[11]

Later that day, Parliament debated the new security measures at some length. Willie Gallacher, one of the two Communists then in Parliament, suggested that the purge had been prompted by the United States and mentioned a case of political discrimination that had already occurred in private employment.[12] Most of the members who spoke, however, conceded the need to take steps to protect the security of the State, but many were concerned about the process and whether there would be sufficient protection for the rights of the employees. In reply, Attlee again stated that there would be 'no general purge, no general witch hunt', and that most of those affected would be transferred to other work. He set out the

[11] PRO, CAB 128/12, CM 25 (48).
[12] 448 *Hansard* 3398 (25 Mar 1947).

procedure that would be followed, as described at the Cabinet meeting, pointing out that the final authority in every case would rest with the Minister in charge.[13]

While most newspapers supported the government, the *New Statesman and Nation* ran a column on the purge that included the following:

Past experience of MI5 . . . suggests it would be administered by people lacking any of the necessary 'intelligence or fair-mindedness.' MI5 found it difficult in the last war to pay attention to Fascists because they had always been trained to watch Communists. If given their heads now, these custodians of our liberties will readily start the kind of witch-hunt which has recently disgraced American public life. . . . It won't be long before Labour Ministers will find their own pasts raked over, to the delight of newspapers which always declared that Socialism and Communism are the same thing.[14]

The reaction of groups outside Parliament was mixed. The Co-operative Party Conference met on 28 March, and a resolution opposing the purge was defeated.[15] The Conference of the Clerical and Administrative Workers Union held a special session on the same day, at which they passed a resolution drawing a distinction between civil servants who 'accept the democratic premises' and those 'prepared to endanger the security of the State in the interest of a foreign power', and determined that the latter group should be withdrawn from positions affecting security, although they were concerned about securing the full protection of civil rights for those involved.[16] In September of that year, the Trades Union Congress (TUC) defeated a motion demanding that civil servants under investigation should have the right to be represented by officers of their union. The Institution of Professional Civil Servants, on the other hand, went on record against the purge in May 1948.[17]

There was no ambiguity in the National Council for Civil Liberties' (NCCL) response to the Prime Minister's statement. At their Annual General Meeting on 20 March 1948, the following resolution was passed: 'The National Council for Civil Liberties expresses unqualified condemnation of the Prime Minister's pronouncement of political discrimination which imperils the freedom not only of civil servants but of all other employed persons. It calls for its complete withdrawal as entirely alien and repugnant to the British tradition of civil liberties for 250 years.'[18]

The primary objections to negative vetting, as it was called, both within and outside Parliament, were what was perceived as a lack of fairness in the procedure, rather than to the theoretical principle of barring certain people from secret work. Other than the NCCL, which opposed the purge as discriminatory, most other groups and Members of Parliament were concerned that there would be mistakes

---

[13] Ibid 3421–3.

[14] *New Statesman and Nation* (20 Mar 1948), 229.

[15] D. N. Pritt, *The Labour Government, 1945–51* (London: Lawrence and Wishart, 1963), 165–6. The Co-operative Party was at that time an affiliated organization of the Labour Party.

[16] Ibid 165–6.

[17] Ibid 166.

[18] NCCL archives, Box 18, File 4. The NCCL passed resolutions condemning the purge and the subsequently imposed positive vetting procedures at every AGM from 1952 to 1957. Box 33, File 9.

made because of the inability to be represented or to know the evidence that was being used.

As Attlee had announced to Parliament, retired civil servants were appointed to act as a tribunal, known as the Three Advisers. If, after a check of MI5 and Special Branch files, or as a result of information passed on to them, Ministers had reason to doubt the loyalty or reliability of employees in their departments, the employees would be informed that there was a prima-facie case against them and that they had a right to a hearing before the Three Advisers. Employees would be told only the charges against them, but neither the evidence for the charges nor its source.

The terms of reference of the Three Advisers were to advise the Minister on a question of fact: whether the civil servant in question is a member of the Communist Party or a Fascist organization or associated with either in such a way as to raise legitimate doubts about the employee's reliability.[19] At the hearing, then, the employee could challenge the factual basis of the findings but not whether he or she was actually likely to be a security risk. For example, one civil servant, a scientist, was told that the charge against him was that he had been a member of the Communist Party until 1943, and he was informed that if he *denied* the charge he could request a hearing, but presumably if he admitted membership he would be dismissed or transferred, regardless of any other considerations he might have been able to raise.[20]

Employees could request that character witnesses testify on their behalf, but they were not permitted to be represented by a lawyer or a representative of the union. Employees were not informed of the results of the hearing, but would be told only what the Minister had decided about their future employment.

The procedural aspect to which the unions most objected was the denial of trade union representation at the hearing, and a delegation was sent to Attlee to discuss that issue in July 1948. The government claimed that it would be a breach of security to allow a union representative to be present, to which the delegation responded that since the civil servant himself was allegedly a Communist, his presence was as prejudicial to security as that of a union official who might or might not be a Communist. The government replied that by attending a series of hearings, the union official would build up 'a far clearer insight into security methods than a Civil Servant at a single hearing'.[21]

At a second meeting, in December 1948, the deputation from the TUC made two requests: representation at the hearing and the appointment of a person from the trade union movement to the panel. The Prime Minister again turned down the first request, but agreed to the latter. In a brief prepared for the Prime Minister before the meeting, it was pointed out that the TUC had narrowly defeated the call for trade union representation of civil servants at their Congress in September, and though the same security issues that had been raised earlier were still a consideration, there was no objection to the appointment of an appropriate trade union

---

[19] PRO, PREM 8/948.
[20] NCCL archives, Box 18, File 4, undated statement from the Civil Service Branch of the NCCL.
[21] PRO, PREM 8/948.

person as a member of the Three Advisers.[22] Accordingly, J. W. Bowen, former General Secretary of the Union of Post Office Workers, was appointed to replace Sir Maurice Holmes, who had been given a position in the West Indies.

Had the new procedure caught those few spies who were later revealed to be operating within the civil service, and no one else, there might have been little cause for civil libertarians to object. As it turned out, however, it did neither. Most of the people who were transferred or dismissed were clearly not spies, and many of them appear not to have been involved in sensitive work. On the other hand, Burgess, Philby, and Maclean continued to serve within the security forces long after the purge was initiated.

One of the victims of the purge was an employee of the Ministry of Education, and it is hard to imagine that she had access to highly classified documents. She had been employed in the same Minister's office for over five years and had apparently never made a secret of her left-wing views. Nonetheless, the Minister was sufficiently impressed with her ability and trustworthiness that when he was moved from Labour to the Ministry of Works, and again when he was switched to Education, he insisted that she go with him.[23]

The NCCL newsletter, *Civil Liberty*, indicates that as early as 1948 the purge had been applied to industrial workers. Although the Prime Minister had never said that the security measures would be confined to the higher levels of the civil service, the emphasis on access to secret documents implied such a limitation. Nonetheless, four workers at the Post Office Dollis Hill research station at Willesden were suspended for 'association with the Communist Party',[24] as well as a shop steward at Maltby Royal Ordnance Factory, who was a member of the Communist Party; a shop steward at the Royal Ordnance Depot, Enfield; and a capstan operator at Woolwich Arsenal. The capstan operator was ultimately reinstated.[25]

Other employees who reported action against them include a mechanic examiner at the Inspectorate of Fighting Vehicles, Ministry of Supply, Royal Ordnance Factory, Nottingham, who was given the choice of accepting a lower paying job or resigning, after allegations were made that he was a Communist Party member; a cashier at the Government Communications Club, Cheltenham, who was fired in 1954 because her husband was a member of the YCL; a woman who was dismissed in 1954 from a job carrying boxes at the Ministry of Supply for being a Communist; and a man who was dismissed from a job at the Colonial Geological Surveys, Imperial Institute, South Kensington in 1954 for membership in the Communist Party.[26] In addition, a letter in the NCCL files from George Holland of the Fire Brigades Union in July 1955 reports the discharge of a porter at British Railways Morpeth Dock, Birkenhead because of Communist Party membership.

[22] Ibid.
[23] NCCL archives, Box 18, File 4, undated statement from the Civil Service Branch of the NCCL.
[24] *Civil Liberty* (Nov 1948), 1.
[25] Ibid 4.
[26] NCCL archives, Box 18, File 5.

He believed that there had been other incidents as well but was unable to supply the details.[27]

On 7 November 1948, a civil servant wrote to the NCCL to express her concern about her job security. She had recently been elected to a position in her union, the Civil Service Clerical Association, following which two members of the union had alleged that she was unfit to represent the association because of her 'Communist sympathies'. Her fear was that the public allegation by the union members would have a negative effect on her employment.[28] There is no follow-up letter in the file, so there is no way of knowing whether this particular civil servant was sacked, transferred, or left where she was, but her letter indicates the relationship between red-baiting in the unions and the purge. An employee who was sacked for left-wing activities or sympathies would no longer be an active member of the union, thus diminishing the number of left-wingers at the very time that, for example, the Civil and Public Services Association was going through a struggle between the left and the moderates.[29]

Although the purge, as described by Attlee, was to apply only to civil servants, there were also incidents of employees of private firms being sacked, usually because of pressure from the government. Unlike civil servants, private employees had no access to the Three Advisers, so there was no procedure available to them at all to question their dismissals or the information upon which it was based, except whatever protection was offered by their unions.

In July 1948, D. N. Pritt asked the Prime Minister what steps he proposed to take to procure alternative employment for people dismissed by private employers, so that they would not be worse off than civil servants who were most often transferred to other work. In a written answer, the Prime Minister replied, 'The position of a civil servant dismissed from his post is no different from that of any other person who has become unemployed. In both cases the machinery of the Ministry of Labour and National Service is available to help him find other employment.'[30] Pritt followed up the next day with a more specific question, asking about a call by MI5 on the engineering firm where S. J. Manley was a draughtsman. Chuter Ede, the Home Secretary, replied that a police officer had visited the firm 'for the purpose of making certain enquiries', but that he had not made representations to the firm concerning Manley as Pritt had suggested in his question.[31]

---

[27] Ibid.

[28] Ibid.

[29] E. Wigham, *From Humble Petition to Militant Action: A History of the Civil and Public Services Association, 1903–1978* (London: Civil and Public Services Association, 1980). See also Weiler at 221–3 for the links between the purge and struggle between the Communist and anti-Communist wings of the civil service union: P. Weiler, *British Labour and the Cold War* (Stanford, Calif: Stanford University Press, 1988). Conflicts within the unions concerning Communists and sympathizers are not within the scope of this work, in that non-governmental discrimination does not implicate civil liberties in a traditional sense. Nonetheless, one should not ignore the parallels between governmental and private actions during these years.

[30] 454 *Hansard* 4 (19 July 1948).

[31] Ibid (20 July 1948), 35.

A minute sent to the Prime Minister before his meeting with the TUC delegation, referred to above, dealt also with the question of private employees, as follows.

Communist propaganda is suggesting that the Government's policy in regard to Communists is extending beyond the Civil Service to general industry. Mr. Pritt's two Questions in the House this week are directed at establishing this contention. It is unfortunately the case that private contractors engaged on secret work for the Defence Department are required by a clause in their contracts not to employ persons in respect of whom objections are raised by the Departments. This is a long standing practice and is no new development.[32]

In other words, while it was true that private employees were being sacked at the behest of the government, and therefore hardly 'Communist propaganda', it was not true that it was connected with the purge, since it had actually been going on before the security restrictions were imposed on the civil service.

The dismissal of private employees was raised again in the House in 1954, after Mr Chambers of Rolls-Royce was sacked following instructions by the Minister of Supply not to give him access to information about secret defence projects.[33] Mr Warbey asked the Minister of Supply, Duncan Sandys, whether Chambers would be compensated for his loss of earnings. Sandys responded that any claim for compensation lay against the company, not against the government. He added that the power to instruct a firm to deny an individual access to secret information had been a part of standard form government contracts since before the war and had been used seven times since the war, three times by Sandys and four times by his predecessor in the Labour government. Sydney Silverman then pointed out that had Mr Chambers been a government employee, he would have had the right to be heard before the removal took place and he would have been removed to other employment at a comparable rate of pay.[34]

In some cases, of course, employment was denied before the fact. The *Daily Herald* on 8 March 1954, reported that Canon Christopher Francis Harmon, the vicar of South Marston, had been appointed to a post in East Harptree, Somerset, but the offer was withdrawn by the Secretary to the Duchy of Cornwall on the ground that Harmon was a Communist (which he was not) and a pacifist (which he was). The NCCL wrote to the Socialist Christian League on 9 March 1954, expressing 'alarm' because the Duke of Cornwall is, in effect, a public officer.[35]

Another instance concerned a journalist, Mervyn Jones, who was offered a job writing pamphlets for the Central Office of Information, 'a job which, so far from being secret, consisted entirely in making things public', but the offer was withdrawn when it came out that Jones had been a member of the Communist Party, even though it was five years since he had left the Party.[36]

[32] PRO, PREM 8/948.
[33] *Daily Herald* (9 Mar 1954).
[34] 525 *Hansard* 23 (15 Mar 1954).
[35] NCCL archives, Box 18, File 4.
[36] K. Martin and I. Gilmour, *The Secret Police and You* (London, 1958), 9.

Joan Mahoney

Serving as a retired officer of the armed forces is not precisely employment, but the government determined in 1952 to remove Edgar Young's name from the list of retired naval officers because of his activities in the various friendship societies and other 'Communist front' groups. The action led to an uproar in Parliament. On 19 March 1952, Ian Mikardo addressed a question to the First Lord of the Admiralty, asking why Young's name had been removed from the Navy list.[37] The answer, from Mr J. P. L.Thomas, was that the Admiralty had no further use for his services.

His activities on behalf of the Communist Party are proving such a source of embarrassment and distress to the Royal Navy at home and abroad that it has been found necessary to make it clear that the Admiralty do not hold themselves responsible in any way for his conduct, and that he is not entitled to call himself Commander R.N. (retired) or to wear naval uniform.[38]

Mikardo pointed out that another retired officer who had urged Fascist opinions, and been interned during the war as a result, was still on the list, while Young had been struck off. Thomas's answer was that the Sir Barry Domvile was not *currently* engaged in political activities.[39] The question was raised again on 24 March, at which time a number of MPs, Conservative as well as Labour, suggested that the purpose was to restrict Young's right to express his political views, and, as such, the action was inappropriate. Brigadier Terence Clark wondered whether, if the Bevanites were to obtain power, he might be deprived of his rank because of his Tory views.[40] Thomas argued that they were not depriving Young of his right to speak, but were removing the additional weight his title gave his speech, although he admitted that there was no way Young could be prohibited from using his title, if he were to choose to do so.[41]

Despite the protests in Parliament and a deputation from the NCCL, the Admiralty maintained that Young was not entitled to use the designation of retired naval officer, but Young continued to use his title nonetheless. As Thomas had admitted during the debate on the issue, the only remedy open to the Admiralty was to inform those people to whom Young communicated that he was no longer on the retired list. In December of 1952, the British Information Services sent a letter to the *Pakistan Times* indicating that Young had signed articles that he wrote for them with his title, which he was not entitled to use.[42] One wonders whether Young spent the rest of his life signing articles and letters as a retired naval officer, and whether the British Information Services followed his letters around the globe with the disclaimer about his use of the title.

Like Young, Monica Felton was fairly well-known in Britain during this time, her political views having caused controversy on a number of occasions, including

---

[37] 497 *Hansard* 2313.
[38] Ibid.
[39] Ibid 2314.
[40] 498 *Hansard* 56 (24 Mar 1952).
[41] Ibid. 59–62.
[42] NCCL Files, Box 25, File 5.

most particularly her visit to Korea which was one of the triggering factors in the consideration by the government of new legislation to prevent such trips. Although Mrs Felton was not prosecuted for her trip to Korea, she was fired from her job as Chairman of the Stevenage Development Corporation. Hugh Dalton, then the Minister of Local Government and Planning, assured Parliament that her sacking was not due to her political views, but to her absence for four weeks during the time she was in Korea.

When Anthony Eden raised a question in the House about Mrs Felton's position, Dalton replied that he had dismissed her from her post because, 'in my judgment, she is unfitted to continue to hold this appointment'.[43] She had apparently been told in March that she would be required to appear before a House Committee in June, but she did not return to the country in time for the hearing. He added that when she left in April for Korea, she had failed to inform anyone in authority of her absence, nor made plans for the carrying on of her duties. The last point was contradicted by G. McAllister, who pointed out that she had informed the General Manager of the Stevenage Corporation that she was leaving.[44]

Eden was apparently not satisfied that Mrs Felton had been fired, and asked Dalton whether she had received any assistance from the Foreign Office in making her trip. Dalton's response was that the last question should be addressed to the Foreign Secretary. His only concern, he stated, was the administration of the new towns. 'From that point of view it is a matter of total indifference to me whether Mrs. Felton was absent in Hollywood or the Riviera or anywhere else. The point to me is that she was absent and neglected her functions.'[45]

The question of Mrs Felton's dismissal was raised again on 14 June, in the debate on the adjournment. Again, there was discussion of her political views and the controversy caused at home by her trip to Korea. Sir Frank Soskice, the Attorney General, suggested that he ought not to answer questions on the issue, because he had referred the papers regarding Mrs Felton's activities to the Director of Public Prosecutions.[46] Mr McAllister again pointed out that Mrs Felton had informed both the General Manager and the Deputy Chairman of the Stevenage Corporation of her plans to go abroad, that she had arranged for the latter to take the chair while she was gone, and that she had cabled the appropriate person regarding the delay in her travel plans and the fact that she would miss the scheduled committee meeting. He stated that it was clear that her dismissal was not based on the grounds given by Dalton, as was obvious from the tenor of the debate on her dismissal.[47]

Monica Felton's successor was Sir Thomas Bennett, who was also in charge of Crawley, another new town. Tom Driberg pointed out in his column, in *Reynold's News*, that Sir Thomas Bennett had announced that he was going to Australia for three months, but he had not been sacked.[48] The NCCL requested a meeting with

---

[43] 488 *Hansard* 2308 (13 June 1951).
[44] Ibid 2311–12.
[45] Ibid 2309
[46] Ibid (14 June 1951), 2680.
[47] Ibid 2684.
[48] *Reynold's News* (29 July 1951).

Dalton to discuss the situation, but his office responded that since he had already appointed a successor, no useful purpose would be served by such a meeting.[49]

The Prime Minister had stated that Fascists as well as Communists would be barred from sensitive employment, but there was in fact very little interest in Fascists at that time and, presumably, minimal efforts were made to discover those in the civil service. Hennessy and Brownfeld write, again basing their information on private sources, 'The security authorities were overjoyed when they eventually found a fascist in one of the service departments. It made the whole operation look genuinely evenhanded. Union leaders have always reckoned, with some justification, that the inclusion of fascists in the prime minister's March, 1948 statement was a piece of window-dressing.'[50]

The security measures introduced in 1948 were the first step in attempting to prevent access to secret information by Communists or those associated with them, but there were additional procedures adopted over the years. Following the arrest of Klaus Fuchs, in 1950, further measures were deemed to be required, and the system of 'positive vetting' was introduced. Rather than starting and ending with a check of the files, positive vetting, which was used for jobs requiring extraordinary secrecy, began with a check of the files, but went on to require the filling out of a questionnaire by the employee or applicant, a personal interview, and a check on the references listed. In November 1950, Norman Brook prepared a brief for the Prime Minister based on a report of the committee chaired by A. J. D. Winnifrith, stating that in the future a conscious effort would be made to confirm the reliability of candidates for certain sensitive posts, estimated to number about 1,000. He then asked:

Are Ministers prepared to accept the possibility—the probability, according to the Home Office and the Security Service—that the institution of special enquiries, even in a very few cases, will eventually become known and will put Ministers under the necessity of making a public announcement? The answer to this depends on how Ministers judge the present temper of Parliament and the extent to which Members of Parliament are willing to reconcile demands for more stringent security measures with concern for the traditional liberties of the subject.[51]

It was intended that the programme of positive vetting was to be kept secret and was only to apply to approximately 1,000 positions, or those people engaged in particularly sensitive work.[52] Sir Percy Sillitoe suggested, in a note to the Prime Minister, that informing civil servants that they were suspect would only encourage them to keep Communist Party membership secret. He proposed that, at least in London, active cases be discouraged and that civil servants who were suspected of being members of the Communist Party should be transferred from secret to non-secret work 'whenever a plausible opportunity presents itself', but that when

[49] NCCL Files, Box 25, File 4.
[50] Hennessy and Brownfeld, above n 2, 969. See also, D. G. T. Williams, *Not in the Public Interest* (London: Hutchinson, 1965), 170. 'Fascists were also included within the loyalty programme—but this was merely to ensure that there was no discrimination.'
[51] PRO, CAB 21/2248 (10 Nov 1950).
[52] Draft circular from Sir Edward Bridges to heads of various departments, PREM 8/1522.

the risk was not great, Departments 'will be asked to continue to tolerate the continued presence of Communists'.[53]

The way in which positive vetting worked is illustrated by the case of Robert Haslam, who was an engineer at an establishment concerned with the peaceful uses of atomic energy. After three years of employment and two previous security checks, Mr Haslam was interviewed again. He was asked what schools he had attended since the age of four, the addresses of all previous employers, and the names of all trade unions, societies, associations, and allotment clubs to which he belonged. He was questioned about his political beliefs and his church attendance, when he was married and who the guests at his wedding had been. His interviewers wanted to know about his brothers and sisters and asked his wife about *her* brothers and sisters. He was asked for his opinion about the head of his department and how they got on, what political discussions went on at the office and whether anyone expressed 'extreme views'. Inquiries were made by phone to his two referees, and when one was out, the interviewers spoke to his wife instead. The other referee was a Unitarian minister, Mrs Vallance, who was sufficiently upset about the incident to contact the press and preach a sermon on the process.[54]

The number and type of questions and the way in which the referees were interviewed led Will Griffiths to raise the incident in the House, and in January 1954, he asked whether any disciplinary action would be taken against the security officer responsible for the investigation. The Minister of Works replied that the officer had been reprimanded 'for errors made in the course of the investigation', and Griffiths added that this was not the only objectionable case, mentioning an instance in which a woman executive officer's newsagent was questioned as to what papers she read and her tradespeople to find out if she owed them money.[55]

Subsequent changes in the procedures followed the defection of Burgess and Maclean. They had actually left Britain in 1951, but the defection of Vladimir Petrov from the Russian Embassy in Canberra in 1954 revealed previously unknown information about their role. Following a debate in Parliament in November 1955, concerning the defects in the security procedures that had allowed Burgess and Maclean to continue in their positions and then to flee, a committee of privy councillors was appointed to conduct an inquiry into the matter. Although the full report was not released, a White Paper on their findings was issued in 1956.[56] The White Paper pointed out that in the past the chief danger to the security of the State came from espionage carried out by professional agents, while now the primary risks 'are presented by Communists and other persons who for one reason or another are subject to Communist influence'. Although the chief risk was deemed to come from Communists, the 1948 arrangements had been directed at Fascists as well, and therefore, in the paper, 'for convenience and brevity the term Communism is used to cover Communism and Fascism alike'. While the White

[53] PREM 8/1522.
[54] Martin and Gilmour, above n 36, 9.
[55] 522 *Hansard* 1583 (26 Jan 1954).
[56] Statement of the Findings of the Conference of Privy Councillors on Security (Cmnd, 9715, 1956).

Paper concluded that the structure of the security service was basically sound, one major change was the suggestion that the investigation include attempts to discover 'character defects' such as homosexuality, drunkenness, or drug addiction that might make a person unreliable or expose him to blackmail attempts. The report also indicated that, 'It is right to continue the practice of tilting the balance in favour of offering greater protection to the security of the State rather than in the direction of safeguarding the rights of the individual'.

The NCCL had been opposed to the purge since 1948, and, as has been seen above, questions concerning various aspects of both the purge and positive vetting were raised in Parliament from time to time. It was, however, an incident in 1956 that led to the formation of a group specifically concerned with investigations of civil servants and employees of firms engaged in business with the government. The group was called the Campaign for the Limitation of Secret Police Powers and it was headed by Benn Levy and Will Griffiths.[57]

John Lang was a solicitor with Imperial Chemical Industries, who had married a former member of the Communist Party in 1951. Because he handled confidential documents relating to work done by ICI for the Ministry of Supply, the Government expressed concern about his wife's political record, and in 1956, the Treasury Solicitor informed ICI that they would receive no further government contracts unless Mr Lang was denied access to secret information. He was therefore sacked, but the event led to something of an uproar.

Griffiths and Levy formed the Campaign, with a sponsoring council that included MPs such as Aneurin Bevan and Jennie Lee, Barbara Castle, Michael Foot, Tony Benn, Ian Mikardo, and Sydney Silverman, and non-politicians such as Kingsley Martin, Sybil Thorndike, Henry Moore, and J. B. Priestley. On 18 July 1956, a rally was held at Caxton Hall, at which Aneurin Bevan was a speaker,[58] described in the foreword to a pamphlet entitled, 'The Secret Police and You' by Kingsley Martin and Ian Gilmour as follows:

This spontaneous concern about an issue of civil liberty is encouraging. People quickly understood what was at stake. They suddenly realised that it was possible in the England of 1956 for men and women to be penalised, not as a result of any due process of law, but in deference to denunciation by unidentified informers and allegations by the secret police. They could lose their jobs without even knowing what charge was made against them, without evidence being called, and in defiance of all the legal safeguards of which England has boasted since the 17th century.[59]

It is curious that this sudden realization of the dangers of the purge occurred eight years after it was announced by Attlee, and one wonders whether there was something about Mr Lang's case in particular to distinguish it from those that had happened earlier, or whether by 1956, the mood had changed sufficiently in England, as it had in the United States, to permit the formation of such a group. They did not, however, suggest that security screening by the government should be abandoned,

[57] Williams, above at n 50, 177.
[58] M. Foot, *Aneurin Bevan* (London: Davis-Poynter, 1973), 508.
[59] Martin and Gilmour, above n 36, 1.

but they did suggest a five-point plan intended to protect the subjects of the purge, as follows:

(1)   Rules governing employment on security work should be approved by Parliament and made known to every person engaged upon it.

(2)   No person should be removed from their employment on a pretextual charge, ie, if they are considered a security risk, they should not be discharged for inefficiency.

(3)   Any person considered a security risk should be informed of the charges, the right to appeal, and the right to be supported by either legal or trade union representation.

(4)   There should be an appeal to three High Court judges, sitting *in camera*, whose proceedings would be protected by the Official Secrets Act.

(5)   If the Court should find evidence of misconduct, it should be reported through the Lord Chancellor to the Privy Council.[60]

The issue of the purge was also raised at the Fifty-Fifth Annual Conference of the Labour Party at Blackpool in October 1956, when the National Executive Committee introduced a document entitled 'Personal Freedom'.[61] G. Cornes, of the Association of Engineering and Shipbuilding Draughtsmen, while conceding that there may have been good reasons for the security measures introduced in 1948, stated that since then 'the ramifications of the Act have gone much wider' and that now employees of private industry were more exposed to 'what is happening' than highly placed civil servants. He mentioned that a number of union members had been dismissed because of pressure put on the employers by government departments, even though some of those dismissed were neither Communists nor Fascists, but were thought to have sympathies 'in one direction or another'.[62]

R. Leonard, the MP from Harrow, expressed concern about the recommendation in the document to continue to tilt the balance toward the security of the state, as had been suggested in the White Paper. 'What appalls me about this', he said, 'is that this sentence might very well have been written by Senator McCarthy.'[63] Benn Levy then moved an amendment to the document which consisted, essentially, of the five-point plan proposed by the Campaign for the Limitation of Secret Police Powers, adding, 'I would lay odds that there are dossiers in MI6 files about a great many more of you here than you suppose.'[64] Will Griffiths supported the amendment, citing the cases that had been detailed in the pamphlet published by the Campaign.[65] G. R. Strauss, who was Minister of Supply in the Labour government and one of the signers of the Privy Councillors Report, defended the existing system, stating that an average of only seven civil servants a year had been removed

[60]   Ibid 15.
[61]   Report on the Fifty-Fifth Annual Conference of the Labour Party (Blackpool, 1956).
[62]   Ibid 83.
[63]   Ibid 84.
[64]   Ibid.
[65]   Ibid.

from their posts and that an average of only one person a year in private industry had been affected.[66] The Levy amendment was defeated by a vote of 3,478,000 to 2,625,000.[67]

One result of the uproar over Mr Lang's dismissal was that employees in private industry were given access to the Three Advisors if they chose to contest their dismissals.[68] Nonetheless, the Minister of Supply stated that this option would not be available to Mr Lang himself, 'Because the responsible Ministers considered this case with great care, at great length, and with all the information at their disposal, and there does not seem to be any object in going over the same ground again'.[69]

The Radcliffe Report, which came out in 1962, suggested that civil servants be permitted to bring a representative with them to the hearing before the Three Advisors, although also suggesting that Departments refuse to carry on negotiations with trade union officials who were believed to be Communists.[70] Other than that, the procedures continued relatively unchanged from their initial structure in 1948, until well after 1956,[71] and debate continues to this day on whether they are sufficient or not.[72]

With all the questions that were raised about the fairness of the procedures, it is important to determine how many people actually lost their jobs as a result of the purge. Between 1948 and 1954, a total of 124 civil servants were removed from their posts, of whom the majority were transferred to other positions. Between twenty and thirty civil servants were dismissed in those years and almost as many resigned.[73] In the year 1950, for example, forty-three civil servants were suspended: seven were reinstated, seventeen were transferred, four resigned, and eleven were dismissed. Four were still on special leave by July 1951.[74] The positive vetting procedures led to even fewer dismissals, as would be expected. Generally, positive vetting took place before a person was employed, and the only time it was likely to occur in circumstances that could lead to discharge was where a civil servant was about to be promoted. There were, therefore, only four persons dismissed for security reasons from highly sensitive posts between 1952 and 1955.[75]

These figures do not, of course, reveal the number of people who were refused jobs in either the civil service or private industry because they were deemed to be a security risk, nor does it indicate how many either resigned or failed to apply for certain positions because they wished to avoid the security clearance procedure. There is, in addition, reason to believe that Mr Strauss's estimate of the number of

---

[66] Ibid 91.
[67] Ibid. None of those who spoke on either side mentioned the list of proscribed organizations maintained by the Labour Party, membership in which was grounds for expulsion from the Party. See Appendix X attached to the report.
[68] Williams, above n 50, 178.
[69] 555 *Hansard* 9 (25 June 1956).
[70] Security Procedures in the Public Services (Cmnd 1681, 1962).
[71] Williams, above n 50, 179.
[72] See the concerns raised about Sir Maurice Oldfield, former head of MI6, who was revealed to be a homosexual after his retirement. The *Guardian* (24 Apr 1987).
[73] Williams, above n 50, 171.
[74] Ibid 176.
[75] Ibid 180.

employees in private industry who were sacked is quite low; although the evidence is anecdotal, rather than statistical, there would appear to be more than eight cases of private employees who were fired, based on the NCCL files and the statement of Mr Cornes at the Labour Party Conference. Nonetheless, even if the figures are low, they simply do not compare with the numbers who lost their jobs in the United States during that period. David Caute estimates that there were 2,700 dismissals and 12,000 resignations from the federal civil service alone, which does not take into account those who were fired from positions with state and local governments, nor those who lost their jobs in private industry.[76] It is quite likely that fewer than 200 people were either transferred or dismissed by the central government, or at their instigation, in the years between 1948 and 1956, and when viewed in light of what was happening in the United States, the effect of the purge in Britain was minimal indeed.

Much of the mechanism for the McCarthy period in the United States was in place long before the Cold War really started. The Dies Committee (which was later to become the House Committee on Un-American Activities—known generally as HUAC) was set up before World War II and was charged with investigating Fascists as well as Communists. The Smith Act, making it a crime to advocate the desirability of overthrowing the government of the United States by force and violence, among other things, was passed in 1940.[77]

Nonetheless, there was a change after World War II, though the change occurred sometime before the appearance of Senator McCarthy, after whom the era got its name. In fact, it was during the Truman administration that the first steps toward a search for Communists in the corridors of power, as well as in Hollywood and academia, began. On 25 March 1947, the President issued Executive Order 9835, providing procedures for a programme to determine the loyalty of employees in the executive branch of government. The order required the investigation of all civilian employees entering the executive department through the use of the files of a number of agencies, including the FBI, the House Committee on Un-American Activities (HUAC), military and naval intelligence, and local law enforcement groups. If any derogatory information was found relating to the employee's loyalty, a full field investigation was to take place. Existing employees were also to be investigated, but unlike applicants, employees were entitled to hearings before a loyalty board in the agency in which they were employed and could appear personally, accompanied by counsel or the representative of their choice. The employee was also entitled to appeal an adverse decision of the loyalty board to the head of the department or agency involved.[78]

---

[76] D. Caute, *The Great Fear; The Anti-Communist Purge under Truman and Eisenhower* (London: Secker and Warburg, 1978), 275.

[77] Internal Security Control Act, 18 USC 2384–6 (1948).

[78] Truman's Order was much more complex, far-reaching, and intensive than Attlee's purge announcement of the following year. The British scheme provided that if the government were to obtain information suggesting that an employee engaged in security work was a member of the Communist Party, or associated with it in such a way as to raise doubts about his or her reliability, the employee would be transferred, if possible, and only fired as a last resort. The American programme

The standard for refusal of employment or termination was stated as follows: 'that, on all the evidence, reasonable grounds exist for belief that the person involved is disloyal to the Government of the United States'.[79] This finding could be based on acts of sabotage, or espionage, treason, sedition, or the advocacy thereof, disclosure of documents or information under circumstances that might indicate disloyalty, or membership in or 'sympathetic association with' any group designated by the Attorney General as totalitarian, Communist, Fascist, or subversive. Although the presumption was in favour of continued employment, this was reversed by Executive Order 10241, in 1951, providing for dismissal if there was reasonable doubt about an employee's loyalty, thus making the presumption in favour of dismissal rather than retention.

Following Truman's executive order, the Justice Department updated and expanded the Attorney General's list, which was then published in March 1948. It included seventy-eight organizations, listed in six categories. The list was revised periodically until 1955, after which some groups were removed, but no further organizations were listed. Although individuals who were accused of disloyalty, as evidenced perhaps by their membership in organizations that were on the list, were entitled to a hearing before losing their government jobs, the organizations designated as subversive were not entitled to hearings either before they were put on the list or afterwards. The lack of due process was challenged in the courts, and in *Joint Anti-Fascist Refugee Committee v McGrath*,[80] the Supreme Court held that it was unconstitutional to list these groups without a hearing, although there was no immediate change in the procedures used by the Attorney General.[81]

By and large, the civil service unions went along with the loyalty programme. The American Federation of Government Employees and the National Federation of Federal Employees both expressed confidence that the programme would be fair and that those with nothing to hide would have nothing to fear. Only the United Public Workers, which was affiliated with the CIO, expressed fear that the loyalty programme was in reality a witch hunt.[82]

The powers provided by the issuance of executive orders were strengthened by a statute in 1950,[83] which permitted a number of federal agencies to dismiss employees on national security grounds, without reference to their loyalty. Someone who was perfectly loyal might be considered a security risk based on the possibilities of blackmail, such as homosexuals and others who might engage in activities they would not want to have publicly known. In 1953, the security risk concept was expanded in Executive Order 10450 and essentially supplanted the loyalty programme.

---

applied to *all* executive department employees, required positive investigation of their loyalty, and provided for termination of employment if there were doubts about an employee's loyalty.

[79] 12 CFR 1938 (1947).
[80] 341 US 123 (1951).
[81] Caute, above n 76, 170.
[82] Caute, above n 76, 270.
[83] Act of August 26, 1950, ch 803, 64 Stat476 (1952) (current version at 5 USC 7531–3 [1980]).

Most federal jobs, at least in the executive branch, were covered by one programme or another, and files were kept at one point on almost every federal employee. According to David Caute, a total of 2,700 federal employees were dismissed between 1947 and 1956 and 12,000 resigned.[84] There is no way of determining how many people were denied government jobs during this period because they failed to establish their loyalty or that they would not be security risks, and there is no question that there were numbers of people who avoided government employment because either they feared that they would not be found acceptable or simply because they did not want to go through the process.

So how did the processes in the two countries compare? The British programme was adopted in two stages, starting with negative vetting and only adopting the broader provision for positive vetting in 1950, while in the United States, both applicants and current employees were investigated thoroughly from the inception of Truman's executive order in 1947.[85] In both countries, existing employees, but not applicants, were entitled to hearings. And the United States allowed the employee to bring a representative to the hearing, which the British government did not. On the other hand, the hearing in the United States was before the 'Loyalty Board' of the agency that employed them, with an appeal to the head of the agency. In Britain, the hearing was before the Three Advisors, who were retired civil servants, and after the unions protested the process, a former union official was appointed to the Three Advisors. While their role was, as the title suggests, advisory, and the Minister in charge had the final decision, the British system incorporated a more independent voice in the process.

There were also differences in the presumptions that operated in the two processes. In Britain, previous membership in the Communist Party was presumed to make a person unreliable, but that presumption could be rebutted. In addition, the preference, with both positive and negative vetting, was to transfer the person away from classified work, rather than firing the employee. The American programme applied to all employees of the executive branch, not just those involved in secret work, and made no provision for transfer rather than termination. Although the presumption in Truman's original executive order was in favour of continued employment, the presumption was reversed in 1951. And, finally, membership in any group on the Attorney General's List was deemed to be sufficient evidence of disloyalty to justify discharge.

If, then, we define due process (or natural justice) as requiring notice, the opportunity to be heard, and decision by a neutral fact-finder, the British system seems considerably closer to the ideal than the system in the United States, where the hearing was before a committee of the agency where the accused was employed. Especially in light of Senator McCarthy's attack on the State Department and other branches of government for 'harboring Communists', heads of departments were unlikely to err in favour of the employee. Probably the easiest way to compare

---

[84] Caute, above n 76, 274.
[85] Harold Rome wrote a song about the process, said to be inspired by Alger Hiss, the chorus of which went, 'Who's Going to Investigate the Man Who Investigates the Man Who Investigates Me?' *New York Times* (31 July 2008).

the processes is to look at the numbers: in Britain, 124 people were removed from their jobs between 1948 and 1954, of which 20–30 were fired and the remainder were transferred. In the United States, 2,700 were dismissed and 12,000 resigned.

If the United States was less protective of civil liberties, despite the written Constitution and the Bill of Rights, then how do we account for the difference? The difference is almost certainly based on political differences between the two countries. By politics, we mean both the political culture and the actual workings of government.

Many people have written about American Exceptionalism—the lack of a viable left-wing party, the absence of a political party with ties to and commitment to the labour movement, and the prevalence of red-baiting of one sort or another over the years.[86] The different experiences of the American and British Left during the early Cold War period exemplify that difference in political culture, and it is clear from the comments made within Attlee's cabinet, as well as in Parliament, that the kind of anti-Communism prevalent in the United States was simply politically impossible in Britain. Even the head of MI5 was afraid that trying to purge too many members of the civil service would create a backlash.

But the difference also extends to politics as it describes the working of government. The American system of separation of powers is meant to provide checks and balances, to keep any one branch of government from amassing too much power. But it also isolates the branches from one another. When Truman promulgated the executive order that began the civil service purge, there was no way for Congress to respond, short of a proposed statute to overrule the executive order, or, even more drastic, a motion of censure. In the British system, on the other hand, the Prime Minister is answerable to Parliament. Attlee announced the proposed negative vetting in Parliament and faced an immediate reaction from members of his own party, who set the matter down for discussion a few days later. It was political pressure from the unions that led to a change in the make-up of the Three Advisors, and it was fears about the political repercussions that kept the second stage of the programme, the positive vetting introduced in 1950, so limited in its scope. The only formal way to challenge the programme in the United States was through a constitutional action, and the only case that involved the security purge was *Joint Anti-Fascist Refugee Committee v McGrath*,[87] and that dealt with the manner in which groups were added to the Attorney General's List (membership in which was deemed to be proof of disloyalty), rather than the purge itself.

Similarly, in recent years the Bush administration used executive power to restrict civil liberties and avoid congressional oversight. By statute, the government is required to obtain a warrant before, or a reasonable time after, intercepting phone calls between Americans and people overseas. In fact, the Bush administration began a programme of secret, warrantless, wiretapping, and when it was revealed, claimed that it was necessary for national security.

---

[86] See, just as one example, R. Hofstadter, 'The Paranoid Style in American Politics', *Harper's Magazine* (Nov 1964).
[87] 341 US 123 (1951).

In addition, Bush used signing statements, issued when he approved legislation, to indicate that instead of using the veto, which could be overridden by Congress, he was intending to interpret a statute in a way that was different than intended, or was refusing to enforce a provision of the statute. When, for example, the McCain amendment prohibited torture, President Bush signed the act, but indicated that he would continue to take the action that he believed would protect national security.

There are many other examples of the ways in which the Bill of Rights failed to contain anti-Communism in the United States during the early Cold War period and the ways in which politics did in Britain what constitutionalism did not do in the United States, but the differences in the way in which Communists and fellow travellers were removed from security work in both countries serves as an excellent example of the differences. Obviously, constitutionalism alone cannot contain violations of civil liberties, when the political culture is not supportive. Only later in the period, as our longer work will demonstrate, did the political culture in the United States change sufficiently to allow the Supreme Court to adopt the role of protector of civil liberties.

8

The Cold War, Civil Liberties, and the House of Lords

K. D. Ewing

I. Introduction

It is a striking feature of the Cold War that it did not lead to the banning of the Communist Party in the United Kingdom, as it did in many other countries (notably the United States, Australia, and South Africa). Nor did it lead to the introduction of repressive legislation to constrain the activities of the Communist Party. As Joan Mahoney has shown, the response of the British State was much more low key, though deliberate, and was based on three strategies of exclusion of Communists from sensitive positions in government and elsewhere; surveillance of Communist Party members and sympathizers; and the prosecution of those who were found to have committed offences of espionage or related activities. It is possible to speculate about the reasons for such restraint in a country in which there was not only a significant Communist presence, but also an absence of constitutional protection of rights which might operate as a barrier to such restrictions (though the existence of such a measure in the United States proved to be less than inadequate). Possible explanations include the existence of a strong culture of liberty that pervaded the political classes (or at least some of them), a theme to which Mahoney draws attention and which can also be seen to some extent (though perhaps in a diluted form) in the background documents that are considered in this chapter. A second possible explanation is the existence of a Labour government in Britain at the time key decisions were taken about strategy for dealing with the Communist Party. Although it is true that the Labour Party had no time for the Communist Party, and although it is true that the Labour Party proscribed the Communist Party, there are serious questions about whether a Labour government could secure the passing of legislation to proscribe the Communist Party of Great Britain (CPGB), for although there may have been loathing at the highest levels of party organization, this would not necessarily translate to local level, where activists would work together in communities and in trade unions. A third possible explanation is that the CPGB had parliamentary and local government representation, in the context of which it would be inconceivable to impose a ban on a party with a parliamentary mandate, even if there was the stomach to do so.

The lack of any direct legal attack on the CPGB meant that the British courts were denied the opportunity to make their own contribution to winning the Cold War. Indeed it is an equally striking feature of the period that it left no legacy of jurisprudence, though the treatment of communists did raise questions about the application of constitutional principle, the strategies of exclusion and surveillance without formal legal authority revealing again a weak conception of the rule of law in the British system of government. It is not until the 1960s that the courts began gradually to be engaged with Cold War issues, though the evolving jurisprudence related not to the activities of the Communist Party but to the activities of the peace movement, and in particular the large-scale demonstrations that they organized.[1] It was at this point that the patience of the State snapped, the commitment to liberty was sacrificed, and the courts used as instruments of repression, a role which some of the judges at least appeared to relish. The historical record also reveals the close relationship between the judicial and executive arms of government and the close involvement of the government in the first case relating to the Cold War to reach the House of Lords. The case in question is *Chandler v DPP*,[2] a case which is well-known but which has attracted little contemporary academic interest.[3] It is the case in which the State went to war with a militant peace organization—the Committee of 100—founded by Bertrand Russell, operating a strategy of civil disobedience alongside the more traditional and law-abiding strategies adopted by CND, which had been founded three years earlier. The Committee of 100 was looking for something more than 'walking from Aldermaston every 12 months, something better than sending letters to the Prime Minister or to sundry MPs, something more worthwhile than meaningless political manoeuvres in deserted Labour Party wards'.[4] This chapter is concerned to assess the *Chandler* decision in its historical context, with a view to revealing the deep roots that continue to nourish the courts when called upon to reconcile human rights with questions of national security. The issues considered by that decision continue to trouble the authorities as a new generation of peace protestors use the tactics deployed by the Committee of 100, albeit in a modified form. These tactics continue to give rise to prosecutions in which the Human Rights Act makes little difference to the ways in which these cases are dealt with, albeit under less draconian and intimidating laws.

II. The Committee of 100 and Trafalgar Square

The Committee of 100 was formed in October 1960 to further the aims of CND by acts of civil disobedience. One of its first acts was a sit-down protest outside the Ministry of Defence in February 1961. This activity elsewhere (such as outside the US Embassy) led to arrests and legal proceedings for obstruction against

---

[1] Judges were also involved extra-judicially in Cold War security issues. See Cmnd 1681, 1962.
[2] [1964] AC 763.
[3] But for a superb contemporary critique, see D. Thompson, 'The Committee of 100 and the Official Secrets Act, 1911' [1963] *Public Law* 201.
[4] Independent Labour Party, *The 100 versus The State* [nd], BLPS, CND/2008/3/5, 5.

the organizers.[5] The first major brush with the law was to arise, however, with the proposed demonstration in Parliament Square on 17 September 1961, for which permission was sought from the Minister of Works to have a rally in Trafalgar Square. Remarkably, the request was considered by the Cabinet on 1 August 1961, where the Home Secretary expressed concern that the previous activities of the Committee of 100 'suggested that it was their intention on this occasion also to obstruct the public highway by sitting down and declining to move if challenged by the police'. The point was made that the demonstration earlier in the year had led to over 800 arrests, and concern was expressed that 'a repetition on an even larger scale would throw an unacceptable strain on the police'. It was therefore proposed that the application should be refused, leading to discussions in which 'some misgivings were expressed on the ground that refusal would amount to an interference with the traditional rights of freedom of assembly and freedom of speech'. These misgivings appear to have been reinforced by the fact that '[n]o application from an organisation for the use of Trafalgar Square had been refused (except when the Square had already been booked) since 1916, when permission had been refused for a demonstration against continuing the war'. In breaking with precedent, the Cabinet decided that 'the grant of permission on condition that the demonstrators did not break the law would certainly be ineffective', while the fact that the RAF Association was already planning to hold a demonstration in the neighbourhood on the same day also had to be taken into account. The minutes also record that

The danger of consequent public disorder was a sufficient justification for refusing the present application, although it would be preferable to offer no reasons for the refusal. If, however, it were possible to obtain evidence, as distinct from a presumption, of a definite intention on the part of the organisers to commit breaches of the law, the Government would be in a stronger position to refuse any application they might make for the use of Trafalgar Square on an alternative date. It might even be appropriate to apply to a magistrate, under an Act of 1301, to require the organisers to show cause why they should not be bound over to keep the peace.[6]

(a) Preparing for Battle—the Role of the Government

Raising nice questions about the fettering of ministerial discretion, the Minister of Works was 'invited' by the Cabinet 'to refuse' the application for the use of Trafalgar Square for a demonstration in favour of nuclear disarmament on Sunday 17 September. The invitation having been accepted, it is simply unknown what would have happened to the Minister of Works had he declined. The Cabinet also 'invited' the Attorney General 'in consultation with the Home Secretary' to assess 'such evidence as could be obtained of the precise intentions of the organisers of the proposed demonstration'. This could mean only one thing, namely the assessment of evidence obtained by surveillance of the Committee of 100 by the police and the security service, about which there was a fair body of circumstantial evidence,

[5] *The Times*, (15 Sept 1961).
[6] TNA, CAB128/35/CC46 (61).

albeit produced by the Committee itself.[7] Further evidence of close surveillance was provided when the police moved not simply to ban the rally but to remove its organizers. On 12 September 1961, 32 members and supporters of the Committee of 100 (including Lord and Lady Russell) were jailed by the Bow Street Magistrates' Court for refusing to be bound over. The summons alleged

you are a disturber of the peace in that you have incited members of the public to commit breaches of the peace and breaches of the law, and in particular have incited divers persons unknown unlawfully to obstruct the highway in the vicinity of Parliament Square, Westminster, SW1 on September 17, 1961, and that you are likely to persist in such unlawful activity.

Information about the plan to block Parliament Square with a demonstration of 10,000 people was provided by a number of police officers, including a Sergeant R. Oakley who said he had attended a meeting at St Pancras Town Hall on 2 July 1961; the meeting was attended by about 300 people and reference was made to the Trafalgar Square rally and the Parliament Square demonstration. Asked in cross-examination by George Clark (who was to feature as a defendant in several cases),[8] about why he had been at the meeting of Committee of 100 supporters, Oakley said that he had been directed to attend (by his superiors), 'which was usual if a meeting was of interest to the police'.

A full report of the proceedings in *The Times* suggests that the trial of the 32 was little short of a pantomime, with another of the 32 popping up when Clark sat down to ask sergeant Oakley if he was a 'police spy', at which point the magistrate intervened to announce that he was not going to let all and sundry jump up again, for otherwise the trial would be interminable. He also slapped down one of the accused, in a vain attempt to prevent him using the machinery of the court for political 'advertising'.[9] Such was the nature of the events that both the Home Office and 'ministerial circles' were said to have gone 'to some lengths' on the day of the trial to dissociate the Home Secretary and the government from the action of the police in prosecuting the anti-nuclear campaigners.[10] But although the government was at pains to claim that the Home Secretary had not interfered in any way, as the *The Times* pointed out it was the Minister of Works who had banned the rally, and as we now know the possibility of securing binding over orders had been actively considered by the Cabinet only six weeks earlier. It was also the government that put in place a number of contingency arrangements to frustrate the event which was going ahead despite the ban. Thus, it was reported that the police planned to blockade the roads, and divert buses and tube trains away from Trafalgar Square, and that police restrictions would cover a square mile around Trafalgar Square. These steps were presumably taken under

---

[7] Hampstead Group, Committee of 100, *Mail Interception and Telephone Tapping in Britain* [nd], BLPS, CND/2008/8/119.
[8] See eg *R v Clark (No 2)* [1964] 2 QB 315.
[9] *The Times* (13 Sept 1961).
[10] *The Times* (14 Sept 1961).

the authority of the Metropolitan Police Act 1839 which provided by section 59 that

> It shall be lawful for the commissioners of police from time to time, and as occasion shall require, to make regulations for the route to be observed by all carts, carriages, horses, and persons, and for preventing obstruction of the streets and thoroughfares within the metropolitan police district, in all times of public processions, public rejoicings, or illuminations, and also to give directions to the constables for keeping order and for preventing any obstruction of the thoroughfares in the immediate neighbourhood of Her Majesty's palaces and the public offices, the High Court of Parliament, the courts of law and equity, the theatres, and other places of public resort, and in any case when the streets or thoroughfares may be thronged or may be liable to be obstructed.[11]

And as the day drew nearer, the Metropolitan Police Commissioner invoked the Public Order Act 1936 (this time with the necessary authority of the Home Secretary) to ban marches and processions by the Committee of 100 for 24 hours from midnight on 16 September.

(b) The Battle of Trafalgar [Square]

The preparation before the events of 17 September thus revealed strategies of (i) surveillance (attending meetings, though there was also known to be interception of communications); (ii) removal of key activists by imprisonment in circumstances which they predictably dubbed 'political trials'; and (iii) restraint by bans of various kinds (the rally, the assembly of people, the procession of people). The event itself was to reveal (iv) a pattern of police brutality that had been a feature of earlier events and which was to be seen at other high profile policing events in London in the 1960s and beyond, but which nevertheless was said to have been shocking in the level of its ferocity. Concern about the policing of the peace protestors had led to a number of MPs volunteering to act as observers. Such was the level of brutality encountered by Arthur Greenwood that he raised it in an Adjournment Debate in the House of Commons at the earliest available opportunity (the House was not sitting in September). A Labour MP, Greenwood strongly disapproved of civil disobedience as a method of political expression, but believed equally strongly that 'every citizen should be protected from any abuse of police powers'.[12] In common with other observers, Greenwood watched the scene from the roof of St Martin-in-the-Fields Church, from where he 'clearly saw men and women dragged along the ground by one arm and one man dragged along by his legs with his head scraping the ground'. Although he had no reason to doubt that the great majority of the officers on duty lived up to the best traditions of the police service, Greenwood thought that there was 'certainly a case for an impartial inquiry into the behaviour of the minority'.[13] Much of the evidence assembled by Greenwood strongly reinforced the case, with a *Daily Telegraph* reporter describing how a number of

[11] On which, see *Papworth v Coventry* [1967] 2 All ER 41.
[12] HC Debs, 17 Oct 1961, col 155.
[13] Ibid.

demonstrators making their way quietly out of the Square 'were thrown to the pavement, dragged forcibly to vans and coaches and manhandled', while a university lecturer from Wales 'described how women and girls were dragged head downwards across the paving stones and slammed down in the gutters', and Lord Kilbracken reported seeing 'a woman in her forties being dragged face downwards by one leg through deep puddles of water'.[14]

Other independent witnesses whose accounts were also placed on the record by Greenwood highlighted two features of the police response. The first was the tactic of throwing demonstrators into the fountain. Lord Kilbracken reported also that he saw 'a group of constables carrying three demonstrators, two of them women, and throw them into the deep water surrounding one of the fountains', the same fate befalling another participant whose statement as read by Greenwood records that 'a couple of policeman picked [him] up, carried [him] over to the fountain nearby and dropped [him] in the water'. The second complaint was of police kicking and punching demonstrators, with one participant telling the NCCL that he saw a police officer approach 'an inert man and deliver two well aimed kicks to his ribs, before being dragged the diagonal of the Square on his back at express speed, carted up the steps and thrown into the gutter below the National Gallery where almost immediately a young woman landed on top of him. Another participant claimed to have been 'punched or kicked in the face with sufficient force to break [his] nose and cause it to bleed so profusely that the police seemed alarmed'; while yet another claimed that a police officer 'deliberately raised his foot above [him] and kicked [him] in the stomach near the kidneys', the individual then being carried, dragged and kicked and apparently taken by bus to a police station where he was 'dragged out of the bus, kicked, told to get up against the railing' before a 'police sergeant came with a hose to drench [him and others]'. Medical evidence was said to corroborate this particular story which included allegations of further ill-treatment while in custody, where after being told to take the victim to a place where there were no witnesses, two policemen restrained him by painful arm locks while another four kicked to the tune of a well-built police woman who urged them to kick him harder. This was not an isolated example of ill treatment in custody, with Greenwood telling the story also of a 16-year-old girl who refused to give her name and address on arrest, following which she was questioned about whether she was pregnant, whether she had been in a remand home, and whether she had slept with men, subject thereafter to other predictable forms of institutional bullying, even after she provided the information demanded.

III. From Trafalgar Square to Wethersfield

The events at Trafalgar Square were a reminder of the power of the State. The overwhelming use of force was to be seen also at the other major event planned for 1961, namely the demonstrations at a number of airfields, including RAF

---

[14] Ibid, col 156.

Wethersfield, which were planned for 9 December. This event clearly troubled at least some government departments, with the Secretary of State for Air (Julian Amery) writing to the Prime Minister on 5 December 1961 about the three demonstrations anticipated to take place at Ruislip, Wethersfield, and Brize Norton. Ruislip was thought not to present any special problem, with some 2,000 expected to turn up.[15] According to Amery, 'the police were confident of being able to keep the entrances open'. The demonstrations at Wethersfield (with an estimated 3,000–5,000 demonstrators) and Brize Norton (with an estimated 800–1,000) on the other hand were said to 'raise more serious problems'. According to Amery, '[n]uclear weapons are stored in these stations and a proportion of aircraft is held at instant readiness with nuclear weapons on board. These aircraft, and the bomb stores, are guarded by armed American sentries'. The concern was not only that the demonstrators would block the entrances, but that they intended 'by means of "commandos" of 30 men and women, to invade the airfield and immobilise the aircraft by sitting around them', with the added concern that some of these activities were to take place in the dark. The real concern, however, was explained in the following chilling terms

The USAF have made it clear that they cannot permit the demonstrations to impair the operational capability of the bases. They have said that if demonstrators persist in approaching sensitive areas, and disregard the orders of the sentries, the latter will be compelled to open fire. They cannot take the risk that there might be saboteurs or secret agents among the demonstrators.

Amery then outlined a number of steps he proposed to take in order to 'avoid a direct clash between demonstrators and USAF personnel'. With 'the concurrence of the Home Secretary and the Attorney General', he proposed to use an 'unarmed force of RAF personnel and Air Ministry Constabulary to protect the airfields', with 6,000 men being used to surround the perimeter. He also anticipated the possibility that some demonstrators might breach the security, in which case they would be evicted or arrested as the case may be by RAF police, 'with the use of not more than the minimum force necessary'. Airfield commanders were also to be authorized to use fire hoses (rather than firearms which would be used only by the Americans) to keep the runways clear, while a small number of police dogs would be used as a last resort 'to avoid a clash between demonstrators and armed American guards'.

(a) The Attorney General and the Defence Minister Intervene

On the following day (Wednesday the 6th, only four days before), matters were warmed up significantly when the Attorney General (Sir Reginald Manningham-Buller) intervened in a letter to the Prime Minister to inform the latter that after discussion with the DPP, 'the time has come for the institution of serious criminal proceedings against the organisers of the demonstrations planned for next Saturday

---

[15] TNA, PREM 11/4284 (Prime Minister's Office: Correspondence and Papers, 1951–64).

if necessary evidence can be secured and the organisers identified'.[16] Sir Reginald advised the Prime Minister that search warrants were being executed that morning, with the hope that the searches would 'reveal who are really the people behind this and sufficient evidence to justify charging them'. It was proposed that if evidence did become available, arrests would be made on Friday 'on charges either of contravening the Official Secrets Acts or of conspiracy to contravene them, or both'. The Attorney continued in a passage that was to reveal a significant concern, by pointing out that 'This is likely to lead to a trial at the Old Bailey before a jury and apart from anything else, there is the risk that the jury will contain one or more sympathisers'. Sir Reginald suggested nevertheless that such a risk 'should now be run', though quite why the Prime Minister needed personally to be briefed in this way is far from clear. The Attorney was, however, careful to point out that the government had no responsibility for the institution of the prosecution, but that he had consulted the Home Secretary before deciding whether to prosecute, as he was 'entitled to do'. The Home Secretary's views are not recorded, though it seems unlikely that he would have been strongly opposed. For his part, Sir Reginald was on the way up the greasy pole, being appointed to the office of Lord Chancellor in the following year, a position which he held as Viscount Dilhorne until the general election in 1964, sitting thereafter as a Law Lord.

This note from the Attorney was copied to a number a senior ministers, including the Minister of Defence, who on the same day wrote separately to the Prime Minister (copying in the Attorney General among others) to alert him to the diplomatic consequences of the proposed demonstration.[17] Raising the temperature still higher, Watkinson advised Macmillan that he supported the Air Ministry's plan to use 'as many men as [they] judge necessary to try to protect at least the sensitive areas of the American bases', and also supported the proposal that although unarmed, RAF personnel should be authorized to use fire hoses on the demonstrators, and 'any other passive means of carrying out their duty'. He continued with some concern in the following terms:

Unless you take some action with the President or I telephone Mr McNamara, it is possible that we shall have a serious incident in which an American serviceman will have shot one of the demonstrators. If this happens, it will make the political position, I would have thought, extremely difficult to hold as regards all American bases in this country. I hope therefore that the Secretary of State is authorised to use all possible means short of shooting to stop the American Forces getting directly involved with the demonstrators.

Continuing to express these concerns, the Defence Minister questioned whether 'a message should not go to the President or the Secretary of Defense asking them to instruct their commanders over here to act under the orders of the senior RAF officer who will be in charge of the general task of protecting the airfield, the aircraft and their nuclear weapons, and not to act independently of such orders'. In view of these 'very serious political implications', Watkinson offered to raise the

---

[16] TNA, PREM 11/4284 (Prime Minister's Office: Correspondence and Papers, 1951–64).
[17] TNA, PREM 11/4284 (Prime Minister's Office: Correspondence and Papers, 1951–64).

matter at the following day's cabinet meeting, and to have the Secretary of State for Air present, an offer which appears to have been accepted.

(b) The Committee of 100 Considered in Cabinet

So it was that the Wethersfield demonstration was considered by the Cabinet only two days before it was due to take place,[18] with the Secretary of State for Air advising that elaborate precautions had been taken in consultation with the United States authorities. In particular, it had been agreed that the RAF should be responsible for guarding the perimeter fence, and that large numbers of the RAF Regiment would be deployed for this purpose. Amery also reported that if 'any of the demonstrators succeeded in gaining access to the airfield, forceful action (including the use of fire houses and police dogs) would be taken to prevent them from approaching bombed-up aircraft or bomb stores'. And it was only 'if they attempted to interfere with these that United States personnel would be directly involved', though it was also pointed out in discussion that the 'United States Ambassador in London had undertaken to see that the officers in charge of the United States squadrons at [the] two air stations [Wethersfield and Brize Norton] were aware of the political dangers of any direct clash between their men and the demonstrators'. The other main report was from the Attorney General (whose views are minuted at length), according to whom 'the installations were prohibited places under the Official Secrets Act', and the demonstrations planned by the Committee of 100 involved offences under the Act. He continued by saying that as a result of searches made by the police on the previous day at the headquarters of the Committee and at the homes of some of its leading members, 'evidence might become available which would warrant the immediate arrest of some of the main organisers of the demonstrations on charges of conspiracy to commit those offences'. The Attorney also said that 'he had advised the local police that he would be ready to authorise proceedings under the Act against persons who tried to force their way into these air stations; and he hoped that, with this knowledge, police might be able to arrest some of the ringleaders at an early stage in the demonstrations'.

Following the discussion after these two contributions, it was also pointed out that a statement was to be made in the House later that day to the effect that the demonstrations would involve a breach of the Official Secrets Act 1911. The matter was addressed that afternoon by a Minister of State at the Home Office who not only assured the House that all necessary steps would be taken to prevent any unauthorized entry of the airfield, but also drew attention to section 1 of the 1911 Act for the benefit of the organizers of the demonstrations so that there 'should be no failure on [their part] to appreciate the gravity of the offences for which those participating in them may render themselves liable to be prosecuted'.[19] Offering the Opposition's supine support, George Brown did not wish to prevent people from 'taking every legal opportunity to demonstrate their feelings', but he drew the

[18] TNA, CAB 128/35/ CC68 (61).
[19] HC Debs, 7 Dec 1961, col 1534.

line at 'infiltrating into an airfield under modern conditions', which he described as 'a highly dangerous operation' and a 'declared intention to disrupt the forces of law and order' which 'cannot be permitted in a modern democratic state'.[20] With the voice of loyal Opposition thus offering support for the government, only two voices of dissent were to be heard, with both Emanuel Shinwell (a former Secretary of State for War in the post-war Labour government) and Judith Hart (soon to be a junior minister in the government) raising civil liberties concerns. The latter was moved particularly by the junior minister's reference to the Official Secrets Act asking first if he was aware that it was open to him to 'institute charges against any-one who breach the peace on Saturday under other enactments than the Official Secrets Act', and rhetorically if it is 'not as grave as possible an interference with civil liberties that that the Official Secrets Act should be invoked'.[21] The matter was easily sidestepped by the minister, on the ground that it was not for him to institute charges against anyone, because he was not the prosecuting authority, such matters being the responsibility of the DPP.[22]

IV. The Arrest and Prosecution of Committee of 100 Activists

So far as the demonstration itself was concerned, it all went smoothly for the gov-ernment. *The Times* report on Monday 11 December was headlined 'Minister Sums up Invasion of Wethersfield—A Flop'. Referring to the government's 'mas-sive protection screen', the newspaper reported that 'Not a single "commando" penetrated the defence screen, which included 5,000 RAF regiment men, 60 RAF and WRAF police, 850 civilian police and Special Branch officers, 75 Air Ministry

---

[20] Ibid, col 1535.

[21] Ibid, col 1537.

[22] It is unclear what effect Mr Renton's statement would have had on those planning to join the demonstration, though probably very little. It did, however, have a profound effect on those planning to take them to Wethersfield. An anonymous note sent to the Prime Minister on Friday 8 December records that Sir James Dunnett (a senior official in the Ministry of Defence) had rung to say that 'they' had spoken to the manager of a bus company (Eastern National) that had been planning to take demonstrators to Wethersfield. According to the note, the Managing Director of the parent company had on his initiative instructed the bus company to withdraw from the venture, a state of affairs which was said to be 'satisfactory as far as it goes'. It meant that it would be difficult for about 900 of the demonstrators to get there, though it would be difficult to stop the others who were going by car or rail, or by separate coaches hired from 'small local men'. This action had been taken by the managing director 'on the strength of Mr Renton's reply yesterday afternoon', though it is not clear whether the businessman was moved by a spirit of patriotism or fear of possible legal consequences for his firm. The latter is perhaps not a fanciful concern, with the Cabinet having concluded on the morning of Mr Renton's reply that 'Many of the demonstrators were to travel to London by motor buses. It might be possible to prevent this, either by warning the owners of the buses that they would be contributing to the commission of offences under the Official Secrets Act or by dispersing the buses from their pre-arranged assembly points in London'.

The conclusions then record that the Home Secretary and the Minister of Transport were invited to consider 'what steps could be taken to discourage the 'bus companies concerned from transport-ing persons intending to take part in these demonstrations'. At least in the case of Eastern National, no such steps were necessary, though the *Daily Telegraph* reported on the morning of the 9th that 'Traffic Commissioners had withdrawn the operator's licence from the coach company that was to carry the demonstrators to the NATO base at Wethersfield'.

constabulary men, 12 RAF police Alsatian dogs, two Belvedere helicopters, and six and a half miles of barbed wire fence'. In what has been described as the biggest display of force by a government in peacetime since the General Strike,[23] the projected thousands of demonstrators were outnumbered by about 10 to 1, with a 'bedraggled' 300 or so squatting 'damply in the fog outside the two gates for about four hours'. It was also reported, however, that 73 foot-soldiers and officers in 'Lord Russell's army' were arrested, most of whom were dealt with in a Braintree school which had been converted into a court for the occasion. Most of the arrests were for obstruction of the highway or obstructing a police officer in the execution of his duty (though quite how a breach of the peace could reasonably be anticipated by a bunch of pacifists at a remote airbase is difficult to imagine). Only one arrest was for assaulting a police officer. It seems, however, that more arrests could have been made, with a senior police officer telling *The Times* that 'administrative considerations' had governed the number of arrests, these considerations most probably being the capacity of the court and the police to process the numbers involved. Of those arrested, 69 were charged, of whom 34 were jailed, the other 35 released on payment of fines. The ease with which the police appeared able to deal with the operation had led some to question its cost, to which the minister (who had arrived at the scene by helicopter) replied that they had made this 'considerable effort' because the American Air Force were 'our guests on an RAF base and it is our duty as the host country to ensure that nothing happens to the equipment of our allies or to prevent their operational capability'. The purpose of the large numbers of troops and police officers was to ensure 'overwhelming strength', paradoxically in order to 'prevent violence'.

(a) The Official Secrets Act 1911

Although the security of the bases was thus not breached, six members of the Committee of 100 were arrested and charged under the Official Secrets Act 1911 in connection with the events at Wethersfield. Consistently with the Attorney General's note to the Prime Minister on 6 December 1961, they did not include figureheads such as Lord Russell, but six leading activists in the form of Helen Allegranza (who was to die in Holloway prison), Terence Chandler, Ian Dixon, Trevor Hatton, Patrick Pottle, and Michael Randle. The charges related to organizing the events at Wethersfield, and they were each charged with conspiracy to commit and conspiracy to incite others to commit a breach of the Official Secrets Act 1911, section 1.[24] This provides that it is an offence for 'any person for any purpose prejudicial to the safety of the state' to approach or be

<hr />

[23] Independent Labour Party, *The 100 versus The State* [nd], BLPS, CND/2008/3/5, 11.

[24] Crucial evidence appears to have been obtained by the police raids authorized by Manningham-Buller (and criticized in Parliament by Shinwell). A letter written on 7 November 1961 provided as follows:

> The working group at this end has finally decided in favour of a demonstration that will involve an attempt to occupy the base at Wethersfield. However the plan is for only a number of trained people to do this. The bulk of the demonstrators will squat by the entrances on the roadway. Our leaflet about the demonstration will simply state that we

in the neighbourhood of, or enter any prohibited place within the meaning of the Act. According to Lord Devlin, these provisions of the statute are 'far wider and vaguer than those usually employed in the definition of criminal offences', with 'terms such as "purpose", "interests" and "State" being unfamiliar in the criminal law and [having] no settled meaning in connection with it'.[25] The Wethersfield base was clearly a prohibited place within the meaning of the Act, but it is far from clear that Parliament contemplated that the Act might be used in this way. A clue as to the purpose of this provision is provided by the side-note which refers to penalties for spying, while the parliamentary record provides little evidence that this was a mistake, though it is true that the only real evidence of parliamentary intention was out of bounds to the courts by their self-denying ordinance that they would not look at Hansard. If they had, they would have discovered from the House of Lords debates that the notoriously rushed through 1911 Act was designed to apply to British citizens as well as to those of other countries, but that the furthest it was designed to go was to deal with those furtive individuals who found themselves on military establishments not necessarily to spy on behalf of foreign powers, but to obtain information that they could then sell on to such powers.[26]

The point was made even more clearly by the proceedings in the House of Commons (the bill started life in the Lords), where concerns were raised about the bill 'upset[ting] Magna Carta'; about its 'rather stringent provisions'; and about it being 'extremely drastic'.[27] The then Attorney General (Sir Rufus Isaacs) intervened to say that 'there was nothing novel in the principle of the Bill', supported by a backbencher who volunteered that 'the change in the law is slight'.[28] This is a view readily supported by the long title of the 1911 Act which is declared to be 'An Act to re-enact the Official Secrets Act 1889, with amendments'. This throws us back to the 1889 Act, which declares unequivocally that it is 'An Act to prevent the Disclosure of Official Documents and Information'. This purpose is to be found clearly and unequivocally in section 1 of the 1889 Act (though not clearly and just as unequivocally enough for the Court of Appeal);[29] this states that 'where a person for the purpose of wrongfully obtaining information' is found in the wrong place, then an offence would be committed. Apart from making clear that the Act was designed to deal with surveillance rather than sabotage (for which there were no doubt other laws available),[30] it was also made clear that anyone who had the grave misfortune to

intend to immobilise the base and this is the information that will be released to the Press. (*Chandler v DPP* [1964] AC 763, at 787–8)

[25] [1964] AC 763, at 804.
[26] HL Debs, 25 July 1911, cols 642–4.
[27] HC Debs, 18 Aug 1911, cols 2253, 2253, and 2258 respectively.
[28] Ibid, cols 2253–4; and 2258 respectively.
[29] [1964] AC 763, at 772. This was not a matter 'sufficient to justify any limitation on the plain words of section 1(1)', words said by Lord Devlin to be 'far wider and vaguer than those usually employed in the definition of criminal offences' (804).
[30] On this, see also Thompson, above n 3, where a number of other points are made to the same effect, dealing with assurances given at the time of the enactment of the Official Secrets Act 1920.

be in a prohibited place would have ample opportunity to explain himself, with the Secretary of State for War (Viscount Haldane) announcing that

under this Bill what has to be shown is that there was a purpose prejudicial to the safety or interests of the State, and if your Lordships will look at Clause 1, subsection (2), you will see that it is enacted that a person's motive may be inferred if from the circumstances of the case or his conduct or his known character he may be taken to have been there to no good purpose. Of course, he has the opportunity of clearing his character in the fullest way, but the circumstances are such as to throw the burden of proof on him.[31]

(b) The High Court Convicts

The trial was conducted before the 72-year-old Sir Cecil Havers, father of Sir Michael Havers who became Lord Chancellor in a Conservative government, and Baroness Butler Sloss who became President of the Family Division. The main strategy of the accused was to challenge the whole basis of the government's policy of nuclear deterrence. Thus, they planned to show that their purpose was not prejudicial to the interests of the State, that the aircraft carried nuclear bombs, and that it was not in the interests of the State to have aircraft armed in this way. It was also proposed to argue secondly, that the accused reasonably believed that it was not prejudicial but beneficial to the interests of the State to immobilize the aircraft, and that the jury were entitled to hold that no offence had been committed. This was the nightmare that had been anticipated by Manningham-Buller in his note to the Prime Minister on 6 December 1961 that the matter might end up before a jury at the Old Bailey, with 'the risk that the jury will contain one or more sympathisers'.[32] Although the risk could be managed to some extent by the process of jury vetting (which according to the Committee of 100 would take place in the potential juror's home),[33] there was also the apparently unanticipated risk that a jury that did not contain sympathizers would be influenced by the case presented by the defence, with significant political consequences if the accused were to be acquitted as a result. This second risk now had to be addressed, which meant that the argument about 'the futility of nuclear warfare'[34] had to be kept away from the jury which, despite being vetted, might not be obliging in the light of unpredictable expert evidence and evidence of fact that the defence intended to call, which would deal with the effect of exploding a nuclear bomb, no doubt to the discomfort of the squeamish. Hence the vigour of the government's argument (presented by the Attorney General who appeared for the Crown) that 'an objective test must

[31] HL Debs, 25 July 1911, col 643. Viscount Haldane also said that 'the criminal purpose under this Bill is any purpose prejudicial to the safety or interests of the State, and if a person is in a place where prima facie his presence is prejudicial to the safety or interests of the State, he has to satisfy the jury that his purpose was a right one. That, as I have said, is nothing new. It is a section taken from the Prevention of Crimes Act, 1871. Under that section certain classes of offenders have to justify themselves when their character and conduct raise suspicion'.

[32] TNA, PREM 11/4284 (Prime Minister's Office: Correspondence and Papers, 1951–64).

[33] See Committee of 100, Policy and Planning – *Report of National Conference held over weekend 11/12 April at Unity House London* (1964), BLPS, CND/2008/3/1.

[34] [1964] AC 763, at 802.

determine whether the purpose of grounding aircraft was a prejudicial purpose, that the accused's beliefs were irrelevant and so was the reasonableness of their beliefs'.

Apart from anything else, this would mean that the defence could not ask government witnesses in cross-examination whether the aircraft were carrying nuclear weapons. However, accepting the arguments of the Attorney General, the trial judge ruled that the defence were not entitled to call evidence to establish that it would be beneficial for this country to give up nuclear weapons or that the accused honestly believed that it would be.[35] But as Lord Devlin pointed out, the judge's ruling did not stop with the exclusion of the evidence, Mr Justice Havers also directing the jury that 'it was no defence for the appellants to say that they intended to do something which would be beneficial to the State in the long run, namely, to induce or compel the government to abandon nuclear weapons'.[36] It is true that the jury were directed that 'it was for them to say whether they were satisfied that what the accused had conspired to do was prejudicial to the safety or interests of the State', but it was also true that 'the general effect of his summing up was that if they accepted the evidence of Air Commodore Magill they could not do otherwise than find prejudice to the safety or interests of the State'.[37] Magill had said that the base was occupied by squadrons of the US Air Force assigned to the Supreme Commander Allied Forces, Europe, and that these squadrons were combat ready and on constant alert, and that in the event of an emergency, any interference with the ability of the aircraft to take off would gravely prejudice their operational effectiveness.[38] The jury duly did its duty, with Lord Devlin noting in the House of Lords appeal that Mr Justice Havers had 'indicated a fairly strong opinion in the present case, particularly at the end of his summing-up, when he hinted to the jury that there was only one verdict that they could in conscience return'.[39] Having thus secured a guilty verdict (albeit with a request for leniency from the jury), Mr Justice Havers is reported as having said that he had 'to pass a sentence which is adequate to the offences that [the accused had] committed and which will deter others from committing similar offences'.[40] They were each sentenced to 18 months.[41]

V. The House of Lords

An appeal to the Court of Appeal was unsuccessful, and was notable only for enabling the Lord Chief Justice (Lord Parker) to quote his father (Lord Parker of Waddington) as authority.[42] The House of Lords appeal was heard as usual by

[35] Ibid at 788 (Lord Reid).
[36] Ibid at 802–3 (Lord Devlin).
[37] Ibid at 789 (Lord Reid).
[38] Ibid at 788.
[39] Ibid at 804.
[40] Independent Labour Party, *The 100 versus The State* [nd], BLPS, CND/2008/3/5, 12.
[41] BLPS, CND/2008/3/5.
[42] *The Zamora* [1916] 2 AC 77, at 107: 'Those who are responsible for national security must be the sole judges of what national security requires'.

a Bench of five. Sir Reginald Manningham-Buller was not yet Lord Chancellor Dilhorne and appeared again for the Crown in an appeal that was took four days between 30 May and 5 June 1962, with judgment delivered on 12 July. The five men who Manningham-Buller was about to join were from a very different world from that of the six defendants. Lord Reid had been a Tory MP and the Scottish law officer for ten years (1936–45) (first as Solicitor General for Scotland and then as Lord Advocate). He had also seen active service in the machine gun corps during the First World War and had risen to the rank of Major. Unusually, he was appointed as a Law Lord in 1948 without having previously occupied judicial office. Viscount Radcliffe had served in the Ministry of Information during the war, and was appointed as a Law Lord in 1949 after having played a part in the partition of India in 1947. Like Lord Reid, he was appointed as a Lord of Appeal in Ordinary without having previously held judicial office, and became a Viscount in 1962.[43] Lord Hodson was appointed to the House of Lords in 1960, where he served until 1971, having previously served for ten years in the Court of Appeal. Hodson had a distinguished military career, having been wounded twice during the First World War in an incident for which he was awarded the Military Cross for gallantry. Added to the foregoing was a rich educational background likely to encourage loyalty and conformity: Edinburgh Academy and Jesus College, Cambridge (Lord Reid); Cheltenham College and Corpus Christ, Oxford (Lord Pearce); and Stoneyhurst College and Christ's College, Cambridge (Lord Devlin), to which we can add Cheltenham College (Lord Hodson) and All Souls College, Oxford (Viscount Radcliffe). The youngest of the bunch was 58 (Lord Devlin) and the oldest 73 (Lord Reid), at least four were Privy Counsellors, and one (Lord Reid) was to become a Companion of Honour.

(a) The Issues Re-opened

Into this bewildering world of judges with distinguished government, military, and legal service with impeccable social credentials stumbled six peace campaigners. The great political importance of the case was rehearsed by counsel on their behalf who argued that the 1911 Act 'envisages very grave incursions on the liberty of the subject',[44] and that the decision of the Court of Criminal Appeal to uphold Havers J was 'of very great constitutional importance for it decides that where national security is involved, no evidence and no cross examination can be adduced in a criminal case on that matter',[45] and that the

---

[43] According to L. Lustgarten and I. Leigh, *In from the Cold: National Security and Parliamentary Democracy* (Oxford: Oxford University Press, 1994), Lord Radcliffe was 'another favourite choice of the government for such tasks: among several other public duties he chaired a Committee on Security Procedures in the Public Service, a 1921 Act tribunal on the Vassall case, a committee on recruitment to the secret intelligence services, and Privy Counsellors' Committees on D Notices and on ministerial memoirs' (487–8).

[44] [1964] AC 763, at 777.

[45] Ibid at 778.

interpretation placed on the Act by the Court of Criminal Appeal was so wide that

a workman on strike who approached a government establishment, for example, Woolwich Arsenal, in order to induce workers there to come out on strike would be guilty... of being in the neighbourhood of a prohibited place for a purpose prejudicial to the safety and interests of the State.[46]

The appellants also contended that it is not a principle of a criminal case that the executive are the sole judges of what is prejudicial to the State, with Lord Parker having been wrong to have relied on the authority of his father in a civil case, which offered 'no authority for the proposition that in a criminal case evidence cannot be called to challenge the policy of the security of the State'.[47] In arguing that the statute should be limited because of its impact on civil liberties, counsel for the appellants provided many opportunities for this to be done, referring to the parliamentary history, as well as contending that the accused should have been allowed to have been given the chance to give evidence of their beliefs in order to show what their purpose was; and that the evidence should have been at large to enable the jury to decide as a fact whether the appellants' purpose was or was not prejudicial.[48]

Too bad, it seems, with Sir Reginald Manningham-Buller seeking to minimize the importance of the case by claiming that the question for the House of Lords was 'simply as to the admissibility of evidence sought to be adduced by cross-examination and by calling witnesses'. He continued as follows:

Right from the start the Crown emphasised that whether there was a purpose prejudicial to the safety or interests of the State was a question for the jury. But it does not follow that that evidence can be tendered on both sides, but whether evidence can be given on both sides depends on whether the evidence it is sought to call is in law admissible.[49]

However, the Court of Criminal Appeal had unhelpfully drafted the certified point for appeal rather broadly, requiring Manningham-Buller to address more general questions of construction of section 1. This led him to argue for an extremely wide construction of the 1911 Act, as being designed to

Prevent the obtaining and communication of information which should be kept secret, and (ii) to protect certain places, the prohibited places, and to keep them secret and free from damage, obstruction or interference.[50]

As we have seen, this was not the purpose of the Act presented to Parliament in 1911, and in any event it was an explanation which in its own terms was implausible. How could the design of the Act be to keep sites secret when those approaching them would be presented with warning signs that the site was a prohibited place?

---

[46] Ibid.
[47] Ibid at 779.
[48] Ibid at 778–9.
[49] Ibid at 780.
[50] Ibid at 781.

Even more remarkable was his claim that 'If Parliament had intended section 1
(1) to apply only to spying it could have so worded the section'. The reference in
the marginal note to 'penalties for spying' which appeared to do just that was dismissed on the ground that the marginal note cannot limit the plain meaning of
an Act of Parliament. The Attorney General's parallel strategy was to claim that
the issues of judgment under the Act were issues for the exclusive judgment of the
government, not the courts, nor juries, nor anyone else. Thus, Parliament was the
place to challenge defence policy, not the criminal courts, while Air Commodore
Magill's evidence—establishing the role played by the airfield in the defence of the
State—was 'conclusive on the question whether the airfield is required in an operational condition for the safety or interests of the State'.[51]

(b) A Resounding Success for the Attorney General

It would be impossible to place a cigarette paper between the Law Lords and Sir
Reginald, who was about to join their ranks. First, the House of Lords agreed that
the Act was to be read widely and could not be confined to spying: the side-note
referring to penalties against spying was dismissed by Lord Reid as being no use
as an aid to construction, while in any event it was impossible to suppose that
the section did not apply to sabotage as well as spying, though there is nothing
on the parliamentary record to support this construction. According to Viscount
Radcliffe, 'the saboteur just as much as the spy in the ordinary sense is contemplated as an offender under the Act'.[52] Secondly, the House of Lords adopted a narrow approach to the question of purpose, preventing the appellants from having a
jury consider whether their purpose was beneficial rather than prejudicial to the
interests of the State. According to Viscount Radcliffe again, 'if a person's direct
purpose in approaching or entering is to cause obstruction or interference, and
such obstruction or interference is found to be of prejudice to the defence disposi-
tions of the State, an offence is thereby committed, and his indirect purposes or his
motives in bringing about the obstruction or interference do not alter the nature or
content of his offence'.[53] But this was an argument that seemed to be undermined
(as Lord Devlin was to point out) if not fatally weakened by the following passage
in Viscount Radcliffe's speech:

Is a man guilty of an offence, it was asked, if he rushes onto an airfield intending to stop
an airplane taking off because he knows that a time bomb has been concealed on board? I
should say that he is not, and for the reason that his direct purpose is not to bring about an
obstruction but to prevent a disaster, the obstruction that he causes being merely a means
to securing that end.[54]

Thirdly, the House of Lords adopted an equally narrow approach to who determines what is or is not prejudicial to the interests of the State. Here there was little

[51] Ibid at 782–3.
[52] Ibid at 794.
[53] Ibid at 795.
[54] Ibid at 796.

difficulty, with Lord Reid drawing on the royal prerogative line of cases to say that 'the disposition and armament of the armed forces are and for centuries have been within the exclusive discretion of the Crown', and 'no one is entitled to challenge it in court'.[55]

The Attorney General thus succeeded in both construing section 1 widely and in keeping the crucial question away from the jury. A sympathetic court would determine the issue. The only note of criticism was to be heard from Lord Devlin, who was at times excoriating and at others submissive. On the question of purpose, he was unable to accept the Crown's argument accepted by Viscount Radcliffe. Exposing the contradiction in the Crown's position, Lord Devlin argued that if it is permissible for a man who has interfered with the running of an airfield to say that all he was doing was trying to capture a criminal, 'it must also be permissible for him to say that all he was doing was trying to save the State from impending harm'.[56] For Lord Devlin the salient question was whether 'immobilisation of this airfield [could] be regarded as the first step in a general immobilisation of all the country's nuclear weapons and, if so, would that be a good thing for the country'.[57] At this point, Lord Devlin fell into line, rejecting the idea that the trial judge should allow 'hours or days to be spent at the trial in giving an accused the opportunity of expounding his political views', in the process evoking parallel concerns with those expressed by Lord Hoffmann in recent cases about the courts being used as a platform for the continuation of political campaigns as diverse as opposition to the war in Iraq to the re-settlement of the Chagos Islanders.[58] According to Lord Devlin, 'the court is not the forum for such a debate and the jury is not the body to determine what the interests of the State should be'.[59] Although appearing to dispute the view that the interests of the State are to be determined by the government, Lord Devlin nevertheless held simply that there was a rebuttable presumption that it is 'contrary to the interests of the Crown to have one of its airfields immobilised just as it may be presumed that it is contrary to the interests of an industrialist to have his factory immobilised'.[60] So despite the fancy rhetoric, Lord Devlin ended up agreeing with Sir Reginald that '[t]he thing speaks for itself', before uttering the most famous passage in his speech which acquired a significance well beyond its importance for the disposal of the case, and which is not normally quoted in full:

Men can exaggerate the extent of their interests and so can the Crown. The servants of the Crown, like other men animated by the highest motives, are capable of formulating a policy ad hoc so as to prevent the citizen from doing something that the Crown does not want him to do. It is the duty of the courts to be as alert now as they have always been to prevent abuse of the prerogative. But in the present case there is nothing at all to suggest

---

[55] Ibid at 791.
[56] Ibid at 806.
[57] Ibid.
[58] See *R (Bancoult) v Secretary of State for Foreign and Commonwealth Affairs* [2008] UKHL 61; [2009] 1 AC 453.
[59] [1964] AC 763, at 808.
[60] Ibid 811.

that the Crown's interest in the proper operation of its airfields is not what it may naturally be presumed to be or that it was exaggerating the perils of interference with their effectiveness.[61]

VI. The Aftermath

The strategy of decapitation (as revealed by the Attorney General in his letter to the Prime Minister), and show trials for extreme offences, together with the strategy of vastly superior force, appeared to be successful. The role of the House of Lords is also not to be under-estimated. One of the most revealing features of the episode was the role played by the Attorney General, operating in a twilight world between the legal and the political. Having instigated the prosecution after consulting the Home Secretary (and working closely with the police), he was later to claim in the High Court proceedings that

This is not a political prosecution... This is not a prosecution by the Government. They do not prosecute and they have no responsibility for instituting prosecutions. Indeed, the Government cannot direct a prosecution such as this to be instituted. This is the point I want to emphasise once again: the prosecution is brought solely and simply because they have deliberately broken the criminal law of the land.[62]

No doubt an exemplary statement of constitutional fiction; but not widely believed as a political fact. The other revealing feature of the episode was the role played by the courts, which provided a weak form of defence for citizens against a rampant State. The Committee of 100 may well have disturbed the peace and may well have justified punishment. But this means punishment in accordance with the law, and not an abuse of the legal process to secure punishment on a scale that would encourage the others. Lord Devlin's speech was perhaps as disappointing as the others were predictable. Laced with claims that the Attorney General was proposing 'an unconstitutional doctrine', and that the case touched matters of 'some constitutional importance', these were cruelly deflated by corresponding claims that it was 'difficult to see how a sensible jury could have acquitted', and that it was not 'improper' for the trial judge to indicate 'a fairly strong opinion', particularly at the end of his summing up 'when he hinted to the jury that there was only one verdict that they could in conscience return'.[63] Indeed, it is difficult to see what the Devlin approach would allow the jury to consider, for he was prepared to withhold from the jury any consideration of what is or is not prejudicial to the interests of the State, with the jury to focus on the interests of the State only as 'can be proved by an officer of the Crown wherever it may be necessary to do so'.[64]

---

[61] Ibid.
[62] Independent Labour Party, *The 100 versus The State* [nd], BLPS, CND/2008/3/5, 12.
[63] [1964] AC 763, at 803, 809, 803, and 802 respectively.
[64] Ibid 811.

(a) The Airfield Campaign Continues...

Despite the setbacks at Wethersfield and the defeat in the courts, the campaign of the Committee of 100 continued, with a demonstration at RAF Marham in Norfolk, scheduled for 11 May 1963, the success of which was seen by the Committee of 100 as 'being important for the future of their movement'.[65] A letter, dated 25 April 1963, from the Secretary of State for Air to the Home Secretary raised concerns about 'a hard core of extremists' who were expected to attend as part of an anticipated group of 500 Committee of 100 supporters.[66] This was followed by a reply on 6 May 1963 from the Home Secretary who thanked the Secretary of State for Air, noting that his plans 'seem generally to follow the precedent of those made for Wethersfield'. On this occasion, however, the security of the base was breached, with the London Committee of the Committee of 100 reporting that they had twice got onto the base in large numbers. On the first occasion, the police arrested 12 of the protestors and charged them with offences under the Official Secrets Act 1911, section 1 (1). When this became known, another 56 returned to the base and 'occupied one of the main runways for an hour and a half before being arrested and taken away', also to be charged under section 1 of the 1911 Act.[67] It appears, however, that these serious charges were dropped, though an unknown number of charges were brought under the Official Secrets Act 1920. One such case involved Frank Adler, who was charged with obstructing a member of Her Majesty's armed forces in the vicinity of a prohibited place, contrary to sections 3 and 8 (2) of the 1920 Act. He was found guilty by the magistrates at Downham Market and fined £25, as well as being bound over for 12 months. On appeal, Adler argued that, as he had been arrested while on the RAF base, he could not at that time be in the vicinity of the base. This, however, cut little ice with the Lord Chief Justice, who thought that no violence 'is done to the language by reading the words "in the vicinity of" as meaning "in or in the vicinity of" '.[68]

Perhaps buoyed up by the events of 11 May, the Committee of 100 organized a second demonstration at Marham for the following week, leading to another flurry of correspondence. A letter to the Home Secretary from the Secretary of State for Air on 16 May announced that the Committee of 100 were planning yet another demonstration at RAF Marham, having been repulsed again on the 11th. Concern was expressed that if they were unsuccessful, the Committee of 100 would 'continue trying to gain entry to other airfields in the area'. Clearly exasperated, the Secretary of State continued—

I must restate the concern which I expressed to you earlier this week. These demonstrations are aimed at operational airfields, at which armed aircraft are in constant readiness. I can only prevent interference with the operational effectiveness of RAF and USAF bases by providing protection which involves a heavy drain on RAF resources and their diversion from normal tasks. Sooner or later the Committee of 100 will realise that a relatively small

---

[65] TNA, PREM 11/4284 (Prime Minister's Office: Correspondence and Papers, 1951–64).
[66] Ibid.
[67] BLPS, CND/2008/7/21 (Note from the London Committee).
[68] *Adler v George* [1964] 2 QB 7.

effort on their part can impose a significant reduction in the efficiency of our deterrent bases or a disproportionate effect to prevent this. Moreover, if these demonstrations recur (and not all demonstrators appear to act on strictly pacifist principles) there is an obvious risk of ugly incidents.[69]

This letter was copied to the Prime Minister, among others, with an irritated Macmillan then writing to the Home Secretary on 18 May to say that he had seen Fraser's minute of two days' earlier, ending plaintively with the question 'But what does he propose we should do?'[70] But just as the campaign appeared to be making some political progress, so it was brought to an end, for reasons that are not yet clear. The over-anxious Air Ministry had under-estimated the effect of the government's various strategies in response to the activities of the Committee of 100, with the Home Secretary writing to the Prime Minister on 16 June to say that since receiving the Prime Minister's note of 18 May, he had discussed the matter with the Air Ministry and the Attorney General, reporting that

Our confidential information is that the Committee of 100 consider that demonstrations at air bases are 'played out', at any rate for the time being; and they are now concentrating their efforts on planning a demonstration to take place on 29 June at the [Chemical Defence Establishment] at Porton Down in Wiltshire.[71]

(b) ... And then Changes Direction

By 1963, the air base campaign appears to have burned out as suggested, with the attention of the Committee moving to other concerns. Another clash with the Official Secrets Act occurred when the spies for peace revealed the locations of the highly secret Regional Seats of Government, the underground locations (in places such as Brooklands Avenue, Cambridge, and Corstorphine Hill, Edinburgh) that were to keep the country running in the event of a nuclear war.[72] The other major preoccupation in 1963 was the preparation and aftermath of a State visit by the King and Queen of Greece, beginning on 9 July 1963.[73] Questions of course arise as to why a British anti-war movement should be exercised by the soon to be

---

[69] TNA, PREM 11/4284 (Prime Minister's Office: Correspondence and Papers, 1951–64).

[70] TNA, PREM 11/4284 (Prime Minister's Office: Correspondence and Papers, 1951–64).

[71] The Home Secretary continued by saying that he did not think that fresh legislative powers were necessary, but that what was needed was 'some regular means of co-ordinating the action required to deal with particular plans made by the Committee as they come to notice'. He proposed therefore 'to arrange as necessary for the representatives of the Home Office, the DPP, the Service Department concerned and the Police to meet and consider what needs to be done', and to call a meeting of ministers concerned 'when issues of importance had to be decided': TNA, PREM 11/4284 (Prime Minister's Office: Correspondence and Papers, 1951–64). The Porton Down file reveals serious questions about the validity of bye-laws made under the Military Land Act 1842, which were to be used to keep demonstrators off the site, and raises a number of concerns about the limited powers of arrest which were then available to the police. See TNA, TS 50/142.

[72] Independent Labour Party, *Resistance Shall Grow: The Stories of the Spies for Peace* [nd], BLPS, CND/2008/8/119.

[73] The following account draws heavily on Committee of 100, Open Letter to an Old Bailey Court, BLPS, CND/2008/3/5 (a 14-page pamphlet addressed to the judge and jury in the trial of Peter Moule and Terry Chandler who had been arrested during the Greek royal visit. See below).

deposed Greek royal family. The answer, it seems, relates to the banning by the Greek government of an anti-nuclear march the year before. The march had been planned to take place from Marathon to Athens, and the ban led to the arrest of 2,000 who had tried to march, and to the deportation of the British contingent. There was also concern about the murder of Gregory Lambrakis, an independent Greek MP and a member of the Greek anti-nuclear committee. In attempting to hold demonstrations against the royal visit, the Committee of 100 encountered resistance at all levels by the authorities. First, they were refused permission to have a rally in Trafalgar Square on 6 July 1963. Despite assurances that there would be no calls for civil disobedience and despite the fact that the use of the Square by the Committee of 100 had been approved in the past when such assurances had been given, on this occasion the Minister of Works decided that 'it would not be in the public interest to allow the meeting to proceed'.[74] According to the Committee of 100, these previous meetings had been 'completely orderly', the Committee having 'stood by their assurances'. This was not the end of it, for three days later (on 24 June) the offices of the Committee of 100, along with the homes of key members (including Terry Chandler), were searched, with the authority of warrants issued under the Official Secrets Act 1911. A number of documents were removed relating to the forthcoming demonstration at Porton Down, but so too were 'papers and documents referring to the state visit'. This was followed later in the week by a police ban on 'demonstrations in practically the whole of central London', exercising powers under the Metropolitan Police Act 1839, which we have already encountered.

According to the Committee of 100, thereafter, 'the police used their extensive powers to make illegal in London any pickets or protests, any procession or demonstration—even the wearing of black sashes in memory of Gregory Lambrakis was banned by the authorities'.[75] Moreover,

The Committee of 100 was warned by the police that anyone distributing leaflets anywhere within five miles of Charing Cross could be arrested for illegal advertising. One person, Jane Buxton, was not only prevented from distributing leaflets, but was also warned by the police that wearing a black sash with a nuclear disarmament sign on it constituted wearing a uniform and was, therefore, illegal. It was at this stage that Terry Chandler and Peter Moule were warned that they might face serious charges if the demonstrations went ahead.[76]

Predictably, the demonstrations did go ahead, though the demonstrators did not get very far. It had been proposed to meet the royal couple on their arrival at Victoria station, with demonstrators carrying posters and wearing black sashes. But this was disrupted by a police cordon of several thousand officers and by the arrest of a number of demonstrators for obstructing the highway. On the evening of the same day, it had been proposed to march from Trafalgar Square to Buckingham Palace and to hold a silent vigil in memory of Lambrakis. But police cordons blocked the

[74] The letter is reproduced in the foregoing pamphlet.
[75] Committee of 100, Open Letter to an Old Bailey Court, BLPS, CND/2008/3/5, 7.
[76] Ibid.

way, horses were used, and police motorcyclists were alleged to have driven into the crowd, from which 90 people were arrested. On the following day, it was proposed to hold a demonstration at the Guildhall where the royal couple were being entertained to lunch and in the evening at the Aldwych Theatre where they were to be just entertained. But special 12 feet high barriers were erected in the city to block the streets (though again it was the demonstrators who were arrested for obstructing the highway), while three lines of police kept the demonstrators away from the theatre, where the Foreign Office had taken the precaution of booking every seat. On the next day it was planned to march from Trafalgar Square again but this time to hold a vigil outside Claridge's (for reasons unknown, though perhaps because the royal couple were staying or dining there). But this too was disrupted by the police cordons blocking many West End streets. According to the Committee of 100,

Opposite the Mayfair restaurant there were fifty people clapping and waving Greek flags. They were allowed to stay there. Further up the road hundreds of peaceful demonstrators were 'dealt with' by police on motor bikes, police on horseback, and police on foot'.[77]

VII. Back to Court for George Clark and Terry Chandler

Apart from preventing the demonstrations taking place, the Greek royal visit led to a large number of arrests and a number of controversial prosecutions, which led in turn to appeals which in turn added further to the Committee of 100's unique contribution to the Law Reports. These cases reveal the ease with which the criminal law could be applied, and the lack of regard for rights of the accused. A number of complaints were made about the indiscriminate nature of the arrests, which were said to include tourists and others who were not part of the demonstrations. There were also complaints about the planting of evidence on demonstrators, including in one case eight people taken to the West End Central Police Station being presented with bricks on their arrival and then charged with possessing an offensive weapon. One of their number was able to pay for legal representation and was acquitted; the other seven were convicted. The individual who was acquitted then brought civil proceedings against the police officers, leading to an offer of compensation to four of the people concerned, and an inquiry into all eight cases. There were bitter complaints too about police perjury in many of the cases brought following the arrests at the Greek royal family demonstrations.[78]

(a) The Imprisonment and Release of George Clark

George Clark (the field secretary of CND) was charged with public nuisance by obstructing the highway on 9 July, the various locations being Pall Mall, Lower Regent Street, Charles II Street, St James's Square, Piccadilly, and Constitution

---

[77] Ibid 8.
[78] See generally, Committee of 100, Open Letter to an Old Bailey Court, BLPS, CND/2008/3/5, 9.

Hill. The case against him was based on the evidence of two plainclothes police officers who had been mingling with the crowds; according to the police witnesses, the defendant had said to various groups of people gathered in Whitehall

'We can't get through that way. Follow me', and then marched to Trafalgar Square, beckoning the crowd of some 500 people to follow him. The police officers further stated that the defendant and the crowd went along Cockspur Street into Pall Mall and that the crowd, by then numbering about 2,000, spread over Pall Mall. It was further testified that the defendant, on reaching a police cordon at Waterloo Place, told persons near him to turn right before the cordon and walk round behind it, and that the crowd did turn right, later partially blocking Lower Regent Street and completely blocking Charles II Street.

The evidence continued in this vein, with the defendant being said to have shouted encouragement to the crowd (which presumably included the two police officers) as it went into Pall Mall, and that as it turned into Piccadilly after marching up St James's Street, half the road was blocked. It was only when the crowd reached its destination that Clark was arrested, brought in due course before the London Sessions where the jury was directed to consider whether the defendant had unlawfully incited 'various people to commit a nuisance to the public by the unlawful obstruction of various streets'. Although 13 defence witnesses were called on behalf of Clark to contest the police claim that he had incited the crowd, and despite Clark's claim that he was not a ring-leader as alleged,[79] the police evidence was preferred and on 10 September 1963 he was found guilty as charged.

Clark was—remarkably—jailed for 18 months (the same as the Wethersfield six under the Official Secrets Act 1911), and served ten weeks of his sentence before a successful appeal to the Court of Criminal Appeal, where it was claimed that the judge in the lower court had misdirected the jury. In a short decision guided by the Irish decision in *Lowdens v Keaveney*,[80] a case involving the blocking of a Belfast street by a 'band' in which a conviction was quashed because of a failure of the justices to decide 'the real question', which was whether the user of the street was in the circumstances unreasonable, Gibson J said that

A public highway is primarily for the free passage of the public for all reasonable purposes of business or pleasure; but persons using such highway may stop on lawful occasions, as for example for the purpose of taking up or discharging persons or goods at adjoining houses, provided that in doing so they do not unreasonably interfere with corresponding rights of others. Where the use of the highway is unreasonable and excessive, that is a nuisance, irrespective of any guilty or wrongful intent.[81]

The Court of Criminal Appeal heard argument that it was of the essence of the common law offence of public nuisance not that the highway was blocked, but that there had been an unreasonable user of the highway, 'bearing in mind that this procession, on the face of it and unless it did amount to a public nuisance, was under our law perfectly lawful'. The Lord Chief Justice agreed, noting that

---

[79] Ibid.
[80] [1903] IR 82.
[81] Ibid at 89.

'unfortunately in the present case, there was no direction to the jury as to the question of reasonableness or unreasonableness'.[82] Although the defendant may well have been found guilty even if such a direction had been given, the failure to include this information in the direction to the jury was thought to be fatal, and the conviction was overturned. Terry Chandler was not so fortunate.

(b) The Contrasting Fortunes of Terry Chandler

Chandler was charged on four counts of (i) conspiracy to cause a public nuisance by unlawfully obstructing the highway by means of assemblies, demonstrations and processions; (ii) causing a public nuisance on 9 July by unlawfully obstructing the highway in the neighbourhood of Trafalgar Square and Whitehall; (iii) inciting persons unknown to cause a public nuisance on 11 July at Trafalgar Square, Charing Cross Road, Wardour Street and various other places; and (iv) causing a public nuisance on 11 July at these latter locations. He was found guilty of the last three counts and sentenced to nine months, and he appealed on a number of grounds, appearing again before Lord Parker who was no more friendly this time than he had been in the Wethersfield case. One of the issues in the appeal, which casts further light on the activities of the Special Branch at this time, related to the following exchange in cross-examination between Chandler and Chief Detective Inspector Dickinson of the Special Branch:

The defendant: Were any of the officers under your instructions directed to keep an eye on me during the State visit? The witness: May I discuss, My Lord? Judge Rogers: Were any officers under your control given any instructions about this man? The Witness: I believe they were, in fact, my Lord.[83]

But when Chandler then asked for the names of the officers, Dickinson was told that he did not have to answer, a ruling with which the Court of Appeal agreed. Chandler had told the Court of Appeal that 'there were one or two officers he knows whose special duty was to keep an eye on him and who were, in effect, at his elbow metaphorically on these two days and that he would have liked to have known their names in order to call them as witnesses'. In an extraordinary passage, Lord Parker replied:

If he had got to the stage of one or two, then it may be he could ask the names, though in the opinion of this court the better course would have been to say to the judge: 'Will you please ask the prosecution to tender these two men as witnesses then I can cross-examine because I have now shown they were present at the time and must be able to give relevant evidence'.[84]

Such sophistry would be bad enough at the best of times; for it to be deployed against a litigant in person facing a lengthy jail sentence was inexcusable. However, the case was dominated by another issue, namely the selection of the jury,

---

[82] [1964] 2 QB 315, at 321.
[83] [1964] 2 QB 323, at 325.
[84] Ibid at 339.

about which the Committee of 100 was especially exercised. In a lecture to the Committee by a spokesman from the NCCL (Geoffrey Clark), it was reported that the *Chandler* appeal had challenged the

very fairness and legality of the present jury system which allows the prosecution too much rope in its questioning of jurymen, but because of lack of knowledge, time and money is denied to most defendants. Potential jurors can be sifted by being questioned in their own homes—a right open to the defendant if he has the above-mentioned things![85]

When the first nine jurors were brought forward, Chandler challenged peremptorarily seven of them, and thereafter asked others to 'stand by, until he had gone through all the "panel". This "somewhat novel procedure" nonplussed the judge "somewhat"', having never heard of it until Chandler referred to a passage in Halsbury's Laws of England in which the was stated that 'The Crown has no peremptory challenge in any case, but may challenge by asking that the juror "stand by for the Crown" as the names are called over, and is not bound to show the cause of challenge until the panel is gone through'. It is then said that 'A defendant whose peremptory challenges have been exhausted may follow the same course'. The trial judge then permitted Chandler to continue, as a result of which another 18 jurors were 'stood by' (for reasons unknown), until such time as clerk of the court rose to announce that 'My Lord, that exhausts the panel I have available'. Although disputed by Chandler, who argued that others should be brought, the trial judge then allowed some of those who had been stood by to be sworn, over the objections of the accused. The Court of Appeal held, nevertheless, that the magistrate had not acted improperly, remarking that 'luckily this kind of thing does not happen very often in this country'.[86] According to the Court of Appeal, the defendant had no such right, and the awkward authority the other way was dismissed as *obiter*.

VIII. Conclusion

Apart from the campaign against the airfields and the demonstrations against the Greek royal visit, prominent Committee of 100 activists made a number of other contributions to the Law Reports. Andrew Papworth tested the scope of the Metropolitan Police Commissioner's powers under the Metropolitan Police Act 1839 to impose restraints on the freedom of assembly of the people of London when he was arrested while conducting a peaceful demonstration at the junction of Whitehall and Downing Street;[87] while Farmer Cheney tested the ability of the Inland Revenue (as it then was) to raise money by taxation that would then be used to finance nuclear weapons, allegedly in breach of the Geneva Conventions.[88] In none of these cases could the activists plead that the authorities in question were

---

[85] National Committee of 100, *Policy and Planning* (1964), BLPS/CND/2008/3/1, 2.
[86] [1964] 2 QB 323, at 333.
[87] *Papworth v Coventry* [1967] 2 All ER 41.
[88] *Cheney v Conn* [1968] 1 All ER 779.

violating constitutionally protected rights (such as freedom of assembly or freedom of conscience), as they might do in a number of other countries. Just as Joan Mahoney has pointed out in relation to the early stages of the Cold War, it is striking that even as matters warmed up on the streets of London, constitutional principle remained a contested departure point at all levels of government. We have seen how 'traditional rights' troubled the Cabinet in advance of the proposed Trafalgar Square meeting in September 1962; and we have seen how a number of civil liberties concerns were raised in the House of Commons on the eve of the Wethersfield demonstration on 9 December 1961. Similar concerns were also raised in a slightly different context in the House of Lords when Sir Reginald Manningham-Buller in his form as Viscount Dilhorne introduced a Public Order Bill in June 1963 to raise the penalties following conviction. Introduced to deal mainly with fascists rather than peace campaigners following the decision in *Jordan v Burgoyne*,[89] concerns were nevertheless expressed that because this was a bill affecting freedom of speech, it was thus a bill of a constitutional character and ought to have started in the House of Commons, to which the Lord Chancellor was compelled to reply in the following terms—

At that time the noble Lords were at a disadvantage since they had not had an opportunity of seeing the Bill. Now that they have done so, they will, I hope, agree that it is so framed that it does not alter the limits of freedom of speech at all. It does no more than increase the penalties that may be imposed on those who infringe the existing law. No constitutional question is involved.[90]

The courts were also alert or alerted to civil liberties issues, with Lord Hodson acknowledging in *Chandler* that the case before the House had been referred to as one of those cases 'which it is said raises a grave constitutional issue'.[91] The point was made more forcefully by Lord Devlin who said that the arguments presented in the case

Embraced big constitutional questions concerning the right to trial by jury and not by judge, and the extent to which the courts can question statements on political matters by the executive. All such questions which concern the liberty of the subject need great care in their consideration. It is for me a special inducement to the exercise of care that these appellants have not traded their liberty for personal gain but for what they sincerely, and however mistakenly, believe to be the safety of the world.[92]

However, the courts were also to be revealed as instruments of the political constitution, whose members moved effortlessly between politics and law, even while they were in office. Indeed a few months before sitting in the *Chandler* case. Viscount Radcliffe had produced his report on Security Procedures in the Civil Service.[93] But not only were the lines between legal and political activity blurred, so were the lines between political and legal principles. So while it is true that there

---

[89] [1963] 2 QB 744.
[90] HC Debs, 20 June 1963, cols 1386–7.
[91] [1964] AC 763, at 799.
[92] Ibid 811–12.
[93] Cmnd 1681, 1962. See Lustgarten and Leigh, above n 43, pp 131–2.

was some acknowledgement of constitutional principle in the jurisprudence, this was outweighed by considerations of the kind that we saw expressed in the other great event of this period. This was the Vassall spy inquiry in which Lord Parker memorably found it 'quite impossible to say' that the interests of journalists should 'as a matter of policy be preferred to the overriding public policy of Parliament',[94] a view most probably shared by his counterpart in Moscow at the time. His counterpart in Moscow might probably also share the view of the House of Lords in *Chandler* that the nature and scope of that duty is to be determined by the government of the day, or in his case by the military establishment in the form of the evidence by Air Commodore Magill, whose views the courts would not permit the accused to challenge. And while the lines between political and legal principles were blurred and although some judges appeared comfortable in both domains, they were nevertheless content not to challenge the fundamentals of government policy on behalf of those who by their actions had done just that. The answer was provided by Lord Reid, who said with impeccable constitutional propriety that 'Anyone is entitled, in or out of Parliament, to urge that policy regarding the armed forces should be changed; but until it is changed, on a change of Government or otherwise, no one is entitled to challenge it in court'.[95]

What of course Lord Reid did not add with the same logic was that the opportunity for change was rendered impossible as a matter of constitutional practice by the position adopted by all the main parties and other sources of opinion. Nor was there any challenge to the absurd statement by Sir Reginald Manningham-Buller, who in response to the suggestion that section 1 'involved a wide infringement of basic liberties', replied in legal argument that 'the requirement of the Attorney General's fiat is a safeguard against oppressive action'.[96] As the *Chandler* case revealed, this is not much of a safeguard when the Attorney General is the cheerleader or instigator of these restrictions on liberty rather than their defender. But what *Chandler* also revealed is the depth of the challenge for those who would rescue human rights by legal instruments and judicial power, the affair vividly illuminating a number of issues relating to the protection of civil liberties and human rights. These include the deep intrusion of the Special Branch and its various surveillance activities, and the extensive power of the police empowered whimsically to ban marches, processions, meetings, and demonstrations; in addition to the highly politicized role of the Attorney General who appeared to use his office as a political platform, to the role of the courts which appeared willing to do the government's bidding. The commitment to a constitutional principle of liberty that runs through much of the background to these events was to buckle very quickly in the face of serious challenge. Popular protest was met with brute force, with the public authorities showing little respect for the values they were purporting to uphold. In the protection of liberty, the defence of national security became the rule of law—the core constitutional principle of government, Parliament and

---

[94] See *Attorney General v Clough* [1963] 1 QB 773, at 793.
[95] [1964] AC 763, at 791.
[96] Ibid 781.

the courts, with neither Parliament nor the courts willing to operate as a source of restraint. These are matters that continue to have a contemporary resonance as latter-day defenders of liberty step forward to replace Helen Allegranza, Terry Chandler, Ian Dixon, Trevor Hatton, Patrick Pottle, and Michael Randle. It is true that matters are now very different: the judges have more power (though it was not a want of power that was the problem in *Chandler*), and there are more formal lines that separate the legal and the political (with judges some steps removed from the political classes they now scrutinize). It seems unlikely, however, that the justiciability of the aforementioned constitutional principles in the form of constitutional rights would have made any difference to the outcome of *Chandler* or the other cases, or the legacy that they left. On the contrary, what recent cases confirm is that when national security is challenged (however weak the challenge), judicial power does not provide a sufficient restraint on the power of a government which has lost its sense of responsibility for safeguarding liberty, government self-restraint being the ultimate defence of civil liberties. When that is lost, it is time to change the government, as happened in 1964, and again in 2010.

9

Lessons from the Past? Northern Ireland, Terrorism Now and Then, and the Human Rights Act

Aileen McColgan

Recent years have seen a sustained assault within Great Britain and by its government on civil liberties and human rights. There have been actual and attempted terrorist atrocities, many of the latter doubtless outside the sphere of public knowledge. But the period 2000 to the present has witnessed a catalogue of extraordinary measures perpetrated by the state, largely in the name of 'national security'. These measures include (but are not limited to):

- the use of internment;[1]
- the normalization of long periods of pre-charge detention;
- the direct and indirect use of torture by agents of the state;
- the use by the police of deadly force against those suspected of terrorist involvement and of highly coercive methods of control, including the use of significant levels of violence, against protestors and others and the extensive use of arbitrary stop and search powers;
- the criminalization of forms of expression and of organizations regarded as hostile to the interests of the state.[2]

The parallels with the British approach to decades of civil and political unrest, and the associated terrorist threat, in Northern Ireland are perhaps particularly striking to one who grew up there in the 1970s and 1980s. What is surprising is that the British state has apparently failed to learn the lessons of its recent past, and that the government's public commitment to a human rights-based approach to governing, trumpeted by its adoption of the Human Rights Act 1998, does not appear

---

[1] I include the system of control orders which, in 2005, replaced the system originally introduced in 2001.

[2] See eg C. Walker, 'Clamping Down on Terrorism in the United Kingdom' [2006] *Journal of International Criminal Law* 1137; A. Tomkins, 'Legislating Against Terror: The Anti-terrorism, Crime and Security Act 2001' [2002] *Public Law* 205.

to have acted as a meaningful counterweight to the exigencies of events in shaping responses to the current terrorist threat.

In this chapter I do no more than sketch a history of some of the human rights abuses perpetrated by the British state in Northern Ireland between 1967 and the mid-1980s, and of the judicial failures in responding to those abuses. So numerous and varied were the human rights breaches that I have selected only a few, concentrating for the most part on the early years of the period and indicating in cursory form the criminal 'justice' developments in the period after the imposition by London of direct rule in 1975. In recounting this history, I have three aims. The first is to tell the story for its own sake, and to draw attention to the ongoing failures on the part of the state to remedy, even to acknowledge, past wrongs. The second is to underline that nothing that is done now is done for the first time, this with a view to countering the tendency to see human rights abuses carried out by the state as understandable, even justifiable, responses to extreme, perhaps 'unprecedented', situations of crisis. I do not suggest that there are direct parallels between the events I discuss and those of recent years, or between the nature of the threat to the state then and now, but some of the similarities are striking. My third aim in writing this chapter has been to cast the spotlight on judicial failures in the face of state abuses of human rights, by introducing some of the Northern Irish decisions and suggesting that the record of the British judiciary post-Human Rights Act has been for the most part similarly supine. This pessimistic conclusion is tempered to some degree, however, by what may prove to be a trend towards the demand for transparency. Notwithstanding a very patchy record on the part of the judiciary, there have in the last few months been a number of judicial decisions which may yet prove significant in calling the executive to account for alleged human rights violations, in particular in the context of Iraq. So what is for the most part a fairly bleak account is not entirely so, though whether this is for the most part the result of a natural tendency to optimism on the part of the writer remains to be seen.

I. The Background: The Demand for Civil Rights in Northern Ireland

In 1967 Catholics in Northern Ireland were suffering under multiple yokes of oppression, being subject to the uneven application of special powers legislation which permitted, *inter alia*, arrests without warrant or charge and internment (see further below), the wholesale by-passing of normal criminal justice safeguards, and the banning of any organization, meeting, or publication;[3] policed in part by the predominantly Protestant RUC, otherwise by the exclusively Protestant, sectarian part-time 'B Specials'; their votes gerrymandered and their needs for jobs and

---

[3] See L. Donohue, 'Regulating Northern Ireland: The Special Powers Acts, 1922–1972' (1998) 41 *Historical Journal* 1089.

housing discriminatorily denied.[4] That year saw the inauguration of the Northern Ireland Civil Rights Association (NICRA), which set out to challenge the status quo. One of the first steps taken by Northern Ireland's establishment (which at the time boasted its own Parliament and Prime Minister, Captain Terence O'Neill) was the imposition of a ban on republican clubs, which had been active in the establishment of NICRA, viewed by then Home Secretary William Craig as an IRA front.[5] Already banned under the SPAs were a large number of republican organizations, but not until 1969 was a single loyalist paramilitary organization (the Ulster Volunteer Force) banned, this despite the fact that that organization had been involved in a bombing campaign since 1966.[6]

Establishment hostility to NICRA did not stop with the banning of republican clubs. Early civil rights marches were greeted with resistance by loyalist organizations and soon with bannings and violence. Marchers in Derry in October 1968 were baton-charged by the RUC and the rioting which ensued is regarded by many as marking the start of 'the Troubles'. Limited reforms announced by O'Neill in November 1968 were insufficient to lance the boil of nationalist/Catholic dissatisfaction and further marches resulted in attacks on civil rights demonstrators by extremist unionists during which the forces of law and order stood idly by as demonstrators were set upon by armed thugs[7] and, on occasion, joined in the assaults.[8] Rioting spread across the North with the establishment of 'Free Derry' (a no-go area for the police) and the election of 21-year-old Bernadette Devlin to the British Parliament in April 1969. August 1969 saw the 'Battle of the Bogside', which resulted in the deployment of British troops on the streets, and in Devlin's conviction for riot and incitement to riot in December of that year.[9] The Irish Taoiseach, Jack Lynch, announced that field hospitals would be set up on the border, called on the British government to request a UN Peacekeeping Force, and declared that the Irish government would 'no longer stand by and see innocent people injured or even worse'.[10] Nationalist hopes of troop movements across the border from the South came to nothing and many Catholics fled the North for the safety of the Republic, having been burnt out of their homes.

British soldiers were first greeted with enthusiasm by many nationalists and were seen to protect Catholics from attack by Protestant extremists. But an absence of action on civil rights commitments, coupled with a failure by the state to take

[4] See eg J. Whyte, 'How much Discrimination was there under the Unionist Regime, 1921–68?', in T. Gallagher and J. O'Connell (eds), *Contemporary Irish Studies* (Manchester: Manchester University Press, 1983), 30.

[5] See *McEldowney v Forde* [1971] 1 AC 632, discussed below.

[6] Donohue, n 3 above.

[7] Including the rout at Burntollet Bridge in 1969: see B. Egan and V. McCormack, 'Burntollet' (1969), available at <http://cain.ulst.ac.uk>.

[8] See P. Berresford Ellis, *A History of the Irish Working Class* (London: Pluto Classics, 1996); 'Disturbances in Northern Ireland: Report of the Commission appointed by the Governor of Northern Ireland' (1969) Cmnd N Ir 532, ch 6; E. McCann, *War and an Irish Town* (London: Pluto Press, 1993), 108.

[9] See *Battle of the Bogside* (2004), V. Cunningham (dir), <info@northlandbroadcast.net>; *Devlin v Armstrong* [1971] NI 13.

[10] <http://www.politics.ie/history/93598-jack-lynch-troubles-2.html>.

any action in respect of the amount of weaponry in loyalist hands,[11] skirmishes between troops and nationalists, and the issue of a 'shoot to kill' warning by the Army GOC (General Officer Commanding) resulted, historian Peter Berresford Ellis records, in a chilling in relations and:

Following the election of Edward Heath's Conservative Government [in June 1970], the role of the army significantly changed. British troops now turned a 'blind eye' to 'loyalist' extremists and the Catholic and Nationalist communities found themselves the object of harassment and searches by the army.[12]

In January 1970 the IRA had split between the Provisionals (who maintained a republican line and advocated the aggressive use of force against British rule) and the Officials, who wanted only to use force defensively in support of those under siege in Catholic areas. The Provisional IRA were responsible for 170 bomb attacks in 1970, a figure which almost doubled to 298 in the first six months of 1971.[13] In July 1971 IRA ranks swelled after the killing of two young men by British troops in Derry[14] and the imposition by British troops of a curfew in the Falls Road area of Belfast which resulted in three days of gun battles and rioting, five deaths, and 60 injuries.[15] 1971 also saw the re-invigoration of SPA powers relating to the publication and circulation[16] of 'any document advocating: (a) an alteration to the constitution or laws of Northern Ireland by some unlawful means, (b) the raising or maintaining of a military force, (c) the obstruction or interference with the administration of justice or the enforcement of the law, or (d) support for any organization which participates in any of the above.'[17] 'Further, any individual who was reasonably believed by a member of the security forces to have such a document in his or her possession would be found guilty of an offence if he or she failed to turn the document over to the security forces on demand'.[18]

II. Internment

In March 1971 Brian Faulkner became Northern Irish Prime Minister after first O'Neill then his successor Chichester-Clark had resigned in the face of an increasingly hard-line unionist rump. Faulkner wanted internment, largely as a

[11] Berresford Ellis states, n 8 above, 320, that 'Westminster had been told that there were 102000 *licensed* weapons in the hands of the Unionists alone…'.
[12] Ibid.
[13] K. Jeffrey suggests, in T. Bartlett and K. Jeffery (eds), *A Military History of Ireland* (New York: Cambridge University Press, 1996), 452, that at the time the IRA had 'a fairly sound popular basis'.
[14] P. Taylor, *Brits: The War Against the IRA* (London: Bloomsbury Publishing, 2001), 83.
[15] General Sir Michael Jackson, a captain in the paras in Northern Ireland in January 1972, acknowledged in a BBC Spotlight programme broadcast on 29 May 2007 that the imposition of the curfew had been a 'mistake'.
[16] See Donohue, n 3 above, 1104–6.
[17] Reg 8 (originally 4) as amended in January 1971.
[18] Donohue, n 3 above, 1102–3.

sop to those even more hardline than he.[19] On 5 August, Faulkner and a British delegation which included Prime Minister Heath and Home Secretary Reginald Maudling agreed on the introduction of internment. Historian Ronan Fanning reports that the British Conservative government took the view that internment should precede any imposition of direct rule because ' "we might well be creating subsequent political embarrassment for ourselves if we needed, under direct rule, to use a weapon which we had earlier denied to the Northern Ireland Government" [citing Cabinet papers] ... The corollary was that if, as so many in Whitehall predicted, internment was a disaster, then the blame would fall on Faulkner's administration rather than on Heath's'.[20]

On 9 August 1971, in 'Operation Demetrius', 342 men were arrested in predawn raids on Catholic/nationalist areas by members of the British Army. Not one of those arrested was a loyalist, this despite the fact that the UVF had been actively involved in terrorist activities for five years. One unaffiliated Protestant man living in a Catholic area was inadvertently included in the swoop and a number of non-Catholic nationalists were also interned.[21] It was not the first time that internment had been used in the North, similar tactics having been deployed against nationalists in 1921–4, 1938–45 and 1956–6.[22] The arrests were made under Regulation 12(1) of the Special Powers Regulations, which allowed the relevant minister to issue detention orders against anyone 'who is suspected of acting or being about to act in a manner prejudicial to the preservation of the peace and the maintenance of order in Northern Ireland'. Northern Irish Prime Minister Brian Faulkner declared in a televised statement that:

This is not action taken against any responsible and law-abiding section of the community. Nor is it in any way punitive or indiscriminate ... The main target ... is the IRA which has been responsible for recent acts of terrorism ... They are the present threat. But we will not hesitate to take strong action against any other individuals or organisations who may present such a threat in future ...

It is with understandable reluctance that one uses these exceptional powers ... I ask those who will quite sincerely consider the use of internment powers as evil ... 'Is it more of an evil than to permit the perpetrators of these outrages to remain at liberty?'

I cannot guarantee that the action we have now taken will bring this campaign swiftly to an end. We may yet have to endure as a community. But if we endure with courage and steadiness, the utter defeat of terrorism is sure.[23]

---

[19] See R. Fanning (Professor of Modern History at University College Dublin), 'Fateful Steps on the Road to Internment', (6 Jan 2002) *The Independent*, discussing Cabinet Papers released at the end of 2001, available at <http://irelandsown.net/fatefulsteps.html>.

[20] Ibid.

[21] Among them John McGuffin, of whom more below, and Ivan Barr, the Ulster Scots chair of NICRA.

[22] R. J. Spjut, 'Internment and Detention without Trial' (1986) 49 *Modern Law Review* 712, 713.

[23] <http://news.bbc.co.uk/onthisday/hi/dates/stories/august/9/newsid_4071000/4071849.stm>.

It is a matter for speculation whether Faulkner would have regarded the present settlement as indicating 'the utter defeat of terrorism'. As to his suggestion that internment was carefully targeted, historian Tim Pat Coogan records that:

Operation Demetrius... relied on lists drawn up by the RUC Special Branch... The lists were weighted towards the Officials, who, despite being the more pacific of the two IRA wings, were regarded by MI5 as the more dangerous adversaries because of their Marxist orientation. Hence their potential was assessed in cold-war terms, rather than in an Irish context. The names included... people who had never been in the IRA, including Ivan Barr, chairman of the NICRA executive... What they did not include was a single Loyalist. Although the UVF had begun the killing and bombing, this organisation was left untouched, as were other violent Loyalist satellite organisations such as Tara, the Shankill Defenders Association and the Ulster Protestant Volunteers. It is known that Faulkner was urged by the British to include a few Protestants in the trawl but he refused.[24]

The Diplock Commission, of which more below, concluded in December 1972 that 'the scale of the [internment] operation led to the arrest and detention of a number of persons against whom suspicion was founded on inadequate information', but the suggestion that this was down to (ill) luck rather than deliberate judgment has been challenged.[25] R. J. Spjut, who interviewed former Northern Ireland Secretaries Willie (then Lord) Whitelaw and Merlyn Rees in 1984, suggested in the *Modern Law Review* that the internment of the innocent was not inadvertent, being used in response to political pressure from unionists and in order to taint those 'suspected of marginal involvement with the P.I.R.A. [Provisionals]... so that they... once released... would not be readily accepted by the P.I.R.A.'.[26]

In the two days following 'Operation Demetrius', 17 people were killed, ten of them Catholics shot by the army, including a Catholic priest shot dead by the army while he was administering the last rites to a dying man.[27] In the same period an estimated 7,000 Catholic families fled across the border as a result of loyalist violence, including the firebombing of Catholic homes. Support for the IRA increased and a widespread campaign of civil disobedience ensued, with barricades erected around 'Free Derry' for a period of almost a year and a rents and rates strike which, according to the government's own figures, attracted the support of some 26,000 households. Violence soared, with 140 deaths in the remainder of 1971 compared with 34 in the seven months before the introduction of internment, and 1972 witnessing the highest number of deaths in any year of the Troubles (467, with a total of 10,628 shooting incidents and 1,853 explosions or defusions of bombs, this in an area about 5 per cent the size of Britain and with a population of around 1.5 million at the time).[28]

---

[24] *The Troubles: Ireland's Ordeal 1966–1996 and the Search for Peace* (London: Hutchinson, 2002), 126.

[25] 'Report of the Commission to Consider Legal Procedures to deal with Terrorist Activities in Northern Ireland' (1972) Cmnd 5185, para 32.

[26] n 22 above, 731.

[27] CAIN chronology of events, <http://cain.ulst.ac.uk/events/intern/chron.htm>.

[28] Fanning, n 19 above, reporting on Cabinet Papers of 1971 released. See also P. Bew and G. Gillespie, *Northern Ireland: A Chronology of the Troubles 1968–1999* (Dublin: Gill and Macmillan,

By 1972 there were 924 internees. The first Protestants deliberately detained were interned on 2 February 1973 and by the end of internment on 5 December 1975, 1,981 people had been detained, 1,874 of whom were Catholic and 107 Protestants. The highest numbers of Catholics and Protestants detained at any one time were, respectively, 809 and 70 in February 1972 and May 1974 respectively. This was despite significant and increasing levels of loyalist violence. Whereas, in 1971, republicans were responsible for 126 deaths and loyalists for 21, rising to 255 and 103 respectively in 1972 and declining to 128 and 80 in 1973, in 1974 and 1975 respectively loyalists were responsible for 104 and 115 deaths to republicans' 98 and 102. Whitelaw told an interviewer in November 1984 that one of the reasons why so few Protestants were interned was that 'Our intelligence about the Protestant community was absolutely nil' because '[t]he Stormont Government [thought] quite reasonably, in their view, if you were a Protestant you were a loyal figure…until proved otherwise. Whereas over the years the exact opposite was regarded of the minority community'.[29]

III. The Use of Torture

From the first days of internment, allegations began to emerge about the abuse of internees. On 31 August the UK Parliament appointed the Compton Commission to investigate 'allegations by those arrested on 9th August under the Civil Authority (Special Powers) Act of 1922 of physical brutality while in the custody of the security forces *prior to either their subsequent release, the preferring of a criminal charge, or their being lodged in a place specified in a detention order*' (emphasis added). John McGuffin, himself detained on 9 August, later charged that:

… by its very nature the committee was intended to be effectively disabled from arriving at the truth, but at the same time give the impression of concern and efficiency… the Inquiry was limited to those arrested on 9 August; many of the worst tortures came after that date when the interrogation-torture centre at Palace barracks, Holywood, became fully operational. In addition, the Inquiry was limited to 'physical' torture, no brief being given for psychological maltreatment.[30]

Amnesty International's report, published on 8 November 1971,[31] recorded the alleged use of electric shocks, injections of hallucinatory drugs, and genital physical abuse on those arrested after 9 August 1971, concluding that 'the authorities have in no way been restrained or intimidated by the Compton Commission…Indeed, those in charge of interrogations may well consider their activities to be insulated

1999), 37; B. Dickson, 'Northern Irish Emergency Legislation—the Wrong Medicine?' [1992] *Public Law* 592.

[29] Spjut, n 22 above, 736.

[30] *Internment* (Tralee, Anvil Books: 1973), ch 12, <http://www.irishresistancebooks.com/internment/intern12.htm>.

[31] 'Report on Allegations of Ill-Treatment Made by Persons Arrested under The Special Powers Act after 8 August, 1971'. For a first-hand account see J. McGuffin, 'When They Came in the Morning' (1971) 52 *New Blackfriars* 532.

from criticism because of the narrow scope of the Commission's mandate and think themselves able to act more freely in regard to persons arrested after 9th August'.

The Compton Commission sat in secret, unable to compel the attendance of witnesses or to demand the production of any document, and with detainees initially denied any legal assistance and thereafter, 'after public and professional outcry...allowed a lawyer [who was, however] barred from even seeing or hearing, let alone questioning, the defence witnesses (army and police witnesses were legally represented)'.[32] Of the 342 men arrested on the first day of internment, only one spoke to the Inquiry team which, further, refused to accept any evidence from Amnesty International or other organizations which had themselves gathered evidence about the mistreatment of internees, interviewing 11 doctors and no fewer than 95 army, 26 police, and 11 prison personnel. The Commission, which reported on 3 November 1971[33] (a mere nine weeks after its appointment), accepted that detainees had been subjected to:

- in-depth interrogation with the use of hooding, white noise, sleep deprivation, and prolonged wall standing, together with a diet of bread and water;

- prolonged periods of enforced physical exercise ('these compulsory exercises must have caused some hardship but do not think the exercises were thought of and carried out with a view to hurting or degrading the men who had to do them');

- blindfolding and being thrown out of helicopters hovering around 4 feet above the ground, detainees being deceived into believing that they were to be thrown from high-flying helicopters (the 'physical experience of these men' characterized by the report as 'constitute[ing] a measure of ill-treatment');

- being forced to run an obstacle course over broken glass and rough ground whilst being beaten (the report states that 'the men concerned may have suffered some measure of unintended hardship').[34]

It did not accept, however, that the treatment amounted to 'brutality':

We consider that brutality is an inhuman or savage form of cruelty, and that cruelty implies a disposition to inflict suffering, coupled with indifference to, or pleasure in, the victim's pain. We do not think that happened.[35]

On 8 November 1971 Amnesty reported that 'Definite patterns emerge from an analysis of the allegations' made by internees, with the majority of those released after 48 hours reporting (only) 'severe beatings usually about the head and shoulders with truncheons', 'being made to run barefoot for several hundred yards over stony ground strewn with broken glass, rough boards and other debris', 'indignities...including verbal abuse ridiculing the presumed religious beliefs of the

---

[32] McGuffin, *Internment*, n 30 above.
[33] 'Report of the Enquiry into Allegations against the Security Forces of Physical Brutality in Northern Ireland Arising out of Events on the 9th August, 1971' (1971) Cmnd 4823.
[34] Ibid, ch VIII 'Summary'.
[35] Ibid, para 105.

persons in custody', having dogs set on them, being denied sleep, and forced to undertake vigorous exercise for prolonged periods. It is testament to the severity of other forms of abuse that Amnesty categorized the men thus treated as 'not severely brutalised...but...subjected to calculated cruelties, imposed on them solely for the entertainment of their captors'.

But on selected testimonials the pattern alters radically. Apparently pre-designated persons were arrested and not mal-treated until processed and transferred to a special interrogation centre [Palace Barracks, Holywood], where they were then subjected to severe beatings and physical tortures in the nature of being forced to stand in a 'search position' (legs apart, hands against wall) for hours at a time. When they would collapse, severe beatings were again administered. This pattern was followed by prolonged interrogation, often over several hours. The prisoners were offered money to give information relating to Irish Republican Army activities in Northern Ireland. During these tortures, the prisoners were first stripped naked, their heads covered with an opaque cloth bag with no ventilation. They were then dressed in large boiler suits (one-piece coverall garments). They were forced into the search position in a room filled with the high pitched whining sound of a air compressor or similar device. This went on in some cases for 6 to 7 days. Many prisoners felt they were on the brink of insanity—one alleges he prayed for death, another that he tried to kill himself by banging his head against some metal piping in the room.[36]

Notwithstanding the excusatory tone of the Compton report, Prime Minister Edward Heath reacted with fury to the Commission's acknowledgement that any wrongdoing had occurred. In a memo written in advance of the report's publication Heath protested that:

It seems to me to be one of the most unbalanced, ill-judged reports I have ever read...the number of incidents involved in the arrest of 300 odd men were small and, in the conditions of war against the IRA, trivial...nowhere is this stated loud and clear and a clean bill of health given to the army...they seem to have gone to endless lengths to show that anyone not given 3-star hotel facilities suffered hardship and ill-treatment...What, above all, I object to—and I think many others will share this view to the point of driving themselves into a lesser or greater degree of fury—is that the unfounded allegations made for the most part by outsiders are put on exactly the same level as tested evidence from the Army and the RUC. This I believe to be intolerable.[37]

On the day the Compton report was published, Home Secretary Reginald Maulding established a Committee of Privy Councillors under the Chairmanship of Baron Parker of Waddington, Lord Chief Justice of England, to consider guidelines for future interrogation methods.[38] That report was adopted on 31 January 1972 but not published until 2 March 1972. The opening address of Counsel to the Baha Mousa Inquiry (see further below) records very extensive behind-the-scenes efforts on the part of the government to manage the military evidence flowing to the Committee with a view to maximizing the room for manoeuvre to be

[36] Ibid, 'Brief Summary'.
[37] According to a BBC Report of 2 January 2005.
[38] McGuffin, n 30 above ch 12: 'Denis Healey, the former Labour Minister, indignantly denied that "our boys" had done anything like that in Aden—although the "guidelines for interrogation methods" date to 1967—and a Labour Government.'

left by the final report.[39] The Committee formed the view that the methods used
in Northern Ireland had been unlawful under domestic law, though the majority
concluded that their use, subject to 'proper safeguards', was not to be ruled out 'on
moral grounds'. In a comment which was later to find its echo in the now notorious 'torture memos' (in which US administration lawyers denied the applicability
of the Geneva Conventions to suspected al-Qaeda and Taliban prisoners),[40] the
majority Parker report further suggested that the Geneva Conventions, to which
the Directive made reference, might not apply 'in the emergencies which we are
considering and the same can be argued in respect of our other international obligations under the European Convention for the Protection of Human Rights and
Fundamental Freedoms (Article 3) and under the Universal Declaration of Human
Rights (Article 5)'.

On the day the Parker report was published, Edward Heath declared in the
House of Commons that 'The Government, having reviewed the whole matter
with great care and with particular reference to any future operations, have decided
that the techniques which the Committee examined will not be used in future
as an aid to interrogation'.[41] What looks like, and has been generally regarded as
amounting to, a commitment to the total abandonment of the techniques was, in
fact, rather more limited. According to evidence before the Baha Mousa Inquiry,[42]
the words 'as an aid to interrogation' were in fact highly significant, much discussion having been devoted as to the presentation of the techniques as, on the one
hand, measures designed for security purposes (hooding to disguise prisoners from
each other, wall-standing to make them easier to guard, white noise to prevent
their identification of and communication with each other). The same undertaking was to be given by the UK Attorney General before the ECHR on 8 February
1977, in the *Ireland v UK* proceedings (the Court finding in the event that the
UK had breached Article 3 of the Convention by imposing inhuman and degrading treatment on the internees).[43] Events following the death of Baha Mousa, an
Iraqi hotel receptionist kicked and/or suffocated to death by British soldiers in
Iraq in September 2003, however, made it clear that Heath's undertaking, however
it might have been interpreted, had ceased to regulate British behaviour at least

[39] <http://www.bahamousainquiry.org/hearings/transcripts.htm>.
[40] The Yoo Delahunty Memorandum of 9 Jan 2002, <http//en.wikipedia.org/wiki/File:20020109
_Yoo_Delahunty_Geneva_Convention_memo.pdf>; the Rumsfeld Order of 19 Jan 2002 <http://
www.lawofwar.org/Rumsfeld%20Torture%20memo_0001.jpg>; the Bybee Memo of 22 Jan 2002
<http://www.washingtonpost.com/wp-srv/nation/documents/012202bybee.pdf>; the Gonzales
Memo of 27 Jan 2002, <http://www.gwu.edu/~nsarchiv/NSAEBB/NSAEBB127/02.01.25.pdf>,
and the Bush Order 7 Feb 2002, <http://lawofwar.org/Bush_memo_Genevas.htm>.
[41] HC Deb, vol 832, col 743 (2 Mar 1972).
[42] Baha Mousa Inquiry opening statement of Counsel to the Inquiry on 14–15 July 2009, n 39
above.
[43] (1980) 2 EHRR 25. As Lord Hope pointed out in 'Torture' [2004] *International and
Comparative Law Quarterly* 807, 826, in light of the ECtHR decision in *Selmouni v France* (1999)
29 EHRR 403, para 10, 'It seems likely that the mixture of physical and psychological pressures that
were used in the case of the IRA suspects would now be regarded as torture within the meaning of
Article 3 of the Convention'.

overseas as, apparently, had even the most minimal commitment to the humane treatment of prisoners.[44]

IV. Bloody Sunday

The introduction of internment was coupled with blanket bans on demonstrations, first for six months from 9 August 1971, then for 12 months in January 1972. Notwithstanding the August ban, there had been a series of marches since Christmas 1971, and right-wing loyalists had warned Faulkner on 16 January that, if 'drastic' action were not taken to curb these illegal demonstrations, 'There will be determined Loyalist action to sweep weak leadership away'.[45] On 22 January, anti-internment marches in Armagh and Magilligan, the site of an internment camp near Derry, were broken up by British force, the paratroop regiment being deployed in Magilligan. Tim Pat Coogan describes the Magilligan incident through the eyes of Nigel Wade, then a junior reporter at the *Daily Telegraph*. Having noted the paper's attitude to the army ('"Our boys would not do anything like that"—i.e. anything brutal or untoward, as in the case of internment'), Coogan continues:

He was horrified at what he saw. The march proceeded without incident until it drew near the camp. Then, from behind sand dunes emerged a squad from the First Paratroop Regiment armed with batons and rubber bullet guns. They began shooting these at the marchers, driving many of them into the sea...Some of the paras used their batons with a ferocity that appalled Wade. Eventually it also appalled their NCOs, who tried to call off the Dogs of War. The paratroopers' initial reaction was to ignore their superiors and continue their onslaught. They were only brought back to a sense of discipline when the NCOs began wielding their batons fiercely on their own men.[46]

The events that took place in Derry on 30 January 1971 remained in dispute at least until the report in June 2010 of the Saville Inquiry some 11 years after its appointment.[47] What is perhaps not widely known is that the area within which all the killings and all but two of the woundings occurred was no bigger than about 500 square metres (the minimum size of a football pitch and 40% of the size of an Olympic pool). What could, prior to the report of the Saville Inquiry, have been said with reasonable certainty about that day was that:

- a decision had been taken by the IRA, both Provisional and Official, to attend the march unarmed, this decision almost certainly being known to British Army Intelligence;[48]

---

[44] This having been required since at least 1965: see the Joint Directive on Military Interrogation, 17 Feb 1965, discussed in the opening statement of Counsel to the Baha Mousa Inquiry, 14–15 July 2009, n 39 above.

[45] E. McCann, 'Bloody Sunday—Time for the Truth' (Feb 1998) 216 *Socialist Review*.

[46] n 24 above, 158.

[47] The report of the Inquiry post-dated the writing of this chapter.

[48] M. Sayle, 'Bloody Sunday Report' (11 July 2002) *London Review of Books*.

- the march had largely passed off with no more than the normal levels of stone throwing and taunting by the 'Derry Young Hooligans';
- in a space of no more than ten minutes, over 100 bullets were fired by 15 paratroopers[49] and seven men and six boys (five aged 17 and the other 16) lay dead or dying. A further man died of his injuries within weeks;
- not a single soldier was injured despite claims to the subsequent Widgery Inquiry that they had come under intense fire;[50]
- no civilians were injured other than by military fire (again despite allegations made by the military about intensive gunfire in a very small, crowded, area);
- no wounded survivors of the shootings were searched, nor were any placed under guard in hospital, a fact which sits oddly with military assertions at the time that all those shot at by troops were gunmen or bombers;[51]
- there were multiple eye-witness accounts, including many from journalists and others unconnected with the civil rights movement or nationalist politics, but no evidence of non-military fire except one shot after the killings were over;[52]
- there were many journalists and photographers in the area, but no photographs taken of gunmen or bombers;
- on the eye-witness accounts, on the medical evidence then available, and even on the evidence of soldiers to the Tribunal, some shootings had been of persons who were not on any account posing any immediate threat to anyone, being evidently unarmed (Jack Duddy,[53] Michael Bridge, Gerald McKinney), and/or prone on the ground (Pat Doherty), and/or completely incapacitated by a previous shot when killed (Jim Wray);
- no guns or traces of bombs were found on any of the dead or wounded with the sole exception of Gerald Donaghy, discussed below, forensic evidence which suggested otherwise having been withdrawn before the Saville Inquiry.[54]

---

[49] D. Walsh, 'The Bloody Sunday Tribunal of Inquiry: A Resounding Defeat for Truth, Justice and the Rule of Law', available at <http://cain.ulst.ac.uk> on the shortcomings of the Widgery Report. It was significantly as a result of Walsh's work that the Irish government pressurized the UK to reopen the Bloody Sunday matter.

[50] As A. Hegarty points out ('Truth, Law and Official Denial: The Case of Bloody Sunday' (2004) 15 *Criminal Law Forum* 246, n 41), 'One soldier accidentally shot himself in the foot but lied about how the injury had come about'. See 'Bloody Sunday Inquiry Transcript, day 305, 27–31' (4 Mar 2003) and Statement of Soldier Inq No 1255, paras 12–13.

[51] Sayle, n 48 above.

[52] Ibid: 'no evidence that any shots, petrol or nail bombs were fired at the Army, or that any of the crowd of civil rights marchers were armed'.

[53] Whose death is described by Father Edward (later Bishop) Daly in *Mister, Are You a Priest?* (Dublin: Four Courts Press, 2000).

[54] The many eye-witness accounts of the events include F. Grimaldi's *Blood in the Street* (Derry: Guildhall Press, 1998); Civil Rights Movement, *Massacre at Derry* (Derry: Civil Rights Movement, 1972); R. McClean, *The Road to Bloody Sunday* (Swords, Dublin: Ward River, 1983); D. Mullan, *Eyewitness Bloody Sunday* (Dublin: Wolfhound, 1997); and see also P. Pringle and P Jacobson, *Those are Real Bullets, Aren't They?* (London: Fourth Estate, 2000) and D. Walsh, *Bloody Sunday and the Rule of Law in Northern Ireland* (Dublin: Gill and Macmillan, 2000). See also British Irish Rights Watch, *'Bloody Sunday' Submission to the UN Special Rapporteur on Summary and Arbitrary*

Before the Saville Inquiry the MOD accepted that none of those shot on Bloody Sunday had been armed.

Murray Sayle, who travelled to Derry as part of the *Sunday Times*' Insight team and conducted extensive investigations on the ground, recounts the movement of people towards 'Free Derry Corner' for a meeting after the main part of the march, at which point armoured vehicles then began to accelerate towards the crowd, followed by foot soldiers and Jack Duddy (17) was fatally shot.[55] In his account of the events Edward, later Bishop, Daly recalls 'the revving up of engines... three or four Saracen armoured cars moving towards me at increasing speed', and a mass flight of civilians away from the troops towards Free Derry Corner:

I ran with the others but veered to my left towards the courtyard of Rossville Flats... As I was entering the courtyard, I noticed a young boy running beside me. I was running and he was running and, like me, looking back from time to time. He caught my attention because he was smiling or laughing. I do not know whether he was amused at my ungainly running or exhilarated by nervous excitement. He seemed about 16 or 17. I did not see anything in his hands. I didn't know his name then, but I later learned that his name was Jackie Duddy. When we reached the centre of the courtyard, I heard a shot and simultaneously this young boy, just beside me, gasped or groaned loudly. This was the first shot that I had heard since the two or three shots I had heard some time earlier in the afternoon. I glanced around and the young boy just fell on his face. He fell in the middle of the courtyard, in an area, which was marked out in parallel rectangles for car parking. My first impression was that he had been hit by a rubber bullet... I could not imagine that he had been struck by a live round...[56]

At about the same time as Jack Duddy was fatally shot, mother of 15 Peggy Deery was wounded so severely by a high velocity bullet that she almost lost her leg. The armoured troop carriers continued at speed towards Free Derry Corner and, on Sayle's account, 'Within the next few minutes a dozen more people were shot down and many wounded. Civilian witnesses describe a scene of horror in which the Saracens pulled up, apparently at random, soldiers jumped out and began shooting, apparently indiscriminately, at the panic-stricken crowd running frantically for their lives':

Executing the normal fire-and-movement tactic taught to British infantry (the trained and the untrained witnesses agree exactly on this, using different terms) the Paratroopers cleared the barricades in Rossville Street by shooting everyone on it or near it. [Michael] Kelly [17], William Nash [19], [John] Young [17] and [Michael] McDaid [17] were killed here—ex-Sergeant-Major Chapman saw three people hit and slump on the barrier. Everyone at the barrier, considered by Bogside people to be their main line of defence, was either dead or wounded... A section of Paratroopers running through the Little Diamond to link up with their comrades at the barricade got behind it—there was no one left alive to stop them—and began laying down a field of fire behind Rossville Street flats. In this shooting [Hugh] Gilmore [17] was killed; [Barry] McGuigan [41] who ran up to him was

---

Executions: The Murder of 13 Civilians by Soldiers of the British Army on 'Bloody Sunday', 30th January 1972 (1994), <http://cain.ulst.ac.uk/events/bsunday/birw.htm>.

[55] n 48 above.
[56] n 53 above.

killed, and [Pat] Doherty [31], crawling along at some distance to escape, was shot dead in the same line of fire.

Paratroopers leading the Little Diamond pincer movement ran into Glenfada court-yard, where a handful of demonstrators had taken refuge, and began shooting—a normal street-fighting tactic when entering a possible ambush area; in this shooting [Jim] Wray [22] was killed and [Joe] Friel [20] wounded. This section continued through to Abbey Park and repeated the clearing fire, killing Gerald Donaghy [17], Gerald McKinney [35] and William McKinney [26] . . . [57]

Eye-witness and medical evidence was that Jim Wray was shot in the back as he lay, helpless, on the ground. Dr Raymond McClean, a former medical officer in the RAF who tended to many of the dead and dying and attended the post mortems in the city's hospital, reports that Wray had been paralysed by the first bullet which hit him which 'did not damage the spinal canal, but could have created shock waves sufficient to have caused a temporary paralysis of both legs. The trajectory line of the second upper wound was consistent with his having been shot while lying on the ground with his head raised, apparently talking to others who were in hiding'.[58] And in the case of Gerald McKinney, who according to eye-witnesses had both his arms raised above his head when he was shot: 'Forensic evidence showed that this man was shot through the chest from left to right on the mid axillary line. It was very clear from the trajectory line of this bullet that this man must have had both arms raised, otherwise the fatal bullet must have penetrated one or both arms'.

[Kevin] McElhinney [17] was shot dead…in the centre of the [Rosville Flats car park]…medical evidence is that a high-velocity bullet entered his left buttock an inch from the anus and carried the length of the body and exited at the right side of the shoulder—a wound only possible if he was shot on hands and knees while crawling.

As McElhinney fell, Michael Bridge [25], a Civil Rights steward wearing a white arm-band, ran up to him, saw he was dead and, overcome with rage, turned towards the Saracen standing at the entrance of the parking lot, raised his arms and shouted: 'You murdering bastards.' A soldier standing next to the Saracen, he says, shot him in the thigh. We have studied a photograph of this incident taken by an amateur photographer; Bridges can be clearly seen with his arms outstretched in the attitude of someone shouting abuse. His hands are visible and they are empty.[59]

Meanwhile the Paras were blocking the entrance to Chamberlain Street. A young French photographer, Gilles Peress, who works for the famous Magnum photo agency, was running up Chamberlain Street behind fleeing demonstrators when, as he passed Eden Street, he saw a Paratrooper kneeling by a burned-out car. He raised his camera over his head and shouted: 'Press!' The soldier fired a single round at him. We have paced out this incident described by Peress and discovered a bullet-hole in the front of the house on the corner of Harvey Street and Chamberlain Street, which confirms his story and indicates the bullet went a few inches wide of his head…

After the shooting stopped, the Paratroopers began loading the dead, dying and wounded into the Saracens; lining up demonstrators against walls and searching them; and leading arrested groups away at gunpoint, accompanied by, in some cases, blows from

---

[57] n 48 above.
[58] n 54 above. See also accounts of Jim Wray's death in *Massacre at Derry*, n 54 above.
[59] This is consistent with the account in Edward Daly's 2000 book, n 53 above.

gun-butts and batons. These activities were all overlooked by Rossville Flats, where IRA snipers, had there been any, would have had easy targets. No eye-witness reports any shooting at the soldiers at this stage...[60]

On Sayle's account a handful of armed IRA men arrived on the scene after the shootings stopped: 'One of these men fired one pistol shot at long range towards the Army, but does not claim he hit any soldiers. This shot was the last one fired in the engagement and we believe the only one fired at the Army—we can find no witnesses, among dozens, who heard or saw any other'.

A few days after the slaughter in Derry, a public inquiry was established under the chairmanship of Lord Widgery, Lord Chief Justice, and a former British Army officer, to inquire into 'the events on Sunday 30 January which led to loss of life in connection with the procession in Londonderry on that day'.[61] The Tribunal, which sat in Coleraine (a Protestant town some 24 miles from Derry), held 20 sessions in February to March 1972 and interviewed 117 witnesses, as well as considering photographic evidence and over 200 statements, 'did not visit the scene of any of the shootings, nor did it commission any engineers' reports of the locations of any of the shootings, nor did it take evidence from victims who were still in hospital'.[62] The Treasury Solicitors acted as solicitors to the Inquiry and also instructed the barristers representing the Army. And particular difficulties were created by the fact that Widgery managed what should have been an inquisitorial inquiry as an adversarial contest between counsel for the army, on the one hand, and the two barristers representing not only all the deceased and the wounded, but the interests of the 'nationalist citizenry of Derry'. The most acute problem resulting from this judicial mismanagement was that, coupled as it was with non-disclosure to those barristers of crucial evidence upon which the soldiers could have been cross-examined to devastating effect, it sabotaged any proper fact-finding process.

The evidence which was withheld from barristers representing the victims of Bloody Sunday consisted of 41 statements made by the soldiers to the Military Police on the night of the shootings and, in some cases, on following days. When these statements were eventually released in 1996, it became apparent that there were very significant contradictions between them and the evidence given to the Inquiry. Those contradictions would have been evident to the Inquiry itself, Widgery and the Inquiry's counsel being in possession of the statements. But counsel for the Inquiry played almost no role in the soldiers' cross-examination and 'Even when the solicitor for the Army asserted in his closing address that the evidence given by the soldiers to the Tribunal did not differ from their original

[60] See also *Massacre at Derry*, n 54 above.
[61] Walsh, n 49 above, remarks that the memo of the meeting between the Prime Minister, the Lord Chancellor, and Lord Widgery actually records the Prime Minister telling Lord Widgery that: '[i]t had to be remembered that we were in Northern Ireland fighting not only a military war but a propaganda war'. See Hegarty, n 50 above, 211, on the fact that the rapid announcement of the Inquiry was 'at that time so stringently interpreted that the institution of the Tribunal silenced public debate about the matter in the United Kingdom'. As British Irish Rights Watch pointed out in 1994 (n 53 above, paras 5.2–5.6), Minister of State for Defence Lord Balniel and the Ministry of Defence made statements on the Army's version of events just prior to the announcement of the inquiry.
[62] Walsh, n 49 above.

statements, apart from one admitted instance, counsel for the Tribunal remained silent...'.[63] This also, as Walsh points out, makes all the more surprising Widgery's conclusion that 'in general the accounts given by the soldiers of the circumstances in which they fired and the reasons why they did so were ... truthful', a conclusion premised in significant part on their performance under cross-examination in which (as Widgery knew) the questioner had none of the cards. This conclusion was, further, only possible in view of the Tribunal's failure to take into account any civilian evidence: Eamonn McCann states that:

Widgery confined himself to the evidence of some eyewitnesses, refusing to hear the evidence of others. In writing his report, he then ignored much of the evidence which he had heard, and distorted a great deal of the rest—an examination of the text rules out the possibility of this having come about through misunderstanding, carelessness or unconscious bias.

In the days after Bloody Sunday...NICRA...gathered more than 700 eyewitness statements from civilians in Derry. Copies of these were presented to Widgery on 9 March. But instead of welcoming this reservoir of relevant information, Widgery, according to an internal tribunal memorandum dated 10 March, 'considered that the statements...had been submitted at this late stage to cause him the maximum embarrassment'. In fact the three inch thick file of statements had been delivered to the Treasury solicitor's office in London on 3 March, only 34 days after the event.

The 10 March memorandum records that 'only 15' of the statements were 'drawn to (Widgery's) attention'. It is not clear whether Widgery himself actually read any of these 15 statements. But on the basis of this knowledge, he is recorded saying of all 700 statements that 'he did not think that the people who wrote them could bring any new element to the proceedings'. The statements were discarded.[64]

Widgery published ten weeks after the Tribunal was established, and ran to a mere 36 pages. As Dermot Walsh later commented, the speed and brevity were very surprising given that the Tribunal's remit was 'to investigate the most serious allegations that had ever been made in peace time against the British Army since it was established'.[65] Widgery concluded, on 10 April 1972, that '[t]here is no reason to suppose that the soldiers would have opened fire if they had not been fired upon first'; and that '[s]oldiers who identified armed gunmen fired upon them in accordance with the standing orders in the Yellow Card', which orders were 'satisfactory'.[66] In reaching his conclusions, Widgery overlooked serious conflicts between the evidence of various of the military personnel, and such bizarre incidents as soldier F's having 'forgot[ten] to mention having shot dead [an] alleged gunman' and soldier H stating that he fired no fewer than 19 shots at a gunman who was standing behind a window which 'did not shatter during this barrage so that he did not get a clear picture of the gunman', the clear glass window at which

---

[63] Walsh, n 49 above.

[64] n 45 above.

[65] Ibid.

[66] 'Report of the Tribunal appointed to inquire into the events on Sunday, 30 January 1972, which led to loss of life in connection with the procession in Londonderry on that day' (HL 101, HC 220, April 1972).

he claimed to have shot displaying a single bullet hole. McCann records reports by soldiers of extended periods of gunfire during which they took refuge behind an armoured personnel carrier ('a bulkier vehicle than, say, a Ford Transit van') which, however, was unscathed (as were they) by the 'blizzard of bullets'.[67]

A further bizarre element of Widgery's conclusions related to Gerald Donaghy (17), on whose body it was alleged at the time that that four nail bombs had been recovered by the Army. The boy had been seen at the site of his shooting by a doctor, who found that he was still alive and, having searched his pockets for identification, recommended that he be taken to hospital at once. The car carrying Gerald Donaghy was stopped by the army who drove him to an Army medical post where he was pronounced dead by an army medical officer who had, according to Walsh, 'examined the body twice, actually opening the front of the trousers in the process'. Shortly after this, it was alleged that Soldier 127 found Donaghy to be carrying four nail bombs (one in each of the front pockets of his tight jeans and another in each of the breast pockets of his jacket, the right of which was so tight around said bomb that the bomb had to be cut out). One of the bombs 'found' on Donaghy was sticking visibly out of his pocket. Soldier 150, who had driven the boy to the Army medical post, later testified to the Saville Inquiry that he did not see any bombs on the boy and that he was 'sure that if there had been a nail bomb or bombs in the man's pocket I would have seen them'.[68] Widgery concluded nevertheless that the bombs had been in Donaghy's pockets all the time.[69]

V. The Aftermath

Direct rule was imposed on Northern Ireland in March 1972. Among the early actions taken by London were the replacement of the 1922 Act as the legal basis of internment with the Detention of Terrorists (Northern Ireland) Order 1972[70] and the establishment of the Diplock Commission to consider 'what arrangements for the administration of justice in Northern Ireland could be made in order to deal more effectively with terrorist organisations by bringing to book, otherwise than by internment by the Executive, individuals involved in terrorist activities'.[71] Publishing within seven weeks of appointment, the Commission took its evidence in London except for two two-day visits by Lord Diplock to Northern Ireland

---

[67] n 45 above.

[68] BBC Northern Ireland News (19 June 2000).

[69] The Saville Inquiry concluded, perhaps surprisingly in view of the evidence detailed at chapters 126–44 of the report, that (para 3.110) 'We have considered the substantial amount of evidence relating to this question and have concluded, for reasons that we give [chapter 145], that the nail bombs were probably on Gerald Donaghey when he was shot [though] we are sure that Gerald Donaghey was not preparing or attempting to throw a nail bomb when he was shot; and we are equally sure that he was not shot because of his possession of nail bombs. He was shot while trying to escape from the soldiers.'

[70] See Spjut, n 22 above for details at 719 and 728–31.

[71] 'Report of the Commission to Consider Legal Procedures to deal with Terrorist Activities in Northern Ireland' (1972) Cmnd 5185, para 1.

'during which he met members of the security forces on the ground'.[72] Neither the evidence received nor the names of those who submitted it were published.

Diplock concluded, in December 1972, that internment remained necessary to re-establish order given the difficulties presented to conviction by the intimidation of witnesses, and that the dangers of juror intimidation and the possibilities of perverse jury decisions necessitated the establishment of jury-less ('Diplock') courts. As Greer and White pointed out, these conclusions were not based on any systematic data and Diplock himself acknowledged that 'we have not had our attention drawn to complaints of convictions that were plainly perverse and complaints of acquittals which were plainly perverse are rare'.[73] But to complaints made at the time about the (lack of any) evidential base for his recommendations, Lord Diplock responded that 'When I see a fire starting...I send for the fire brigade, not a statistician'.[74]

The Diplock report recommended that, in such (juryless) trials as would occur, the burden of proof should be placed on the accused to disprove membership of an illegal organization or being in the vicinity of explosives or weapons discovered by the security forces. The courts should continue to accept the evidence of un-named and often absent security personnel and informers who would not be available for cross-examination on the part of the accused. Further:

A confession made by the accused should be admissible as evidence in cases involving the scheduled offences unless it was obtained by torture or inhuman or degrading treatment; if admissible it would then be for the court to determine its reliability on the basis of evidence given from either side as to the circumstances in which the confession had been obtained.[75]

Diplock's conclusions were immediately accepted by the Conservative government and the Northern Ireland (Emergency Provisions) Act 1973, later the Prevention of Terrorism (Temporary Provisions) Act 1974, passed.[76] The 1973 Act provided a new legal basis for internment, replacing the 1972 Order which had in turn replaced the Special Powers Act and Regulations. Neither the Act nor the Order which preceded it required anything more than suspicion that the person to be interned had been 'concerned in the commission or attempted commission of an act of terrorism or in the direction, organisation or training of people for the purposes of terrorism', there being no requirement that the suspicion be reasonable.[77]

The publication of the Diplock report marked the start of the policy of 'criminalization', that is, the removal of any legal distinctions between politically motivated and other criminal behaviour. Resistance to that policy culminated in the hunger strikes of 1980 and 1981. Over 300 cases a year were dealt with by Diplock

---

[72] Ibid, para 4.

[73] Ibid, paras 35 and 36.

[74] HL Debs, vol 344, col 706, cited in S. Greer and A. White, 'A Return to Trial by Jury', in A. Jennings (ed), *Justice under Fire: Abuse of Civil Liberties in Northern Ireland* (London: Pluto Press, 1990), 47, 58.

[75] n 71 above, conclusion, para 7k.

[76] See D. Bonner, 'Responding to Crisis: Legislating Against Terror' (2006) 122 *Law Quarterly Review* 602.

[77] In *Re McElduff* [1972] NI 1, dealing with the materially identical SPA provision.

courts at the peak of their activities, a figure which declined dramatically over the last decade, though as recently as June 2009 Derry solicitor Manmohan 'Johnny' Sandhu pleaded guilty before a Diplock court to inciting loyalist terrorists to murder in a case which resulted from covert police recordings of Sandhu in interviews with paramilitary suspects at a police station.[78]

The number of those detained began to fall immediately after the imposition of direct rule, but internment continued until Christmas 1975, this in part as a sop to loyalists.[79] The end of internment increased the pressure on courts to secure convictions of suspected terrorists. In addition to providing a new statutory basis for internment, the 1973 Act, like the special powers legislation which it replaced, provided a power of arrest on suspicion of being a terrorist. Suspects could be held for up to 72 hours, seven days with the sanction of the Secretary of State (the successful challenge to this in *Brogan v UK* resulted in an Article 15 derogation upheld by the ECtHR in *Brannigan v UK*[80]). Nor did the suspicion have to relate to any particular offence: in *McKee v Chief Constable for Northern Ireland*, the House of Lords ruled that an instruction from a superior officer was sufficient to satisfy the suspicion requirement under the emergency provisions legislation, thus insulating arrest decisions from judicial review and facilitating arrests for the purposes of interrogation (as distinct from charge).[81] Further, suspects were required to answer questions as to their identity and movements, and to provide any information they had relating to recent life-threatening terrorist incidents, and had no right to a solicitor for three days and until charged with a specific offence.

The Diplock courts relied heavily from the start on confession evidence (which, following Diplock's recommendation, was admissible unless proven to have been secured in breach of Article 3 of the ECHR). Interrogation centres opened at Castlereagh police station in Belfast and Gough barracks and, unsurprisingly perhaps, allegations of the continued use of the five techniques, as well as of beating and ill-treatment, continued to emerge throughout the 1970s. These were initially dismissed as 'mere propaganda' until the Bennett Inquiry, which reported in 1979, was triggered by an Amnesty International report in 1978 and concerns expressed by police surgeons as to the ill-treatment of prisoners. Bennett's Committee of Inquiry into Police Interrogation Procedures in Northern Ireland, whose remit precluded investigations into individual complaints, nevertheless reported in 1979 that

---

[78] *Limavady Chronicle* (11 June 2009): see *McE v Prison Service for NI & Anor* [2009] 1 AC 908, discussed by M. Requa, 'Defence Rights in the Shadow of RIPA: Covert Surveillance of Privileged Consultations after Re McE' (8 May 2009) 4 *Archbold News* 6. For discussion of the Diplock courts, see C. Carlton, 'Judging without Consensus: The Diplock Courts in Northern Ireland', (1981) 3 *Law and Policy* 225.

[79] Spjut, n 22 above, 717, citing his discussions with Whitelaw.

[80] Respectively (1989) 11 EHRR 117 and (1993) 17 EHRR 539.

[81] [1984] 1 WLR 1358, applying s 11(3) of the Northern Ireland (Emergency Provisions) Act 1978 (formerly s 10 of the 1973 Act), which allowed arrest on suspicion of terrorism. See more recently *O'Hara v Chief Constable of the RUC* [1997] AC 286 and see D. Walsh, 'Arrest and Interrogation', in Jennings, n 72 above, 27, 33. Legislative tightening after the Baker Report of 1987 was (see Walsh) largely thwarted by the decision of the Northern Ireland Court of Appeal in *ex p Lynch* [1980] NI 126. See also J. Finn, *Constitutions in Crisis: Political Violence and the Rule of Law* (Oxford: Oxford University Press, 1991), 89.

'Our own examination of medical evidence reveals cases in which injuries, whatever their precise cause, were not self-inflicted and were sustained in police custody'.[82] It also drew attention to the fact that 'Solicitors are not in practice admitted to see terrorist suspects before they are charged'[83] and noted that 'fully two-thirds of those detained under Section 11[[84]] were subsequently released without charge, thus indicating that the security forces used the provision primarily to detain individuals for whom they lacked enough evidence to charge, much less to convict'.[85]

Bennett made a number of recommendations as to prisoner treatment whose introduction, Hadden, Boyle, and Campbell record,[86] 'led to a dramatic decline in the number and seriousness of complaints... But, for the most part, the confessions obtained by prolonged interrogation continued to be accepted as the sole or primary basis for convictions', and such confessions continued to be admissible even if involuntarily provided, in the absence of proof of 'torture, inhuman or degrading treatment'.[87] According to Finn, writing in 1990: 'In over half the cases...the only significant evidence was the defendant's confession'.[88] Arrests for the purposes of interrogation remained the norm, the 1984 Review of the Operation of the Northern Ireland (Emergency Powers) Act 1978 (the Baker Report)[89] finding on the RUC's own figures that '76 percent of those arrested were released without charge. Indeed, the individual detained often was not the target of the investigation'.[90] And although the RUC agreed, post-Bennett, to let suspects see a solicitor after eight hours if practical, the force in fact 'cautioned its officers not to tell suspects that they could see their solicitors', the view being taken that access to legal advice 'would disrupt its efforts to create an environment conducive to intensive questioning', and 'The form attached to the front of each prisoner's file specifically instructed constables: "Under *no* circumstances must the Prisoner be asked 'Do you wish to have a Solicitor?' ".'[91]

VI. The Judicial Record

It is clear from the above that the judiciary did little to mitigate the draconian impact of the emergency provisions, even leaving aside the outrage of Widgery and the shortcomings of Parker and Diplock (Compton being ombudsman to the

[82] Cmnd 7497, paras 404 and 163, cited by T. Hadden, K. Boyle, and C. Campbell, 'Emergency Law in Northern Ireland: The Context', in Jennings, n 74 above, 1, 16.
[83] Ibid, para 404, cited by Hadden et al, ibid 13.
[84] EPA 1978, by this stage the provision permitting the arrest of those suspected of terrorism.
[85] Finn, n 81 above, 89.
[86] n 81 above, 9.
[87] As Finn, n 81 above, points out (71) 'The purpose... "was clearly to authorize the admission of statements obtained in breach of the common law rules..."'.
[88] n 81 above, 102. See also C. Walker and and B. Fitzpatrick, 'Holding Centres in Northern Ireland, the Independent Commissioner and the Rights of Detainees' (1999) *European Human Rights Law Review* 27.
[89] Cmnd 9222.
[90] Finn, n 81 above, 89.
[91] Ibid 88.

Northern Ireland Parliament at the time of his appointment). The ban on republican clubs, mentioned above, was challenged on the grounds that it was void for uncertainty (there being no definition of such clubs nor any requirement that they had any unlawful or seditious purpose). The challenge failed before the House of Lords in *McEldowney v Forde*,[92] this notwithstanding the fact (pointed out by Lord Peace, in dissent) that the inclusion of republican clubs within the banning regulation of necessity applied to associations whose activities were lawful 'since a[ny] club whose activities were unlawful was already dealt with under the previous regulations'.[93] In *in re McElduff*, the High Court in Belfast allowed a challenge to the legality of internments arising out of a failure to specify the provision of the Special Powers Act Regulations under which arrests were made,[94] but although this gave rise to multiple damages claims, no one was released as a result who was not immediately re-arrested on suspicion of terrorism and re-interned.[95] This was made possible by that court's refusal to read any requirement of reasonableness into the requirement for 'suspicion' in the power of arrest on suspicion of terrorism, this despite its acknowledgement that 'a person completely innocent [of] any crime could be arrested on the merest suspicion and then, since no time factor is imposed and no right of appeal or resort to the courts provided for in the regulations, held for an indefinite duration of time'.[96]

Finn points out that: 'the absence of a reasonable suspicion requirement... preclude[d] *habeas corpus* [or] ... effective review by *any* independent body on any question other than the good faith of the officer'. But '[p]erhaps more surprising has been the temerity of Northern Irish judges even in those cases where the relevant statutory provision itself specifies that suspicion must be reasonable'.[97] In a precursor to the long-discredited decision of the House of Lords in *Liversidge v Anderson*,[98] the Northern Irish High Court in *R (O' Hanlon) v Governor of Belfast Prison* had interpreted 'reasonable suspicion' under the Special Powers Act to mean *subjectively* reasonable suspicion.[99] And although arrest without warrant under the emergency provisions legislation required the arrestee to be informed promptly of the reason for his arrest,[100] in *ex parte Lynch* the High Court of Northern Ireland ruled that it was sufficient that a person arrested on suspicion of terrorism under the Prevention of Terrorism Act 1984 be notified that he was being arrested under that provision on suspicion of involvement in terrorist activities, and that the

---

[92] [1971] 1 AC 632. See more recently *R v Z (AG for Northern Ireland's Reference)* [2005] 2 WLR 1286, discussed by C. Walker in 'Terrorist Offences: Terrorism Act 2000 s.11(1)—belonging to proscribed organization' [2005] *Criminal Law Review* 985.

[93] Ibid 652.

[94] n 77 above.

[95] Finn, n 81 above, 90 and see McGuffin, *Internment*, n 30 above and K. Boyle, 'Internment and Natural Justice' (1971) 23 *Northern Ireland Legal Quarterly* 331.

[96] Boyle, ibid 334. See G. Marcus, 'Secret Witnesses' [1990] *Public Law* 207.

[97] Finn, n 81 above, 91.

[98] [1942] AC 206.

[99] (1922) 56 ILTR 170.

[100] This by virtue of the common law rules laid down by the House of Lords in *Christie v Leachinsky* [1947] AC 573.

reasonable suspicion which was required by that provision did not have to relate to any particular crime.[101]

There were occasional judicial stands against the executive. In February 1972, for example, in *Moore v Shillington and Ministry of Defence*, Judge Conaghan awarded the maximum sum possible for unlawful detention and ill-treatment to two of those interned in August 1971. The sum was only £300, but following the award a further group of 15 detainees achieved settlements in respect of assaults ranging between £250 and £15,000.[102] But this example is relatively isolated, and the judicial record relating to involuntary confessions was less than impressive. In *R v McCormick*, the High Court in Northern Ireland confirmed that a 'moderate degree of physical maltreatment for the purpose of inducing a person to make a statement' did not result in the inadmissibility of any resulting confession.[103] And:

In *R v. Tohill*[104] the trial judge accepted in evidence a statement taken from a 15-year-old who had been arrested at 3.30 a.m. and, in the judge's words, subjected to four hours of intensive interrogation during which the detectives became angry, expressed their disbelief in forceful language, and reduced the boy to tears on several occasions. Also in *McKearney*[105] the trial judge excluded a confession of membership of the IRA made by the accused in the first 14 interviews because he found that the accused had been subjected to torture and inhuman and degrading treatment [but] proceeded to admit a confession of attempted murder made in interviews 15 and 16 on the grounds that the effects of the earlier treatment had dissipated by this stage—despite the fact that only a few hours had elapsed between the confessions and that the accused remained in the same police station under the custody and control of the same police officers... [and in] *R v Culbert*[106] the Court of Appeal ruled that the failure of the police to comply with the Bennett recommendations, which were aimed at protecting those in police custody against physical ill-treatment, was not sufficient to take the resulting confession into the grey area where the judge might exercise his discretion to exclude.[107]

The Gardiner report of 1975 concluded that 'so long as the judicial discretion remains, we think the chances of...an unjust trial or an unsafe verdict are remote'.[108] Dermot Walsh, however, declared in 1990 that 'The reluctance of judges to accept that a confession may have been extracted by torture or inhuman or degrading treatment renders it virtually pointless for defendants even to attempt a challenge... 10,000 individuals have been convicted mainly on confession evidence in the Diplock courts', and condemned a 'supine' judiciary for creating 'by

---

[101] [1980] NILR 126.

[102] Ibid.

[103] (1977) NI 105, decision of McGonigal J, discussed by D. Walsh, n 79 above, 38; also discussing *R v O'Halloran* (1979) 2 NIJB (CA); *R v Hetherington* (1975) NI 160; *R v Milne* (1978) NI 110. See also P. Duffy, 'English Law and the European Convention on Human Rights' (1980) 29 *International and Comparative Law Quarterly* 585, 588–9.

[104] (1974) NIJB.

[105] Unreported, 1978.

[106] (1982) NIJB (CA).

[107] Walsh, n 81 above, 38–42 and see also Finn, n 81 above, 103–5.

[108] 'Report of a Committee to consider, in the context of civil liberties and human rights, measures to deal with terrorism in Northern Ireland' (1975) Cmnd 5847.

default...an environment in which the security forces can call the shots in the criminal process'.[109]

Concern over the coercive methods of interrogation and convictions based on ensuing confessions was to give way to consternation over the use of 'supergrasses' (mass informers) in the early to mid-1980s. The government always denied the existence of a supergrass 'system',[110] but by the end of 1982 at least 25 potential supergrasses had been recruited by the security forces and almost 600 people arrested on their evidence. The following year saw the first mass 'supergrass' trial, that involving Christopher Black. The trial, which lasted 120 days, involved 38 defendants of whom 22 were convicted in August 1983 and sentenced to more than 4,000 cumulative years in prison. Eighteen of these convictions were overturned on appeal in July 1986, as were the April 1983 convictions on the evidence of loyalist Joseph Bennett, in the latter case in December 1984. Also overturned on appeal were the convictions arising from the evidence of the last of the supergrasses, Harry Kirkpatrick, after those concerned had spent a year in prison post-conviction (this in each case in addition to long periods on remand). Stephen Greer records that 'Several of these defendants were shunted from one supergrass to another either as a result of having been acquitted in one case or the evidence against them having been retracted. Three of the accused in the *Kirkpatrick* trial, for example, were implicated by five successive supergrasses and spent nearly four years in custody before being found guilty of any offence'.[111] Greer and others pointed out that the supergrass system 'facilitated a form of "internment by remand"'.[112]

In 1985, in a House of Lords Debate on the use of supergrasses,[113] Lord Longford called for the immediate termination of 'the system [which is] totally contrary to ordinary ideas of legal justice and...calculated to bring the whole legal system of Northern Ireland into disrepute', relying on the extraordinarily high rates of retraction by supergrasses (15 of 25 in the preceding four years), the lack of corroborative evidence in supergrass cases; 'the grant of complete immunity to dangerous criminals who have committed very serious crimes'; 'the lack of disclosure of the arrangements made between the authorities and supergrasses'; the absence of juries in supergrass trials, this having the bizarre effect that the judge had to issue a warning to himself as to the unreliability of accomplice evidence); the delays associated with the enormous supergrass trials, and the amount of time that those charged ended up spending in custody (generally on no evidence other than the word of the supergrass, in the vast majority of cases being eventually freed after acquittal at

---

[109] n 81 above, 40 and 44. S. Greer, '"Supergrasses" and the legal system in Britain and Northern Ireland' (1986) 102 *Law Quarterly Review* 198, 233. Cf B. Dickson 'Protection of Human Rights—Lessons from Northern Ireland' (2000) *European Human Rights Law Review* 213, 219.

[110] See eg Parliamentary Under-Secretary of State for Northern Ireland, Lord Lyell, in HL Debs, vol 462, cols 330–1 (3 Apr 1985).

[111] n 109 above, 230.

[112] Ibid, citing Greer, 'Internment with a Judge's Stamp' (Apr 1984) *Fortnight*; D. Walsh, *The Use and Abuse of Emergency Legislation in Northern Ireland* (London: The Cobden Trust, 1983), ch 5.

[113] HL Debs, vol 462, cols 306–35 (3 Apr 1985).

trial or on appeal, having undergone years of quasi internment), and 'the sheer size of many recent supergrass trials'.[114]

Supergrass trials ended in December 1986 with a settlement in the appeals from the Kirkpatrick convictions. By this stage it had become apparent that any convictions relying on the evidence of such witnesses were vulnerable to appeal, and so it could be said that the judiciary caused the system to collapse. It should not be forgotten, however, that this collapse did not happen without significant loss of liberty on the part of those who were acquitted either at trial or on appeal in circumstances such that the only evidence against them was the say-so of a witness with every motive to lie. Among those convicted were the seven found guilty by Lord Chief Justice Lowry in October 1983 on the evidence of supergrass Kevin McGrady, despite his own declaration that McGrady's evidence was 'bizarre, incredible and contradictory'.[115]

VII. The Final Solution: State Killings and the Absence of Accountability

Shortly after the abandonment of supergrasses came the abolition of the right to silence in Northern Ireland,[116] this, Steven Greer suggests, as a by-product of the requirement that Diplock courts produce reasoned judgments, thus impeding the covert drawing of inferences from silence.[117] But perhaps most alarming of all the events in Northern Ireland have been the allegations of state involvement in executions of suspected terrorists both directly (through the alleged 'shoot to kill' policy of the 1980s) and by collusion between the security forces and loyalist terrorists in the murders, *inter alia*, of solicitors Rosemary Nelson and Pat Finucane. The incidents are too numerous and most of the facts too unclear as yet to detail here, but from 1982 there were a significant number of cases in which the security forces appear to have been involved in the deliberate execution of suspected republicans. The first six deaths (Gervaise McKerr, Sean Burns, Eugene Toman, Michael

---

[114] Ibid, cols 306–8. See also Lord Gifford, cols 313–16.

[115] *Fortnight: An Independent Review For Northern Ireland* (2–15 June 1986) 5. See also Greer, n 109 above, 235 who points out that '88 per cent of the 64 accused in th[e first] three trials were found guilty. This seemed to indicate that the courts were prepared to co-operate with the supergrass strategy more or less as it stood, thereby making it a highly efficient method of obtaining convictions…61 per cent. of these convictions were secured on the uncorroborated evidence of the supergrasses…[and] judges were prepared to trust the supergrasses' uncorroborated evidence despite the fact that both it and other aspects of the prosecution case in each trial contained specific flaws, in addition to those generally associated with the evidence of supergrasses.'

[116] By the Criminal Evidence (NI) Order 1988, a precursor to similar action taken in Great Britain by the Criminal Justice and Public Order Act 1994.

[117] *Supergrasses: A Study in Anti-terrorist Law Enforcement in Northern Ireland* (Oxford: Clarendon Press, 1995), 209. Greer also notes, at 206, that 'In May 1993 the then Chief Constable of the RUC outlined seven measures, including making accomplice evidence more readily admissible against the accused, that he said were being considered at a senior level within the Northern Ireland Office and which were necessary to tackle terrorism more effectively.' On 29 December 2008 the *Times* reported that the Metropolitan Police 'have turned to "supergrasses" once again in the fight against organised crime'.

Tighe, Seamus Grew, and Roddy Carroll) took place within a period of a month in late 1982.[118] The killings have resulted in numerous applications to the European Court of Human Rights, which has made repeated findings as to the inadequacy of domestic investigations;[119] a report by Amnesty which expressed concern that 'some of the killings by the security forces may have resulted from a deliberate policy at some official level to eliminate, or permit elimination of, rather than to arrest individuals whom they identified as members of armed opposition groups';[120] the highly publicized Stalker affair (the then Assistant Chief Constable of Manchester was removed from the inquiry on disciplinary charges, which were subsequently dismissed, just at the point at which he believed he would obtain access to a tape recording of one of the killings);[121] and the longest running inquests in history.

The alleged 'shoot to kill' tactics were exported to Gibraltar in March 1988 where they resulted in the deaths of three IRA activists, an inquest of considerably wider scope than would have occurred in Northern Ireland, and eventual findings on the part of the European Court of Human Rights that the UK had breached the substantive Article 2 rights of the dead.[122] The following year Pat Finucane, a very prominent criminal defence solicitor, was shot dead by loyalist paramilitaries. Finucane had received death threats from the RUC via his clients prior to his death and allegations of collusion between security forces and loyalist paramilitaries were made at the time of his death and since.

The inquest into the deaths of Gervaise McKerr and other early alleged 'shoot to kill' victims was opened in August 1984 after three RUC men had been acquitted of the murder of Eugene Toman[123] (Lord Justice Gibson commending the three, who had killed unarmed men by firing at least 109 rounds of ammunition into the car in which the men were travelling, 'for their courage and determination in bringing the three deceased men to justice, in this case to the final court of justice'[124]). The inquest was adjourned pending completion of the Stalker/Sampson investigation and two sets of judicial review proceedings which reached

---

[118] For the legal background to these killings see R.J. Spjut 'The "Official" Use of Deadly Force by the Security Forces against Suspected Terrorists: Some Lessons from Northern Ireland' [1986] *Public Law* 38.

[119] *McKerr v UK* (2002) 34 EHRR 553; *Kelly v UK* (*App no 30054/96*) [2001] *Inquest Law Review* 125; *Jordan v UK* (2003) 37 EHRR 2; *Shanagan v UK App no 37715/97* [2001] *Inquest Law Review* 149. See also *McShane* (2002) 35 EHRR 23. For discussion see F. Aolain, 'Truth Telling, Accountability and the Right To Life in Northern Ireland' (2002) *European Human Rights Law Review* 572.

[120] Amnesty International, *Northern Ireland: Killings by the Security Forces and 'Supergrass' Trials* (1988), 59 cited in Jennings, n 74 above, p xix.

[121] Stalker later wrote in his account of the events that 'There was no written instruction, nothing pinned up on a notice board. But there was a clear understanding on the part of the men whose job it was to pull the trigger that that was what was expected of them', J. Stalker, *Stalker* (London: Penguin, 1988).

[122] See *McCann v UK* (1996) 21 EHRR 97. The same year (1988) saw the imposition of the broadcasting ban later (unsuccessfully) challenged before the House of Lords and the ECtHR in the *Brind* litigation (*R v Secretary of State for the Home Department, ex p Brind* [1991] 1 AC 696; *Brind and McLaughlin v United Kingdom* 77-A DR 42 (1994), E Com HR).

[123] *R v Robinson, Montgomery and Brannigan* (1984), unreported.

[124] *McKerr v UK*, n 119 above, para 20.

the House of Lords;[125] resumed and was adjourned again in May 1992; was closed in January 1994 and reopened in March 1994, but abandoned six months later after the Secretary of State issued a public interest immunity certificate stating that disclosure of the Stalker/Sampson report would cause serious damage to the public interest. In March 1993 Gervaise McKerr's mother lodged an application with the European Court of Human Rights, which ruled in May 2001 that the UK had breached the procedural obligations arising under Article 2 and awarded her £10,000 as just satisfaction in respect of frustration, distress, and anxiety. The government took no steps to hold a further investigation and in June 2002 McKerr's brother sought judicial review of the continuing failure to provide an Article 2-compliant investigation. The application was dismissed by the High Court in Northern Ireland, an appeal allowed by the Northern Ireland Court of Appeal, but the first instance decision was reinstated by the House of Lords in 2004, which ruled that the procedural breach of Article 2 found by the ECtHR in the *McKerr* decision was brought to an end by the payment made by the UK government to the family, and that the Human Rights Act did not apply in respect of deaths predating its implementation.[126] As Aidan O'Neill QC has pointed out, this decision[127] is inconsistent with the House's earlier case law[128] and, further, with the subsequent decision in *Brecknell v United Kingdom* in which the ECtHR ruled that the procedural obligations imposed by Article 2 were of a continuing nature.[129]

The coroner at Pat Finucane's inquest did not permit his widow to make a statement recounting the alleged RUC threats to her husband's life, this on the basis that they were not relevant to the 'how' of his death.[130] Despite no fewer than three reports by John, now Lord, Stevens of Kirkwhelpington, into the allegations of collusion over a period of some 14 years, and his eventual conclusions that there was collusion both in the murder of Pat Finucane and in that of Brian Adam Lambert (a 19-year-old Protestant student shot by loyalist paramilitaries in 1987 having been mistaken for a Catholic[131]), no convictions have resulted. In July 2003 the ECtHR ruled that the UK had breached the procedural obligations imposed by Article 2 of the Convention in connection with Pat Finucane's death, this because it had failed to carry out an independent, effective, and public investigation into the killing in respect of which allegations of state involvement had been made.[132] In 2000 Amnesty International had called for a public inquiry into the affair, as (in 2004) did retired Canadian Judge Peter Cory, who was appointed by the British and Irish governments to investigate collusion.

---

[125] *McKerr v Armagh Coroner* [1990] 1 WLR 649 and *R v Attorney General for Northern Ireland, ex p Devine* [1992] 1 WLR 262.

[126] *In re McKerr* [2004] 1 WLR 807.

[127] Like those in *Jordan v Lord Chancellor* [2007] 2 AC 226, and *R (Hurst) v London Northern District Coroner* [2007] 2 AC 189.

[128] *R (Amin) v Secretary of State for the Home Department* [2004] 1 AC 653, *R (Middleton) v West Somerset Coroner* [2004] 2 AC 182 and *R (Sacker) v West Yorkshire Coroner* [2004] 1 WLR 796.

[129] 'The European Court and the Duty to Investigate Deaths' (21 Sept 2009) *The Journal Online*.

[130] See similarly *Shanaghan*, n 119 above, para 31.

[131] 'Stevens Enquiry 3' (17 Apr 2003), para 4.7.

[132] *Finucane v UK* (2003) 37 EHRR 29. The case was the first of its kind. See also *Brecknell v UK* (2008) 46 EHRR 42, *McCartney v UK App no 34575/04* and *Reavey v UK App no 346040/04*.

The Cory recommendations resulted in the ongoing inquiry into the death of Robert Hamill, a Catholic man kicked to death in a sectarian attack in April 1997, allegedly under the noses of RUC, but Pat Finucane's family have rejected the inquiry offered into the solicitor's death because it would be carried out under the Inquiries Act 2005, which allows the executive to determine the inquiry's terms of reference and whether, and to what extent, it is held in public; to appoint its chair, to decide to block disclosure of evidence, and to dismiss any member of the inquiry. Also by contrast with the position under the previous Tribunals and Inquiries Acts of 1971 and 1992, 2005 Act inquiries report to the Minister rather than to Parliament, and the Minister can alter their terms of reference at will and can decide whether or not to publish any report.[133] Ironically, the introduction of the 2005 Act was justified in part by reference to the extraordinary expense and length of the Saville Inquiry, whose Chairman is on record as stating that the 2005 Act 'Makes a very serious inroad into the independence of any inquiry; and is likely to damage or destroy public confidence in the inquiry and its find-ings...As a Judge, I must tell you that I would not be prepared to be appointed as a member of an inquiry that was subject to a provision of this kind.' These criti-cisms are perhaps all the more interesting given the criticisms which were made of Saville's apparent tendency himself to favour the executive over others involved in the Bloody Sunday Inquiry.[134]

Both Justice Cory and Amnesty International have reiterated the call for a fully independent inquiry, the former stating that 'the new Act would make a meaningful inquiry impossible' in the Finucane case and the latter calling on the British judiciary to boycott any inquiry under the Act which in its view 'empow-ers the UK authorities to block public scrutiny of state actions'.[135] And in May 2006 the US House of Representatives called on the UK government to widen the scope of the 2005 Act and hold an independent public inquiry into Finucane's death, a move welcomed by Irish Minister for Foreign Affairs, Dermot Ahern.[136] On 6 June 2007 the Council of Europe Ministers reiterated a call made in 2005 to the UK to take all necessary steps to 'achieve concrete and visible progress' in the alleged shoot to kill and collusion cases,[137] including that of Pat Finucane. But on 26 June 2007 the *Independent* reported allegations of a 'scandalous cover-up after a decision not to prosecute police officers or soldiers in connection with [his] assassination'.

---

[133] For critiques see <http://www.birw.org/Summary%20and%20Critique.html>; <http://www. publicinquiries.org/introduction/the_inquiries_act_2005>.

[134] See in particular his committal for contempt of court of the only person yet to have been jailed as a result of Bloody Sunday: 'PIRA 9', a republican who was jailed in January 2005 for refusing to give evidence to the Inquiry. This action has been contrasted with Saville's tolerance of dissembling by former Prime Minister Edward Heath and the refusal of a number of military personnel to answer questions or even enter the witness box: see Hegarty, n 50 above, 230–43.

[135] <http://www.wraytimes.com/group27/collusion.html>.

[136] RTE (Friday, 19 May 2006).

[137] CM/ResDH(2007)73, see <https://wcd.coe.int/ViewDoc.jsp?id=1423217&Site=CM> and also see CMRes/DH(2005)20 (23 February 2005). All of the cases concerned killings by the police or armed forces in Northern Ireland or alleged collusion between the security forces and the killers.

In July 2007 it was reported that the British government had asked Northern Ireland police ombudsman to re-open the *McKerr* ('shoot to kill') investigation, but it became apparent almost immediately, however, that there were questions as to her jurisdiction to investigate. In March of that year the House of Lords had ruled, in *McCaughey v Chief Constable of PSNI*,[138] that police were placed by the Coroners' Act 1959 under a continuing duty to supply to the coroner such information as they had at the time of notifying him of the death or were thereafter able to obtain. Coroner John Leckey reopened the inquests but had to adjourn in October 2007 after Sir Hugh Orde, by this stage Chief Constable of the Police Service for Northern Ireland (PSNI), refused to hand over the Stalker/Sampson reports. On 3 December 2007 Leckey announced that Orde had agreed to allow him to see the reports in their 'entirety'. A subsequent challenge by the PSNI to Leckey's order, that the force disclose redacted copies of the reports to the families of the deceased, failed in the High Court in 2010.[139]

VIII. Conclusions

It is difficult to avoid a sense of pessimism given the fact that many of the sores described above are still weeping. The record of the judiciary post-Human Rights Act has been no better than patchy. Grandstanding decisions such as that in *A v Secretary of State for the Home Department*, however satisfying at the time, have had limited impact in practice given the replacement of internment with a system of control orders which, in some cases and in some respects, have been even worse.[140] Most of the challenges to control orders failed in the lower courts even after the decision of the House of Lords in *Secretary of State for the Home Department v JJ*, in which that court ruled that control orders imposing 18-hour curfews, amongst other restrictions, breached Article 5 of the Convention.[141] In *MB*, decided on the same day as *JJ*,[142] the House effectively gave a clean bill of health to the Orwellian special advocate system, an approach with which the ECtHR was to disagree in *A v UK*, with the result that many of the control order cases have been re-opened given the reliance of the courts on closed evidence.[143]

In *A v Secretary of State for the Home Department (No 2)*, the House of Lords confirmed (as the Court of Appeal had failed to do) that evidence extracted by means of torture was inadmissible in the domestic courts.[144] By a majority, however, the House went on to rule that evidence alleged to result from torture

---

[138] [2007] 2 AC 226.

[139] *Re Chief Constable of PSNI's Application* [2010] NIQB 66.

[140] [2005] E AC 68 and see K. D. Ewing and J. Tham, 'The Continuing Futility of the Human Rights Act', [2009] *Public Law* 668, 670–8.

[141] [2008] 1 AC 385 and cf *Secretary of State for the Home Department v E* [2008] 1 AC 499, *MB* [2008] AC 440. See Ewing and Tam, ibid 678–85 for discussion. For lower court decisions see eg *SSHD v AU* [2009] All ER (D) 93 (Mar); *SSHD v AR* [2009] All ER (D) 125 (Jan).

[142] [2008] AC 440.

[143] *App no 3455/05*, (19 Feb 2009).

[144] [2006] 2 AC 221.

should be excluded only if the relevant court was satisfied on inquiry that it had been so obtained. As Lord Bingham pointed out, dissenting on this point, the burden imposed by the majority:

> ...is a test which, in the real world, can never be satisfied. The foreign torturer does not boast of his trade. The security services, as the Secretary of State has made clear, do not wish to imperil their relations with regimes where torture is practised. The special advocates have no means or resources to investigate. The detainee is in the dark. It is inconsistent with the most rudimentary notions of fairness to blindfold a man and then impose a standard which only the sighted could hope to meet. The result will be that, despite the universal abhorrence expressed for torture and its fruits, evidence procured by torture will be laid before SIAC because its source will not have been 'established'.[145]

Also worthy of note in the judicial roll of shame are the decisions in *R (Gillan) v Commissioner of Police of the Metropolis* in which Lords Brown and Hope appeared to go out of their way to express approval for racial profiling,[146] and *Austin & Anor v Metropolitan Police Commissioner* in which the House of Lords ruled that the detention by police, for a period of up to seven hours, of protestors and members of the public for the purposes of crowd control did not engage Article 5 of the Convention as long as the measures were not 'arbitrary', were resorted to in good faith, were proportionate and were enforced for no longer than was reasonably necessary.[147] That decision, apparently based on the view that those who had assembled at the relevant demonstration were 'up for trouble', or at least aware that trouble was likely, was seized upon by the Metropolitan Police to justify its tactics at the 2009 May Day demonstrations which resulted in the death of newspaper vendor Ian Tomlinson and the recorded use of arbitrary violence by police against peaceful protestors.

Such cause for optimism as there may be is limited, and has arisen, perhaps perversely, out of alleged murders of Iraqi civilians by British troops in 2004. In *R (Al Sweady) v Secretary of State for Defence*, a three-judge Administrative Court awarded interim costs of £1,000,000 against the respondent, which had made false PII claims in respect of material which was already in the public domain by virtue of having been disclosed at the court martial arising from the death of Baha Mousa. The court further declared that 'until such time as the MOD has demonstrated that its procedures have remedied the risk of the kinds of errors occurring that occurred in this case it will, in our view, be incumbent on the Courts to approach the content of any [PII] Certificate...with very considerable caution'.[148] When the defendant was unable to produce the material required of it, the relief sought by the claimants, the promise of a Convention-compliant investigation, was obtained. The court went out of its way, however, to emphasize the importance of disclosure by the state in human rights cases in which the facts were in dispute, this because of its

---

[145] Ibid, para 59. Lords Nicholls and Hoffmann also dissented on this point (there being a panel of seven).
[146] [2006] 2 AC 307. See the decision of the ECtHR in *Gillan & Quinton v United Kingdom, App no 4158/05* (12 Jan 2010).
[147] [2009] 1 AC 564.
[148] [2009] EWHC 1687 (Admin), para 48, [2009] EWHC 2387 (Admin).

recognition that the application to such claims of the normal approach to judicial review (in which disclosure and cross-examination are rare and factual disputes are resolved in favour of the respondent) 'would have the ... far-reaching consequences that a defendant would always succeed if sued for an infringement of human rights which was disputed'.[149] This being the case, cross-examination would be necessary in cases where '"*hard-edged*" questions of fact' were at issue, with disclosure 'to enable effective and proper cross-examination to take place'. Whereas 'In practice, orders for disclosure in judicial review cases have usually been unnecessary [in part] ... because the defendant normally complies with this well-recognised duty to make disclosure',[150] the defendant's approach in the instant case, in which the duty of candour was particularly high given the breaches of Articles 2 and 3 alleged, had been lamentable and the witness upon whom the defendant sought to rely 'most unsatisfactory'.[151]

It may be that the *Al-Sweady* judgments indicate a judicial appetite to hold the executive to account. Such appetite has been noticeably lacking at many points in the past and is all the more necessary in view of the changes made by the Inquiries Act 2005 to the framework for public inquiries. Had the courts adopted a different approach in Northern Ireland, it may be that we would not have had to wait almost 40 years for a legal response to Bloody Sunday.

[149] [2009] EWHC 2387 (Admin), para 18.
[150] Ibid, para 23.
[151] Ibid 52.

10

Constitutional Law Meets Comparative Politics: Socio-economic Rights and Political Realities

Ran Hirschl and Evan Rosevear

It is obviously contrary to the law of nature, however it may be defined, for a child to command an old man, for an imbecile to lead a wise man, and for a handful of people to gorge themselves on superfluities while the starving multitude lacks necessities.[1]

Three-quarters of the world's written constitutions make reference to a right to education, and nearly half to a right to health care.[2] Most also include a generic protection of 'the right to life' or of 'human dignity'. And, several key regional and international human rights regimes purport to protect a variety of subsistence rights. This has brought about an expanding corpus of, and an increasing interest in, socio-economic rights jurisprudence at both the international and the domestic levels. As one comprehensive collection has recently put it: 'in the space of two decades, social rights have emerged from the shadows and margins of human rights jurisprudence'.[3]

Despite this flurry of constitutional innovation, little attention has been given by legal academics to questions such as what prompts countries to constitutionally entrench socio-economic rights, the place of such rights in a larger scheme of the welfare state, or the non-idealist, 'realpolitik' factors that explain the variance in judicial interpretation of socio-economic rights provisions or divergence in the actual distributive consequences of social rights regimes. In this chapter, we suggest that the variance in constitutional protections of socio-economic rights— either through constitutionalization or through judicial interpretation—cannot be understood in isolation from the political and economic contexts within which such protections evolve, function, and mutate. We argue that to facilitate the

---

[1] J. Rousseau, 'Discourse on the Origins of Inequality Part I', in M. L. Morgan (ed), *Classics of Moral and Political Theory*, 3rd edn (Indianapolis: Hackett Publishing, 2001), 755.

[2] V. Gauri and D. Brinks (eds), *Courting Social Justice: Judicial Enforcement of Social and Economic Rights in the Developing World* (New York: Cambridge University Press, 2008), 1.

[3] See eg M. Langford (ed), *Social Rights Jurisprudence: Emerging Trends in International and Comparative Law* (New York: Cambridge University Press, 2008).

realization of socio-economic rights it is necessary to go beyond the largely insular constitutional discourse concerning such rights to identify the political and judicial conditions that are conducive to such realization. To truly 'rescue' socio-economic rights, a more realist approach is required, one that goes beyond idealist normative accounts or insular constitutional discourse to understand these rights as part of a larger matrix of public policy, economics, and politics.

A promising departure point for such a realist account is provided by Mark Tushnet's recent book, *Weak Courts, Strong Rights*.[4] In the first section of this chapter, we assess Tushnet's politically sober account of the forms of judicial review that are likely to be most conducive to the realization of socio-economic rights. In the second section, we explore several other extra-judicial—'realpolitik'—factors and political macro-variables that ought to be taken into account when assessing the prospects for advancing the status of such rights. Specifically, we argue that there seem to be multiple paths and trajectories to the realization (or neglect) of social welfare rights, of which constitutionalization is merely one aspect. In the third section, we examine the possible impact of 'strategic' behaviour by courts on judicial interpretation of socio-economic rights, for example attempts to avoid confrontation with powerful political stakeholders or to expand the ambit of judicial influence by acting on a salient social issue when elected officials will not.

Taken as whole, the examples we discuss herein raise interesting questions concerning the extra-judicial (eg historical, cultural, economic, ideological, or political) determinants of a given polity's commitment to a relatively generous welfare regime. In particular, they illuminate the inexplicable gap between the well-developed body of comparative politics scholarship, qualitative and quantitative, concerning the determinants and effects of the welfare state on the one hand, and the generally inward-looking, court-centric literature on the constitutional protection of positive rights on the other. Not only does the latter type of scholarship overlook (or remain unaware of) the theoretical claims and empirical findings of pertinent political science literature, it also tends to operate under the assumption that constitutional protection of social welfare rights is a predominantly constitutional issue, not instrumental or reflective of social and political trends within the polity, either at present or at the time of constitutional entrenchment. We conclude by suggesting that the possibilities for a fruitful dialogue between comparative constitutional law and comparative politics seem quite promising. No account of the prospects for progressive realization of socio-economic rights is complete without such a non-doctrinal, inter-disciplinary conversation.

I. The 'Weak Courts, Strong Rights' Argument

One of the more interesting features of the global convergence towards constitutional supremacy and active judicial review has been the emergence of innovative mechanisms designed to address and mitigate the tension between rigid

[4] M. Tushnet, *Weak Courts, Strong Rights: Judicial Review and Social Welfare Rights in Comparative Constitutional Law* (Princeton: Princeton University Press, 2007).

constitutionalism and judicial activism on the one hand, and fundamental demo-cratic governing principles on the other. This bundle of institutional means has been loosely termed 'weak-form' judicial review.[5] Whereas under 'strong-form' judicial review (the approach established in the United States) judicial interpret-ations of the constitution are binding on all branches of government, 'weak-form' review allows the legislature and executive to limit or override constitutional rul-ings by the judiciary—as long as they do so openly and explicitly.

Two oft-cited examples of such mechanisms are found in the Canadian Charter of Rights and Freedoms: the 'limitation clause' (section 1) and 'override' or 'not-withstanding' clause (section 33). Section 1 carries an inbuilt emphasis on judicial balancing between rights provisions and other equally important imperatives. Very few constitutional catalogues of rights reflect, in such a clear fashion, the notion that no constitutional right is 'absolute'. Rights litigation and jurisprudence in the shadow of section 1 are inherently attentive to public policy considerations that are 'demonstrably justified in a free and democratic society' and that in most other constitutional democracies would fall beyond the purview of rights jurisprudence per se. The embedded subjection of Canadian rights jurisprudence to broad public policy considerations has led to sound, middle-of-the-road SCC judgments on a host of potentially divisive issues.

However, Canada is not alone in this trend towards weak-form, dialogi-cal review. Persisting political traditions of parliamentary sovereignty were also taken into account by the framers of the new constitutional arrangements in other Westminster-style political systems such as Britain, Israel, South Africa, and New Zealand (to mention only a few examples). A noteworthy example of a weak-form review is provided by the British Human Rights Act, 1998 (entered into effect in October 2000), which effectively subjects British public bodies to the provisions of the European Convention on Human Rights (ECHR). The Act requires the courts to interpret 'as far as it is possible to do so' existing and future legislation in accord-ance with the Convention. If the higher courts in Britain decide that an Act of Parliament prevents someone exercising their ECHR rights, judges make what is termed a 'declaration of incompatibility'. Such a declaration puts Ministers under political pressure to change the law (or so it is hoped). Formally, it does not override existing Acts of Parliament; however, Ministers must state whether each new piece of legislation that they introduce complies with the ECHR. What is more, the Act also provides for a fast-track procedure that allows Parliament to repeal or amend legislation found incompatible with the ECHR.

At the core of Mark Tushnet's rich and thought-provoking book, *Weak Courts, Strong Rights*, stands the juxtaposition of the idea of weak-form judicial review with the problems of legitimacy deficit, injusticiability, and lack of enforcement capacity that are so often drawn upon to explain judicial passivity in matters con-cerning social welfare rights. Tushnet argues, quite counter-intuitively, that a

---

[5] See eg M. Tushnet, 'Weak-Form Judicial Review and "Core" Civil Liberties' (2006) 41 *Harvard Civil Rights—Civil Liberties Law Review* 1; J. Waldron, 'The Core Case Against Judicial Review' (2006) 115 *Yale Law Journal* 1346, at 1354–9; S. Gardbaum, 'The New Commonwealth Model of Constitutionalism' (2001) 49 *American Journal of Comparative Law* 707.

weak-form judicial review may be more suitable and effective than a strong review model for advancing progressive notions of subsistence rights and, by extension, of distributive justice more generally.

To fully appreciate this intriguing argument, a few words on the status of social welfare rights in the United States are warranted. Unlike other countries (notably South Africa, Belgium, Spain, and Brazil), the United States has no explicit constitutional guarantees of subsistence rights such as basic income, education, housing, or health care. Moreover, unlike in other countries (eg India), such rights have not been protected under more generic provisions such as those of human dignity and/or security of the person. Indeed, the struggle for realization of subsistence social welfare rights through constitutional litigation in the United States has long sunk into constitutional oblivion. Liberal and progressive American constitutional scholars—perhaps with the exception of Mark Tushnet himself—have given up on any attempt to advance progressive notions of distributive justice through constitutional jurisprudence. As Sotirios Barber suggests, the most common view on both the right and the left in America is that the federal constitutional duties of public officials are limited to respecting negative liberties and maintaining processes of democratic choice.[6]

The concept of a judicially enforceable right to minimum welfare was somewhat more prevalent in American constitutional discourse a few decades ago, before the 'chastening' of such aspirations during the 1980s.[7] In the American experience, subsistence rights have, at best, been judicially 'under-enforced' norms.[8] Americans have thus been forced to pursue other, extra-judicial, means of enforcing these constitutional norms. Because many Americans believe that the courts cannot possibly enforce subsistence rights guarantees, Tushnet argues that a weak-form judicial review, which leaves the final word to legislatures, may actually allow for de facto stronger social welfare rights protection under American constitutional law.

Arguably, one of Tushnet's main achievements is his ability to go beyond the traditional call common among progressive activists to formally constitutionalize socio-economic rights or to (judicially) interpret them in a more generous fashion. Instead, Tushnet advances a more nuanced and politically sober account of the institutional conditions that are likely to be most conducive to the realization of such rights. This reflects the transition from a principled yet unrealistic approach

---

[6] S. A. Barber, *Welfare and the Constitution* (Princeton: Princeton University Press, 2003), 23–41. It does, however, bear mentioning that some scholars have argued against the dichotomous construction of rights as 'negative' and 'positive', instead arguing that the substantive enforcement of all rights has the potential to impose obligations, fiscal and otherwise, on the state and distinctions between different rights being matters of degree rather than fundamental. See eg S. Holmes and C. R. Sunstein, *The Cost of Rights: Why Liberty Depends on Taxes* (New York: W.W. Norton, 1999); M. Tushnet, above at n 4.

[7] M. Tushnet, 'Foreword: The New Constitutional Order and the Chastening of Constitutional Aspiration', (1999) 113 *Harvard Law Review* 29, 33.

[8] L. G. Sager, *Justice in Plainclothes: A Theory of American Constitutional Practice* (New Haven: Yale University Press, 2004), 88.

to the realization of social welfare rights, to a more pragmatic, realist, and even consequentialist way of dealing with them.[9]

Tushnet is a prominent constitutional theorist and one of the last genuine leftist-progressive Mohicans in mainstream American legal academia. As with several other prominent figures of the Critical Legal Studies movement of the 1970s and 1980s, his more recent scholarship has undergone a pragmatic turn. Accordingly, his efforts in this book to salvage social welfare rights discourse in the United States through concrete and practical means (weak-form judicial review) seem to reflect a results-driven, 'realpolitik' approach to the issue.[10] Ultimately, Tushnet makes a positivist, empirically testable argument about the possible effectiveness of weak-form judicial review in advancing the status of socio-economic rights. This in turn may serve as a springboard for engaging in a comparative cross-disciplinary exploration of the intersection of socio-economic rights and political realities.

II. Comparative Rights and Realities

Although the formal constitutional protection of positive social rights is supposed to advance their actual status, there is no readily apparent correlation between the two. Some countries (eg Brazil) have unqualified subsistence rights provisions in their constitutions, whereas other countries (eg South Africa) have qualified provisions (progressive realization, subject to available resources, etc.). In yet other countries (eg India), such rights have been protected under more generic provisions such as those of human dignity and security of the person. Despite these differences, measurements of income inequality and standardized development indicators (eg Gini coefficients, UNDP HDI scores) are roughly similar in Brazil, South Africa, and India. And these values are not substantially different from those in other developing world countries such as Mexico, where no subsistence rights are granted constitutional status.

Consider Canada, where an inexplicable gap exists between the polity's long-standing commitment to a relatively generous version of the Keynesian welfare state model and the outright exclusion of subsistence social rights from the purview of rights provisions. During national and provincial election campaigns, Canadians consistently refer to health care as the public policy issue about which they care the most. Moreover, a viable, publicly funded health care system is repeatedly cited by Canadians as one of the most important and distinctive markers of Canadian collective identity, compared with the lack of such a system in Canada's neighbour to the south. The Canada Health Act enjoys near-sacred status in public discourse.

---

[9] Such consequentialist arguments for and against social rights are also advanced by K. Lane Scheppele, 'A Realpolitik Defense of Social Rights' (2004) 82 *Texas Law Review* 1921; and by C. Sunstein, 'Against Positive Rights' (1993) 2 *East European Constitutional Review* 35.

[10] A recent attempt to give this approach a more principled take is provided by R. Dixon, 'Creating Dialogue about Socio-Economic Rights: Strong v. Weak-Form Judicial Review Revisited' (2007) 5 *International Journal of Constitutional Law* 391. Similarly, Roux has argued that the success of the South African Constitutional Court has been a result of the 'principled-pragmatic' approach it has taken to socio-economic rights adjudication. See T. Roux, 'Principle and Pragmatism on the Constitutional Court of South Africa' (2009) 7 *International Journal of Constitutional Law* 106.

This status was reiterated by the overwhelming public reaction to the landmark SCC ruling in *Chaoulli v Quebec (AG)*[11] concerning the provision of private health care services in Quebec.[12] And, not too far behind health care are issues such as education, child care, welfare benefits, and affordable housing—all of which fall under the umbrella of subsistence rights.

Yet, despite the centrality of these issues on Canada's public agenda, as well as Canada's long-term commitment to a relatively generous version of a Keynesian welfare state, subsistence social rights are not protected by the Charter of Rights of Freedoms and have been altogether excluded from its purview by pertinent Supreme Court of Canada jurisprudence. The Court has repeatedly rejected claims that would have required the state to provide benefits to rights holders, either directly through a social programme (eg health care, unemployment benefits) or indirectly through social legislation that imposes obligations on private actors (eg minimum wage, pay equity, rent control). According to Chief Justice Lamer in *R v Prosper*,[13] 'it would be a very big step for this court to interpret the Charter in a manner which imposes a positive constitutional obligation on governments'.[14] In its landmark ruling in *Gosselin v Quebec (AG)*,[15] the Court rejected the argument of an unemployed Montreal resident that section 7's 'right to security of the person' prohibits cuts to welfare that would deny recipients basic necessities and that the Charter's equality right provision entails substantive obligations to provide adequately for disadvantaged groups relying on social assistance. By a five-to-four decision, the Court held that the 'right to security of the person' does not guarantee an adequate level of social assistance by the state. In her majority opinion, Chief Justice McLachlin stated that section 7 restricts the state's ability to deprive people of their right to life, liberty, and security of the person but does not place any positive obligations on the state. Two years later, in *Auton v British Columbia (AG)*, the Court unanimously held that provincial health care plans are not required to fund special treatment regimes for autistic children.[16] In *Newfoundland v NAPE*, the Court of Canada gave preference to the province of Newfoundland and Labrador's budgetary difficulties over the implementation of pay equity laws aimed at equalizing remuneration to women employees in the provincial public sector.[17] In *British Columbia v Christie*, the Court went on to rule that provincial tax on legal services did not infringe the right to access to justice of low-income persons.[18] And it was not until its ruling in *Health Services v British Columbia* in 2007, after 20 years of a distinctly neo-liberal approach to the matter, that the Court recognized the right

[11] [2005] 1 SCR 791.
[12] The court ruled that limits on the delivery of private health care in Quebec violated Quebec's Charter of Human Rights and Freedoms. Three of the judges also ruled that the limits on private health care violated section 7 of the Charter of Rights and Freedoms. The decision could have significant ramifications on health care policy in Canada and may be interpreted as paving the way to a 'two-tier' health care system.
[13] [1994] 3 SCR 236.
[14] Ibid at para 31.
[15] [2002] 4 SCR 429.
[16] *Auton (Guardian ad litem of) v British Columbia (AG)* [2004] 3 SCR 657.
[17] *Newfoundland (Treasury Board) v NAPE* [2004] 3 SCR 381.
[18] *British Columbia (Attorney General) v Christie* [2007] 1 SCR 873.

to collective bargaining as protected by the Charter.[19] In other words, a paradigmatic model of weak-form protection of rights has failed to yield effective constitutional protection of social welfare rights.

More puzzling still are the differential impacts of judicial interpretation. Section 7 of the Canadian Charter of Rights and Freedoms reads: 'Everyone has the right to life, liberty and security of the person and the right not to be deprived thereof except in accordance with the principles of fundamental justice'. Section 21 of the Constitution of India reads: 'No person shall be deprived of his life or personal liberty except according to procedure established by law'. Despite the near identical wording of these provisions, in their interpretation two very different paths with respect to constitutional protection of subsistence rights have been taken. Such rights are appreciated in Canadian public discourse, but have been consistently pushed beyond the purview of section 7 by the Supreme Court of Canada. India, by contrast, features vast socio-economic gaps; yet its Supreme Court has consistently declared claims for subsistence social rights justiciable and enforceable through constitutional litigation that draws on section 21.[20] It is clear, then, that the extent of constitutional protection of subsistence rights in a given polity does not necessarily reflect the prevalence of such rights in that polity's public discourse.

Nor does the list of curious cases end with these examples. In Scandinavia, Sweden, Finland, and Denmark—three of the most developed and prosperous nations on earth—have long adhered to a generous notion of the welfare regime and a relatively egalitarian conception of distributive justice. At the same time, however, they have demonstrated themselves to be less than enthusiastic (to put it mildly) toward the notions of constitutional rights and judicial review. Until a constitutional amendment in 2000, judicial review of legislation was explicitly forbidden in Finland. In Denmark and Sweden, judicial review has almost never been practised. The Danish courts have set aside legislation only once in the past 160 years—the *Tvind* case (1999)—and the Danish Constitution is silent on the issue.[21] The picture is similar in Sweden. In short, a long-standing tradition of rights and judicial review is not a necessary condition for achieving high levels of human development.

In contrast, government policy—in turn shaped by political factors—seems to matter a great deal when it comes to the realization of socio-economic rights. Luiz Inácio Lula da Silva became President of Brazil on 1 January 2003. Lula, as he is known popularly, has been advocating a socialist-progressive agenda. His administration introduced a series of social policies and new spending priorities aimed at eradicating poverty and illiteracy in Brazil. The results have been nothing short of staggering. From 2002 to 2009, the number of poor people in Brazil dropped from

---

[19] *Health Services and Support-Facilities Subsector Bargaining Assn v British Columbia* [2007] 2 SCR 391.
[20] See eg *Olga Tellis v Bombay Municipal Corporation*, AIR 1986 SC 180; *Unni Krishnan, JP v State of Andhra Pradesh*, AIR 1993 SC 2178. Note that in 2002, a new section (21A) was added to the Indian Constitution. It warrants that '[t]he State shall provide free and compulsory education to all children of the age of six to fourteen years in such manner as the State may, by law, determine'.
[21] The *Tvind Case* (U 1999 841H).

58.2 million to 41.5 million, while the overall population increased from 176 million to 198 million. The Gini-coefficient fell from 0.581 to 0.544; the illiteracy rate dropped from 13.6 per cent to less than 10 per cent and the infant mortality rate per 1,000 live births fell from 35.8 to 22.6.[22] The social and economic rights provisions in the Constitution of Brazil have not changed since 1988. Akin to the Nordic experience, the impressive improvements in alleviating poverty in Brazil have been achieved by targeted government policies, not by constitutional reforms or by more progressive constitutional jurisprudence as compared to jurisprudence in the pre-Lula years.

A rigorous assessment of poverty-reduction in Brazil, China, and India authored by the director of the World Bank's Development Research Group suggests that Brazil's main cash-transfer program, called Bolsa Familia, provides help to 11 million families, or 60 per cent of all those in the poorest tenth. In contrast, social security in China is still provided largely through the enterprise system (government-owned companies), so it tends to bypass those not in work. And government interventions in India are extraordinarily perverse. People in the poorest fifth are the least likely to have any kind of ration card (the key to public handouts), whereas the richest fifth are the most likely to.[23]

In polities where leftist political forces have historically been influential, such as Brazil, India, or Spain, constitutional support for social welfare rights can be discerned. Conversely, the United States lacks any meaningful constitutional support for social welfare rights. However, much like Brazil and India, the United States features one of the most unequal distributions of income among advanced industrial societies. Unlike Brazil, India, or Spain, however, a true socialist political agenda has never garnered any meaningful popular support in 20th-century United States.

Countries in the post-communist bloc vary considerably with respect to their constitutional protection of welfare rights despite the fact they all share a strong communist past. While in several of these countries pro-welfare rights constituencies were in a distinctly stronger political position at the time of transition to democracy, they have been virtually wiped out in other post-communist settings. And there are numerous other variations among countries that may be derivative of differences in hegemonic cultural propensities or demographic trends, historical and institutional path dependence, domestic and international political economy factors, or strategic behaviour by constitutional courts vis-à-vis other political actors or the public.

The political-economic literature on the welfare state is quite insightful in this regard.[24] One key factor in explaining cross-country variance in redistribution

---

[22] Data drawn from the *CIA World Factbook 2010*.

[23] M. Ravallion, 'A Comparative Perspective on Poverty Reduction in Brazil, China and India,' World Bank Policy Research Working Paper 5080 (Oct 2009); cited in 'Fighting Poverty in Emerging Markets: Lessons from Brazil, China and India', *The Economist* (26 Nov 2009).

[24] For a more comprehensive overview of this vast body of literature see, T. Iversen, 'Capitalism and Democracy', in B. Weingast and D. Wittman (eds), *Oxford Handbook of Political Economy* (Oxford: Oxford University Press, 2006), 601–23; D. Swank and C. J. Martin, 'Employers and the Welfare State: The Political Economic Organization of Firms and Social Policy in Contemporary Capitalist Democracies' (2001) 34 *Comparative Political Studies* 889; I. Mares, 'Firms and the Welfare State: When, Why, and How Does Social Policy Matter to Employers?', in P. A. Hall and D. Soskice (eds), *Varieties of Capitalism* (Oxford: Oxford University Press, 2001), 184–212; A. Hicks

of resources is the organizational and political strength of labour. The 'power resources approach' emphasizes the historical strength of the political left as a key determinant of redistribution. Union strength reduces income inequality by virtue of increasing the power of workers relative to employers through collectivization and organization. Left-oriented government results in greater egalitarian redistribution as a result of their ideological basis and the firm grounding of their support with individuals of lower income.[25] 'Neo-corporatist' theory focuses on the organization of labour and its relationship with the state, most notably the degree of centralization of unions and their incorporation into (some might say cooptation by) public decision-making processes.[26]

Other theories focus on the median voter's preferences, voter turnout among the poor (the greater it is, the greater the redistribution level is expected), and so on. Vincent Mahler, for example, suggests that both the centralization of wage coordination and voter turnout are positively correlated with reduced income inequality, but that union density per se is a less significant catalyst of redistribution or reduced inequality.[27] Yet another theory—often referred to as 'Varieties of Capitalism'—focuses on business interests as shaped by the structure of the economy. So, for example, relatively small industrial countries, say the Scandinavian polities, are likely to have a more generous welfare state so as to insure themselves against the vicissitudes of the global economy. Likewise, industries that are highly exposed to risk will favour a relatively generous social insurance system so as to share costs and risks with the state. It has also been argued that the burden of contemporary welfare 'retrenchment' is unequally borne, in a systematic manner that is conditioned by the relative (collective) strength of those who benefit from specific programs.[28] If benefits do not cut across economic and/or social cleavages, it is argued, they tend to lack broad-based support, and are more susceptible to elimination.

Determining which theory or theories are most convincing is not a simple matter; the causal links that underpin the workings of modern welfare states are complex. Further, the descriptive—and to a lesser degree, prescriptive—properties of these often conflicting models of comprehending distribution and redistribution

and C. Zorn, 'Economic Globalization, the Macro Economy, and Reversals of Welfare: Expansion in Affluent Democracies, 1978–94' (2005) 59 *International Organization* 631; T. Skopcol and E. Amenta, 'States and Social Policies' (1986) 12 *Annual Review of Sociology* 131.

[25] D. Bradley, Evelyne Huber, Stephanie Moller, Francois Nielsen, and John D. Stephens, 'Distribution and Redistribution in Postindustrial Democracies' (January 2003) 55 *World Politics* 193.

[26] The relative size and type of national economy have also been suggested as important factors shaping such coordinated bargaining arrangements, particularly via the greater or lesser degree of perceived shared exposure to risk on the international market by business and labour. P. J. Katzenstein, *Small States in World Markets: Industrial Policy in Europe* (Ithaca, NY: Cornell University Press, 1985). See also D. R. Cameron, 'The Expansion of the Public Economy: A Comparative Analysis' (1978) 72 *American Political Science Review* 1243.

[27] V. Mahler, 'Economic Globalization, Domestic Politics, and Income Inequality in the Developed Countries: A Cross-National Study' (2004) 37 *Political Studies* 1025.

[28] P. Pierson, 'The New Politics of the Welfare State' (1996) 48 *World Politics* 143, 176–8; S. Bashevkin, 'Rethinking Retrenchment: North American Social Policy during the Early Clinton and Chrétien Years' (2000) 33 *Canadian Journal of Political Science* 7; G. Esping-Andersen, *Social Foundations of Postindustrial Economies* (Oxford: Oxford University Press, 1999).

through the welfare state have been operationalized and tested to reasonable success. What is clear, however, is that a sizable body of academic research relating to the interrelationship of the state and socio-economic inequality that incorporates a broad swath of political economic variables exists, but, that little or no provision is made for the impact of the law in general or constitutional rights and jurisprudence in particular in the conduct of that research. This literature, although marked by internal disagreement, represents a wealth of data and analysis which could be fruitfully incorporated into the comparative study of constitutionalism, particularly with regard to the analysis of the impacts of constitutional rights guarantees and constitutional jurisprudence. Both the qualitative and quantitative elements of this field have much to offer by way of a more holistic approach to the comparative analysis of constitutionalism and its effects.

When we turn our attention to measuring the actual impact of socio-economic rights, the picture becomes even more inconclusive. As an astute observer has recently noted, 'the transformative potential of rights is significantly thwarted by the fact that they are typically formulated, interpreted, and enforced by institutions that are embedded in the political, social and economic status quo. This is so even in relation to socio-economic rights.'[29] There is little doubt that the canonical interpretation of rights as predominantly negative freedoms has not done much to reduce the widening disparities in fundamental living conditions within and among polities. It has proven virtually futile in mitigating, let alone reversing, wide-ranging social and economic processes of deregulation, privatization, reduced social spending, and the removal of 'market rigidities'.[30] It has failed to promote the notion that no man, woman, or child can fully enjoy or exercise the classic civil liberties in a meaningful way if they lack the basic essentials for a healthy and decent life in the first place.[31] In fact, in most post-communist countries, for example, the constitutionalization of rights has been associated with precisely the opposite ethos, placing private ownership and other economic freedoms beyond the reach of majoritarian politics and state regulation, thereby planting the seeds for greater, not lesser, disparity in essential life conditions. Clearly, then, the constitutionalization of socio-economic rights per se—however morally compelling its premise is or however significant its symbolic value may be—is limited in its independent capacity to alleviate pre-existing inequalities in living conditions. And even that much progress in a given polity very likely depends upon the existence of what Charles Epp terms a 'support structure for legal mobilization' that allows groups and individuals to invoke rights provisions through strategic litigation in the first place.[32]

---

[29] M. Pieterse, 'Eating Socioeconomic Rights: The Usefulness of Rights Talk in Alleviating Social Hardship Revisited' (2007) 29 *Human Rights Quarterly* 796, 797.

[30] R. Hirschl, *Towards Juristocracy: The Origins and Consequences of the New Constitutionalism* (Cambridge, Mass: Harvard University Press, 2004), 100–48.

[31] This notion is based on Amartya Sen's 'capabilities' or 'basic needs' approach to human development. It has been adopted by the UNDP and numerous other international human development agencies. See A. Sen, 'Equality of What?' in S. McMurrin (ed), *Tanner Lectures on Human Values* (Cambridge: Cambridge University Press, 1980); and *Inequality Reexamined* (Cambridge, Mass: Harvard University Press, 1992).

[32] See C. Epp, *The Rights Revolution: Lawyers, Activists and Supreme Courts in Comparative Perspective* (Chicago: University of Chicago Press, 1998).

A central problem faced by democratic regimes is that of balancing competing rights claims with long-term sustainability. As Cass Sunstein argues, '[t]here
should be little question that people who live in desperate conditions cannot lead
good lives. People who live in such conditions are also unable to enjoy the status
of citizenship. On the other hand, legislatures in poor nations, and perhaps in less
poor nations, cannot easily ensure that everyone lives in decent conditions.'[33] The
complexity and incremental nature of public policy suggest that the pursuit of an
immediate and full realization of socio-economic rights is an unrealistic endeavour. Rights, all rights, come with a price tag and the finite resources available to
government cannot be so radically shifted from year to year, either legally, practically, or politically.[34]

Evidence of these limitations is readily available. Unlike in the United States,
the question of social and economic rights has been a central theme in the constitutional renewal that has taken place in South Africa over the last fifteen years.
Ignoring the issue is unthinkable given the vast social and economic gaps in post-
apartheid South Africa, the dismal living conditions in the densely populated
shantytowns, and the ever-accelerating HIV–AIDS pandemic. For starters, the
new South African constitutional catalogue of rights explicitly protects positive
social and economic rights, such as the rights to housing, health care, food, water,
social security, and education. None of these positive rights provisions, however,
implies an unqualified right to housing, health care, or education per se; instead,
they merely assert that reasonable state measures must be taken to make further
housing, health care, and education progressively available and accessible. This
innovative construction of 'weak' rights requires the government to take reasonable measures, within its available resources, to achieve the progressive realization
of each of these rights by establishing practicable programmes of land reform,
housing, education, and health care.[35] This approach therefore strikes a balance
between constitutional commitments and political and economic realities.

Since the adoption of the new South African Constitution in 1996, the South
African Constitutional Court has released several landmark rulings interpreting the scope and nature of protection under this innovative constitutional
framework.[36] Two of those rulings—the *Grootboom* case[37] and the *Nevirapine*

---

[33] C. R. Sunstein, 'Social and Economic Rights? Lessons From South Africa' (2001) 11
Constitutional Forum 130.

[34] Accepting the finite nature of public resources, a reasonable expectation could involve some
type of indexation of a nation's social assistance levels with a measure or measures that are indicative
of that country's economic circumstances. This might take the form of establishing a basic income
floor at a certain percentage of median income or per capita GDP. This would ensure that as the
economic fortunes of a given country rose or fell, state fiscal obligations to social services and welfare
transfers would vary accordingly.

[35] See eg M. Tushnet, 'Social Welfare Rights and the Forms of Judicial Review' (2004) 82 *Texas
Law Review* 1895, 1902–6.

[36] See eg *Minister of Health v Treatment Action Campaign* 2002 (5) SA 721 (CC); *Government of
RSA v Grootboom* 2001 (1) SA 46 (CC); *Soobramoney v Minister of Health (KwaZulu-Natal)* 1998 (1)
SA 765 (CC).

[37] *Government of RSA v Grootboom* 2001 (1) SA 46 (CC).

case[38]—have generated extensive commentary both in South African and in foreign media outlets and law reviews. However, the actual reality of social and economic rights in South Africa is, alas, quite appalling. In the *Grootboom* case, for example, the Court dealt with the enforceability of social and economic rights and redefined the scope of the state's obligations under section 26 of the South African Bill of Rights. A group of 900 homeless people were living in dismal circumstances in Wallacedene, an informal and unrecognized settlement in the Western Cape Province.[39] The Court held that, 'there is, at the very least, a negative obligation placed upon the State... to desist from preventing or impairing the right of access to adequate housing'.[40] The Court went on to note that the new South African Constitution obliges the state to act positively to ameliorate the plight of the hundreds of thousands of South Africans living in deplorable conditions throughout the country. The state must also foster conditions that enable citizens to gain access to land on an equitable basis.

Four years later, a report in the South African *Sunday Times* described the *Grootboom* ruling in these terms: 'Squatters' precedent-setting victory in the Constitutional Court has gained them only stinking latrines...Leaking sewage and piles of rotting rubbish smell so bad in Grootboom that you can actually taste the stench'.[41] The article continues: 'the Grootboom victory made headlines around the world, as noted by former Judge Richard Goldstone, who went on to serve the International Court of Justice in The Hague. The "uniqueness" of the Grootboom decision, Judge Goldstone told Harvard University's Kennedy School of Government, would be remembered as the first building block in creating a jurisprudence of socioeconomic rights. As far as the people of Grootboom are concerned, however, Goldstone's "building block" is the only building material they have seen since the court ruled in their favour on 4 October 2000.'[42] Such protracted implementation of arguably a *Brown v Board of Education*-like decision in the comparative socio-economic rights domain is a sobering reminder that Gerald Rosenberg's 'constrained court' thesis remains quite relevant in questioning the hyperbolic assertions on the efficacy of litigation.[43] Indeed, in two recent rulings, the South African Constitutional Court itself resorted to a pragmatic, perhaps even restrictive approach to the realization of socio-economic rights, giving considerably more weight than in the past to the practical challenges of implementing new anti-poverty policies in a country plagued by socio-economic gaps and limited state capacity.[44]

---

[38] *Minister of Health v Treatment Action Campaign* 2002 (5) SA 721 (CC) (holding that the South African enumerated constitutional right to access to health care obliged the state to remove restrictions on Nevirapine—a drug that reduces the risk of mother to child transmission of HIV—and to take steps to make the drug more readily available.)

[39] *Government of RSA v Grootboom* at 53–4, 88.

[40] Ibid at 66.

[41] B. Schoonakker, 'Treated with Contempt' (21 Mar 2004) *Sunday Times*.

[42] Ibid.

[43] See G. Rosenberg, *The Hollow Hope: Can Courts Bring About Social Change?*, 2nd edn (Chicago: University of Chicago Press, 2008).

[44] *Mazibuko v Johannesburg* 2010 (4) SA 1 (CC); *Nokotyana v Ekurhuleni Metropolitan Municipality* 2010 (4) BCLR 312 (CC).

The measurement of impact may also take a more quantitative and comparative direction.[45] The recent inequality data made available by Frederick Solt in his Standardized World Income Inequality Database (SWIID) is of particular note, as it broadens the scope of comparison possible by combining the three principal data sets utilized in the measurement of socio-economic conditions over time.[46] This is accomplished by employing a complex missing-data algorithm that maximizes comparability and compensates for the variation and difficulty of comparison between data sets.[47] Caution must be employed when attempting to quantify the nature and generosity of a government welfare state as the potential for distortion and inaccuracy has been clearly pointed out.[48] Nonetheless, a reasonably comprehensive proxy measure can serve as a starting point for investigation, and, when informed by qualitative or otherwise contextually rich investigation, can serve as a powerful aid in assessing the actual impact of constitutionalization or progressive jurisprudence on the realization of socio-economic rights.

Consider the following data on income inequality in South Africa. Figure 10.1 presents three different measures of income inequality and government redistribution. The first two (net and gross Gini) are explicit measures of inequality, while the third (redistribution) reflects the degree to which a given national government reduces market income inequality via taxation and transfers to lower income individuals. The Gini coefficient is a measure of economic inequality that reflects the overall distribution of income in a society. It also has the merit of being one of the most widely used measures of inequality across disciplines.[49] It is an interval measure with a range of 0 to 100, with 0 representing perfect equality—income is evenly distributed across the society—and 100 representing perfect inequality—one individual receiving all of a society's income, while the remainder receive none.[50]

Solt's data set is particularly useful as it contains two Gini measures, net and gross. Gross Gini represents income prior to the levying of taxes or the disbursement of social assistance or other government transfers, while net Gini measures income post tax and transfers.[51] Via comparison of the two, a reasonably reliable

---

[45] In this vein, Harvey and Rooney have recently contemplated the potential utility of several forms of economic analysis (specifically: Cost-Benefit; Cost-Effectiveness; and Multi-Criteria) in the development of public policy that accurately considers socio-economic rights performance. There too, as they aptly note, there is a good deal of work to be done in order to reform these extant tools for application to socio-economic rights analysis and there are significant possibilities for invalid measurement and discursive cooptation. See C. Harvey and E. Rooney, 'Integrating Human Rights? Socio-Economic Rights and Budget Analysis' (2010) *European Human Rights Law Review* 266.

[46] Namely, the Luxembourg Income Study's, the World Bank's, and the World Institute for Development Economics Research of the United Nations University's (UNU-WIDER).

[47] F. Solt, 'Standardizing the World Income Inequality Database' (2009) 90 *Social Science Quarterly* 231, (SWIID Version 2.0, July 2009).

[48] See eg G. Esping-Andersen, *Three Worlds of Welfare State Capitalism* (Princeton: Princeton University Press, 1990), 19–26; P. Pierson, above at n 28; additionally, Bashevkin points out the potentially differential impacts of social welfare expenditures in terms of gender, see above at n 28.

[49] The other being the share of gross domestic product (GDP) possessed by various sub-groups of the population. See E. Glaeser, 'Inequality', in B. Weingast and D. Wittman (eds), *The Oxford Handbook of Political Economy* (Oxford: Oxford University Press, 2006), 624.

[50] It is, however, worth noting that it may also be represented as a decimal of 0-1 by dividing each measured result by a factor of 100.

[51] Solt, see above at n 47, 4.

and cross-nationally comparable measurement of government redistribution can be ascertained. Herein this has been done by calculating the net Gini as a percentage of gross Gini in order to provide a rough measure of redistribution in which a higher number represents greater redistribution.[52]

It can be reasonably assumed that if efficacious the entrenchment of justiciable socio-economic rights will reduce income inequality, by either slowing trends toward increased inequality or quickening trends to the reverse resulting in a more equal distribution of income as measured by net Gini coefficient as a result of increased government transfers to the less advantaged. Moreover, the substantive adjudication of welfare rights claims should lead to an increase in government redistribution as a proportion of gross Gini due to the increasing progressiveness of government taxation and transfers. This would be reflected herein by an increase in 'redistribution'.

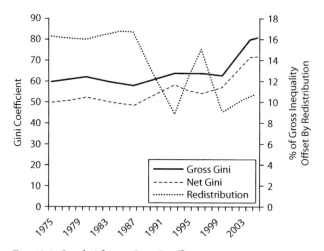

Fig. 10.1 South African Gini Coefficients

The data, however, paint a somewhat opposite picture. In particular, both net and gross inequality have dramatically increased since the entrenchment of the Constitution. Moreover, the redistributive tendencies of the South African government have significantly declined. Although it is noteworthy that since roughly 2000, the proportion of inequality offset through government redistribution has begun to improve, the proportion of inequality offset through redistribution is still

---

[52] Specifically, 'Redistribution' as conceived here would be the value of [(1—(net gini/gross gini))*100] for a given year. This hypothetical variable is, in essence, a measure of the proportion of market inequality of income—gross Gini—that is offset through taxation and social transfers—net Gini—in a given year. For example, if gross Gini is 50 and net Gini is 40 for a given case in a given year, then the value of the variable 'Redistribution' would be 20. The motivation behind calculating the variable as a proportion is to allow comparison across countries while, to a large degree, controlling for disparities in their respective levels of inequality and/or levels of per capita GDP.

nearly 50 per cent below what it was during the years leading up to the 1993–6 constitutional experience.[53]

A comparative analysis of the redistributive tendencies of states reveals a similar trend. When measured across their constitutionalization periods, Canada, Israel, New Zealand, and South Africa all exhibit a similar lack of improved redistributive tendencies in their post-constitutional periods.[54] After the adoption of Canada's Charter of Rights and Freedoms in 1982, no substantial variation in the general trend towards improved redistribution is evident. In fact, as a coherent jurisprudence of Charter rights began to evolve throughout the 1980s, a gradual decline is evident.[55] This trend is even more closely correlated with the enactment of the New Zealand Bill of Rights Act (1990) and with Basic Law: Human Dignity and Liberty and Basic Laws: Freedom of Occupation (1992/1994) in Israel. And, as discussed above, while redistribution in South Africa shows some signs of improvement, its level of redistribution is still well below what is was during the apartheid era—something that is especially troubling from a welfare rights perspective in light of its hugely increased levels of net and gross inequality. While causality remains ambiguous with such a simple analysis, it does seem that bills of rights may have little effect on rights provision.

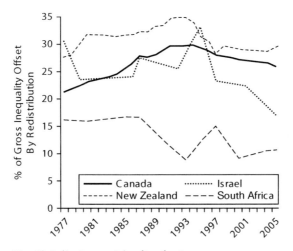

Fig. 10.2 'Juristocratic' redistribution

---

[53] To be sure, these measures and analysis should not be considered indicative of causation. The political, economic, and social forces impacting constitutional processes are far too complex to be captured via the type of univariate analysis outlined above. Instead, we present this data and analysis as an example (and hopefully, a signpost) of the potential utility of incorporating extra-legal analysis into the discussion of positive rights.

[54] Solt, see above at n 47. Case selection for this examination was motivated by a desire to complement an earlier, primarily qualitative work of one of the authors. See, Hirschl, above at n 28.

[55] Although it must be recognized that this decline in redistributive tendencies was mirrored in a large number of developed democracies as, *inter alia*, the effects of a decade or more of neo-liberal governance, public policy, and discourse came to fruition.

Another way of assessing the significance of constitutional provisions is by looking at their contribution to human development. A common definition of that concept emphasizes access to adequate standard of living, basic needs, services, protections, and meaningful life opportunities.[56] It is premised on the notion that no one can fully enjoy or exercise any classic negative civil liberty in any meaningful way if they lack the essentials for a healthy and decent life in the first place. According to this notion, basic needs such as access to food and safe water, housing, education, and health care are both morally and practically more fundamental than any given classic negative right. One's ability to live a decent life, to be adequately nourished, and to have access to basic health care, education, and shelter are essential preconditions to the enjoyment of any other rights and freedoms.

According to many sources—such as Nobel Laureate Amartya Sen, the Universal Declaration on Human Rights (UDHR), the International Covenant on Economic, Social and Cultural Rights (ICESCR), and the United Nations Human Development Programme (UNDP)—assessing human development in terms of decent living conditions, substantive equality, and access to real opportunities for education, health care, income, employment, and so forth is quite germane. Indeed, what these authorities demonstrate is that it is as analytically justifiable for studying the effects of constitutionalization on human development as any other definition of the ultimate indicators of human development, including the prevalent liberal mix of procedural justice, formal equality, and classic civil liberties (often bundled with the libertarian addition of property rights).

The Human Development Index (HDI) is a widely recognized metric combining standardized measures of life expectancy, literacy, educational attainment, and GDP per capita for countries worldwide. The basic use of HDI is to rank countries by level of 'human development' on a scale of 0 to 1 (based on a complicated yet reliable formula). The most recent Human Development Report (2009) ranks Norway at the top with a score of 0.971, followed by Australia, Iceland, Canada, Ireland, the Netherlands, Sweden, France, Switzerland, Japan, Luxemburg, Finland, and the United States at 15th place with a score of 0.956.

Other countries in the top 30 include the European powerhouses (Germany, Spain, Italy, and Britain) alongside smaller polities such as Greece, Portugal, Belgium, Cyprus, Slovenia, Israel, Singapore, New Zealand, Korea, and Hong Kong. With the exception of Japan (humble constitutionalism and limited judicial review) and the United States (extravagant constitutionalism and great judicial visibility), none of the world's most populated countries is among the world's leaders in terms of human development. Highly populated countries such as Mexico, Nigeria, Brazil, Indonesia, Bangladesh, Pakistan, let alone India and China, have made strides but do not excel in terms of HDI.[57] Alongside population size and stable electoral processes, the existence of a developed market economy, combined with centralized planning that cherishes public investment in science, education,

---

[56] See eg A. Sen, above at n 31.

[57] United Nations Development Programme (UNDP), *Human Development Reports* (United Nations, 2009), <http://hdr.undp.org/en/>.

and health care, appears to be the winning formula here. A large middle class and a well-developed civil society are key societal factors. And what is the impact of the variance on the constitutionalism axis? Quite negligible, frankly. So rights alone certainly do not do the trick when it comes to human development.

III. Strategic Judicial Behaviour

Whereas in many other respects, the world has witnessed a profound judicialization of politics and policy-making, in matters of broad economic and social policies this has not been the case.[58] With few exceptions, courts have been less active in areas such as income distribution, eradication of poverty, or subsistence rights, all of which require wider state intervention and a change to public expenditure priorities, than in areas of classic civil liberties. Judicial enforcement of socio-economic rights requires either additional public expenditure or the reallocation of extant resources. Either approach requires head-on scrimmages with government officials or powerful economic interests. It is therefore quite plausible to assume that judicial decision-making in this area is not free of various extra-judicial, 'realpolitik' or strategic considerations.

An emerging area of scholarship in political science treats the conventional legal doctrine view of judges as precedent followers (eg the *stare decisis* doctrine) or framers of legal policies and interpretive approaches (eg textualist or purposive interpretation) as a benchmark against which to develop its antithesis: judges do not reach decisions in a way that is qualitatively different from any other branches of government. Courts are political institutions not merely because they are politically constructed, but also because the determinants of judicial behaviour are not fundamentally different from determinants of decision-making by other public officials. Judges as individual decision-makers may be driven by their personal attitudes and ideologies, by cognitive psychological biases (social and/or physiological), by career-related considerations, or simply by their quest to cater to their epistemic communities.

More generally, courts and judges may be viewed as strategic actors to the extent that they seek to increase their policy-making influence, or maintain or augment the court's independence and institutional position vis-à-vis other major national decision-making bodies. They may also wish to enhance the court's symbolic power and international prestige by fostering its alignment with a growing community of liberal democratic nations engaged in judicial review and rights-based discourses. Strategic judges may recognize the changing fates or preferences of influential political actors or gaps in the institutional context within which they operate; such events might allow them to strengthen their own position by extending the ambit of their jurisprudence and fortifying their status as key national policy-makers. Constitutional courts seek institutional legitimacy and may thus be responsive to

---

[58] See R. Hirschl, 'The Judicialization of Mega-Politics and the Rise of Political Courts' (2008) 11 *Annual Review of Political Science* 93.

public opinion and preferences; judges seem to care about popular perceptions of the court and its landmark rulings.[59]

And there are possibly other instrumentalist factors to consider. Judges may vote strategically to minimize the chances that their decisions will be overridden;[60] if the interpretation that the justices most prefer is likely to elicit reversal by other branches, they will compromise by adopting the interpretation closest to their preferences that could be predicted to withstand reversal. What's more, because justices do not have the institutional capacities to enforce their rulings, they must take into account the extent to which pertinent political decision-makers will support their rulings.[61] Strategic judges must gauge the prevailing winds that drive political stakeholders and make decisions accordingly. In short, courts and judges may engage in strategic decision-making either due to the variety of costs that judges as individuals or courts as institutions may incur as a result of adverse reactions to their unwelcome decisions, or because of the various benefits that they may acquire through the rendering of strategically tailored decisions.[62]

When political pressure, tacit or explicit, on the courts does not achieve the intended objectives of those who appoint and promote judges, these actors may take harsher measures. As the recent history of comparative constitutional politics shows us, the recurrence of unsolicited judicial intervention in the political sphere in general and unwelcome judgments concerning contentious political issues in particular, have brought about significant political backlashes, targeted at clipping the wings of over-active courts. The most common of these reactions is the executive override of controversial or unwelcome rulings, generally via counter-legislation or executive ordinances. Among other more common power-constraining strategies are the following: political tinkering with judicial appointment and tenure procedures to ensure the appointment of compliant judges and/or to block the appointment of undesirable judges; court-packing attempts by those who hold political power; disciplinary sanctions against 'overly independent' judges; impeachment or removal of objectionable or over-active judges; or the introduction of serious jurisdictional restrictions that limit the boundaries and powers of judicial review.[63] In some instances (eg Russia in 1993, Kazakhstan in 1995, Zimbabwe in 2001, Thailand in 2006, Pakistan in 2007, on three occasions in Ecuador from 2004 to 2007, and most recently in Niger in 2009), such a backlash has ended in constitutional crisis,

---

[59] See eg W. Mishler and R. S. Sheehan, 'The Supreme Court as a Countermajoritarian Institution? The Impact of Public Opinion on Supreme Court Decisions' (1993) 87 *American Political Science Review* 87; W. Mishler and R. S. Sheehan, 'Public Opinion, the Attitudinal Model, and Supreme Court Decision Making: A Micro-analytic Perspective' (1996) 58 *The Journal of Politics* 169; B. Friedman, *The Will of the People: How Public Opinion has Influenced the Supreme Court and Shaped the Meaning of the Constitution* (New York: Farrar, Strauss and Giroux, 2009).

[60] See eg J. Ferejohn and C. Shipan, 'Congressional Influence on Bureaucracy' (1990) 6 *Journal of Law, Economics, and Organization* 1.

[61] K. McGuire and J. Stimson, 'The Least Dangerous Branch Revisited: New Evidence on Supreme Court Responsiveness to Public Preferences' (2004) 66 *Journal of Politics* 1018.

[62] This in a nutshell is the take-home message of the 'strategic' approach to judicial behaviour. See, P. T. Spiller and R. Gely, 'Strategic Judicial Decision-Making', in K. Whittington, R. D. Kelemen, and G A. Caldeira (eds), *The Oxford Handbook of Law and Politics* (Oxford: Oxford University Press, 2008), 35–45; L. Epstein and J. Knight, 'Towards a Strategic Revolution in Judicial Politics: A Look Back, A Look Ahead' (2000) 53 *Political Research Quarterly* 625.

[63] See Hirschl, above at n 58.

leading to the reconstruction or dissolution of the high courts. To this we may add another political response to unwelcome rulings—more subtle, and possibly more lethal to the court's influence: bureaucratic disregard, or protracted or reluctant implementation,[64] thus putting into effect Andrew Jackson's famous words, '[t]he Chief Justice has made his decision and now let him enforce it'.[65]

Overactive courts and judges do learn the lesson. A wide array of empirically grounded studies suggest that harsh political responses to unwelcome activism or interventions on the part of the courts, or even the credible threat of such a response, can have a chilling effect on judicial decision-making patterns. Variations on the same logic explain prudent and/or strategic judicial behaviour in countries as disparate as Argentina, Germany, Pakistan, Russia, and Japan.[66]

Courts may act in the area of socio-economic rights when elected officials won't, or when they view the distributive justice agenda as a fertile terrain for expanding the ambit of their influence or enhancing their public legitimacy or popularity.[67] Whereas governments actually have to fund and provide social services, judicial declarations in support of socio-economic rights maximize the courts' symbolic status without actually paying much for it. In settings where issues of widespread poverty, illiteracy, socio-economic inequality, or the excessive rollback of the welfare state occupy the public agenda but are not adequately addressed by elected officials or government agencies, constitutional courts may sense an opportunity to bolster their public legitimacy, and thus may jump in and address the issue. This impulse may explain the rise of progressive constitutional socio-economic rights jurisprudence in countries such as India, Brazil, or Colombia. A paradigmatic illustration of legitimacy enhancing judicial behaviour in this context is the Hungarian Constitutional Court ruling of 1995 that declared unconstitutional an unpopular government 'austerity plan' to retroactively terminate welfare entitlements and pension plans.[68] It was estimated at the time that over 90 per cent Hungarians supported the continuation of social programmes. The Court's disqualification of the plan earned it a lot of credit among Hungarians.

[64] See Rosenberg, above at n 43; G. Rosenberg, 'Judicial Independence and the Reality of Political Power' (1992) 54 *Review of Politics* 369; Geoffrey Garrett, R. Daniel Kelemen, and Heiner Schulz 'The European Court of Justice, National Governments, and Legal Integration in The European Union' (1998) 52 *International Organization* 149; L. Conant, *Justice Contained: Law and Politics in the European Union* (New York: Cornell University Press, 2002).
[65] S. Goldman, *Constitutional Law and Supreme Court Decision-Making* (New York: Harper and Row, 1982), 33; cited in K. Roach, *The Supreme Court on Trial: Judicial Activism or Democratic Dialogue* (Toronto: Irwin Law, 2001), 17.
[66] See eg G. Helmke, *Courts under Constraints: Judges, Generals, and Presidents in Argentina* (New York: Cambridge University Press, 2005); G. Vanberg, *The Politics of Constitutional Review in Germany* (New York: Cambridge University Press, 2005); J. M. Ramseyer and E. Rasmusen, 'Why are Japanese Judges So Conservative in Politically Charged Cases?' (2001) 95 *American Political Science Review* 331; L. Epstein, J. Knight, and O. Shvetsova 'The Role of Constitutional Courts in the Establishment and Maintenance of Democratic Systems of Government' (2001) 35 *Law and Society Review* 117.
[67] P. Frymer, 'Acting When Elected Officials Won't: Federal Courts and Civil Rights Enforcement in US Labor Unions, 1935–85' (2003) 97 *American Political Science Review* 483.
[68] *Austerity Package Decisions* 1995 (the so-called 'Bokros cases'). An English translation of this case is available in L. Sólyom and G. Brunner (eds), *Constitutional Judiciary in A New Democracy: The Hungarian Constitutional Court* (Ann Arbor: University of Michigan Press, 2000), 322–32; see also, Scheppele, above at n 9.

Another telling illustration of judicial response to the changing socio-political preferences surrounding it is the near-miraculous change of heart of the Israeli Supreme Court with respect to socio-economic rights. The question of constitutionalizing positive subsistence rights was on the table during the negotiations leading up to the constitutional revolution of 1992. In fact, it was only at the last minute that provisions protecting a number of subsistence social and economic rights (as well as workers' rights to unionize, bargain collectively, and strike) were excluded from the purview of the two new Basic Laws adopted in 1992. Reacting to an outcry by several leading academics committed to a traditional Keynesian welfare state agenda, the initiators of the constitutional reform added tentative provisions protecting workers' freedom of association and the unqualified right to humane social and economic living conditions to the proposed laws. However, an 'invisible hand' eliminated the added provisions just before the final versions of the new laws were submitted for legislative approval. Responding to criticism by leftist intellectuals, the government pledged to amend the new laws at a later stage so as to include the eliminated provisions or even to enact a complementary law, Basic Law: Social Rights. However, none of these proposals has come to fruition thus far.

In 1994, Chief Justice Barak specified guidelines for the interpretation of the new Basic Law: Human Dignity and Liberty.[69] According to Barak, fundamental human dignity in Basic Law: Human Dignity and Liberty should be understood to include formal equality of opportunity, due process of law, freedom to pursue one's own life plan, the right to own property, freedom from state intrusion into one's physical and mental privacy, and the recognition that each individual is a moral being. Under this definition, however, the protection of basic human dignity translates primarily into a legal right to non-interference—a negative right. Barak explicitly noted that '[s]ocial human rights such as the right to education, to healthcare, and to social welfare are, of course, very important rights, but they are not, so it seems, part of "human dignity." '[70]

This position was reflected in the Court's rights jurisprudence during the 1990s. In 1995, for example, the Court explicitly declared that the rights to basic education and child care (pertaining to developmentally challenged children) have no constitutional grounding in Basic Law: Human Dignity and Liberty, or in any other constitutional source in Israel for that matter.[71] The Court held that the state is not constitutionally obliged to provide its citizens with any sort of basic education or even any equality of opportunity in education. Likewise, the Court excluded collective workers' rights, such as the right to collective bargaining and the right to strike, from the purview of the two new Basic Laws.[72] At the same time, in its historic ruling in *United Mizrahi Bank*, the Court drew upon the constitutional entrenchment of the right to property, as specified in Article 3 of the Basic Law: Human Dignity and Liberty, to virtually invalidate—for the first time

---

[69] A. Barak, 'K'vod HaAdam K'z'chut Chukatit [Human Dignity as a Constitutional Right]', (1994) 41 *Ha'Praklit* 271.

[70] A. Barak, *Parshanut Be'Mishpat* [Interpretation in the Law], (Jerusalem: Nevo, 1994), vol 3, 419.

[71] HCJ 1554/95 *Amutat Shokharey Gilat v Sar Ha-Khinukh, Ha-Tarbut V'Ha-Sport* [*Shocharei GILAT Assoc v Minister of Educ, Culture and Sport*] [1996] IsrSC 50(3) 2.

[72] HCJ 1074/93 *Attorney-General v Nat'l Labour Court* [1995] IsrSC 49(2) 485.

in Israel's constitutional history—a Knesset law that was aimed at erasing the heavy financial debts owed to major banks by collective agricultural settlements in Israel.[73]

This neo-liberal, business-friendly interpretation of human dignity prompted fierce criticism by prominent legal academics in Israel. Some have even described the Court's jurisprudence as 'Lochnerisation' of Israeli Constitutional Law.[74] The ever-widening social and economic gaps within Israeli society, as well as the explicitly neo-liberal economic policies implemented in Israel over the last decade, have started to take their toll. A recent National Insurance Institute report suggests that over 1.5 million Israelis (roughly 20 per cent of the population), including one in three children, live below the poverty line. Inequality levels have reached new heights. Single mothers and low-income families have become vocal in demanding government support. Issues such as homelessness, the living and employment conditions of foreign workers, or the legal status of their children have found their way to the centre of the public agenda. Most importantly, the Zionist centre-left—the Court's main community of reference and bastion of public support—became tired of dealing with the never-ending Israeli-Palestinian struggle. Social activists and leftist intellectuals have gradually turned their attention to issues such as poverty, homelessness, the rights of foreign workers, and, above all, welfare rights. The politically astute Aharon Barak was quick to rethink his position concerning the meaning of human dignity and the constitutional status of subsistence rights: Israel's constitutional landscape, he suggested in 2004, should be inspired by the South African model of protecting social rights.[75] A new jurisprudential line was born.

A high point of this new approach to social rights came in late 2009, when the Israeli Supreme Court drew upon Basic Law: Human Dignity and Liberty to block a 2004 government plan that would have allowed a private contractor to build and operate a new prison near the southern city of Be'er Sheva. The arguments for such privatization replicated the economic rationale of similar initiatives in the United States, Germany, and elsewhere. Essentially, the state would pay the franchisee $50 per day for each inmate, but would be spared the cost of building new prisons and expanding the Israel Prison Service's staff. In 2005, a petition was filed against the constitutionality of the prison privatization plan.

In 2009, a panel of nine justices ruled (8:1) that a transfer of authority for managing a prison from the state to a private contractor whose sole aim is monetary profit would severely violate the prisoners' basic human right to dignity and freedom.[76] The Court held that the proposed plan to privatize prisons granted a private corporation an invasive authority over prisoners. For example, the manager of the private prison would have been authorized to sentence a prisoner to solitary confinement for as long as 48 hours, to order invasive inspections of a prisoner's naked

---

[73] CA 6821/93 *United Mizrahi Bank v Migdal Coop. Village* [1995] IsrSC 49(4) 195.

[74] A. Gross, 'The Israeli Constitution: A Tool for Distributive Justice, or a Tool which Prevents It?', in M. Mautner (ed), *Distributive Justice in Israel* (Tel Aviv: 2000), 79.

[75] A. Barak, 'Social Rights and their Constitutional Status, Address at the Environment, Society, and Human Rights Symposium', (Mar 16, 2004).

[76] HCJ 2605/05 *Academic Center of Law and Business, Human Rights Division v Minister of Finance* (Privatization of Prisons Case; decision released on 19 Nov 2009).

body, and to authorize the use of reasonable force in order to search the prisoners. In light of this, the Court held that '[w]hen the power to incarcerate is transferred to a private corporation whose purpose is making money, the act of depriving a person of his liberty loses much of its legitimacy. Because of this loss of legitimacy, the violation of the prisoner's right to liberty goes beyond the violation entailed in the incarceration itself'. While the Court acknowledged the economic benefits of the privatization plan, the material aspect itself, it ruled, was not a key factor that the Court must consider when exercising its judicial review powers. As important a value as efficiency may be, C.J. Beinisch wrote, it is not an absolute value when the most basic and important human rights for which the state is responsible are at stake. In a prison run by a private company, prisoners' rights are undermined by the fact that they are transformed into a means of extracting profit. Who would have thought that such a powerful statement (perhaps the first of its kind in the context of privatized prisons) against the pervasive 'cult of efficiency' that drives commodi-fication of social services would come from the Supreme Court of Israel of all con-stitutional courts worldwide. The Court's change of heart may be explained by the increasing challenges to its early neo-liberal interpretation, the alarming inequality in the Israeli society, and perhaps most importantly, by the changing expectations of the Court's epistemic community and camp of avid supporters.

IV. Conclusion

Most accounts of socio-economic rights focus on the constitutional or jurispruden-tial aspects of such rights. However, such rights are not constituted, interpreted, or implemented in an institutional, ideological, or political vacuum. Specifically, the prospects for advancing socio-economic rights in a given polity cannot be ana-lysed in isolation from the concrete fiscal realities, political interests, legacies of welfare provision, or patterns of executive-judiciary relations. This chapter has examined several possible 'extra-constitutional' explanations for tremendous vari-ance in constitutional protection of social and economic rights and our analysis suggests that are multiple paths and trajectories to the realization (or neglect) of social welfare rights, of which constitutionalization is only one aspect. Moreover, a significant body of scholarship in comparative politics and political economy attempts to determine the primary causal factors involved in shaping the form and strength of social protections regarding inequalities in living conditions, redis-tribution of wealth, and provision of welfare services. We make no pretence that this literature offers a comprehensive list of key causal factors, nor are we suggest-ing that simply grafting a broad 'constitutionalism' variable onto existing socio-economic data is appropriate. We do, however, submit that this literature and the empirical data upon which it draws could serve as an effective point of departure for investigating the relationship of constitutionalization of socio-economic rights and their actual provision. Likewise, an exclusively doctrinal-legalist examination of socio-economic rights jurisprudence is of limited utility if it does not take into account the extra-judicial determinants of judicial behaviour, particularly as socio-economic rights jurisprudence often has crucial fiscal and political ramifications.

11

Business Rights as Human Rights

Danny Nicol

The orthodox way to have considered the interplay between human rights and business rights would have been to have catalogued the use of human rights—as we conventionally understand them—by corporations, as exemplified in the notorious *RJR Macdonald* case in Canada in which a company invoked freedom of expression to overturn a ban on tobacco advertising.[1] I intend however to eschew this approach because I have become increasingly convinced that if we restrict ourselves to the received definition of human rights, we unduly limit our field of enquiry and thereby fail to see the full picture of the 'new constitutionalism'. What I propose to do, therefore, is to call into question the conventional definition of 'human rights'.[2] The essence of this contribution is that there are compelling reasons to be sceptical about the very distinction between classical human rights and those business rights which have, in effect, been constitutionally entrenched by supranational agreements. The idea of 'human rights' has such a high degree of indeterminacy—indeed it is almost criterionless[3]—that such rights can attach to the protection of an economic status quo just as they can attach to what we conventionally deem to be civil liberties.[4] The supranational agreements which I have in mind are such agreements as the European Union Treaties, the World Trade Organization Agreements, and the North American Free Trade Agreement.

I would like to pursue this argument through the lens of my own state, the United Kingdom. We have of course our Human Rights Act, which, at a formal level, creates a balance between courts and Parliament such that, in theory, it is possible to propose how both legislature and judiciary might contribute to the interpretation of rights.[5] In practice, however, the ethos of judicial interpretative monopoly appears to be pervasive, irrespective of constitutional design, as

---

[1] *RJR-Macdonald Inc v Canada (Attorney General)* [1995] 3 SCR 199.

[2] The idea that 'human rights' has an array of alternative meanings is pursued in M. B. Dembour, *Who Believes in Human Rights?* (Cambridge: Cambridge University Press, 2006).

[3] J. Griffin, *On Human Rights* (Oxford: Oxford University Press, 2008), 14.

[4] M. Graziadei, 'Rights in the European Landscape: A Historical and Comparative Profile', in S. Prechal and B. van Roermund (eds), *The Coherence of EU Law* (Oxford: Oxford University Press, 2008).

[5] See eg J. Hiebert, *Charter Conflicts* (Montreal: McGill–Queen's University, 2002), 218–28; D. Nicol, 'Law and Politics After the Human Rights Act 1998' [2006] *Public Law* 722; C. Gearty, *Principles of Human Rights Adjudication* (Oxford: Oxford University Press, 2004).

shown by Janet Hiebert in her contribution to this book. As in the United States of America,[6] it has proven difficult in the United Kingdom to resist a general cultural willingness to accept a theory of judicial supremacy. In any event, we have, above and beyond the HRA, an international obligation in the form of compliance with the European Convention on Human Rights, and the ECHR is based uncompromisingly and explicitly on the judicial interpretative monopoly of the European Court of Human Rights. At the same time, the United Kingdom is also a member of various mainly economic organizations, some of which also have their own juridical bodies empowered to delineate and enforce the rights which those organizations protect. Chief amongst these organizations are the European Union and the World Trade Organization.

These three systems—ECHR, EU, and WTO—would appear to have much in common. Each was founded in the wake of the Second World War. Each not only laid down obligations for the states involved, but also established permanent institutions charged with developing those obligations. Each has very significantly widened its remit over time, in part through the legislation or jurisprudence of its own institutions. In each, the task of enforcement has been taken out of the hands of the states themselves, and has been given to powerful juridical bodies: the European Court of Human Rights, the European Court of Justice (ECJ), and the WTO Appellate Body and WTO panels. Thereafter, however, we witness a conceptual and disciplinary parting of the ways: the official wisdom would be that the ECHR concerns itself with human rights, whereas the EU and WTO deal predominantly (though in the case of the EU, by no means exclusively) with economic matters.

These latter two organizations commit us to free trade, but political leaders often deploy the rhetoric of free trade to disguise other objectives. In reality free trade is inextricably linked to private sector domination of our services and industries. This is because, in a legal system based on free trade in goods and services, it is not possible to keep private enterprise out of economic sectors, since market participants from other states have been accorded a fundamental right to trade or to establish branches or subsidiaries in the national territory.

Thus in the United Kingdom, in fact, there can be no state takeover of gas, electricity, water, postal services, banking etc, since to bring these sectors into public ownership would contravene the free movement rights of corporations from other states. To focus on the EU, EU provisions do not actually preclude nationalization. Indeed, there is a provision of the Treaty on the Functioning of the European Union (TFEU) which grandly proclaims that the Treaty shall in no way prejudice the system of property ownership in the Member States.[7] But the EU's defence of privatization is all the more effective for being somewhat more subtle than a crude ban on public ownership. Since the 1980s it has become increasingly clear, by virtue of the jurisprudence of the ECJ and EU legislation, that any public sector actor must, in the normal run of things, be run *as if it were a private sector undertaking,*

---

[6] M. Tushnet, *Taking the Constitution Away from the Courts* (Princeton: Princeton University Press, 1999), 25.

[7] Article 345 TFEU.

within a market which is open to private enterprise.[8] There can be no blocking-off of the free market in the different sectors of the economy. Thus the only permissible form of public ownership is competitive public ownership, with the state participating in the market on equal terms to privately owned undertakings, rather than replacing the market. This contrasts with the situation some 30 years ago when the UK government and Parliament assumed that they were entitled to a free choice in the various economic sectors between state and market.

Traditionally, of course, human rights law has been seen as a wholly different field of law from this kind of international or supranational economic law. But this rigid separation, whilst deeply engrained within legal culture, is nonetheless unreal. My key argument is as follows: that there is no compelling basis on which these business rights can be disentangled from political human rights—above all, because they all share the same basic characteristic of fundamentality, in the sense that they prevail over 'ordinary' laws which a parliament is entitled to enact. To be sure, one could sit in some academic ivory tower and construct a theoretical distinction between economic policy which should be contestable and classical political rights which ought not to be. Common law constitutionalists famously try to do so. They differentiate between policy and principle,[9] between positive rights and negative rights.[10] But this does not correspond to legal reality, where business rights are protected as strongly as, if not more strongly than, classical political rights, by force of what amounts to supranational constitutional law.

My thesis is therefore that it is mistaken to keep these different species of rights in hermetically sealed containers. To do so is to cling to the myth of liberal constitutionalism in the face of a legal reality within which these rights run into each other. And in any event, considered in the round, they create a design for life which is very difficult to change by democratic means. One does not discern the full measure of the crimes against democracy wrought by fundamental rights until one looks at the full picture; not just the classical civil liberties, but the free movement and competition regimes too. If this analysis were to be more widely adopted, the perceived division between business rights and human rights would start to fall away and we would begin to see the new constitutionalism in its full, unmitigated horror of entrenchment and judicialization. This might serve to strengthen the arguments in favour of a more general move towards the contestability of rights.

I am aware that I might be adding a jarring note by muddying the 'high politics' of human rights with the 'low politics' of economic policy. It might be argued that in focusing on economic rights, away from the holy grail of classical political rights, I am dealing with things that are not really of the first importance. This I emphatically refute. The free trade rights and competition rights entrenched in the EU treaties and WTO Agreements cannot be dismissed as merely an erosion of national sovereignty 'at the edges'. They restrict national activity in very important spheres of economic life. These constraints, however, have been obscured and

---

[8] See generally E. Szyszczak, *The Regulation of the State in Competitive Markets in the EU* (Oxford: Hart, 2007).

[9] R. Dworkin, *Law's Empire* (London: Fontana Press, 1991), 221–4.

[10] Sir J. Laws, 'The Constitution: Morals and Rights' [1996] *Public Law* 622, 627–35.

camouflaged by the seamless succession of neoliberal governments. British governments of all three parties have embraced neoliberalism with vim and vigour. This
consensus has helped to achieve two things. First, it has served to bring about a
degree of constitutionalization of neoliberal policy. Secondly, however, consensus
has served to *mask* the very constitutionalization which has occurred. Since all
major parties have broadly pursued constitutionally compliant economic policies,
neither party has had occasion to come up against the force of the new constitutional law in any significant way.

The purpose of this constitutionalization is, I would argue, to serve as a sort of
insurance policy, aimed at creating a legacy of endless neoliberalism, and therefore
entrenching the business stability craved by corporations. The idea of constitutionalism as a commitment-device is well chronicled in the literature on the North
American Free Trade Association: as Kahler observes, NAFTA's precision was part
of the Mexican government's strategy to bind successor governments to its policies of economic openness, and this exemplifies how 'legalization' may provide an
institutional solution to ensure the fulfilment of commitments over an extended
period of time. Kahler also points out that the creation of judicial or quasi-judicial
agencies within such legalized regimes may serve similar purposes, by restricting
future freedom of action by politicians.[11]

Now let me anticipate a likely objection to my argument. In the current crisis, we
appear to be living in an era of massive state intervention and therefore seemingly
a resurgence of the primacy of elected politicians over the leaders of business. One
might think, therefore, that the free market rights entrenched in EU law and WTO
law do not matter very much. I would contend, however, that such an argument
misreads the true nature of neoliberalism. To be sure, one way of viewing neoliberalism would be to relate it to the Hayekian 'grand design' involving a perfect system
of competition with strict limitations on state interference in the activities of private
enterprise.[12] However, the second, and more convincing interpretation of neoliberalism, sees it as a project to restore the power of economic elites.[13] On this reading, neoliberal principle is essentially window-dressing, to be cast aside whenever
it interferes with that project. During the crisis the majority of neoliberals adhered
to this second version of neoliberalism: those who stuck to the Hayekian utopian
design proved to be in the minority. On this reading, the bank bail-outs were perfectly in conformity with the dominant interpretation of neoliberalism, and were
therefore wholly permissible under neoliberal constitutional law.

Why are business rights inextricably linked to human rights? We are told that
human rights are human rights because they are something owed to the individual in their capacity as a human.[14] But what is owed to one by virtue of being

---

[11] M. Kahler, 'Conclusion: The Causes and Consequences of Legalization', in J. Goldstein,
M. Kahler, R. Keohane, and A. M. Slaughter (eds), *Legalization and World Politics* (Cambridge,
Mass: The MIT Press, 2001), 279 (emphasis added).
[12] Hayek insisted that state intervention *was* legitimate to establish and maintain a system of competition, but not to replace that system. See F. Hayek, *The Road to Serfdom* (London: Ark Paperbacks,
1986); and F. Hayek, *The Constitution of Liberty* (Chicago: The University of Chicago Press, 1976).
[13] D. Harvey, *A Brief History of Neoliberalism* (Oxford: Oxford University Press, 2005), 19.
[14] Griffin, above n 3, 2.

a human is ideologically driven, not ideologically neutral. It depends on one's vision of the good life. I would argue, therefore, that what makes a right a human right is actually constitutionalization, that is, the decision to make something supra-legislative, to elevate it to the constitutional plane and to that extent to disable the legislature. It is precisely because certain rights are conceived as the basic rights owed to human beings that these rights are accorded a fundamental status. I think we should beware, therefore, of the fact that some rights are *labelled* human rights whereas others are *labelled* free movement rights or competition law. If a decision is made to fundamentalize a business right, that decision in itself necessarily presupposes that that right is an essential element of human existence. *It is, in other words, constitutionalization itself which elevates something into a human right.*

It might, however, be argued that the concept of 'classical' human rights nonetheless enjoys an extra layer of legitimacy which supranational economic law lacks. This is no doubt the case as a matter of popular culture. But in this regard popular culture and judicial practice bifurcate. In the eyes of the courts such extra legitimacy as is possessed by human rights as conventionally conceived, is largely immaterial. The courts will accord supremacy to fundamental economic law over ordinary law just as much as they will in the case of 'classical' human rights—and arguably more so. Thus it is those rights which a society elects to entrench which truly constitute that society's 'fundamental human rights', regardless of their substantive content.

There has been much discussion about the rise of judicialization in the wake of the Human Rights Act. However, it would be wrong to say that judicial supremacy was wholly alien to Britain before 2000. The erosion of British parliamentary legislative authority did not start with the Human Rights Act but with our membership of the European Community, now European Union. EU membership, in fact, makes the United Kingdom, at least in legal terms, more like a state or province of a federal entity than some may realize. In particular, the EU's court, the ECJ, fashioned a federal-type constitution early on in the lifetime of the Community. The ECJ made it clear that EU law was more than just a contract between states. Rather, its free movement and competition rights are rights which can be invoked by any natural and legal person. Moreover they are rights which it is the task of *our national courts* to enforce.[15] For good measure the ECJ also proclaimed a supremacy doctrine whereby it is the duty of every national court and tribunal to set aside any national statute which prevents EU law being given its full force within the Member States.[16]

Although theoretical debate persists over whether Member States can ultimately legislate contrary to EU law, this debate is, in the grand scheme of things, almost entirely hypothetical. The ordinary day-to-day experience is that in our courts, EU law reigns supreme. British courts and tribunals, even at the lowest

---

[15] Case 26/26 *Van Gend en Loos* [1963] ECR 1.
[16] Case 4/64 *Costa v ENEL* [1964] ECR 585, Case 106/77 *Amministrazione delle Finanze dello Stato v. Simmenthal SpA* [1978] ECR 629.

instance, routinely accord supremacy to EU law over British statute.[17] In other words, if Parliament passes a law which is contrary to EU law, then litigants can come before the *British* courts and tribunals, and get those courts and tribunals to accord primacy to EU law over British Acts of Parliament. In addition the ECJ has a system of preliminary references allowing it to pinpoint what kind of laws Britain and the other Member States are permitted to have within the European construct.[18]

Thus the free trade and competition rights of the EU do indeed enjoy a fundamental status. Our courts, the British courts, ensure this primacy. So it is a much simpler arrangement than under the HRA. Unlike the HRA, there is no theoretical invitation for Parliament to deliberate on the rights or wrongs of a court's judgment concerning a statutory provision.[19] Rather, the offending provision is automatically rendered ineffective by the court delivering the decision. Furthermore if the court holds that an Act of Parliament contravenes one of the articles of the EU Treaties, these articles can only be amended by common accord of the 27 Member States, each approving the amendment in conformity with its respective constitutional requirements.[20] Thus the degree of entrenchment is profound. It is small wonder, then, that the ECJ frequently draws attention to the *fundamental* nature of the substantive EU rights which it delineates.[21]

I have argued that the characterization of certain rights as intrinsically 'owed to "humanity"' is in fact not universal but rather ideological. Thus, when dwelling on what is a 'human' right, we have to consider the type of society which is being created. In the European construct, democracy was not intended to be the highest constitutional value.[22] Instead the idea was that the European Community would entrench substantive values, primarily those of market liberalism. If the EC/EU is premised on market liberalism, then this inevitably affects its conception of the human being, and accordingly of what is owed to each of us as a human.

I. Corporate Free Movement as a Fundamental Right

Moreover the *analysis* involved in *adjudicating* business rights is strikingly similar to the analysis employed for adjudicating classical, liberal human rights with which we are more familiar. The most important case which the European Court of Justice ever decided with regard to the free movement rights was the *Cassis de*

---

[17] See eg D. Nicol, 'The Industrial Tribunals—Disapplying with Relish?' [1996] *Public Law* 579. There is little indication that British MPs comprehended the change in relations between Parliament and the national courts which would be likely as a result of EC membership. See D. Nicol, *EC Membership and the Judicialization of British Politics* (Oxford: Oxford University Press, 2001).

[18] Article 267 TFEU.

[19] s 4 HRA 1998.

[20] Article 48 TEU.

[21] R. Lane, 'The Internal Market and the Individual', in N. Nic Shuibhne (ed), *Regulating the Internal Market* (Cheltenham, UK: Edward Elgar, 2006), 257–8.

[22] J. Alder, *Constitutional and Administrative Law* (Basingstoke: Palgrave Macmillan, 2007), 219.

Dijon case in 1979.[23] The case involved the free movement of a French blackcurrant liqueur, Cassis de Dijon, in the face of a German law which prohibited the marketing of *all* fruit liqueurs, domestic as well as imported, with an alcohol content of less than 25 per cent. *Cassis* was a landmark judgment because the ECJ declared that EU law could prohibit even those national trade restrictions which did not actually discriminate against products from other Member States. The ECJ could thereby override even those rules which applied equally to domestic products and to products from other Member States. The *Cassis* decision thereby constituted a very important expansion of the substantive scope of EU law. Most significantly for our purposes, the ECJ went on to hold that such rules could only be successfully defended by the Member States if they (a) helped to achieve certain imperative requirements in the public interest and (b) were proportionate to the legitimate objective pursued. This is essentially the same analysis as a classical human rights analysis, where a court starts with the assumption that a right enjoys fundamental status and therefore can only be restricted under very limited circumstances. To that end, the court then has to consider whether the competing aim to be served by restricting the right is legitimate and sufficiently important. Hence the state's limitation of the right must correspond to a 'pressing social need'. The court then analyses the proportionality of the limitation on the right, to see if it is 'necessary in a democratic society' to achieve the legitimate aim.

The *Cassis* form of analysis has been extended to the free movement of services, freedom of establishment, and free movement of persons.[24] As Joseph Weiler has observed, the application of the doctrine of proportionality in these contexts cannot be value-neutral: rather, the ECJ is obliged to enter into the policy merits of the national measure, and to impose a European Union value-choice on the Member State.[25] The need to strike a balance between competing public interests means that courts cannot protect rights without becoming deeply involved in the social context and in legislative decision-making. In so doing the ECJ has predominantly favoured the interests of the creation of a single market over competing considerations.[26] In particular, as Judy Fudge explains in her contribution to this book, the ECJ has in recent years made it clear that it will privilege the free movement rights of corporations over social and labour rights. To this end it has further reinforced the fundamentality of free movement rights by indicating that they enjoy 'horizontal direct effect'—allowing private parties (notably corporations) to enforce them against other private parties (notably trade unions). In *Viking*, the ECJ held that corporations could rely on their free movement rights against trade unions when industrial action threatened employers' exercise of those rights.[27] In *Laval*, the ECJ

---

[23] Case 120/78 *Rewe-Zentrale AG v Bundesmonopolverwaltung für Branntwein* [1979] ECR 649.

[24] Case 33/74 *Van Binsbergen v Bestuur van de Bedrijfsvereniging voor de Metaalnijverheid* [1974] ECR 1299; Case C-384/93 *Alpine Investments BV v Minister van Financiën* [1995] ECR I-1141; Case C-55/94 *Gebhard v Consiglio dell'Ordine degli Avvocati e Procuratori di Milano* [1995] ECR I-4165; Case C-281/98 *Angonese v Cassa di Riparmio di Bozano SpA* [2000] ECR I-4139.

[25] J. Weiler, *The Constitution of Europe* (Cambridge: Cambridge University Press, 1999), 122–3.

[26] A. Stone Sweet, *Governing with Judges* (Oxford: Oxford University Press, 2000), 99.

[27] Case C-438/05 *International Transport Workers' Federation v Viking Line ABP* [2007] ECR I-10779; [2008] 1 CMLR 51.

held that free movement rights precluded a trade union from using a blockade of sites to force an employer from another Member State to sign a collective agreement containing terms which were more favourable than those laid down in the relevant legislation.[28] In *Rüffert*, the ECJ made it clear that national public authorities could not require public works contractors to comply with prevailing collective agreements which had not been declared universally applicable.[29] In *Commission v Luxembourg*, the ECJ declared that Member States lack the power to require all employers posting workers to comply with relevant collective agreements, notably those not declared universally applicable.[30]

It should be emphasized that in all these cases the ECJ was essentially interpreting provisions of the EU Treaties: Article 49 TFEU on freedom of establishment in *Viking*, and Article 56 TFEU on freedom to provide services in *Laval*, *Rüffert*, and *Commission v Luxembourg*. Accordingly the only certain way to overturn the ECJ's prioritization of corporate interests over social interests would be for all 27 Member States to amend the Treaty.[31] Therefore it would only require a single Member State to veto any such reprioritization of EU values.[32] Thus the ECJ's interpretation of the relevant Treaty provisions in these cases enjoys a high degree of entrenchment.

The ECJ's methodology also highlights the extent to which the free movement rights are accorded a supreme status over competing concerns. In *Viking* and *Laval*, the ECJ accepted that the right to take collective action, including the right to strike, was a fundamental right which formed an integral part of the general principles of EU law.[33] The ECJ was confronted, therefore, with a conflict between two rights, both ostensibly of a fundamental nature—free movement on the one hand, the right to collective action on the other. Normally the effect of such a conflict would be to expand the margin of appreciation enjoyed by the state authorities. The European Court of Human Rights so held in *Otto-Preminger Institut v Austria*,[34] and the ECJ appeared to take the same position in *Schmidberger*,[35] and

---

[28] Case C-341/05 *Laval un Partneri Ltd v Svenska Byggnadsarbetareförbundet* [2007] ECR I-11767; [2008] 2 CMLR 9.

[29] Case C-346/06 *Rüffert v Land Niedersachsen* [2008] 2 CMLR 39.

[30] Case C-319/06 *Commission of the European Communities v Grand Duchy of Luxembourg* [2008] ECR I-04323.

[31] The European Trade Union Confederation appears to recognize that only Treaty revision will change the situation, proposing a draft protocol to the Treaty on European Union to the effect that 'nothing in the Treaties, and in particular neither economic freedoms nor competition rules, shall have priority over fundamental social rights and social progress...In case of conflict fundamental social rights shall take precedence'.

[32] It is true that three of the cases also involved the interpretation of the Posted Workers' Directive (Directive 96/71/EC). However, in *Laval*, the ECJ appeared to endorse the Advocate General's view that the sole relevance of the directive was that it might shed light on the interpretation of the Treaty article. There can be no certainty, however, that the ECJ would change its interpretation of Articles 49 and 56 TFEU if the Council and European Parliament changed the secondary legislation. Whilst the ECJ is not formally bound by its previous decisions, it reverses them rarely.

[33] *Viking* [44], *Laval* [91].

[34] *Otto-Preminger Institut v Austria* (1994) 19 ENRR 34, E Com HR.

[35] Case C-112/00 *Schmidberger, Internationale Transporte und Planzuge v Austria* [2003] ECR I-5659.

in *Omega*,[36] the thinking being that when a state is faced with a conflict between two fundamental rights, the scales are evenly balanced and a difficult choice has to be made, so it makes sense to give the state considerable leeway. The ECJ, however, took a strikingly different approach in *Viking* and *Laval*, adopting its normal test that a restriction on free movement could only be accepted if it pursued a legitimate aim compatible with the Treaty, and was justified by overriding reasons of public interest. The ECJ went on to hold that even if this was the case, the restriction would still have to be suitable for securing the attainment of the objective pursued, and—crucially—must not go beyond what is necessary in order to attain that objective.[37] It was on that final limb of the proportionality test that the trade unions' case collapsed.

As Anne Davies observes, the proportionality test is commonly used as a way of assessing the state's limitations on the right to strike, whereas in *Viking* and *Laval*, the right to strike was not the starting point for analysis. Rather, the ECJ's reasoning begins with the employer's assertion of its free movement rights under Article 49 TFEU or Article 56 TFEU against not the state but a trade union. The union's industrial action then had to be tested for proportionality in relation to the employer's fundamental freedom of movement. The ECJ's recognition of the right to strike is therefore *conditional* on the satisfaction of the proportionality test. Furthermore, in *Viking* in particular, the ECJ emphasizes the 'least restrictive alternative' version of the proportionality test. This directs national courts to consider whether there was any other form of action open to the unions which would have been less restrictive of the employer's free movement rights. Yet industrial action is *intended* to cause harm to the employer: the more harm it causes, the more effective it is likely to be in persuading the employer to make concessions.[38] To put it crudely: the more disproportionate it is, the better. Davies observes that, for an English lawyer, the introduction of proportionality is a remarkable new development. Our domestic law has sought to avoid 'politicizing' the courts, by preventing them from considering the merits of the dispute and the harm caused to the employer. By contrast, the EU law approach involves the courts in a much more politically sensitive analysis involving the application of the proportionality test to industrial disputes.[39] Malmberg and Sigeman observe that the rulings compromise the freedom of Member States such as Denmark, Finland, and Sweden to preserve their favoured 'variety of capitalism', whereby it is almost entirely the responsibility of trade unions to safeguard high levels of wages and conditions of employment.[40] Loïc Azoulai criticizes the ECJ for having imposed a choice in favour of a model of industrial relations which privileges the interests

---

[36] Case C-36/02 *Omega Speilhallen-und Automate naufstellungs-GmbH v Oberbürgermeisterin des Bundesstadt Bonn* [2004] ECR I-9609.

[37] *Viking* [75], *Laval* [101].

[38] A. Davies, 'One Step Forward, Two Steps Back? The *Viking* and *Laval* Cases in the ECJ' (2008) 37 *Industrial Law Journal* 128, 141–3.

[39] Ibid 146.

[40] J. Malmberg and T. Sigemann, 'Industrial Actions and EU Economic Freedoms: The Autonomous Collective Bargaining Model Curtailed by the European Court of Justice' (2008) 45 *Common Market Law Review* 1115, 1117.

of undertakings, when an alternative model was available which would look to the interests of workers and be more respectful of the divergent requirements of national social models.[41] Thus the ECJ's vaunted commitment to the right to collective action as a fundamental right cannot be taken at face value. In practice it emphatically subordinates this right to its 'right of right', the free movement of economic actors.

For good measure, a fundamental right to free trade is also guaranteed by the juridicial bodies of the World Trade Organization. The WTO's Appellate Body has made it clear that non-trade policies, for example environmental policies, fall within the scope of WTO law, enabling it and the WTO panels to delineate a 'line of equilibrium' between trade and non-trade policies.[42] In other words, the WTO judiciary has assumed jurisdiction to determine whether WTO members are adopting a lawful balance between free trade and other concerns such as the environment, or whether their pursuit of competing policies at the expense of free trade is unlawful. Once again this is reminiscent of ECJ jurisprudence, where fields that fall outside the ambit of the EU Treaties have nonetheless been held to be affected by EU law.[43] In this way the Appellate Body, like the ECJ, performs a function of constitutional adjudication, balancing the interests of private enterprise against social priorities.

It might be argued that the WTO does not accord free movement quite the same degree of fundamentality as EU law, since WTO law has not adopted a *Cassis de Dijon*-style presumption against non-discriminatory obstacles to trade. Rather, the WTO Appellate Body purports to adopt a neutral balancing between trade and non-trade considerations. In reality, however, neutrality is not possible. Whatever the formal position pronounced by the Appellate Body, the WTO case law appears to show that, not unnaturally, juridical bodies charged with free trade favour solutions which privilege free trade, irrespective of the test they officially profess.[44] In any event Joseph Weiler regards it as inevitable that before too long the *Cassis* form of reasoning will find its way into WTO jurisprudence, since it is in fact the only way of excluding the unnecessary restrictions on trade which are forbidden by the text of the Agreements.[45] In any event it is noteworthy that the task of balancing free trade concerns against competing public interests has once again been transferred to non-accountable institutions, in the form of the Appellate Body and WTO panels. In this regard, interpretations of WTO law by the Appellate Body and panels

---

[41] L. Azoulai, 'The Court of Justice and the Social Market Economy: The Emergence of an Ideal and the Conditions for its Realization' (2008) 45 *Common Market Law Review* 1335.

[42] *United States—Import Prohibition on Certain Shrimp and Shrimp Products* WTO case nos 58 (and 61) WT/DS58/AB/R, paras 152–3.

[43] eg national systems of property ownership, though formally falling outside the Treaties, cannot be exercised so as to impede free movement of goods in the field of intellectual property. Case 15/74 *Centrafarm v Sterling Drug* [1974] ECR 1147, [1974] 2 CMLR 480.

[44] I. J. Sand, 'Polycontextuality as an Alternative to Constitutionalism', in C. Joerges, I. J. Sand, and G. Teubner (eds), *Transnational Governance and Constitutionalism* (Oxford: Hart, 2004).

[45] Article XX of the GATT. See J. Weiler, 'Epilogue: Towards a Common Law of International Trade', in J. Weiler (ed), *The EU, the WTO and the NAFTA* (Oxford: Oxford University Press, 2000), 230–1.

set important precedents for all to follow.[46] Whilst there is no formal doctrine of *stare decisis*, nonetheless the WTO judiciary itself employs a fairly powerful use of precedent.[47] From the point of view of private companies, the body of law enshrined in precedent provides the rules and certainty which can lower the 'risk premium' for international transactions.

To a large extent the constitutional enormity of decision-making through WTO dispute settlement is concealed. No doubt political leaders were anxious not to raise concerns for democracy: after all, they would have been at pains to avoid problems over ratification. They were aided by the terminological baggage which accompanies trade policy. Thus decisions affecting the freedom of action of states are made not by courts but by 'Panels' and by an Appellate 'Body'. The esoteric trade law 'spin'—the idea that complex matters are being hived off to specialist technocrats —obscures the profound centrality of WTO decision-making. The constitutional reality is that, on behalf of almost the entire world, the Panels and Appellate Body determine the balance between the interests of the free market on the one hand, and competing policies on the other. This role, inherent in the logic of the WTO text, has made the WTO not a mere 'specialist' trade treaty but more an instrument for world governance.[48]

II. The Right to Compete in a Market as a Fundamental Right

Not only do corporations benefit from a fundamental right to transnational trade, but they also enjoy a fundamental right to 'undistorted competition', and the effect of this is once again to improve the hand of the private sector against the public sector. Thus the European Union has a well-known competition regime. Article 106 TFEU mandates the Member States not to act contrary to the Treaty rules, in particular the competition rules, in respect of their public undertakings. In a series of cases in the 1990s, the ECJ was called upon to consider whether Article 106 permits Member States to reserve certain activities to their public sectors and thereby shelter them from competition. In interpreting Article 106, the ECJ case law moved discernibly in the direction of a presumption of illegality of special or exclusive rights for the public sector, unless the Member State could show that these were indispensable. In *Höfner and Elster* and in *Job Centre*, the ECJ held that where the public sector may well be unable to satisfy demand for services, it is contrary to Article 106 for a Member State to prohibit rival undertakings from operating in the relevant market.[49] And in *Corbeau*, the ECJ instructed the national

---

[46] Paradoxically, however, and in contrast to proceedings before the European Court of Justice, WTO Members which are not party to a case have no right to submit their observations.

[47] J. Jackson, *Sovereignty, the WTO and Changing Fundamentals of International Law* (Cambridge: Cambridge University Press, 2006), 10.

[48] Hand in hand with the substantive expansion of WTO law, the WTO enforcement machinery has become progressively more effective. See D. Nicol, 'Britain's Transnational Constitution' (2008) 61 *Current Legal Problems* 125.

[49] Case C-41/90 *Höfner and Elser v Macrotron GmbH* [1991] ECR I-1979, [1993] 4 CMLR 306; Case C-55/96 *Job Centre coop arl* [1997] ECR I-7119.

courts to carefully examine the particular tasks assigned to the public sector with a view to deciding which tasks could be dissociated from it and made subject to competition.[50]

Thus not only are courts assuming the power to determine the balance between public ownership and private enterprise, but attempts at even-handedness have gone by the board. As Craig and de Búrca put it, 'agnosticism as to forms of economic organization has been replaced by a more strident belief in the operation of free markets, unless the State can provide special justification for the privileges accorded'.[51] Monti suggests quite simply that 'today, under EC law, state intervention in the economy is suspect'.[52] Gardner characterizes the case law as revolutionary, since it 'has reversed the decades-old presumption—reflected in the very text of [Article 106]—that public monopolies and privileged undertakings are compatible with the EC Treaty and that Member States are free in principle to determine their preferred system of property ownership'.[53]

The Article 106 jurisprudence was merely a prelude. By eroding the legitimacy of public monopolies, the ECJ prepared the ground for a far more comprehensive assault on the public sector. The 1990s witnessed a wave of liberalization through *legislative* intervention at EU level.[54] EU legislation has made a far more comprehensive contribution than ECJ jurisprudence in opening up the public monopolies, because legislation is general rather than piecemeal.[55] Thus the Council and European Parliament have enacted directives to open up the markets in gas, electricity, and postal services.[56] Legislation on rail services is presently in the pipeline.

It might well be argued that the liberalization legislation is the product of democracy, since it has been enacted after due deliberation by the Council and the

[50] Case C-320/91 P *Procureur du Roi v Paul Corbeau* [1993] ECR I-2533.

[51] P. Craig and G. de Búrca, *EU Law—Text, Cases and Materials* (Oxford: Oxford University Press, 2007), 1079.

[52] D. Chalmers, C. Hadjiemmanuil, G. Monti, and A. Tomkins, *European Union Law* (Cambridge: Cambridge University Press, 2006), 1115.

[53] A. Gardner, 'The Velvet Revolution: Article 90 and the Triumph of the Free Market in Europe's Regulated Sectors' (1995) 16 *European Competition Law Review* 78.

[54] D. Geradin and C. Humpe, 'The Liberalization of Postal Services in the European Union: An Analysis of Directive 97/67', in D. Geradin (ed), *The Liberalization of Postal Services in the European Union* (The Hague: Kluwer Law International, 2004), 91.

[55] J. Baquero Cruz, 'Beyond Competition: Services of General Interest and European Community Law', in G. De Búrca (ed), *EU Law and the Welfare State: In Search of Solidarity* (Oxford: Oxford University Press, 2005), 211.

[56] Directive 2003/55/EC of the European Parliament and of the Council of 28 June 2003 concerning common rules for the internal market in natural gas and repealing Directive 98/30/EC, OJ L176, 15.7.2003, p 57; Directive 2003/54/EC of the European Parliament and of the Council of 26 June 2003 concerning common rules for the internal market in electricity and repealing Directive 96/92/EC, OJ L176, 15.7.2003, p 37, Directive 97/67/EC of the European Parliament and of the Council of 15 December 1997 on common rules for the development of the internal market of Community postal services and the improvement of quality of service, OJ. L015, 21.01.1998, p 0014–0025, Directive 2002/39/EC of the European Parliament and of the Council of 10 June 2002 amending Directive 97/67/EC with regard to the further opening to competition of Community postal services. OJ L175, 5.7.2002, p 21, Directive 2008/6/EC of the European Parliament and the Council of 20 February 2008 amending Directive 97/67/EC with regard to the full accomplishment of the internal market of Community postal services OJ. L52/4, 27.2.2008.

European Parliament, and so there can be little objection to its legitimacy. True enough, no one forced the EU institutions to pass this legislation. Yet at the same time the Council and Parliament do not operate in an ideologically impartial constitutional environment. Since the Treaties entrench the free movement rights, it is far easier for the EU institutions to liberalize sectors than for them to permit Member States to renationalize them. A fictitious scenario may help prove the point. Imagine that a national government sought the introduction of EU legislation to permit Member States to renationalize in their totality their postal, gas, and electricity services. One would have to depend on the Commission putting forward such a proposal to the Council and European Parliament. One would also require the identification of a convincing legal base—an article authorizing the creation of such legislation—in the Treaties. The most obvious possibility would be Article 352 TFEU, which requires the Council to act unanimously.[57] Thus any Member State could veto the legislation (perhaps, for example, at the prompting of a transnational corporation providing public services on its territory and in other Member States). Even if legislation emerged, it might well be struck down by the EU judiciary for its incompatibility with the fundamental freedom to provide services between Member States.[58] If this were the case, then only Treaty amendment, requiring the common accord of all Member States, could guarantee the constitutionality of such legislation. By contrast, when the EU legislates to liberalize public utilities, this is subject to a far lower hurdle, the approval of a qualified majority of the Council.[59] Thus liberalization, which brings an inevitable degree of privatization in its wake, enjoys a high degree of entrenchment within the EU, consolidating the fundamental status of the right to private enterprise.

The process whereby EU secondary legislation expands the interpretation of the freedoms enshrined in EU primary legislation—the Treaties—is intriguing. One can discern a process whereby secondary legislation upgrades and rachets-up the Treaty rights of freedom of establishment and freedom to provide services. Once the political institutions have legislated, entrepreneurs can then invoke not only the relevant directive but also their expanded Treaty rights in order to prevent their exclusion from the relevant markets. Yet it is seemingly not open to the EU's political institutions to do the opposite. Having enlarged the scope of the free movement rights through secondary legislation, it would seem unlikely that they could effectively deploy secondary legislation to contract the scope of these rights once again, to the point of permitting Member States

---

[57] 'If action by the Union should prove necessary...to attain one of the objectives set out in the Treaties, and the Treaties have not provided the necessary powers, the Council, acting unanimously on a proposal from the Commission and after obtaining the consent of the European Parliament, shall adopt the appropriate measures....'

[58] It might be argued that in this context the EU Charter of Fundamental Rights 2000 might prevail over the freedom to provide services. In fact Article 36 of the Charter protects access to services of general interest only in accordance with the Treaties. Article 16 of the Charter protects the freedom to conduct a business in accordance with EU law.

[59] Article 114 TFEU.

to reintroduce state-owned monopolies. It would appear that nothing short of Treaty amendment could authorize this.

III. Corporate Property as a Fundamental Right

Just as orthodox business rights need to be seen as fundamental human rights, so too orthodox human rights can be seen as buttressing the business system. There are, to be sure, some very visible points of contact between the conventional conception of human rights and the business rights. Bizarrely the 'human' rights of the ECHR can be invoked not only by individual human beings but also by corporations.[60] The right to the peaceful enjoyment of one's possessions is a traditional human right, enshrined in Article 1 of Protocol 1 of the ECHR. During the 1970s and early 1980s this right developed into a right to compensation, and the case law of that era suggested that states had a wide margin of appreciation as regards the quantum of compensation to be paid.[61] But this case law was decided before the global political 'herding' towards neoliberalism became readily apparent. A more robust approach by the European Court of Human Rights is likely today. If the case law of the Court were to require the payment of full compensation, this might well have the practical consequence of restricting public ownership to bankrupt companies, such as the banks during the crisis of 2008. This would represent a very significant restriction of national economic policy discretion.

However, even accepting the likelihood that the ECHR property right has evolved into a right of full compensation, it is nonetheless arguable that the EU and WTO free movement and competition rights still in fact provide stronger 'human rights' protection for corporate property than does the 'official' human right itself. The EU or WTO right to participate in the market in a given economic sector actually precludes the bringing of that sector into public ownership, so that questions of compensation normally need never arise.

Significantly, some international economic lawyers explicitly articulate the inseparability of business law and the fundamental property right. We must be thankful in particular for the candour of Ernst-Ulrich Petersmann, one of the leading academics in the field of WTO law. For Petersmann, WTO provisions can strengthen, and give precision to, the *human* right to free trade which ought to be protected by every national constitution; WTO law can also serve the important domestic constitutional function of restricting broad governmental discretion over trade policy. Petersmann argues that international economic law rightly exists to protect the property rights of those engaged in international transactions. In his view it is therefore preferable to the many national constitutions which afford weak

---

[60] Article 34 ECHR.
[61] See eg *Lithgow and others v United Kingdom* (Application nos 9006/80, 9262/81, 9263/81, 9265/81, 9266/81, 9313/81, 9405/81) judgment of 8 July 1986.

protection to property rights, and which give too much freedom to governments to intervene in the economy.[62]

IV. Conclusion

The received wisdom is that the authors of international human rights law disowned the idea that human rights could be the expression of any single conception of human good, and that they aspired to a notion of human rights which could be endorsed from many political points of view.[63] Yet at base a 'human right' is a right which is considered of the first importance, because it constitutes an essential element of the way life should be lived. However, judgments regarding the way in which life should be lived are not arrived at by some universalist alchemy. They are made by those who enjoy ideological hegemony in a given era, and for the past 30 years it is neoliberals who have enjoyed this hegemony. Neoliberals have done much to fashion today's supra-constitution: a higher-order law prevailing de facto over traditional British parliamentary sovereignty, by force of increasingly powerful supranational regimes.[64] This *entrenchment* has allowed the judiciary and quasi-judiciary to assume a similar role to that of the American courts during the notorious *Lochner* era, and to transform the entrepreneur's right to pursue his business into a constitutional or human right.[65] Against this background we cannot really get the true measure of the 'new constitutionalism' and the judicialization of rights if we restrict our analysis merely to the 'classical' liberal political rights, and leave out of the reckoning the corporate rights which have likewise been accorded the status of fundamental human rights. In fact there is no compelling reason to separate these rights from each other: it is more instructive to consider the entire constitutional construct. If one does so, such an analysis reveals that the need for a general move towards contestability and democratization is far more pressing than might otherwise be assumed.

---

[62] E.U. Petersmann, *Constitutional Functions and Constitutional Problems of International Economic Law* (Fribourg, Switzerland: University Press, 1991); E. U. Petersmann, 'European and International Constitutional Law: Time for Promoting "Cosmopolitan Democracy" in the WTO', in G. de Búrca and J. Scott (eds), *The EU and the WTO* (Oxford: Hart, 2001).

[63] C. Beitz, *The Idea of Human Rights* (Oxford: Oxford University Press, 2009). For an opposing argument see D. Nicol, 'Original Intent and the European Convention on Human Rights' [2005] *Public Law* 152.

[64] See generally D. Nicol, *The Constitutional Protection of Capitalism* (Oxford: Hart, 2010).

[65] In *Lochner v New York* 198 US 45 (1905), the United States Supreme Court held by 5 to 4 that state legislation restricting working hours for bakers unconstitutionally restricted their freedom of contract which was implicitly enshrined in the Constitution. The case lent its name to an era of case law which emphasized market liberty, private property, and judicial intolerance of legislation promoting the 'special interests' of particular groups. For an account of the *Lochner* jurisprudence and its impact, see eg W. Forbath, *Law and the Shaping of the American Labor Movement* (Cambridge, Mass: Harvard University Press, 1989). For a comparative study see D. Nicol, 'Europe's *Lochner* moment' [2011] *Public Law* (forthcoming).

12

Constitutionalizing Labour Rights in Europe

Judy Fudge

I. Introduction

Since the mid-1990s, constitutionalizing labour rights has typically referred to the goal of securing the recognition of labour rights as fundamental human rights at the transnational and national levels.[1] The idea is that once there is general recognition of the status of labour rights, especially the rights to bargain collectively and to strike, as fundamental human rights, then they can be used as a counterweight to global competition, which, when combined with neo-liberal economic policies, threatens to lower both labour standards and workers' standards of living. Labour rights can achieve this fundamental status either through negotiated constitutional amendment or via judicial recognition. Although fundamental rights can take a variety of institutional forms, justiciable and legally enforceable rights are regarded as the most powerful.

Harry Arthurs juxtaposes labour rights in the 'formal constitution' with what he refers to as labour's 'real constitution', a key component of which are the transnational free trade regimes and neo-liberal policies.[2] He argues that labour rights are subordinate to the real constitution, the legitimacy of which ultimately depends 'on its promises to make life better by facilitating the operation of markets'.[3] If the real constitution fails to make good on this promise, then, according to Arthurs, it may be possible for 'labour to assert its rights', although he cautions that these rights cannot be realized by constitutional negotiation or litigation.[4]

In this chapter, I want to explore the relationship between these dual processes of constitutionalism by combining Stephen Gill's notion of new constitutionalism,[5] which refers to the process by which markets have expanded throughout the globe and market rules have been embedded in transnational agreements, with Karl Polanyi's idea of the 'double movement', whereby 'society protects itself against the

[1] R. Dukes, 'Constitutionalizing Employment Relations: Sinzheimer, Kahn-Freund, and the Role of Labour Law' (2008) 35 *Journal of Law and Society* 341, at 342. See also footnote 1 in which Dukes refers to a number of articles advocating the constitutionalization of labour rights.

[2] H. W. Arthurs, 'Labour and the "Real" Constitution' (2007) 48 *Les Cahiers de Droit* 43, at 61.

[3] Ibid 63.

[4] Ibid 63–4.

[5] S. Gill, 'Globalization, Market Civilization, and Disciplinary Neoliberalism' (1995) 24 *Millennium: Journal of International Studies* 399.

perils inherent in a self-regulating market economy'.[6] The renewed emphasis on labour rights as fundamental human rights since the mid-1990s is part of a broader movement to recognize the social dimension of globalization and to re-embed the labour market, and, thus, it is a response to neo-liberalism.[7]

The big question is the extent to which the attempts to constitutionalize labour rights reflects rather than challenges the basic tenets of neo-liberalism.[8] Since the goal of many human rights advocates is to have human rights legally recognized, by either the appropriate court or international institution, there is a tendency for human rights to map strongly onto civil and political rights. However, many human rights advocates also want to broaden the prevailing conception of fundamental right to include social rights with a collective dimension.[9] It is an open question the extent to which constitutionalizing labour rights marks a substantive return to social protection.

The specific focus in this chapter is the role of the courts in constitutionalizing labour rights. Not only is judicial review a key feature of both processes of constitutionalization, unions, especially those in common law countries, historically have viewed courts with suspicion since courts historically have subordinated labour rights to bargain collectively and to take collective action to the rights of employers to trade. However, prominent courts in Europe have begun to characterize key labour rights as fundamental human rights. In 2007, the European Court of Justice released two decisions that recognized the right to strike as a fundamental right to be considered when interpreting the European Community Treaty.[10] In 2008, the European Court of Human Rights overruled its earlier decisions on the matter to hold that the right to freedom of association in the European Convention on Human Rights includes collective bargaining.[11] Moreover, the decision by the European Court of Human Rights (ECtHR) does not appear to be an isolated event, but rather a harbinger of a trend; in four subsequent decisions, the ECtHR confirmed that the freedom of association in Article 11 of the European Convention of Human Rights included collective bargaining[12] and collective action.[13] Both the Luxembourg and Strasbourg courts referred to the ILO

---

[6] K. Polanyi, *The Great Transformation: The Political and Economic Origins of Our Time* (Boston: Beacon Press, 1944), 76.

[7] J. Fudge, 'The New Discourse of Labour Rights: From Social to Fundamental Rights?' (2007) 29 *Comparative Labor Law and Policy Journal* 29.

[8] D. Harvey, *A Brief History of Neo-liberalism* (Oxford: Oxford University Press, 2005), 175–6.

[9] Ibid 178–82.

[10] Case C-438/05, *International Transport Workers' Federation, Finnish Seamen's Union v Viking Line ABP, OÜ Viking Line Eesti*, Opinion of Advocate General Miguel Poiares Maduro, 23 May 2007, ECJ decision, 11 Dec 2007 (referred to as '*Viking*'); Case C-341/05, *Laval un Partneri Ltd v Svenska Byggnadsarbetareförbundet, Svenska Byggnadsarbetareförbundet, avd. 1, Svenska Elektrikerförbundet*, Opinion of Advocate General Paolo Mengozzi, 23 May 2007, ECJ decision, 18 Dec 2007 (referred to as '*Laval*').

[11] *Demir and Baykara v Turkey*, Application no 34503/97, 12 Nov 2008 (referred to as '*Demir*').

[12] *Danilenkov v Russia*, Application no 67336/01, 30 July 2009.

[13] *Enerji Yapi-Yol Sen v Turkey*, Application no 68959/01, 21 April 2009; *Saime Özcan v Turkey*, Application no 22943/04, 12 Sept 2009; *Kaya and Seyhan v Turkey*, Application no 30946/04, 15 Sept 2009, which are discussed in K. Ewing and J. Hendy, 'The Dramatic Implications of Demir and Baykara' (2010) 39 *Industrial Law Journal* 2–51.

conventions and supervisory body decisions, the Charter of Fundamental Rights of the European Union, and the European Social Charter as a source of law.[14]

However, despite the fact the highest courts in Europe have recognized labour rights such as collective bargaining and collective action as fundamental, the results of the constitutionalization of labour rights are paradoxical. In order to substantiate this claim, the chapter unfolds in three sections, beginning with the conceptual discussion, in which the new constitutionalism, Polanyi's pendulum, and the constitutionalization of labour rights are discussed. The utility of this relational approach to labour rights and constitutionalism is put to the test in a European case study, which begins by briefly describing the two-step process of constitutionalization, although it concentrates upon the recent court decisions that have recognized labour rights as fundamental at a constitutional level. The chapter concludes by explaining why the results are paradoxical.

II. The Dual Process of Constitutionalism

(a) New Constitutionalization

Constitutions set limits on the legitimate use of state power and they 'are intended to have a level of fixity outside of politics, that is, they are intended to standardize enduring rules of the game.'[15] Although traditional notions of constitutionalism are associated with political rights, obligations, freedoms, and procedures that give institutional form to the state, the term has also been used to describe the international institutional arrangements and agreements that nation states have adopted that circumscribe the exercise of their legislative or regulatory power.[16] Constitutionalism is a process that has both transnational and national dimensions.

Globalization refers to the process of greater economic integration across national boundaries and it has been promoted and accompanied by neo-liberal political discourse that prioritizes markets over politics and emphasizes market mechanisms and individual approaches to solving or handling economic or social problems. Neo-liberalism is 'in the first instance a theory of political economic practices that proposes that human well-being can best be advanced by liberating individual entrepreneurial freedoms and skills within an institutional framework characterized by strong private property rights, free markets, and free trade'.[17] Neo-liberal restructuring at the national level is closely associated with international economic agreements, such as free trade agreements, which 'serve as a restructuring tool or, put differently, as a conditioning framework that promotes

---

[14] See discussion below.
[15] D. Schneiderman, 'Investment Rules and the New Constitutionalism' (2000) 25 *Law and Social Inquiry* 757.
[16] Gill, above n 5.
[17] Harvey, above n 8, at 2.

and consolidates neo-liberal restructuring'.[18] These conditioning agreements can be bilateral, regional, or international. Stephen Gill coined the term 'new constitutionalism' to refer to the quasi-legal process whereby nation states cede their authority to interfere with the market.[19]

A key element of this process of new constitutionalism is the separation of powers and judicial review.[20] At the transnational (eg the European Community Treaty and North American Free Trade Agreement) and international (the World Trade Organization, for instance) levels, courts and tribunals have the jurisdiction to hear complaints brought by corporations against social and economic policies of national governments.[21] At the national level, 'new constitutionalism' refers to the entrenchment of justiciable bills of rights and it marks a transformation in the relations between courts and representative institutions.[22]

The object of new constitutionalism is to embed disciplinary neo-liberalism, which seeks to insulate 'key aspects of the economy from the influence of politicians or the mass of citizens by imposing, internally and externally, binding constraints on the conduct of fiscal, monetary, trade and investment policy'.[23] The international agreements are designed to bind future governments (since they are so difficult to amend) and thus foreclose certain options that the populations of nation states may want to preserve or adopt in the future. The key feature of the new constitutionalism is the discipline imposed on state institutions both to prevent national interference with an extended suite of property rights and to provide entry and exit options for holders of mobile capital with regard to political jurisdiction. But, as Isabella Baker and Stephen Gill remark, 'missing from this policy framework are measures to guarantee and secure the rights of workers, and in consequence greater rights and freedoms for capital may result in greater exploitation and economic insecurity for workers'.[24]

(b) The Double Movement

The political economist Karl Polanyi's insight was that 'every period of economic reconstruction, associated with major technological change and the renewed

---

[18] R. Grinspun and R. Kreklewich, 'Consolidating Neoliberal Reforms: "Free Trade" as a Conditioning Framework' (1994) 43 *Studies in Political Economy* 33.

[19] Gill, above n. 5.

[20] I. Bakker and S. Gill, 'Ontology, Method, and Hypotheses', in I. Bakker and S. Gill (eds), *Power, Production and Social Reproduction: Human Insecurity in the Global Political Economy* (Houndmills, Basingstoke: Palgrave, 2003), 17–18 at 31. Christine Kaufman discusses the process of integrating constitutional ideas into international obligations, and identifies five key principles: the rule of law, separation of powers, fundamental rights, democratic participation, and social justice. See *Globalisation and Labour Rights: The Conflict between Core Labour Rights and International Economic Law* (Oxford and Portland: Hart, 2007).

[21] Arthurs, above n 2, 63.

[22] J. Fudge, 'Legally Speaking: The Courts, the Market, and Democracy' (2003) 19 *Supreme Court Law Review* (2nd series) 111, at 119.

[23] Gill, 5 n 5, 412. In this collection, Danny Nicol has referred to these agreements, in particular, the EU Treaties and the World Trade Agreement, as bringing about a 'degree of constitutionalism of neo-liberal policy'.

[24] Bakker and Gill, above n 20, 31.

pursuit of flexibility, has eventually induced a counter-movement to provide new systems of social protection compatible with new structures and processes'.[25] This double movement between market expansion and social protection is the motor of institutional change, and it springs from the fact that labour is not a real commodity. Human beings are not conceived and raised as commodities to be sold on the market; instead, we are embedded in a series of natural social relationships that are deeply incompatible with market institutions and impersonal exchange.[26] Thus, the extension of the self-regulating market provokes resistance in part because it overturns established and widely accepted social compacts on the right to livelihood. Those whose traditional livelihoods and living standards are dislocated by the market will use the state to protect themselves from the consequences, and it is this dynamic, according to Polanyi, which leads to large-scale institutional change.

For Polanyi, the force behind the pendulum is a widely held sense of 'injustice'.[27] Each extension of the market is countered by mobilization for state regulation through social legislation, factory laws, unemployment insurance, and trade unions.[28] Thus, the poor laws of the first industrial revolution in the United Kingdom in the 1830s and the welfare state associated with the Fordist production regimes of advanced capitalist countries from the mid-1940s to the early 1980s are both instances of this dynamic in action.[29] Similarly, the current crisis of new constitutionalism and neo-liberalism may mark a turn towards social protection; 'the world wide dislocation of established ways of life and livelihood caused by this late-twentieth century swing towards unregulated markets is once again producing a deep crisis of social legitimacy for world capitalism'.[30]

(c) Labour Rights as Human Rights

The project of embedding labour rights in transnational instruments and national constitutions is part of an attempt to swing the pendulum back towards social protection.[31] A core component of this project has been to recast labour standards as international human rights[32] and thus transform 'the legal matter at hand into a moral one—the moral and unjust denial of human dignity',

[25] G. Standing, *Global Labour Flexibility: Seeking Distributive Justice* (Houndsmill, Basingstoke: Macmillan Press, 1999), 50.
[26] M. Blythe, *Great Transformations: Economic Ideas and Institutional Change in the Twentieth Century* (Cambridge: Cambridge University Press, 2002), 3.
[27] B. J. Silver, *Forces of Labor: Workers' Movements and Globalization since 1879* (Cambridge: Cambridge University Press, 2003), 18.
[28] Polanyi, above n 6, 176–7.
[29] S. Deakin and F. Wilkinson, *The Law of the Labour Market: Industrialization, Employment, and Legal Evolution* (Oxford: Oxford University Press, 2005).
[30] Silver, above n 27, 178. Silver notes that Polanyi, unlike Marx, does not account for power in his discussion of the motor behind the pendulum; ibid 18.
[31] P. Macklem, 'The Right to Bargain Collectively in International Law: Workers' Rights, Human Rights, International Rights?' in P. Alston (ed), *Labour Rights as Human Rights* (Oxford: Oxford University Press, 2005), 61, 82–4.
[32] Ibid 70.

placing them on a new symbolic plane.[33] Accompanying this shift in discourse has been a change in institutions, away from the traditional vehicles for labour rights, such as social citizenship, the welfare state, trade unions, and collective bargaining, which are in decline in many parts of the world, to legal and constitutional mechanisms.[34]

The campaign to have labour rights recognized as fundamental human rights operates at three levels—the international, the regional, and the national—and uses different, but connected, methods, such as political negotiation, institutional reform, and litigation. The International Labour Organization best exemplifies the first level. Long the champion of labour rights at the international level, in 1998, the International Labour Conference issued the *Declaration on Fundamental Principles and Rights at Work* and its follow-up, which is known as the *Social Declaration*.[35] The *Social Declaration* identifies four categories of fundamental rights at work, amongst them freedom of association and the effective recognition of collective bargaining, and it has what Bob Hepple aptly describes as a 'unique legal character'.[36] The obligations are placed on all member states not by reason of ratification of the named conventions, but 'from the fact of membership. This is, therefore, a constitutional obligation not one which rests upon voluntary acceptance.'[37] The ILO has adopted a promotional mechanism to monitor member state recognition of the *Social Declaration,* instead of utilizing the existing supervisory machinery.[38]

At the regional level, one of the most significant steps in the constitutionalization of labour rights was the proclamation of the *Charter of Fundamental Rights of the European Union* in Nice in 2000, which includes the rights to collective bargaining and to strike.[39] Initially, the *Charter* was a proclamation by the European Parliament, Council, and Commission, and did not establish any new power or task for the Commission or member states of the Union, or modify the powers or tasks defined by the Treaties.[40] The adoption of the Treaty of Lisbon gave the Charter legal effect, but, like the ILO's Declaration, the Charter is not directly enforceable by individual complaints resolved through adjudication.[41] Moreover,

---

[33] B. de Sousa Santos, *Toward a New Common Sense: Law, Science and Politics in the Paradigmatic Transition*, 2nd edn (London: Butterworths, 2002), 483.

[34] S. Deakin, 'Social Rights in a Globalized Economy', in P. Alston (ed), *Labour Rights as Human Rights* (Oxford: Oxford University Press, 2005), 25, 52.

[35] International Labour Conference, *Declaration on Fundamental Principles and Rights at Work and its Follow-Up*, 18 June 1998, 37 ILM 1233, online: International Labour Organization <http://www.ilo.org/declaration/thedeclaration/textdeclaration/lang--en/index.htm>.

[36] B. Hepple, *Labour Laws and Global Trade* (Oxford: Hart, 2004), 59.

[37] Ibid.

[38] Ibid 59–60.

[39] S. Fredman, 'Transformation or Dilution: Fundamental Rights in the EU Social Space' (2006) 12 *European Law Journal* 41, 56.

[40] J. Kenner, 'Economic and Social Rights in the EU Legal Order: The Mirage of Indivisibility', in T. Hervey and J. Kenner (eds), *Economic and Social Rights under the EU Charter of Fundamental Rights* (Oxford and Portland: Hart, 2003), 1, 14; Fredman, above n 39, 56.

[41] T. Novitz, *International and European Protection of the Right to Strike: A Comparative Study of Standards Set by the International Labour Organization, the Council of Europe and the European Union* (Oxford: Oxford University Press, 2003), 228.

several member states have made constitutional reservations to it, and great care was taken to assure member states that it did not grant greater labour rights than already conferred.[42]

International and transnational labour rights may also have legal effect indirectly when constitutional courts rely on them when interpreting other fundamental rights in constitutional instruments that provide individuals with access to judicial review of state and private action. Freedom of association is a central component of many constitutions that protect civil and political rights, and a key question is the extent to which these first generation rights can accommodate labour rights, which are typically categorized as part of the second generation.[43]

III. Europe, Constitutionalization, and Labour Rights

(a) The European Double Movement

The European Community Treaty, the 1957 Treaty of Rome, was designed to create an integrated common market by guaranteeing the free movement of factors of production—goods, persons, services, and capital—and prohibiting member state action that distorted competition. Member states bore principal responsibility for social policy in general, and labour law in particular, with only limited European competence provided in the Treaty of Rome, which was given effect through directives and regulations.[44] Differences in labour regulation across the member states were not regarded as distorting the common market or segmenting the market along national lines. According to the theory of competitive advantage that influenced the architects of the common market, wage differentials and social and fiscal charges, like labour regulation, reflected differences in productivity and could be accommodated by differences in national exchange rate fluctuations.[45] The prevailing wisdom was that differences between states' labour law and industrial relations would be absorbed in the process of creating a common market, which would result in increased prosperity for all the member states.[46]

It is important to place the balance between labour and economic rights that was struck in the 1957 Treaty of Rome in its context. In the mid-1950s, the six original member states were all committed to maintaining strong

[42] P. Syrpis, 'The Treaty of Lisbon; Much Ado…But about What?' (2008) 27 *Industrial Law Journal* 219–35; B. Bercusson, *European Labour Law*, 2nd edn (Cambridge: Cambridge University Press, 2009), ch 11.

[43] Fudge, above n 7.

[44] C. Barnard, *EC Employment Law*, 3rd edn (Oxford: Oxford University Press, 2006); J. Kenner, *EU Employment Law: From Rome to Amsterdam and Beyond* (Oxford: Hart, 2008); B. Bercusson, above n 42.

[45] D. Ashiagbor, 'Collective Labour Rights and the European Social Model' (2009) 3 *Law and Ethics of Human Rights* 223; S. Deakin, 'Regulatory Competition after Laval' (2007–8) 10 *The Cambridge Yearbook of European Legal Studies* 581.

[46] Ashiagbor, above n 45, 229.

welfare states, provided legal support for collective bargaining, and had closely aligned cost levels. Moreover, most had adopted post-war constitutions that treated labour rights on a par with civil and political rights. Thus, as Simon Deakin notes, under these conditions it was plausible to believe that levelling up of wages and social standards was possible, without the need for labour law harmonization.[47]

However, the expansion of the common market shook these assumptions. In response to litigation brought by traders against state regulation, the ECJ extended the scope of the internal market and, in this way, embarked on the path of negative integration.[48] The Single European Act (SEA), which came into force on 1 July 1987, added new momentum to European integration and the completion of the internal market. It was fundamental to securing a constitutional priority for economic freedoms and subjecting social rights to challenge; it also shifted power to employers.[49] The Maastricht Treaty, which came into effect in 1993, provided for a single currency, reduced member state powers, and further strengthened European Community institutions. By 2007, the initial six member states had grown to 27. The adoption of the euro and the accession of member states with wages costs and social entitlements that were not aligned with those of existing members created the conditions for a race to the bottom for wages and labour standards.

The response to the growing loss of legitimacy of the European social model was to constitutionalize it;[50]

from an initial silence on the issue of human rights or general principles of law in the founding treaties, the gradual development of human rights jurisprudence and human rights instruments in the EU, as well as the development of free standing social policy mark the evolution of the Union from an 'elite-driven liberal trade regime,' toward something akin to a constitutional polity.[51]

There have been a variety of attempts more fully to embed the social dimension within the European Union, the most recent of which was the Treaty of Lisbon, which took effect as the European constitution on 1 December 2009.[52]

From the perspective of collective labour rights, one of the most significant developments was the adoption of the European Charter of Fundamental Rights at Nice, which combined the fundamental rights and basic procedural rights with

---

[47] Deakin, above n 45, 604.

[48] P. Davies, 'Market Integration and Social Policy in the Court of Justice' (1995) 24 *Industrial Law Journal* 49.

[49] F. Scharpf, 'Negative Integration and Positive Integration in the Political Economy of European Welfare States', in G. Marks, F. W. Scharpf, P. C. Schmitter, and W. Streeck (eds), *Governance in the European Union* (London: Sage, 1996). My thanks to Ruth Dukes to bringing this work to my attention. Bercusson, above n 42, 390.

[50] As Claire Kilpatrick notes, 'constitutionalism both explains and enhances the legitimacy of the EU', 'New EU Employment Governance and Constitutionalism', in G. de Búrca and J. Scott (eds), *Law and New Governance in the EU and the US* (Oxford and Portland: Oxford, 2006), 121 53, 142.

[51] Ashiagbor, above n 45, 238, footnotes omitted.

[52] Barnard, above n 44, 28.

economic and social rights.[53] Although the Charter protects collective labour rights, upon inspection, the extent of the protection offered is meagre.[54] Some member states did not want the Charter to create justiciable labour rights, and their concerns are reflected in both the Charter and the Treaty that implements it. Article 28 of the Charter only guarantees the rights to collective bargaining and to collective action to the extent that they are in accordance with Community laws and national laws and practice. The Charter neither empowers the Community nor requires member states to create a right to strike. The Treaty of the European Union also makes it clear that the provisions of the Charter shall not extend in any way the competence of the Union. In a Protocol accompanying the Charter, both Poland and the UK specify that the chapter of the Charter in which labour rights are located does not create justiciable rights applicable in their countries except in so far as they have provided for such rights in national law. Thus, the Charter of Fundamental Rights does not create justiciable collective bargaining and strike rights, although it can be used as a source of norms by other courts, such as the ECJ.[55]

The ECJ can also play an important role in the constitutionalization of labour rights, although in a direction that is not protective. The free flow of goods and services within the single market may 'restrict the freedom of Member States to adopt whatever labour law regime they prefer (in those areas where no conflict arises between the national provisions in question and the Community rules adopted under the specific social competence)'.[56] The Court's interventions in the area of employment and labour law have been particularly contentious, and commentators have questioned whether the ECJ's process of decision-making, decision-makers, and methods of gathering information are appropriate for the task of balancing fundamental labour rights against market freedoms.[57] However, the preliminary reference process, does, as Siofra O'Leary notes, avoid the disadvantages of a bipolar dispute, 'since the Commission and member states are entitled to intervene and the Advocate General is on hand with an independent opinion'.[58]

The extent to, and the ways in, which the ECJ balances social goals and market freedoms will, in large part, influence the ability of member states to respect and to protect collective labour rights. The Court's legitimacy rests primarily upon its ability to provide convincing reasons for its decisions.[59] Thus, the

---

[53] Ibid.

[54] Ibid 29; Syrpis, above at n 42, 232; Fredman, above at n 39, 56 7; D. Ashiagbor, 'Economic and Social Rights in the European Charter of Fundamental Rights' (2004) 9 *European Human Rights Law Review* 62; B. Ryan, 'The Charter and Collective Labour Law', in T. Hervey and J. Kenner (eds), *Economic and Social Rights under the EU Charter of Fundamental Rights—A Legal Perspective* (Oxford and Portland: Hart, 2003); Dukes, above n 42; Bercusson, n 42.

[55] Barnard, above n 44, 31–2; Ashiagbor, above n 45, 71–2; Fredman, above n 39, 58; Hepple, above n 36, 141–5.

[56] Davies, above n 48, 50.

[57] See the summary in S. O'Leary, *Employment Law and the European Court of Justice: Judicial Structures, Policies and Processes* (Oxford and Portland: Hart, 2002), 1–4.

[58] Ibid at 4.

[59] See also Davies, above n 48, 76.

onus is on the ECJ to provide 'a truly constitutional answer concerning how to settle the existing—and possible future—conflicts between social structures in Member States that still remain within their own areas of competence and the dynamics of EC law seemingly favouring the liberal spirit of free movement to the detriment of the social arrangements of ... countries with a strong welfarist tradition'.[60]

(b) The EJC at Work: *Viking* and *Laval*

The uneasy balance between economic and social rights at the European level was profoundly disrupted by the accession of several low-wage former-Soviet states in 2004, which, as Brian Bercusson remarked, confronted 'the legislative and judicial processes ... simultaneously ... with the same issues'.[61] The Services Directive was an attempt to remove obstacles to economic activity within Europe. Since services account for the majority of employment in Europe, the Directive proved to be a focal point for the conflict between market integration and labour rights. Initially, the Directive was premised on the country of origin principle, which would subject service providers only to the laws applying in the country in which they were based. Trade unions feared that service providers based in Eastern European and Baltic States that had low wages and labour standards, as well as ineffective trade union representation, would use this comparative advantage to compete with service providers in member states with strong regimes of labour regulation. Unions lobbied to exclude labour law from the provisions of the Directive, so that the labour law of the host state, instead of home country, would apply to service providers. They also wanted to carve out a space that protected trade union collective action from judicial scrutiny for compliance with the Directive. The final version of the Directive that came into effect in 2006 dropped the country of origin principle for labour law.[62] However, its characterization of collective labour rights was equivocal;[63] 'the compromise position reflected in the Services Directive was not to spell out the legitimate scope of collective action in the event of conflict with the free movement provisions of the EC Treaty, but rather to delegate the decision to the Court'.[64]

In 2006, two national courts asked the ECJ to determine the extent to which trade union collective action may operate as a legitimate constraint on employers'

---

[60] N. Reich, 'Free Movement v. Social Rights in an Enlarged Union—the Laval and Viking Cases before the ECJ' (2008) 9 *German Law* 126, 127.

[61] B. Bercusson, 'The Trade Union Movement and the European Union: Judgment Day' (2007) 13 *European Law Journal* 279, 279–80.

[62] The Services Directive has continued to be politically charged. Only one-third of EU member states had successfully implemented it, despite the passing of the 28 December 2008 deadline (three years after the Directive was adopted). A. Willis, 'EU States Miss Services Directive Deadline' (3 Feb 2010), <http://euobserver.com/9/29369?print=1>.

[63] Ashiagbor, above n 45, 252–5; P. Syrpis and T. Novitz, 'Economic and Social Rights in Conflict: Political and Judicial Approaches to their Reconciliation' (2008) 33 *European Law Review* 411, 416–18.

[64] Syrpis and Novitz, above n 63, 418.

freedoms under Community law. Thus, it fell to the ECJ to develop an approach
that balanced the interests of workers in older member states, workers in newer
member states, and businesses and service providers in both old and new member
states. However, it did so in a context in which employers, and not unions, would
be posing the questions, and market access was the primary objective.[65]

The first case, *Viking*, concerned a Finnish company wanting to reflag its
ferry, the *Rosella*, under the Estonian flag so that it could use an Estonian crew
to be paid considerably less than the existing Finnish crew.[66] At the request of
the Finnish Seaman's Union, the International Transport Workers' Federation
(ITF), which is based in the United Kingdom, told its affiliates to boycott the
Rosella in support of its Flag of Convenience policy, which sought to prevent
shipping companies from reflagging vessels in order to ratchet down labour
standards. Viking sought an injunction in the English High Court restraining
the ITF and the Finnish Seaman's Union (FSU) from anticipated strike action,
which, although lawful under Finnish labour law, Viking alleged beached Article
49 [43] of the EC Treaty, which guarantees freedom of establishment. The High
Court readily granted the injunction; however, the Court of Appeal was not as
confident that the unions had breached the Treaty, and referred the case to the
ECJ. *Viking* is a classic case of an establishment moving across borders in order to
gain access to cheaper labour.

Laval, by contrast, is a case of a service provider crossing borders and using home
state workers who are paid at lower rates. In *Laval*, a Swedish subsidiary of a Latvian
company won a contract to refurbish a school in Sweden using its parent's Latvian
workers who earned about 40 per cent less than comparable Swedish workers. The
Swedish construction union wanted Laval to apply the Swedish collective agreement but Laval refused, in part because the collective agreement was unclear as to
how much Laval would have to pay its workers. There followed a union picket at
the school site, a brief blockade by construction workers, and sympathy industrial
action in the form of a boycott by the electricians' union. Although this industrial
action was lawful under Swedish law, Laval brought proceedings in the Swedish
labour court, claiming that this action was contrary to Community law, specifically the Article 56 [49] freedom of services, and raised the issue of the Posted
Workers Directive, which stipulated which country's labour laws were to apply to
(posted) workers who were accompanying service providers.[67] The Swedish Court
referred the case to the ECJ.

---

[65] Ashiagbor, above n 45, 261.
[66] *Viking*, above n 10, paras 6–12. The Court placed a great deal of significance on the fact that
the shipping country promised that all of the Finnish workers would retain their jobs.
[67] A complicating factor in *Laval* was the Lex Britannia provisions in the Swedish collective bargaining legislation, which provided that a trade union has a right to take industrial action to set aside
or amend a foreign collective agreement such as a collective agreement entered into by a foreign service provider in a home state. The Swedish peace obligation that prohibits trade unions from taking
industrial action when there is a collective agreement does not apply in cases in which the collective
agreement is foreign. M. Rönnmer, 'Free Movement of Services versus National Labour Law and
Nordic Industrial Relations Systems: Understanding the Laval Case from a Swedish and Nordic
Perspective' (2007–8) 10 *Cambridge Yearbook of European Legal Studies* 493, 504. See C. Woolfson,

Both cases involved opinions from the Advocates General, and were decisions of the Grand Chamber.[68] Essentially, they raised four main issues for the ECJ to decide. The first concerned the material scope of the EC Treaty; do Articles 49 [43] and 56 [49] apply to fundamental social rights such as the right to industrial action? The second focused on whether Articles 49 [43] and 56 [49] had direct horizontal legal effect against trade unions. The third revolved around the question of breach of the EC Treaty; does collective action by trade unions constitute a restriction on free movement? Whether the breach was justified, and if so, whether the action was proportionate comprised the final issue. In both *Viking* and *Laval*, unions asserted the fundamental nature of the right to take industrial action in order to defend themselves from corporations that asserted their freedom of movement against them. Although the old and new member states split over the answers to these legal issues, there was a consensus over the existence of a fundamental right to take collective action.[69]

The trade unions along with the Danish and Swedish governments submitted that the right of trade unions to take collective action should fall outside of community law.[70] For the purposes of this chapter, the argument that fundamental rights, including the right to strike, were outside Community law, is the most important. Referring to the European Social Charter, ILO Convention 87, the Community Charter of the Fundamental Social Rights of Workers, and the Charter of Fundamental Rights of the European Union, in *Viking* the Court recognized the right to take collective action, including the right to strike, as 'a fundamental right which forms an integral part of the general principles of Community Law'.[71] However, it went on to hold that the exercise of the right was subject to certain restrictions, 'and must be reconciled with the requirements relating to rights protected under the Treaty and in accordance with the principle of proportionality'.[72] The restrictions the Court identified were those set out in Article 28 of the Charter of Fundamental Rights of the European Union—those imposed by national law and practices and Community law. Thus, the Charter was used to limit, rather than to expand, labour rights. Although the ECJ recognized the right to strike as fundamental, it did so in what Anne Davies characterized as a 'defensive' context.[73]

C. Thörnqvist, and J. Sommers, 'Labour Migration and the Future of Labour Standards after Laval' (2010) 41 *Industrial Relations Journal* 333–50.

[68] C. Kilpatrick, 'The ECJ and Labour Law: A 2008 Retrospective' (2009) 38 *Industrial Law Journal* 180, 181–2. In this chapter, I will focus exclusively on the decisions of the ECJ and not the opinions of the Advocate General.

[69] Bercusson, above n 61, 305–6.

[70] Together they provided three arguments: that the EU lacked competence as a result of Article 145(f) [(137(5)] of the EC Treaty to regulate with respect to the right to strike; that, by analogy with *Albany* [1999] ECR I-5751, collective worker action leads to an inherent restriction of the freedom of establishment and freedom to provide services and thus falls outside the scope of the EC Treaty; and the fundamental nature of the right to strike.

[71] *Viking*, above n 10, para 44.

[72] Ibid, para 46.

[73] A. C. L. Davies, 'One Step Forward, Two Steps Back? The Viking and Laval Cases in the ECJ' (2008) 37 *Industrial Law Journal* 126, 139.

The second issue the Court dealt with was whether Articles 49 [43] and 56 [49]
had direct horizontal effect against a trade union. This was a particularly controversial question. Instead of bringing their actions against the governments of
Finland and Sweden for having labour law regimes that permitted the trade union
action, in both cases the employers who sought to use lower paid labour and avoid
host country collective agreements brought the actions directly against the trade
unions. Relying on cases that stood for the proposition that private associations
that exercised regulatory functions (such as sporting and professional associations)
were directly bound by the Treaty, the Court held where trade unions 'participate
in the drawing up of agreements seeking to regulate paid work collectively'[74] they
are covered by the free movement provisions. In doing so, the Court expanded the
scope of Articles 49 [43] and 56 [49] beyond quasi-public organizations exercising
a regulatory function and emphasized the close link between collective bargaining and collective action. However, the Court did not seem to appreciate that the
difference between collective bargaining and regulation is that the former depends
upon the balance of power between unions and employers. Nor did it provide a
basis for limiting the scope of Articles 49 [43] and 56 [49] when it came to private
action.[75]

Having established that Community law applied to the trade union action in
both cases, the Court followed the standard market access approach analysis of
breach, justification, and proportionality. Given the Court's conclusions about the
scope of the EC Treaty and the direct application of Article 49 [43] to trade unions,
it was almost inevitable that the Court would conclude that the FSU's and ITF's
actions were in breach of the Article: 'in the present...case it cannot be disputed
that collective action such as envisaged by FSU has the effect of making less attractive, or even pointless, as the national court has pointed out, Viking's exercise of
its freedom of establishment, inasmuch as such action prevents both Viking and
its subsidiary, Viking Eesti, from enjoying the same treatment in the host Member
State as other economic operators established in that state'.[76]

Although the Court also found a breach of Article 56 [49] in the *Laval* case,
its analysis was complicated by the Posted Workers Directive, which attracted
more attention from the Court than did Article 56 [49]. The Court's focus on the
Posted Workers Directive was somewhat surprising given that the provisions of the
Directive are not capable, in themselves, of having direct effect in a case involving
private parties.[77] However, the Court simply stated that the Directive had to be
taken into account when giving a ruling on Article 56 [49].[78] The Court concluded

[74] *Viking*, above n 10, paras 64 and 65.
[75] Davies, above n 73, 136–7; C. Barnard, 'Viking and Laval: An Introduction' in (2007–8) 10
Cambridge Yearbook of European Legal Studies 463, 472–4; T. Novitz, 'A Human Rights Analysis of
the Viking and Laval Judgments' (2007–8) 10 *Cambridge Yearbook of European Legal Studies* 541,
551–4.
[76] *Laval*, above n 10, para 72. The Court also said that the ITF's policy of combating the use of
flags of convenience 'must be considered as at the least liable restrict Viking's exercise of freedom of
establishment'. Ibid, para 73.
[77] Barnard, above n 75, 477.
[78] *Laval*, above n 10, para 61.

that the Posted Workers Directive does not permit a member state to impose on foreign-service providers the obligation to conduct on-site negations with trade unions to determine the rates of pay. Nor, according to the Court, does it allow trade unions to force a foreign-service provider to accept better conditions than the bare minimum standards allowed in the Directive. Thus, the Court found that industrial action by trade unions that was aimed at forcing a service provider established in other member states to agree to terms that are more favourable than those provided in the Posted Workers Directive 'is liable to make it less attractive, or more difficult, for such undertakings to carry out construction work in Sweden, and therefore constitutes a restriction on the freedom to provide services within the meaning of Article 56 [49] EC'.[79] As Deakin pointed out, 'the Directive was needed in order to bring Laval within Article 56 [49] in the first place; Article 56 [49], in its turn, supplied the context for the Court's pre-emptive reading of the Directive'.[80]

Thus, having found the unions' collective action in the two cases to have breached the Treaty, the Court turned to the issues of justification and proportionality. In both cases, the Court adopted a strict approach to proportionality: a restriction on a fundamental freedom 'can be accepted only if [1] it pursues a legitimate aim compatible with the treaty and [2] is justified by overriding reasons of public interest. But even if that were the case, it would [3] still have to be suitable for securing the attainment of the objective pursued and [4] must not go beyond what is necessary in order to attain it.'[81] The Court recognized that 'the right to take collective action for the protection of the workers of the host state against possible social dumping may constitute an overriding reason of public interest'.[82] It also accepted that the secondary action (the blockades) by the unions fell within the objective of protecting workers.[83] However, because the obligations that the unions were seeking to impose on the service provider exceeded the nucleus of minimum rules provided in the Posted Workers Directive, the collective action could not be justified.[84] Moreover, the fact that the Swedish construction union sought to compel the service provider to adhere to a collective agreement that would have provided a framework for pay negotiations was not justified because it did not provide sufficient transparency for the service provider to determine its obligations.[85] Since the Swedish trade unions' actions were not justified, it was not necessary for the Court to consider whether they were proportionate.[86] It sent the case back to the Swedish

---

[79] Ibid. para 99.

[80] Deakin, above n 45, 599, footnotes omitted. In this chapter I am not going to develop an analysis of the ECJ's interpretation of the PWD and its implications. For a collection that looks at the impact of *Laval* from the perspective of member states, see A. Swiatkowski (ed), *The Laval and Viking Cases: Freedom of Services and Establishment v. Industrial Conflict in the European Area and Russia* (Alphen aan den Rijn: Kluwer Law International 2009).

[81] *Viking*, above n 10, para 75.

[82] *Laval*, above n 10, para 103.

[83] Ibid, para 107.

[84] Ibid, para 108.

[85] Ibid, para 110.

[86] The ECJ also held that the Lex Britannia provision in the Swedish collective bargaining legislation discriminated against the foreign service provider and that it was not justified; Rönnmer, above n 67, 517–18.

Labour Court, which had to apply the ECJ's decision. On 2 December 2009, one day after the Treaty of Lisbon came into effect, the Swedish Labour Court handed down its decision, which awarded damages against the construction workers' and electricians' unions.[87]

By contrast, the Court engaged in a more detailed analysis of justification in *Viking* in order to provide the national court with detailed guidance about how to answer the question of proportionality. The Court stated that 'the right to take collective action for the protection of workers is a legitimate interest which, in principle, justifies a restriction of the fundamental freedoms guaranteed by the Treaty' and 'that the protection of workers is one of the overriding reasons of public interest recognized by the Court'.[88] According to the ECJ, 'it is for the national court to ascertain whether the objectives pursued by the FSU and ITF by means of the collective action which they initiated concerned the protection of workers'.[89] However, it gave the national court very strict guidance about the legitimate scope of worker protection; the ECJ made it clear that the FSU's actions could only be justified 'if the jobs and conditions of employment of members of that union [were] liable to be adversely affected by the reflagging of the Rosella'.[90] Once the justification was established, the national court 'would then have to ascertain whether the collective action initiated by the FSU is suitable for ensuring the achievement of the objective pursued and does not go beyond what is reasonably necessary'.[91] Citing two ECtHR decisions in support, the ECJ noted that collective action 'like collective negotiations and collective agreements, may, in the particular circumstances of a case, be one of the main ways in which trade unions protect the interests of their members'.[92] Thus, collective action could be suitable for protecting workers. However, the Court's approach to necessity further narrowed the remit of the right. The national court was instructed to examine whether, on the one hand, under the national rules and collective agreement law applicable to that action, the 'FSU did not have other means at its disposal which were less restrictive of freedom of establishment in order to bring to a successful conclusion the collective negotiations entered into with Viking and, on the other, that the trade union had exhausted those means before initiating such action'.[93] As regards the ITF's policy of requesting solidarity action against any ship owner that registered a ship in a state other than that of which it was a national, the Court doubted that it could be justified because the policy 'automatically opposes business relocation without regard to whether such relocation would actually be detrimental to the workforce'.[94] These

---

[87] Woolfson et al, above n 67.
[88] *Viking*, above n 10, para 77.
[89] Ibid, para 80.
[90] Ibid, para 81.
[91] Ibid, para 85.
[92] Ibid, para 86, referring to *Syndicat National de la police belge v Belgium*, 27 Oct 1975, Series A No 19 and *Wilson v UK*, 2 July 2002, 2002-V, para 44.
[93] Ibid, para 97.
[94] Ibid, paras 88–9.

questions were never answered since the parties settled the action before the case was sent back to the UK Court of Appeal.

Thus, although the ECJ recognized that the right to take collective action in order to protect workers from social dumping constituted a legitimate objective that could constitute a restriction of the freedom of establishment or services, the limitations it imposed on the right's exercise almost completely nullified it. The ECJ did not recognize a right to strike per se, only collective action for a wider approved purpose—worker protection, which it interpreted very narrowly. By implication, as Tonia Novitz noted, collective action for other purposes, such as to protest government policy or policies for workers in the future, was not legitimate.[95] The Court also placed the burden on the union to find the least restrictive method to protest social dumping. Social considerations, including the right to strike, are recognized as legitimate but they are conceptualized as derogations from economic rights, which are regarded as truly foundational. Classifying this right to strike as fundamental is paradoxical.

Moreover, in *Laval*, the ECJ seemed deeply suspicious of collective bargaining as a legitimate form of norm setting. The Court compared collective autonomy unfavourably—too messy, too uncertain, too disruptive—with judicially enforced legislation as means of setting and protecting standards for posted workers.[96] The Court's preference for a juridified means of determining and implementing standards is a threat to certain types of social models, such as in Sweden and Denmark, in which civil society organizations such as trade unions play a more prominent role in establishing workplace norms than do legislatures and courts.[97]

The ECJ's decisions in *Viking* and *Laval* do not demonstrate much appreciation for the distinctive context of industrial relations.[98] By deciding that the Treaty applied directly to trade unions, it clearly placed unions on the defensive. In the UK, employers are more likely to seek and to obtain injunctions to prevent unions from organizing and participating in transnational collective action.[99] Unions in

---

[95] Novitz, above n 75, 554–9.

[96] *Laval*, above n 10, para 110.

[97] Some member states are amending the legislation that implements the PWD; T. van Peijpe, 'Collective Labour Law after Viking, Laval, Rüffert, and Luxembourg' (2009) 25 *The International Journal of Comparative Labour Law and Industrial Relations* 81, 81–107; C. Kilpatrick, 'Laval's Regulatory Conundrum: Collective Standard-Setting and the Court's New Approach to Posted Workers' (2009) 34 *European Law Review*, 844.

[98] Davies, above n 73, 148; C. Kilpatrick, 'British Jobs for British Workers? UK Industrial Action and Free Movement of Services in EU Law', *LSE, Law, Society and Economy Working Papers* 16/2009, 20; Rönnmer, above n 67, 519–23.

[99] Shortly after the decisions were released, British Airways sought an injunction in the United Kingdom to stop collective action threatened by the union representing its airline pilots that was called to protest the airline's decision to start a new service, called Open Skies. BA proposed to fly passengers from mainland Europe to the United States using BA planes, support staff, and BA management, but not BA pilots. The pilots union took a vote of its members to determine their support for a strike to protest Open Skies, and BA claimed that, following *Viking*, the union was in violation of Article 43 of EC Treaty. The union went to the UK national court and successfully obtained an order for a speedy trial to determine the question of the Treaty violation in order to avoid having the question answered in the context of BA's application for an interim injunction. However, the union

Sweden have been found liable in damages to employers for breaching Article 56 [49].[100] Although the question of union liability for damages for industrial action in breach of protection of free movement of establishment in Article 49 [43] is an open one, employers are able to exploit this uncertainty when unions threaten industrial action that has a transnational focus.[101]

(c) The European Court of Human Rights and the Swing to Protection

The 2008 decision of the ECtHR in *Demir and Baykara v Turkey* stands in marked contrast to the approach adopted by the ECJ in *Viking* and *Laval* to collective labour rights. The Grand Chamber of the European Court of Human Rights explicitly overruled its earlier decisions to hold that Article 11 of the European Convention of Human Rights includes the right to collective bargaining.[102] In the 1970s, the ECtHR took a formal and individualized approach to the interpretation of freedom of association under Article 11 of the Convention, treating it as a civil and political right, and contrasting it to the social rights protected under the European Social Charter.[103] It excluded collective bargaining and strikes from its scope.[104] However, in the 1990s, as part of its broader and 'integrated' approach to the interpretation of social right claims under the Convention, the ECtHR began to invoke the interpretation of freedom of association provided by the ILO's supervisory bodies in order to justify a change in approach to labour rights and freedom of association.[105]

At issue in *Demir and Baykara* was the lack of express statutory provisions in Turkey recognizing a right for trade unions formed by civil servants to enter into legally enforceable collective agreements.[106] The trade union, which was founded by civil servants, entered into a collective agreement with a municipal council. When the municipality failed to fulfil certain obligations, the union brought civil proceedings against it. The municipality claimed that the union did not have the legal capacity to enter into and to enforce the collective agreement under Turkish law, and asked the District Court to dismiss the action. Referring to international law, specifically ILO conventions, the District Court filled in the legal gap and granted the union capacity to enforce its agreement. The Court of Cassation granted the municipality's appeal and quashed the District Court decision on the

---

withdrew its action in the face of BA's claim for damages and the prospects of a lengthy and expensive litigation. Barnard, above n 75, 489–90; Ewing, and Hendy, above n 13.

[100] Woolfson et al, above n 67.

[101] K. Apps, 'Damage Claims against Trade Unions after Viking and Laval' (2009) 34 *European Law Review* 141. Moreover, it is not clear what gives a particular dispute its transnational dimension. Is national action caught only if there is an actual obstacle to a transnational market relationship, or is it sufficient if it merely (potentially) impedes market access?

[102] *Demir*, above n 11, para 154.

[103] Novitz, above n 75, 544.

[104] Ryan, above n 54.

[105] V. Mantouvalou, 'Is there a Human Right not to be a Trade Union Member? Labour Rights under the European Convention on Human Rights', *LSE Law, Society and Economy Working Papers* 8/2007, 4–5.

[106] *Demir*, above n 11, paras 13–53.

ground that the union had no authority to enter into collective agreements. The issue was re-litigated with the same results before both courts. The Turkish Audit Court ordered the union members to repay the benefits they had secured under the now defunct collective agreement. A seven-judge panel of the ECtHR held that there had been a violation of Article 11 'so far as the domestic court had refused to recognize the legal personality of the trade union … and had considered null and void the collective agreement between that trade union and [the Council]'.[107] The Turkish government asked that the matter be referred to the Grand Council.

The ECtHR applied its traditional two-step test to Article 11; the first step is to establish whether there is an interference with a Convention-protected right. If so, the second step is to determine if the interference can be justified. To be justified, an interference must be prescribed by law, serve a legitimate aim, and be necessary to achieve that aim.[108] The ECtHR took a broad, integrated approach to the interpretation of rights under the Convention. It referred to ILO Convention 98 and the European Charter of Fundamental Rights as the basis for understanding the right to collective bargaining in the context of the freedom of association.[109] The Court also made it clear 'that in searching for common ground among the norms of international law it has never distinguished between sources of law according to whether or not they have been signed or ratified by the respondent State'.[110] The Court decided,

having regard to the developments in labour law, both international and national, and to the practice of Contracting States in such matters, the right to bargain collectively with the employer has, in principle, become one of the essential elements of the 'right to form and to join trade unions for the protection of [one's] interests' set forth in Article 11 of the Convention, it being understood that States remain free to organise their system so as, if appropriate, to grant special status to representative trade unions. Like other workers, civil servants, except in very specific cases, should enjoy such rights, but without prejudice to the effects of any 'lawful restrictions' that may have to be imposed on 'members of the administration of the State' … —a category to which the applicants in the present case do not, however, belong.[111]

The Court adopted an approach that simultaneously confirmed the freedom of states to develop their own collective bargaining systems, and identified ILO standards and jurisprudence as providing minimum labour rights for the 47 members of the Council of Europe.

That *Demir* marks an important development in the ECtHR's approach to the freedom of association was confirmed by four subsequent cases that dealt with the right to take collective action.[112] The first, *Enerji Yapi-Yol Sen v Turkey*,[113] involved

---

[107] Ibid, para 8.
[108] J. Gerards, 'Judicial Deliberations in the European Court of Human Rights', in N. Huls, M. Adams, and J. Bomhoff (eds), *The Legitimacy of Highest Courts' Rulings* (The Hague: T.M.C. Asser Press, 2009), 407–36, 421.
[109] Ibid, paras 37–52.
[110] Ibid, para 77.
[111] Ibid, para 154.
[112] None of the subsequent cases was a decision of the Grand Chamber.
[113] *Enerji Yapi-Yol Sen v Turkey*, Application no 68959/01.

an executive order that prohibited public servants from taking part in a one-day national strike as part of their campaign for a collective agreement. Some of the union's members participated in the strike and they were disciplined. After the Turkish courts dismissed the union members' appeals of their disciplinary penalties, they brought a complaint to the ECtHR. The Court noted that strike action constitutes an important aspect of the protection of trade union members' interests, is recognized by ILO supervisory bodies as 'an indissociable corollary of the right of trade union association that is protected by ILO Convention 87', and is enshrined in the European Social Charter as 'a means of ensuring the effective exercise as the right to collective bargaining'.[114] It held that strike action was protected under Article 11(1). Although it acknowledged that the right to strike was not absolute and that a restriction could be justified if it answered a pressing social need and was not disproportionate, the Court held that the Turkish government failed to demonstrate the general and absolute ban on all public sector workers from striking was a necessary restriction.

The second decision, *Danilenkov v Russia*,[115] which was released in July 2009, dealt with a complaint by a group of dockworkers that they had been discriminated on the basis of union membership because they were members of a union that had engaged in industrial action against their employer. The dockworkers were unhappy because the only method of legal redress for the discrimination they suffered was criminal proceedings against the employer, which was ineffective. After exhausting all of the national courts, the union complained to the ECtHR. The ECtHR invoked ILO conventions and jurisprudence both to emphasize the fundamental status of the right to be free from discrimination on the basis of union membership and to suggest some minimum standards for the effective protection of the right.[116] The Court found that it is 'crucially important that individuals affected by discriminatory treatment should be provided with an opportunity to challenge it and to have the right to take legal action to obtain damages and other relief. Therefore, the States are required under Articles 11 and 14 of the Convention to set up a judicial system that would ensure real and effective protection against anti-union discrimination'.[117] It held that Russia had 'failed to fulfil its positive obligations to adopt effective and clear judicial protection against discrimination on the ground of trade union membership' and that there was a 'violation of Article 14 of the Convention taken together with Article 11'.[118] Moreover, in two subsequent cases, the ECtHR found that penalties imposed on striking workers constituted a violation of Article 11.[119]

[114] Ibid, para 32.
[115] *Danilenkov v Russia*, Application no 67336/01, 30 July 2009.
[116] Ibid, paras 102–8.
[117] Ibid, para 124. Article 14 provides: 'The enjoyment of the rights and freedoms set forth in this Convention shall be secured without discrimination on any ground such as sex, race, colour, language, religion, political or other opinion, national or social origin, association with a national minority, property, birth or other status'.
[118] Ibid, para 136.
[119] *Saime Özcan v Turkey*, above n 13, involved criminal sanctions imposed against an individual worker, whereas in *Kaya and Seyham v Turkey*, above n 13, the striking workers were disciplined (in

(d) The Status of Labour Rights: The ECJ versus the ECtHR

The difference in approach taken by the two European courts to collective bargaining, collective action, and trade unions is stark. While both courts refer to many of the same human rights instruments, their treatment of international law is very different. The ECtHR, for example, engaged with ILO supervisory body jurisprudence and used it to explore the positive obligations of states to protect collective bargaining, whereas the ECJ simply invoked ILO Conventions at the level of general rights and neglected nuance and detail.[120] The two courts also started from opposite premises of the legitimacy of trade union collective action. The analysis at the ECtHR under the Human Rights Convention began with the assumption that collective bargaining and collective action are protected, and the obligation is on the state to show that its restriction is necessary. Before the ECJ, where the task is primarily to protect the freedoms under the EC Treaty, the union has to justify why industrial action was justified in restricting fundamental freedoms. At the ECJ, unions are asserting fundamental rights as a defence against claims brought against them by employers, whereas, at the ECtHR, unions are asserting fundamental rights in order to challenge restrictive state action.

The extent to which the European Court of Human Rights can operate as a restraint on its Luxembourg cousin is an open question. Like the ECJ, the ECtHR is a supranational court with a constitutional stature.[121] The EU Charter refers to the ECHR and Article 52(3) accords deference to the ECtHR jurisprudence on Convention rights. Although the EU is not a party to the ECHR, individual member states must comply with the Convention.[122] Moreover, the Lisbon Treaty commits the union to accession to the European Convention for the Protection of Human Rights.[123] Assuming that accession means that EU institutions would, for the first time, be subject to the jurisdiction of the European Court of Human Rights, it may be possible to argue that the ECJ's decisions in *Viking* and *Laval* infringe Convention rights.[124] Moreover, the ECJ has stated that it will take full account of the European Court of Human Right's jurisprudence and Article 6(2) of the EC Treaty already provides that the EU must respect fundamental rights guaranteed by ECtHR.[125]

Keith Ewing suggested that the 'decision in Demir . . . creates the alluring possibility of complaint being made in the Strasbourg Court against an EU member State about the latter's failure to comply with the ECHR because of obligations arising under EU law'.[126] However, the precise legal process for bringing such an

---

the form of written warnings) for participating in the strike. For a discussion of these cases see Ewing and Hendy, above n 13.

[120] Novitz, above n 75, 559.

[121] Gerards, above n 108, 40910.

[122] Woolfson et al, above n 67.

[123] On 3 October 2009, the second Irish referendum on ratification of the Treaty of Lisbon was successful.

[124] Syrpis, above n 42, 231–33.

[125] Ibid 234.

[126] K. D. Ewing, preface in Bercusson, above n 42, p x.

action is not obvious.[127] Another problem is the ECtHR's limited remedial power. Although individuals can pursue actions against their governments for violating their fundamental rights, the ECtHR does not have the power to amend, repeal, or modify legislation or individual decisions by a competent state actor. It can issue a legally binding judgement determining whether a domestic act, court decision, or law is in breach of the ECHR, and it can specify the state's obligations.[128] But it has no direct power to enforce. Using *Demir and Baykara* and the subsequent violations of the rights of Turkish workers by the Turkish state as an object lesson, Ewing and Hendy caution 'even great legal triumphs can produce such little progress'.[129]

Europe's two transnational constitutional courts have taken quite different approaches to the question of fundamental labour rights. In part, this difference is attributable to the different contexts in which the question is raised; the legal regimes in which the courts operate, although they overlap, are quite distinct, having different institutions, members, and orientations.[130] But, despite these differences, it is now, after *Demir and Baykara*, even more important for their legitimacy and the project of European integration for the two courts to come to a shared understanding and a common approach to the status and role of labour rights in the European Union.[131] The ECtHR has greater legitimacy than the ECJ when it comes to the interpretation of human rights.[132] It is also beginning to develop a more nuanced and sophisticated approach to treating the ILO conventions and supervisory body decisions as an important legal source for identifying labour rights and the scope of their legitimate restriction. The Luxembourg Court has recognized 'the need to reconcile the requirements of the protection of fundamental rights in the Community with those arising from a fundamental freedom enshrined in the Treaty and, more particularly, the question of the respective scope of freedom of expression and freedom of assembly, guaranteed by Articles 10 and 11 of the ECHR, and of the free movement of goods, where the former are relied upon as justification for a restriction of the latter'.[133] Although not bound by them, the ECJ cites relevant ECtHR decisions with deference and respect. The problem is

---

[127] Ewing and Hendy, above n 13.

[128] Gerards, above n 108, 409–10. For a discussion of the processes for lodging complaints at the ECtHR and the Court's 'judicial restraint' regarding remedies, see E-U. Petersmann, 'Human Rights, International Economic Law and "Constitutional Justice"' (2008) 19 *The European Journal of International Law* 769, 777–8. Petersmann contrasts access to the ECtHR with access to the ECJ at 776.

[129] Ewing and Hendy, above n 13. The Court of Appeal dismissed union's claim that the strike ballot requirements violated Article 11 in *Metrobus v Unite The Union* [2009] EWCA Civ 829. For a discussion of the case, see Ruth Dukes, 'The Right to Strike under UK Law: Not Much More than a Slogan?' (2010) 39 *Industrial Law Journal* 82–91.

[130] The differences between the ECJ and ECtHR are discussed in G. de Burca, 'The Future of Social Rights Protection in Europe', in G. de Burca and B. de Witte (eds), *Social Rights in Europe* (Oxford: Oxford University Press, 2005), 3, 12.

[131] Syrpis, above n. 42, 234.

[132] R. C. A. White, 'Judgments in the Strasbourg Court: Some Reflections', at 8, <http://ssrn.com/abstract=1435197>.

[133] Case C-112/00, *Eugen Schmidberger, Internationale Transporte und Planzüge v Republik Österreich*, 12 June 2003, para 77.

that the ECJ follows its traditional template, and treats the fundamental rights as an exception to the fundamental market freedoms such that their exercise must be justified and proportional.[134] This problem is compounded by the direct application of the Treaty to trade unions; unions must persuade the Court that they used the least restrictive means that was suitable for achieving a legitimate objective. In this way, the ECJ reverses the approach of the ECtHR, which is to determine whether the state's restrictions on the right to collective action are proportionate.

The ECJ plays a constitutional role in the European Union, and it is charged with balancing fundamental rights and market freedoms. But the balance it has struck not only encroaches substantially on workers' fundamental freedoms, it narrows the right of member states to determine their national labour regimes. Given the evolution of, and changes to, the European Union, the recognition and protection of a core set of labour rights that is not subjugated to the free movement provisions of the EC Treaty is, as Hepple noted, crucial if 'mutual recognition—as an alternative to harmonizing legislation—is [to be] workable in respect of labour'.[135] The ECJ needs to reconsider its approach to fundamental labour rights. Instead of placing the onus on unions to justify the interference to fundamental freedoms caused by their exercise of fundamental labour rights, the ECJ should place the onus on the entity claiming that it is appropriate to restrict a fundamental labour right to justify the restriction as legitimate, suitable, and proportionate. In determining the scope of fundamental labour rights and legitimate restrictions on their exercise, the ECJ should follow the approach of the ECtHR and adopt the international labour law *acquis* that is composed of the ILO conventions and decisions by supervisory bodies. But, the problem is that such a profound realignment of the ECJ's approach to labour rights calls into question the capacity of the ECJ as it is currently constituted to protect a core of fundamental labour rights.[136] Establishing a specialist tribunal of the ECJ, with the power to exclude competence to override fundamental rights to collective action protected in member states and to authorize the social partners to intervene in cases before the ECJ, would increase the legitimacy of the ECJ's decisions when it comes to fundamental labour rights.[137]

IV. Conclusion

The paradox of labour rights as international rights is that, for the task they assign to both international labour law and international human rights law, we have globalization and flexible production to thank.[138]

---

[134] Barnard, above n 75, 492; A. Hinarejos, 'Laval and Viking: The Right to Collective Action versus EU Fundamental Freedoms' (2008) 8 *Human Rights Law Review* 714, 727–9.

[135] Hepple, above n 36, 223.

[136] Ashiagbor, above n 45, 206.

[137] B. Bercusson, 'The European Trade Union Movement and the European Court of Justice', British Institute of International and Comparative Law Seminar, Internal Market, Social Policy and Protectionism, 6 May 2008.

[138] Macklem, above n 31, 84.

Although a paradox is not an impossible political condition, according to the political scientist Wendy Brown, it is a demanding and frequently unsatisfying one.[139]
This description captures the tension in the double movement of constitutionalism
that we are witnessing. The perils of neo-liberalism are obvious. In Europe, employers can use their right to move freely throughout the common market to discipline
unions that have the political and economic clout to prevent social dumping on
a transnational basis. Countries with strong corporatist arrangements that give
unions a great deal of political and economic strength are particularly vulnerable
to attack. Recourse to fundamental labour rights as a counter to capital mobility
rights is defensive. Law replaces politics as the vehicle for articulating needs in the
public setting. Neo-liberalism is not only about constructing markets; it is also
about restructuring political power. It involves a shift from parliamentary to judicial and executive power. In the context of Europe, it means that the ECJ is 'the
most juridically powerful and...least democratic institution in the EU'.[140]

The promise of constitutionalizing labour rights is that it will help to restore the
legitimacy of the European Union and to preserve distinctive national social models. With the new political geography of Europe[141] it is difficult to achieve a political consensus about how to balance the fundamental freedoms that favour capital
against workers' fundamental rights. Thus, to a large extent, it falls to the ECJ to
balance these competing freedoms and rights. Hence, Alain Supiot's claim that
'juridical devices specific to democracy, whether electoral freedoms or freedom of
association, make it possible to process the stuff of political and social unrest and
to convert tests of strength into test cases'.[142]

That the current balance set by the European Court of Justice does not have
much social legitimacy is illustrated by two high profile industrial disputes that
occurred in 2009 (at Total, an oil refinery in the north of England, and Alsom,
at a power station in the south) in which British workers mobilized to halt sub-
contracting arrangements in which UK contracts were awarded to businesses from
other EU member states. The key issue in both disputes was the use of posted
workers. While some portray this protest as narrow protectionism, the unions,
supported by the European Parliament, argued that their dispute is not against free
movement of persons, but against the inappropriate balance currently being struck
between business and workers and between the social and economic dimensions of
the EU project.[143]

[139] W. Brown, *States of Injury* (Princeton: Princeton University Press, 1995), 430.
[140] A. Supiot, 'Possible Europes' (2009) 57 *New Left Review* at 3, <http://www.newleftreview.org?A2780>.
[141] Kilpatrick, above n 98, referring to the accession of 12 new member states since 2004 with vastly different wages, labour law regimes, and standards of living.
[142] A. Supiot, 'Viking-Laval-Rüffert: Economic Freedoms versus Fundamental Social Rights—Where Does the Balance Lie?', ETUI-REHS, 4–5. The original version of this article, in French, was published in the *Revue Permanente du Mauss*, <http://www.journaldumauss.net/spip.php?article283>.
[143] Kilpatrick, above n 98, 6; G. Meardi, 'Strikes against Foreign Contractors' (2009) 16 *International Union Rights*.

These strikes demonstrate that the contest of expectations in the daily 'lived world' of industrial relations is the true arbiter of whether developments in labour standards are in a regressive or progressive direction. Although framed and endorsed by the legal system, expectations in the arena of industrial relations are *socially* legitimized in the ongoing conflict of social classes over distributional issues.[144] In a similar way, 'legitimacy among the citizenry is the binding agent [that] sustain[s] such societal contracts as constitutions'.[145] The legitimacy of the Lisbon Treaty and the European Union are jeopardized by the lack of democratic accountability regarding both its ratification and ramifications.

The ECtHR's recent decisions on labour rights must be put in the context of the public dissatisfaction with the European Court of Justice's decisions in *Viking* and *Laval*. The promise of the constitutionalization of labour rights is that it provides an opportunity to build a social model that extends protections to all workers rather than excludes some from the benefits of integration. The problem is, as Polanyi recognized, 'No mere declaration of rights can suffice; institutions are required to make the rights effective'.[146] In Europe, the courts have become key institutions to which the future of labour rights has been entrusted. While judicial recognition of collective bargaining and the right to strike as fundamental human rights are important, the specific court's orientation and function—its mandate to protect fundamental human rights or to build a common market—as well as its remedial powers and authority, are crucial in determining the extent to which labour rights will be effective in protecting the European social model from expanding markets and competition.

[144] Woolfson et al, above n 67.
[145] S. Clarkson, 'Global Governance and the Semi-peripheral State: The WTO and NAFTA as Canada's External Constitution', in M. Griffin Cohen and S. Clarkson (eds), *Governing under Stress: Middle Powers and the Challenges of Globalization* (London: Zed, 2004), 153–75, 165.
[146] Polanyi, above n 6, 276.

13

Freedom, Security, and Justice in the European Court of Justice: The Ambiguous Nature of Judicial Review

Sionaidh Douglas-Scott

It is generally conceded that the EEC (as it then was) did not come into being with the primary aim[1] of protecting human rights.[2] The main aim of the treaty of Rome, signed in 1957, was to set up a 'Common Market'. The goal of economic prosperity was central to the new Community and its treaties contained no Bill of Rights.

However, there is a story to be told, too long to be recounted here, of how human rights came to play their part in EU law, first as 'general principles of law',[3] integrated by the case law of the European Court of Justice (ECJ[4]) into the EU legal order, and then given explicit treaty protection, for example in Article 6 of the treaty on European Union (TEU),[5] and most recently by the incorporation and binding effect of the Charter of Fundamental Rights. Opinions differ as to the reasons underlying this integration of human rights into EU law—the more cynical might argue this came about only under necessity, otherwise the primacy of EU law over national law would be at stake if EU law did not guarantee observance of crucial human rights standards protected under national law.[6] Those of a more optimistic nature might, however, be tempted to agree with a recent opinion of

[1] Unless we understand human rights protection as a collateral effect of the EEC treaty's declared aim of preserving peace in Europe.

[2] Andrew Williams, for example, asserts that to claim human rights as a force for the founding of the EEC is a 'myth' (A. Williams, *The Ethos of Europe: Values, Law and Justice in the EU* (Cambridge: Cambridge University Press, 2010)).

[3] See eg Case 11-70, *Internationale Handelsgesellschaft* [1970] ECR 01125.

[4] Since the coming into force of the treaty of Lisbon, the EU Court has been known as the Court of Justice of the European Union but still appears to be shortened to the 'ECJ'.

[5] Article 6(2) of the TEU, prior to the treaty of Lisbon amendments, formerly read, 'The Union shall respect fundamental rights, as guaranteed by the European Convention for the Protection of Human Rights and Fundamental Freedoms signed in Rome on 4 November 1950 and as they result from the constitutional traditions common to the member states, as *general principles* of Community law.' (Emphasis added.)

[6] See eg J. Coppell and A. O'Neill, 'The European Court of Justice: Taking Rights Seriously?' (1992) 29 *Common Market Law Review* 669, at 689.

Advocate General Maduro in the *Centro Europa 7* case, in which he asserted that, 'Protection of the common code of fundamental rights accordingly constitutes an existential requirement for the EU legal order'.[7]

This contribution does not share a faith in human rights as occupying a central role in the EU order, however desirable such a role might be. This chapter will explore some ways in which human rights have not been granted as much 'respect'[8] as they should under EU law. It will focus in particular on that area of EU law known as the Area of Freedom, Security and Justice, and on the role which the ECJ has played.

I. The Area of Freedom, Security and Justice

In 1997, in the context of the Treaty of Amsterdam, the EU created an 'Area of Freedom, Security and Justice' (AFSJ). This was supposed to make the EU citizen feel closer to the EU and more included by it. It also aspires to be an 'an area of rights' according to the European Commission.[9] Within the scope of the AFSJ, the EU is able to adopt all sorts of measures which people do not usually associate with EU action, including measures on terrorism, migration management, visa policies, asylum, privacy and security, the fight against organized crime, and criminal justice.

Unfortunately, it has become almost a commonplace to state that, in the context of the EU's AFSJ, freedom and justice are being sacrificed to the needs of security. This means, among other things, that important human rights are sacrificed. Although, since the Lisbon treaty came into force on 1 December 2009, the EU's Charter of Fundamental Rights at last has binding force, the EU has generally been slow to adopt measures on rights,[10] and too quick to adopt more coercive and potentially rights-violating measures such as the European Arrest Warrant, or the extremely broad EU definition of terrorism.

The nature of all of this activity undermines the claim made by some theorists that legitimacy of EU action should not be of primary concern because the EU lacks the competences of a traditional state and its powers are mainly economic. Andrew Moravscik, for example, has suggested that any perceived democratic deficit is of less concern in the EU context because the EU still falls far short of what a nation state can do—it has very little coercive power and does not tax and

---

[7] Case C-380/05 *Centro Europa 7* [2008] ECR I-349 at para 19.

[8] 'Respect' for human rights being a key term in the Court's case law and Art 6 TEU.

[9] See Commission, 29/04/2009, 'Report on the practical operation of the methodology for a systematic and rigorous monitoring of compliance with the Charter of fundamental rights' COM(2009) 205 final.

[10] For example, eight years after its first proposal for a 'procedural rights directive', the EU finally adopted Directive 2010/64/EU of 20/10/2010 on the right to interpretation and translation in criminal proceedings. However, an EU Framework Decision on data protection was adopted in 2009 after years of discussion, as well as the EU's Framework Decision on combating certain forms and expressions of racism and xenophobia by means of criminal law which renders criminal intentional public acts designed to incite violence or hatred, or trivializing genocide and similar atrocities.

spend: 'Of the 5 most salient issues in most west European democracies—health care provision, education, law and order, pension and social security policy and taxation—none is primarily an EU competence'.[11] Similarly, Ulrich Haltern suggests that those who aim to create 'foundation narratives' of the constitutional sort for the EU 'will be prone to making a laughing stock of themselves rather than suiting the Union's purpose', proposing instead that the EU be celebrated for what it is—'a shallow' and 'superficial' entity engineered for the 'privileging of the commercial above all else'.[12]

Yet within the scope of the AFSJ are matters that are crucial, indeed almost at the heart of constitutional law, namely, the relation between the individual and public authorities. Bradley and Ewing refer to constitutional law in this context as 'one branch of human learning that helps make life in today's world more tolerable and less brutish that it might otherwise be'.[13] However, a significant question is whether, in the context of the EU, life has actually been made less 'brutish'. It is crucial, if the AFSJ is to be further developed, that this be achieved in the spirit of a 'constitutional moment', as a space of hope, rather than what Pocock has called a 'Machiavellian moment'[14] (ie an attempt to remain stable by any means in the face of a stream of irrational events). To this end, human rights should play an important role.

The example of data collection may be given to illustrate the nature and import of this recent flurry of activity by the EU—and why we should be concerned about it. The EU has long considered control and exchange of information to be a necessary weapon in the fight against terrorism. For example, the European Union's former counter-terrorism co-ordinator, Gijs de Vries, has written, 'Timely and accurate information—its collection, analysis and dissemination—is essential to prevent acts of terrorism and to bring terrorist suspects to Justice'.[15] There are already diverse EU-wide databases in existence. For example, states exchange immigration and crime-related information through the Schengen Information System. Crime-related information is also exchanged through the Europol Information System to which the Europol Convention applies. The Eurojust Information System applies to national prosecutors and courts exchanging information and the Customs Information system applies to data, for example, of smuggling collected by customs officers.[16] It seems in fact that the only domain of European social

[11] A. Moravscik, 'In Defence of Democratic Deficit: Reassessing Legitimacy in the EU' (2002) 40 *Journal of Common Market Studies* 603.

[12] U. Haltern, 'Pathos and Patina: The Failure and Promise of Constitutionalism in the European Imagination' (2003) 9 *European Law Journal* 14.

[13] A. Bradley and K. D. Ewing, *Constitutional and Administrative Law*, 14th edn (London: Longman, 2007), 4.

[14] J. Pocock, *The Machiavellian Moment: Florentine Political Thought and the Atlantic Republican Tradition*, revised edn (Princeton: Princeton University Press, 2003) .

[15] G. de Vries, 'The European Union's Role in the Fight Against Terrorism' (2005) 16 *Irish Studies in International Affairs* 3.

[16] Convention Implementing the Schengen Agreement of 14 June 1985 between the Governments of the States of the Benelux Economic Union, the Federal Republic of Germany, and the French Republic on the Gradual Abolition of Checks at Their Common Borders, tit IV, 22 Sept 2000, 2000 OJ L239/19; Convention Based on Article K.3 of the Treaty of European Union, on the

life that is still untouched by EU data protection law is intelligence-gathering by national intelligence agencies. National agencies such as Germany's Office for the Protection of the Constitution and Federal Intelligence Service generally do not come within the reach of EU law at all. There is no equivalent of the FBI, CIA, or MI5 and 6 at EU level.

The Italian philosopher Giorgio Agamben sparked a debate when he published an article in the *Süddeutsche Zeitung* (and later in the *German Law Journal*[17]) describing how he had cancelled his trip to New York University to give guest lectures in 2004. Agamben's ground for doing this was his unwillingness to subject himself to new biometric measures applying to foreign citizens travelling to the United States. These now familiar measures require non-US citizens to undergo data registration, as well as have fingerprints and iris records taken. Agamben said that his protestations went beyond individual sensitivity, claiming that this involved the appropriation of the most private and unsheltered element of human beings—the biological life of bodies. This, said Agamben, was nothing more than *normalization of a biopolitical status,* in so-called democratic states, of procedures previously considered exceptional and inhumane. He saw this as a key step over the threshold of what Foucault had described as the progressive animalization of man—the taking of fingerprints, electronic tattoos. This, he stated, should not be confused with security reasons.

Yet the EU and its member states are right behind the United States. A noteworthy development at EU level concerns the requirement of biometric information in passports. In 2004 the EU Council adopted a regulation[18] on standards for security features and biometrics in passports and travel documents issued by member states. This regulation requires member states to introduce biometric identifiers for passports issued by them. The aim is to establish a reliable link between the document and its genuine holder and to facilitate checks at external borders.

This EU action on biometrics is a significant step—the 'normalizing' of biometric requirements such as fingerprinting connotes a rather dystopian vision. This regulation may well lead to an EU-wide database containing biometric information of passport applicants and probably other relevant data needed for a proper management of the system. The risk is that such a centralized EU database could become a mass surveillance operation tracking the movements of all residents and citizens. Plans to give access to all law enforcement and internal security agencies also risk the misuse of sensitive personal information. At the very least, such action should be matched by countervailing data protection measures

Establishment of a European Police Office, Arts 2–3, 1995 OJ C316/2; Decision 2002/187/JHA of 28 Feb 2002 Setting Up Eurojust with a View to Reinforcing the Fight Against Serious Crime, Art 5, 2002 OJ L63/1, 3; Council Regulation 515/97, On Mutual Assistance between the Administrative Authorities of the Member States and Cooperation between the Latter and the Commission to Ensure the Correct Application of the Law on Customs and Agricultural Matters, Art 30, 1997 OJ L82/1.

[17] G. Agamben, 'Bodies without Words: Against the Biopolitical Tatoo' (2004) 5 *German Law Journal* 168.
[18] Council Regulation (EC) No 2252/2004 of 13 Dec 2004 OJ L385/1.

by the EU.[19] This, however, is just one example of EU activity with potentially far-reaching implications for rights, a sampler to indicate cause for concern. The remainder of this chapter will develop this investigation further.

II. Untransparent, Undemocratic Lawmaking Leads to Violations of Rights

The EU has not declared itself to be in a state of emergency in response to the terrorist events of September 11, nor to any terrorist or other sort of threat. Former EU Justice and Home Affairs Commissioner, Antonio Vittorino, declared at the announcement of the EU's Hague Programme (which detailed a five-year plan for the field in Justice and Home Affairs in 2004[20]) that the EU had not taken any exceptional measures, that there had been no state of emergency.[21] There has been no comprehensive anti-terrorist legislation in the EU—no equivalent of the Patriot Act in the United States, or the Terrorism Act in the United Kingdom. And yet there has been a great deal of activity, and much of it not by way of what we would think of as 'normal' legislative processes.

  Much of this action took place under the so-called 'Third Pillar' of the TEU, which dealt with police and judicial cooperation in criminal matters. Since the treaty of Lisbon came into force, the EU's 'pillar' system has ceased to operate and Title v of the newly consolidated version of the treaty on the functioning of the EU now deals with the AFSJ. However, not every aspect of the new treaty structure's lawmaking procedures is satisfactory, and transitional provisions mean that the

---

[19] After several years of discussions and debates with the EU institutions, the Framework Decision on the protection of personal data processed in the framework of police and judicial cooperation in criminal matters was adopted by the Council on 27 Nov 2008 (Council Framework Decision 2008/977/JHA of 27 Nov 2008 on the protection of personal data processed in the framework of police and judicial cooperation in criminal matters (OJ 2008/977/JHA L 350/60)). This is a step forward, if not totally satisfactory in the protection it provides. We may look to the European Data Protection Supervisor for informative critical comment, who after having noted that he welcomed its adoption, as an important first step forward in a field where common standards for data protection are very much needed, also stated that he did not see the level of data protection achieved in the final text as fully satisfactory. (European Data Protection Supervisor (EDPS): Press release: 28 Nov 2008.)

[20] See Council of the European Union, Brussels, 13 Dec 2004, 6054/04 JAI 559 Hague Programme: strengthening freedom, security and justice in the European Union. For an analysis of The Hague Programme see S. Carrera and T. Balzacq (eds), *Security versus Freedom: A Challenge for Europe's Future?* (Hampshire: Ashgate, 2006). The Hague Programme has now been superseded and replaced by the Stockholm Programme—'An open and secure Europe serving and protecting the citizens, the next EU plan for Justice and Home affairs', adopted in autumn 2009 (EU doc no: 16484/09, dated 23 Nov 2009).

[21] Cited by Tony Bunyan in Statewatch report no 42, 'The exceptional and draconian become the norm: The emerging counter-terrorism regime: G8 and EU plans for "special investigative techniques", the use of "intelligence information" in court and new "preparatory" offences' (July 2005); In not having declared a 'state of emergency', the EU is unlike the UK, which specifically declared one in order to derogate from Art 5 ECHR in the context of Art 23 ACSTA, which declaration was upheld by House of Lords in *A v Home Secretary* [2004] QB 335.

old procedures will apply to existing Third Pillar acts until 2014,[22] and, in any case, it is important to understand how many of the EU's anti-terrorist measures came about. One reason why the EU's often rather extraordinary measures may not have been noticed is that the way in which these actions have been taken is not especially different from the way in which other Third Pillar measures were taken—that is, those which do not relate to a perceived terrorist threat. Indeed, the whole of the Third Pillar had the appearance of one big state of exception in which the exceptional has become the norm.

A commonly used lawmaking provision previously under the old Third Pillar was that of Article 34 TEU (in effect from 1993 until 30 November 2009) by which the Council adopted legally binding acts (framework decisions, decisions, common positions, or conventions). However, under Article 39 TEU, the European Parliament only had a right to be consulted on these measures, and no right, unlike under the EC Pillar, to table any amendments, nor any possibility of vetoing any measures. The role of the Court of Justice was similarly curtailed under the Third Pillar, with only limited possibilities for judicial review, which were dependent on member states' explicit acceptance of the Court's jurisdiction.

So the whole Third Pillar for all this time, when these key liberty-constraining measures were adopted, lacked many of the safeguards of democratic and legal accountability which existed within the EC Pillar. This is because the Third Pillar was traditionally seen as intergovernmental in nature and the EU states wanted to control it. But this was highly undesirable given the nature of the measures taken under the Third Pillar, which frequently involved intrusions into the liberty and private life of the individual. Neither the European Parliament, nor EU Courts, nor the national parliaments or courts, had any great input in their generation or review.

This had the result that the perceived need for swift, efficient action resulted in a deplorable lack of scrutiny and transparency, throughout all of EU and EC law, suggesting that the rule of law has been scarcely observed in some areas of activity. This secrecy and lack of transparency within the AFSJ was berated by the European Court of Justice in the case of *Heinrich*.[23] This concerned a disgruntled passenger who brought a case against airport authorities, who forced him off a plane he had boarded with tennis racquets (not permitted under EC safety regulations on prohibited articles). However, in breach of the EC treaty, the relevant measures had not been published by the EU Commission. The ECJ (in its Grand Chamber, this formation indicating it was considered to be an important case) held that an act adopted by a Community institution cannot be enforced against individuals before they have had the opportunity to learn of its existence. The ECJ stated that '[i]n particular, the principle of legal certainty requires that Community rules enable those concerned to know precisely the extent of the

---

[22] There will be a five-year transitional period relating to ECJ jurisdiction (ending 1 Dec 2014), in which the 'old' rules on that jurisdiction apply—meaning no infringement actions, and references only from the national courts of 17 member states which agreed to give it jurisdiction under Art 35 TEU.

[23] Case C-345/06, *Gottfried Heinrich*, judgment of 10 Mar 2009.

obligations which are imposed on them. Individuals must be able to ascertain unequivocally what their rights and obligations are and take steps accordingly.'[24]

In addition to the untransparent and undemocratic lawmaking procedures previously operating under the Third Pillar (as if that were not enough!), there are the 'extra-EU' mechanisms for law creating, such as those of the treaty of Prüm, or agreements within the G6,[25] meetings which take place usually in secret, in an utterly untransparent, impenetrable way, but which often end up informing, or even penetrating, the EU criminal justice action. The treaty of Prüm, for example, was signed by a group of EU states (initially Belgium, Netherlands, Luxembourg, Germany, and Austria, later joined by France, Spain, and Italy) in order to further closer cooperation and the exchange of information, including DNA profiles, fingerprints, and vehicle registration data, and later, during the German Presidency of the EU Council, incorporated into the EU's *acquis communautaire* in 2007. Indeed, just a brief mention in the European Council Presidency Conclusions of June 2007 noted the Prüm treaty's transformation from a Schengen-area agreement to a codified European law,[26] without, it is submitted, adequate regard for either human rights or democratic input. Although all of its signatories were EU member states, the treaty was signed outside the EU framework and is seen by many as working against the goal of EU-wide legislation in this area, thereby undercutting the trend towards 'Community method' decision-making. For example, Elspeth Guild writes, '[T]ransferring privately negotiated treaties into the EU *acquis* does not fulfil the requirements of legitimacy. It appears underhanded and dishonest.'[27]

The EU G6 is comprised of the United Kingdom, Germany, France, Italy, Spain, and Poland. At a meeting in Heiligendamm in March 2006, the G6 ministers discussed their joint response to terrorism, illegal immigration, and organized crime.

---

[24] *Heinrich* at para 44. Regrettably, the court undermined the effect of these words by considering that, notwithstanding its inability to impose obligations on individuals, the measure in question could still be considered valid.

[25] The EU G6 is comprised of UK, Germany, France, Italy, Spain, and Poland. G6 ministers have discussed their joint response to terrorism, illegal immigration, and organized crime. The House of Lords European Union Committee, was extremely critical of the G6 decision to press forward with the 'availability principle' and disregard data protection issues:

'A G6 meeting is not a forum in which ministers of some only of the Member States can purport to change EU policy, or even to make formal proposals for changes to EU policy (as opposed to expressing a hope or expectation that such policy will change). It is not clear that the ministers recognise this. The Conclusions record that other Member States "will be fully informed about proposals made by the G6 countries and can participate in their implementation". This is an extraordinarily patronising way of referring to the interests of three quarters of the Member States. There is no suggestion that those States might have views of their own about the desirability of these proposals, and so far from being grateful for being allowed to participate in their implementation, might even be opposed to them.' (House of Lords European Union Committee, 40th Report of Session 2005–6. 'Behind Closed Doors: The Meeting of the G6 Interior Ministers at Heiligendamm'.)

[26] <http://www.consilium.europa.eu/ueDocs/cms_Data/docs/pressData/en/ec/94932.pdf>. The one sentence in the conclusions of the Brussels European Council, 21–2 June 2007, Presidency Conclusions, 11177/1/07 REV 1, is: 'The recent decision to integrate the essential provisions of the Prüm treaty into the Union's legal framework will help to intensify cross-border police cooperation' (see <http://consilium.europa.eu/ueDocs/cms_Data/docs/pressData/en/ec/94932.pdf>, p 7, accessed 18 Oct 2008).

[27] See eg Elspeth Guild, written evidence to House of Lords Select Committee on the European Union, 18th Report 2006–7, 'Prüm: An Effective Weapon Against Terrorism and Crime?' HL 90.

The House of Lords European Union Committee was extremely critical of the G6 decision to press forward with the 'availability principle' (which concerns making information from one member state available in others) and disregard of data protection issues.[28]

So many EU, or EU-backed, initiatives in this area lack the safeguards of democratic and legal accountability which exist at national level or even within the former EC Pillar. This is highly undesirable given the nature of the measures taken, which frequently involve intrusions into the liberty and private life of the individual.

Even more complex and unnoticed is the fact that many of the sorts of actions which have been taken within the Third Pillar occur at a sub-state and operational level, agreed by groups of experts and professionals—almost acts of private law creating with little state input (certainly none from any parliament). In the context of international commercial law, Günther Teubner described a similar development as a new global 'lex mercatoria'.[29] Within criminal law and justice a parallel 'lex vigilatoria'[30] seems to have developed, but in this context, such a phenomenon not only suffers problems of accountability but also human rights and justice concerns, where coercive law is enforced in private. This development has been apparent in the context of national executive and operational agencies and police forces, and also in the creation and strengthening of EU agencies such as Europol and Eurojust. It is just this sort of arrangement that traditional constitutional law (or even national criminal law) is liable to miss—however, there are considerable consequences of this growth of executive power—both for individual liberty and for a lessening of democratic accountability. Such lawmaking processes are of course not singular to the EU, but are a notable feature of norm creation in late modernity, in an era which has seen a growth in the power of the private sphere and much deregulation and devolution of function from the public to the private sphere, along with an increasing premium on 'flexible', 'responsive'[31] law creation.

All of this is to suggest that 'normal' legislative processes—that is, those in which parliaments play an important part, which comply with requirements of democracy, rule of law, and human rights—have not been well respected within

[28] 'A G6 meeting is not a forum in which ministers of some only of the Member States can purport to change EU policy, or even to make formal proposals for changes to EU policy (as opposed to expressing a hope or expectation that such policy will change). It is not clear that the ministers recognise this. The Conclusions record that other Member States "will be fully informed about proposals made by the G6 countries and can participate in their implementation". This is an extraordinarily patronising way of referring to the interests of three quarters of the Member States. There is no suggestion that those States might have views of their own about the desirability of these proposals, and so far from being grateful for being allowed to participate in their implementation, might even be opposed to them.' House of Lords European Union Committee, 40th Report of Session 2005–06. 'Behind Closed Doors; the meeting of the G6 Interior Ministers at. Heiligendamm'.

[29] See G. Teubner, ' "Global Bukowina": Legal Pluralism in the World Society', in G. Teubner (ed), *Global Law without a State* (Aldershot: Dartmouth, 1997).

[30] T. Mathiesen, 'Lex Vigilatoria—Towards a Control System Without a State?', European Civil Liberties network, *Essays for Civil Liberties and Democracy in Europe*, available at <http://www.ecln.org/essays/essay-7.pdf>.

[31] G. Teubner, 'Substantive and Reflexive Elements in Modern Law' (1983) 17 *Law and Society Review* 239; P. Nonet and P. Selznick, *Law and Society in Transition: Toward Responsive Law* (New York: Octagon, 1978).

the EU's Third Pillar (although to say this is not necessarily to imply that they were well-respected within the former EC Pillar of course, nor that the changes brought by the treaty of Lisbon will necessarily bring great improvements).

In the context of this critique, it has been traditionally suggested that greater communitarization or 'normalization' of EU actions, such as the amendments of the treaty of Lisbon, which have resulted in an increased role for the European Parliament and Court of Justice, would be an improvement. It is to be hoped that the profile and status of human rights in EU law will now be ameliorated. The amended Article 6(1) of the TEU now states that:

The Union recognises the rights, freedoms and principles set out in the Charter of Fundamental Rights of 7 December 2000, as adapted at Strasbourg, on 12 December 2007, which shall have the same legal value as the Treaties.[32]

A binding Charter of Fundamental Rights may help to clarify the somewhat ambiguous status of human rights as 'general principles of law'.[33] Furthermore, Title v of the TFEU now deals with the AFSJ, and Article 67(1) TFEU specifically states that,

The Union shall constitute an area of freedom, security and justice with respect for funda-mental rights and the different legal systems and traditions of the Member States.

The TFEU's provisions on judicial and police cooperation in criminal matters now provide that 'the ordinary legislative procedure', that is, the procedure in which the European Parliament plays its most substantial role, and enjoys the possibility of a veto, shall be used for virtually all of the laws to be adopted. The Court of Justice now enjoys jurisdiction over nearly all of the ASFJ.[34]

III. The Disappointment of Judicial Review?

So we might see some hope for improvement of AFSJ measures, given the amend-ments of the Lisbon treaty, and most particularly those which make greater provi-sion for ECJ jurisdiction in this area. Yet how certain can we be that judicial review by the ECJ will indeed be of benefit to the AFSJ? In 1975, AG Trabucchi famously stated, 'If we want Community law to be more than a mere mechanical system of economics and to constitute instead a system commensurate with the society

---

[32] Article 6(2) TEU as amended by the Lisbon Treaty also provides the authorization for the EU to accede to the ECHR with the effect that acts of the EU, including those of the ECJ, could be sub-jected to the review of the European Court of Human Rights.

[33] See wording of n 5 above.

[34] Although with the important caveat that, according to Art 276 TFEU (as was also previously the case pre-Lisbon):

'In exercising its powers regarding the provisions of Chapters 4 and 5 of Title v of Part Three relating to the area of freedom, security and justice, the Court of Justice of the European Union shall have no jurisdiction to review the validity or proportionality of operations carried out by the police or other law-enforcement services of a Member State or the exercise of the responsibilities incum-bent upon Member States with regard to the maintenance of law and order and the safeguarding of internal security'.

which it has to govern, if we wish it to be a legal system corresponding to the concept of social justice and European integration, not only of the economy but of the people, we cannot fail to live up to what is expected of us'.[35]

However, the case law of the European Court of Justice does not necessarily give grounds for great confidence. The record of the ECJ in this field has so far been ambivalent, to say the least, in areas where it has been able to carry out a judicial review of measures.

The remainder of this chapter will examine some areas of AFSJ activity in which the ECJ has already been able to deliver judgments. It has not necessarily improved the protection of human rights.

IV. Human Rights Challenges to the European Arrest Warrant

The results of less than democratic lawmaking procedures, and the dangers of pressing ahead with measures which strengthen security without considering too deeply fundamental rights implications, can be seen in the operation of the European Arrest Warrant (EAW) and in the many legal actions brought once the EAW was implemented into national law. Nor have the problems necessarily been remedied by judicial review.

The EAW is the key mutual recognition initiative in EU criminal law. This was adopted by the EU as a framework decision in 2002[36] and implemented (more or less) by member states by 1 January 2004.

The EAW is used to secure the arrest and surrender of an individual for the purpose of conducting criminal proceedings against them in another member state. The requesting state does not have to show that there is a case to answer and the merits of the request are taken on trust—there are limited grounds for refusing enforcement. Traditional exceptions for political, military, and revenue offences have been abolished. Further, for a long list of 32 offences, the Framework Decision removes the principle of double criminality, that is, the usual requirement that the act in respect of which extradition is sought is recognized as criminal in both the requesting and surrendering states. EAWs have been widely used—in 2007, for example, EAWs were used in over 9,400 cases.

However, the operation of the EAW illustrates deep problems in the EU regarding lack of mutual trust in each other's legal systems and in the lack of protection of individual rights. A specific problem concerns member states surrendering their own nationals. Some EU member states have provisions in their constitutions restricting the extradition of their own nationals and the EAW has come under attack in a number of national courts on this basis. In April 2005 the Polish Constitutional Tribunal found that the EAW offended the Polish Constitution's

---

[35] Opinion of Advocate General Trabucchi in Case 7/75, *Mr and Mrs F v Belgium* [1975] 6 ECR 679.
[36] Framework Decision 2002/584/JHA 1 of the Council of the European Union of 13 June 2002.

ban on extraditing Polish nationals.[37] In July 2005 the German Constitutional Court annulled Germany's law transposing the EAW framework decision because it did not adequately protect German citizens' fundamental rights.[38] The Supreme Court of Cyprus has found the EAW to fall foul of a clause in the Constitution of Cyprus prohibiting their citizens from being transferred abroad for prosecution.[39] This meant that, for quite some time, the EAW procedure was not operative in these countries and old cumbersome extradition procedures had to be used instead. On the other hand, the EAW has survived challenge in the Greek Constitutional Court.

But of critical importance was a challenge brought to the legality of the EAW in the ECJ, because, unlike these other challenges, this was the only action challenging the actual validity of the EU measure itself, rather than specific national implementing measures, and so could have proved fatal to the EAW. In *Advocaten voor de Wereld*,[40] a preliminary reference was made to the European Court of Justice from the Belgian Supreme Court (Court of Arbitration) on 13 July 2005, on the issue of whether the EAW framework decision itself was null and void for violating human rights, and more specifically the principles of legality, equality, and non-discrimination, because it abolishes the double criminality requirement.

The ECJ, following Advocate General Ruiz-Jarabo, took the view that the European Arrest Warrant did not breach the fundamental rights to equality and to legality in criminal proceedings. However, this was hardly a very satisfactory judgment. An overall impression is that, considering its huge importance (illustrated by the fact that ten member states gave opinions), it was remarkably brief—a judgment of only 62 paragraphs, a mere 18 of which dealt with the submissions on the fundamental rights points,[41] although the ECJ at least explicitly mentioned the Charter of Fundamental Rights.[42] More specifically, the reasons the Court gave for finding the EAW not to breach fundamental rights were unsatisfactory.

The first set of human rights challenges to the EAW in *Advocaaten* concerned the principle of legality. The Court simply stated that the EAW did not infringe the principle of legality (ie the claim that it would be uncertain what the specific elements of the offences were because the EAW itself does not define them, leaving this task to the member states, which of course all do so in different ways) because it was not the intention of the EU to harmonize criminal law. It stressed that the responsibility for defining offences rested with the member states, which must comply with fundamental rights, and other states would therefore recognize

[37] An unofficial translation, provided by the Polish Constitutional Tribunal, has been published by Common Market Law Reports: *Re Enforcement of a European Arrest Warrant* [2006] 1 CMLR 36.
[38] Decision of 18 July 2005, upon an application by a German national, Mamoun Darkazanli, whose extradition was sought by the Spanish authorities on alleged al-Qaida terrorist charges.
[39] Decision of 7 Nov 2005.
[40] Case C-303/05, *Advocaten voor de Wereld v Leden van de Ministerraad* [2007] ECR I 3633.
[41] See eg on this F. Geyer, 'European Arrest Warrant: *Advocaten voor de Wereld VZW v. Leden van de Ministerraad*' (2008) 4 *European Constitutional Law Review* 149.
[42] For the first six years of the Charter's existence, the ECJ failed to make any explicit reference to it, preferring to cite instead the ECHR or national human rights provisions. The Court of First Instance and Advocates General, did, however, specifically cite the Charter.

these laws on the basis of trust. The Court also stated its belief that there was a high level of mutual trust between the member states.

Mutual trust and recognition is a familiar thread in EU law, and has also been frequently cited by the Court as the basis for the enforcement of the *ne bis in idem* or double jeopardy system on forbearance of prosecutions.[43] Yet, does such mutual trust actually exist? Further, how should we measure its existence? One would have thought that some kind of empirical evidence would be necessary, but no such data was used by the Court in its judgment. Criminal laws and procedures differ substantially between EU states, particularly between common law and civil law groups. EU states adopt different approaches to offences such as abortion, euthanasia, blasphemy, and inciting race hatred. Criminal investigations may also take different procedural forms within different EU states. The harmonization of such different approaches would take many years, is generally seen as undesirable, and in any case further (and much contested) treaty changes would need to be introduced to EU law to allow for such harmonization. Yet, the existence of continued differences between systems leads to a lack of mutual trust. For example, advocates of common law systems sometimes complain that the civil law emphasis on written evidence does not give defendants adequate rights and protections. Conversely, civil law proponents allege that the adversarial nature of the common law prejudices those defendants who cannot afford expensive lawyers to act for them.

The *Ramda*[44] case, decided before the coming into operation of the EAW, illustrates this lack of mutual trust. In *Ramda*, the English High Court initially refused to surrender, in extradition proceedings, a suspect wanted for the Paris metro bombings, on the basis that evidence against him might have been obtained oppressively—thus illustrating a lack of faith in the French justice system. On the other hand, a willingness to take other states' legal systems at face value was demonstrated in the case of *Osman Hussain*. Hussain, a suspect for the attempted London bombing attacks on 21 July 2005, was sought in Italy by the British authorities. Hussain had argued that the prosecution and the issued warrant infringed his fundamental rights. The Italian court however found that a violation of the fundamental rights must be deduced from objective circumstances, and the traditions of the issuing state, in this case the United Kingdom, excluded the existence of such breaches. This judgment demonstrates mutual trust even in such a sensitive case, in which political issues were at stake.

---

[43] The *ne bis in idem* principle is to be found in Art 54 of the Schengen Implementing Convention. The ECJ has had to determine a number of cases on this article, for example, Cases C-187/01 and C-385/01, *Hüseyin Gözütok and Klaus Brügge* [2003] ECR I-5689. Mutual recognition is also the basis of other measures. For example, Council Framework Decision 2008/909/JHA of 27 Nov 2008 on the application of the principle of mutual recognition to judgments in criminal matters imposing custodial sentences or measures involving deprivation of liberty (OJ L327/27, 5.12.2008) which will enable sentenced persons to be transferred to another member state for enforcement of their sentences.

See also Council Framework Decision 2008/947/JHA of 27 Nov 2008 on the application of the principle of mutual recognition to judgments and probation decisions with a view to the supervision of probation measures and alternative sanctions (OJ L337/102, 16.12.2008).

[44] *R v Secretary of State for the Home Department ex p Ramda* [2002] EWHC 1278. See also *Irrastorza Dorronsoro* (No 238/2003), judgment of 16 May 2003, Cour d'Appel de Pau (France).

The abolition of double criminality still presents a problem. Double criminality is no longer required for the list of 32 categories of offences in Article 2(2), as long as they are punishable in the issuing state by a custodial sentence for a period of at least three years. Following the ECJ's *Advocaaten* judgment, it seems that the definition given by the domestic law of the issuing state should control. However, there are a number of acts listed in Art 2(2) which are not defined as crimes in every member state. For example, Belgium has stated that abortion and euthanasia are not to be considered 'murder' for the purposes of the execution of the warrant.[45] However, abortion in Poland is prohibited as murder (and Poland issues about a third of all European arrest warrants received in the United Kingdom, for example).[46] So the ECJ's approach does not in any way remedy the lack of certainty in criminal law. The only issue of importance is, according to the Court, the law of the issuing state, which is supposed to be safeguarded or supervised by the general notion of human rights in the EU and, more specifically, by the Charter.

The second rights-based challenge in *Advocaaten* was on the basis of non-discrimination, that is, the claim that in departing from dual criminality there was an unjustified difference in treatment, dependent on whether individuals were acting in the executing member states or elsewhere. In this regard, the ECJ's approach was even less satisfactory. The ECJ stated that comparable situations must not be treated differently but did not take the time to establish whether there was in fact a risk of different treatment. It simply referred to the seriousness of the offences at issue, as a justification for the dropping of double criminality. In effect, the Court's approach was one of proportionality—it saw the measure as no more than necessary, given the serious nature of the crimes, but overall, the ECJ did not address the underlying rationale, if any, for abandoning dual criminality.

The problems with the ECJ's approach and remaining lack of legal certainty can be further illustrated in the specific context of the *Toben* case.[47] Many of the offences set out in Article 2(2) EAW are uncertain. What constitutes 'racism' or 'xenophobia'? Would it encompass Holocaust denial? In *Toben*, a European arrest warrant was issued in Germany in an attempt to detain Frederick Toben, who lived in Australia but was arrested while changing planes at Heathrow. Toben was accused of Holocaust denial in Germany (on the basis of material posted on an Australian website but accessible in Germany). Holocaust denial falls under the category of racism or xenophobia in the EAW, and is one for which dual criminality has been abolished. However, Toben had not committed an offence under British law, nor indeed under the law of 17 of the 27 European Union member states. The UK magistrates' courts expressed doubt as to their duty to execute the warrant, and Toben was released when the German government discontinued the prosecution.

[45] Article 5(4) Belgian Law implementing the European Arrest Warrant—Loi du 19 December 2003, see *Moniteur Belge* (22 Dec 2003).

[46] However, it should be noted that the main problem arises when a member state seeks to assert an *extra-territorial* jurisdiction for something which is not an offence in the executing member state—see J. R. Spencer, 'The European Arrest Warrant', in J. Bell and C. Kilpatrick (eds), *Cambridge Yearbook of European Legal Studies: Volume 6* (Cambridge: Cambridge University Press, 2003–4), at 201.

[47] See eg *The Times* (20 Nov 2008), 'Holocaust Denier Fredrick Toben Wins German Extradition Fight'.

Given the lack of common definitions, and weak mutual trust, there will continue to be problems with the EAW in its current form (although it should be acknowledged that, in terms of its extremely wide usage and the vast increase in speed of surrender of suspects, compared to the old process of extradition, the EAW has been considered by many to be a great success). It has been suggested that the list of crimes contained in Article 2(2) be reduced to a few core offences, that is, those for which common criteria for definition and punishment can be more easily found.[48] The litigation over the EAW illustrates that even if the EU does press ahead with legislation, human rights issues will not go away, and that even ECJ judgments do not necessarily resolve these matters.

One way to resolve some of these problems and strengthen faith in fairness of proceedings in other EU states, and thus mutual confidence, would be to have certain minimum common standards throughout the EU. Such a set of basic procedural safeguards operating throughout the EU would also of course strengthen the protection of the individual. In 2004, the Commission proposed that minimum safeguards for criminal proceedings be agreed by member states by way of a framework decision on procedural rights.[49] The rights contained in the original draft framework decision included the right to legal assistance, the right to interpretation and translation, and the right to communicate with consular authorities. The provision of such rights, it was suggested, would bring benefits to citizens facing justice abroad and enhance perceptions of criminal justice systems across the EU. Unfortunately, progress has been slow and the shape and content of the draft framework decision changed quite radically as concerns emerged in the Council. Amendments to the proposal provided for exceptions to rights in cases of terrorism and serious crime, the removal of certain rights, and alleged difficulties in ensuring compatibility with the European Convention on Human Rights also provoked modifications. All of this consequently caused disagreement among member states and calls for further amendments to modify and tone down the proposal to a non-binding resolution indicating slight engagement with the importance of individual rights. More recently, however, in October 2010, the EU at least adopted a directive setting common minimum standards on the right to interpretation and translation in criminal cases throughout the EU.[50]

It has been suggested that adequate protection of suspects' procedural rights already exists under the European Convention on Human Rights and therefore no further action by the EU is really necessary. However, within the ECHR, the standards set are inevitably aimed at securing minimum safeguards at a level acceptable to all its members (which are very diverse in nature—from Russia and Turkey to

---

[48] See eg M. Fichera, 'The European Arrest Warrant and the Sovereign State: A Marriage of Convenience?' (2009) 15 *European Law Journal* 70.

[49] Commission Proposal for a Council framework decision on certain procedural rights in criminal proceedings throughout the European Union Brussels, 28.4.2004 COM(2004) 328 final 2004/0113 (CNS).

[50] Directive 2010/64/EU of 20/10/2010 on the right to interpretation and translation in criminal proceedings.

Sweden and Ireland). In contrast, EU cooperation is at a far more advanced stage than that within the members of the Council of Europe. The agreement of a number of measures in the criminal justice sphere on surrender proceedings, organized crime, and terrorism, has illustrated that action can be achieved across the EU at a level which could not currently be achieved in the Council of Europe and puts the EU in a position to set higher standards. It is therefore disappointing that, six years after announcing the Hague Programme, measures envisaged therein are lacking support from member states. The European Arrest Warrant was agreed in just three months, but eight years on, there is still no agreement on suspects' rights. In the meantime, agreement has been secured on the European Evidence Warrant, which may cause problems of its own.[51] While governments stressed their commitment to the Hague Programme, they nonetheless emphasized a need for what they call 're-prioritization'—which usually means favouring swift adoption of those measures which prioritize security as a concern.

However, there were problems with the thrust of the Hague Programme itself, which tended to stress the balancing of freedom and security (an approach not taken by its predecessor, Tampere). The danger is that the use of balance can marginalize fundamental rights and freedom.[52]

V. The PNR Agreement between the EU and United States

Another case illustrates the unhelpful attitude of the ECJ to human rights issues. After the September 11 terrorist attacks, the US authorities determined that airlines flying into the United States should be required to give the US Bureau of Customs and Border Protection (CBP) access to the passenger name records (PNR data) in their computer systems. The PNR data was to be extracted by the CBP and stored in the CBP's own computer system. This was designed to allow the CBP to check on any terrorist connections of passengers before their arrival in the United States, as well as preserving the data for future investigations. However, this system placed EU airlines in a difficult position, given the extensive nature of the data required—details of up to 35 types of passenger information—including for example, the passenger's choice of in-flight meals. They could submit to the US rules—but at the risk of a breach of data protection rules of individual EU states, some of which provide greater protection of individual data than does US law. Alternatively they could refuse to provide the information—and find themselves in breach of US law, and subject to heavy fines or even unable to land in the United States.

In order to remedy this awkward situation, it was determined that the EU should adopt an agreement with the United States on the handover of PNR records, thus binding the airlines at EU level, as well as setting certain standards

---

[51] Council Framework Decision 2008/978/JHA of 18 Dec 2008 on the European Evidence Warrant, OJ L 350/72.

[52] D. Bigo, S. Carrera, and E. Guild, 'What Future for the Area of Freedom, Security and Justice? Recommendations on EU Migration and Borders Policies in a Globalizing World' (March 2008) *CEPS Policy Brief.*

as to types of data which could be handed over. The low level of data protection in the United States had been subject to criticism, so, after some investigation of the matter, the Commission adopted a decision on the adequacy[53] of US standards of protection of data on 14 May 2004—a decision that was highly controversial, given widespread criticism of US levels of protection of personal data. This in turn enabled the EU Council to adopt the agreement of 17 May 2004 on the exchange of PNR between the EC and US.[54] The legal basis for these acts was EC Data Protection Directive 95/46,[55] in force since 1998, which standardizes data protection rules for all market actors in the EC.

The European Parliament challenged in the ECJ both the Commission's and the Council's decisions on PNR with the United States. There were numerous legal grounds for the Parliament's challenge, most of which were human rights based and went to the inadequate protection of privacy, but which included a challenge on the competence of the EC to adopt the agreement under the First Pillar, rather than under the Third Pillar, which more specifically dealt with criminal laws which might apply to a terrorist threat.

The Court of Justice, in its decision of 30 May 2006, found for the European Parliament.[56] However, the ECJ chose not to ground its judgment on lack of data protection and violations of privacy by the PNR agreement. The Court of Justice did not consider any of the privacy-related claims. Instead, it found that neither the Commission nor the Council had the power to enter into the PNR agreement under the EC treaty. It determined the case on the issue of EC competence.

Since the PNR agreement involved private, commercial European air carriers, the Commission and the Council believed they could adopt the measure under the EC Pillar, which is used as a basis for such regulation of air transport as there is in the EU. However, the Court of Justice disagreed—stating that since the text of the Data Protection Directive expressly does not cover '[data] processing operations concerning public security...and the activities of the State in areas of criminal law' (ie matters that fall under the Third Pillar) and since the PNR agreement covers 'processing operations concerning public security and the activities of the State in areas of criminal law', the Commission's decision could not be based on the Data Protection Directive. It applied a similar logic to annul the Council's decision. The Court therefore clearly regarded these measures concerning the transfer

---

[53] Commission Decision 2004/535/EC of 14 May 2004 on the adequate protection of personal data contained in the Passenger Name Record of air passengers transferred to the United States Bureau of Customs and Border Protection (OJ L235, 2004, 11).
[54] Council Decision 2004/496/EC of 17 May 2004 on the conclusion of an Agreement between the European Community and the United States of America on the processing and transfer of PNR data by Air Carriers to the United States Department of Homeland Security, Bureau of Customs and Border Protection (OJ L183/83, 2004 and corrigendum at OJ L255/168, 2005).
[55] Directive 95/46/EC of the European Parliament and of the Council of 24 Oct 1995 on the protection of individuals with regard to the processing of personal data and on the free movement of such data (OJ L281, 23.11.1995, pp 0031–0050).
[56] C-317/04, *Parliament v Council*, C-318/04, *Parliament v Commission* ECR [2006] I-4721. However, not to cause too much turmoil for the governments and the airlines, the Court of Justice allowed the Commission's decision—and, therefore, the PNR agreement too—to stay effective until 30 Sept 2006.

of PNR data as squarely in the Third Pillar, stating that the data transfer covered by that agreement was 'not data processing necessary for a supply of services, but data processing regarded as necessary for safeguarding public security and for law enforcement purposes'.[57]

However, what is disappointing is the refusal of the ECJ to address the Parliament's arguments based on human rights, as well as the total absence in the ECJ's judgment of any reference to fundamental rights outside of the data protection directive—that is, no reference to the ECHR Article 8, nor to the Charter of Fundamental Rights (which it had not yet referred to at all at this date).[58] Indeed, the practical result was that a new PNR agreement was adopted in October 2006,[59] this time under the Third Pillar, which is even less protective of personal data than the one annulled by the Court. For example, under the new agreement, data can be shared with third countries. There have also been practical problems in the accessing of data from the US Department of Homeland Security—individual requests in the United States for such PNR data have typically taken more than a year to answer—many times longer than the legal time limits in the US Privacy Act and Freedom of Information Act. Further, when individuals have requested 'all data' about them held by the DHS, often they have not been given any of their PNR data.[60] This lack of a clear remedy for wrongful use and transmission of personal information under PNR sits very uncomfortably with the right to an effective remedy under Article 47 of the EU Charter of Fundamental Rights. It has also proved very difficult to establish if records such as PNR do in fact contribute to the fight against terrorism or organized crime—the House of Lords EU Select Committee complained that it was not given enough information of counter-terrorism operations in which PNR data had been relied on.[61]

However, since the EU-US agreement, the EU has proposed its own Framework decision on the retention of PNR data.[62] If adopted, this measure would establish immense databases tracking the travel of every individual, by logging details of every individual flight. Such information could be retained for 13 years. The information could also be accessed by other EU countries without prerequisite of individual suspicion, or of warrant or prior permission. The proposal envisages using this information for 'profiling' of all passengers. As originally proposed, the database would apply only to international flights (ie entering or leaving the EU), but

---

[57] Ibid, para 57.

[58] It should be noted that such a response was not unique from the ECJ—it similarly failed to respond to human rights concerns in addressing the legality of the Family Re-Unification Directive—C-540/03, *Parliament v Council* (family reunification) [2006] ECR I-5769.

[59] Agreement between the European Union and the United States of America on the processing and transfer of passenger name record (PNR) data by air carriers to the United States Department of Homeland Security (OJ L298/29, 27.10.2006).

[60] <http://www.papersplease.org/wp/2008/12/24/dhs-admits-problems-in-discl...>

[61] EU/US Passenger Name Record (PNR) Agreement, House of Lords European Union Committee, 21st Report of 2006/07, HL Paper 108.

[62] Proposal for a Council framework decision on the use of Passenger Name Record (PNR) for law enforcement purposes {SEC(2007) 1422} {SEC(2007) 1453} COM(2007) 0654 final. Since then, the EU Commission has stated a further intention to propose a new PNR Directive early in 2011.

some EU states wish to extend this to include all flights within the EU. Indeed the UK seeks to expand on this by creating a database of all ferry and rail traffic within the EU. The Commission's proposal has already been the subject of criticism across Europe from, for example, the European Data Protection Supervisor, who stated that it did not represent: 'a proper balance between the need to combat such illegality and the rights of the innocent majority to go about their daily lives without undue interference by the State'.[63]

To reiterate: what is surprising is the total absence in the ECJ's judgment of any reference to fundamental rights outside the Data Protection Directive—that is, no reference to the ECHR Article 8 nor to the Charter of Fundamental Rights (to which the Court had actually never referred at that time). The practical result was that the new PNR agreement, although adopted under the Third Pillar, is even less protective of personal data than the one annulled by the Court.

VI. Terrorist Blacklists

These have caused consternation. Has the European Court of Justice ameliorated the situation from a human rights perspective?

The EU's involvement in challenges to the legality of terrorist lists arose in the following way. The UN Security Council blacklisted certain persons and groups as terrorists, or terrorist associates, requiring all states to take steps to freeze the financial assets of individuals and entities associated with Osama Bin Laden, Al-Qaida and the Taliban. In order to implement Security Council (SC) resolutions, the EU, as successor to the member states in certain areas of foreign policy, including such 'smart' sanctions, implemented the measures. This situation presents a problem for those who wish to challenge these EU measures as wrongly listing them in breach of their rights. Such situations have been described as notorious 'black holes', with those listed finding it very hard to find a forum to challenge their blacklisting. The *Kadi* case,[64] decided by the ECJ in September 2008, arises out of such a background set of circumstances, and is often represented as a triumph and victory for human rights and judicial review, with one prominent commentator writing, 'In the EU's flawed system of governance, democracy finds solace in judicial review'.[65]

Mr Kadi, a Saudi Arabian national, with substantial assets in the EU (in fact some $9M), had been listed in an EU regulation[66] implementing an EU common position which in turn implemented a UN SC resolution. Kadi contested his listing, arguing

---

[63] Opinion of the European Data Protection Supervisor on the draft Proposal for a Council Framework Decision on the use of Passenger Name Record (PNR) data for law enforcement purposes, DPS/07/14.

[64] Joined Cases C-402 and 415/05P, *Kadi & Al Barakaat Int'l Found v Council & Commission*, [2008] ECR I-6351.

[65] T. Tridimas, 'Terrorism and the ECJ: Empowerment and Democracy in the EC Legal Order' (2009) 34 *European Law Review* 103.

[66] Council Regulation 881/2002, Annex 1, 2002 OJ L139/9 (EC), available at <http://eur-lex.europa.eu/LexUriServ/LexUriServ.do?uri=OJ:L:2002:139:0009:0022 :EN:PDF>.

that he had never been involved in terrorism or the financial support of it, and was wrongfully named. He claimed, *inter alia,* that the EU measure violated his fundamental right to property, the right to a fair hearing, and right to judicial redress. It was not possible for him to petition the UN Sanctions committee directly as it does not accept direct representations from individuals but only from member states. So he approached the EU courts in Luxembourg. At first, the EU's Court of First Instance (CFI) held that the primacy of the UN prevented review of the measure on the basis of EU standards, given that all that the EU was doing was implementing a UN measure, and had no discretion in how it implemented the measure.[67] The Court stated that any review according to EU standards would cause serious disruption to the international relations of the Community. The only possible review would be on the basis of *jus cogens,* not autonomous freestanding EU fundamental rights standards, and on the basis of *jus cogens,* the CFI considered no breach of Kadi's rights to have taken place. A bad day for access to justice, one might think. The best the CFI could do was to say that national courts could provide judicial review of any wrongful refusal by national authorities to submit his case to the UN Sanctions committee for reconsideration. The reasoning of the CFI was unconvincing and leaves not just merely a lacuna but a huge *abyss* in effective judicial protection.

Mr Kadi appealed his case to the ECJ, which, contrary to the CFI, found that his rights had been violated.[68] This decision of the ECJ is usually treated as a victory for rights, which it probably is. The ECJ proclaimed the constitutional autonomy and hegemony of the EU legal order, stating that the EU is a community based on the rule of law, and that respect for fundamental rights is an integral part of the EU legal order. It also held that the obligations of an international agreement could not prejudice the constitutional principles of the EC treaty. Therefore, it was less concerned than the CFI about the primacy of the UN SC resolutions. From there, it was able to go on to review the measure under EU rights standards and to find that Mr Kadi's right to effective judicial process had been violated by the failure to communicate to him the reason for his listing. The failure to observe due process standards also resulted in a violation of his right to property.

So far so good, one might think. A victory for Mr Kadi and human rights. Yet there are aspects of the ECJ's judgments which might trouble us. The real concern of the ECJ seems to be the autonomy of the EU legal order. The ECJ relies very heavily on EU 'constitutional principles' in its judgment. This illustrates a very strong constitutional emphasis on the part of the ECJ on a par with that of its early pathbreaking cases of *Van Gend en Loos* and *Costa v Enel*, which set out the basic principles of the direct effect and supremacy of EEC (as it then was) law. The Court in *Kadi* was also keen to equate EU law with national and with constitutional, rather than international law. Yet what about the EU's commitment to international law, namely the UN resolutions? This judgment shows less respect for international law than is usual from the ECJ. It also rejects the notion

---

[67] See Case T-315/01, *Kadi v Council & Commission* [2005] ECR II-3649; Case T-306/01, *Yusuf & Al Barakaat Int'l Found v Council & Commission* [2005] ECR II-3533.

[68] Joined Cases C-402 and 415/05P, *Kadi & Al Barakaat Int'l Found v Council & Commission* [2008] ECR I-6351.

that the regional EU is in a subordinate relation to the UN.[69] In this respect, the reasoning of the ECJ might be compared with that of the US Supreme Court in recent cases such as *Medellin v Texas*,[70] in which the US Supreme Court found a judgment of the ICJ not to be enforceable in the United States without prior congressional action. In *Kadi*, the ECJ treated the UN Charter as nothing more than any other international treaty. In this respect, the ECJ's judgment is much less deferential than that of the CFI,[71] or that of the European Court of Human Rights in *Behrami*,[72] in which the Strasbourg Court held that it did not have jurisdiction *ratione personae* over actions or failure to act by agents of member states of the Convention where this action or failure to act was attributable to the UN alone. It may also be contrasted with the *Al Jeddah*[73] decision in which the (then) House of Lords found that the relevant Security Council resolution authorizing British forces to operate in Iraq displaced Article 5 of the ECHR to the extent that a conflict arose between the two instruments, and that the contested detention in that case was consequently lawful. This is not to suggest that the approaches of the CFI, European Court of Human Rights, and House of Lords are preferable from a rights perspective. It is rather to suggest that, while justice may have been done in the individual *Kadi* case, this may be storing up problems for the future observance by the EU of international law. Ziegler, for example, suggests that the Court's approach in *Kadi* may lead to a fragmentation of international law, and even ultimately to the insulation of the ECJ from any international human rights standards, because of its choice to look instead to autonomous EU standards.[74]

A further noteworthy observation concerns the eventual outcome of the *Kadi* litigation. Despite the ruling of the European Court of Justice in *Kadi* that the Council Regulation freezing their assets was unlawful, the European Commission decided to maintain Mr Kadi and the Al Barakaat International Foundation on the EU terrorist list on the grounds that 'the listing of [the parties] is justified for reasons of its association with the Al-Qaida network'. In response to the ECJ's ruling, the European Commission 'communicated the narrative summaries of reasons provided by the UN Al-Qaida and Taliban Sanctions Committee, to Mr Kadi and to Al Barakaat International Foundation and [gave] them the opportunity to comment on these grounds in order to make their point of view known'. Mr Kadi's lawyers duly responded in a letter dated 10 November 2008, which the European Commission simply dismissed on the grounds that the 'preventive nature of the freezing of funds

---

[69] See on this, G. De Búrca, 'The ECJ and the International Legal Order after Kadi' (2009) 51 *Harvard Journal of International Law* 1.

[70] *Medellin v Texas* [2008] 552 US 491.

[71] However, see a later blacklisting case *Omar Mohammed Othman v Council and Commission* [2008] ECR I 0000 in which the CFI followed the ECJ's reasoning.

[72] *Behrami and Behrami v France* [2007] 45 EHRR SE10.

[73] *R (Al-Jedda) v Secretary of State for Defence* [2007] UKHL 58.

[74] K. S. Ziegler, 'Strengthening the Rule of Law, but Fragmenting International Law: The *Kadi* Decision of the ECJ from the Perspective of Human Rights' (2009) 9 *Human Rights Law Review* 288.

and economic resources' justifies the ongoing violation of Mr Kadi's fundamental rights.[75]

VII. The Ambiguity of Judicial Review

In this respect, the *Kadi* decision may be seen in the context of a line of cases in which the ECJ, while delivering a judgment apparently rights-friendly on the face of it, in fact merits closer scrutiny for other motivating factors. Such ulterior agendas may be traced back to the early and seminal case of *International Handelsgesellschaft*,[76] in which the ECJ, in order to ensure the supremacy of EC law, read into the fabric of EC law an unwritten bill of rights by which it, rather than national courts, could review EC measures for their compatibility with human rights. In describing the European Court's resolution in *Handelsgesellschaft*, Joseph Weiler has written: 'the surface language of the Court is... the language of human rights. The deep structure is all about supremacy...'.[77] Nearly 20 years ago, Coppell and O'Neill, in a seminal article, suggested that the European Court had instrumentalized rights as tools for European integration.[78] The ECJ's strategy in these cases may be criticized for utilizing forms of legality which are supposedly liberating in nature, such as civil liberties or judicial review, while in fact participating in an all-determining instrumentalization of social control, normalization, and governance. Gaete, for example, suggests that the libertarian project of human rights is trapped as 'the instruments of liberation tend to become the means of manipulation'.[79] And so human rights become a means to the legal system's self-aggrandisement and success.[80]

Kadi may be linked with other recent case law of the ECJ. In *Pupino*,[81] the ECJ held that Third Pillar measures, although explicitly lacking direct effect according to the wording of the TEU, could be interpreted as having indirect effect, thus giving it the jurisdiction to review the ability of national measures to be interpreted in conformity with them. *Pupino* has been interpreted as a very bold finding by the

---

[75] See Commission Regulation 1190/2008/EC of 28 Nov 2008.

[76] Case 11-70, *Internationale Handelsgesellschaft* [1970] ECR 01125.

[77] J. H. Weiler, A. Cassese, and A. Clapham (eds), *Human Rights and the European Community* (Baden-Baden: Nomos, 1991), vol II at 58.

[78] Coppell and O'Neill, above n 6. Coppell and O'Neill claim that their conclusion is backed up by their survey of outcomes—ie that in very few of the cases where the Court boldly uses the rhetoric of fundamental rights does the applicant actually succeed in their assertion of that right. The vehemence of the Coppell and O'Neill claim is only matched by those who seek to defend the European Court against such accusations of bad faith, such as Weiler and Lockhart in their article '"Taking Rights Seriously" Seriously: The European Court and its Fundamental Rights Jurisprudence—Part I' (1995) 32 *Common Market Law Review* 51; Part II (1995) 32 *Common Market Law Review* 579.

[79] R. Gaete, 'Postmodernism and Human Rights: Some Insidious Questions' (1991) 2(2) *Law and Critique* 149.

[80] See M. Foucault, *Power/Knowledge* (New York: Pantheon, 1980); K. Marx, *On the Jewish Question* (reprinted in J. Waldron (ed), *Nonsense on Stilts* (London: Methuen, 1987).

[81] Case C-105/03, *Pupino* [2005] ECR I-5285.

Court, raising the issue of whether the Court would take further steps with Third Pillar law, finding it to be capable of primacy over national law.[82]

The cases discussed in this chapter illustrate an ambiguity in the ECJ's attitude toward human rights. They are not explicitly unfriendly to rights, and yet they do not afford the centrality and attention to rights reasoning which one might hope for. In the *PNR* case, the rights argument is sidelined altogether, whereas, in *Advocaten voor de Wereld* and *Kadi,* even where the questions of rights are be addressed, the approach is still less than satisfactory. In *Advocaten*, the reasoning is thin and inadequate, leaving many questions unaddressed, and in *Kadi*, what on the face of it appears to be a rights-friendly judgment results in a pyrrhic victory for the claimant and raises problems for the relationship of EU law to international law.

It has, however, been suggested, that contrary to this somewhat sceptical thesis, the ECJ has shown a more positive, productive relationship with human rights, specifically in cases such as *Carpenter, Omega,* and *Schmidberger*.[83] These three cases concerned free movement within the Internal Market, rather than the type of AFSJ measures on which this chapter focuses, and as such are beyond the scope of this contribution, but they do necessitate a brief discussion to rebut the suggestion that they provide strong evidence of a rights-friendly jurisprudence.

Carpenter was an immigration case. Mrs Carpenter, a Philippine national who was married to an English citizen, had been denied a right to reside in the UK under UK law. Mr Carpenter claimed that EU law also applied to this case on the basis of his (rather intermittent) provision of services to other EU states. This right would be restricted if his wife (who helped care for his children) were forced to leave the UK. The ECJ accepted that EU law was implicated and held that, given that this was so, the Carpenters' right to family life would be restricted if she were deported, and so held the interference with the right to provide services to be disproportionate. This case appears to be a victory for human rights, especially in the strong interpretation of the right to family life, but is nonetheless unsatisfactory in that it provides EU law with huge jurisdiction over matters which seem to be very distant from its usual scope, hardly leaving any room for national regulation of immigration matters. It lacks a *de minimis* approach, the worrying implications of which became evident in the later *Viking* and *Laval* litigation.

It has been suggested that *Omega* and *Schmidberger* provide examples of cases in which the Internal Market was subordinated to fundamental rights. If this were so, it would be a remarkable and rare urge on the part of the ECJ, but it is submitted that this is to read too much into these cases. In *Omega*, an imported British laser game had been banned in Germany on the basis that 'playing at killing' with laser games infringed the concept of human dignity. It was argued by the importers that banning the game infringed the free movement of goods and services. In

---

[82] On this see, T. Corthaut and K. Lenaerts, 'Of Birds and Hedges: The Role of Primacy in Invoking Norms of EU Law' (2006) 31 *European Law Review* 287.

[83] Case C-60/00, *Mary Carpenter v Secretary of State for the Home Department* [2002] ECR I-6279; Case C-36/02, *Omega* [2004] ECR I-09609 14; Case C-112/00, *Schmidberger* [2003] ECR I-5659.

this case, the ECJ held the ban not to be disproportionate, recognizing the right to dignity as inherent in EU law. It might seem that this judgment shows great deference to member states' fundamental rights standards, and yet it is unlikely that the concept of dignity would be stretched beyond the circumstances of this case. The Court did not engage in any in-depth analysis of the concept of dignity,[84] but rather focused instead on the concept of proportionality. Similarly *Schmidberger*, a case in which a trader's right to the free movement of goods, which had been blocked by an environmental protest on the Brenner motorway, was overridden by the right of the protesters, was decided on the basis of proportionality. What is, however, of particular concern in *Schmidberger*, is the Court's categorization of the free movement of goods and freedom of expression as 'equal interests'.[85]

The equivalence of fundamental market freedoms and fundamental rights was raised once again in the cases of *Viking* and *Laval*,[86] this time with no positive result for fundamental rights. These cases illustrate the downsides of both *Carpenter* and *Schmidberger*. In both *Viking* and *Laval*, it was claimed that the applicant undertakings' market freedoms had been restricted by trade union collective action. Although the right to take such action was at least acknowledged by the Court as a 'fundamental right', in both cases it was outweighed by the fundamental market freedom. As in *Carpenter*, the Court took a broad approach to the application of EU law, holding that collective action could restrict market access. It then went on to weigh the freedom to provide services against this fundamental right to strike, in effect interpreting the right to strike as a *restriction* on the market freedom. Such reasoning is antipathetic to fundamental rights and has been strongly criticized. The Court found that the right to strike had not been exercised proportionately.

The discussion above is of course not a comprehensive discussion of these cases, but it aims to sketch out how the reasoning in the first three cases, while apparently protective of rights, has its undersides which can be used to undermine them. Once more the effect of judicial review is ambiguous. Therefore, *Carpenter, Omega*, and *Schmidberger*, in their way, set the scene for the unfavourable results in *Viking* and *Laval*, by first, allowing a very wide concept of restricting market access to give rise to EU jurisdiction, and then by allowing fundamental rights to have an equal status to so-called 'fundamental' market freedoms in EU law. As has so often been the case in the EU, the Internal Market lies at the centre of things, and proportionality's essential function is to ensure that market integration is not too greatly compromised.

The ambiguity of the Court's reasoning becomes even more critical in the context of the AFSJ. Whereas, in the past, there were fewer occasions for fundamental rights issues to come before the ECJ in a context dominated by free market language, in the context of the AFSJ, which concerns matters which may intrude greatly into liberty and justice, it is crucial that fundamental rights play less of a sideline role.

---

[84] See eg A. Williams, *The Ethos of Europe* (Cambridge: Cambridge University Press, 2010), at 134.
[85] *Schmidberger*, at para 81.
[86] Case C-438/05, *Viking* [2007] ECR I-10779; Case C-341/05, *Laval* [2007] ECR-I 11767.

VIII. Human Rights in the Future of the AFSJ

The EU has declared no 'state of emergency', but I have suggested that, over the past decade, by means of its undemocratic legislation processes within the former Third Pillar, and the draconian measures it has adopted, it is proceeding as if there were such a state of emergency. This is a critical state of affairs—what possibilities are there for improvement?

(a) Repatriate the EU's Area of Freedom, Security, and Justice

I have suggested that within the EU, or at least within AFSJ, there exists little, or no, respect for the rule of law and freedom and justice. Indeed the EU is in breach of its own treaty—for example, Article 6 TEU, by which it is bound to respect human rights, democracy, and the rule of law. The AFSJ was perceived at the time of the treaty of Amsterdam as the next big initiative for the EU, to give it momentum after the completion of the 1992 Single Market project, to provide the EU with a sense of identity and its citizens with a sense of belonging, and to make the new EU competences in certain matters of justice and home affairs seem more meaningful. But in fact it has resulted in a disastrous misuse of democracy, giving reign to the worst excesses of member states, which, in the intergovernmental Council, have been free to pursue their own gain, free from parliamentary scrutiny.

Given this state of affairs there is at least some sense in the (albeit extreme) notion of the repatriation of these areas to the member states—at the very least, the criminal law provisions which had their place in the former Third Pillar could be repatriated. While it is the case that the member states themselves do not have a great record on human rights protection, in time of emergency (witness successive terrorist legislation in the United Kingdom since 2000) at least, much national legislation is still subject to parliamentary scrutiny and Parliament sometimes takes this scrutiny seriously— for example, as in the case of the UK Terrorism Acts, in which the government was unable to get its desired 90-day pre-charge detention provisions through.

(b) 'Normalization' of the AFSJ

Realistically, such a repatriation is unlikely to happen. This jurisdiction is unlikely to be returned to the member states. There is a consensus (including the opinion of the European public it seems) that there is a need to fight crime on a broader scale and that it is appropriate for the EU to be active here. However, if this is to be the case, then the EU must 'normalize' its activities in this area to more standard democratic methods of lawmaking.

Terrorist legislation is incompatible with the protection of human rights—a point that Conor Gearty has made.[87] He suggests that the ordinary criminal

---

[87] Per C. Gearty, *Can Human Rights Survive?*, Hamlyn lectures 2005 (Cambridge: Cambridge University Press, 2006).

justice system will do the job for us—we do not need a special regime—indeed, we cannot have one, if we are to uphold human rights. If this is the case—if there is no need for a special exceptional regime to fight terrorism—then how much more so is it the case in the pursuit of ordinary crime fighting actions? Yet, the EU uses abnormal methods for these as well.[88]

What would 'normalization', or the removal of these abnormal or emergency-like procedures, involve in the context of the EU's AFSJ? It would require the 'ordinary' Community method to be applied—that is, a legislation process in which the European Parliament played a strong part (usually by means of the co-decision procedure), and the availability of individual access to judicial review in the ECJ for all actions. Much of this process has in fact been achieved by the Lisbon treaty, and this is at least one reason to welcome yet another overly complex EU treaty with all of the inconvenience of re-numbering.

Yet, the discussion of this chapter suggests that normalization is no panacea for human rights protection. The EU has never given human rights a sufficiently central place in its order. The Internal Market continues to provide it with its *raison d'être*. Even where judicial review is available, and human rights claims may be asserted in the ECJ, the results are at best ambiguous. Any system in which fundamental rights fall to be justified as 'restrictions' on apparently equal status fundamental market freedoms, as in *Viking* and *Laval*, cannot be satisfactory. Nor is it at all clear that the European public would be satisfied with giving the ECJ a mandate as a human rights court in any case. So we must look for solutions elsewhere.

How did this abnegation of Justice and Freedom happen? How did we, the citizens of Europe, allow our governments, through the Council of Ministers, to get away with this large-scale appropriation of so many coercive measures with so little public attention? Remedying the situation requires not only normalizing the AFSJ through the 'Community' method but also *rethinking* the AFSJ. This would involve seeing 'security' less as a good and more as a means towards freedom and justice. This in turn requires thought about what freedom and justice could mean in this context. Justice in this context should not be interpreted in a very narrow way to mean administration of justice, with a concomitant prosecutorial bent (in some translations of the EU treaty, ie Dutch and German, 'justice' is translated as 'Recht'—ie 'law', encouraging such an interpretation, but this is not the only way to see it). Justice must surely at least incorporate the rule of law. How should the rule of law be understood? A most basic and minimal interpretation of the rule of law is that law should be capable of guiding the behaviour of its subjects and to do this must be prospective, general, clear, public and relatively stable, and also comprise mechanisms of an independent judiciary, open and fair hearings without bias, and some review of legislative and administrative officials and limits to police discretion.[89] 'Freedom' also incorporates human rights, including those of

---

[88] eg most of the crimes for which a European Arrest Warrant may be issued are not terrorist measures at all, but ordinary crimes, although it was the terrorist events of 9/11 which provided the conditions of possibility for the EAW's adoption.

[89] Per J. Raz, 'The Rule of Law and its Virtue' (1977) 93 *Law Quarterly Review* 195. Raz in fact gives a rather minimal account of the rule of law, and others have given it more substantive content—

minorities and suspects, a fact which is being lost in the pursuit of security across the EU.

Such an interpretation, with a strong emphasis on justice, human rights, and the rule of law, could encourage a sense of belonging and commonality among European peoples. The EU should take freedom and justice seriously—this might involve taking action against member states to show it is serious about human rights—for example, proceedings under Article 7 TEU[90] against those states who allowed 'rendition' on their territory, or even more controversially, against states like the UK who engage in flagrant breach of ECHR in long periods of pre-trial detention, or against any state that would admit evidence under torture. In this way, the AFSJ could gain a high profile and become meaningful to all EU citizens. Otherwise, the future looks very bleak, and Agamben's predictions would seem to be coming true—and most people would not even have noticed.

but we can see that the EU Third Pillar has been deficient, even according to Raz's rather formal account.

[90] Art 7 TEU allows the suspension of EU voting rights of those states which have breached eg EU fundamental rights standards:

1. On a reasoned proposal by one third of the Member States, by the European Parliament or by the European Commission, the Council, acting by a majority of four fifths of its members after obtaining the consent of the European Parliament, may determine that there is a clear risk of a serious breach by a Member State of the values referred to in Article 2. Before making such a determination, the Council shall hear the Member State in question and may address recommendations to it, acting in accordance with the same procedure.

The Council shall regularly verify that the grounds on which such a determination was made continue to apply.

2. The European Council, acting by unanimity on a proposal by one third of the Member States or by the Commission and after obtaining the consent of the European Parliament, may determine the existence of a serious and persistent breach by a Member State of the values referred to in Article 2, after inviting the Member State in question to submit its observations.

3. Where a determination under paragraph 2 has been made, the Council, acting by a qualified majority, may decide to suspend certain of the rights deriving from the application of the Treaties to the Member State in question, including the voting rights of the representative of the government of that Member State in the Council. In doing so, the Council shall take into account the possible consequences of such a suspension on the rights and obligations of natural and legal persons.

PART II

POLITICIZING HUMAN RIGHTS

14

The Political Institutions of Rights-Protection

Mark Tushnet[1]

What institutions best protect fundamental rights? The default modern answer is, the courts. Legislatures and executives are too easily diverted from deliberative consideration of fundamental principle by the passions of the moment, it is said. And, more important, legislatures and executives respond to majority will when fundamental rights are typically imperilled by political majorities; indeed, it is often said that one basic point of identifying fundamental rights in a constitutional document is to ensure that those rights are not overridden by political majorities.[2] However imperfect they are in executing the duty to enforce fundamental rights, courts are ordinarily no more influenced by political majorities than are legislatures and executives, and are ordinarily less influenced by them.

The argument just sketched certainly has elements of truth to it. It has two flaws. First, it implicitly assumes that threats to fundamental rights come primarily from government action rather than inaction. That (traditional liberal) assumption has to be supplemented by the view associated with social democracy that threats to fundamental rights come from exercises of private power to which legislative action might respond.[3] The second flaw lies in the argument's overly general depiction of legislatures and executives. After making one preliminary conceptual point, this chapter argues that there are many 'legislatures' and 'executives', and these institutions vary in the degree to which they are susceptible to the deliberative distortions arising from majoritarian pressure at the core of the default answer. I argue that under some reasonable assumptions, legislatures and executives may develop defensible *specifications* of fundamental rights, the displacement of which by alternative specifications emanating from the courts is not justified by the argument supporting the default answer. By *specification* I mean the identification in a reasonably concrete setting of whether some government action is compatible or inconsistent with recognizing the set of fundamental rights we have. The key

---

[1] Thanks to Adrian Vermeule for helpful comments on an earlier version of this chapter.

[2] One point, but not the only one: A nation's lawmakers might want to enumerate fundamental rights as a way of expressing their nation's commitment to the actualization of those rights.

[3] The social democratic perspective is a development of liberal premises. It recognizes that 'government action' is ever-present, and particularly, for the social democrat, in the legal entitlements—a form of government action—that place non-government actors in a position to threaten interests that even traditional liberals recognize as fundamental.

298 *Mark Tushnet*

elements of my argument are institutional—variations in government structure, in the nature of legislation, and, importantly, in party structure. The chapter concludes with two observations, one about the relation between its argument and the distinction between traditional liberalism and social democracy I have mentioned, and one about institutional design for rights-protection in a liberal and social democratic world.

I. The Role of 'Specification' in Institutional Choice

The notion of 'specification' plays an important part in my argument, so I begin with a discussion of why specification matters. The discussion identifies two ways in which problems of specification can arise, but they share a common structure resting on uncertainty about whether a specific piece of legislation actually violates fundamental rights. Uncertainty arises at the individual level in the first, at the level of group disagreement in the second.

Suppose a person holds firm views about the specific content of some fundamental right (hence the term 'specification')—for example, not merely that the right of free expression is a fundamental one, but that that right requires that newspapers be allowed to publish false defamatory statements about public officials if the newspapers have adhered to prevalent journalistic standards in attempting to verify the statements' accuracy. That person should allocate the protection of that right to whatever institution is more likely to protect it—and similarly for all the other rights the person believes worth protecting. There is no systematic reason for that person to choose only the courts or only the legislature as the venue for rights-protection. Perhaps the courts are more likely than legislatures to protect every right the person believes worth protecting, but perhaps legislatures are more likely than courts to protect some rights, less likely than legislatures to protect others. The person should assign protection of the first set to the courts and protection of the second to the legislature. The decision will have to be made on a right-by-right basis.

Perhaps, though, rights-protection is cumulative. That is, what could be wrong with assigning the power to protect rights to legislatures in the first instance, and then using courts as a back-up institution to protect those rights that legislatures for whatever reasons fail to protect? The answer is that a person with firm views about what rights should be protected under which circumstances should know that courts make mistakes. Perhaps the legislature enacts a rights-protecting statute. Constitutional review gives the courts a chance to strike that statute down—erroneously, from the perspective we are assuming.[4]

Of course no one could hold views about every possible specification of rights he or she holds to be fundamental. New technologies will generate new problems, for

---

[4] Even advocates of constitutional review acknowledge the possibility of error when they defend adding one layer of review beyond the legislature and not two, three, or more. Each additional layer adds direct costs, of course, but also increases the risk of error. I have never seen a cogent argument showing that a constitutional system's performance is necessarily improved by adding one layer of review, with its associated direct costs and risk of error, but not by adding two layers.

example, and changes in society may produce novel forms of older problems, which might—or might not—suggest that older answers should be reconsidered. Again, if the person knows (to her own satisfaction) immediately how the fundamental right should be specified in connection with these new problems, the institutional solution is the same: Give the institution most likely to protect the right the power and duty to do so. More often, though, the person will not have firm convictions about the right answer to the specification question, that is, will not know whether the new problem involves a rights-violation or not. She could of course deploy her intellectual resources to develop her own convictions on the specification question. Alternatively, and more efficiently, she could rely on the answer provided by some other institution. If she takes that approach, she cannot ask herself the question she asks when she knows what the answer is. She cannot ask, that is, Which institution is more likely to produce the answer I already know is the right one? Rather, she must ask herself a question roughly like this: Which institution is more likely to produce an answer that I would give if I had full information? Here too, though, it seems unlikely that any general answer will be available. One piece of information that I will have is the specification offered by the institution to which I have assigned the task, and so the question probably can be reposed as, Which institution is more likely to produce an answer that I will find acceptable on reflection after the event? Courts might be better at generating answers acceptable on ex post reflection to questions about specifying free expression rights, legislatures better at doing so about specifying equality rights.

The ex post inquiry introduces another complication. Assigning the specification question to the courts might generate an answer that is acceptable on ex post reflection, and yet had the question been assigned to the legislature, that institution might have produced a directly contrary answer that would also be acceptable on ex post reflection. The reason is precisely that specification questions typically involve conflicts among competing interests and values, including conflicts among fundamental rights. Publication of true facts about a person's private life implicates the fundamental right of free expression, but also the fundamental right of privacy or human dignity.[5] Courts and legislatures might produce different answers to the specification question here: A legislature might create a cause of action for intrusion on privacy by publishing true facts whose publication adds little to public knowledge or understanding about any matter with which the public is rightly concerned; a court might reject liability for publishing such facts unless the publisher disseminated them with the specific intention of offending the victims of the intrusion; and a person might on reflection think that both answers are adequately respectful of fundamental rights. An individual concerned about rights-protection might then be indifferent about the assignment of that task to one or another institution.

The same is true at the level of groups, which is plainly more important for the issues of institutional design of interest here. An individual can be uncertain about

---

[5] Protection of human dignity is not treated as fundamental in a constitutional sense in the United States, but the individual citizen we are dealing with here might accept the view prevailing in most other advanced democracies that protection of human dignity is indeed a fundamental right in the normative sense even when it is not so treated as a matter of positive law.

what the correct rights-specification is, but she cannot disagree with herself about that question. In contrast, groups can be uncertain *and* in disagreement. And disagreement about rights-specification has been at the heart of contemporary arguments against giving courts the final word on rights-protection.[6] The structure of those arguments is simple. Well-ordered legislatures can be committed to the protection of fundamental rights for many reasons: principle, national or legislative culture, concern about election and re-election. In the cases of interest, legislation necessarily takes a position on rights-specification. Those who oppose constitutional review by courts—judicial review, as it is termed in the United States—assert that the first question we must ask when legislation is challenged, whether in the courts or elsewhere, as violating fundamental rights is, Is this statute a reasonable specification of rights in the settings to which it applies? They object to a system in which the courts jump over that question and ask only, Should we—the judges—find that the statute is incompatible with fundamental rights, that is, is not a permissible specification of rights?[7]

The institutional design issue here parallels that for the individual-level case. Taking the existence of disagreement about rights-specification as pervasive, can we determine whether courts or legislatures are better venues for rights-protection? The answer will depend on the institutions' characteristics, and it seems as unlikely here as at the individual level that a one-size-fits-all answer will be appropriate. In particular, the answer may depend on variations in the institutional characteristics of legislatures, which is the topic of the remainder of this chapter. It seems worth observing at the outset, though, that differences in institutional detail may have relatively little effect on the overall levels of rights-protection: Once the basic and minimal institutions of liberal democracy are in place, variations in detail may not matter much: In gross, rights are protected to pretty much the same levels in Great Britain and the Netherlands, and not protected to pretty much the same degree in Pakistan and The People's Republic of China.

II. The Many Dimensions of Institutional Choice

A standard division in institutional design is between parliamentary systems and separation-of-powers systems. According to standard definitions, the executive in a parliamentary system is directly dependent on support from a parliamentary majority, whereas the executive in a separation-of-powers system has a source of authority independent of the legislature. Although formally correct, it is a bit misleading

---

[6] Disagreement is one and probably the most important form that uncertainty can take at the group level.

[7] Opponents of what I have called strong-form constitutional review, in which courts have the final word in the short to medium run on the permissibility of legislative rights-specifications, can support weaker forms of constitutional review, in the form of a relatively easy power to override judicial determinations or in the form of a standard for constitutional review in which courts can reject rights-specifying statutes only if the courts are firmly convinced that the specification is an objectively unreasonable one.

to describe the executive in modern parliamentary systems as dependent on the parliamentary majority, because in the ordinary course of events the chief executive (or prime minister) actually leads the parliament. The chief executive must of course retain the confidence of a majority in parliament, but the ordinary way in which he or she loses that confidence is by losing an election.[8] Separation-of-powers systems have a similar characteristic. Chief executives in such systems are elected separately from the legislature, but they ordinarily are associated with political parties that compete for legislative majorities. A separation-of-powers system in which the chief executive and the legislative majority are affiliated with the same political party—generally referred to as a situation of unified party government—resembles a parliamentary system, the more strongly so if the chief executive exercises a strong leadership role within the majority political party.

What consequences does the choice between these two systems have for rights-protection? First, the legislature and the executive in a separation-of-powers system can compete for public support over rights issues. Especially when the legislature and the executive are controlled by different political parties, in cases of divided rather than unified government, the legislature can point out the executive's rights 'abuses', and sometimes can enact rights-protective legislation over the executive's objections. The executive has parallel powers. Separating powers means that legislation can become effective only with the support of legislators and executives with different bases of political support,[9] and the general view is that this makes it difficult to enact all sorts of legislation, including rights-abusive laws. This virtue of separation-of-powers systems, if it is one, is weakened when a single party controls both the executive branch and the legislature. Unified party government in a separation-of-powers system resembles what occurs in a parliamentary system.[10]

Competition over rights-protection can occur, and the multiple 'veto points' in separation-of-powers systems are an obstacle to the enactment of rights-abusive legislation when one or the other branch takes rights-protection as a subject for political competition. But, of course, some laws are rights-protective, and separation-of-powers systems make enactment of all laws, including rights-protective ones, more difficult. The general view of parliamentary systems is that they are more 'efficient' than separation-of-powers systems, in the sense that the program of the chief executive is more likely to be enacted. This can include rights-protective legislation.

---

[8] There are recent examples of chief executives losing the confidence of a parliamentary majority before an election occurs, but even then the loss of confidence is typically associated with the majority's fear that under the existing chief executive it will lose an impending election.

[9] Or with substantial enough majorities to allow enactment by one branch only.

[10] It may be more difficult to sustain unified party government if the legislature and the executive are elected at different times than if they are elected at (roughly) the same time. Perhaps enough voters will be willing to alter the composition of the legislature if they are able to do so while continuing with the sitting chief executive, when not enough would be willing to 'split their tickets' to vote for one party to control the legislature and another to control the executive branch. Making ticket-splitting effective is particularly difficult when the chief executive is elected in a nation-wide constituency and legislators are elected from districts.

The fact that separation-of-powers systems can in some configurations of party power resemble parliamentary ones helps identify another dimension of institutional variation. The executive government in a parliamentary system can be formed by a single party with a majority or by a coalition of parties. As I have said, the legislature in a separation-of-powers system can serve as a counterweight to the executive, challenging what legislators believe to be rights-threatening executive initiatives (but, of course, blocking rights-promoting initiatives as well). Minority parties in a governing coalition can do the same. They can insist that the executive government withdraw what they regard as rights-threatening proposals as the cost of their continuing as members of the coalition—but, of course, they can equally insist that the executive government pursue rights-threatening initiatives for the same reason.

Some further complications should be introduced. The rules governing office-holding in parliamentary systems create the possibility that some party members will be 'permanent backbenchers', that is, party members who hold no hope of becoming members of the executive government, and who can occasionally disagree, even vehemently, with the party leadership but who cannot be dismissed from the party or the legislature because they have built an independent base of support within the party. Sometimes a permanent backbencher will oppose the executive government on a rights issue, functioning within the party in the way a minority party within a coalition government can. Of course a single backbencher cannot credibly threaten to bring down the government by withdrawing her support for the government, but her support within the party, which makes it impossible for the party leadership to expel her from the party, means that her opposition will cause the leadership political embarrassment. More generally, backbenchers and even more some aspirants for positions within the executive government can form factions within a majority party. A faction that is large enough can make compliance with its demands a condition for continuing to support the party leadership in power. Here too, factions within a majority party can serve some of the functions that the legislature does in a separation-of-powers system. Once again, though, the contrast between parliamentary and separation-of-powers systems cannot be drawn too sharply. Return to the case of unified party government in a separation-of-powers system. That 'unified' party can itself be a coalition of factions, which means that sometimes a government unified in form is divided in practice.

The foregoing analysis indicates that questions of institutional design have some implications for the ability of political institutions to protect rights, but that the more important questions revolve around the orientations of political parties toward rights. I suggest that, roughly put, an important inquiry asks under what conditions a political party or its leadership, or a party faction of large enough size, or permanent backbenchers with a significant base of support within a party will orient itself or themselves to rights-protection, that is, will take protecting rights as an important component of its overall political agenda.[11]

---

[11] I use the phrase 'orient itself to rights protection' to indicate that there will always be controversy over whether particular legislative proposals are specifications of rights, violations of rights, or mere policy proposals unrelated to rights-promotion or impairment.

The structure of political parties depends in large measure on a nation's election system. Where legislators are chosen from single-member districts pursuant to a rule awarding each seat to the candidate in the district who receives more votes than any other—so-called 'first past the post' systems—political scientists have shown, and evidence confirms, that the systems tend to have two major political parties and no more than one or two minor parties.[12] Proportional representation with legislators chosen from national lists tends to proliferate parties, although the higher the threshold for gaining seats in the legislature, the smaller the number of parties with a significant political role.[13] The effective number of significant political parties is important because some parties in a true multiparty system can take rights-protection (or rights-violation, although they will rarely put it that way) as the main element in their platforms. In a two- or three-party system, in contrast, party platforms necessarily range across public policy generally, with rights issues being no more than one of many to which the party addresses itself. With a smaller number of significant parties, those who take rights-protection as their primary concern must become or have a strong influence on a faction within one of the major parties if they are to achieve their goals. From the perspective of party leaders, what matters is the net strength of rights-promoting parties (as members of a coalition government) or factions within one of the major parties. Facing a significant rights-promoting faction, party leaders have incentives to package their substantive and rights-related policies as reasonable specifications of rights. The overall effects of these aspects of party structure are in general indeterminate, particularly because a large party may be less likely to take rights-protection as an important part of its platform but more likely to implement rights-protection when it does. Detailed analysis of particular nations is likely to be more productive than attention to general questions about party structure.

Mechanisms of candidate selection can also affect the strength of rights-oriented factions within major political parties. In systems with national party lists, party leaders typically have a great deal of control over candidate selection. They identify and, perhaps more important, rank their candidates on the list with an eye to securing strong support for the leaders' programmes. Party leaders' preferences about rights will then be translated into the party's support for rights in the legislature. Leaders are not entirely unconstrained, though, because some potential candidates may have enough support within the party—may lead party factions—with the effect that they must be placed relatively high on the party's national list. In other systems party leaders may play a smaller role in candidate selection. Historically candidate selection in the United States took place at the local level, over which national party leaders had rather little control. Over the

---

[12] Blended systems like Germany's, with some seats allocated by district and some pursuant to the national vote, and systems with 'instant runoffs', second-round votes, and the like appear to have the same tendency toward two major parties. I am unaware of scholarly literature explaining this tendency as the parallel tendency in 'first past the post' systems has been explained.

[13] The experience in Germany suggests that a threshold of slightly more than 5 per cent reduces the number of significant parties quite a bit, making systems with thresholds at that level quite similar to 'first past the post' systems.

course of the twentieth century, power over candidate selection flowed to the national parties, although some candidates today remain 'self-nominated', using their personal resources of money and celebrity to attract support within the constituencies they seek to represent. As I suggested earlier, in systems with elections from single-member districts, incumbents can carve out some protected space for themselves by providing services and voting for policies about which their constituents are especially concerned, thereby opening up the possibility that the incumbents can oppose their national party leadership on issues the incumbent cares a great deal about.

Finally, the methods by which parties finance their activities can affect their commitments to rights-protection. Roughly speaking, publicly financed parties are free to choose whatever position they want on rights (and other) issues. Parties that depend on their members for financial support will of course be responsive to their members' views, whatever they happen to be. Parties in the United States are not truly membership organizations. Rather, they are organizations supported by private donors. Some donors give relatively small amounts, which they regard as their party 'dues', but otherwise participate very little in party activities. The party leadership must ensure that the party's actions overall generate continuing support from these donors. During the 1990s and the early 2000s the Republican party developed dramatically effective mechanisms of obtaining support from donors of small amounts who were interested in socially conservative positions, and the party's need to retain their support shaped the party's platform—and, perhaps, limited the party's ability to expand beyond this donor base. Even so, the donors have relatively little direct input into the development of party policy. Other donors give rather large amounts, supposedly limited by campaign finance regulations that are, however, easily evaded. These donors can have large effects on the development of party policy. These donors are often properly disparaged as seeking benefits for special interests, particularly businesses, but they can be concerned about rights policies as well. For example, large donors from the entertainment industry have had an important effect in making the rights of gays and lesbians a significant priority for the Democratic Party.

Among the interest groups to which party leaders might respond are rights-oriented NGOs such as the American Civil Liberties Union, Amnesty International, and Liberty, to name only those prominent in the United States and Great Britain. Of course party leaders care most about the extent to which these groups can offer electoral support or opposition—how many people they can influence at the polling booths. I think the general view is (a) that most party leaders believe that the NGOs' electoral influence is small relative to all the other influences affecting voters' choices, and (b) that this belief is correct. Still, concerns about the NGOs' political influence may play a role in elections that are expected to be particularly close. And, as always, party leaders may simply agree with the NGOs' positions, or some of them, as a matter of principle.

Another dimension of interest involves the significance and character of legislation. I have argued that in situations of uncertainty or disagreement, statutes themselves can be specifications of rights. When they are, the case for treating legislatures as appropriate venues for rights-protection is strength-ened.[14] Whether they are may depend on what I call the legislation's character. Some statutes are almost exclusively about rights: the statute described earlier providing a cause of action for invasion of privacy, or nearly every significant anti-terrorism statute adopted in recent decades. Chief executives and legisla-tors who propose and approve such laws will typically have views about whether the laws are rights-protective or rights-violative.[15] That a legislature has adopted a statute about rights should have some bearing on the specification question, giving some reason, though not necessarily a conclusive one, to think that the specification the statute makes is a reasonable one. In contrast, sometimes con-stitutional issues lurk in the details of a statute about something else. A statute imposing new regulations on disclosures by banks of their investments might include a provision that raises questions about consumers' informational privacy. The importance of the legislation overall, or the obscurity of the provision, might mean that legislators do not attend to the constitutional issue. Any inference that the provision is a reasonable specification of the right at issue would be accord-ingly weaker.

Legislation's importance, and more particularly the importance of particular proposals to legislative leaders, plays a more general role in assessing whether the legislature is sufficiently attentive to rights that its actions should be treated as specifications of rights and evaluated for their reasonableness. Importance points in two directions, unfortunately. Legislators might be willing to ride roughshod over rights in the rush to enact an important piece of legislation. Or, leaders' desire to enact the statute might give a group of legislators significant leverage on rights-issues with which they are concerned. Such legislators might be able to force com-promises on those issues in exchange for their votes on overall package.

III. The Implications of Differing Incentives on Institutional Performance

To some, I think large, extent whether party leaders, factions, or backbenchers ori-ent themselves to rights will depend on simple individual preference and will not be affected by choices among institutional design. That, though, does not in itself undermine the case for legislative rather than judicial protection of fundamental rights, for the same could be said about individual judges: The degree to which judges orient themselves to rights depends to a large degree on individual prefer-ence. Are there, then, institutional differences that affect the preferences legislators

---

[14] But not established: On reflection we might conclude that a legislative rights-specification is unreasonable.

[15] In systems where statutes are subject to constitutional review, these officials may take the pub-lic position that their job is to determine what is good policy, leaving questions of constitutionality to the courts. This possibility is reduced in systems with rights-vetting institutions that advise execu-tives or legislatures about the constitutionality of proposed legislation, especially when the advice is made available to the public.

and judges have? One often-mentioned candidate is that judges are imbued with a culture that tells them that rights-protection is inherent in their role. I believe that this is an unpromising route. Certainly legislators could be imbued with a culture telling them that rights-protection is inherent in the legislative role. In addition, I am sceptical about the possibility that legal cultures that tell judges that they are to protect rights will not also tell legislators to do so.[16] Perhaps, though, something operates to weaken legislators' rights-orientation that does not operate on judges.

The obvious candidate is that legislators must seek election and judges typically do not.[17] Legal scholars seem to believe that the need to be elected skews legislators' incentives against rights-protection. The analytic case for that proposition is weaker than scholars' intuitions about it.[18] Perhaps most obvious, the claim that legislators will ignore or undervalue rights because of their concerns about election is parasitic on the view that voters ignore or undervalue rights. Here it is important to distinguish between rights that accrue to all members of society, such as free expression rights and rights with respect to procedural fairness in civil and criminal proceedings, and equality rights that accrue to members of minority groups.[19] It is not at all clear why voters should ignore or undervalue rights from which they can expect to benefit. Further, in the cases of most interest—where the right at issue is not fully specified prior to legislative action—it is unclear what should count as undervaluing a fundamental right, as distinguished from supporting one of numerous possible specifications.

The phenomenon illustrated by permanent backbenchers brings out another facet of the supposed electoral incentive to ignore or undervalue rights. As noted earlier, permanent backbenchers have a political base independent of their party leadership. That allows them to disagree with the leaders on questions of rights. So too with a legislator's disagreement with her constituents on such questions. A legislator who provides constituents with services and policies they strongly prefer may have some 'slack' on rights-issues: Having received the important services and policies, constituents will put up with their representative's pursuit of rights policies with which they disagree.

Additional complexities arise when we shift from the individual legislator to the party system.[20] Consider a well-organized minority group entitled to participate

[16] The point can be made by reference to the US Constitution, which requires the same oath of 'Senators and Representatives [in the national legislature]..., the Members of the several State Legislatures, and all executive and judicial Officers, both of the United States and of the several States' that they will 'support this Constitution'. US Constitution, Art 6.

[17] Some judges in the United States are elected. One would expect elected judges to respond to the incentives created by a system in which they are elected much as legislators do.

[18] For a more detailed development of the points made here, see M. Tushnet, *Weak Courts, Strong Rights: Judicial Review and Social Welfare Rights in Comparative Constitutional Law* (Princeton: Princeton University Press, 2008), 87–9.

[19] There may be an overlap between the two types of rights if voters think themselves free of substantial risk of being subjected to criminal proceedings.

[20] J. Hart Ely, *Democracy and Distrust: A Theory of Judicial Review* (Cambridge, Mass: Harvard University Press, 1980), remains the best-developed argument for constitutional review relying on the points discussed here. For my more extended comments on Ely's approach, see M. Tushnet, *Taking the Constitution Away from the Courts* (Princeton: Princeton University Press, 1999), 157–61;

in a nation's electoral system. The mere fact that it is a minority has no necessary implications for the incentives parties have to ignore or undervalue the group's fundamental rights, including their right to equal treatment. A stylized example makes the point. Suppose a nation has a majority group with 90 per cent of the nation's population and a single minority group with 10 per cent. Suppose in addition that the majority group is divided into two parties, one supported by 48 per cent of the population, the other by the remaining 42 per cent. If the minority group is well-organized politically, it can be the 'king-maker'. Whichever party it votes for will win the election. The minority group can then insist on protection for its rights as a condition of gaining its political support.

Disfranchisement of the minority group would of course deprive this argument of any force, and constitutional review of disfranchisements might be appropriate. Further, some groups are pariahs in particular societies, unable to form political alliances with anyone in the majority, even when such an alliance would allow one party to displace another. The problem posed by pariah groups might be generalized to justify constitutional review when groups are informally or practically excluded from political participation, or when their level of participation is lower than their numbers warrant for reasons of social disapproval or de facto legal impairment.

Here too the problem of specification arises. It is relatively easy to identify a formal disfranchisement, effectuated by force of law. It is more difficult to identify pariah groups. And, when we reach the question of informal exclusions or de facto undervaluation, the issue of specification is likely to be so troubling that the case for taking a judicial specification that a group is informally excluded as authoritative is probably no stronger than the case against doing so. The best candidate for identifying when informal exclusions exist is that the disfavoured groups face difficulties in organizing themselves politically. The standard method of doing so asks whether the group is a 'discrete and insular minority', to use the phrase introduced to constitutional theory by US Supreme Court Justice Harlan Fiske Stone.[21] As Bruce Ackerman observed, this has things backwards: Discrete and insular minorities are able to organize effectively because the costs of doing so are relatively low in light of the interactions among members of the groups; it is dispersed minorities (and majorities) that face difficulties in organizing.[22]

Legislatures may adopt policies that have the effect of disfavouring the interests of some minority group, often though not always in pursuit of some other social goal. In such circumstances the legislative decision to distribute some social good in a way that disfavours the minority group—the specification the legislature adopts—may result from selective indifference to the group's interest. Authorizing constitutional courts to set aside legislation when they perceive selective indifference at work is quite a bit bolder than authorizing them to set

---

M. Tushnet, *Red, White, and Blue: A Critical Analysis of Constitutional Law* (Cambridge, Mass: Harvard University Press, 1988), ch 2.

[21] *United States v Carolene Products Co*, 304 US 144, 152–3 n 4 (1938).

[22] B. A. Ackerman, 'Beyond *Carolene Products*' (1985) 98 *Harvard Law Review* 713.

aside formal disfranchisements. More than a general reference to the problems minority groups face is needed to explain why such a broad power should be lodged in constitutional courts, and the explanation, if it be available, is likely to depend on the particular circumstances of specific minority groups in each nation.

Something similar can be said about the second main strand of accounts that identify legislators' electoral incentives as a reason for preferring constitutional review. As US Supreme Court Justice Oliver Wendell Holmes wrote, 'If you have no doubt of your premises or your power and want a certain result with all your heart you naturally express your wishes in law and sweep away all opposition'.[23] Legislators are elected so that they can enact laws their constituents believe will advance the social good. And, having made a judgment that a particular law does so, legislators might well think it sensible—Holmes used the word 'logical'—to protect that law against criticism. Yet, laws adopted by legislatures responsible to the voters that prohibit criticism of existing policies entrench those policies in a way inconsistent with the idea that citizens always have the power to alter their laws through elections.

Here too the basic insight is correct but the implications for constitutional review are narrower than is often thought. As Robert Bork famously argued—to his later disadvantage when he was nominated for a seat on the US Supreme Court—the basic insight justifies constitutional review of only a rather small slice of the universe of expression.[24] Only political speech, not literary or artistic expression for example, is covered by this principle, and perhaps not all political speech. More important, and as then-Professor Bork also argued, modern democratically responsible legislatures rarely have outlawed speech critical of existing policy on the simple ground that it *is* critical of that policy. Rather, they contend that the dissemination of such speech makes it more likely that some listeners will break the law, having heard and been persuaded by arguments that the law being criticized is unjust, unwise, and the like. Legislatures contend, that is, that speech critical of existing policies has what historically has been known as a bad tendency. Defenders of constitutional review sometimes contend, I think mistakenly, that speech critical of existing policy has no tendency to induce breaches of the law. A better argument is that experience has shown that legislatures and executive officials regularly exaggerate the threat that such speech poses to social order, and that courts are needed to protect against such exaggerations. Note, though, that the justification for constitutional review rests on real historical experience, not on deep principles about what constitutionalism requires. And it does so precisely because of the specification issue: Has the legislature properly specified that fundamental principle permits them to protect their substantive enactments against law-breaking caused to some degree by speech critical of those enactments?

---

[23] *Abrams v United States*, 250 US 616, 630 (1919) (Holmes, J, dissenting).
[24] R. Bork, 'Neutral Principles and Some First Amendment Problems' (1971) 47 *Indiana Law Journal* 1.

For all these reasons, a more finely grained analysis of particular societies is needed to know whether elections give legislators incentives to ignore or promote both widely distributed rights and the rights of minority groups.

IV. Conclusion: Liberalism, Social Democracy, and Institutional Choice Revisited

I now return to the distinction between traditional liberalism and social democracy. It would misread the foregoing discussion to say that it focuses on what some political scientists call veto points in the political process. Veto points are, as the term suggests, institutions that have the power to stop a policy initiative from moving forward toward enactment and implementation. True, a separation-of-powers system typically has more veto points than a parliamentary system, a system with coalition governments more than one with a disciplined one-party majority. And, were threats to fundamental rights to arise only from completed legislative action, the more veto points, the fewer the threats to rights.[25] But, the existence of veto points is not an unalloyed good for liberal social democrats. They want to enact legislation that addresses threats to rights emanating from private actors put in a position to threaten rights by their legal entitlements. The difficulty of enacting rights-promoting legislation increases as veto points proliferate. Determining how many veto points are enough and how many too many requires careful judgments about particular contexts. Doing so cannot be reduced to some general rule.

Finally, the very existence of the permutations that can arise within a single domestic legal order might suggest a general preference for courts as the better institution for rights-protection. Some variations, such as those associated with parliamentary versus separation-of-powers systems, are probably irrelevant because those institutional choices once made are unlikely to be unmade absent massive institutional redesign. Some variations, though, might be consequential. Consider a parliamentary system in which an election changes the governing majority from a formal coalition among parties to a single and disciplined party. The efficacy of the parliament as an institution for rights-protection might decline. Courts in that system will be more stable. That stability will over time 'dominate' the variation that occurs in legislative protection of rights.[26]

Although I do not want to get too formal about the question, one might think of the choice between institutions as one involving consideration of the variance

---

[25] For a defence of constitutional review on the ground that it inserts another veto point into the policy-making process, see R. H. Fallon, Jr, 'The Core of an Uneasy Case *for* Judicial Review' (2008) 121 *Harvard Law Review* 1693.

[26] Perhaps we can make some stabs at assessing the likely effects of large-scale choices that will probably remain stable. A nation's history of ethnic division, for example, might have some implications for large-scale institutional choice. The literature on this question is maddeningly ambivalent: People agree that persistent ethnic division has some implications for institutional design, but disagree wildly on what those implications are. A nation's history of assimilating or not assimilating immigrants might have implications for institutional choice as well.

and the mean in the level of rights-protection each affords. If legislatures have a higher mean level of rights-protection but a greater variance than courts, over time the rights-protection afforded by courts might be larger overall than the rights-protection afforded by legislatures. And, even if that is not true, variance in legislative protection might lead to spectacular performance at times but disaster at other times. Those who are risk-averse with respect to rights might accept that judicial protection of rights might eliminate the possibility of spectacular legislative performance in exchange for avoiding disasters.[27]

This might be true even if, as is the case, there are relevant variations in the design of constitutional review. As I have noted, many aspects of institutional design are likely to be stable, and this is true about the design of constitutional review, such as the choice to locate constitutional review in a specialized court, or the choice of centralized over diffused constitutional review. Some design choices can produce the kinds of variation in the level of rights-protection I have just described, though. The mechanisms for choosing judges for constitutional courts and the rules regulating their tenure might be particularly important. For example, suppose the terms of all the judges on a constitutional court expire at the same time in a system where those judges are chosen by the parliament.[28] In such a system the variation in the rights-protection afforded by the courts will replicate the rights-variation in the legislature at the two relevant times—when the judges were initially appointed and when they are replaced—although not variations within the period of judicial tenure. As these conditions are weakened, for example in systems in which judges are replaced one or a few at a time, variation in judicial rights-protection will diminish but not disappear.[29]

A final variation in institutional design must be introduced. Constitutional review can be quite modest or limited to only a short list of judicially protected rights (and not necessarily all or only fundamental rights), as in the present Australian constitution. It can consist primarily of a judicial negative on legislation, as the idea that constitutional courts can serve as an additional veto point suggests. Or it can be action-forcing, either through various remedial forms courts can develop or through a provision allowing for a declaration of unconstitutionality by omission, as in the Portuguese and Hungarian constitutions. The choice among these forms of constitutional review will depend on one's assessment of the risks posed by legislative underperformance with respect to rights.

---

[27] It is worth emphasizing that giving the courts the power to specify rights does pose the possibility that the courts will prevent spectacular performance by, for example, finding unconstitutional legislative efforts to protect particular rights on the ground that those efforts violate other rights. On the most general level, this is the concern associated in the United States and by analogy elsewhere with the *Lochner* line of decisions. For a discussion, see S. Choudhry, 'The *Lochner* Era and Comparative Constitutionalism' (2004) 2 *International Journal of Constitutional Law* 1.

[28] As I understand it, this was true of the Hungarian constitutional court. For a discussion, see K. Lane Scheppele, 'The New Hungarian Constitutional Court' (1999) 8 *East European Constitutional Review* 81.

[29] Recent controversies in the United States over nominations to the Supreme Court have arisen precisely because each nomination raises the question of what level of rights-protection the Court with its new member will afford, that is, over what I have called variation in the level of rights-protection afforded by the courts.

I believe that intuitions about institutions are all we have to go on at this point. We must of course take into account the variations in the level of rights-protection afforded by legislatures and courts. My intuitions are, first, that the variance in rights-protection will probably be lower when courts have the power to specify rights; secondly, that courts are unlikely to avert the disasters the risk-averse fear;[30] and, thirdly, that we cannot say anything systematic about the mean level of rights-protection. I suspect that, in the end, scholars can say only three things about questions dealing with the institutions of rights-protection. First, those questions must be answered with reference to the design of a nation's political and judicial system as a whole. Secondly, they must be answered with reference to the particulars of a nation's history.[31] Thirdly, normative recommendations are likely to be overwhelmed by the political facts at the time design choices are made.[32] Modesty in scholars' prescriptions should be the order of the day.

---

[30] The standard citations for this proposition in US constitutional discourse are *Plessy v Ferguson*, 163 US 537 (1896), upholding state laws requiring racial segregation, and *Korematsu v United States*, 323 US 214 (1944), upholding the federal government's internment of Japanese-Americans during World War II.

[31] Two examples: Nations with histories of rights-disasters might properly be quite risk-averse with respect to rights, and can design their constitutional courts in ways that capitalize on the lower variance associated with constitutional courts. Nations with histories of robust rights-protection by legislatures might limit their constitutional courts quite severely so as to capitalize on the possibility that the legislature will sustain its higher mean level of protection. Germany and New Zealand or Australia might be examples in the two categories, with some qualification added to address the latter nations' dealings with aboriginal peoples. The passage of time might dissipate the relevance of these histories to questions of institutional design.

[32] For some elaboration on this point, see M. Tushnet, 'Some Skepticism About Normative Constitutional Advice' (2008) 49 *William and Mary Law Review* 1473.

15

Reclaiming the Political Protection of Rights: A Defence of Australian Party Politics

Joo-Cheong Tham

I. Introduction

More than six decades ago, Elmer Schattscheider famously observed that 'modern democracy is unthinkable save in terms of (political) parties'.[1] The literature on the bills of rights, however, does not seem to have fully absorbed the compelling force of Schattscheider's statement. Two distinct strands of thought can, in fact, be detected in this literature: a neglect of political parties and the role they can play in protecting rights; and a jaundiced view of political parties that views them as either indifferent to questions of rights or, worse, tending to undermine the protection of rights.

This chapter takes aims at these tendencies by, first, critiquing what are perhaps the key reasons for the wrongful neglect of political parties in the bills of rights literature. In doing so, it emphasizes the centrality of political parties to the process of protecting rights in Australia. The second part of this chapter provides a critical examination of views that portray political parties as institutions that are indifferent or hostile towards the protection of rights and explains how political parties can advance the protection of rights in Australia.

Many of the chapter's arguments will be illustrated by reference to the recent debates accompanying the passage of the Fair Work Act 2009 (Cth) ('Fair Work Act'). The Fair Work Act has been chosen as a case study for two reasons. First, it is a highly significant piece of legislation. Not only does it lay down the framework for Australian industrial regulation, it does so by effecting a partial reversal of changes made by the Workplace Relations Amendment (Work Choices) Act ('Work Choices Act'); an Act that effected the most radical changes to the Australian industrial system for more than a century.[2] Secondly, opposition to the Work Choices policy and support for the Australian Labor Party's Forward with

---

[1] E. E. Schattschneider, *Party Government* (New York: Holt, Reinhart and Winston, 1942), 1.
[2] See the articles in (2006) 19(2) *Australian Journal of Labour Law*.

Fairness election policy were key, perhaps even decisive, factors explaining the defeat of the then Coalition government and the victory of the ALP Opposition.[3]

II. Party Politics Not a 'Forum of Principle'?

One reason for the wrongful neglect of party politics in the bill of rights literature can perhaps can be traced to Ronald Dworkin's influential view that courts are '(t)he forum of principle'.[4] According to this characterization, courts are better suited than legislatures to determining questions of principles, that is, rights-based issues, as distinct from questions of policy.

While this characterization simply argues for the superiority of legal over political processes in deciding these questions of rights, it seems to have transformed into something much stronger. Take, for example, the arguments made by former Australian High Court Chief Justice Sir Anthony Mason in support of a federal Charter of Rights. According to Mason, a Charter would mean that 'principled judicial decision-making would replace political compromise'.[5] This is all the more important, according to Mason, because parliamentarians are 'primarily concerned with the exercise of government power and policy' and not questions of human rights.[6] The thrust of these arguments is not only that parliaments are less able than courts to adequately deal with questions of rights but, going even further, these institutions are not even capable of principled debate, especially when it comes to questions of rights. It would follow from this extreme view that Australian party politics, being an aspect of parliamentary politics, is inept at handling questions of rights. If so, then party politics are rightfully ignored when it comes to discussions of the protection of rights.

There are many difficulties with this extreme position. It rests on the problematic distinction between principles/questions of rights and power/questions of policy.[7] Why can't parliaments and government be pursuing a *policy* of protecting *rights* and in doing so, adopt arrangements that confer *power* upon government agencies to prevent and detect abuses of rights? For example, how can this distinction make sense of the Australian Federal Government's current consultation on the protection of human rights which, according to the Government, is based on

---

[3] See eg M. Warren, 'IR Again the Issue that Cost—Election 2007: Making History' (26 Nov 2007) *The Australian*; L. Shanahan, 'Selling of WorkChoices Tops Blame List' (26 Nov 2007) *The Age*; P. Hartcher, 'Witness to an Execution: All Labor had to Do was Turn up' (26 Nov 2007) *The Sydney Morning Herald*.

[4] R. Dworkin, *A Matter of Principle* (Cambridge, Mass: Harvard University Press, 1985), ch 2.

[5] Sir A. Mason, 'Why Do We Need a Bill of Rights?' (14 Dec 2005) *NewMatilda.com*, at <http://newmatilda.com/2005/12/14/why-we-need-australian-bill-rights> (last visited 3 Nov 2008).

[6] Ibid.

[7] Dworkin, n 4 above, 24–5. Dworkin explains the distinction between policy and principle in this way: 'Arguments of policy try to show that the community would be better off, on the whole, if a particular program were pursued. They are, in that special sense, goal-based arguments. Arguments of principle, on the contrary, that particular programs must be carried out or abandoned because of their impact on particular people even if the community as a whole is in some way worse off in consequence. Arguments of principle are right-based': ibid 2–3.

its commitment to 'the promotion of human rights—a commitment that is based on the belief in the fundamental equality of all persons'.[8] Is this not a policy of respecting rights? Would consideration of how best to protect rights in Australia not involve the question of whether appropriate power has been conferred upon various government agencies?

The extreme position is also refuted by many examples where the political process and parliaments, in particular, have clearly debated questions of rights and principles. The debates accompanying the passage of the Fair Work Act provide a case on point. In the 2007 federal election, the industrial relations policy of the Liberal-National Coalition ('Coalition'), which then held federal office, was based on the Work Choices Act[9] while the Opposition Australian Labor Party's ('ALP') was entitled Forward with Fairness.[10] The latter policy formed the basis of the Fair Work Act which was passed in May 2009.

While Graeme Orr would correctly describe these titles as legislative slogans,[11] slogans do have meaning beyond their public relations value and, in this case, did signify crucial differences in principles. At the risk of oversimplification, the choice between the Coalition and the ALP positions can be understood as one between freedom from state restraint or a formal freedom to strike individual agreements on one hand, and fairness in the sense of all workplace agreements, individual or otherwise, being subject to community standards on the other. The Second Reading Speech to the Work Choices Bill, for example, stated that it was aimed at securing the 'future prosperity of Australian individuals and families' 'by accommodating the greater demand for choice and flexibility in our workplaces'[12] while the Second Reading Speech to the Fair Work Bill emphasized that the Bill was 'based on the enduring principle of fairness while meeting the needs of the modern age'.[13]

At the centre of this debate concerning deep questions of principle was the role of collective bargaining. Under the Work Choices regime, individual bargaining was prioritized with statutory individual contracts, 'Australian Workplace Agreements', overriding other industrial instruments, notably awards and collective agreements.[14] The Fair Work Act reverses this priority. Statutory individual

[8] See <http://www.humanrightsconsultation.gov.au/www/nhrcc/nhrcc.nsf/Page/TermsofReference_TermsofReference>, (last visited 27 May 2008).
[9] Coalition Government, *Election 2007 Policy: Employment and Workplace Relations—Targeting Full Employment: 'Go for Growth'* (2007).
[10] K. Rudd and J. Gillard, *Forward with Fairness: Labor's plan for fairer and more productive Australian workplaces* (Apr 2007).
[11] See G. Orr, 'Names without Frontiers: Legislative Titles and Sloganeering' (2001) 21 *Statute Law Review* 188; G. Orr, 'From Slogans to Puns: Australian Legislative Titling Revisited' (2001) 22 *Statute Law Review* 160.
[12] Workplace Relations Amendment (Work Choices) Bill 2005, *House of Representatives Official Hansard,* No 18, 2005, (Wednesday, 2 Nov 2005) 4 at 17.
[13] Fair Work Bill 2008, Second Reading Speech, *House of Representatives Official Hansard,* No 17, 2008, (Tuesday 25 Nov 2008) 11189 at 11189.
[14] Workplace Relations Act 1996 (Cth), ss 348(2), 349 as per compilation prepared on 27 Mar 2006, taking into account amendments up to Act No 153 of 2005 (Workplace Relations Amendment (Work Choices) Act 2005).

contracts can no longer be offered,[15] with the Act stating as one of its objects that it is aimed at 'ensuring that the guaranteed safety net of fair, relevant and enforceable minimum wages and conditions can no longer be undermined by the making of statutory individual employment agreements given that such agreements can never be part of a fair workplace relations system'.[16] The Act further states that one of its objects is to achieve 'productivity and fairness through an emphasis on enterprise-level collective bargaining'.[17]

The questions surrounding collective bargaining further demonstrate how the debates relating to the Fair Work Act were not only debates of principles but also of rights. The ability to collectively bargain is clearly recognized by International Labour Organization Conventions as an aspect of freedom of association;[18] a matter acknowledged by the Senate committee that inquired into the Fair Work Bill.[19] More than this, freedom of association is considered by the International Labour Organization as one of the four fundamental rights at work.[20]

III. An Analytical Preoccupation with the Branches of Government

Another reason for the wrongful neglect of political parties in the bills of rights literature is that politics is often analysed through the lens of the branches of government. This is common to analysis by legal academics and is clearly reflected in 'dialogue' theories of bills or charters of rights. For instance, prominent 'dialogue' theorists, Peter Hogg and Allison Bushell, couched their understanding of 'dialogue' said to result from the Canadian Charter of Rights, as one between the courts and legislatures.[21] The notion of 'dialogue' has also been quite influential in the Australian debates. Speaking of the Victorian Charter of Human Rights and Responsibilities,[22] one academic commentator described it as providing for

---

[15] This is the effect of Workplace Relations Amendment (Transition to Forward with Fairness) Act 2008 (Cth), sch 1 (Workplace agreements and the no-disadvantage test) and sch 7A (Transitional arrangements for existing AWAs) (sch 1 repeals s 326 of the Workplace Relations Act 1996 (Cth), which had provided for employers to make AWAs; sch 7A notes, with respect to the continuing operation of AWAs, that 'To avoid doubt, nothing in this Schedule permits an agreement made after the Commencement of this Schedule to be treated as an AWA').

[16] Fair Work Act, s 3(c).

[17] Fair Work Act, s 3(f).

[18] ILO Convention 87: Freedom of Association and Protection of the Right to Organize Convention, 1948; ILO Convention 98: Right to Organize and Collective Bargaining Convention, 1949. See, in particular, Article 4 of latter convention.

[19] Senate Standing Committee on Education, Employment and Workplace Relations, *Fair Work Bill 2008 [Provisions]* (2009), para 1.16.

[20] ILO Declaration on fundamental principles and rights at work, International Labour Conference, 86th Session, Geneva, June 1998, 2, available at <http://www.ilocarib.org.tt/portal/images/stories/contenido/pdf/InternationLabourStandards/ILO%20declaration%20on%20fundamental%20principles%20and%20followup.pdf> (last visited 22 June 2009).

[21] P. W. Hogg and A. A. Bushell, 'The *Charter* Dialogue between Courts and Legislatures (Or Perhaps the *Charter of Rights* Isn't Such a Bad Thing After All)' (1997) 35 *Osgoode Hall Law Journal* 75. For another example, see K. Roach, 'Constitutional and Common Law Dialogues between the Supreme Court and Canadian Legislatures', (2001) 80 *Canadian Bar Review* 481.

[22] *Charter of Human Rights and Responsibilities 2006* (Vic).

an 'institutional dialogue about rights between three arms of government'.[23] Similarly, in the Second Reading Speech to the Charter of Human Rights and Responsibilities Bill, the Victorian Attorney General, Rob Hulls, emphasized that the Bill is based on:

(a) dialogue model of human rights that seeks to address human rights issues through a formal dialogue between the three branches of government while recognising the ultimate sovereignty of Parliament to make laws for the good government of the people of Victoria.[24]

The lens of the various branches of government, however, leaves party politics largely out of the picture and, thus, provides a distorted view of Australian politics. In his major study of Australian political parties, Dean Jaensch correctly observed that:

There can be no argument about the ubiquity, pervasiveness and centrality of party in Australia. The forms, processes and content of politics—executive, parliament, pressure groups, bureaucracy, issues and policy making—are imbued with the influence of party, party rhetoric, party policy and party doctrine. Government is party government. Elections are essentially party contests, and the mechanics of electoral systems are determined by party policies and party advantages. Legislatures are party chambers. Legislators are overwhelmingly party members. The majority of electors follow party identification. Politics in Australia, almost entirely, is party politics.[25]

In the context of the preoccupation with the branches of government and its accompanying neglect of political parties, the following observation made by Maurice Duverger decades ago bears repeating:

Knowledge of classic constitutional law combined with ignorance of the part played by parties give a false view of contemporary political regimes; acquaintance with the part played by parties combined with ignorance of classic constitutional law gives an incomplete but accurate view of contemporary political regimes.[26]

The correct approach, as Duverger perceptively understood, is to understand the role played by the branches of government *and* party politics for the '(r)eal separation of power... (is) the product of party system and constitutional setting'.[27]

---

[23] J. Debeljak, 'Balancing Rights in a Democracy: The Problems with Limitations and Overrides of Rights under the Victorian *Charter of Human Rights and Responsibilities Act 2006*' (2008) 32 *Melbourne University Law Review* 422, 423. See also J. Debeljak, 'Rights and Democracy: A Reconciliation of the Institutional Debate', in T. Campbell, J. Goldsworthy, and A. Stone (eds), *Protecting Human Rights: Instruments and Institutions* (Oxford: Oxford University Press, 2003), 135, 154–6.

[24] Victoria, *Parliamentary Debates*, Legislative Assembly, 4 May 2006, 1293 (Rob Hulls, Attorney General). The Attorney General also stated that '[t]his bill promotes a dialogue between the three arms of government—the Parliament, the executive and the courts—while giving the Parliament the final say': at 1290.

[25] D. Jaensch, *Power Politics: Australia's Party System* (St Leonards: Allen & Unwin, 1994), 1–2.

[26] M. Duverger, *Political Parties: Their Organization and Activity in the Modern State*, rev edn (London: Methuen & Co, 1959), 353.

[27] Ibid 354.

IV. A Simple/Simplistic View of Political Representation

Possibly another reason for the wrongful neglect of political parties in the literature on bills of rights lies in understanding political representation as an unmediated relationship between citizens, on one hand, and their elected representatives, on the other; an understanding fostered perhaps by the powerful but misleading mantra, 'government by the people'.[28]

This simple view of political representation tends to write off the role of intermediary political organizations, in particular, political parties. It fails to recognize how political parties fundamentally transform the character of political representation. As Duverger remarked:

elections, like the doctrine of representation, have been greatly changed by the development of parties. There is no longer a dialogue between the elector and the representative, the nation and parliament: a third party has come between them, radically modifying the nature of their relations.[29]

The transformative effect of political parties in mediating politics can be understood as the interaction of various functions.[30] Political parties have responsive functions, that is, functions aimed at these groups reflecting public opinion. Foremost, they perform an electoral function whereby political parties, in their efforts to secure voter support, respond to the wishes of the citizenry. They also have a participatory function as they offer a vehicle for political participation through membership, meetings, and engagement in the development of party policy.

The relationship between political parties and the citizenry is not, however, one way. As Sartori has noted, '(p)arties do not only *express;* they also *channel*'.[31] Alongside their responsive functions, political parties also perform an agenda-setting function in shaping the terms and content of political debates. For example, the platform of a major party is influenced by as well as influences public opinion.

Political parties further perform a governance function. This function largely relates to parties who succeed in having elected representatives. These parties determine the pool of people who govern through their recruitment and pre-selection processes. They also participate in the act of governing. This is clearly the case with the party elected to government and also equally true of other parliamentary parties as they are involved in the law-making process and scrutinize the actions of the executive government.

There are, of course, many other intermediary organizations; many of which perform one or more of these functions that have been ascribed to political parties. The media, for example, clearly performs an agenda-setting function and, to a

---

[28] See discussion in Schattschneider, n 1 above , 13–16.

[29] Duverger, n 26 above, 353.

[30] The following functions have been distilled from various sources, including G. Sartori, *Parties and Party Systems: A Framework for Analysis: Volume 1* (Cambridge: Cambridge University Press, 1976), 20–3, 27; J. Blondel, *Political Parties: A Genuine Case for Discontent?* (London: Wildwood House, 1978), ch 2.

[31] Sartori, n 30 above, 28 (emphasis in original).

lesser (and controversial) extent, a responsive function. Non-government organizations, like interest groups, also perform responsive and agenda-setting functions, while the public service obviously has a governance function. But no other institution or group *combines* these various functions. That is why Sartori was correct to argue that '(p)arties are *the* central intermediate and intermediary structure between society and government'.[32]

Specifically, in the context of *party government*, that is government by political parties, parties through their governance function are central to the operations of *responsible government* whereby the executive is held responsible to the legislature. The combination of their governance and responsive functions further means that political parties are the key mechanism for translating responsible government into *responsive government*, that is, government that is responsible to the electorate.[33] It is such responsiveness that allows us to describe a political system as one of *representative government*.[34] It is no understatement to say that political parties perform a constitutional role in Australian politics.

This point is even stronger with major parties, parties that are serious contenders for national government. Nancy Rosenblum has identified three defining characteristics that give major American political parties their 'unique *normative* status'.[35] These characteristics, which can be seen as an elaboration of the responsive, agenda-setting, and governance functions of political parties, similarly apply to the major parties in Australia.

According to Rosenblum, major parties, first play a role in bridging local and national citizenship. Secondly, major political parties are ideally inclusive and integrative. The former alludes to the process of drawing support from various and disparate groups, while the latter refers to process of balancing and accommodating the wishes of the various groups as well translating these wishes into a coherent programme. Thirdly, major political parties have a function of comprehensiveness in that their policies should have a broad national agenda and not merely be based on a narrow set of issues.[36] These three characteristics explain why, of all membership groups, major political parties are *primus inter pares*, a first among equals.[37]

The central mediating role of Australian political parties can be illustrated by the role of the ALP in the process leading to the enactment of the Fair Work Act. As noted earlier, the ALP's election policy that gave rise to the Act was developed in

[32] Ibid, p ix.
[33] See ibid 20–3.
[34] H. F. Pitkin, *The Concept of Representation* (Berkeley: University of California Press, 1967), 233.
[35] N. Rosenblum, 'Political Parties as Membership Groups' (2000) 100 *Columbia Law Review* 813, 824 (emphasis in original).
[36] Ibid 824–5.
[37] Ibid 826. Schattschneider has forcefully argued for the superiority of political parties over pressure and interest groups. According to Schattscheider, '(t)he parties are superior (to interest groups) because they must consider the problems of government broadly, they submit their fate to an election, and are responsible to the public. By every democratic principle the parties, as mobilizers of majorities, have claims on the public more valid and superior to those asserted by pressure groups which merely mobilize minorities': Schattschneider, n 1 above, 193.

an electoral context as an alternative to the Coalition's Work Choices policy.[38] The formulation of this policy was influenced by public opposition to the Work Choices regime; opposition that partly came about as a result of the Australian Council of Trade Union's ('ACTU') 'Rights at Work' campaign.[39] The policy was also subject to input from the party organization through the party platform,[40] which, in turn, was the result of deliberation by party members, including affiliated trade unions.[41] The result of these various processes was the Forward with Fairness election policy[42] and its implementation plan.[43] Upon being elected, the ALP government began drafting the Fair Work Bill; a process which involved it consulting State and Territory ministers as well as business and trade union representatives.[44] After the Bill was tabled in the Commonwealth Parliament, it was subject to an inquiry by the Senate Education, Employment and Workplace Relations Committee, which received public submissions.[45] Some of the recommendations of the Committee, which had a majority of ALP Senators, were subsequently adopted as amendments to the final Bill.[46]

This brief account makes obvious the mediating role of the ALP in the enactment of the Fair Work Act. Through a complex interplay of its various functions, the ALP was clearly pivotal to the process culminating in the adoption of the Act. The election policy giving rise to the Act, Forward with Fairness, resulted from its discharge of its electoral and participatory functions. The policy itself was an instance of the ALP performing an agenda-setting function. The process of drafting the Fair Work Bill also underlined the significance of the ALP's responsive function, this time through the consultations that the ALP government undertook, but also through the Senate inquiry which provided an avenue for public opinion to be directly expressed to the Commonwealth Parliament. Further, the

[38] See Coalition Government, n 9 above.

[39] See K. Muir, *Worth Fighting For: Inside the Your Rights at Work Campaign* (Sydney: University of NSW Press, 2008).

[40] Australian Labor Party, *National Platform and Constitution 2007* (2007), para 27.

[41] On the power of trade unions within the ALP, see Kathryn Cole, 'Unions and the Labor Party', in K. Cole (ed), *Power, Conflict and Control in Australian Trade Unions* (Ringwood: Pelican Books, 1982), where it was concluded that 'the power of unions within the ALP is far more circumscribed than is commonly believed and the process which each of the party's two sections (ie industrial and political wings) accommodates to the demands and needs of the other is complex and tortuous': ibid 100.

[42] K. Rudd and J. Gillard, *Forward with Fairness: Labor's plan for fairer and more productive Australian Workplaces* (Apr 2007).

[43] K. Rudd and J. Gillard, *Forward with Fairness: Policy Implementation Plan* (Aug 2007).

[44] For detail, see Explanatory Memorandum to Fair Work Bill 2008, pp vii–viii.

[45] Senate Education, Employment and Workplace Relations Committee, *Fair Work Bill [Provisions]* (2009) available at <http://www.aph.gov.au/Senate/committee/EET_CTTE/fair_work/report/index.htm> (last visited 29 May 2009).

[46] For example, Senate Committee Report Recommendation 2 recommended that the Fair Work Information Statement include information on individual flexibility agreements, incorporated into s 124(2) of the final Bill; Recommendation 3 recommended that Fair Work Australia conduct investigations into the operation of individual flexibility arrangements, incorporated into s 653 of the final; and Recommendation 6 recommended that the Bill provide for a fourteen-day time limit (rather than a seven-day limit) for appeals against unfair dismissals to be lodged with Fair Work Australia, incorporated into s 394 of the final Bill: see Senate Education, Employment and Workplace Relations Committee, *Fair Work Bill [Provisions]* (2009), at 30, 38, 70.

Committee's report was an example of the governance function in action, as was the eventual enactment of the Fair Work Act.

V. The Question of Party Discipline

The preceding two sections give rise to the conclusion that party politics are central to Australian politics because of the functions that Australian political parties perform. This means that translation of parliamentary sovereignty in this country into popular sovereignty crucially depends on political parties. Put in another way, Australian party politics can promote rights in the fundamental sense that they advance what Jeremy Waldron has dubbed the 'right of rights', the right to participate in public decision-making.[47]

But are political parties in Australia able to advance the protection of rights beyond their contribution to the realization of democratic rights? If, as Tom Campbell correctly argues, 'the articulation and defence of human rights ought to be a central task of any democratic process which regards the equal right of all to participate in political decision-making as fundamental',[48] can political parties positively contribute to this task? The remaining sections of this chapter will consider two sets of arguments that suggest that the answer is no. This section will consider the supposed problem of party discipline, while the following section will examine the danger of 'faction' posed by political parties.

Party discipline can be understood as rules or practices that require parliamentarians belonging to parties to vote according to the policies of their parties whether they agree with them or not. This understanding of party discipline is compatible with a range of practices. For instance, it can accommodate a variety of power relations within political parties from highly centralized political parties with power concentrated in the hands of the leadership, to more decentralized organizations where rank-and-file members having a greater say over party policies or where different branches of the party possess more autonomy.

It is not, however, the intent of this discussion to identify which types of political parties that abide by party discipline are more or less fitted to the task of protecting rights. It focuses on a prior concern: Why is party discipline considered to be *necessarily* problematic from the perspective of protecting rights?

This is not an easy question to answer because party discipline is often condemned with little elaboration. Arguably, party discipline is seen as incompatible with the deliberative duties of legislators and legislative assemblies; duties that would extend to their deliberation of questions concerning rights.

One way to assess this argument is to do so through the views of Edmund Burke, in particular, his famous speech to the Electors of Bristol.[49] This speech has been

---

[47] J. Waldron, *Law and Disagreement* (Oxford: Clarendon Press, 1999), ch 11.
[48] T. Campbell, 'Democracy, Human Rights, and Positive Law' (1994) 16 *Sydney Law Review* 195, 199.
[49] E. Burke, 'Speech to the Electors of Bristol', in *The Works of the Right Honourable Edmund Burke: Volume II* (London: Oxford University Press, 1926), 159.

pivotal to the debate as to proper role of legislators, in particular, whether legislators should be seen as trustees or delegates. At the risk of oversimplification, legislators as trustees are to act according to their own judgments of the public interest and not to be bound by the instructions or views of the constituents who elected them. Legislators as delegates, on the other hand, are bound by the instructions (and even, according to some understandings, the views) of their constituents. Burke's speech is often seen as a powerful argument for legislators acting as trustees[50] and may seem then to provide support for the view that party discipline is contrary to the proper role of legislators.

This impression is, however, misleading as a closer analysis of Burke's views will reveal. There are three key principles in Burke's speech to the Electors of Bristol. First, parliament is a national assembly. As Burke puts it:

Parliament is not a *congress* of ambassadors from different and hostile interests; which interests must maintain, as an agent and advocate, against other agents and advocates; but parliament is a *deliberative* assembly of *one nation*, with *one interest*, that of the whole; where, not local purposes, not local prejudices ought to guide, but the general good resulting from the general reason of the whole.[51]

After noting the diverse interests of a nation, Burke further stated that '(a)ll these widespread interests must be considered; must be compared; must be reconciled if possible'.[52]

The second principle is that elected representatives are obliged to reach their own judgments. Speaking of these representatives, Burke said:

his unbiassed (sic) opinion, his mature judgment, his enlightened conscience, he ought not to sacrifice to you; to any man, or to any set of men living. These he does not derive from your pleasure; no, for from the law and the constitution. They are a trust from Providence for the abuse of which he is deeply answerable. Your representative owes you, not his industry only, but his judgment; and he betrays, instead of serving you, if he sacrifices it to your opinion.[53]

The third principle is that elected representatives should vote according to their own judgments. Of the three principles, the scope and meaning of the third is least clear. In his speech, Burke clearly condemned 'authoritative instructions, mandates issued, which the member is bound blindly and implicitly to obey, to vote, and to argue for, though contrary to the clearest conviction of his judgment and conscience'.[54] According to Burke, such instructions and mandates 'arise from a fundamental mistake of the whole order and tenor of our constitution',[55] in particular, a failure to recognize that 'parliament is a *deliberative* assembly of *one nation*, with *one interest*, that of the whole'.[56]

---

[50] See H. Pitkin, *The Concept of Representation* (Berkeley: University of California Press, 1967).
[51] Burke, n 49 above, 159, 165 (emphasis in original).
[52] Ibid 159, 166.
[53] Ibid 159, 164.
[54] Ibid 159, 165.
[55] Ibid. 159, 165.
[56] Ibid 159, 165 (emphasis in original).

It is unclear in these passages whether Burke is saying that elected representatives should *always* vote according to their own judgments or whether abiding by instructions and mandates are permissible so long as it is not through blind obedience or clearly contrary to the conscience of the representative. Another possibility that arises from Burke's reference to parliament being a national assembly is that Burke's condemnation of instructions and mandates rested on the nature of their *source*, namely, the electors of the particular constituency that elected the representative. According to this interpretation, if the source of instructions and mandates was a national body, Burke's objection may fall away.

Is party discipline then incompatible with these principles? Far from being incompatible with the principle that parliament is a national assembly, party discipline as it relates to major parties is, in fact, essential to advancing this principle. As may be recalled, the three defining features of major parties are that they ought to bridge local and national citizenship; be inclusive and integrative; and, lastly, have the function of comprehensiveness.[57] The last feature, in particular, should issue in an agenda for governing the nation. Party discipline within these parties would require their elected representatives to vote according to these national agendas and, in doing so, supports the role of parliament as a national assembly.

Further, party discipline is not incompatible with the principle that elected representatives reach their own judgments. They clearly need to do so in deciding to join a political party. There is also a strong deliberative aspect to the participatory function of political parties. This function implies that political parties are themselves sites of deliberation, with members including elected representatives having to decide for themselves how they choose to participate within intra-party fora, for instance, caucus meetings.[58] Moreover, party discipline, as understood above, applies to votes but not necessarily to speech. While ALP members of the Senate Education, Employment and Workplace Relations Committee would, because of party discipline, be bound to vote according to the party line, they could, and did, in their report, recommend changes to the Fair Work Bill that diverged from the party's position.[59]

In sum, there are two reasons why party discipline is not incompatible with the principle that elected representatives reach their own judgment. Party discipline is, first, founded upon an assumption of internal deliberation. This would clearly allow elected representatives to exercise their own judgments. Secondly, there are limits to party discipline in that it is restricted to voting and does not dictate all aspects of the behaviour of elected representatives.

Indeed, in an essay entitled 'Thoughts on the Cause of the Present Discontents', Burke strongly suggests that the duty of elected representatives to reach their own

---

[57] See discussion above accompanying nn 36–7.

[58] J. Teorell, 'A Deliberative Defence of Intra-Party Democracy' (1999) 5 *Party Politics* 363. On the deliberative potential of associations more generally, see J. Cohen and J. Rogers, 'Secondary Associations and Democratic Governance', in E. O. Wright (ed.), *Associations and Democracy: The Real Utopias Project: Volume 1* (London: Verso, 1995), ch 1.

[59] See eg Senate Standing Committee on Education, Employment and Workplace Relations, *Fair Work Bill 2008 [Provisions]* (2009), ch 4.

judgment implies an obligation to combine in political parties, groups he understood as comprising 'a body of men united for promoting by their joint endeavours the national interest upon some particular principle in which they are all
agreed'.[60]

A crucial step in Burke's reasoning is that the duty of elected representatives
to reach their own judgment comes with the duty to take steps to put those judgments into effect. In his words, public duty 'demands and requires that what is
right should not only be made known, but made prevalent; that what is evil should
not only be detected, but defeated'.[61] In another passage, he says '(p)ublic life is a
situation of power and energy; he trespasses against his duty who sleeps upon his
watch, as well as he that goes over to the enemy'.[62]

There is then, according to Burke, a duty to contend for positions of power.[63]
This duty, however, could not be properly fulfilled unless elected representatives
combined into groups as 'no man could act with effect, who did not act in concert;
no man could act in concert, who did not act with confidence; and no man could
act with confidence, who were not bound together by common opinions, common affections, and common interests'.[64] It followed for Burke that '(o)f such a
nature are connexions in politics; essentially necessary for the full performance of
public duty'.[65] If so, and if these connections typically take the form of combining
into political parties, Burke's reasoning would seem to imply an obligation to act
through political parties and further embrace the incidents that attach through
such combination, most notably, party discipline.

Of the various principles in Burke's speech to the Electors of Bristol, it is the
third principle that poses the greatest challenge for party discipline. The extent
to which party discipline comports with this principle will, of course, depend on
the meaning ascribed to it. If the principle allows for instructions or mandates
provided that they are not blindly obeyed or clearly contrary to the conscience
of the elected representative, it can still accommodate party discipline, especially
if such discipline follows from robust internal party deliberation. If the principle
rests upon an objection to instructions issuing from particular constituencies then
it would not appear to be incompatible with party discipline within major parties.

The real difficulty results if the principle is that elected representatives should
always vote according to their own judgments. There is no escaping the conclusion
that a principle of this kind would be incompatible with party discipline in most
respects. This principle, however, amounts to a profound objection to acting collectively to further political objectives. The clear advantage of collective action is
strength in numbers. This advantage can only be sustained if members of a group
act as a group. This means that members are bound by the decision of the group

---

[60] E. Burke, 'Thoughts on the Cause of the Present Discontents', in *The Works of the Right
Honourable Edmund Burke: Volume II* (1926), 2, 82.
[61] Ibid 2, 79.
[62] Ibid 2, 86.
[63] Ibid 2, 82.
[64] Ibid 2, 81–2.
[65] Ibid 2, 80.

even when they disagree. In many ways, party discipline is simply the application of this logic to political parties.

The notion that elected representatives should always vote according to their judgments, regardless of the policies of the party which endorsed them, also comes close to expressing contempt for the decisions made by the voters. Citizens, when voting for a candidate standing on a party platform, tend to be expressing support for the policies of the party and, hence, would seem to have a legitimate expectation that the candidates, if elected, will implement party policies. It is this expectation that provides the basis for saying that an elected party has a mandate to govern according to its policies.

Party discipline is, therefore, necessary for a party to implement its electoral mandate. In other words, such discipline is essential to the proper discharge of the electoral function of parties. Therefore, a principle that elected representatives should always vote according to their judgments is not only hostile to party discipline but also to responsiveness to the electorate.

The case of the Fair Work Act is illustrative. The ALP government, of course, insisted that it had a mandate to enact this Act. But so did the Liberal Party, by repeatedly proclaiming that 'Work Choices is dead'.[66] The Coalition Senators' Minority Report to the inquiry of the Senate Education, Employment and Workplace Relations' Inquiry into the Fair Work Bill put this in emphatic terms:

The right of the Government to abandon much of the *WorkChoices* architecture, based on its commitments in the lead up to the 2007 Federal election, is clear and beyond challenge. *Coalition senators acknowledge that **WorkChoices** is dead;* only the makeup of its successor remains to be determined.[67]

If an ALP parliamentarian voted against the Fair Work Bill on the ground that she believed that the policy that the ALP brought to the election was flawed, many of us would see this as a deep insult to the electorate and the political process. Moreover, in this instance, the insult is not only an affront to democratic principles but also expresses disrespect for the commitment to rights held by those who voted for the ALP. As shown earlier, the debates concerning the Fair Work Bill implicated rights through questions surrounding collective bargaining. Many of those who supported the ALP's Forward with Fairness industrial policy would have done so in support of a greater role for collective bargaining and, most likely, for freedom of association.

Lastly, it is also worthwhile reflecting on what is likely to happen if parliamentarians were not bound to vote according to party policies but regularly cast so-called 'conscience' votes. The superficial appeal of 'conscience' votes is that they seem to contrast principled voting with the supposedly blind voting that results from party discipline. This is a deeply flawed contrast. As we have now seen, voting that stems from party discipline can be the result of robust and considered deliberation.

---

[66] See eg M. Keenan, Shadow Minister for Employment and Workplace Relations, 'Speech to the Australian Industry Group PIR' (9 Dec 2009), 1.

[67] Senate Standing Committee on Education, Employment and Workplace Relations, *Fair Work Bill 2008 [Provisions]* (2009) Coalition Senators' Minority Report, 1 (emphasis original).

More to the point, parliamentarians who vote according to their 'conscience' are not free from electoral pressures that are experienced by parliamentarians bound by party discipline. In the absence of party discipline, these pressures will, however, express themselves in different ways. Generally, these parliamentarians will tend to vote according to the wishes of those who can secure their election. They may vote according to the wishes of the voters of their particular constituencies; a path that would lead to more parochial politics. They may also vote according to the wishes of their financiers, giving rise to the risk of plutocratic politics. Or they may vote according to the positions of the pressures groups that can support their re-election (or are able to threaten it). This would lead increasingly to issue-based politics rather than broad-based politics for an entire nation.[68]

VI. Parties and the Danger of Faction

According to Madison's famous formulation, a faction is:

a number of citizens whether amounting to a majority or minority of the whole, who are united and actuated by some common impulse of passion, or of interest, adverse to the rights of other citizens, or to the permanent and aggregate interests of the community.[69]

From Madison's definition, we can specify two ways in which parties risk becoming factions, thereby, undermining the protection of rights: as a minority acting for itself; and as a vehicle for majority views. These risks will be discussed in turn.

The danger of political parties becoming a minority faction stems, of course, from the self-interest and ambition that is inherent in the competition for political power. Being central to this competition, political parties, of course, squarely raise this danger. That in itself is not necessarily antithetical to the protection of rights. As Sartori acutely observed: 'The power-seeking drives of politicians remain constant. What varies is the processing and the constraints that are brought to bear on such drives.'[70]

The key for Sartori is understanding that 'parties are *functional* agencies—they serve purposes and fulfill roles'.[71] Ideally, their electoral function shapes and channels their self-interest into a rivalry as to what notion of the 'public interest' should prevail. Elections do not simply involve competitions for political power. At their best, they involve a competition for power to *put principles or agendas into effect*. This is what Edmund Burke elegantly described as 'a generous contention for power'; a process that can 'be easily distinguished from the mean and interested struggle for place and emolument'.[72] This generous contention for power reduces the danger of

---

[68] Schattschneider, n 1 above, 196–7.
[69] J. Madison, 'Paper No 10', in A. Hamilton, J. Madison, and J. Jay, *The Federalist Papers* (New York: A Mentor Book, 1961), 77, 78.
[70] Sartori, n 30 above, 25.
[71] Sartori, n 30 above, 25 (emphasis in original).
[72] Burke, 'Thoughts on the Cause of the Present Discontents', n 60 above, 2, 82–3.

political parties becoming a minority faction. Madison, for example, believed this danger was ameliorated by regular votes based on the majority principle.[73]

It is appropriate here to recall that some of the historic achievements of party government in Australia, in fact, concern the mechanisms for robust electoral competition. Amongst others, proportional representation in the Senate, the extension of franchise and compulsory voting were all the result of legislation enacted through party government. Through these achievements, Australian political parties demonstrate some capacity to self-regulate in reducing the risk of them becoming a minority faction.

What then of the danger of political parties becoming a majority faction? For Madison, 'the superior force of an interested and overbearing majority' might mean that 'the public good is disregarded in the conflicts of rival parties, and that measures are (not) decided…according to rules of justice and the rights of the minor party'.[74] Expressing similar sentiments, Ronald Dworkin argued that '(m)embers of entrenched minorities have in theory most to gain from the transfer (of power to judges), for the majoritarian bias of the legislature works most harshly against them, and it is their rights that are for that reason most likely to be ignored in that forum'.[75]

It will follow from such views that, in a country like Australia where there is party government, political parties may, because of their majoritarian bias, neglect (or even violate) the rights of minorities. Or, to couch it in that often-used phrase, political parties raise the danger of the tyranny of the majority.

It is sometimes hard to resist the conclusion that arguments invoking the tyranny of the majority are just clichés passing off as analysis, with conclusions assumed rather than reasoned through. These arguments, first, overstate the danger of the tyranny of the majority. They do so by failing to adequately recognize that whether an electoral system produces a result in accordance with a majority principle (ie whoever secures a majority of votes wins) clearly depends on its features. With the Australian federal parliament, for example, there is no reason to assume that the party (or parties) that control the parliament has secured the support of the majority of voters for two reasons. The Upper House, the Senate, is composed of an equal number of representatives from each State. Moreover, control of the House of Representatives requires a majority of seats but not a majority of votes. In the 2001 federal election, for example, the Coalition was elected government after winning a majority of seats even though the ALP Opposition secured 50.98 per cent of votes on a two-party preferred basis while the Coalition parties secured 49.02 per cent.[76]

---

[73] Madison, n 69 above, 77, 80.

[74] Ibid 77, 77.

[75] Dworkin, n 4 above, 27–8. Various meanings can be attributed to the phrase, 'the tyranny of the majority', other than a reference to a numerical majority oppressing a minority; see G. Sartori, *The Theory of Democracy Revisited: Part One: The Contemporary Debate* (Chatham: Chatham House Publishers, 1987), 133–7.

[76] See Australian Electoral Commission, *Election 2001: Election Results* (2001) at <http://www.aec.gov.au/Elections/federal_elections/2001/results/index.html> (last visited 26 Feb 2009).

Another fundamental reason why the danger of the tyranny of the majority is overstated is that there is very rarely a cohesive majority acting with a common impulse. It is true that the application of the majority principle produces a numerical majority, but this majority is usually composed of disparate and shifting elements: 'the referent "majority" is a set of *ephemeral aggregations*'.[77] As Sartori correctly argued, the application of the majority principle does not usually produce majority rule in terms of 'a numerical, concrete majority "ruling" in the literal and strong sense of the term'.[78]

The other difficulty with arguments invoking the tyranny of the majority has support from an unlikely source. In *A Matter of Principle*, Ronald Dworkin says this:

> It is no doubt true, as a very general description, that in a democracy power is in the hands of the people. But it is all too plain that no democracy provides genuine equality of political power. Many citizens are for one reason or another disenfranchised entirely. The economic power of large business guarantees special political power for its managers. Interest groups, like unions and professional organizations, elect officers who also have special power. Members of entrenched minorities have, as individuals, less power than individual members of other groups that are, as groups, more powerful. These defects in the egalitarian character of democracy are well known and in part irremedial.[79]

This passage suggests that the problem facing 'entrenched minorities' is not the power of the majority; after all '(m)any citizens are for one reason or another disenfranchised entirely'.[80] Rather the problem is one of powerful minorities like large business and interest groups that have the wherewithal to overwhelm not only the 'entrenched minorities' but also the majority of citizens.

This account, which focuses on powerful minorities, is quite compelling. As Dahl puts it:

> of course a majority might have the power or strength to deprive a minority of its political rights. In practice, though, I would guess that a powerful minority strips a majority of its political rights much more often than the other way around.[81]

It may well be that it is not the tyranny of the majority that is to be feared but rather the tyranny of powerful minorities.

The final difficulty with arguments based on the tyranny of the majority is that they fail to properly appreciate that the views of the majority are not necessarily or even usually antithetical to the rights of vulnerable minorities. It is true that majorities can act against the rights of vulnerable minorities but it is not clear why it is assumed that they will tend to do so. On the contrary, the views of the majority, including those articulated by political parties, can clearly be imbued by a concern for vulnerable minorities.

---

[77] Sartori, *The Theory of Democracy Revisited*, n 75 above, 136 (emphasis in original).
[78] Sartori, *Parties and Party Systems,* n 30 above, 17.
[79] Dworkin, n 4 above, 27.
[80] Ibid.
[81] R. Dahl, *Democracy and its Critics* (New Haven: Yale University Press, 1989), 171.

Take, for example, the previous federal election where the ALP was elected on its Forward to Fairness industrial policy. Those that supported the ALP constituted a majority of voters[82] and, according to conventional political wisdom, would have supported the ALP's industrial policy (or, more accurately, opposed the Coalition's Work Choices policy). This support would mean broad endorsement of the idea that workplace agreements should be subject to community standards, whether through legislative standards, collective agreements, or other industrial instruments. Such endorsement implies concern for vulnerable workers who would not fare well in what Justice Higgins described as 'the higgling of the market',[83] where the 'pressure for bread'[84] means that workers stand in a 'usual but unequal contest'[85] with employers. This example demonstrates majority views can clearly include a concern for vulnerable minorities.

VII. Concluding Remarks

This chapter has argued that political parties are not only central to the protection of rights but can also advance the protection of rights in Australia because of their functions. This is not equivalent to an unqualified endorsement of Australian party politics. 'Can' does not mean 'will' or even 'likely will'. It is obvious that Australian political parties do not naturally, let alone always, promote the protection of rights. In the end, this chapter is best seen as a ground-clearing exercise. The challenge remains to foster virtuous party politics that advances the protection of rights in Australia.

Meeting this challenge, first, requires an identification of the salient aspects of the party system in Australia.[86] Secondly, it requires a normative framework to evaluate these aspects. Space does not permit an elaboration of this framework, but the functions of parties should clearly underpin such a framework. The normative framework should not, however, rest upon these functions alone. These functions can be performed well or poorly and some criterion (or set of criteria) needs to be in place to evaluate these matters. The principles of democracy would seem to be a natural source of such criteria. Thirdly and fourthly, there needs to be a diagnosis of the strengths and limitations of current Australian party system in relation to protection of rights and an agenda for reform.

---

[82] The ALP secured 52.7 per cent of votes on a two-party preferred basis: see <http://results.aec. gov.au/13745/Website/HouseStateFirstPrefsByParty-13745-NAT.htm> (last visited 4 June 2009).
[83] *Ex p H v McKay* (1907) 2 CAR 1, 3.
[84] Ibid.
[85] Ibid.
[86] See Mark Tushnet's chapter in this collection.

16

Messages from the Front Line: Parliamentarians' Perspectives on Rights Protection

Carolyn Evans and Simon Evans

[W]e are not asking about legislative efficiency in the abstract. We are asking: does Parliament take its legislative responsibilities seriously enough to make it inappropriate for Judges to undertake the sort of close scrutiny of statutes that gets attacked as 'judicial activism'. A deserted chamber, Bills rushed through under urgency, members subservient to the executive, constant closure motions, no second chamber, no checks and balances—is that the sort of process that can reassure us that judicial scrutiny is not necessary?[1]

I. Introduction

The case against human rights-based judicial review of legislation combines both theoretical and empirical claims. Sometimes the theoretical claims appear to predominate in the literature. Nonetheless, many of those who defend the legislature as the best forum for the resolution of debates about contestable rights do so, at least in part, because they claim that actually existing non-idealized democratic institutions are capable of adequately protecting rights. While Jeremy Waldron's influential analysis of legislatures, legislation, and the legislative process is 'philosophically, rather than empirically, based'[2] (as Adrienne Stone puts it), it depends on a series of assumptions that are capable of being tested, at least to some extent. Increasingly, there has been a call for a turn to empirical method to test the capacity of actual democratic institutions to protect rights given their often significant democratic and deliberative deficits compared with any 'ideal' legislature.[3] The philosophical debate has continued despite the call for empirical verification of its assumptions,

---

[1] J. Waldron, 'Compared to What? Judicial Activism and New Zealand's Parliament' [2005] *New Zealand Law Journal* 441, 443.

[2] A. Stone, 'Disagreement and an Australian Bill of Rights' (2002) 26 *Melbourne University Law Review* 478, 493.

[3] See eg M. Tushnet, 'Interpretation in Legislatures and Courts Incentives and Institutional Design', in R. W. Bauman and T. Kahana (eds), *The Least Examined Branch: The Role of Legislatures in the Constitutional State* (Cambridge: Cambridge University Press, 2006), 355, 377 ('The basic question is empirical, and one on which we have relatively little systematic information. Systematic

and it has taken some time for scholars to take up the challenge of critically assessing the performance of the legislatures in protecting human rights.[4]

In this chapter we seek to contribute to the growing body of empirical work on the performance of legislatures by presenting the results of a series of interviews carried out with Australian parliamentarians. The voices of ordinary parliamentarians are rarely heard on these issues, which is perhaps strange given the weighty role that is attributed to them in protecting rights in a system such as Australia's. When politicians do enter the public debate on bills of rights, it is (perhaps predictably) current or former members of the executive, such as former (ALP)[5] Premier of New South Wales Bob Carr, former (coalition)[6] Commonwealth Treasurer Peter Costello and former Commonwealth Attorney General Daryl Williams whose voices are heard most consistently. Even then, their treatment of the topic is rarely much more than twin assertions that elected representatives do a better job of rights protection than unelected judges and that a government that defies human rights may be voted out of office. That is, they largely repeat a simplified version of the arguments made by those scholars who oppose enactment of a bill of rights. They have not provided much in the way of 'inside information' about the way in which the current system operates and how effective the mechanisms for protecting rights through democratic means are in practice. Carr, for example, who has been one of the most prominent critics of the idea of a Bill of Rights in Australia, has argued:

Parliaments are elected to make laws. In doing so, they make judgments about how the rights and interests of the public should be balanced. Views will differ in any given case about whether the judgment is correct. However, if the decision is unacceptable, the community can make its views known at regular elections. This is our political tradition. A bill

studies of nonjudicial decision makers are ... more likely to be productive than additional conceptual inquiry.').

   [4] See eg D. Feldman, 'Parliamentary Scrutiny of Legislation and Human Rights' [2002] *Public Law* 323; D. Feldman, 'The Impact of Human Rights on the Legislative Process' (2004) 25 *Statute Law Review* 91; D. Feldman, 'Can and Should Parliament Protect Human Rights' (2004) 10 *European Public Law* 635; J. Hiebert, 'Interpreting Human Rights: The Importance of Legislative Rights Review' [2005] *British Journal of Political Science* 235; J. Hiebert, *Charter Conflicts: What is Parliament's Role?* (Montreal: McGill-Queen's University Press, 2002); J. Hiebert, 'A Hybrid Approach to Protect Rights? An Argument in Favour of Supplementing Canadian Judicial Review with Australia's Model of Parliamentary Scrutiny' (1998) 26 *Federal Law Review* 115; J. Kelly, *Governing with the Charter: Legislative and Judicial Activism and the Framers' Intent* (Vancouver: University of British Columbia Press, 2005); D. Kinley, 'Human Rights Scrutiny in Parliament: Westminster Set to Leap Ahead' (1999) 10 *Public Law Review* 252; Lord Lester of Herne Hill QC, 'Parliamentary Scrutiny of Legislation under the Human Rights Act 1998' [2002] *European Human Rights Law Review* 432; M. Tolley, 'Parliamentary Scrutiny of Rights in the United Kingdom: Assessing the Work of the Joint Committee on Human Rights' (2009) 44 *Australian Journal of Political Science* 41; J. Uhr, 'The Performance of Australian Legislatures in Protecting Rights', in T. Campbell, J. Goldsworthy, and A. Stone (eds), *Protecting Rights Without a Bill of Rights* (Oxford: Oxford University Press, 2006). For our contribution to this debate, see C. Evans and S. Evans, 'Evaluating the Human Rights Performances of Legislatures' (2006) 6 *Human Rights Law Review* 545; C. Evans and S. Evans, 'Scrutiny Committees and Parliamentary Conceptions of Human Rights' [2006] *Public Law* 785.
   [5] Australian Labor Party. Where relevant we indicate parenthetically the political affiliation of interviewees and commentators.
   [6] In government (and sometimes in opposition) the Liberal and National parties operate as a coalition in parliaments where both are represented.

writing to, and following up with telephone interviews, parliamentarians who were members of a parliamentary committee that had some role in scrutinizing legislation. We also issued several more general invitations to participate in interviews to other parliamentarians (including former members of parliamentary standing committees) to which we received a small number of responses.

Among the parliamentarians interviewed were members of the Australian Labor Party (21), the Liberal Party (16), the Nationals (3), the Australian Greens (4), the Australian Democrats (1), and the Country Liberal Party (1). Our sample thus encompassed all Australian parliaments, the five main political parties together with independents, and included people who had been ministers or were shadow ministers, but no then-serving members of the executive. We also interviewed several employees of the parliament or parliamentary committees.

The main distorting factor present in our selection of interviewees is that our primary targets were current or former members of the parliamentary committees with responsibility for scrutinizing legislation—sometimes with a specific mandate for human rights but other times for more general administrative law and justice compliance.[12] We did target and interview some people who had never belonged to such committees, often because they had been identified as having a particular interest in rights. Nonetheless the overwhelming majority of those who agreed to be interviewed had been committee members. As a result, the group that we interviewed—on their own assessment—were more informed about and more likely to be interested in rights issues than most parliamentarians. Several said that their time on the committees had raised both their awareness of and commitment to rights issues.

The interviews followed a semi-structured format covering several groups of issues. The first group of questions was about the nature of rights—their definition, their source, their comparative importance, and the importance of particular rights to the interviewee. We then asked interviewees to discuss some of the parliamentary processes for protecting human rights that they had experienced and to assess the strengths and weaknesses of those processes. In addition, we asked for examples of legislation passed during their time in parliament that demonstrated parliament's capacity to pass legislation that was protective of rights and to identify legislation that raised concerns about human rights. Finally, we asked them if there were any changes to parliamentary processes that they thought would strengthen the ability of parliament to protect human rights.

III. The Nature of Rights

(a) The Origin of Rights

When asked what human rights were and where they came from, respondents frequently started by referring to the leading international human rights

---

[12] For further discussion of the role of standing committees, see C. Evans and S. Evans, 'Legislative Scrutiny Committees and Parliamentary Conceptions of Human Rights' [2006] *Public Law* 785.

instruments, particularly the Universal Declaration of Human Rights.[13] An even more frequent position was that human rights were *inherently* possessed by all people; 33 of 52 parliamentarians took this approach. Three Liberal parliamentarians expressly linked their belief in human rights to their Christianity. Some of the most common examples that respondents gave of human rights were freedom of expression, freedom of association, and freedom of movement.

Only five of 52 parliamentarians were sceptical about the very notion of human rights (although this may be influenced by the sample's bias towards those with a greater interest in the area). One Victorian Opposition (Liberal) front-bench MLC,[14] for example, said 'I have a problem with human rights *per se*'. His main concern was that statements of human rights are a 'fashion statement of the day. Establishment of a human right at a particular point in time doesn't allow for changing values and expectations.' For this reason, he expressed strong concerns about the Victorian Charter.[15] Several others who were more supportive of some notion of rights were concerned about the abuse of rights language in the political process. One Federal Opposition (ALP) Senator for Queensland was concerned that rights were sometimes tainted 'when people deliberately misconstrue statements of rights for their own political purposes' and that this had become a more common problem as rights rhetoric had become more pervasive.[16]

(b) The Scope of Rights

When asked if there were rights that they considered particularly important or relevant to their work, interviewees gave a mixture of answers. Several identified particular rights that were of concern to them, for example the rights of children or gay and lesbian people,[17] but several others rejected the notion that certain rights were more important than others, with one interviewee describing the question as 'leading' and another saying, 'You can't put one category above another—you need an overall appreciation of impacts'.[18]

The questions that we asked about rights deliberately avoided using preconceived legal conceptualizations of rights, such as asking about the relative

---

[13] GA Res 217A, UN GAOR, 3rd sess, 183rd plen mtg, UN Doc A/Res/217A (1948) ('UDHR'). In total, 13 of 52 parliamentarians referred to international instruments. The UDHR was referred to by five interviewees; the International Covenant on Civil and Political Rights, opened for signature 19 Dec 1966, 999 UNTS 171 (entered into force 23 Mar 1976) ('ICCPR') was referred to by three interviewees; and other international treaties were referred to by six interviewees.

[14] Member of the Legislative Council (the second chamber in all State parliaments except Queensland—which has a unicameral parliament).

[15] Charter of Human Rights and Responsibilities Act 2006 (Vic).

[16] Several others discussed the problem of rights language being abused for political purposes, including a Federal Government (Liberal) MP and a State Green MLA.

[17] A State Independent MLA, for example, said that she was mainly concerned with children's rights and the rights of victims of crime. She said that the $6.5 million spent to implement the Charter would be better spent on the Corrections Office.

[18] State Green MLA. Another said that it was impossible to grade one human right above another and that 'human rights are a package of inalienable rights, a growing and living set of concepts that changes and improves over time': Federal Democrat Senator.

importance of civil and political or economic and social rights. This allowed for more individual responses identifying interviewees' ideas about the origins, scope, significance, and ranking of human rights. The protection of social and economic goods was raised by 27 of 52 parliamentarians, but there was a significant divergence as to whether these were considered to be rights or not.[19] Some parliamentarians saw economic and social rights as additional to civil and political rights (eg a State Independent, a Federal Independent MP, a NSW Government (ALP) Member of the Legislation Review Committee, and a Queensland Government (ALP) Member of the Justice Ministerial Legislation Committee). Four others saw 'basic needs' as separate from, and more important than, 'human rights'. For example, a State Independent, when asked about how important human rights were, relative to other concerns, replied, 'People have more pressing concerns; where will you get your next feed? How do you protect your family from the elements?' The right to food and shelter are classic socio-economic rights and are protected in the International Covenant on Economic, Social and Cultural Rights,[20] yet for at least five of those interviewed, these types of socio-economic concerns were contrasted with rights and sometimes argued to be more important than 'rights' as the parliamentarian conceived of rights.

(c) The Importance of Human Rights to the Working Life of Parliamentarians

With respect to questions about the relevance of rights protection to their work as parliamentarians, the responses varied greatly. Two-thirds of parliamentarians saw it as an essential part of their role. For example, a Tasmanian front-bench Opposition (Liberal) MLA[21] said that human rights come up on a daily basis in State politics. A Federal Queensland (ALP) Senator said that there was 'rarely a piece of legislation that doesn't have a human rights element'. An Independent MP said that he did not see himself as a politician 'but as a member of Parliament and a journalist. It's my job to investigate human rights issues.'

Two-fifths spoke about human rights as providing a base-line or framework for their roles. A Federal Opposition Senator for Queensland said that 'you start from a human rights based approach—policy and human activity flow within that construct'. A Federal Opposition Senator for South Australia spoke of human rights as a 'framework for a civilised, inclusive society' and a Federal Government MP similarly noted that human rights 'must be the base-line for our work'.

At the opposite end of the scale, six of those interviewed did not see their parliaments having a particularly strong role in the protection of rights. For some State politicians, human rights were a Federal government concern. For example,

[19] By way of interesting contrast, a relatively small series of interviews with members of Congress and non-governmental organizations in Washington, carried out for another part of this project, demonstrated a high level of consensus that the only 'real' rights were those that were protected in the United States Constitution.
[20] Opened for signature 16 Dec 1966, 999 UNTS 3 (entered into force 3 Jan 1976) art 11.
[21] Member of the Legislative Assembly (the lower house of State parliament).

a State Independent parliamentarian argued that human rights issues are not very pressing in Australia, but that they are very important internationally. As such, human rights issues are mainly dealt with by the Federal government, which can address worldwide matters. '[People from my state] don't connect human rights with their own personal issues. They see human rights as something relevant to less fortunate people in other parts of the world.' Similarly, a Federal Government (coalition) Senator for South Australia was mainly concerned with international human rights issues—he said that domestically there were adequate government structures and institutions to protect human rights. A number of other interviewees made similar comments about human rights issues really being an issue that was more important in other countries. These parliamentarians were not hostile to rights; on the contrary, many of them felt that rights were an important issue in many foreign countries and they were keen to see improved protection of rights in those countries. They simply felt that the type of serious violations that were seen in other countries were more aptly described as human rights problems than the sort of problems that occurred in Australia.

A third group of those interviewed were more nuanced in their response to questions about the relevance of rights and noted the compromises and competing interests that are an inevitable part of political life; this group comprised one-third of parliamentarian interviewees. A Queensland Government (ALP) Member of the Justice Ministerial Legislation Committee recognized that even if one accepts a rights framework, there is still room for debate: 'Anyone who says that human rights should transcend politics is missing the point. It's about balancing rights.' Some MPs identified the need to balance broader social needs with human rights as the 'key challenge': rights are 'fundamental, but not so fundamental that they always deserve primacy'.[22] In addition, even when human rights are considered important, that does not mean that they always receive protection. A Federal Opposition (ALP) Senator for New South Wales claimed that 'I think in general that MPs have a strong view that human rights are central to political structures and should be protected to the greatest extent possible. But in day to day politics you get forced to compromise.'

(d) The Importance of Rights to Constituents

Thirty-one per cent of parliamentarians interviewed emphasized the critical nature of constituents' perceptions of rights in ensuring that rights are protected in Australia. A number of parliamentarians expressed the view that, as a Victorian Opposition (coalition) MLC put it, respect for rights 'has to be a part of culture'—'the fact that it's written means nothing'. Several of them identified this as the critical factor in whether rights-protective changes to legislation can be forced through parliament or not.[23]

---

[22] Federal Government Senator for Queensland. A Victorian Government MLA made similar comments.

[23] eg a Federal Government MP, a Federal Opposition Senator for Queensland, a NSW Government MP, a NSW Opposition front-bench MLA.

It is enormously important that the public participates—this can be very powerful. I don't think that members can bring change contrary to government policy without the weight of public opinions (or sectors of the public). Sometimes the government can be persuaded through intellectual argument; sometimes, but not often.

It was also recognized that public opinion could stimulate members of parliament who might otherwise not have had a particular commitment to human rights to become interested in them. As a NSW Opposition (coalition) front-bench MLA succinctly put it, 'Parliamentarians tend to respond to concerns expressed by constituents'. A slightly more complicated nexus of factors was identified by a NSW Government (ALP) Member of the Legislation Review Committee, who said that parliamentarians are motivated to raise rights issues by 'personal ideology, to some extent'; 'what sort of community they represent'; and 'also what is seen to be acceptable within the broader community'. Nonetheless, both those who were supportive of rights and those who were more sceptical about them were clear that strong public sentiment for or against human rights is politically potent.

However, one-fifth of those interviewed were doubtful that human rights were a priority for their constituents. This included a number of those who were committed strongly themselves to the protection of rights, but felt that their constituents' support for rights protection was weaker than their own.[24] A State Independent, for example, saw 'human rights' as something divorced from the day-to-day concerns of the people living in his electorate. He said that human rights were not high on the agenda of his constituents, who were more concerned with things like roads, education, job opportunities, debt, the hospital system, and the economy. He explained that, in considering legislation, 'human rights' were not at the front of his mind. Instead, he thought about how legislation would impact on people's lives, from a common-sense perspective. Similarly, a Queensland Government Member of the Justice Ministerial Legislation Committee said that the majority of people were not concerned with human rights (they are more concerned with matters such as the security of their suburb). 'If we said we would introduce a Bill of Rights, that's not something that would win us the next election.' He said that Parliamentarians often have to stand in the way of demands from constituents to breach human rights; 'motivation to defend human rights is largely a matter of conscience'.[25] Similarly, a State Independent said that '[c]onstituents rarely come to us with human rights issues. They are more concerned about what happens in their street.'

This was of concern to four of those interviewed who emphasized the necessity of vigilance, particularly about the dangers of erosion of rights protection by incremental change (the sort of incremental change that was unlikely to spark serious public criticism). A Federal Opposition (ALP) MP for Tasmania made the point that Australian politics is fairly short-term, whereas 'issues of human rights are

---

[24] Twelve interviewees held this view, including two Federal Opposition Senators for Queensland, a Federal Opposition MP for Tasmania, a Federal Government MP, two State Independent MPs, four State Opposition MPs, and two State Government MPs.

[25] On a similar footing, an NT MLA memorably stated: 'I stick to my own core beliefs, even against the will of the electorate'.

essentially long-term; even measures that are expeditious in the short-term may chip away at rights over the long-term. We proceed in a way which presumes that small changes won't make a difference to society. I'm afraid that they often do.'

In addition, the need to create public interest influenced the way in which parliamentarians who were committed to protecting rights went about this role. The role of formal parliamentary debate or committee reports in generating responses from the government was often subsidiary to being able to convince the media of the importance of an issue. Over a quarter of parliamentarians touched on the importance of the media in protecting human rights. Thus, experienced politicians often by-passed the parliament as a forum for the protection of human rights and went directly to the people through the media. For example, a NSW Government (ALP) MLC said 'perceptions of competing rights present challenges; understanding in the general community is limited, so it's a media-driven debate', and a Victorian Opposition (coalition) MLC saw 'pressure from the media, the community and other parliamentarians' leading to legislative amendment as a viable and desirable alternative to enforcement of rights in the courts. A NSW Opposition (coalition) MP noted that 'a lot of our concerns are initially raised in the media', and admitted that parliamentarians are 'sensitive to negative comments in the newspaper'.

IV. The Capacity of Parliament and Parliamentarians to Protect Rights

(a) Identification of Rights Issues

Nearly 60 per cent of parliamentarians noted that there were real strengths in their parliaments' capacity to identify rights. Parliamentary committees were particularly respected for their capacity to bring rights issues to light. However, even those who were supportive of the role and effectiveness of parliamentary committees in bringing rights issues to the fore were less sanguine about their effectiveness in having their concerns taken seriously or acted upon. A Queensland Government (ALP) Member of the Justice Ministerial Legislation Committee distinguished between the effectiveness of parliamentary process in identifying rights issues and the effectiveness of processes in adequately addressing or responding to rights issues. He was positive about the capacity of parliament to identify rights issues, but thought that aversion to argument ('reluctance to have the argument') and considerations of political expedience compromised parliament's capacity effectively to respond to and address rights concerns. Others pinned the problems on the fact that the parliament as a whole tended not to take the concerns of the committee very seriously. '[The scrutiny committee] is very thorough, but most members of Parliament don't pay enough attention to reports—often they don't read or internalise them.'[26]

---

[26] A State Independent MLC. A similar comment was made by a Federal Government Senator for Western Australia: 'There is appropriate account taken [of rights issues]—whether it is adhered to is totally different'.

Those who felt that committees were capable of being effective in actually changing legislation so that it better protected human rights commonly pointed to informal mechanisms that allowed this. For example, the chair of the committee could play an important role (if he or she had the trust of the committee and members of the executive) by obtaining some involvement in pre-vetting legislation or having a 'quiet word' outside the official committee report to persuade the government to change legislation in order to avoid a negative committee report.[27] This tended to work best for technical or relatively minor changes rather than on issues where the government had a strong commitment to the policy and felt that it had already done what was needed to balance rights against other interests. Similarly, government members of the committee were sometimes able to exert influence behind the scenes. In speaking about the operation of the Victorian Scrutiny of Acts and Regulation Committee, one member said that 'Committee members sometimes take concerns to individual Ministers outside the process and other parties take concerns to the Committee or directly to ministers. This is often more effective than formal processes, which are locked into their own time scales.'

However, some parliamentarians were concerned about the capacity of parliamentarians to identify human rights problems in legislation and many were frank in their own admissions that they did not always have the relevant skills to do so. A Liberal Senator commented that many parliamentarians without legal training are not aware of the actual consequences of certain forms of legislation and therefore cannot anticipate how laws will work in practice. Concern about parliamentarians without legal training was echoed by a number of other interviewees. 'From a general perspective, a lot of parliamentarians don't have legal training—it makes concepts [relating to rights] difficult to grasp', said a NSW Government MLA. A State Independent said that, because he has no legal training, he privately hires a lawyer to analyse legislation for him and an ACT MLA said that she has a final-year law student read legislation for her.

Several added that being on a committee assisted them in developing a knowledge and understanding that other parliamentarians who are not lawyers would lack:

> Many Parliamentarians without legal training are not aware of the actual consequences of certain forms of legislation, and can't anticipate how they'll work in practice. Committees look at these things. If parliamentarians are not on those committees, they remain ignorant. They don't learn how to critically analyse legislation from a human rights perspective.[28]

However, the importance of independent and expert advice from the committee's adviser was identified by many as critical for their success in issue identification.

---

[27] For example, a Victorian National Party MLA said that when in government, a bill would go through four to five stages, including ministerial consideration, the party room, the SARC, the bill committee, and a series of informal 'chats' with the relevant Minister. Although he admitted that there are fewer chances in opposition, he said opposition members have a professional working relationship with the government and can talk to Ministers: 'we fight before the media, but we can talk in private'.

[28] A Federal Government Senator for Western Australia. This is consistent with a Victorian Government MLA's statement that 'being on the SARC has heightened my awareness for things I have always taken for granted'.

A Federal Greens Senator, for example, emphasized the importance of 'having a clear analysis from authoritative people; having people who can look through complex legislation and explain what it means'.

In addition to the adviser to the parliamentary committees (and the reports of the parliamentary committees), which many interviewees identified as sources of useful information, the parliamentary libraries were favourably mentioned by 30 per cent of those interviewed. A Federal Government MP noted the lengths to which the Commonwealth Parliamentary Library will go. (For example if parliamentarians approach the Library, it will run lunchtime forums on particular topics. The library also specially prepared a paper for her about disability rights issues.) She commented that the Library is sometimes underutilized. However an interview with a staff member at the Library revealed that the discussions about Bills of Rights, which were gaining some prominence in Australia at the time, had led to a significant increase in questions from members about rights-related issues.

There were several other sources of information that parliamentarians used with respect to human rights issues, including non-government organizations, personal contacts, notably including constituents, lobbyists, and even reports of international organizations. However, quite a significant proportion (fully half of the parliamentarians interviewed) did not use any source of information other than their own knowledge and insights or the advice of the parliamentary committee and its experts. There was surprise from some interviewees at the notion that there would be any need for advice or information about human rights implications of legislation, despite recognizing the difficulty in understanding all the legislation and human rights issues that come before parliament.

(b) Ways in which Rights Issues Could be Raised

Once a parliamentarian had identified rights issues, there were a variety of ways that those issues could be pursued (some more effective than others). The use of scrutiny committees (discussed above) was one such mechanism, although often the report of the committee was not particularly effective in influencing legislative outcomes. Four parliamentarians, including one State parliamentarian, also mentioned the Human Rights Subcommittee of the Commonwealth Parliament's Joint Standing Committee on Foreign Affairs and Trade as a possible parliamentary forum for discussion of human rights issues.

Debate on legislation in parliament itself was mentioned by only three interviewees as an effective mechanism for protecting rights, seemingly because, as one Victorian National Party MLA put it, 'once a Bill hits the floor, you can do nips and tucks at best'. However, five parliamentarians commented that Private Member's Motions and speeches provide an opportunity for people to speak on human rights issues.[29]

---

[29] A Federal Government MP, NSW Opposition MLA, and three Independent MPs. The NSW Opposition front-bench MLA wanted to see more time allocated for Private Members' Motions.

A few less formal and more creative options for raising the profile of human rights issues also emerged. A NSW Opposition (coalition) front-bench MLA spoke about how the creation of a shadow portfolio can lead to government action on a human rights issue. In NSW, the Liberal Party appointed a Shadow Minister for Mental Health. This put pressure on the Labor government—it 'forced them to deal with the mental health crisis'; in response to the creation of the shadow port-folio, the Labor government appointed its own Minister Assisting the Minister for Health (Mental Health). Another less common approach to manifesting a com-mitment to human rights was taken by a Federal Opposition (ALP) MP, who con-tinues to practise as a barrister and was involved in a successful challenge to the constitutional validity of amendments to the Migration Act that purported to oust judicial review of certain decisions;[30] he also writes academic articles on rights issues.

(c) Party Discipline and Political Compromise

Despite having a variety of ways to pressure governments into better protecting human rights, parliamentarians acknowledged real limits on their capacity to effectively promote rights. Among the key limitations were the demands of the party and the necessity to compromise for political reasons unrelated to rights. The high levels of discipline in the major parties in Australia presented another formidable obstacle; as one State parliamentarian put it, 'you're on the team or you're not' is the basic party philosophy at least in the major parties.[31] Participants noted that even dissent on issues of rights in the privacy of the party room was increasingly being branded as disloyal and resulting in personal and political con-sequences for those who did so,[32] although many of those interviewed agreed that backroom bargaining was one of the most effective ways to get through minor amendments to legislation and far more effective than the floor of parliament. The most experienced and effective political players focused on getting rights consider-ations addressed by minor changes to legislation in as non-visible a way as possible; sometimes a victory for substantive human rights outcomes, but more question-able from a democracy and transparency point of view.[33]

Interviewees tended to be more critical of the political constraints placed on those in other parties rather than in their own. For example, a Federal Democrat Senator noted that 'the ALP doesn't even allow conscience votes' and the same point was made by a State Independent MLA. Another State Independent MLA said that, in the Victorian Parliament,

Majority members try to suppress debate. The two presiding officers are members of the Labor Party. Until they are independent, we do not have a democratic Parliament. They are

[30] *Plaintiff S157/2002 v Commonwealth* (2003) 211 CLR 474.
[31] A Victorian Opposition MLC.
[32] Federal Democrats Senator, Victorian Opposition MLC, and two State Independent MPs.
[33] See the discussion above regarding the work of committee chairs and members in informally raising rights issues outside the committee structure.

bound by very strict Labor Party rules and regulations. That's the sword that hangs over their head.

She also noted that government members constituted a majority on each committee, including a scrutiny committee. Conversely, one Labor Senator for Queensland argued that 'for us, an argument relating to a violation of human rights is a very powerful argument. For the Coalition, pragmatism and political experience over the last five to six years has diminished the power of those arguments'.

However, there were also acknowledgements of the imperfections of the party system to which interviewees belonged. One Western Australian Labor MLC, for example, identified as a problem for their capacity to engage effectively with human rights the ALP stipulation that bills remain confidential at caucus stage, preventing them from seeking external advice.

(d) Executive Dominance

The problem of executive dominance of Westminster-style parliaments, which has been identified by scholars in the past,[34] was identified by many parliamentarians we interviewed as a substantial obstacle to the capacity of parliament to protect rights. Interestingly, even government MPs were prepared in some cases to speak critically of the role of the executive in controlling parliament. One Government Senator noted the 'creeping degree of executive power over issues of rights. I have concerns over the leeching away of individual rights, and the intrusion of the executive.'

However, one interviewee, a NSW Government (ALP) Member of the Legislation Review Committee, did note that executive control could be a double-edged sword depending on the context. Asked what sort of factors make it more likely that human rights issues will have an impact on legislation, he pointed to the 'personality' of the NSW Attorney General Bob Debus: 'Debus provided a very real human rights focus in Cabinet, which led to the moderation of extreme proposals coming out of Canberra'. He also pointed to the influence of leading parliamentary lawyers in other jurisdictions. This was an important reminder that members of the executive could also have a positive impact on human rights protection and were not simply opposed to human rights protection.

A particular variation on the executive power issue was raised in the context of the Australian federal system. On some of the most contentious rights issues—most notably some anti-terrorism legislation—national responses were developed and agreed to by the Commonwealth and State and Territory governments. The proposed legislation, and the agreement of the State and Territory governments, was predicated on classified assessments of the terrorist threat level. This legislation was presented to the parliaments on a 'take it or leave it' basis, without the security assessments that were said to warrant the extreme measures contained in

---

[34] See eg R. A. W. Rhodes, J. Wanna, and P. Weller, *Comparing Westminster* (Oxford: Oxford University Press, 2009); D. Savoie, *Governing from the Centre: The Concentration of Power in Canadian Politics* (Toronto: University of Toronto Press, 1999).

the legislation. Several parliamentarians, even a couple of conservative State parliamentarians who were generally supportive of national security legislation, expressed concern that they were being asked to limit traditional rights and freedoms without adequate information to assess the necessity of these measures and without a real opportunity to calibrate the legislative response at the level of threat. The purported need for a unified national response and the assessment of confidentiality dramatically restricted the opportunity for deliberation.[35]

(e) Time and Resources

The final significant constraint that parliamentarians identified as constraining the capacity of parliament to protect rights effectively was a lack of time and resources, particularly for committees with responsibility for legislative scrutiny. The issue was raised by numerous parliamentarians:

The main thing that would make parliamentary scrutiny more effective is more time. The time scale is too short and there is not enough time between scrutiny and the debate (especially for contentious bills). (SARC member)

The work load is horrendous, especially when combined with the need to review regulations which can be more dangerous. (former SARC member)

Generally speaking, parliamentary debate is much shorter than it should be. Small opposition makes for lazy politicians. (Queensland MP)

The Chair of LegCon [Legal and Constitutional Affairs Committee] has an almost impossible role. The workload is too heavy. I can't remember a chair who was married or had children—you just couldn't do it. (Commonwealth Parliament employee).

The degree to which committees were given sufficient time to carry out their role did differ from jurisdiction to jurisdiction. Similarly the amount of time given to debate of contentious bills in parliament depended on both the issue and the parliament. Some scrutiny committees were sometimes given so little time to report that their reports came out at the same time as—or sometimes even after—the parliament began debating legislation. This significantly decreased the impact of the committee report and was a source of irritation for committee members who felt (with some justification) that their role was not being respected.[36]

V. Recommendations for Reform

When parliamentarians were asked about whether there were any reforms that would make it easier for parliament to be effective in protecting rights, there were two broad clusters of answers.

---

[35] For example, a Victorian Government MLA noted that where legislation is drafted for COAG, one State takes the lead in legislating. While that State's Scrutiny of Acts and Regulations Committee can scrutinize this legislation, it is 'effectively ineffective', and a national scrutiny committee for such situations would be a useful improvement.

[36] Federal Greens Senator, two Victorian Government MLAs, and two State Independent MPs.

The first was around whether a statutory or constitutional bill of rights would be helpful. As might be expected, opinions were divided. While Labor parliamentarians were more likely to express support for a bill of rights than conservative party parliamentarians, political party was not determinative of viewpoint on the issue; of the 17 parliamentarians in favour of a bill of rights at either the state or federal level, 10 were Labor (representing just under half of Labor respondents), three were Green, two were Independent, one was Democrat, and one was Liberal.

A greater degree of consensus emerged around reform of parliamentary processes themselves. First, there was a need for parliamentarians, and parliamentary committees, to be given sufficient time to carry out their role seriously and responsibly. The substantial amount of legislation passed by the parliaments, the complexity of much of that legislation, and the very short timelines adopted by some parliaments for reports or debates meant that legislation was often not properly scrutinized.

Secondly, there was a desire expressed by many of those interviewed to have more explicitly rights-oriented analysis of legislation. Some thought that the best mechanism was to require the Attorney General or minister introducing the Bill to produce and table a statement of compatibility with rights. Others suggested that a formal rights impact statement should be produced and a parliamentary committee given a more explicit mandate to scrutinize legislation for compliance with rights than many of the current committees possess.

VI. Analysis and Conclusions

Most of the parliamentarians who were interviewed for this project believed that parliaments could make a real contribution to the protection of human rights. Many spoke with approval of the scrutiny committees of their parliaments; others pointed to the variety of ways in which parliamentarians could bring human rights issues to the attention of the public or the parliament. Nonetheless, there was a widespread acknowledgement of limitations on the capacity of Australian parliaments to protect human rights effectively.

The fact that different parliamentarians had different conceptions of the nature, scope, limits, and importance of rights is not in itself a limitation of parliamentary mechanisms for protecting rights. Indeed, it could be said to be a strength. One criticism of bills of rights is that they can entrench a single, limited understanding of the definition of rights and thus implicitly devalue other rights (for example, the importance of economic and social rights can be undermined if only civil and political rights are formally protected). Parliaments that do not operate under a canonical bill of rights can consider and act on a wide range of conceptualizations of rights. This can be a healthy form of pluralism and allow for a more open debate about the relevance of rights in particular circumstances than the more constrained and legalistic arguments that tend to be made under bills of rights.

However, the very diverse range of understandings of rights can be a danger at another level. Rights can come to mean everything or nothing. Meaningful debate over rights protection can fizzle out when there is no agreement on the basic parameters of rights. Rather than embracing a wide variety of rights, this can lead to parliamentary institutions such as the scrutiny committees taking a 'lowest common denominator' definition of rights for fear of sparking intractable debate over the meaning of rights.

The lack of consensus over all but the most basic rights fed into another problem noted by interviewees: lack of expertise in evaluating rights problems. Scholars sceptical about the judicialization of rights have criticized the notion that lawyers have a monopoly of wisdom in evaluating rights issues. They have emphasized the moral reasoning involved in articulating and evaluating the interests that under-gird human rights; they have also noted that moral and empirical dimensions of determining the correct or preferable balance to strike between rights-protection and other important social values. But before these issues are reached, there are technical aspects to determining the rights-compliance of legislation. These tech-nical aspects should not be underestimated.

First, parliamentarians must be capable of understanding complex legislation. Unless a parliamentarian understands what the legislation does, it is impossible to evaluate its rights-compliance. This task requires the capacity to read legislation, including legislation that is difficult even for those with legal training to under-stand. In addition, parliamentarians need to understand enough of the particular subject matter of the legislation to make sense of how the bill would operate in practice. Moreover, this can include a requirement that they understand enough about the structure and processes of government to identify some techniques (such as 'Henry VIII' clauses) that have the potential to undermine rights even though they may appear to the untrained eye to be merely technical provisions. Finally, they need to have the time and ability to read carefully through thousands of pages of legislation every year.

In the Commonwealth Parliament, at least, the notion that parliamentarians would have time to read all the bills presented to the parliament is unrealistic. In 2006–8, for example, more than 500 Acts were passed. In 2008, there was a total of 3,411 pages in the bills introduced to the parliament. Bills recently before the parliament address topics as diverse as changes to the tax system to discour-age under-age alcohol consumption, the abolition of a commission that regu-lates the building industry, the power of the Australian Security and Investments Commission to investigate some fees charged by banks, greenhouse gas emission reduction, and the regulation of political donations. All of these topics are ones where rights issues might be relevant, but reading the legislation, isolating those rights issues, and engaging in a serious deliberation about the rights at stake are complex and time-consuming tasks.

If post-enactment judicial review of legislation against human rights standards is not available, parliamentary scrutiny and deliberation about the rights implica-tions of bills ought to be comprehensive and effective. There is ample evidence in the cases, corroborating the interviews we undertook, that the complexity and volume of proposed legislation introduced into Australian parliaments is such that scrutiny and debate on occasions fail to meet this standard.[37] The problems of complexity and volume are only exacerbated when government insists on proposed legislation being moved through the parliamentary process urgently.[38]

There are bills on certain topics where it will be clear to all that human rights issues will be at stake—anti-terrorism, police powers, or asylum seeker regulation are areas where rights issues are commonly raised in Australia. In those circumstances, identifying that rights issues are raised by the bill is usually not difficult, although a detailed understanding of how particular provisions engage particular rights or whether the limitation on rights is justified may be more complex. Legislation on these topics tends to be subjected to at least some media attention and parliamentarians expect to grapple with rights issues when debating it. However, while a number of parliamentarians noted anti-terrorism laws in particular as laws that breached human rights, others pointed to the ways in which more mundane or technical-sounding legislation, which raised little public, media, or parliamentary interest, could have a significant impact on rights. Major events such as the Commonwealth or Olympic Games[39] lead to significant powers being vested in ministers and officials; extensive search and seizure powers are often given to regulatory bodies with far less outcry than if the same powers were given to police or intelligence forces. Parliamentary committees regularly pull up governments over retrospectivity, 'Henry VIII' clauses, changes to the burden of proof, and other technical rights problems that rarely excite the press, public, or human rights bodies. Thus, parliamentarians cannot afford to assume that any legislation has no implications for human rights, nor to assume that human rights violations only occur in legislation that deals with issues that are linked substantively with currently popular human rights causes.

Even assuming that parliamentarians have the skills necessary to read and understand legislation (a robust assumption given the complexity of much contemporary regulatory legislation), it is a time-consuming task for people who also have substantial responsibilities to their constituents, to their parties, to the community, and to other aspects of the parliamentary process. These are not trivial

---

[37] In *R v Hughes* (2000) 202 CLR 535, Kirby J referred to 'the unpleasant task of examining an almost incomprehensible network of federal, State and Territory laws': at 560. In *Byrnes v The Queen* (1999) 199 CLR 1, 13, four justices wrote in apparent dismay: 'Bentham viewed with disfavour "the dark Chaos of Common Law", favouring the prescription of rules of conduct by statute. This, Bentham said, would "mark out the line of the subject's conduct by visible directions, instead of turning him loose into the wilds of perpetual conjecture". By that criterion, the legislative scheme, the subject of these appeals, is a failure. It does not go so far as to bind the citizen by a law, the terms of which the citizen has no means of knowing. That, as Barwick CJ put it in *Watson v Lee* (1979) 144 CLR 374, "would be a mark of tyranny". However, the legislative scheme does require much cogitation to answer what, for the citizen, should be simple but important questions respecting the operation of criminal law and procedure.'

[38] This appears to be a regular occurrence in relation to 'law and order' measures, responding to particular events and public attention. The Law Enforcement Legislation Amendment (Public Safety) Act 2005 (NSW) was introduced and passed on the same day. The Legislation Review Committee's report on the bill was not tabled until two months later. The Dangerous Prisoners (Sexual Offenders) Act 2003 (Qld) was introduced and enacted in the course of two days. The Scrutiny of Legislation Committee's report was tabled more than a month after the Act received assent.

[39] And World Youth Day: see *Evans v NSW* (2008) 250 ALR 33.

obligations and for most of those interviewed, obligations such as looking after their constituents' interests was their first priority. Service on scrutiny committees was simply not as high a priority for most parliamentarians as other political and parliamentary roles.

The solution to the problem of insufficient time and insufficient expertise to read and analyse legislation was resolved by many parliamentary committee members by relying on the advice of the expert adviser to the committee.[40] It became clear from the interviews that even many members of scrutiny committees felt they did not have sufficient time to examine all bills in detail;[41] some interviewees suggested that the committees needed more members and staff—perhaps leading to an inference that not all committee members currently scrutinize all legislation for themselves. The committee members certainly debated the appropriate balance to be struck and determined what should be said in the report in terms of the substantive recommendations to parliament, but they did rely, at least to some degree, on the analysis and information provided by the adviser. They certainly relied on the advisers' identification of the relevant human rights issues, something that is rather problematic given the wide variety of definitions of human rights that parliamentarians were demonstrated to have during the interviews. The identification of issues is not simply a technical task, it requires some degree of evaluation and insight and an appropriate standard against which issues to be brought to the attention of the committee should be judged. The adviser was typically legally trained and generally approached the issues from a legal viewpoint (indeed, it would arguably be inappropriate for an adviser to insert their own political or moral value judgements into the debate).

In short, then, parliamentarians have diverse conceptions of human rights; many regard deliberation on human rights implications of proposed legislation as an important aspect of their role; but the non-legislative dimensions of their role and the complexity and volume of legislation produce pressures on their time and capacity to engage in effective scrutiny. The result is that in these (non-idealized) legislatures, effective scrutiny is more tied to legal expertise than is usually acknowledged. An ongoing challenge for any who want legislatures to be at the heart of the rights-protection project is to identify how legal expertise can *serve* legislative deliberation on human rights issues rather than define its parameters.

---

[40] For many of those who were not committee members, there was reliance on the report of the committee.

[41] A Victorian Government MP, two New South Wales Government MPs, a Federal Opposition Senator, and a Federal Greens Senator.

17

Human Rights and the Global South

Gavin W. Anderson

I. Introduction

The current state of debate between legal and political constitutionalism might suggest that a sceptical approach to the transformation of human rights is self-contradictory. As numerous chapters in this collection demonstrate, the intensity of the case against the judicial enforcement of bills of rights as a means of holding power to account has not greatly dissipated in the decade since *Sceptical Essays on Human Rights*[1] was published. However forcefully this argument has been put though, it has not deterred the further rise of 'juristocracy',[2] which itself rests, at least in its public justification, on a deep scepticism as to whether political constitutions, based in majoritarian practices, can avoid self-interested decision-making and effectively promote the interests of minorities.[3] The cumulative effect of an often trenchant criticism on each side tends to be a mutual cancelling out of the supposed advantages of either legal or political constitutionalism: if this is a zero sum game, what is being fought over barely amounts to zero itself. Furthermore, although the debate ostensibly focuses on the respective merits of various models for protecting human rights, there is a growing sense that this is a cipher for a different debate over relative judicial and legislative institutional capacities to effect particular political outcomes. Thus, one is likely to be a rights-sceptic if one sees courts as a barrier to redistributive economic policies. Accordingly, we may have good grounds for being sceptical as to whether some versions of human rights scepticism are being sceptical about *human rights* at all.

In short, scepticism, broadly conceived, may well be a victim of its own success, rendering highly problematic the question of where we might turn to develop alternative strategies for refashioning human rights. One response could be that current debates do not exhaust the range of possibilities, and that experience elsewhere

---

[1] T. Campbell, K. D. Ewing, and A. Tomkins, *Sceptical Essays on Human Rights* (Oxford: Oxford University Press, 2001).

[2] See R. Hirschl, *Towards Juristocracy: The Origins and Consequences of the New Constitutionalism* (Cambridge, Mass: Harvard University Press, 2004), chs 1–3.

[3] For an overview of the debate, see A. Tomkins, *Our Republican Constitution* (Oxford: Hart, 2005), ch 1.

reveals innovative institutional solutions to the protection of human rights.[4] This chapter adopts a different approach, and considers how we can extricate the debate from this apparent deadlock by considering the prospects for reconnecting rights discourse with emancipatory politics as elaborated in a different literature, namely the human rights discourse of the global South.[5] At first glance, this might seem an unlikely starting point. It is doubtful whether the chastening effects of scepticism should be felt anywhere more keenly than in the South, whether on account of the collective memory of the use of rights in justifying colonialism, or their instrumental deployment in the developing world as a continuation of Cold War politics, or the more recent linkage of rights with structural adjustment programmes and their attendant social costs, which, for some, amounts to new forms of imperialism.[6] However, notwithstanding this historical, and in most cases justified, suspicion of rights discourse, over the past fifteen years or so we have witnessed—often to the puzzlement of critical scholars—the emergence of human rights in the South 'as the language of progressive politics'.[7]

For our purposes, the significance of these developments is that they represent an alternative approach to engaging with human rights. We can identify three ways in which this approach can be distinguished from the debate outlined above. First, it self-consciously, and unashamedly, places human rights to the fore. Accordingly, this approach seeks to redirect debate to the necessarily prior question of what human rights are for. Secondly, that addressing this question requires us to revisit prevailing accounts of human rights which, often implicitly, underpin Western debates to rediscover what lies at the core of human rights as a motivational force for emancipatory politics. Thirdly, for many in the South, the most propitious route to rethinking human rights may take us outside the familiar structures of either legal or political constitutionalism. We discuss these themes in the three sections of this chapter. In the first, we outline the key elements of a Southern perspective on human rights, and highlight how this presents a different critical perspective to that characteristic of Western debates, problematizing issues of universalism, progress, and the latter's limited parameters. The second section elaborates how a Southern-based approach reconstructs our knowledge of human rights to encompass genuine intercultural dialogue, the central duty of addressing suffering, and a non-institutional framework for action. The third substantive section addresses the argument that this task is well under way through various initiatives associated with

---

[4] See chapters in this volume by Bull and Tuori.

[5] As reflects the argument to be made in this chapter, reference to 'the South' here evokes as much an attitude of mind as a specific location. Accordingly, while many writers cited as articulating a Southern perspective are scholars *from* the South, the perspective adopted here also includes scholars *of* the South, whose research focuses on the human rights implications of North-South relations. However, it should also be made clear that there is no presumption in this chapter to speak *for* the South (except to the extent of drawing human rights arguments which originate in the South to the attention of, perhaps, a new audience).

[6] A. Anghie, *Imperialism, Sovereignty and the Making of International Law* (Cambridge: Cambridge University Press, 2004).

[7] B. de Sousa Santos, 'Human Rights as an Emancipatory Script? Cultural and Political Conditions', in B. de Sousa Santos (ed), *Another Knowledge is Possible: Beyond Northern Epistemologies* (London: Verso, 2008), 3 at 3.

modernity first coined the term 'human rights', what is in dispute is the further claim that this was their only possible source *and* its corollary that non-Western cultures were devoid of any conception of human rights.[10] Accordingly, the equation of Western rights with universal rights is said to obscure the many ways in which non-European cultures have generated distinctive approaches to the protection of human dignity.[11]

The second form of this critique highlights the ideological functions served by attaching the label 'universal' to human rights.[12] This goes further than the often-voiced complaint that the actual protection of rights falls short of the rhetoric of universalism, and instead argues that so-called universal rights were always intended to be limited in their reach. For Upendra Baxi, the 'human' of universal human rights was constructed as the rational, self-maximizing individual of Western liberal theory, who would necessarily exercise their reason and will to choose the path of development outlined by Western modernity. Such an individual was entitled to the protection of universal human rights; but others, who would exercise their reason and will differently, or indeed would not recognize this vocabulary, were not yet human enough to bear these rights.[13] Accordingly, where projects such as colonialism, and more recently neoliberalism, impose Western practices on non-European conceptions of human nature, this is not seen as a violation of human rights, but compatible with their advance.[14] On this basis, it is argued that attaching the label 'universal' to human rights does not only seek to confer legitimacy upon the outcome of geopolitical struggles with suspect ethnocentric origins, but crucially does so by conflating 'universal' with 'non-ideological', and so removes these struggles from the sphere of political debate.[15]

Challenges to the universal nature of human rights raise for some the spectre of cultural relativism, as linked with controversies such as the Asian values debate, which sought, in part, to defend authoritarian regimes on account of their supposed capacity to promote economic growth.[16] As we will discuss, this challenge need not lead to the view that all expressions of cultural difference are equally justified. But for the present, it is important to emphasize that the critical Southern literature we are tracking here does not locate its objection to universalism on the transcendental plane, but instead focuses on the material consequences of the appropriation of universalist language by Western discourse. While other approaches to the universal nature of human rights could be imagined, the major problem facing those who adopt this terminology is

[10] U. Baxi, *The Future of Human Rights*, 3rd edn (New Delhi: Oxford University Press, 2008), 34 and 37.
[11] Ibid 40–1.
[12] See T. Evans, *The Politics of Human Rights: A Global Perspective* (London: Pluto, 2001), 14–35.
[13] Baxi, above n 10, 44.
[14] Ibid. 252–261; see also P. O'Connell, 'On Reconciling Irreconcilables: Neo-liberal Globalisation and Human Rights' (2007) 7 *Human Rights Law Review* 483.
[15] M. Mutua, 'The Ideology of Human Rights' (1995–6) 16 *Virginia Journal of International Law* 589.
[16] Y. Ghai, 'Human Rights and Governance: the Asian Debate' (1996) *Australian Yearbook of International Law* 21.

here presented as overcoming the path dependency whereby universal rights are those which are often most antithetical to the interests of the non-West.[17]

A Southern perspective also questions the narrative of progress which underpins Western human rights discourse. According to this narrative, human rights have generally contributed to improving the conditions of social life, and have often been at the fore of social transformations. This idea of progress is well captured in T. H. Marshall's famous account of the evolution of citizenship from the eighteenth century and the emergence of civil rights, through the gains for political rights in the nineteenth century, culminating in the social rights of the twentieth-century welfare state.[18] While legal and political constitutionalists may disagree over how far the other's realization of rights represents progress in practice, there is nonetheless broad acceptance, even from the strongest critics, that each embodies a bona fide account of how human existence can be enhanced.[19] For scholars of the South, this narrative is necessarily partial, as progress for some often deliberately entailed suffering for others. This argument accordingly goes further than the objection that the priority of certain rights over others necessarily involved an incidental loss of benefit for some groups: instead, it directly links progress in the name of human rights to the systematic perpetration of violence against non-Western peoples. For Baxi, this was always entailed by the justification of colonialism in terms of the 'collective human right to colonize the less well-ordered peoples and societies for the collective "good" of both'.[20] This rested on a logic of exclusion: as those being colonized had not exercised their reason and will to follow the same path of development as the colonizers, they did not count as fully human—and because of this, they could be forcibly yoked to Western modernity, and its attendant practices of suffering, such as the slave trade, without this being considered a violation of their human rights.

It may be countered that as human rights have evolved, the force of this critique has been weakened as former colonies are now included as beneficiaries of human rights in international law, and in particular enjoy the right to self-determination. However, for some, the post-colonial era served to usher in new forms of exclusion. For example, it is argued that self-determination excluded visions of societal development which did not meet the approval of the former rulers—and in the Cold War era, new centres of influence—under whose tutelage it was in effect exercised.[21] Balakrishnan Rajagopal contends that there is still a limited conception

[17] For example, Susan Marks has demonstrated how the spread of the universal right to democracy over the past few decades, which has been the cause for great celebration in the West, has in practice maintained what is described as 'low intensity democracy' in non-Western countries, which ensures that newly democratized states do not challenge the right of the West to promote economic liberalization: S. Marks, *The Riddle of All Constitutions* (Cambridge: Cambridge University Press, 2000), 53–61.

[18] T. H. Marshall, *Citizenship and Social Class* (London: Pluto, 1992).

[19] See eg A. C. Hutchinson, 'The Rule of Law Revisited: Democracy and Courts', in D. Dyzenhaus (ed), *Recrafting the Rule of Law: the Limits of Legal Order* (Oxford and Portland, Ore: Hart, 1999), ch 10.

[20] Baxi, above n 10, 45.

[21] See I. Shivji, 'Constructing a New Rights Regime: Promises, Problems and Prospects', (1999) 8 *Social and Legal Studies* 253, at 258; J. Tully, 'On Law, Democracy and Imperialism',

of the 'human' at the heart of modern human rights regimes, but now an '*homo oeconomicus*' whose potential is only fully realized in 'the material conditions of the global market'.[22] This in itself, he suggests, rests on an underlying account of scarcity, which supports a particular role for the state, for example in providing infrastructure for the management of finite resources. Performing these functions entails committing acts of violence; however, human rights discourse is not only indifferent to forging strategies of resistance thereto, but actively legitimizes such conduct which is seen as necessary to effective governance and promoting human rights which conform to the market model.[23]

The third distinctive line of critique we can identify in the Southern literature questions the extent to which the institutional debates which occupy Western human rights discourse are debates at all. This will no doubt appear a jarring claim to some protagonists in those debates, for whom much rests on the likely judicial or legislative propensity to favour negative or positive liberty.[24] For example, according to advocates of greater social equality, it matters whether social and economic rights have the same degree of institutional protection as civil and political rights.[25] To a Southern audience though, it is the common assumptions underpinning these apparently antithetical contributions to the debate which stand out. Thus, for some, it is not the different liberal and communitarian emphases in the political versus legal constitutionalism debate over the protection of rights which is most important, but rather the fact that they each reflect universalist aspirations[26] (for example, the case for social and economic rights is sometimes presented as 'completing' the universal protection of human rights). Accordingly, the debate it produces is said to oscillate within a relatively narrow frequency, which moreover does not exhaust the options available.[27]

This argument takes an interesting, and in some ways, unanticipated turn, in terms of its analysis of civil and political, and social and economic, rights. Rather than presenting these, as is often the case, as a central cleavage of debate, and moreover one which reflects different priorities between North and South,[28] what

in E. Christodoulidis and S. Tierney (eds), *Public Law and Politics: The Scope and Limits of Constitutionalism* (London: Ashgate, 2008), 69, at 91.

[22] B. Rajagopal, *International Law from Below, Development, Social Movements and Third World Resistance* (Cambridge: Cambridge University Press, 2003), 199.

[23] Ibid 199–200.

[24] See eg Hirschl, above n 2, ch 5.

[25] See eg K. D. Ewing, 'The Charter and Labour: The Limits of Constitutional Rights', in G. W. Anderson (ed), *Rights and Democracy: Essays in UK-Canadian Constitutionalism* (London: Blackstone, 1999), ch 4.

[26] J. T. Gathii, 'Neoliberalism, Colonialism and International Governance: Decentering the International Law of Governmental Legitimacy', (1999–2000) 98 *Michigan Law Review* 1996, at 2015–16.

[27] Ibid 2016. Gathii argues that in practice it can be difficult to distinguish between (what he characterizes as) conservative and liberal perspectives: '[t]he rhetoric of self-reliance is conservative; that of sharing, liberal. The rhetoric of self-realization is liberal; that of communal authority, conservative.': ibid, quoting D. Kennedy, *A Critique of Adjudication: Fin de Siècle* (Cambridge, Mass: Harvard University Press, 1997), 54.

[28] See Shivji, above n 21, 257–8.

is instead highlighted is their shared understanding of the role of the state in protecting human rights. Thus, while the two UN covenants gave voice to liberal capitalist and state socialist preferences in terms of economic management, in a post-Cold War world, it is their common statist frame which endures, rendering certain functions as natural and exclusive to the state, such as maintaining security.[29] This has led, it is argued, to the pervasiveness of a human rights discourse in which only those claims which can be prosecuted against, or advanced through, the state are to be recognized. For example, while a right to employment may be accepted, this excludes employment in the informal economy, and so presumes the current institutional arrangements of the state and, given its coalescence around neo-liberal policies, the market.[30] While these assumptions may unite those who debate the relative merits of legal and political constitutionalism, it separates them from others, particularly in the South, who recognize a more pluralistic account of social life. Accordingly, it is necessary to step outside these assumptions before human rights discourse can regard itself as a form of progressive politics for many in the South.[31]

Undergirding all three challenges is the sense that any significant transformation of human rights is unlikely to be achieved so long as we take as our starting point the extant discourse. Indeed, the message of the foregoing is that this discourse may have less to do with human rights than advancing Western interests, and furthermore, that its hold in the collective imagination may impede opening up rights discourse to a broader range of values. Accordingly, a different approach is needed, one which moves beyond the often dogmatic insistence that the Western canon, and the modernist institutional framework which it assumes, exhausts the possible understandings of human rights. Instead, it is proposed that we adopt a broader understanding of the normativity of human rights, which moves beyond analysing them simply, or primarily, as legal norms within formal structures. Rather, in the words of anthropologist Mark Goodale, their normativity should be understood as 'the means through which the idea of human rights becomes discursive, the process that renders human rights into social knowledge that shapes social action'.[32] This discursive approach not only returns the question of what human rights are for to the centre of the inquiry, but also suggests that the limits of Western discourses can only be overcome by engendering an alternative knowledge of human rights. It is perhaps unsurprising that it is in the South that the discursive turn has been most pronounced—in the remainder of this chapter, we consider the extent to which the knowledge of human rights which this advances can provide a more promising basis for an emancipatory project of human rights.

---

[29] See Rajagopal, above n 22, 200.
[30] Ibid 201.
[31] Ibid.
[32] M. Goodale, 'Locating Rights, Envisioning Law between the Global and Local', in M. Goodale and S. E. Merry, *The Practice of Human Rights: Tracking Law between the Global and the Local* (Cambridge: Cambridge University Press, 2007), 1, at 8.

III. A Southern Knowledge of Human Rights

The first way in which a Southern perspective seeks to reconstruct human rights discourse is by broadening the knowledge base to include those non-Western traditions previously discounted. At a sociological level, this emphasizes that, while cultures may express their most prized values in universal terms, the very plurality of cultures means that each such expression is necessarily incomplete.[33] This leads to a normative argument which has both a negative and positive limb: first, that there should be no arbitrary privileging of any one culture's human rights discourse on account of its provenance; and second, that 'rais[ing] the consciousness of cultural incompleteness' should be regarded as central to redirecting human rights to more emancipatory ends.[34] In practical terms, such consciousness raising is to be achieved through a critical hermeneutics, variously described as 'dialogism',[35] 'opening the doors of interpretation',[36] or 'a cross-cultural dialogue'.[37] Undertaking such an exercise is said to reap numerous rewards: it enables us to see that conceptions of human dignity are multifarious, not confined to the cultural assumptions or timelines of the West, nor restricted to those discourses which self-consciously adopt the terminology of human rights. Santos, for example, argues that comparing the concept of human rights with those of *dharma* and *umma* in Hindu and Islamic culture respectively reveals some useful insights, such as the limitations of the Western mindset that every right requires a correlative duty: thus, from a Hindu perspective, with its focus on the individual's place in the cosmos, the idea that nature has no rights (because it can bear no duties) is necessarily incomplete.[38] Moreover, such hermeneutics show that Western assumptions about the monolithic nature of some cultures are often unfounded, highlighting, for example, an ongoing and rich debate among Islamic scholars over the relation between the Shari'a and human rights.[39]

Proponents of this approach take pains to emphasize that while their starting point is that all cultures are relative in terms of their conceptions of human dignity, this does not equate to a position of cultural relativism in which all cultural

[33] B. de Sousa Santos, 'Human Rights as an Emancipatory Script? Cultural and Political Conditions', in B. de Sousa Santos (ed), *Another Knowledge is Possible: Beyond Northern Epistemologies* (London: Verso, 2008), 4, at 15.
[34] Ibid.
[35] Baxi, above n 10, 86
[36] A. Supiot, *Homo Juridicus: On the Anthropological Function of Law* (London: Verso, 2007), 203.
[37] Santos, above n 33, 15.
[38] Ibid 16. Santos's 'diatopical hermeneutics' also highlights incompleteness in non-Western approaches to human dignity. Thus, while he argues that a 'fundamental weakness' of Western society is that its strict delineation between the individual and society often leads to a 'possessive individualism', in Hindu and Islamic cultures, he finds a failure 'to recognize that human suffering has an irreducible individual dimension' and so they can 'condone otherwise unjust inequalities': ibid 17.
[39] Ibid 18–19. Discussing the work of Abdullahi Ahmed An-na'im, Santos distinguishes between the (earlier) Mecca and (later) Medina stages of Islamic thought. The first, which emphasized 'the inherent dignity of all human beings, regardless of gender, religious belief, or race', was considered too advanced for earlier times, but for some Islamic scholars, it is now appropriate to consider its implementation.

positions on human rights are equally valid, and which could justify, for example, the continuing repression of women in some societies.[40] Rather, they stress that it is still possible to develop criteria for distinguishing between reactionary and progressive politics of rights.[41] The key to this is seen as the construction of a genuinely multicultural dialogue, but one which both eschews multiculturalism as a bland search for the lowest common denominator or as a latent means of maintaining Western ascendancy.[42] Instead, it is acknowledged that no cultures are reducible to each other; however, and crucially, this does not mean we cannot translate between them. For Alain Supiot, it is through this insight that we can 'avoid the insoluble dilemma of absolute versus relative values', as human rights now become 'a resource for all humanity'.[43] A number of points follow from this. First, that a multicultural dialogue emerges from the ground up: rather than replacing one imposed 'false universalism' with another, the content of human rights derives from 'isomorphic concerns' shared between cultures.[44] Secondly, this dialogue entails a degree of reflexivity among the participating cultures, as they come to see that their own contribution to the debate is necessarily partial—for example, current debates on the 'war on terror' would be enriched by an admission of the extent to which Western states have employed terror to political ends.[45] Accordingly, multiculturalism here is not simply a more cosmopolitan form of liberalism, providing a broader range of material from which (Western) human rights discourse can pick and choose.[46] Thirdly, the choice between equality and difference which often attends cultural relativist debates should now be seen as a false one. While all cultures may participate in the debate, no one culture is entitled to impose its dogmatic notion of human rights upon another: equality *and* difference co-exist. Thus, Santos argues that people have the right to be equal when difference makes them inferior, but they also have the right to be different when equality jeopardizes their identity.'[47]

The second way in which adverting to the global South innovates upon Western knowledge of human rights emerges from the unsettling effects of opening up a genuine dialogue with those voices previously excluded. In particular, this highlights the important constituency of the global poor, and the correlation between lack of wherewithal and enjoyment of human rights.[48] Accordingly, the challenge here is whether the deprivations visited upon large parts of the world's population, currently invisible in much of the dominant discourse, can be not just translated

---

[40] See eg Baxi, above n 10, ch 6.

[41] Santos, above n 33, 14.

[42] B. de Sousa Santos, J. A. Nunes, and M. P. Menese, 'Opening up the Canon of Knowledge and the Recognition of Difference', in Santos (ed), above n 7, p xix at pp xxi–xxiv. See also Baxi, above n 10, 190.

[43] Supiot, above n 36, 204.

[44] Santos, above n 33, 14.

[45] Supiot, above n 36, 215.

[46] Ibid 205.

[47] Santos, above n 33, 28.

[48] See T. Pogge, 'Recognized and Violated by International Law: The Human Rights of the Poor' (2005) 18 *Leiden Journal of International Law* 717, at 718.

into, but 'named' as human rights violations.[49] For some, this is a helpful reformulation of the problem facing human rights discourse as it reminds us that human rights are 'quintessentially ethical articulations',[50] bringing us back to the question of what they are for, which necessarily prefigures their taking institutional form. In response, a number of commentators have argued that, as a matter of urgency, we need to reorient our understanding of human rights according to an ethic based, in Upendra Baxi's words, on 'taking suffering seriously'.[51]

Making the alleviation of human suffering central to rights discourse is here posited as crucial to rediscovering the latter's emancipatory character. At the heart of this argument is the claim that the durability of human rights in the progressive imagination, including that of the South, notwithstanding the critique outlined in the first part of this chapter, derives first and foremost from their capacity to galvanize action in response to practices of suffering.[52] Accordingly, the intercultural dialogue highlighted above is not simply an end in itself, concerned solely with syntactical questions of the meaning of particular rights, but a means of closing the gap between those for whom suffering is a daily feature of their lives and the human rights discourse from which they have hitherto been disenfranchised. Moreover, regarding the alleviation of suffering as the core criterion which emerges from this dialogue adds a conceptual clarity some find absent from current debates, thus enhancing their practical value in political struggle.[53] The extent to which this approach entails a shift of mindset from mainstream discourses is not underestimated by its advocates: the corollary of this argument is that the Western canon, with its focus on institutional debates, is prepared to tolerate, or indeed, justify suffering.[54] However, it is argued that if the primary task is to problematize the occlusion of suffering within human rights discourse, a 'revolution in human sensibility' can be achieved in which 'the illegitimacy of the languages of immiseration becomes the very grammar of international politics'.[55]

Emphasizing the connections between human rights and human suffering questions the relevance of some of the deeply held tenets of a Western-based knowledge of human rights, and, it is argued, can transcend some of the more intractable issues of contemporary debates.[56] The division between different generations of rights, or between individualist and collectivist conceptions of rights, now seems less critical than previously imagined. For Andrew Williams, it is 'the relief of suffering [that] courses through the whole language of human rights', and which highlights an opposition expressed throughout the history of human rights to both physical and spiritual oppression, and a commitment to a different alignment of power

---

[49] See Baxi, above n 10, 8.
[50] A. Sen, 'Elements of a Theory of Human Rights', 32 *Philosophy and Public Affairs* 315, at 321.
[51] Baxi, above n 10, 49 (emphasis omitted). See also, A. Williams, 'Human Rights and Law: Between Sufferance and Insufferability' (2007) 123 *Law Quarterly Review* 133.
[52] See Williams, ibid 136.
[53] Ibid 134.
[54] Ibid 146–55. See also Baxi, above n 10, 48
[55] Baxi, above n 10, 58 and 49.
[56] Ibid 49.

which seeks to redress systematic violence.[57] Furthermore, enthralment with the analytical distinctions between different types of rights distracts us from the very practical (and increasingly acknowledged) responsibility to take action to reduce suffering wherever it arises. This response further suggests that the significance accorded to cultural relativism may be overstated. Without denying that cultures may retain important differences in terms of what constitutes suffering, it is argued that an intercultural dialogue is more likely to realize common ground on the more obvious indicia of suffering than, for example, a shared vision of economic development.[58] Moreover, if a knowledge of human rights based in the primacy of suffering is adopted, attention shifts from issues relating to the location of a possible violation of rights to 'whether a particular form of suffering is experienced that dictates action'.[59]

The third contribution of a Southern-based rights discourse seeks to expand our knowledge of human rights to include a broader range of actors and practices than is the norm in mainstream debates. This takes issue with the tendency to focus exclusively on rights in their institutional settings, whether in national, regional, or international instruments and protection mechanisms, and highlights two problems in particular. The first is that for most people in the South, their experiences of human rights take place 'outside of the 'traditional "institutional architectures"'[60] of modern Western discourses. Accordingly, it is argued that our knowledge needs to be reshaped to include these 'extra-institutional spaces'[61] generally unnoticed by mainstream discourses. What is proposed here is a broader conception of the politics of rights which highlights that human rights struggles are directed to 'private, social, economic and cultural arenas in addition to the formal arenas'[62] provided by institutionalized rights. For some, we can therefore only fully comprehend the operation of institutional forms of human rights by acknowledging that they exist in a dynamic relationship with non-institutional sites, and that the latter may be the critical factor in explaining the success or otherwise of the former.[63]

This more expansive version of the terrain of rights discourse provokes a further question, namely whether institutional approaches constitute a barrier to developing a counterhegemonic discourse of human rights? Those who highlight this question identify two potential inhibiting factors in this regard. The first is the continuing hold of ideas of legal centralism and legal instrumentalism for advocates of human rights, that is, that the best form of human rights protection entails their legalization, which then operates in a linear manner to shape conduct and prevent abuses. The difficulty here is that this model cannot explain the well-documented

---

[57] Williams, above n 51, 140.
[58] Ibid 143.
[59] Ibid.
[60] M. Goodale, 'The Power of Right(s): Tracking Empires of Law and New Modes of Social Resistance in Bolivia (and Elsewhere)', in Goodale and Merry, above n 32, 130 at 143.
[61] Rajagopal, above n 22, 235.
[62] Ibid 244.
[63] Ibid 234–5.

failures of human rights instrumentality,[64] and as such lack sufficient depth to provide a plausible account of the relation between human rights and social change. The second flows from the suggestion that an institutionalist mindset also frames critical scholarship on human rights. While this is more concerned with demonstrating the power interests served by rights discourse, it quickly moves to the position that institutional mechanisms simply reflect prevailing power relations.[65] In other words, an institutional approach tends to steer debate between ungrounded optimism and structural fatalism. Accordingly, institutional approaches are found to be unpromising in terms of fashioning a theory of transformative agency which can redirect human rights discourse towards more emancipatory outcomes.

Neil Stammers suggests that there is a 'paradox of institutionalisation' facing any attempt to construct a progressive politics of human rights.[66] This can be stated as follows: while much critical scholarship is directed to seeking a different, and better, form of institutional protection of rights, it has also demonstrated that once rights take institutional form, they are often put in the service of hegemonic interests. This paradox is exacerbated when applied to questions of strategy: few human rights activists accept that we can live without institutions, and moreover, they are unlikely soon to disappear as the principal focus of human rights struggles. If truly a paradox, these dilemmas may therefore be unavoidable features of any enterprise of reworking human rights. However, the key question is what significance is attached to this paradox within the prevailing knowledge of human rights. Thus, in contrast to mainstream approaches which simply assume the current institutionalization of rights as a given, a counterhegemonic approach places this paradox to the fore of the inquiry. For Stammers, the crucial question is whether, and if so how, we might achieve the 'institutionalisation of activism'.[67] In the following and concluding section, we consider the argument that this requires the rejection of 'top-down' analytical frameworks, said to typify not just Western human rights discourse, but critical approaches to social science in general.[68] Instead, what is proposed is a reversal of the North to South transmission of knowledge by elaborating a social theory of grassroots politics which emerges from the human rights struggles conducted by social movements of the South. For some, these forms of political experimentation represent the most likely catalyst for bringing about the necessary shift of mindset in human rights thought.

---

[64] See G. W. Anderson, *Constitutional Rights after Globalization* (Oxford and Portland, Ore: Hart, 2005), ch 5.

[65] See N. Stammers, *Human Rights and Social Movements* (London: Pluto, 2009), 103.

[66] Ibid, ch 4.

[67] Ibid 125.

[68] See B. de Sousa Santos and C. A. Rodríguez-Garavito, 'Law, Politics and the Subaltern in Counterhegemonic Globalization', in B. de Sousa Santos and C. A. Rodríguez-Garavito (eds), *Law and Globalization from Below: Towards a Cosmopolitan Legality* (Cambridge: Cambridge University Press, 2005), 1 at 5–12.

IV. Social Movements and Counterhegemonic Human Rights

In this section of the chapter, we consider the prospects for advancing an emancipatory strategy as outlined above in light of an emergent literature which draws attention to the connections between human rights and the activities of social movements, in particular those whose origins are in the South. While these connections have generally been downplayed in mainstream debates, it is argued that this risks overlooking the potential significance of grassroots struggles as 'a key originating source of human rights'.[69] In terms of our present focus on constructing an alternative account of human rights, adverting to social movements is seen to bring two advantages. Methodologically, it confronts questions of the relation of human rights to social change which are often undertheorized in the human rights literature, but which are necessary to fashioning a response to the institutional impasse discussed at the end of the previous section.[70] Furthermore, when such issues are addressed, it is claimed that social movements represent the plausible transformative agency for effecting a shift in human rights discourse which many find absent from the debates over legal and political constitutionalism. Against this more optimistic outlook, we can contrast a more sceptical view which tests these claims against the argument that they may both exaggerate what social movements can achieve, and underestimate the scope for reworking mainstream discourses. By juxtaposing these arguments, we can clarify the contribution which social movements can make to the issues under discussion.

The crucial claim which we explore here is that the counterhegemonic knowledge of human rights outlined in Section II is not just an aspiration, but is being engineered in practice through the various struggles in which social movements are participating. As such, this situates our analysis of human rights within a broader series of developments described as 'globalization from below'. According to this view, the past decade or so has witnessed the emergence of a rival paradigm to neoliberal globalization through a 'vast set of networks, initiatives, organizations and movements'[71] engaging in counterhegemonic resistance. The focus for much of this activity has been the World Social Forum (WSF) through its meetings in Porto Allegre and Mumbai, which has become the embodiment of an alternative political vision as enunciated by its slogan that 'another world is possible'. The World Social Forum itself is not readily captured by conventional organizational typology: it is not an NGO, and no one is authorized to speak on its behalf, nor does it have a formal decision-making process. It is precisely this lack of institutional pedigree on the part of social movements which for some makes them best suited to act as a catalyst for change. They do not take Western models as their point of departure, and specifically do not regard formal rights as the default mode of engagement.[72]

---

[69] Stammers, above n 65, 1.
[70] Ibid 102.
[71] B. de Sousa Santos, 'Beyond Neoliberal Governance: The World Social Forum', in Santos and Rodríguez-Garavito (eds), above n 68, 29 at 29.
[72] Rajagopal, above n 22, 248.

In the following paragraphs, we consider the argument that social movements can, and do, effect the necessary mindshift in human rights thought and practice to accord with the tenets of a Southern-based knowledge of rights.

On one view, it is the interaction between the different cultural traditions often represented by social movements which best explains their emancipatory promise. According to Rajagopal, it is through the 'unique' form of cultural politics practised by social movements that we can advance alternative societal visions on a geo-political scale.[73] For some, the breadth of this claim will appear counterintuitive, particularly given the association of social movements with identity politics. On this account, what characterizes the 'new' social movements is a concern, if not obsession, with 'lifestyle issues' in contrast with the more material focus of older movements, such as trade unionism—as such, human rights struggles carried out in their name are more likely to lead to a narrowing of politics. We can identify two responses to this argument: the first sees this argument as itself hegemonic, returning us to the privileging of some suffering over others, which has historically favoured those constituencies and causes championed by the West. Secondly, it is contended that this argument misunderstands the political nature of the 'cultural' within a multicultural conception of human rights. Rather than seeing culture as uninterested in the distribution of resources, it is argued that for all social movements—old and new—issues of identity are tied up with strategies for survival.[74] Thus, social movements take seriously the idea that 'culture is political', as it is through the different 'meanings and practices' which emerge from the intromissions between social actors that we define and redefine social power.[75]

We can gain some sense of how debates about 'identities and values' implicate debates about 'strategies and resources'[76] by considering the example of the U'wa indigenous people in Colombia.[77] Here, the U'wa sought to maintain rights in lands which formed part of their ancestral homes against the endeavours of a US petroleum corporation to obtain drilling concessions from the Colombian state. On one level, this could be read as the U'wa defending rights integral to their cultural identity, but at another, the case highlights the connections which social movements have forged between local cultural politics and those acted out on the global stage.[78] Following the U'wa's public threat to commit collective suicide were any licences to be granted, their cause was taken up by international environmental and indigenous rights movements, and soon became imbricated in campaigns against oil exploration, and resistance to neo-liberal globalization more generally. Perhaps the most symbolic interface between local cultural struggles

---

[73] Ibid 244.

[74] Ibid 243.

[75] Ibid 244, quoting S. Alvarez, E. Dagnino, and A. Escobar (eds), *Cultures of Politics/Politics of Culture: Re-visioning Latin American Social Movements* (1998), 7.

[76] Ibid 249.

[77] See C. A. Rodríguez-Garavito and L. Arenas, 'Indigenous Rights, Transnational Activism, and Legal Mobilization: The Struggle of the U'wa People in Colombia' in Santos and Rodríguez-Garavito (eds) above n 68, 241.

[78] L. C. Arenas, 'The U'wa Community's Battle Against the Oil Companies: A Local Struggle Turned Global', in Santos (ed), above n 7, 120 at 121.

and the geopolitical plane took the form of the demonstrations highlighting the U'wa's plight which were held against Al Gore at the 2000 Democratic National Convention on account of his alleged links with the company.[79]

Turning to the second tenet of a Southern-based knowledge of human rights, social movements are also regarded as conducive to expanding the range of human rights discourse to include those previously marginalized, thereby making the occlusion of certain forms of suffering more difficult to sustain. In this regard, the decentred and pluralistic nature of cultural politics is held to provide the necessary conditions for developing alternative politics of rights.[80] The World Social Forum emerges as a key site for such politics: operating on non-hierarchical lines, it has been described as a 'meta-cleavage'[81] between the political cultures of the South and North, providing the space in which social movements and human rights activists can exchange differing views on political strategy. Accordingly, it is perhaps best captured as the 'movement of movements'.[82] Its constituencies are generally those groups, such as peasants, indigenous peoples, migrant workers, and the poor, who have been traditionally under-represented in, or even invisible to, mainstream human rights discourse, and whose lack of social and political power is often in inverse proportion to the hardship and suffering they endure.

The result of this activity, according to Stammers, has been significantly to extend the range of conduct which human rights discourse now contests. He suggests that social movements have played an instrumental role in identifying oppression beyond the exercise of economic and political power to include issues of gender and sexuality, ethnicity, and the links between knowledge, power, and information.[83] He argues that in doing so, social movements should not be seen as uncovering new types of oppression; rather, in rediscovering sites of power which pre-date contemporary organizational forms, they are reconnecting rights discourse to its 'trans-historical' and 'trans-cultural' purposes in rendering visible all forms of oppression.[84] Thus, in contrast to the asceticism of institutionalist approaches, which accommodate only those violations of human rights which fit relatively narrow categorizations, social movements, on this account, advance a broader conception of rights, targeting all forms of arbitrary power, so making them a credible medium for placing the alleviation of suffering at the heart of rights discourse.

For some, expanding human rights discourse to include social movements is a risky enterprise, as such movements also include those of a reactionary disposition, such as fundamentalist groupings of ultra-nationalists or militant religious organizations. This is a serious issue, as the actions of xenophobic or misogynist movements are liable to endanger often hard-won rights on the part of, for example, minorities

[79] Rodríguez-Garavito and Arenas, above n 77, 254.
[80] Rajagopal, above n 22, 248–9.
[81] Santos, above n 71, at 46 and 49.
[82] Ibid 46.
[83] Stammers, above n 65, 148–9.
[84] Ibid 149.

and women.[85] This danger is directly acknowledged in the social movements literature,[86] and the question of whether we can differentiate between progressive and regressive movements raises some of the difficult questions we encountered in the context of cultural relativism. However, as with that debate, to the extent these questions can be satisfactorily answered, this rests on emphasizing what can be, and has been, achieved, with the 'creative praxis' of social movements upheld as an important resource for counterhegemonic politics throughout history.[87] A second objection may argue that broadening our conception of oppression to include non-material aspects undermines what has been the central focus of critical scholarship on the need to address material inequality. However, breadth need not entail dilution: following the non-hierarchical WSF Charter of Principles, where economic conditions are the major cause of suffering, this is where action should be taken, and global social movements have been at the fore of campaigns to eradicate global poverty. Moreover, a broader approach often highlights the connections between what might seem disparate campaigns—for example, peasant workers claiming that violations of their rights can be seen as challenging both traditional social hierarchies as well as capitalist relations of production—enhancing the counterhegemonic potential of each.

A further claim made on behalf of social movements, and highly significant in terms of the question of the agency of social change, is that in expanding the field of contestation in human rights discourse, they have secured some signal victories for counterhegemonic causes. To return to the challenge to oil exploration in Colombia, following the various actions taken by transnational advocacy networks in support of the U'wa, the corporation withdrew their operations.[88] Heinz Klug has documented how the mobilization of transnational health and development movements to campaign for affordable anti-retroviral drugs in South Africa led to various multinational pharmaceutical companies abandoning their intellectual property rights in respect of patented medicines which were protected under the WTO's TRIPs regime.[89] Other examples highlighted in the literature include the gains made by the *Movimento Sêm Terra* for land reform in Brazil,[90] or the resistance to Western models of development undertaken by the Working Women's Forum in India.[91] In each case, the contingent nature of any victory won is acknowledged,

[85] Rajagopal suggests that even where social movements constitute a reaction against some societal change, taking a longer-term view may show that they contributed to a 'collective questioning of what went wrong. He gives as an example the Iranian revolution, arguing that 'while it proved to be violent and dictatorial, it has enabled Iranians to attempt to develop culturally legitimate ways of conceiving social and political progress that do not replicate the mistakes of the Shah regime, including a total alienation from Islam and a violent modernization process.': Rajagopal, above n 22, 236.

[86] See e.g. R. Munck, *Globalization and Contestation: The New Great Counter-Movement* (London: Routledge, 2007), ch 7.

[87] Stammers, above n 65, 4.

[88] See Rodríguez-Garavito and Arenas, above n 68, 259–60.

[89] See H. Klug, 'Campaigning for Life: Building a New Transnational Solidarity in the Face of HIV/AIDS and TRIPs', in Santos and Rodríguez-Garavito (eds), above n 68, 118.

[90] L. J. de Oliveira Neves, 'The Struggles for Land Demarcation by the Indigenous Peoples of Brazil', in Santos (ed), above n 7, 105.

[91] Rajagopal, above n 22, ch 9.

and moreover located as part of a broader struggle.[92] However, the involvement of social movements is crucially seen to have opened up the possibilities for political change in ways that seemed beyond the reach of exclusively institutional processes.

For some, it is the social movements themselves which should answer the charge of a lack of effective political engagement.[93] This scepticism over the viability of non-institutional approaches as the most likely to ground an account of transformative agency can be expressed in various ways. At one level, this objection emphasizes the continuing importance of the state, which here, as the author of many of the more enduring instances of oppression, is regarded as the necessary mechanism for reversing the same.[94] Linked to this, and returning us to the institutional paradox discussed above, is the argument that law is an inescapable feature of human rights discourse, and that accordingly our energy should be directed to constructing new legal approaches which overcome law's traditional indifference to suffering.[95] A further variation might be that given the hegemonic audience to which strategies of change are directed—and whose cooperation is required if a different conception of rights is to be implemented—then a more judicious starting point would to emphasize the radical potential in making existing institutional structures live up to their highest ideals.[96]

While such points are not lightly dismissed in the social movement literature,[97] and nor is the pursuit of alternative strategies necessarily inconsistent with the pragmatic pluralism of the Porto Allegre principles, they do raise the question of what counts as effective political engagement. In terms of a social movement perspective, the concern remains that the forms of political engagement outlined in the preceding paragraph remain closely tied to institutional engagement, and as such are more likely to operate within, rather than transcend, orthodox understandings of human rights. Accordingly, some commentators emphasize that social movements represent a more innovative form of political engagement, one which is not primarily geared to capturing state or institutional forms, but rather to transforming the very character of politics and law.[98] In this connection, following Santos, we might describe the bottom-up human rights struggles in the South as a nascent type of 'subaltern law', reshaping normative worlds in ways apparently beyond the capabilities of institutional mechanisms.[99] In political terms,

[92] While this may have brought the involvement of the US corporation to an end, this was not the end of the story as the state-owned oil company continued with exploratory drilling. For some, this suggests the importance of maintaining a reflexive transnational dimension to cultural politics if they are to produce counterhegemonic outcomes: Rodríguez-Garavito and Arenas, above n 68, 262.

[93] D. Chandler, 'Deconstructing Sovereignty; Constructing Global Civil Society', in C. Bickerton, P. Cunliffe, and A. Gourevitch (eds), *Politics without Sovereignty: A Critique of Contemporary International Relations* (London: UCL Press, 2007).

[94] See D. Schneiderman, *Constitutionalizing Economic Globalization: Investment Rules and Democracy's Promise* (Cambridge: Cambridge University Press, 2008).

[95] Williams, above n 51, 155.

[96] See T. Pogge, *World Poverty and Human Rights*, 2nd edn. (Cambridge: Polity, 2008), ch 4.

[97] Stammers, for example, is clear that the argument canvassed here as to their counterhegemonic potential does not suggest that they are the only means of transforming human rights: above n 65, 4.

[98] See Stammers, above n 65, 141.

[99] See B. de Sousa Santos, *Toward a New Legal Common Sense* (London: Butterworths, 2002), 465–80.

this transformational quality stems from their arm's-length operation from institutional processes, which protects them to a certain degree from the latter's gravitational pull and the compromises this may require of their more radical approach to human rights. In terms of the substantive content of human rights, they have pursued an agenda of democratization which extends beyond the traditional focus on political institutions to include all sites of social power. And, in strategic terms, by engendering a broader dialogue between social movements and present institutional approaches, they open up the possibility for bringing about a counterhegemonic outcome 'which neither assumes top-down governance nor the complete abolition of the institutional world as it currently exists'.[100]

V. Conclusion

In this chapter, we have considered the prospects for overcoming the impasse resulting from the mutually debilitating critiques of legal and political constitutionalism by turning to the human rights experiences of the global South. The principal advantage of this approach is that it does not seek to revisit, or state more precisely or forcefully, the stances in this tried and tested debate, but instead comes to the issues discussed above from a perspective unfamiliar to many involved in the mainstream debates. According to this view, to the extent that the rescue of human rights is possible, this can only be brought about by reorienting some of our basic assumptions by engaging the tenets of a Southern knowledge: this emphasizes the roots of human dignity in a multiplicity of cultures, the core imperative of (re)harnessing rights discourse to the relief of suffering, and the need to adjust our knowledge to the non-institutional and unofficial settings in which many struggles unfold. As such, adverting to the South should not be regarded as an exotic distraction; rather, the alternative knowledge of human rights outlined above is of relevance to struggles *both* within *and* outside the South. In this regard, Santos and Rodríguez-Garavito suggest that it is important to give an expansive interpretation to the initiatives spawned by human rights movements so as to publicize and lend credibility to their emancipatory potential. It is perhaps through such a 'sociology of emergence'[101] that a Southern approach can make its most powerful contribution to constructing an emancipatory future for human rights.

---

[100] Stammers, above n 65, 248.
[101] Santos and Rodríguez-Garavito, above n 68, 17.

18

Judicial Constitutional Review as a Last Resort

Kaarlo Tuori*

I. Europeanization and Constitutionalization

In the conventional account, one of the main differences between common-law and Continental European legal cultures relates to the role of the courts in the functioning of the legal system and in development of the legal order. Many differences exist between the United States and the United Kingdom—including the tenacious English principle of parliamentary supremacy—but, when compared with Continental Europe, they are united by the central locus of the courts. Only somebody raised and socialized in a common-law culture could write as eloquently as Ronald Dworkin of courts as the capitals of law's empire and judges as its princes.[1] But the differences between common-law and Continental systems may be narrowing: courts have acquired a new prominence in Continental European legal systems as well. Indeed, the enhanced status of the courts seems to be a global phenomenon, levelling down differences which have previously set legal cultures apart. And, not surprisingly, a critical debate on the advance of a jurisdiction state[2] has flared up in many countries and in many and divergent legal-cultural contexts; criticism of judicialization is a global phenomenon, too. Finland has not been spared this global phenomenon either.

In Europe, current judicialization is related to two more general tendencies which have coloured recent legal developments: Europeanization and constitutionalization. These have left their impact on Finnish development too.

The *Europeanization* of law has proceeded at a very fast pace. By Europeanization, I refer to both branches of European law: both EU law and Council of Europe rule-work, centred around the European Convention on Human Rights. In the legal-cultural regard, EU law is a peculiar amalgamation of Anglo-American and Continental European influences. The Luxembourg Court's pivotal position in articulating and further developing EU law bears resemblances to a common-law system. Thus, the general principles of EU law largely derive from the court's

* The chapter has been completed through the research programme of the Centre of Excellence Foundations of European Law and Polity, financed by the Academy of Finland.

[1] R. Dworkin, *Law's Empire* (London: Fontana, 1986), 407.
[2] The term *Jurisdiktionsstaat* was coined by Carl Schmitt in his *Legalität und Legimität*, published shortly before the collapse of the Weimar Republic.

case-law. This holds, first, for general determinations of the character of EU law and its relation to municipal legal orders, such as its status as an independent legal order, its direct applicability in Member States' courts, its direct and indirect effects, and its supremacy over conflicting domestic law. Here, the failed Constitutional Treaty would only have confirmed the existing legal situation. Even the Charter of Fundamental Rights, included in the Constitutional Treaty and to which the Lisbon Treaty has expressly assigned legal effects, to a great extent merely codifies norms which the European Court of Justice has already treated as general legal principles. In its case-law, the Court has also formulated such substantive principles as proportionality, legal certainty, and protection of legitimate expectations. If the active role of the Court points to Anglo-American common-law culture, the main inspiration for substantive principles stems from the Romano-Germanic legal family.

EU law is a strange normative entity. As the Luxembourg Court has characterized it, it is both an independent legal order and part of the Member States' national legal orders. Its impact on national legal orders is not confined merely to the surface level of explicit legal material but reaches down to the legal-cultural underpinnings, such as legal concepts, principles, and theories of diverse branches of law. Furthermore, EU law has influenced national legal systems in the institutional respect as well.

The European Court of Justice holds a prominent position in the development of EU law, epitomizing judicialization at the EU level. By the same token, the interplay between the Luxembourg Court and the national judiciary, primarily within the framework of the preliminary-ruling procedure, has reinforced the latter's role within national legal systems: the courts contribute to the development of EU law, bypassing the intermediary of the legislature. The independence of national courts from the national legislature is further boosted by their obligation to interpret domestic law consistently with EU law and, above all, the principle of supremacy which obliges them to ignore all national law conflicting with EU law, including national law with *lex posteriori* or constitutional status. This principle has been hard to swallow, in particular in Member States where legislative supremacy has enjoyed an almost sacrosanct status, such as the United Kingdom with its doctrine of parliamentary sovereignty and France with the Rousseauian notion of legislation embodying the General Will.[3]

In the Nordic countries, resistance has not been as strong, although here too the legislature, not the judges, has traditionally been considered to occupy the throne of law's empire. In Finland, for instance, no evidence exists of defiance on the part of the Finnish courts against such basics of EU law as its direct and indirect effect or supremacy. The courts' subjection to the legislature has been manifest in the high legal source value of not only legislation but *travaux préparatoires* as well. In EU law, *travaux préparatoires* do not enjoy a corresponding status, the case-law of the European Court of Justice being a much more important legal source. EU law

[3] P. Craig, 'Report on the United Kingdom', in A. M. Slaughter, A. Stone Sweet, and J. H. H. Weiler (eds.), *The European Court and National Courts—Doctrine and Jurisprudence: Legal Change in its Social Context* (Oxford: Hart Publishing, 1998), 195–224; J. Plotner, 'Report on France', in Slaughter et al, ibid 41–76.

will probably affect the Nordic doctrine of legal sources by raising the rank of prec-edents and lowering that of *travaux préparatoires*. At least in the long run, it is not very plausible that the courts would apply a significantly divergent doctrine of legal sources in EU-law and domestic-law cases.

The European Convention on Human Rights constitutes the core of the other branch of European law. While the Convention entered into force in 1950, even in some of the original Signatory States its domestic applicability was explicitly affirmed only in the 1990s. As is typical of international human-rights treaties in general, the provisions of the Convention are quite vague and leave much lee-way for specification through the Court's jurisprudence. Consequently, the Court has played a crucial role not only in monitoring the Convention but also in elab-orating its precise normative contents. In so far as the Convention is applied in national courts—either directly or by way of interpreting domestic law—an inter-play occurs between a transnational court and national courts, influencing the development of both transnational and national law without intervention by the national legislature.

This interplay can be illustrated through the Finnish case. The prevalent view is that Finland's international-law obligation pertains to the Convention as speci-fied by the case-law of the Strasbourg Court. The Convention has been incorpo-rated into the domestic legal order through an Act of Parliament, and in domestic law, too, it possesses the content which the Strasbourg Court has assigned to it. Hence, a transnational court is constantly redefining the normative substance of Finland's national legal order. Furthermore, according to the prevailing doctrine, Convention rights define the base-line of the protection offered by corresponding constitutional provisions. Therefore, the jurisprudence of the Strasbourg Court has an immediate impact on national constitutional law as well. Consequently, the Constitutional Law Committee of Parliament in its *ex ante* constitutional review routinely invokes the case-law of the Strasbourg Court. In some of its recent precedents, the Supreme Court has also referred to Strasbourg jurisprudence, for instance when weighing and balancing the right to privacy and the freedom of the press as interpretive principles in applying the criminal-law provision on violation of privacy. The Supreme Administrative Court, too, has in several rulings invoked the Convention and Strasbourg case-law when specifying the bearing of constitu-tional basic-rights provisions.[4]

So the case-law of the Strasbourg Court directly affects the law applied by national courts, without intervening decisions by the legislature. European human-rights law, analogically to EU law, increases national courts' independence from the legis-lature. Quite probably, it will also leave its imprint on the doctrine of legal sources, at least in the Nordic countries. National courts' obligation to interpret domestic law consistently with human rights supports the primacy of the Strasbourg Court's jurisprudence over *travaux préparatoires*, whose traditionally strong position has expressed legislative supremacy and the Nordic parliament-centred conception of

---

[4] See, from the case-law of the Supreme Court, KKO 2005:82, 2005:132 and 2006:20 and from that of the Supreme Administrative Court for instance KHO 2002:91; 2003:24; 2004:21; 2006:77.

democracy. In many respects, human-rights law's mechanism of influence resembles that of EU law. However, national courts play a more passive role in human-rights law than in EU law; given European human-rights law's mere base-line effect, they may be active enough in determining the level of domestic constitutional protection, but with regard to transnational legal development they tend to be simply recipients.

Europeanization is intimately linked to the other general development which has added to the authority of the courts even in Continental Europe: *constitutionalization* of the legal order and the legal system as a whole. Constitutionalization of the *legal order* is epitomized by the increasing significance of basic-rights arguments in all fields of law, including criminal law and such core areas of private law as property and contract law. The diffusion of basic-rights considerations beyond their traditional domain of public law has strengthened the role of principles in legal argumentation and decision-making. Basic- and human-rights norms not only establish individual or group rights but also function as *legal principles* with a wide range of application, not only in *vertical* relations between individuals and public authorities but in *horizontal* relations between private subjects as well. Many established principles of diverse fields of law have obtained supplementary support from national constitutional provisions and international human-rights treaties. In Continental European legal systems, including Finland, rule orientation has at least partly retreated, while principle orientation, often regarded as typical of common-law culture, has gained ground. This cultural transformation has repercussions in relations between different legal practices and the institutions responsible for them.

Arguably, the novel emphasis on legal principles strengthens the status of adjudication and legal science at the expense of lawmaking. Principles may be expressly confirmed in legislation, as are basic-rights principles in countries with a formal constitution, but often enough they derive from other legal sources, such as precedents or legal-cultural principles as articulated by legal scholars. And even when a legal principle finds institutional support in the constitution or a human-rights treaty, norm-formation transpires outside the regular democratic legislative process. The expanded role of principles in legal decision-making augments the weight of judges' and legal scholars' interventions in ongoing discourse on the contents of the legal order.

Moreover, legal principles in general possess a weaker steering power than rules. Typical of principles is both-and applicability: conflicting principles must be weighed against each other, with the respective weight of principles and counter-principles depending on the facts of the case. Weighing occurs on a case-by-case basis and requires the judge's discretion. In doctrinal theories, the principles of a field of law are arranged in a prima-facie order of preference. Legal scholarship assists judges in their discretion but cannot substitute for the reasoning presupposed by weighing principles in the light of the facts. Thus, the particularities that legal principles display in both their formation and application and that set them apart from legal rules tend to boost the status of the courts in the legal system. In addition, recalling the role of scholars in articulating and elaborating principles, principle orientation has the tendency of augmenting the significance of legal science as well.

Constitutionalization of the legal order may proceed even in the absence of a system of *constitutional review*. However, the establishment of constitutional review adds an institutional aspect to normative development and leads to constitutionalization of the *legal system*. Indeed, constitutional review has been an integral element in the *new constitutionalism* which has swept around the globe in the post-World War II era, and with renewed momentum since 1989.[5] This is the era of what Duncan Kennedy[6] has termed the third wave of legal globalization. The first wave, in the age of Classical Legal Thought, was dominated by German scholarship, while during the second wave, transpiring under the auspices of a social conception of law, the leadership passed to French legal culture. In Kennedy's account, the third wave has in turn advanced under US cultural hegemony.

In the inter-war years, constitutional review remained primarily a US peculiarity which did not take root in Europe. Constitutional development seemed to have led to two fundamentally different models: the European legislative model and the US judicial supremacy model. It is true, though, that the first constitutional courts were established in Austria and Czechoslovakia in 1920, under the influence of the writings of Hans Kelsen. However, these courts played merely the limited role of what Kelsen called a *negative legislator*. They focused on constitutional conflicts between institutional actors and did not exercise rights-based review of legislation, which, in Kelsen's view, implies natural-law thinking and would inevitably transform the constitutional court into a *positive legislator*; into a third legislative chamber.[7]

After World War II the tide turned, with constitutional review becoming the rule even in Europe. In the institutional respect, the majority of European states have opted for a constitutional court. This has been the choice of countries breaking away from a totalitarian past: Germany, Italy, and Austria in the wake of World War II; Spain, Portugal, and Greece after the collapse of their authoritarian regimes in the 1970s; and the post-socialist countries of Central and Eastern Europe after 1989. But the new constitutionalism has also encompassed European countries which have not been confronted with a similar constitutional *Vergangenheitsbewältigung*,[8] such as the Nordic democracies of Sweden and Finland, or the United Kingdom with the enactment of the Human Rights Act 1998. The most recent manifestation of new constitutionalism is the establishment of concrete *ex post* review of legislation in France, where, ever since the Revolution,

---

[5] The term 'new constitutionalism' is used by eg C. P. Manfredi, *Judicial Power and the Charter: Canada and the Paradox of Liberal Constitutionalism* (London: University of Oklahoma Press, 1993); A. Stone Sweet, *Governing with Judges: Constitutional Politics in Europe* (Oxford: Oxford University Press, 2000); and R. Hirschl, *Juristocracy* (Cambridge, Mass: Harvard University Press, 2007). Ackerman speaks of 'world constitutionalism'; B. Ackerman, 'Rise of World Constitutionalism', (1997) 83 *Virginia Law Review* 771–798.

[6] D. Kennedy, 'Three Globalizations of Law and Legal Thought: 1850–2000', in D. Trubek and A. Santos (eds), *The New Law and Economic Development* (Cambridge: Cambridge University Press, 2006).

[7] H. Kelsen, 'Wesen und Entwicklung der Staatsgerichtsbarkeit', *Veröffentlichungen der Vereinigung der deutschen Staatsrechtslehrer* 5 (Berlin: De Gruyter, 1929), 30–123.

[8] 'Reckoning with the past'.

legislative supremacy has been ideologically propped up by the Rousseauian notion of legislation as the untouchable expression of the General Will.[9]

In Europe, new constitutionalism displays an important *transnational* aspect. The European Court of Human Rights exercises transnational rights-based review of actions by the authorities of Signatory States. It not only complements national review mechanisms, but has also provided an inducement to their development. Thus, even critics of constitutional review might prefer national over transnational control, and considerations of national sovereignty are likely to have played their part, not only in incorporation of the European Convention into the domestic legal order, but also in the adoption or strengthening of institutionalized constitutional review in those Western European countries which have traditionally clung to the doctrine of legislative supremacy, such as the United Kingdom or France. The EC-law system of *preliminary rulings*, where national courts refer the issue of EC law's relevance and interpretation to the European Court of Justice, was designed after the German and Italian model of concrete constitutional review, with the Luxembourg Court in the role of the guardian of 'higher' law. An integral element in the further constitutionalization of EC law was the Court's adoption of the direct effect and supremacy of EC law over conflicting domestic law. Upholding this principle falls not only to the Luxembourg Court but also to national courts, which, in case of contradiction, are supposed to give preference to EU law. These powers of reviewing acts of the legislature in the light of EU law have presumably levelled the ground for introducing a national system of *ex post* constitutional review in such (former?) bastions of legislative supremacy as the United Kingdom and France.

Finland's constitutional development during the last 20 years is a Northern expression of new constitutionalism. The main milestones in the constitutionalization of the Finnish legal order and legal system are the ratification and incorporation into domestic law of the European Convention on Human Rights in 1990; the reform of the Bill of Rights of the Constitution in 1995; and the new Constitution of 2000, which introduced *ex post* judicial review of legislation. In Finland, too, Europeanization has paved the way for domestic constitutionalization. Still in the 1980s, judicial constitutional review was commonly held to be wholly incompatible with Finnish parliamentary democracy and *ex ante* parliamentary monitoring of constitutionality. By contrast, in the debates preceding the adoption of the new Constitution, hardly a voice was raised in opposition to the new, albeit limited, role of the judiciary.

II. The Core Case Against Constitutional Review

Before turning to a discussion of the Finnish model of constitutional review, let me briefly present my position on the general justifiability of external constitutional

---

[9] Michel Troper's argument against *ex post* judicial review is built on a particular combination of Kelsen and Rousseau. M. Troper, 'Constitutional Justice and Democracy', 1995 17 *Cardozo Law Review* 273–297.

review of legislation. My stance is that of a moderate critic: I subscribe to what might be termed a *last-resort defence of constitutional review*, but I also concede the relevance of critical standpoints for staking out the limits of justifiable review.

From its early beginnings in late-eighteenth-century United States,[10] constitutional review and judicial supremacy have been accompanied by critical debates. In the first decades of the twentieth century, the *Lochner*-era jurisprudence of the Supreme Court was a central target in the attack of Legal Realists on Classical Legal Thought. In the post-New-Deal era, the emphasis in rights-based constitutional review shifted from economic to civil rights. The civil-rights rulings of the Warren Court in the 1950s and 1960s reframed the *'counter-majoritarian difficulty'*[11] for post-Realist academic liberals: how could one maintain both judicial protection of civil rights and democratic governance?[12] In subsequent decades, the debates have shown no signs of calming down; the counter-majoritarian difficulty remains the main obsession of American constitutional theory.

Jeremy Waldron has tried to distil the core of the case against judicial review of legislation. He has presented his case at the general level: supposedly, it is not restricted merely to the US variant but claims validity everywhere where his background assumptions are met. If they fail, he concedes that the argument may not hold. He makes four assumptions. We are dealing with

a society with 1) democratic institutions in reasonably good working order, including a representative legislature elected on the basis of universal adult suffrage; 2) a set of judicial institutions, again in reasonably good order, set up on a nonrepresentative basis to hear individual lawsuits, settle disputes, and uphold the rule of law; 3) a commitment on the part of most members of the society and most of its officials to the idea of individual and minority rights; and 4) persisting, substantial, and good faith disagreement about rights (i.e., about what the commitment to rights actually amounts to and what the implications are) among the members of the society who are committed to the idea of rights.[13]

Waldron's case relies on a two-pronged argument. First, judicial review tends to obscure the real issues at stake when citizens hold diverging views about rights and to focus on 'side-issues about precedents, texts, and interpretation'. This might be called the *juridification* of rights-issues. Secondly, judicial review is illegitimate from the democratic point of view: 'By privileging majority voting among a small number of unelected and unaccountable judges, it disenfranchises ordinary

---

[10] Traditionally, *Marbury v Madison*, decided in 1803, has been regarded as the Great Turning-Point, the Foundational Event of constitutional review. However, recent research has shown that, in several states, constitutional review was already well established in the previous decade. L. Kramer, *The People Themselves: Popular Constitutionalism and Judicial Review* (Oxford: Oxford University Press, 2004), 35 ff.

[11] This formulation of the problem stems from Alexander Bickel's *The Least Dangerous Branch* (Indianapolis: Bobbs-Merrill, 1962), one of the canonical contributions to US debates on constitutional review. The title of Bickel's book alludes to Alexander Hamilton's defence of the institution in *Federalist 78*, which can be considered the Foundational Text of the canon.

[12] B. Friedman, 'The Counter-Majoritarian Problem and the Pathology of Constitutional Scholarship', (2001) 95 *Northwestern University Law Review* 933, at 934.

[13] J. Waldron, 'The Core of the Case against Judicial Review' (2006) 115 *Yale Law Review* 1346–1407, at 1360.

citizens and brushes aside cherished principles of representation and political equality in the final resolution of issues about rights'.[14]

Let us start examining Waldron's case from the latter point of view. This is the familiar argument about the judiciary exceeding the range of its legitimacy principle and violating such constitutional fundamentals as *democracy* and *separation of powers*. This standard criticism emphasizes the inevitability of political choices in rights-based constitutional adjudication. Critics argue that even when the written constitution includes a Bill of Rights, the provisions are vague and leave room for varying, even contradictory, interpretations; the favourite reference is to heated constitutional debates on abortion in many Western countries. The problem does not consist in the abstract text of the Bill of Rights as such but in its application, which presupposes weighing and balancing, either between opposing rights or between rights and policy considerations justifying their limitation. In striking down a law, the court as a non-elected and democratically non-accountable body substitutes its own value or policy preferences for those of the legislature. If reasonable people may reasonably disagree on issues of rights, these should be decided in democratically organized political rather than judicial procedures and by representative rather than judicial bodies. Constitutional review and judicial supremacy unavoidably contradict the principles of democracy and separation of powers. The counter-majoritarian difficulty proves impossible to solve.[15]

At first glance, the attack on constitutional adjudication on the grounds of its policy orientation may seem inconsistent: constitutional review is reproached for both too little and too extensive policy-making. The Realists condemned the conceptual deductivism of the *Lochner*-era courts and called for open policy argumentation. In the same vein, present-day critics claim that the courts tend to turn moral and ethical or political controversies into conceptual and doctrinal problems and so camouflage the real issue. This is the first prong of Waldron's case against judicial review. Another line of criticism claims that the inescapable weighing and balancing politicizes constitutional adjudication and involves judges in choices of a political nature for which they lack democratic legitimacy. The two seemingly

---

[14] Ibid 1353.

[15] In addition to Waldron's article, representative criticisms employing the democracy argument include M. Tushnet, 'Policy Distortion and Democratic Debilitation: Comparative Illumination of the Countermajoritarian Difficulty', (1995) 94 *Michigan Law Review* 245–301; M. Tushnet, *Taking the Constitution away from Courts* (Princeton: Princeton University Press, 1999); R. Bellamy, *Political Constitutionalism: A Republican Defense of the Constitutionality of Democracy* (Cambridge: Cambridge University Press, 2007); and R. Hirschl, *Juristocracy* (Cambridge, Mass: Harvard University Press, 2007). Learned Hand, in his much-cited Oliver Wendell Holmes lecture, put the democracy argument very eloquently: '...it certainly does not accord with the underlying presuppositions of popular government to vest in a chamber, unaccountable to anyone but itself, the power to suppress social experiments which it does not approve... For myself it would be most irksome to be ruled by a bevy of Platonic Guardians, even if I knew how to choose them, which I assuredly do not. If they were in charge, I should miss the stimulus of living in a society where I have, at least theoretically, some part in the direction of public affairs. Of course I know how illusory would be the belief that my vote determined anything; but nevertheless when I go to the polls I have a satisfaction in the sense that we are engaged in a common venture. If you retort that a sheep in the flock may feel something like it; I reply, following Saint Francis, "My brother, the Sheep"'. L. Hand, *The Bill of Rights: The Oliver Wendell Holmes Lecture* (Cambridge, Mass: Harvard University Press, 1958), 74–5.

contradictory claims of too little and too much policy-making are both invoked to renounce the justifiability of judicial review of legislation.

Critics and advocates of constitutional review hold divergent views on the controllability of judicial weighing and balancing. Constitutional doctrine has elaborated devices that are supposed to add to its objectivity or at least inter-subjectivity, the most influential of these being the proportionality test, introduced by the German Constitutional Court and subsequently adopted in many other jurisdictions. But those challenging the justifiability of constitutional review by the judiciary detect in the proportionality test the very root of judicial usurpation of political power.[16] By contrast, the defenders of constitutional review praise the proportionality test as a guarantee of the rationality and controllability of basic-rights adjudication.[17]

Criticism has pointed to the courts' lack of democratic legitimacy as well as the institutional competence indispensable for the policy choices allegedly involved in constitutional adjudication. Both the composition of the courts and judicial procedure reflect the aim of securing a fair trial for concrete parties; by contrast, they make the judiciary ill-suited to policy analysis and argumentation. For the US legal process-school of the 1950s and 1960s, this was a central reason for restricting the role of judicial review,[18] and even today it is frequently called upon.[19]

Waldron's core arguments are related to two general dangers which have worried critical observers of over-constitutionalization in, for instance, Germany: the *politicization of adjudication* and the *juridification of politics*. The former is argued to be a consequence of the judiciary's involvement in policy-making: the judiciary intrudes into areas which, in a democratic *Rechtsstaat* (a constitutional democracy), should be reserved for the democratically elected legislature. The claim of *juridification of politics* is inherent in Waldron's accusation of judicial review transforming political into legal-doctrinal issues. But juridification and the crippling of political discourse can also—perhaps slightly paradoxically—be treated as the reverse side of the politicization of adjudication. Constitutional considerations impose restrictions on the legislature's discretion, and legislation is increasingly seen as constitutionally determined, as the unfolding of the implications of the fundamental value choices already made at the constitutional level. This comes close to what Tushnet has called the distortion and debilitation of majoritarian legislative decision-making, proceeding through the injection of 'too many constitutional norms into the lawmaking process, supplanting legislative consideration of other arguably more important matters'.[20]

---

[16] Manfredi, above n 5; D. Kennedy, *A Critique of Adjudication* (Cambridge, Mass: Harvard University Press, 1997), 316 ff; M. Koskenniemi, 'The Effect of Rights on Political Culture', in P. Alston (ed), *The EU and Human Rights* (Oxford: Oxford University Press, 1999), 99–116, at 107–111; Hirschl, above n 5.

[17] M. Kumm, 'Who is Afraid of the Total Constitution? Constitutional Rights as Principles and the Constitutionalization of Private Law', (2006) *German Law Journal* 341–369.

[18] N. Duxbury, *Patterns of American Jurisprudence* (Oxford: Oxford University Press, 1995), 263–4.

[19] eg Waldron, above n 13, 1377.

[20] Tushnet, above n 15, 247.

In summary, the general case against constitutional review is built upon the principles of democracy and separation of powers, as well as the alleged threat of politicization of adjudication and juridification of politics. Two possible ways are available to confront the criticism: either to continue the discussion at a general level or to question the assumptions on which the case is built and which Waldron—to his credit!—has attempted to spell out. The latter strategy implies changing the discursive level and bringing in examples drawn from particular models or circumstances of constitutional review.

At the general level, we can problematize the notion of democracy adopted in the debate on the counter-majoritarian difficulty and by such prominent contemporary critics of constitutional review as Waldron and Robert Bellamy. It equates democracy with the *majority principle*, applied, first, in elections and, secondly, in decision-making in the elected legislature. On such a view, every deviation from the majority principle violates democracy. Other conceptions of democracy, such as those embraced by Habermas and Dworkin, may lead to divergent appraisals of constitutional review.

Habermas's notion of democracy emphasizes the role of discursive deliberations and the necessity of engaging civil society, particularly in debates on the ethical and moral aspects of legislative issues.[21] In contrast to the majoritarian view, the concept of *deliberative democracy* does not restrict the arenas for democratic processes to the legislature. No conceptual reasons exist why constitutional adjudication could not be surrounded by discourses accessible to civil society and not merely to the legal elite. Indeed, as Dworkin is prone to emphasize, the US experience provides us with illustrations of principled debates on constitutional landmark cases.[22] On the other hand, a defence of constitutional review influenced by the idea of deliberative democracy readily grants the primacy of democratic lawmaking procedures. It regards rights-based constitutional review as merely a last resort, remedying the failure to address rights-issues, related to moral and ethical considerations, at the lawmaking stage.

This view of constitutional adjudication implies a call for *judicial restraint*. As a general rule, the courts should not overturn the legislature's policy choices. The principle of separation of powers, the division of tasks between branches of government, and the corresponding institutional competences entail that, as a rule, policy-making should fall to the domain of the political departments, that is, the legislative and the executive. On the other hand, it is clear that constitutional adjudication is inconceivable without weighing and balancing either between competing rights or between rights and policy grounds calling for limitations to rights. This is not a sufficient argument for rejecting the whole idea of constitutional review, but it imposes on constitutional doctrine the task of elaborating devices which could contribute to the controllability of weighing and balancing, such as the proportionality test. In the eyes of the antagonists of constitutional review, this

---

[21] J. Habermas, *Between Facts and Norms*, tr W. Rehg (Cambridge: Polity Press, 1996), 287 ff.

[22] R. Dworkin, *Freedom's Law: The Moral Reading of the American Constitution* (Cambridge, Mass: Harvard University Press, 2003), 345.

may signal the juridification of constitutional—read: political!—issues. But not all juridification is automatically evil; something may exist which we could term *healthy juridification*, referring to the legitimate tasks of constitutional doctrine in the functioning of the legal and political system.

Yet, despite the efforts of legal doctrine to augment the rationality of judicial decision-making, there are convincing reasons for believing that adjudication inevitably includes an intractable element of fiat; if lawmaking is not all will, neither is adjudication all reason. But in the mature legal system of a consolidated democracy, the impact of fiat is moderated by ongoing legal and public discourse that surrounds constitutional adjudication and where the merits of individual rulings are assessed.

During the *Lochner*-era in the United States, critics—many of them Legal Realists or their precursors—attacked the courts' covert policy-making under conceptualist and deductivist camouflage. After World War II, with the shift in emphasis in constitutional adjudication from economic to civil rights, the focus of criticism has altered. When arguing for his case against judicial review, Waldron alludes to legislative controversies, such as those surrounding abortion, which have a conspicuous ethical or moral nature and where the policy aspect, that is, the instrumentalist dimension of practical reason, plays a secondary role; at issue is what might be called *rights-focused legislation*. When a court strikes down such legislation, it does not invalidate the legislature's policy choices, but, rather, its ethical or moral standpoints. If the lawmaking procedure has already included ethical and moral, rights-focused deliberations and if the legislature has explicitly based its decision on such deliberations, the last-resort argument for constitutional review does not justify the court's intervention.

Abortion cases may be the most heatedly discussed instances of constitutional review, but treating them as paradigmatic examples might be ill-advised. Most legislative projects aim at policy goals and pursue economic or social policies, security objectives, and so on. In standard cases, the legislative motive is primarily pragmatic, with rights-related moral and ethical considerations playing at most the role of side-constraints; the relation of pragmatic to ethical and moral aspects is exactly opposite to their respective significance for the law on abortion. And it is such standard cases that the last-resort argument addresses: the rights-issue may go unnoticed during the legislative phase and be detected only at the stage of application.

Concerns about the politicization of adjudication are warranted; they caution against constitutional review overstepping its legitimate boundaries and reversing the explicit policy or value choices of the legislature. They do not, however, deliver a fatal blow to justifiable judicial review but serve merely as a reminder of its limits. Equally relevant is the threat of juridification of politics which can ensue from an overly 'thick' reading of the constitution. Attempts to nail down controversial policy or value choices in constitutional interpretation are prone to restrict the freedom of democratic political deliberation and decision-making. One should also be aware of the dangers of an ossified constitutional doctrine. Nevertheless, the Legal Realist critique or Waldron's juridification argument should not be allowed to obscure the positive role that doctrine plays in ensuring the consistency and controllability of constitutional adjudication. In constitutional law, just as in other fields of law, general doctrines are needed, but they should not be allowed to petrify into ideological constructions which obstruct, rather than facilitate, the framing of relevant issues.

All in all, even at the general level of discussion, I am not convinced of Waldron's case against constitutional review. He points to considerations which are relevant in examining alternative models of constitutional review, but he does not really tackle its fundamental justification as a last-resort guardian of the law's limits. Such a guardian is needed even in a society that meets Waldron's four assumptions and that roughly corresponds to what I have called a consolidated democracy. Failures to attend to basic-rights issues during the legislative phase are possible in a consolidated democracy too. And if the assumptions do not hold in general, which still largely seems to be the case in, for instance, the new democracies of Central and Eastern Europe, such failures are ever more probable.

A different kind of argumentation is called for in countries still engaged in the process of strengthening democratic institutions, setting up a vigorous civil society, and entrenching a constitutional culture to prop up the provisions of the written constitution. Then, quite simply, Waldron's four assumptions or my own presupposition of a mature legal system in a consolidated democracy do not apply. In those circumstances, a constitutional court may even substitute for a non-functioning representative democracy, safeguarding democratic values enshrined in the constitution. Kim Lane Scheppele[23] has argued that post-communist Hungary, particularly before 1998, exemplified 'democracy through judiciary': it fell to the Constitutional Court to defend democracy in a situation where representative channels were blocked. Constitutional adjudication may also play a crucial role in forming a constitutional culture worthy of a democratic *Rechtsstaat*. Constitutional culture can only evolve through constitutional practices and discourses for which constitutional adjudication provides a central forum and incentive.

In emerging democracies, constitutional adjudication pursues specific tasks that are not equally relevant under the idealized conditions which are, consciously or unconsciously, assumed in supposedly general-level normative debates. These tasks also help to explain why post-totalitarian countries have found themselves on the crest of the post-war wave of new constitutionalism and, as a rule, opted for a strong constitutional court.

General-level discussions usually presuppose, implicitly or explicitly, certain institutional and doctrinal choices, specifying the type of constitutional review under consideration and, by the same token, limiting the reach of the arguments presented. Often enough, the discussion relies on the dichotomy of judicial and legislative supremacy, where the former implies strong constitutional review, exercised by a judicial body. This also holds for Waldron's core case. His arguments

---

[23] K. L. Scheppele, 'Democracy by Judiciary, Or, why Courts can be More Democratic than Parliaments', in A. Czarnota, M. Krygier, and W. Sadurski (eds), *Rethinking the Rule of Law after Communism* (Budapest: Central European University Press, 2005), 25–61.

are relevant, but their weight varies depending on the institutional and doctrinal options adopted in the system under examination. This is an additional reason for questioning the success of Waldron's pleading: even in the institutional and doctrinal respect, his purportedly general case against constitutional review rests on assumptions which do not possess universal validity.

III. The Finnish System Among the Hybrid Models of Constitutional Review

Debates on constitutional review are usually centred around three basic constitutional models: the US model of diffused judicial review; the German centralized model of a constitutional court: and the (pre-1998) British model of parliamentary supremacy which does not accept external review of parliamentary legislation. Although the case against judicial review, based on the counter-majoritarian difficulty or the democracy argument and the juridification of rights-discourse, is argued to have a more general reach, it has primarily been based on the US experience. Nonetheless, claims of politicization of adjudication and juridification of politics are familiar in criticism of the German model too. In addition to Germany itself, this model has been adopted in, for example, Italy and Spain, as well as most of the Central and East European new democracies. It differs from its US counterpart not only in the central institutional choice but also in the powers of constitutional review. Both models include the judiciary's power to strike down legislation. But the US model allows this only *a posteriori* and in the context of a concrete case, the powers of the judiciary being confined to 'cases and controversies'.[24] The legal effects of a ruling finding an inconsistency with the Constitution hinges on whether the statute at issue is considered 'facially invalid' or merely 'invalid as applied', besides the decision's general precedent value. The German model allows both abstract *ex ante* control, preceding the entry into force of the legislation under scrutiny, and *ex post* control, linked to a particular case. *Ex post* control can be initiated in two ways: either by an ordinary court referring a constitutional issue to the Constitutional Court for a *preliminary ruling* or through a *constitutional complaint*, filed by a party to a case after all the ordinary legal remedies have been exhausted. The powers of the Court include declaring the statute at stake ineffective.

Because of the traditional prestige enjoyed by German doctrine, German discussion is of particular interest in examining the Finnish model of constitutional review. In Germany, the debate on over-constitutionalization and the alleged 'transition from a parliamentary legislative state to a constitutional-court state'[25] flared

---

[24] A. M. Bickel, *The Least Dangerous Branch: The Supreme Court at the Bar of Politics* (Indianapolis: Bobbs-Merrill, 1962), 113–16.
[25] 'Übergang vom parlamentarischen Gesetzgebungsstaat zum verfassungsgerichtlichen Jurisdiktionsstaat'. E-W. Böckenförde, 'Grundrechte als Grundsatznormen', in Böckenförde, *Staat, Verfassung, Demokratie* (Frankfurt am Main: Suhrkamp, 1991), 159–199, at 190. See also W. Brohm, 'Die Funktion des BVerfG—Oligarchie in der Demokratie' (2001) 54 *Neue Juristische Wochenschrift*

up quite soon after adoption of the Basic Law in 1949 and establishment of the Constitutional Court. Critics have perceived in the Constitutional Court a third legislative chamber, which has not been content with merely playing the role of a Kelsenian negative legislator but has evolved into a most significant positive legislator. With regard to the parliamentary legislature, it plays the upper hand: it is the Constitutional Court that possesses *Kompetenz-Kompetenz*, so that the German model is that of constitutional-court supremacy.

In Ernst-Wolfgang Böckenförde's judgment, the Constitutional Court no longer confines itself to constitutional interpretation but is engaged in concretizing and balancing the values and principles which it has read into the Basic Law. As a result, constitutional adjudication has undergone a process of politicization. This has entailed a legitimacy problem: the Constitutional Court does not enjoy the democratic legitimacy which the role it has adopted in the legal order's development would require.[26]

Simultaneously with and largely as a consequence of the expansion and politicization of constitutional review, lawmaking, too, has altered its character. Legislation is turned into implementation of basic rights: what state functions or policies are to be carried out through legislation no longer depends on democratic political choices but has been determined in advance by constitutional norms. As both the parliamentary legislature and the Constitutional Court are engaged in concretizing constitutional basic-right norms, the qualitative difference between lawmaking and constitutional adjudication fades away. Separation of powers, which requires organizational disconnection of enactment and application of legal norms, is blurred. The parliamentary legislature and the Constitutional Court find themselves in a situation of rivalry, which the Constitutional Court as final umpire can decide in its own favour.

German critics have attacked the Constitutional Court for disempowering not only the legislature but ordinary courts as well. Particularly through the device of constitutional complaint, the Constitutional Court has allegedly established itself as the highest private-law court.[27]

German constitutional development is not a result of merely institutional but also of doctrinal choices. In addition to the Constitutional Court's general activism, three interrelated doctrines, in particular, have been crucial in enhancing its position vis-à-vis the legislature and ordinary courts: the doctrines of basic-rights norms as legal principles; of basic-rights norms' horizontal effect (*Drittwirkung*); and of the state's protective duty (*Schutzpflicht*). Along with the proportionality test, these doctrines, elaborated by the court in close cooperation with constitutional-law scholarship, have had great success in the advance of the global wave of new

---

1–10, where the term *Richteroligarkie* (oligarchy of judges) is used. W. Brohm, 'Die Funktion des BVerfG—Oligarchie in der Demokratie', (2001) 54 *Neue Juristische Wochenschrift* 1.

[26] Böckenförde, ibid 185–7.

[27] This criticism is summarized in the title of an article by Uwe Diederichsen: 'Das Bundesverfassungsgericht als oberstes Zivilgericht—ein Lehrstück der juristischen Methodenlehre' (The Constitutional Court as the highest private-law court—one element of legal methodological doctrine), (1998) *Archiv für die civilistische praxis* 171–196.

constitutionalism. In Finland, they were adopted in connection with the 1995 reform of the basic-rights chapter in the Constitution.

The German model has attained global prominence as an alternative to US-type constitutional review. However, this should not obscure the fact that post-war developments have brought about new intermediary or hybrid forms which cannot be assimilated to the conventional standard options of the United States and the German variants of judicial supremacy or the traditional British model of legislative supremacy. They are often ignored in critical debates, although they can be seen as attempts to avoid the hazards of which critics have warned, while yet acknowledging the principal need for constitutional review. This holds for the innovations which Stephen Gardbaum[28] has gathered together under the label of *the New Commonwealth Model of Constitutionalism*. He alludes to Canada, New Zealand, and the United Kingdom. These are 'countries that were previously among the very last democratic bastions of traditional legislative supremacy'. Between 1982 and 1998 they 'have created a new third model of constitutionalism that stands between the two polar models of constitutional and legislative supremacy'.[29]

Common to the three examples of the 'Commonwealth model' is the endeavour to engage political actors in constitutional review and to establish a dialogue between political and judicial review. Not only in New Zealand but in Canada and the United Kingdom as well, enactment of the Bill of Rights has entailed an intensification of executive and parliamentary 'rights-vetting' through special bodies, such as the UK parliamentary Joint Committee on Human Rights.[30] However, critical observers have detected signs of advancing judicialization, especially in Canada and the United Kingdom, due to judicial activism and the deference of political actors to judicial views. In practice, the borderline between strong and weak forms of judicial review has proven more fluid than constitutional documents would intimate.[31]

The Finnish model of constitutional review, introduced through the new Constitution of 2000, also finds its locus among hybrid or intermediary forms. Its uniqueness lies in its particular combination of abstract parliamentary *ex ante* and concrete judicial *ex post* review.

In Finnish democracy, as in other Nordic countries too, the parliament has traditionally enjoyed a very prominent status, including vis-à-vis the courts. For instance, its elevated position has been manifest by the high ranking of *travaux préparatoires* in the hierarchy of legal sources; higher than that of precedents of

---

[28] S. Gardbaum, 'The New Commonwealth Model of Constitutionalism', (2001) 49 *American Journal of Comparative Law* 707–760.

[29] Ibid 709.

[30] J. L. Hiebert, 'New Constitutional Ideas: Can New Parliamentary Models Resist Judicial Dominance When Interpreting Rights', (2004) 82 *Texas Law Review* 1963–1987; Hiebert, 'Rights-Vetting in New Zealand and Canada: Similar Idea, Different Outcomes', (2005) 3 *New Zealand Journal of Public and International Law* 63–103.

[31] Hiebert, ibid; M. Tushnet, 'New Forms of Judicial Review and the Persistence of Rights- and Democracy-Based Worries', (2003) 38 *Wake Forest Law Review* 813–838; M. Tushnet, *Weak Courts, Strong Rights: Judicial Review and Social Welfare Rights in Comparative Constitutional Law* (Princeton: Princeton University Press, 2008), 43 ff; A. Geddis and B. Fenton, '"Which is to be Master?"—Rights-Friendly Statutory Interpretation in New Zealand and the United Kingdom', (2008) 25 *Arizona Journal of International and Comparative Law* 733–778.

the supreme courts. Before the constitutional reform of 2000, the Finnish system allowed for no *ex post* control by the courts of the constitutionality of parliamentary legislation. Control of constitutionality consisted exclusively of an abstract *ex ante* review, exercised by the Constitutional Law Committee of Parliament.

The Constitutional Law Committee is a peculiar quasi-judicial body. Like other Committees, it is composed of Members of Parliament and, thus, displays a political character. But its deliberations are based on opinions by constitutional experts—mostly university professors—and, as a rule, the Committee abides by their view. In adhering to a legal rather than political pattern of argumentation, its reports are quite different from those of other Parliamentary Committees. For instance, reports routinely refer to constitutional precedents as settling the issue at hand, although the Committee has by no means bound itself to a strict doctrine of *stare decisis*. The experts of the Constitutional Law Committee have no official status, nor is their role even mentioned in the Constitution or the Rules of Procedure of Parliament. Still, it is quite decisive, and it is hardly conceivable that the Committee would depart from a unanimous expert view. If diversity exists among the experts, the political stance of the Members is given more leeway and voting reflecting the government/opposition division occurs, although relatively seldom; the great majority of the reports are unanimous, which, of course, adds to their acceptance among both the political and legal elite as well as the general public. As a rule, constitutional issues pending before the Committee are excluded from controversies defined through the divisions of party politics: parliamentary groups do not adopt positions on them, nor are the members of the Committee subject to party discipline.

Although the Committee belongs to the institutional organization of Parliament, its deliberations are not part of the regular parliamentary procedure. It is only called on when doubts about the constitutionality of a bill have been raised. In contrast to abstract *ex ante* review by many constitutional courts or a quasi-court like the French *Conseil constitutionnel*, the Committee has not been turned into an instrument of the opposition. On the contrary, in standard cases it is the government which, in the bill it submits to Parliament, advises the latter to consult the Committee. Initiation of constitutional review almost never causes political controversy.

The Committee's assessment of a bill's constitutionality is binding on Parliament. However, ever since the nineteenth century, an essential feature of the Finnish model has consisted in Parliament's power to override the Committee's ruling through a *statute of exception*: a bill which the Committee has found to be unconstitutional can still be enacted under the qualified procedure required for amending the Constitution. The option of a statute of exception bears a resemblance to the Canadian notwithstanding clause. Section 33(1) of the Canadian Charter of Rights and Freedoms grants federal and provincial legislatures the right to declare that an Act or some of its provisions are to operate notwithstanding the Charter's substantive provisions on rights and freedoms. This legislative override is effective for a maximum period of five years but may be re-enacted (s 33(3)–(4)). By contrast, there is no time limit to the effectiveness of Finnish statutes of exception.

In Canada, a convention inhibiting in particular the federal legislature from use of the notwithstanding clause has arisen, and on Gardbaum's view, this 'has prevented Section 33 from tempering the countermajoritarian difficulty posed by an unlimited power of judicial review'.[32] In Finland, development in the use of statutes of exception has taken a similar turn. In the decades preceding the constitutional reforms of 1995 and 2000, some constitutional scholars criticized statutes of exception for weakening the protection of basic rights and for transforming *ex ante* constitutional review into a formal assessment of the required legislative procedure. In fact, the number of statutes of exception diminished considerably even before the constitutional reforms of 1995 and 2000. According to the *travaux préparatoires* to the new Constitution, statutes of exception should be resorted to very sparingly, as a rule merely when they are needed for incorporation of an international treaty or some other international-law obligation. Statutes of exception have lost most of their previous significance, and, when finding a conflict with the Constitution, the Constitutional Law Committee no longer contents itself with pronouncing on the procedural question, but indicates how the bill should be amended in order to remove the conflict.

The new Constitution did not bring about any formal changes to *ex ante* control through the Constitutional Law Committee. The major novelty was the introduction of concrete *ex post* control. Article 106 of the Constitution provides that 'if in a matter being tried by a court, the application of an Act would be in evident conflict with the Constitution, the court of law shall give primacy to the provision in the Constitution'. Nonetheless, it would be hasty to conclude that Article 106 would have epitomized a radical break in Finnish constitutional tradition, a decisive transition from the *ex ante* control of the Constitutional Law Committee in the direction of *ex post* judicial review. The courts have only been entrusted with what might perhaps be called a weaker form of strong judicial review: they have the power merely to set aside a piece of legislation in the case at hand, not to declare it ineffective. As was explicitly emphasized in the *travaux préparatoires*, the primary means for the courts to contribute to implementation of the Constitution remains their duty to construe statutes consistently with constitutional provisions. The *travaux préparatoires* stressed the primacy of *ex ante* control under the new Constitution too. This primacy seems to have been accepted by the courts as well. Thus, in its only ruling invoking Article 106, the Supreme Court stated that 'control of the laws' constitutionality falls mainly to the Constitutional Law Committee, which in the legislative process exercises *ex ante* supervision'.[33] In practice, it may well be that the major alteration induced by the possibility of concrete *ex post* control will be more thorough *ex ante* monitoring. Indeed, the Constitutional Law Committee's workload, as measured by the number of its reports, has significantly increased after the basic-rights reform of 1995 and entry into force of the new Constitution in 2000.

---

[32] Gardbaum, above n 28, 726–7; for an early critical assessment, see Manfredi, above n 5.
[33] KKO 2004:26.

In the *travaux préparatoires* to the new Constitution, the primacy of *ex ante* review was anchored in the requirement of an *evident* conflict established by Article 106. If the Constitutional Law Committee explicitly states in its *ex ante* review that a controversial statute is not in breach of the Constitution, it is hardly conceivable that a court could find an evident conflict with a constitutional provision.

In sum, the Finnish model of constitutional review has retained a notable parliamentary label through the central role of the Constitutional Law Committee. The judiciary has not acquired the dominant role which critics of the US and German models have attacked, but merely accomplishes a complementary function. Still, signs of judicialization and a juridification of politics are detectable in Finnish development as well. After all, the Constitutional Law Committee represents a quasi-judicial element within the legislature, and its increased significance may result in a certain juridification of legislative politics. If the Committee is the capital of constitutional law's empire in Finland, the princes of this empire are not the parliamentarian members of the Committee but, rather, the experts the Committee consults: university law professors. Case-law, precedents, and doctrine play an important role in the practice of the Committee, as they do in judicial constitutional review in other systems, although these are the work not of judges but of constitutional scholars. Nonetheless, I would venture to claim that explicit doctrinal changes, reflecting social and cultural developments, are easier to accomplish in a system where a parliamentary body, instead of a court, retains the ultimate formal decision.

In governmental bills submitted to Parliament in Finland, an augmentation of references to constitutional basic-right provisions is visible. This reflects a heightened awareness of basic rights in the legal and political culture and, hence, in principle can be considered a positive phenomenon. Nevertheless, one should also heed the danger of juridification and unwarranted restrictions imposed on the options available to the democratic legislature inherent in this development.

Intermediary forms, such as those epitomizing the New Commonwealth Model of Constitutionalism or the Finnish after-2000 system, prove that constitutional design is not restricted to a choice between the standard models: the US diffused and the German concentrated model of judicial supremacy and the British pre-1998 model of legislative supremacy. The British example warrants the claim that some sort of constitutional review is needed to resolve the perennial problem of the law's limits, and it is doubtful whether traditional British-type legislative supremacy remains a viable alternative. The hybrid forms discussed above have all in their own way attempted to address threats to democracy and separation of powers, as well as dangers of politicization of adjudication and juridification of politics. They demonstrate that constitutional imagination can come up with innovative solutions. But the menace of *gouvernement des juges* has not vanished: recent developments in, say, the UK, Finland, and France, imply that effective constitutional review is hardly conceivable without *ex post* control and without granting the courts a certain role. These countries were among the last strongholds of unquestioned legislative supremacy, but they have all recently retreated from their previous constitutional positions. In Finland, the *travaux préparatoires* to the new Constitution justified complementary judicial *ex post* control with a last-resort argument:

In the (Constitutional Law) Committee, the constitutionality of laws is examined, as it were, at a general level, *in abstracto*, whereas a court assesses the issue in the context of a concrete case. Hence, it is possible that a court detects a contradiction which the Committee has not addressed at all. In such a situation, the requirement for evident conflict can exceptionally be met although the law has passed the control of the Constitutional Law Committee.[34]

IV. Judicial Activism v Judicial Restraint

The consequences of constitutional review for relations between the judiciary and the legislature turn not only on institutional design but also on constitutional doctrines and other factors of the constitutional culture. Often enough, these factors are discussed through the alternatives of judicial activism and restraint. Though afflicted by a certain conceptual vagueness, these terms may be of assistance in a general characterization of the dominant style in judicial review in a particular jurisdiction at a specific point of time. As the US experience shows, periods of restraint and activism may alternate in accordance, *inter alia*, with the resonance that critical normative points stressed by the opponents of judicial review find in the legal and political culture. Much may also hinge on entrenchment of cultural and sociological prerequisites of a democratic *Rechtsstaat* (a constitutional democracy), as is shown by the activist constitutional courts of the emerging democracies in Central and Eastern Europe. For its part, the activism of the European Court of Justice—the 'constitutional court' of the EU—has clearly been related to the difficulties in transnational political decision-making and the particular requirements of building up an entirely new legal system.[35]

The degree of judicial restraint/activism is also affected by the doctrinal apparatus in use in constitutional adjudication. Even explicit constitutional provisions may play a role, such as the requirement of *evident* conflict expressly spelled out in both the Swedish and the Finnish constitutions. These constitutions have, as it were, positivized the plea for judicial restraint. More specific doctrines also exist that call on constitutional adjudication to show institutional deference to the political branches of government, such as the US *political questions* doctrine, which for instance has largely shielded foreign policy decision-making from judicial interference. The European Court of Human Rights, for its part, has clothed its deference to nation-state sovereignty in the *margin-of-appreciation* doctrine, which operates as a deterrent to the court's second-guessing nation-state authorities' assessment of circumstances warranting limitations to Convention rights.[36]

[34] HE 1/1998, p 164.
[35] A. Stone Sweet, *The Judicial Construction of Europe* (Oxford: Oxford University Press, 2004).
[36] J. Viljanen, *European Court of Human Rights as a Developer of the General Doctrines of Human Rights Law: A Study of the Limitation Clauses of the European Convention on Human Rights* (Tampere: Tampere University Press, 2003).

But, of course, doctrines also exist that have rather justified judicial activism and which, therefore, have been targeted by the critics of judicialization. In the German critique of the *verfassungsgerichtlicher Jurisdiktionsstaat*, much has been blamed on the doctrines of basic-rights norms as legal principles with a general scope, the horizontal effect of rights, and the protective duty of the state. These doctrines left a clear imprint on the *travaux préparatoires* to the Finnish reform of basic rights in 1995, and the Constitution has even positivized the *Schutzpflicht* doctrine through an explicit provision (Art 22). But, as I will argue in the following, the evident-conflict requirement puts brakes on the judicialization which these doctrines might otherwise induce.

V. Extension of the Scope of Liberty Rights

In the standard notion, basic rights are subjective rights that protect private individuals from arbitrary exercise of power by state and other public authorities. This notion is related to the traditional power-limiting understanding of the *Rechtsstaat* and the rule of law. And, as Böckenförde[37] argues, this was also how basic rights were conceived in, for instance, the Weimar Republic and the deliberations leading to enactment of the Basic Law in 1949.

Drittwirkung or horizontal effect extends the protective function of liberty rights to hierarchical power relations where both parties are private persons. Such an extension seems reasonable in the light of the often artificial and even porous boundary between the public and the private. The more private relations distance themselves from the principles of liberty and equality, constituting private law's ideological foundation, the more they obtain features typical of public law and the more warranted it is to include them in the scope of constitutional liberty rights. Not surprisingly, in Germany the *Drittwirkung* doctrine was initially adopted by the Labour Court with a view to protecting employees' political rights against encroachments by employers.[38] The US *state action* doctrine—the American counterpart to the *Drittwirkung*—has also largely evolved through cases involving such hierarchical private relations.[39]

The recent wave of privatization—another global phenomenon!—has endowed with new significance and a novel justification the *Drittwirkung* of basic rights, conceived as subjective rights of deterrence. If administrative tasks are privatized, the protective function of basic rights should also be 'privatized', that is, extended to apply to the recipient private organization. One innovation of the new Finnish Constitution is to provide for such instances of privatization. Article 124 lays down that when public administrative tasks are delegated to those other

---

[37] Böckenförde, above n 25.

[38] U. Preuss, 'The German *Drittwirkung* Doctrine and its Socio-Political Background', in A. Sajó and R. Uitz (eds), *The Constitution in Private Relations: Expanding Constitutionalism* (Utrecht: Eleven International Publishing, 2005), 23–32, at 23–24.

[39] E. Chemerinsky, 'Rethinking State Action', (1985) 80 *Northwestern University Law Review* 503; S. Gardbaum, 'The "Horizontal Effect" of Constitutional Rights' (2003) 102 *Michigan Law Review* 387–459; Tushnet, *Weak Courts, Strong Rights*, above n 31, 161 ff.

than public authorities, the law must guarantee that basic rights, legal protection, and other requirements of good administration are not endangered. When public administrative tasks are delegated under Article 124 to entities of so-called indirect public administration, these entities are included in the public authorities directly bound by basic-right provisions.

In sum, it is reasonable to accord liberty rights a horizontal effect in hierarchically structured private relations. Still, at least in Continental civil-law countries like Finland, it is also warranted to ask who should be entitled to decide on such an extension of the range of basic rights: should it fall to the legislature or the courts? It can be claimed that it is primarily up to the legislature, and not to the courts, to assess what types of private relations should fall under constitutional liberty rights. In delineating the public authorities that are directly bound by basic-right norms, fairly precise formal-organizational criteria are available. By contrast, when determining the reach of the horizontal effect of subjective liberty rights, such formal criteria are not at hand; substantive deliberation is needed, and the legislature may be better suited for it than the courts.

In the Finnish system, I would argue that the courts should not, as a rule, apply their review power under Article 106 to grant direct horizontal effect to a liberty right. Given the horizontal effect's ambiguity, it is doubtful that an ordinary law could be found to be in *evident* conflict with the Constitution because of not providing sufficient protection for a liberty right in private relations. By contrast, the courts' duty to construe statutes in conformity with the Constitution encompasses the protective functions of liberty rights in private relations as well. To take an example, statutory provisions that in Finland grant employers a limited right to breach the confidentiality of their employees' e-mail correspondence should be given a narrow reading.

VI. Basic-Rights Norms as General Legal Principles

In German debates, one of the main culprits responsible for alleged development towards a *verfassungsgerichtlicher Jurisdiktionsstaat* has been seen in the doctrine of basic-rights norms as legal principles with all-encompassing scope and entailing the duty of all state organs to contribute to their realization. Ever since its landmark *Lüth* decision of 1958, the Constitutional Court has argued that basic-rights provisions not only create subjective rights but also express *principle norms* that manifest the legal order's fundamental values and that exert their influence in all fields of law. Basic-rights norms define the foundational order (*Grundordnung*) of not only the state but the entire society and contain, as it were, as germs, the normative substance of the whole legal order. Such a conception is already implicit in the doctrine of *Drittwirkung*, introduced by the *Lüth* decision. Initially, though, reference was made merely to the effect of radiation (*Ausstrahlungswirkung*) which basic rights as an objective value order could wield throughout the law.[40]

---

[40] BVerfGE 7, 1958. The case has been presented by eg Preuss, above n 38, 24–6.

Böckenförde argues that the doctrines of *Drittwirkung* and the state's protective duty (*Schutzpflicht*) derive from the definition of basic rights as the fundamental values or principles of the entire legal order: 'Basic rights as principle norms or value decisions point to ... particular normative contents which call for their realisation; they do not function negatively but require action, the protection of these contents'.[41] Basic-rights norms imply constitutional commissions directed to all state organs and calling for their implementation through legislative, executive, and administrative, as well as judicial action. Application of basic-rights norms is converted from *interpretation* into *concretization*: the realization of basic rights presupposes from both the legislature and the Constitutional Court not only interpretative specification of their contents but creative concretization of constitutional value choices or commands of optimization.[42] The result is juridification of legislative politics and politicization of constitutional adjudication.

Böckenförde has also tried to show that in German doctrine, no clear distinction can be made between indirect and direct horizontal effects of basic-rights principles, but that the former inevitably leads to the latter. Indirect effect is realized through the general clauses of private-law legislation and statutory interpretation in general. If, however, basic rights cannot be implemented through statutory interpretation, this is not the end of their *Drittwirkung*. Thus, the German Constitutional Court has assumed the power to strike down private-law legislation for insufficient attention to basic-rights principles. The Constitutional Court has also allowed for constitutional complaints (*Verfassungsbeschwerde*) to be grounded in basic rights' *Drittwirkung*. The claimant may argue that, in a private-law case, the ordinary courts have not paid due respect to a basic-right norm's indirect or direct horizontal effect. Critics, among them Böckenförde,[43] have been concerned about the Constitutional Court becoming the final court of appeal in private-law cases and of appropriating ultimate interpretive power not only within public law but in private law as well.

The conception of basic rights as general legal principles possessing a comprehensive scope of application and providing all fields of law with their normative basis clearly manifests the constitutionalization of the legal order. A similar tendency has been noted not only in Germany but in many other countries too: for instance, in Spain,[44] France,[45] and, after the 1995 basic-rights reform, even in Finland. It has significantly contributed to the general turn towards argumentation from principle in the previously rule-oriented Continental European legal systems. Should we speak here of over-constitutionalization, leading towards a jurisdiction state? Is threatened or perhaps even partly realized jurisdiction-state development

---

[41] Böckenförde, above n 25, 173.

[42] R. Alexy, *A Theory of Constitutional Rights*, tr J. Rivers (Oxford: Oxford University Press, 2002).

[43] Böckenförde, above n 25, 177–80.

[44] P. Bon, 'La Constitutionnalisation du Droit Espagnol', (1991) *Revue Francaise de droit Constitutionnel*, 35–54.

[45] L. Favoreu, 'Constitutional Review in Europe', in L. Henkin and A. J. Rosenthal (eds), *Constitutionalism and Rights* (New York: Columbia University Press, 1990).

to be localized in this direction? Are proposals to introduce basic-rights-related principles into general doctrines of diverse fields of law—such as criminal law, environmental law, property law, or the law of obligations—accelerating this development? Should these proposals be warded off as lapses endangering the principles of democracy and separation of powers?

The overall consequences of constitutional review result from the interplay of institutional and doctrinal factors. What repercussions the notion of basic-rights norms as 'objective-law principles' will have depends on how constitutional review is organized and how the power of the judiciary is determined. German criticism is premised on the existence of a constitutional court and the constitutional complaint as a legal remedy. The Finnish system does not include a specialized constitutional court nor anything corresponding to the German *Verfassungsbeschwerde*. Nor, too, do the ordinary courts have the power to strike down private-law legislation for its purported contradiction with basic-law principles. Yet the Finnish Constitution does contain an explicit provision on protective duty. Article 22 of the Constitution lays down that 'the public authorities shall guarantee the observance of basic rights and liberties and human rights'. Nonetheless, it is hardly justifiable that a court could find such an *evident* contradiction between a basic-right principle and a statutory provision which would vindicate application of Article 106 of the Constitution. The principles of democracy and separation of powers entail that the protective duty under Article 22 of the Constitution falls primarily to the legislature: it is up to the legislature to guarantee realization of basic-rights principles in the horizontal relations between private persons. Accordingly, the courts should fulfil their protective duty within the legislative framework and grant basic-rights principles merely indirect effects, unfolding through statutory interpretation.

Matthias Kumm has questioned the significance for the German constitution of the distinction between indirect and direct effect, invoking largely similar arguments as Böckenförde. However, unlike Böckenförde, Kumm sees the collapse of indirect into direct effect in mainly positive terms.[46] He portrays opposition to a 'total constitution' and to private law's subordination to constitutional law as the German private-law establishment's campaign to retain the high status it has enjoyed as the guardian of the *Bürgerliches Gesetzbuch*—the climax of German legal scholarship and legal culture.[47] Conversely, scholars from other doctrinal domains may understand expansion of the reach of basic rights as a sign of 'constitutional-law imperialism'. The interlocutors' strategic interests in the power play in the field of law certainly illuminate the context of discursive interventions. But, of course, this does not prevent us from discussing the interventions in terms of the normative credentials of their arguments.

Much can be said in favour of basic-rights principles invading other areas of law. Basic-rights connections fortify the justification of general legal principles

---

[46] M. Kumm and V. F. Comella, 'What is So Special about Constitutional Rights in Private Litigation? A Comparative Analysis of the Function of State Action Requirements and Indirect Horizontal Effect', in Sajó and Uitz (eds), above n 38, 23–32; Kumm, above n 17.
[47] Kumm, ibid 360.

and create conditions for a new kind of cross-boundary dialogue between the law's departments; a dialogue necessitated by the frequent cross-boundary nature of current legal problems. Furthermore, a common basic-rights foundation adds to the law's principle-based coherence. Finally, heightened sensitivity to basic rights and legal principles may lead to more overt argumentation in Continental European legal systems. Even those worried about the consequences of judicialization from the viewpoint of democracy can hardly regard this as other than a positive development: it facilitates discursive monitoring of the court's case-law not only by legal professionals but by the media and the general public as well.

Yet to see all ordinary law as implementation of constitutional law and all adjudication as (potential) constitutional adjudication would be erroneous too. Deference should be shown to the doctrinal traditions of the established branches of law, such as private law with its sub-fields, or criminal law. Basic-rights principles should primarily unfold their effects indirectly, through the intermediary of 'field-specific' principles. Constitutionalization adds to the justification and institutional support of field-specific principles, and may also lead to adjustments in their normative content, but the general doctrines of other fields of law should not be allowed to be replaced by constitutional doctrine. Otherwise, much sedimented legal *ratio* would be lost. Nor should the specialized legal competence and pre-understanding of judges and scholars dealing with other departments of law be allowed to be devalued through over-constitutionalization.

VII. Confrontations between Horizontal and Vertical Effects

The traditional vertical effects of basic rights, related to the liberal *Rechtsstaat* notion, and their *Drittwirkung*, obliging even the legislator, do not always sit comfortably together. Indeed, the recently found horizontal effect may weaken the protection that basic rights offer against the possible abuse of power by the public authorities. Likewise, when basic-rights principles are taken together with the legislator's duty of concretization and implementation, their difference from common goods and policies may be obliterated. I take as my example the right to security. Article 7(1) of the Finnish Constitution states that 'everyone has the right to life, personal liberty, integrity and security'. Correspondingly, Article 5(1) of the European Convention on Human Rights provides that 'everyone has the right to liberty and security of the person'.

'Security' is a tricky concept. It can connote either a collective good—in the sense of 'national security' or 'public safety and order'—or an individualized right to personal security. In its case-law, the European Court of Human Rights has interpreted Article 5(1) of the Convention in line with the latter alternative. Furthermore, it has in general treated security of the person as a non-independent right, auxiliary to the right to liberty. By contrast, the Constitutional Law Committee of Finland has been inclined to understand Article 7(1) of the Constitution in the sense of a collective good, particularly in its early post-1995 case-law. This reading is based on three argumentative steps.

First, the right to security is detached from the rights to personal liberty and integrity, and assigned independent legal relevance. This already points to the direction of a common good: it is hard to see what independent legal meaning, irreducible to the rights to liberty and integrity, could be attributed to an individual right to personal security. Secondly, the Constitutional Law Committee has invoked the horizontal effect of basic rights norms and, thirdly, the legislature's protective duty. On these grounds, the Committee has concluded that the state—in this case, the legislature—is obliged to ensure realization of the independent right to security in horizontal relations between private individuals. In this way, public safety and order as a collective good has been elevated to a basic right with a rank equal to that of individual liberty rights. At the same time, the distinction between policies aimed at collective goods and principles focusing on individual rights has been effaced.

Even without the support of an explicit right to security, a combination of horizontal effect and protective duty can always be employed to justify, say, new powers for the police or other security authorities; such powers can always be claimed to be necessary for guaranteeing realization of basic rights in private relations. On the other hand, police powers usually touch on basic rights purporting to protect individuals in their vertical relations with public authorities, such as rights to personal integrity, privacy, or confidentiality of correspondence. Now, the constitutional acceptability of police powers can be maintained to hinge on weighing of basic-rights principles of equal rank, although with a different locus of application along the horizontal or vertical axes. What, according to liberal constitutionalism and the traditional *Rechtsstaat* notion, was to be restricted through basic rights—executive and administrative power—is, as it were, absorbed within the basic-rights system. In Germany, this point has been raised in criticism of the Constitutional Court's argumentation and Robert Alexy's basic-rights theory as the codification and justification of the Court's case-law.[48]

Although often lumped together, Dworkin's and Alexy's views on principles display significant differences. For Dworkin, the distinction between principles, related to individual rights, and policies, related to collective goods, is crucial; indeed, it provides the very basis for his taking-rights-seriously thesis.[49] Alexy, by contrast, tends to discard it. He has been criticized for equating principles (individual rights) and policies (collective goods) and for according them equivalent normative and argumentative weight. As an example of balancing between principles, Alexy[50] has evoked a Constitutional Court case where the central issue was whether legal proceedings could be launched against a defendant whose health, and even life, could have been endangered if he had been obliged to appear in court. In Alexy's (and the Constitutional Court's) account, decisive for solution of the case, was which of two principles of equal rank was accorded greater weight: the efficiency of criminal justice, or the right to life and

[48] Alexy, above n 42.
[49] R. Dworkin, *Taking Rights Seriously* (London: Ducksworth, 1978).
[50] Alexy, above n 42, 50 ff.

personal integrity. Let me present a rather lengthy citation from Ingeborg Maus's critique:

[T]his artificially induced collision of principles in individual cases...owes its existence to a concept of constitution which is diametrically opposed to the liberal constitutional concept asserted in the 18th/19th centuries. The constitution in the classic sense of the rule of law [the *Rechtsstaat*—KT] always presupposed as a fact the functional efficacy of the organs of the state and criminal prosecution and determined their limitations. This functional efficacy itself need not be guaranteed by a constitution, but is greatest without any constitutional regulation whatsoever....the efficiency of constitutional organs of the state cannot itself be the content of a constitutional principle, because the ratio essendi of the constitution consists precisely in restricting this efficiency....when common goods can also be regarded as principles....constitutional guarantees of freedom compete with principles which are opposite not only in terms of their content, but also in terms of their entire structure, such as the efficiency of criminal justice, the 'efficiency of the Bundeswehr' or the 'efficiency of national defence'..., the 'efficiency of the enterprise and the economy as a whole'... Not only basic rights guaranteeing freedom, but also freedom-limiting state functions themselves are a measure of judicial review....the constitution loses its function of limiting the spread of government powers.[51]

The constitutional *Rechtsstaat* doctrine involves a peculiar dialectic between collective goods and individual basic rights. On the one hand, the main thrust of basic rights—here I am alluding to first-generation liberty rights—is seen in creation of a sphere of private autonomy, secured against infringements by public authorities acting in the name of collective goods, such as public safety and order or national security. But the guarantees that basic rights provide are not—with some important exceptions—absolute: limitations are permitted, in order to promote collective goods similar to those whose purport the rights are intended to restrict. This might seem paradoxical, but the solution to the paradox is quite simple: the limitations may not touch upon the kernel (the *Wesensgehalt* of German doctrine[52]) of the right in question.

Even if we reject Alexy's levelling down of the Dworkinian distinction between principles and policies, we seem to be compelled to concede policies' (re-)entry into constitutional doctrine as grounds for limitations to basic rights. Determining their constitutional relevance certainly involves weighing and balancing, for example in applying the proportionality test. However, this weighing is not internal to the basic-rights system but involves a basic-rights principle and an external policy factor. This portrayal also corresponds to the structure of the European Convention. The Convention refers to policy standpoints, but these define acceptable grounds for limiting rights and not the rights themselves. Article 8(1), for example, guarantees everyone the right to respect for private and family life, home, and correspondence. Paragraph 2 of the same article includes the limitation clause: 'There shall be no interference by a public authority with the exercise of this right except

---

[51] I. Maus, 'Die Trennung von Recht und Moral als Begrenzung des Rechts', (1989) 20 *Rechtstheorie* 191, 197–9.
[52] The Basic Law includes an explicit provision (19(2)) on the *Wesensgehalt*: 'In no case may a basic right be infringed in its essential content'.

such as is in accordance with the law and is necessary in a democratic society in the interests of national security, public safety or the economic well-being of the country, for the prevention of disorder or crime, for the protection of health or morals, or for the protection of the rights and freedoms of others.' In the context of the Convention, abolition of the distinction between principles and policies would amount to eradicating the boundary separating protected rights from the grounds for restricting them.

To sum up the normative message of the preceding discussion, the horizontal effect of basic rights should not be allowed to water down their traditional *Rechtsstaat* function of creating safeguards for individuals against policy-oriented exercise of power by public authorities. When basic-rights norms as legal principles are assigned horizontal effect and when the legislator is ascribed the duty to realize them, principles acquire a policy tinge: along the way, the right to, say, liberty or personal integrity may be transformed in all but name into a policy of law enforcement and public security.

VIII. Conclusion

The Finnish model, based on a combination of abstract parliamentary *ex ante* review and judicial *ex post* control, has managed to ward off at least some of the dangers of which critics of judicial review and the ensuing tendency towards a jurisdiction state have warned. Clear emphasis has been laid on *ex ante* monitoring and courts seem to have accepted the role which the last-resort defence of judicial review assigns to them. An integral part of the present balance between parliamentary and judicial control consists of the evident-conflict requirement established by Article 106 of the Constitution. It has conveyed a general call for judicial restraint and restricted the impact of the German doctrines of basic-rights norms as legal principles with a general scope, the horizontal effect of rights, and the protective duty of the state. Originally, the evident-conflict criterion was borrowed from the Swedish Constitution. At present, constitutional reform is under deliberation in both Sweden and Finland, and voices have been raised for abolishing this restriction on *ex post* judicial constitutional review. This, I think, would be a mistake.

19

Judges without a Court—Judicial Preview in Sweden

Thomas Bull

I. Introduction

The discussion on the legitimacy of judicial control of legislative powers is wide-spread and has deep historical roots. It takes somewhat different routes in different countries, but the main themes are the same: how and when can it be acceptable that unelected judges reject democratically accepted legislation? The answers to this question differ a lot, as can be seen in the European setting, where Constitutional courts with extensive powers to control legislation exist in some countries, while on the other side of the border such powers for courts are considered totally out of the question. Countries like Germany and France come to mind. This essay deals with issues of judicial control from the perspective that such control can possibly be less intrusive in a political system of democracy if the control is not exercised in courts, but instead in institutions that scrutinize legislation before it is enacted. In the constitutional discourse, judicial control of legislation is often divided into judicial review, a system where courts usually get the power to try enacted laws against constitutional provisions in concrete cases where such an issue arises. The archetypical example of such a system is in the United States and the review made by the Supreme Court of the United States. The other system is often called judicial preview, which simply means that legislation is scrutinized before it comes into effect. France, with its well-known institution of the 'Conseil Constitutionnel', is an example of such a system of judicial control.

Sweden has both judicial review and judicial preview. Courts and public authorities are empowered by the constitutional provision in Chapter 11 § 14 of the Instrument of Government not to apply laws (or statutes) that come into conflict with higher law. However, if the Parliament has enacted the legal rule in question, such non-application shall only be made if the conflict is clear. The message is that particular care should be taken before taking such a step. Later, I will return to this power and its impact on the system of preview in Sweden. In Chapter 8 § 20, the constitution provides for a Law Council (*Lagråd*) with the task of scrutinizing government bills for legislation before they are introduced to the Parliament. This preview concerns the relationship to constitutional law as well as other aspects of the proposition. It is this institution I will concentrate on in this essay.

However, the system of preview of legislation is wider than may appear from this provision. The Swedish system of the preview of legislation in order to ensure that constitutional and human rights are respected can be said to consist of four main components: the system of legislative committees in preparing legislation, open access to public documents and the right to publish those, the expert opinions of the Law Council, and scrutiny by the Constitutional Committee of the Parliament. Together, these four components of the preview system make it hard, though not impossible, to legislate in a way that infringes fundamental rights. In this chapter I will give some concrete examples of how these institutions interact and I will attempt to show situations when the system has worked as well as when it has not. The focus will be on the role of the Law Council, as I think this institution might be the one most particular to Sweden and therefore of most interest in a comparative context. Before delving deeper into that subject I will give a brief outline of the other components I have deemed fundamental to the Swedish way of protecting fundamental rights.

II. Legislative Committees, Access to Public Documents, and the Constitutional Committee of the Parliament

(a) Legislative committees

The system of legislative committees is the basis of the Swedish legislative procedure. It is a long-standing tradition to have any issue of upcoming legislation fully examined and deliberated upon by such a committee. The constitutional basis for the system of legislative committees is found in the rather vague provision that all governmental business should be well prepared before the government takes any decision in Chapter 7 § 2 of the Instrument of Government (IoG).[1]

In short, the Swedish system has these basic features: Committees are composed of either MPs from all parties represented in Parliament or an expert on legislative matters (typically a Supreme Court judge with experience in the law department of the government or a professor of law/political science). As a rule, the committee also consists of experts from governmental agencies working in the field to be regulated and other experts (most often professors). The committee will make a public report containing any proposals necessary for new legislation. Every year about 150 such reports are delivered to the government, some of which attract a lot of media coverage.

---

[1] The Swedish constitutional law that deals with institutions, competences, and rights. Sweden has three other constitutional laws; for a comprehensive overview of the Swedish constitutional system, see I. Cameron, 'Protection of Constitutional Rights in Sweden' [1997] *Public Law* 488.

The report is then—once again following the regulation in the IoG—sent for comment to a wide range of institutions and organizations. This includes governmental agencies, courts, and universities, but will also include unions and NGOs. These bodies will be given the chance to make written comments on the proposal, and often the government wants to have such comments within three months. These comments can be of any kind, but often end up approving the proposal (in whole or in part) or in advising the government not to base any bills on the committee's proposal. As there is a constitutional right to petition the government at any time, everyone can comment on a committee report, but of course the government pays more attention to comments from some institutions or organizations than others.

The report and the feedback which the commentators make is then used by the relevant government ministry in the next stage of the process of legislation. A ministerial report with a proposal (in practice often nearly identical to the report of the committee) is produced and presented to the Parliament, which will in due course vote on it. In case a proposal raises constitutional issues (institutional or individual rights), it will be reviewed by the Constitutional Committee of the Parliament and the Committee will produce a written statement to the Parliament on those issues. In that report, comments from the earlier stages of the procedure can reappear, as politicians in Parliament will look for anything that will support their argument about a certain law proposal. Typically, however, Parliament will then adopt the proposal by making it law.

It can be said that this rather cumbersome legislative procedure is the core of the Swedish system of protection of fundamental rights. With any other system of review, it is really too late, that is, the rights have already been infringed. With a legislative process that has mechanisms to ensure that constitutional rules and human rights standards are respected in almost all cases, the need for review in courts is dramatically reduced.

Of course, the benefits of this system should not be overstated. The era of legislative committees working for decades to produce perfect legislation is over and the working conditions of committees are now such that they have fewer staff and less time to do their work. That work has also changed somewhat, from presenting ambitious 'major solutions' with totally new legal regimes to 'patchwork' on the existing legal framework. Furthermore, at times government and Parliament push through constitutionally dubious legislation even in the face of widespread opposition from (more or less) neutral institutions. The ability to respond politically to legal arguments against a certain legislative solution is not always great. Rational discourse can sometimes only go so far, but a system where multiple voices will be heard in multiple arenas before any final decision is made can be more rational and more prone to favour legal arguments than a more closed system of legislation.

(b) Access to public documents

The second part of the system of protection of individual rights in Sweden that we need to look at is the right to have access to public documents. According to the constitutional provisions of the Freedom of Press Act,[2] every citizen has the right to see public documents promptly and to obtain a copy at 'cost price'. The documents can of course be classified as secret according to the Openness and Secrecy Act of 2009 (OSA), but that act is very detailed and quite restrictive on when a document can be withheld on the grounds of secrecy. The presumption is openness and some special circumstances must be present in order to not disclose a public document. The OSA does not give a lot of latitude to public officials and their judgment is subject to appeal in an administrative court of appeal.[3] Apart from situations where a person's identity can be of importance for the application of the Secrecy Act, public bodies are not even allowed to pose questions on who the applicant is and why access is requested.

In the context of rights protection, this system makes it possible for journalists and others to access many government documents prior to the point when the government wants them made public. In that way, access to public documents complements the system of legislative committees, as reports and other materials from such committees will be publicly available. Secondly, open public access to public documents has an important restraining effect on the public administration's opportunities to use its lawful powers in an arbitrary or discriminatory way. Such misuse of public power can often be revealed by delving into the public documents.

As for legislative committees, the Swedish system of access to public documents has some problems when it comes to day-to-day practice. It is well documented that public officials, particularly in local government, are poorly trained in these areas of law and have a tendency to refuse access without any legal support.[4] Furthermore, whether or not the OSA gives a very detailed legal framework for decisions on access, the Act itself is very complicated in structure and also quite extensive. Few lawyers and judges would confidently state that they feel at ease navigating through the Act. Some of these faults may have been fixed by the new OSA that came into force in 2010, but that piece of legislation is even more extensive than the old Act so some issues will become worse. In spite of these critical comments, open access to public documents has played an important role in ensuring that the legislative process and the public decision-making process has been reasonably aware of the limits of public power.

---

[2] The Freedom of Press Act is another of Sweden's four constitutional documents. That access to public documents is regulated therein is a sign of how closely the Swedish constitutional legislators thought that right to be connected to a wide freedom of expression.

[3] That decision can in turn be appealed in the Supreme Administrative Court and these appeals are free of charge. An illustrative case is the judgment of the Supreme Administrative Court in a case (RÅ 1998, ref 42) where a governmental agency denied access due to international relations with the United States. The US government had in fact expressed a certain irritation with the Swedish way of giving access to documents otherwise protected by intellectual property law. In fact, the OSA makes it possible to declare a document secret if its disclosure would seriously affect Swedish international relations. However, the Court found that this provision could not be interpreted so as to include irritation as such, but had instead the purpose of protecting national security, something that was not an issue in the case. The Court struck down the agency's decision on secrecy.

[4] See the Parliamentary Ombudsman's annual report (2008/2009) at 547 and 555 (available at <http://www.jo.se>).

(c) The Constitutional Committee of the Parliament

The last piece of the puzzle in the Swedish system of protection of rights is the role of the standing Constitutional Committee of the Parliament. This Committee was established in 1809 and thus celebrated its 200th jubilee in 2009 and is regulated in Chapter 13 IoG. The Committee is to have ongoing parliamentary control of the government. It consists of 17 members of Parliament, with an MP from the opposition as chairperson. The majority in Parliament also has a majority in the Committee. It is supported by a secretariat of around five persons with a background in law and/or political science.

The controlling function works in two ways in practice: via complaints and investigations.[5] First, the Committee takes on constitutional complaints against individual ministers (or the government as a whole) from members of Parliament. In order to explain these complaints, a brief insight into Swedish constitutional law is necessary. In Sweden, individual ministers have no legal power to govern in the name of the government. Governmental decisions are always collective decisions, taken by at least five ministers and signed by the Prime Minister.[6] Furthermore, the government is constitutionally prohibited from stepping in and affecting any specific decision by the administration in cases concerning the rights or duties of individuals or the application of law.[7] Unlike most countries, in Sweden the government cannot 'pick' an individual case from its administration and decide that itself.[8] Lastly, when the government uses its constitutional prerogative of appointing positions in the public administration (usually the heads of governmental administration), it is constitutionally bound to take such decisions on objective grounds such as merit and experience.[9] At times appointments to public offices are controversial, for example when someone without any prior experience from that field is appointed to head a public administration or when someone with mostly political experience is given such a position. Such appointments may be suspected of being 'rewards' to the individuals involved rather than based on the objective criteria constitutionally required. A complaint can then be filed against the government in the Constitutional Committee on grounds of the unconstitutional use of the power of appointment.

---

[5] This is not wholly true, as the Committee also has the power to prosecute government ministers for grave errors committed in the course of their duties. Such a prosecution is made directly before the Supreme Court, Ch 12 § 3 IoG. This power has, however, not been used since the 1850s, so there is no practical reason to dwell further upon it.

[6] See Ch 7 §§ 3 and 5 IoG.

[7] See Ch 12 § 2 IoG.

[8] This is, however, not as strange as it might seem, as in Sweden the government has been the highest administrative authority for a long time, deciding cases on appeal from the administration. In that way, the government has a tool that can affect the administration's decisions, but only as a correctional instrument. The European influence on the Swedish administrative system (EC law and Article 6 of the ECHR making it necessary to involve courts in many cases that previously were decided in the administrative order), together with a more general wish to free the government from administrative burdens, has led to a diminishing role for the government as an institution for appeals. Naturally this has also led to weakened control over the way administrative justice is done.

[9] Ch 12 § 5 IoG.

Together with the above-mentioned rules on 'well-prepared' governmental decisions, these rules are the legal basis in the Swedish constitution for most of the Constitutional Committee's work with complaints against individual ministers or the government. The Committee will make an inquiry in each case (it has no power not to take up a complaint) and issue a statement to the Parliament in a report. The report can be more or less critical; stating whether the Committee has found any unconstitutional actions by the government and/or actions that are not clearly illegal, yet are not appropriate, and thus should be avoided in the future. Members of the Committee have the right to differing opinions, which are published together with the report. This report can then lead to debate in the Parliament, to unwanted publicity in the press, and—in rare cases—to a vote of no confidence against a certain minister or the government as such.

As the Committee's majority reflects the majority in the Parliament, most complaints against the government or individual ministers will not lead to any criticism or any other consequences. Only in cases where it is absolutely clear that the government has committed an error, will the Committee be united in its evaluation of the constitutional issues. In other cases, the Committee's interpretation of the constitutional provisions will tend to be somewhat coloured by its political relations with the government. But it should be stressed that the Committee seldom interprets the Constitution in a legally unacceptable way. There are three major reasons for this: first of all, most constitutional provisions are open to several interpretations that are equally 'correct' and in most cases no court will ever settle disputes because of a lack of jurisdiction. There is, generally speaking, a certain room for manoeuvre here. Secondly, the Committee has a secretariat with legal expertise of the highest quality. The head of the secretariat has a position almost comparable to a judge in the Supreme Court or one of the Parliament's Ombudsmen. The rest of the secretariat consists of former judges or academic lawyers and political scientists with a doctoral degree. This means that the Committee gets expert legal advice on a continual basis and it is clearly reluctant to go against such advice. Totally outrageous interpretations of the constitution do not often happen.[10]

Thirdly, even if a majority of the Committee were inclined to interpret a constitutional provision in a certain way, the minority has a weapon against the majority in the right for a minority of five members to refer any issue to the Law Council for consultation.[11] In this way, the minority in the Committee can put the majority

---

[10] They do happen, but in those cases it is often not only the politicians of the Committee who are to blame. One such instance was in the interpretation of the time-limit of 'at the most 15 days' for gathering a minority of 35 members of Parliament in order to propose that the Parliament should decide to hold referenda in connection with a revision of the constitution. The Speaker of the Parliament interpreted this as meaning that there was no minimum time to gather the required minority and therefore gave the parliamentarians involved three days, after which the summer break would start. The Committee found that the Speaker's interpretation was in line with the constitution's wording and even if this is true strictly speaking, it means that the Speaker can set any ridiculously short time-limit for such a motion, in practice robbing the minority of their opportunity to take constitutional revisions to the people. It is clear from the preparatory work for the provision in question that this is contrary to the purpose of the regulation, which was to guarantee the minority 15 days, but no more. See 2003/04 KU9, p 103 and prop 1978/79:195, p 64.

[11] In 2009 this has so far been the case on two occasions, but only once on the initiative of a minority of the committee. The issues at hand were the very controversial bill on same-sex marriages

in the awkward situation of having to argue against the Law Council's interpretation of the constitution. A decision to go against the Law Council would generally
generate a lot of media attention and is something that would only occur in specific
contexts.[12] So, in this way, the minority can steer the majority away from the more
exotic interpretations of constitutional law.

III. The Law Council—Some Details

The Law Council celebrated its 100th jubilee in 2009 and over the years it has
remained more or less unchanged as an institution. The current Swedish constitution provides for the existence of a Law Council in Chapter 8 § 20 of the
Instrument of Government. The provision states that the Law Council shall consist
of judges and retired judges of the Supreme Court and the Supreme Administrative
Court. In a special law on the Law Council, the composition of the council is
further specified. To simplify somewhat, the law stipulates that the Law Council
should normally consist of six persons, of whom four should be acting judges of
the Supreme Courts.[13] The remaining two can be retired judges from the same
courts. The Courts choose who to send to the Law Council, not the government,
and this is usually done so that each judge takes his or her 'turn', serving two years
on the Council. The Law Council works in two sections, with three members in
each, and in each section there should be at least one member with experience of
the Supreme Court and one from the Supreme Administrative Court. Additional
members can be appointed for short periods at times of major legislation—making
up a third section—and the Council can also be reduced to only one section at
quieter times.[14] Formally, this is a decision of the government, but in practice it is
the most senior member of the Law Council who either makes a request for additional members or informs the government of a lack of work, to which the government will respond.[15]

---

and a rather technical bill on salaries for members of Parliament. In 2008 there were also two cases
of such referrals, one concerning decisions within the EU on combating organized crime and the
Swedish legislation in relation to that, the other being an issue of documentation of the financial
interests of members of Parliament. A majority supported the referral in both cases. The trend seems
to be that fewer referrals are initiated by a minority and that there are fewer referrals overall.

[12] Such as when there are very complicated political agreements. One example would be the
reorganization of the asylum procedure in Sweden a few years back. At the time, the government
had promised the Green Party such a reform in exchange for support for the budget. When the Law
Council produced a highly critical report on the reform, the government was more or less powerless
to respond in any substantial way, as the deal had to be respected (see opinion by the Law Council,
2005-10-20).

[13] It may be mentioned that the Supreme Courts do not of course let members who have tried legislation as members of the Law Council later take part in a judgment on the constitutionality of that
same law. This is necessary to protect the courts from accusations of partiality just because members
of the court may have been involved in scrutinizing certain legislation at an earlier stage.

[14] During 2007–9 the government appointed a third section several times in order to get large
pieces of legislation through the Law Council.

[15] Of course, at times the government finds that appointing further members would impair the
ability of the courts concerned to function properly and therefore it does not act upon a request to

Furthermore, Chapter 8 § 21 IoG states that the government should grant a hearing to the Council in legislation on a wide ranage of subjects and generally if the bill is of importance to individuals or the public. This 'hearing' takes place prior to the bill being presented to Parliament, but after the wider hearing described above as part of the system with legislative committees. The government is never bound by the opinion of the Law Council and it is specifically stated that the fact that the Law Council has not been heard is no reason for not enacting the law. The Law Council is in this sense only an advisory body, and its opinions have no formal legal effect.[16] As can be seen, the Law Council is a very different creature from the more well-known Conseil Constitutionnel in France, which does not consist of professional judges, cannot scrutinize any bill before it is passed, but does have the power to veto already accepted legislation. In the French case, scrutiny is not made regularly, but rather on demand from a political minority of the Parliament, taking the political struggle into the judicial arena. Because of these substantial differences, one should be careful to draw any parallels between the two institutions. The impact of the Law Council on the legislative process is both more and less than the Conseil Constitutionnel. Less because it cannot veto anything, more because it is able to scrutinize much of the legislation and because its composition of acting and former judges of the Supreme Courts has widespread practical implications.

The Law Council's scrutiny of bills focuses on five specific issues: the relationship to the constitution, the internal relationship of the proposed statutes, the relationship to the principle of legal certainty, whether the law is constructed in a way that will make it able to provide the results sought after, and, finally, to detect issues that may become problematic in practice. It is clear from this brief list that the Law Council can be said to fulfil two very different tasks: the first is quite technical, concerning the logic of law and its effects. This kind of scrutiny can be of value, as it can help the government (and the Parliament) to make better laws as such. Experienced judges—often with experience of legislative work themselves—will try to remove any rough edges in the proposed bill by seeing to it that terms and concepts are consistent with existing law, make suggestions for new wording of individual statutes if they are imprecise or unintelligible, etc. In these instances, one might say that the Law Council works as a highly qualified proofreader.

The second task is quite different; the Law Council should check any upcoming legislation against constitutional law and the principle of legal certainty. This involves the constitutional rules on the delegation of legislative powers to the government and local authorities, the protection of constitutional rights, and the general principle that legislation should be introduced in a foreseeable way.[17] This kind

strengthen the Law Council. This is, however, very unusual and does not occur even once a decade, but much more seldom.

[16] As will be discussed below, the fact that some of the highest judges in the country find a bill to be unconstitutional is a strong argument for not legislating in such a way, as the Swedish constitution contains a provision on judicial review as well (Ch 11 § 14) that empowers courts not to apply a law (or statute) that conflicts with higher law.

[17] See C. Sampford, J. Louise, S. Blencowe, and T. Round, *Retrospectivity and the Rule of Law* (Oxford: Oxford University Press, 2006) for a general discussion of such issues with a certain focus on common law jurisdictions.

of scrutiny comes much closer to the sensitive boundary between law and politics. The idea is of course that the Law Council should make a legal analysis, but there has been a historical discussion in Sweden on whether it sometimes oversteps its role. We will return to this issue below. It is in this context that we can talk about the Law Council as a form of judicial preview, as it will give its opinion on the constitutionality of bills that the government intends to present in Parliament.

As is clear from the above, the Law Council gives a form of expert legal advice that all governments get one way or another from institutions within the government. In that way, there is nothing special about the Law Council. The institutional context of being part of the legislative machinery is made more obvious in the placing of the constitutional provisions on the Law Council, and its place is in the chapter on legislation (Chapter 8) rather than the one on constitutional control (Chapter 12). What marks it out from most other institutions that give legal advice is that because the Law Council consists of the (sometimes retired) highest judges in the country, its advice carries special weight both as being independent advice and as being from 'a source of law' in the Swedish legal system. Furthermore, this advice is given in full view of the public, open to all to peruse and discuss, facilitating informed public debate on complicated legal/constitutional issues.[18] This means that the expert legal opinion from the Law Council has a much wider impact and function than similar legal advice that takes place solely within the government.

I would wish to make a final point on these rather technical issues. First of all, it must be noted that the constitutional provision in Chapter 8 § 21 makes it mandatory to hear the Law Council in any legislative procedure.[19] The provision makes two explicit exceptions: if it would be of no importance or if it would delay the legislation such that major negative consequences would follow. The first of these exceptions concerns situations with very simple legislation. One example might be where certain terminology is changed in a law and because of this, the same changes will have to be made in connected laws, a phenomenon that might be called 'follow-up legislation'. In such a case, scrutiny by the Law Council would be of little value. The second exception concerns all kinds of negative effects and gives the government a certain room for manoeuvre over whether to hear the Law Council or not.[20] In practice, it seems that the government would decline to hear the Law Council in certain cases of tax legislation

[18] I think this might be one of the more important features of this institutional order, as it removes the government's 'monopoly' on expert legal opinion and makes it impossible for government to push through legislation without publicly acknowledging constitutional—or other—problems that might otherwise go unnoticed.
[19] Before 1971, it was obligatory to hear the Law Council in certain areas of legislation, but that requirement was abolished as being too much of an intrusion of judicial power in the political process. In 2010, the rule on mandatory consultation of the Law Council was reintroduced.
[20] Remember that the Constitutional Committee of the Parliament will review the government's practice of hearing the Law Council annually (or bi-annually) and criticize the government if any misuse of this power not to hear it is detected. In extreme cases, this could of course lead to a vote of no confidence in Parliament, but that is somewhat unlikely in practice.

for reasons of the perceived negative effects of such a hearing and the time it would take.[21]

Lastly, it should be mentioned that in its bill to the Parliament, the government will comment on the opinion of the Law Council. This will sometimes be done in order to draw attention to the fact that the Law Council has had nothing to say, which is quite usual. On the other hand, in cases of criticism, the government will want either to let it be known that it has changed the proposition since the Law Council made its comments or it will argue for its own view more substantially.[22] A now-retired judge of the Supreme Administrative Court has expressed the view that only in a handful of cases during his two years on the Law Council did the government go against the opinion of the Council and that only in one or two of these cases did he really regret that they had not been able to persuade the government of their point of view.[23]

IV. Preview in Practice

Now we will turn our attention to the Law Council and its practical role. It is possible to discuss several different themes here, such as constitutional interpretation, political impact, etc. I will organize the text around the content of the Law Council's opinions, with special attention to the type of critique the Law Council expresses. The critique can, simply stated, be non-existent, substantial; and either legal or technical; and minor; and either legal or technical. I will only give concrete examples from the last two groups as the first theme is somewhat empty of substantial content.

Something should however be said about the way the Law Council works in practice. Any bill intended for Parliament that needs to be heard by the Law Council will be sent to the office of the council. Then, some time afterwards, which can vary according to how extensive and complicated the text is, the responsible public official from the government will be called to the Law Council office (close to the Supreme Court's offices in Stockholm) to present the bill orally to the section in question and to answer any questions the members of the council may have. In cases of large legislative products, this 'interrogation' can go on for days

---

[21] It may be noted that members of the Law Council have expressed the view that the government never needs to wait for the Law Council, but that the short time sometimes available to the Law Council makes more sophisticated scrutiny impossible. See the Swedish legal journal *Svensk Juristidning* for a thematic volume on the Law Council (2009, p 201) (R. Lavin, retired judge of the Supreme Administrative Court).

[22] Professor B. Bengtsson in *Svensk Juristidning*, above n 21, 216–60. It is clear that the government has certain techniques for 'disarming' critical opinions from the Law Council that takes legal expertise to see through. For example, statements in a bill that the government 'in principle has followed the opinion of the Law Council' may be nothing other than disinformation. Nevertheless, Bengtsson's conclusion is that the government in general—and particularly the public officials that in practice construct the laws—take the Law Council's arguments seriously and that the system contributes to higher quality legislation than would otherwise be the case.

[23] R. Lavin, *Lagrådet och den offentliga rätten 1999–2001* (Lund: Juristförlaget i Lund, 2001), ('The Law Council and Public Law 1999–2001'), 160.

and it is clear that it can be a less than pleasant experience for the government's civil servant.

(a) Nothing to say

In this context it is enough to establish that many opinions from the Law Council are 'blanks', that is, the Law Council finds no reason to comment on anything in the proposed bill. For 2009 the Law Council has so far given 100 opinions. Of these, 24 have been without any comment whatsoever. In 2008 there were 119 opinions and 38 of these were 'blanks'. From these two years, we can see that around 25 per cent of the opinions contain no comment at all, while in the rest— around 75 per cent—the Law Council will have some minor or major comment. Already from this, we can draw the conclusion that the Law Council makes some kind of difference to the legislative process, as the government will have to consider the comments before presenting a bill to Parliament.

One might mention one factor of importance here, namely that some comments by the Law Council are never put into the official minutes of proceedings or the opinion and thus are not made public. These comments may concern spelling corrections or other 'minor' faults in the text. This practice is of course useful, but has recently been criticized by a member of the Law Council, as it has turned out that the comments—often made in a special paper and given to the governmental official present—are not saved by the government and thus are not available as public documents. There are reasons to believe that such a practice might actually be in conflict with the constitutional provisions on access to public documents. Notwithstanding, it means that there are some critical comments that never see the light of day and that the decision to make an 'important' comment or a 'minor' comment is in the hands of the Law Council itself. This can be criticized for giving too much power to the Law Council concerning what goes public and what does not, even if it certainly saves individual governmental officials from some public embarrassment.

(b) Minor critique

The most common kind of comment in the opinions of the Law Council is on technical issues such as the exact phrasing of a certain paragraph or the structure of a law. The Law Council will try to ensure in such comments that the legislation consistently uses the same words in the same meaning and that laws are structured in a way that is as easy as possible for citizens to grasp. It is quite clear that the Law Council in recent years has become more and more prone not only to pinpoint inconsistencies and room for improvement, but to suggest new wordings in the legislation at hand. These suggestions can at times be rather extensive, but it is clear that they are formulated in a dialogue with the government representative that presents the legislation to the Law Council. In that way, the Law Council's suggestions have a better chance of coming close to the intentions of the government.

Most comments of this kind are not really very exciting and they raise few, if any, democratic issues.

There are types of minor critique that are of more interest to us. In some opinions, the Law Council will voice a general but careful critique on the intended legislation. This can be done in several different ways. In a recent opinion on a law on the Swedish language, the Law Council found that the very vague and abstract statutes in the law, combined with the lack of any instruments for control or sanctions, made it dubious from a legal point of view.[24] Aspects other than what could suitably be legislated on had obviously been decisive in the government's decision to put forward this law, the judges wrote. The government's view, that the Swedish language needed a firmer symbolic position in the law, pointed, according to the Law Council, towards a constitutional amendment instead of an ordinary law. However, a law could in itself lead to greater awareness of the importance of the Swedish language and the Law Council had no further comments.

What we see here is a critique of the means used to achieve a certain goal—greater awareness of our language's importance to our culture and political system. A symbolic manifestation of that kind would, in the view of the Law Council, be more appropriate in the Instrument of Government, which already contains some rather vague paragraphs on the general goals of the public sphere.[25] This is an example of a judgment that is not wholly based on legal considerations and where the Law Council can have no real hope of getting the government to change its mind about having a law on the status of the Swedish language. But the judges cannot abstain from expressing a critical opinion on adopting legislation with no real function other than a symbolic value. In the long run, such use of the law can undermine its normative power and one might suspect that such considerations are behind the opinion of the Law Council.

Another example of such a general and 'soft' critique is the Law Council's opinion on a bill proposing to abolish certain statutes of limitation in criminal law.[26] The intended legislation takes away the period of limitation for murder and some international crimes like genocide and makes such crimes punishable no matter when they were committed. This is rather a dramatic change to Swedish criminal law, which has had periods of limitations for all crimes, and for such serious crimes, of up to 30 or 35 years after the crime was committed. The Law Council notes that the government wants to let this new regulation cover crimes already committed, that is, where the period of limitation is still 'running'. After noting that the constitutional prohibition on retroactive criminal legislation does not hinder such a rule, the Law Council nevertheless states that it has been a generally accepted principle of Swedish criminal law that such legislation should not be adopted. The judges note that the legislation proposed contains a major break with that principle, something that in itself is debatable. On the other hand, in the

---

[24] Opinion 2009-03-02, see <http://www.lagradet.se>.

[25] In Ch 1 § 2, a number of such goals are listed, but with the intention that no legal consequences should follow from that list.

[26] Opinion 2009-10-14, see < http://www.lagradet.se>.

case of international crimes, the change is motivated by adapting Swedish law to the Rome Statute of the International Criminal Court and in other instances, the government argued for the change on the grounds of public opinion, as well as the strong interest of bringing such crimes to justice. The Law Council concluded that it could accept the changes for the reasons given, in spite of the principle objections that were raised.

Once again we see that the Law Council is critical, but does not want to stop or remake a proposition for law. This time it is not the use of legislation as such that draws judges into the grey zone between law and politics, but the clear abandonment of a generally accepted principle in Swedish criminal law. Such a first step—however well motivated—can be the start of a more general undermining of that principle and thus signify something more serious and troubling that the government seems to acknowledge. The Law Council's opinion can be seen as a way of reminding the government (and the Parliament) of the basic principle involved and of the need to have strong reasons for not following it. In such cases it can perhaps not be avoided that the opinion can be interpreted as somewhat 'political'.

(c) Major critique

Let us now turn to more dramatic opinions by the Law Council, in which the judges really act as an instrument for the protection of rights. One such instance was in 2004 when the government wanted to legislate to prohibit the concealment of identity in public gatherings.[27] The proposition was full of legal problems, as the government wanted to make it illegal to wear anything that could conceal the identity of a person whenever a gathering of people was taking place. In practice, it would become criminal to wear a scarf and cap while queuing for a bus in cold weather. Remember, Sweden is still—climate change notwithstanding—a country with cold winters. It would not take any kind of concrete threat to public order to make such acts illegal, and the concealment of identity was in itself considered to be a disturbance of public order by the government. The Law Council made short work of the proposed law and found it unconstitutional as well as contrary to the European Convention on Human Rights (ECHR). The main objection was that in no way was it proportionate to criminalize all concealment of identity regardless of the situation at hand and the concrete threat to public order and that the proposition did not contain any exceptions for situations when concealment could be perfectly legitimate, such as when refugees from a country wished to demonstrate outside their country's embassy in Sweden without putting their relatives at home at risk of reprisals. The government made some substantial changes before going to the Parliament and there the minority of the Constitutional Committee asked to hear the Law Council once again. This time the Law Council found the law constitutional and in accordance with the ECHR, but still voiced some doubts as

[27] Opinion 2004-09-29.

to whether it would really match up to the intentions of the government (securing public order in demonstrations).[28]

In this case we see that the Law Council really did make a difference. The government changed most of its original proposition in order to accommodate the points of view of the judges. It must be remembered that this could be the result of at least three different ways of reasoning. First of all, the government might have been persuaded by the Law Council's arguments and therefore became inclined to change its law. Secondly, the government might dread the media coverage of going to Parliament with a law so thoroughly 'trounced' by the Law Council. Thirdly, the government had to reckon with what would happen if such a law were to be accepted by Parliament and then applied in practice. In such situations, the instrument of judicial review would crop up (Ch 11 § 14 IoG), as, even with the restrictive approach of Swedish courts when it comes to the power of judicial review, the risk of getting the law declared unconstitutional in court proceedings would be considerable.

Not long after, the government wanted to introduce the opportunity to 'bug' with hidden microphones the homes of people suspected of certain crimes, a kind of surveillance technique that the Swedish police had hitherto not been allowed. In its opinion on the proposition, the Law Council had several critical comments.[29] It started off by stating that such intrusions into the privacy of citizens needed very strong reasons, and narrow and precise limits to its application. Furthermore, special procedures were likely to be necessary in order to avoid misuse of the new powers. The Law Council went on to conclude that the same idea had been presented to it in 2000 and had been severely criticized at that time. The new proposition had taken some of the criticism into account, but not all.

The Law Council noted that the government's argument in favour of introducing these instruments was vague and without any deeper analysis. It was unclear if, when, and how this instrument would be of use in solving crimes. The Law Council also noted that the law's field of application was wider than seemed strictly necessary to combat terrorist crimes and international organized crime, which the government argued were the prime targets of the new police powers. Instead, the use of hidden microphones would be possible in 'ordinary' murders, rapes, and economic crimes without any connection to terrorism or organized crime. It was therefore doubtful whether the new legislation could be deemed to be proportional. Furthermore, the Law Council found that the rules did not contain any mechanism in order to live up to the demands in ECHR Article 13 on an effective judicial remedy and that the proposition lacked any discussion on this topic. All together, the Law Council was of the opinion that the law should not be adopted at all and that if it was, some rather substantial changes had to be made in the statutory text to make it more precise and to ensure that no other persons' privacy than that of the 'suspects' was intruded upon. In the end, the government presented the

---

[28] Opinion 2005-11-02.
[29] Opinion 2006-02-24.

proposal to the Parliament in a slightly amended version, and argued for the retention of the rules in most cases.[30] The law was adopted according to the proposed bill.[31]

In this case we can see that the Law Council largely 'failed' to convince the government of the weak parts of its proposition. This can be partly explained by the very general critique made by the Law Council, as it questioned the need for this new instrument and the basis of establishing such a need. One might suspect that this was a need based not on scientific studies of what kind of police powers actually reduce crime, but rather on a 'common sense' opinion on the need to do something about the (alleged) growth of serious crimes; a more or less political judgement that is hard to fit into a legal test of proportionality.[32]

One last example of the work of the Law Council concerns the above-mentioned rights to access to public documents protected by the Freedom of Press Act. In 2007, it became clear that a lot of data had been preserved from the automatic control systems of the government on who was passing in and out of the offices of the government from a period at the end of 2004. This coincided with the world-shaking Tsunami catastrophe in Asia in December 2004. Recordings of this had—by mistake it seems—been kept. At the time, there was a delicate issue in Sweden about who had done what in government—a critique being voiced on the passivity and lack of clear responsibility from the government in times of crisis. The erstwhile Prime Minister Göran Persson was the target of some of the harsher comments. The issues of what he knew and what he had done and what his closest staff knew and had done was of great importance in domestic politics at the time. In that situation, it was timely indeed that the above-mentioned recordings suddenly appeared. Journalists and others immediately asked for access to the recordings in order to verify what the officials in the government had said about their whereabouts at the critical time. Legal confusion broke out. Were the recordings 'public documents'? Could access be denied based on the rules in the Secrecy Act? And so on.

In this situation, the government speedily prepared a new paragraph in the Secrecy Act. The idea was to make the recordings secret and thus unavailable to the public. In the proposal, all of the material was to be regarded as secret and the secrecy restrictions would last for 70 years. The main reason for this was said to be the risks of exposing the working habits of members of cabinet and leading civil servants to foreign powers and persons that could be a threat to their security.[33] The Law Council found the intended legislation to be unconstitutional for the simple reason that the Freedom of Press Act sets out specific criteria for why a public document may be kept secret and while the protection of national security is one

---

[30] Prop 2005/06: 178 .

[31] Law SFS 2007 :978.

[32] And it may be noted that the principle of proportionality in a way contains the seeds of its own undoing, as the greater the threat perceived, the more draconic measures may be proportionate.

[33] One should not forget that the Swedish Foreign Minister Anna Lindh was murdered in Stockholm in 2003 and that the danger to leading political figures against this background was felt to be real.

such criterion, it was inconceivable that *all* the information recorded (consisting of millions of sheets of paper in total) was of that nature. The proposal was changed so that the recordings could be kept secret if certain risks were at hand and this had to be decided case by case.

In this case, the clear rules in the Freedom of Press Act and the well-established principle of open access to public documents were enough to convince the government of the lack of wisdom (and the illegality) in proceeding with its original intentions. Nevertheless, since that time the government has not given up. Recently, the government came back to the issue and presented a new piece of legislation to the Law Council.[34] This time the idea is to make a specific exception in the Freedom of Press Act for such recordings, where they are kept as safety copies, from the concept of a 'public document'. Such data would then never be a public document and thus the constitutional rights to access to such document would never be a problem again. This illustrates that in a constitutional democracy, the political institutions have the last say, if necessary by changing the constitution itself. In such cases, there are no 'supra-constitutional' norms that can be used by the Law Council as arguments against the change.

All in all, we see that the Law Council can 'discipline' the legislative process in several ways when it comes to protecting rights. It can in some cases more or less force the government to make changes, but there are also situations where even highly critical opinions will not stop the government from getting its legislation passed. An educated guess would be that in normal cases, the Law Council will have a good chance of getting the government to accept its opinion, but in cases of 'high politics'—that is, relating to international cooperation or explicit promises made in elections—this does not apply.

V. Preview and Review—A Balancing Approach?

Finally, we come to the point where some kind of general evaluation of the Swedish system of protection of rights can be made. It is important to point out that no single factor determines how this protection works in practice and that looking at the Law Council in isolation is not enough to understand its function and role. The most important parts of this complex role are twofold: one is the way the Law Council's opinions will make a qualified legal analysis available to the public and thus influence public debate and political discourse. The second is the way the opinions of the Law Council interact with the power of judicial review. A law that has passed the Law Council without any criticism on constitutional or human rights grounds will rarely (if ever) be found unconstitutional in a case of judicial review. At the same time, a critical opinion that raises such fundamental issues will put the government in a difficult spot if it does nothing to accommodate the Law Council. The threat of judicial review is then a factor to take into account and something that can—and often does—make a difference. Even cosmetic changes,

---

[34] Opinion 2009-10-12.

made for such reasons, may have some benefits in the end as courts tend to take the wording of laws seriously.

It is thus difficult to say whether the Law Council would have the same position in the Swedish legal system without the balancing existence of judicial reviews. This factor has also been the starting point for the revision of the Swedish constitution that is currently taking place. The Law Council's position will be further enhanced so as to make it possible to avoid judicial review in a legal world that is growing more and more complex and in which the legislator thus runs the risk of 'doing it wrong' all the more often.[35] With a strict judicial preview, the need for judicial review diminishes and courts can generally be kept out of the discussion on the legislation's accordance with higher norms. But, as has been argued above, the mere existence of review is one factor that contributes to making the preview effective.

On the other hand, preview of the Swedish kind, without any acceptance of an institution of judicial review, is something that we have had experience with. The right and duty of courts not to enact unconstitutional laws was codified as late as 1980 and debated until then. During the long period of 1909–80, the Law Council contributed, in much the same way as portrayed here, to the quality and content of legislation without any clear threat of judicial review. Against this background, perhaps the importance of an institution of judicial review as a complement to preview should not be overstated. The authority of the persons serving in the Law Council, its ways of phrasing the opinions in legal and rational terms, and the publicity of those opinions can be quite enough to ensure a major impact on the political process even without the tool of judicial review. Anyhow, we see that it is not only the opinions themselves that matter, but the context in which they are presented.

That being said, is it impossible to export the institution of the Law Council to other countries without exporting the whole package of Swedish legislative process? And maybe the Swedish legal and political culture even has to be exported with those institutions in order for them to function as they do in Sweden. I do not subscribe to the view that institutions or concepts can never be 'transplanted' for the reasons implied by these questions, but it is important to recognize the limits of copying an institution in a totally new context.[36] A Law Council in England or Canada will never be the same as the Swedish institution and its role and function will also be different. This does not have to mean that it will have to be so much different that it will not be at least similar to the institution we know in Sweden. In a year when the Swedish Parliamentary Ombudsman celebrates its 200 years in existence, it is clear that such constitutional exports can be of value to other systems even if they do not end up being 'the same' as the

---

[35] See SOU 2008: 125, pp 377–9. The duty to hear the Law Council will be expanded and the Council will get more resources so as not to be totally in the hands of the government as regards background materials etc.

[36] For a discussion of such problems, see Teubner, 'Legal Irritants' (1998) 61 *Modern Law Review* 11 and contributions in the thematic issue on 'Constitutional Borrowing' of (2003) 1 *International Journal of Constitutional Law* 177, 177–403.

original. Ombudsmen around the world, more or less like the original Swedish Ombudsman, contribute to the protection of individual rights and the idea of the rule of law. The basic idea of having an independent expert, easily accessible and inexpensive, to supervise administration so that it follows the laws and behaves in an acceptable way has caught on. I think that the same can be said for the Law Council. The idea of a highly qualified legal analysis of legislation about to be presented to Parliament, independent of government and in full public view could be exported without using the specific Swedish solutions on the details. I do believe that we can learn from each other and a conversation between the constitutional traditions of the world is, or can be, beneficial. Maybe that could lead to smorgasbord and ombudsman being accompanied by 'lagrad' in the exports of Swedish to our global (legal) language.

20

Rights and the Citation of Foreign Law

Jeremy Waldron

I. *Roper v Simmons* (2005)

In March 2005, the US Supreme Court decided that a state could not execute a man for a crime committed when he was a child. The case is *Roper v Simmons*.[1] Christopher Simmons was 17 in 1993, a junior in High School, when he and a bunch of friends (who were even younger than he was) cruelly murdered a Missouri woman. They burgled her home, they tied her up, they bound her face completely with duct tape, and then they drove her to a railroad trestle and threw her in a river. They told themselves they could get away with it because they were minors.

After bragging about the murder to his friends, Simmons was arrested and confessed to the police. A few months later, once he was 18, he was tried as an adult, convicted, and sentenced to death. He appealed on the ground that execution for a crime committed when he was a minor would be cruel and unusual punishment. His argument was that since minors are, on the whole, less mature than adults, they are less culpable for the offences they commit; and since Eighth Amendment jurisprudence requires the states to reserve the death penalty for their most heinous offenders, it should not be applied to people in this category. The Missouri Supreme Court accepted that argument and overturned the death penalty, substituting life imprisonment without parole. The state appealed to the Supreme Court of the United States.

The Court split 5-4, with a bare majority ruling that the imposition of the death penalty for a crime committed when the offender was a juvenile *was* cruel and unusual punishment. In reaching that decision, Justice Kennedy, who wrote for the Court, noted that the juvenile death penalty was already unusual in the United States; only three states had executed people in this category in the last ten years and eighteen death penalty states explicitly forbade it. Plus—and this was the controversial bit—he said it was also highly unusual by world standards. We ought to consider, he said,

the stark reality that the United States is the only country in the world that continues to give official sanction to the juvenile death penalty.... [O]nly seven countries other than the

---

[1] *Roper v Simmons* 543 US 551 (2005).

United States have executed juvenile offenders since 1990: Iran, Pakistan, Saudi Arabia, Yemen, Nigeria, the Democratic Republic of Congo, and China. Since then each of these countries has either abolished capital punishment for juveniles or made public disavowal of the practice.[2]

Justice Kennedy acknowledged that 'the task of interpreting the Eighth Amendment remains our responsibility'. It is not a job for foreigners. But he said that American courts needed to take the foreign consensus into account for this case, just as they did when they decided in 2002 that states couldn't execute mentally retarded defendants.[3] 'It is proper', said Justice Kennedy, 'that we acknowledge the overwhelming weight of international opinion against the juvenile death penalty... The opinion of the world community, while not controlling our outcome, does provide respected and significant confirmation for our own conclusions.'[4]

II. The Controversy

The citation of foreign law in *Roper v Simmons* exploded in controversy, inside and outside the Court. Justice Scalia blew up. He said 'the basic premise of the Court's argument—that American law should conform to the laws of the rest of the world—ought to be rejected out of hand'.[5]

Outside the court, there were ferocious newspaper editorials, death threats against some of the justices, and ugly talk of impeachment. Legislation was introduced in the Congress which would prohibit any reliance by a federal court on foreign legal materials ('other than English constitutional and common law up to the time of the adoption of the Constitution of the United States').[6]

And the issue has become a staple of legal scholarship in the United States, as American law professors try to make sense of a practice that legal systems everywhere else seem to have no difficulty with whatsoever. There is no time to cite that literature or adduce evidence for the commonplace references to foreign law in other members of the family of legal systems to which the United Sates belongs. Suffice to say—in the latter connection—that every Commonwealth lawyer is intimately familiar with citing to other Commonwealth and American jurisdictions. We do this all the time, and it is part of our training to be familiar with these sources and law reports. I was trained in New Zealand; in a recent decision addressing some difficult questions about the application of the New Zealand Bill of Rights

---

[2] Ibid 575.
[3] *Atkins v Virginia* 536 US 304 (2002).
[4] *Roper v Simmons* 543 US 551 (2005), at 578.
[5] Ibid 624.
[6] eg Constitution Restoration Bill, s 201. 'In interpreting and applying the Constitution of the United States, a court of the United States may not rely upon any constitution, law, administrative rule, Executive order, directive, policy, judicial decision, or any other action of any foreign state or international organization or agency, other than English constitutional and common law up to the time of the adoption of the Constitution of the United States.'

Act to the behaviour-modification regime applied in Auckland prison to prisoners whose conduct was violent or disruptive, the NZ Supreme Court cited twenty-two American cases, nine Canadian cases, eighteen cases decided by the European Court of Human Rights, three South African cases, eight United Kingdom cases (these were in addition to six Privy Council decisions that were cited), ten decisions by the UN Human Rights Commission, as well as seventeen New Zealand cases.[7] New Zealanders find it amusing to hear American lawyers complaining about how they can possibly be expected to cite anything other than American decisions in a disciplined and responsible way.

III. Foreign Law, Democracy, and Judicial Review

Many who oppose the citation of foreign law in cases like *Roper v Simmons* do not question the right of Supreme Court to overrule decisions, though for some it reinforces concerns about the over-use of this power—that is, it reinforces their concerns about what is sometimes called 'judicial activism'.

What about those who oppose strong judicial review? How should they feel about American judges citing foreign law? Well, let's take it step-by-step. The decision in *Roper v Simmons* involved an unelected court modifying the application of a Missouri statute (its legislative provision for the death penalty for murder); accordingly opponents of strong judicial review should be expected to oppose this use of judicial power. The question is: should these opponents be *further* offended by the Supreme Court's citation of foreign law—the absence of the juvenile death penalty elsewhere in the world—to support its decision? Or does it make no difference to their opposition to this exercise of judicial power?

It might seem that they should be further offended. After all, strong judicial review is opposed as undemocratic; the decisions of foreign judges and foreign legislatures have no democratic legitimacy in the United States; so the use of such decisions by American courts seems to aggravate the anti-democratic character of their striking down or modifying American statutes. To put it another way: one of the most persistent and ferocious criticisms of the Supreme Court's recourse to foreign law is that it is undemocratic. The practice allows the decisions of foreign courts to have influence over the fate of Americans, who have neither participated in the election of the politicians who appointed the foreign judges, nor voted for, nor as a people adopted or had any opportunity to amend the charters and constitutions that these foreign judges are supposed to be interpreting.[8] True, it doesn't give the foreign judges direct authority over us, but through the medium of judicial review, it subjects us (in the words of Justice Scalia) to 'the subjective views of five Members of this Court and like-minded foreigners'.[9]

---

[7] *Taunoa v Attorney-General* [2008] 1 NZLR 429.
[8] See eg R. P. Alford, 'In Search of a Theory for Constitutional Comparativism' (2005) 52 *UCLA Law Review* 639, at 709–10 and R. Alford, 'Misusing International Sources' (2004) 98 *American Journal of International Law* 57, at 58–61.
[9] *Roper v Simmons*, 543 US 551 (2005), at 608.

I have no doubt that the existence of strong judicial review in the United States makes the issue of recourse to foreign law more difficult; it certainly makes it politically more volatile. People are already uneasy about judges having the authority to strike down what representative legislatures have done, and that uneasiness is bound to be exacerbated by a sense that this power is being exercised on the basis of law that is not specifically ours. I fear that the background resentment of judges in America translates into an inability to think intelligently about many of the sources of law that judges might use.

Actually, there is no reason in principle why recourse to foreign law should be the monopoly of liberals or judicial activists. Used honestly, it might contribute to judicial restraint or to outcomes that are judged conservative or deferential by American standards. In my Storrs lectures, I cited a South African case that used foreign law (that is, non-South-African law including, notably, American law) to reach a deferential result.[10] In the end, the crucial thing is to figure out whether recourse to foreign law is being used honestly or dishonestly, opportunistically or in a principled manner. Obviously, in order to figure this out, we have to have some account of the theory and jurisprudential principle behind the practice, and that's what I have been trying to arrive at in my recent work on this subject.[11]

I believe that that enterprise is separable from the issue of judicial review. I am inclined to say that if strong judicial review of legislation is an undesirable practice, then it is undesirable *whatever* the courts cite as the basis of their decisions. It is undesirable whether particular exercises of judicial review are grounded in the text of a country's constitution or in foreign law or in the free-standing moral cogitations of the members of its courts.

The logic of this position might work as follows. One can imagine someone opposing the judicial use of foreign law, but accepting that it might still be appropriate as a matter of legislative responsibility. They might say: 'It is perfectly permissible for legislators to cite foreign law in their speeches, to use it to motivate their votes, and to resort to it as a basis of their legislative initiatives'.[12] It would seem odd to criticize *that* practice as undemocratic. We would say, surely, that it may or may not be a good thing for our elected legislators to cite foreign law, but it makes no difference to the political legitimacy of their actions; it leaves their democratic credentials—it leaves the issue of their democratic legitimacy—untouched. Why *similarly* should we not say, then, that the citation of foreign law by judges may or may not be a good idea, but that it leaves the issue of their legitimacy untouched. It makes no difference, we might say, to the legitimacy (or illegitimacy) of their striking down legislation.

---

[10] *President of the Republic v Hugo* (1997) (6) BCLR 708.

[11] J. Waldron, 'Foreign Law and the Modern Ius Gentium' (2005) 119 Harvard Law Review 129; Jeremy J. Waldron, ' "Partly Laws Common to All Mankind": Foreign Law in American Courts', The 2007 Storrs Lectures, Yale Law School, September 2007, available at <http://www.law.yale.edu/news/5408.htm> (forthcoming in a book to be published by Yale University Press).

[12] Justice Thomas said in *Foster v Florida* 123 SCt 470, 472 (2002) at 470: 'Congress, as a *legislature*, may wish to consider the actions of other nations on any issue it likes'.

It will become apparent that I feel the pull of this argument. But it is not a knock-down argument and there is more to be said.

Suppose strong judicial review *is* a desirable or legitimate practice; then there is a further question of what sources of law its exercise ought to be based on. The use of some possible sources might seem to detract from the desirability or legitimacy of strong judicial review. If we thought judges were simply relying on their own subjective moral views or their party-political affiliations, then those inclined to favour judicial review might be tempted to rethink their position. They might say something like: 'Strong judicial review is OK in principle, but not when it is exercised like *this*'. The citation of foreign law might be a factor of this kind. It might tend to intensify any misgivings that one has about strong judicial review. And if it does that (for strong judicial review's wavering supporters), surely it must aggravate or intensify the opposition of strong judicial review's opponents. It may be impossible to aggravate the opposition of a fanatical opponent, but even then you wouldn't expect that opponent to be *indifferent* to the practice of citing foreign law.[13] And certainly a moderate opponent of strong judicial review may find his opposition growing ever stronger as he sees courts continually citing from sources that themselves fall foul of the democratic standards that motivate his position in the first place.

Justice Scalia is not an in-principle opponent of strong judicial review, but he has his doubts about the practice. And his dissent in *Roper v Simmons* does package the two issues together. Scalia thinks it is an outrage that the Court is taking decisions about juvenile death penalty away from state legislatures, and he thinks it is particularly outrageous that this is being done partly in deference to foreign law.

> The Court thus proclaims itself sole arbiter of our Nation's moral standards—and in the course of discharging that awesome responsibility purports to take guidance from the views of foreign courts and legislatures. Because I do not believe that the meaning of our Eighth Amendment, any more than the meaning of other provisions of our Constitution, should be determined by the subjective views of five Members of this Court and like-minded foreigners, I dissent.[14]

Here's another possible route to the same conclusion. Some of us oppose strong judicial review of legislation. But we do not oppose judicial review of executive action (or subordinate legislation or agency rule-making). But we might support these practices because we believe it is important for the executive and its agencies, and other sub-units in the political system, to be held to the standards laid down

[13] Cf J. Allan and G. Huscroft, 'Constitutional Rights Coming Home to Roost? Rights Internationalism in American Courts' (2006) 43 *San Diego Law Review* 1, at 58: 'Our second reason for wariness is that bill of rights adjudication takes place against the backdrop of the countermajoritarian difficulty. It is one thing—and perhaps in itself a difficult thing—to justify the power handed to domestic judges to interpret a domestic bill of rights adopted after debate and disagreement and some sort of head counting exercise sometime in the nation's past. It is a significantly different thing... to try to justify giving a role to the decisions of foreign courts and international tribunals to gainsay elected American legislators. In fact, we have argued that no justifications, alone or together, exist to justify American judges making use of comparative and international rights-based law to trump the American democratic process.'
[14] *Roper v Simmons* 543 US 551 (2005) at 608.

in legislation enacted by an elective national assembly. If the courts begin holding the executive and its agencies, and other sub-units in the political system, to other standards—to standards not laid down democratically—then we might be expected to oppose judicial review in these areas as well.

IV. James Allan's Critique

In an article published in 2005, I defended the citation of foreign law in cases like *Roper v Simmons*, and sought to introduce a general jurisprudential framework for explaining the purpose and desirability of such citation.[15] I also defended it in my 2007 Storrs Lectures delivered at Yale Law School. At various times, people have ventured the observation that it is strange that I of all people should be defending the practice of citing foreign law in constitutional cases, associated as it is with the enhancement of judicial power at the expense of local democracy, and associated as it also is with strong judicial review of legislation, of which I am known as a sworn enemy.[16] Surely if I were consistent, I would associate myself with those like Justice Scalia who denounce recourse to foreign law as undemocratic; surely, like him, I should be 'appalled by the proposition that...the American peoples' democratic adoption of the death penalty...could be judicially nullified because of the disapproving views of foreigners'.[17]

My friend Jim Allan led the charge. Professor Allan is also a fanatical opponent of strong judicial review of democratic legislation. In an article he published in 2008, he said that 'Waldron's underlying thesis in his *Foreign Law* paper is at odds with the core of his own anti-judicial review, anti-bill of rights position'.[18] He speculated that the reason for this (alleged) inconsistency was that I strongly disapproved of the juvenile death penalty (the substantive issue in *Roper v Simmons*) and that I was willing to do whatever was necessary, write in favour of whatever jurisprudence was necessary, to 'support [my] substantive moral opinion on this matter'.[19] And he chided me for this betrayal:

The anti-Bill of Rights Waldron who punctures the pretensions and purported moral superiority of the unelected judiciary...and who emphasizes the fact that dissensus and disagreement on virtually all rights questions is to be expected...—that Waldron lays out a demanding moral path. My understanding has always been that on that Waldronian moral path, when I find that a majority of my fellow citizens disagrees with me in their moral judgments, even as regards the juvenile death penalty, the remedy is not to urge unelected judges to impose my view on the legislature and on all those fellow citizens who disagree with me, even if that urging be indirect and wrapped up in an appeal to the law of

---

[15] J. Waldron, 'Foreign Law and the Modern Ius Gentium' (2005) 119 *Harvard Law Review* 129.
[16] See eg J. Waldron, 'The Core of the Case against Judicial Review' (2006) 115 *Yale Law Journal* 1346.
[17] *Roper v Simmons* 543 US 551 (2005) at 608.
[18] J. Allan, 'Jeremy Waldron and the Philosopher's Stone' (2008) 45 *San Diego Law Review* 133, at 159.
[19] Ibid 160–1.

nations. The Waldronian remedy is for me to spend a few Saturdays a month campaigning for politicians and political parties who share my view, . . . to participate in the democratic process in an effort to change opinions. If Waldron is hinting in his *Foreign Law* paper that the juvenile death penalty issue is somehow idiosyncratically distinct from other rights-based issues, and that disagreement here is in fact unreasonable, then he should tell us why that is. . . . He should avoid erecting an erudite and learned edifice that, at the end of the day, and whatever else it may do, makes less demanding the path of convincing one's fellow citizens to revise their rights-based moral views.[20]

Professor Allan made one conciliatory observation towards the end of his diatribe. He asked what an opponent of judicial review should do if he were actually appointed to the judiciary in a country which had instituted this practice:

[I]t may ultimately be that having accepted the job as a judge one has to do something when confronted with a case involving abstract rights. Indeed, it may well be that such a Waldronian judge is at times sorely tempted, psychologically, to seek guidance or illumination—or at least the comfort of having his or her views confirmed by others. Were that Waldronian judge in those instances to prefer seeking guidance from the musings of other judges around the world rather than in the writings of philosophers like Dworkin, some observers—including me [ie James Allan], perhaps—might find themselves reluctantly resigned to the practice.[21]

But, said Allan, 'that is a world away from actively encouraging and justifying the practice in the way Waldron has done in his *Foreign Law* paper'.[22]

Professor Allan also attacks the jurisprudential grounds on which I defend the practice of invoking foreign law. I shall say something briefly about what those grounds are in Section VI, below. I don't really think Allan understands the argument; maybe this is because I haven't explained it very well. But this is not the place to go into the extent of his misunderstanding. The issue here is the one of inconsistency. Is it inconsistent—is it a betrayal of principle—for an opponent of strong judicial review to support the citation by courts of foreign law?

V. Separating the Issues

My view is that the two issues—strong judicial review and recourse to foreign law—are separable.

Take the Eighth Amendment to the US Constitution, for example. The question of what counts as unacceptably cruel punishment and how we figure that out, ought to be separable from the institutional consequences of a court's finding that a legislated punishment is cruel. In the United States, a finding that a legislated punishment is cruel (and unusual) will lead to the legislation being struck down. In Britain, that finding (or a similar finding that a given legislated punishment is 'inhuman') may lead to a Declaration of Incompatibility, which is likely to be followed by a legislative amendment. In New Zealand, such a finding may lead

---

[20] Ibid 161.   [21] Ibid 160.   [22] Idem.

judges to strain for an interpretation (often a pretty distant one), which is consistent with the NZ Bill of Rights Act. These are three different kinds of response to a
single finding about the cruelty (or inhumanity) of a given legislated punishment.
But the discussion of the place of foreign law in our jurisprudence is not about *that*
choice—strong versus weak versus minimal judicial review. It is about the earlier
stage of the inquiry, which systems of all three types have in common: how do we
determine whether a type of punishment is cruel or inhuman, and what is the place
of foreign law and global consensus in *that* stage of the process?

After all, opposition to strong judicial review does not mean that one denies
the existence or importance of the law that American (or British or New Zealand)
courts administer when they exercise powers of judicial review. I do not deny
the existence of the US Constitution or the importance (as law) of the standards
set out in the Bill of Rights. In Britain, I don't deny the existence of the Human
Rights Act or the European Convention on which it is based or the importance
(as law) of the human rights standards they embody. When I am home in New
Zealand, I do not deny the existence of the New Zealand Bill of Rights Acts or its
importance (as law) or the importance (as law) of the international instruments
on which it is based —notably the International Covenant of Civil and Political
Rights.

When you hang out with opponents of judicial review, you sometimes find
yourself in strange company: supporters of abortion restrictions, hangers and flog-
gers in England, racist supporters of states' rights in America, opponents all over
the world of any restrictions on parents' authority to beat their children, religious
opponents of individual liberty, defenders of torture and extraordinary rendition,
and all sorts of riff-raff. The ones whose company I find particularly unbearable are
those who furiously condemn the whole enterprise of individual rights, whether
in national bills or charters of rights or in international human rights law. I find it
irksome that they think that as a democrat I too will be opposed to this enterprise.
(I am not; my support for democracy is rights-based.)[23] I think the rights enterprise is a massive achievement and that it is very important that it be sustained and
advanced, both at the level of international law and at the level of the national positivization of international law. The only issue on which I disagree with supporters
of strong judicial review of legislation is whether judges or elected legislators ought
to have the final word when there is serious and good faith disagreement about
what the rights-standards should be and how, on important issues, they should be
interpreted.

Whatever the constitutional consequences of its decision, a court asked to address
an issue, such as whether a certain legislated punishment is cruel or inhuman, has
no choice but to return the clearest and most responsible answer it can to that
question. It will no doubt stare at the text of the Bill of Rights for a while; it will
consult its own precedents; it may look up 'cruel' or 'inhuman' in the dictionary. In
America, there might be some felt need to read through the diaries of the Founding

---

[23] See J. Waldron, 'Participation: The Right of Rights', *Aristotelian Society Proceedings* (1998), 307
and J. Waldron, *Law and Disagreement* (Oxford: Oxford University Press, 1999), 232.

Fathers to try to figure out what they had in mind when they used this language. It is perfectly intelligible to me that a court, having done all these things, may still feel that its inquiry is incomplete.[24] It may be aware that it is administering a standard whose wording is similar to—or in some cases an exact echo of—a standard administered in another jurisdiction. The American Eighth Amendment and the Canadian Charter of Rights and Freedoms reproduce, more or less exactly, the words of the English Bill of Rights of 1689 on the issue of cruel punishment. The Human Rights Act in the United Kingdom deliberately reproduces the language of Article Three of the European Convention on Human Rights. The cruelty or inhumanity of punishment is made an issue in the International Covenant of Civil and Political Rights and in the various national bills of rights (like New Zealand's and South Africa's) that draw from it. So a court administering such a standard in any one of these countries might want to examine how the same or closely similar standards are administered in other countries.[25] This may be done out of intellectual curiosity, or because it is thought that there is something to be learned, or because it is thought inappropriate to neglect these sources given that the countries in question, in adopting provisions like these, took themselves to be *engaging in a common enterprise*. A judge might feel that, having been given this question to answer, it would be irresponsible for him to fail to consider this foreign material, just as it would be irresponsible of him to fail to consider historical precedents or dictionary meanings or framers' intentions.

In general, my opposition to judicial review doesn't mean that I am a sceptic about any particular source of law that a constitutional court might draw upon. I have my doubts about some of them: about legislators' or framers' intentions, for example.[26] But what matters is the *argument* for using any particular source of law. This applies to precedent; it applies to any recourse the court might have to framers' intent; it applies to international and foreign law as well. Everything depends on the jurisprudential argument for recourse to a particular source of law.

I can imagine that in some cases, the argument about judicial power might have implications for the argument about the use of a given source of law. There is a great debate in the United States about the place of precedent in constitutional law, particularly in interpreting the Bill of Rights. Should the Supreme Court feel

---

[24] Allan and Huscroft, in *Constitutional Rights Coming Home to Roost*, above n 13, give the impression that, in order to consult foreign law, an American lawyer will have to abandon America's own traditions of constitutional interpretation. They present this as an either/or matter, as though one *either* cited foreign law *or* remained true to one's own constitutional jurisprudence. But the US Supreme Court has shown that it can do both.

[25] Of course in considering these matters, a court will pay attention to differences in the ways in which similar text has been used in other countries. Allan and Huscroft suggest (ibid at 31) that the existence of such differences should have the effect of closing down any reference to foreign law. It does not seem to have occurred to them that courts are adept at drawing analogies that do take proper account of difference. (We *do this all the time in common law*.) They complain that certain constitutional differences might 'combine to create a comparison of apples and oranges'; it doesn't seem to have occurred to them that the life of the law has been comparing apples and oranges and refusing to be blinded to useful analogies simply by the existence of obvious differences. It also does not seem to have occurred to them that reference to foreign law might enable legal systems to learn from one another's traditions of constitutional interpretation and that this may be a good thing.

[26] See Waldron, *Law and Disagreement*, above n 23, 119 ff.

strongly constrained by *stare decisis*, as the plurality opinion suggested in *Planned Parenthood v Casey*?[27] Or should it say that, since *stare decisis* is not a matter of principle but is rather predicated upon certain advantages that are supposed to accrue from stable expectations and since rights are supposed to be able to trump mere considerations of convenience (such as those that accrue from stable expectations), a precedent should not be able to drive us away from an independently supportable conclusion about what respect for rights requires. This is an important debate in constitutional law,[28] and I am not sure which side is winning. I can imagine an opponent of judicial review saying that if we were to adopt a strong principle of *stare decisis*, this would aggravate the problem of judicial power, because it would make (undemocratic) exercises of judicial power harder to overturn, by entrenching them. (On the other hand, I can imagine the opposite argument being made too; judicial review with *stare decisis* makes today's judges a little less powerful than they would otherwise be. So it may be a wash.)

But I do not think that recourse to foreign law is like that. As I said, everything depends on the argument. If the only argument for recourse to foreign law were that the more judges—including foreign judges—we involve in these decisions the better, then one would expect an opponent of judicial power to oppose that. But that was certainly not the position in *Roper v Simmons*: the citation of foreign law in that case was mostly to foreign legislation (on the death penalty) not to foreign judicial decisions.

If the argument, however, is that there is something to be learned from the way in which foreign law has developed, then I don't see how opposition to strong judicial review can generate an argument for opposing recourse to foreign law. For suppose there *is* something important to be learned (and suppose, for the sake of argument, that it cannot be learned in any other way). Then failing to learn it will presumably lead to a decision at home that is *pro tanto* imperfect or flawed. There will be something taken into account that ought not to have been taken into account or there will be something that has not been taken into account that ought to have been taken into account. There will be a line of argument that ought to have been pursued or ought to have been pursued in a different way. Issues will be tangled together which could—if the foreign law had been consulted—have been disentangled and so on. *And someone may die as a result*, because flawed arguments lead to a bad conclusion or considerations favouring a different conclusion might have been given less weight than they ought to have been given and so on.

What do I mean 'someone may die as a result'? Well, suppose the issue is about the cruelty or inhumanity of a particular form of (legislated) capital punishment. Where strong judicial review has been instituted, the system relies on the determinations of judges to save people from cruel or inhuman punishments. A bad argument by a court—bad because it failed to learn (from foreign law) something it needed to learn—may mean it fails to save someone who needed to be saved.

---

[27] *Planned Parenthood of Southeastern Pennsylvania et al v Casey, Governor of Pennsylvania, et al* 505 US 833 (1991), at 854–69.
[28] See eg H. Monaghan, 'Stare Decisis and Constitutional Adjudication' (1988) 88 *Columbia Law Review* 723 and R. Fallon, 'Stare Decisis and the Constitution' (2001) 76 *NYU Law Review* 570.

Where weak judicial review has been instituted, the system relies on judges to give a full and intelligent warning to the legislature (and to the polity at large) that a legislated punishment is cruel or inhuman, and the effect of that warning (eg in bringing about remedial legislative action) may depend on its quality. And again, if the legislation is not amended, because the courts failed to issue a Declaration of Incompatibility because they failed to learn something about the issue that they needed to learn (from foreign law), then someone may be treated cruelly or inhumanly as a result. Where minimal judicial review has been instituted (as in New Zealand), and the capital legislation in question can be interpreted in two different ways (one more draconian than the other), then which interpretation is chosen may depend on the quality of judicial argument; and if the argument is flawed (because the court failed to learn something it needed to learn), then people will be punished under the draconian rather than the non-draconian interpretation of the legislation.[29]

VI. Compelling Reasons for Citing Foreign Law

In the piece I wrote for the *Harvard Law Review*,[30] I said that one of the frustrating things about *Roper v Simmons* was that no one on the Court bothered to articulate a general *theory*—a jurisprudential defence—of the citation and authority of foreign law. The justices who cited foreign law just gave the impression that they thought it was a rather good idea. And those who opposed it simply denounced it, without giving the impression that there was a theory there to be refuted.

If we have heard any sort of theoretical argument in the American debate to justify reference to foreign law, it has mostly been an argument about learning from others. Former US Supreme Court Justice Sandra Day O'Connor has said that 'there is much to learn from other distinguished jurists who have given thought to the same difficult issues we face here'.[31] Justice Ginsburg tells us that '[f]oreign opinions...can add to the store of knowledge relevant to the solution of trying questions'.[32] And Justice Breyer has spoken of 'the enormous value in any discipline of trying to learn from the similar experience of others.'[33] The practice of citing foreign law, said Justice Breyer, 'involves opening your eyes to what is going

---

[29] Of course, New Zealand doesn't have capital punishment; but suppose it did; or suppose that the stakes were similarly high on some other issue of human rights.

[30] Waldron, 'Foreign Law and the Modern Ius Gentium', above n 11.

[31] Sandra Day O'Connor as quoted in R. B. Ginsburg, 'A Decent Respect to the Opinions of [Human]kind: The Value of a Comparative Perspective in Constitutional Adjudication', Address before the Constitutional Court of South Africa, 7 Feb 2006, available at <http://www.supreme-court.gov/publicinfo/speeches/viewspeeches.aspx?Filename=sp_02-07b-06.html>: 'Other legal systems continue to innovate, to experiment, and to find new solutions to the new legal problems that arise each day, from which we can learn and benefit'. See also S. Day O'Connor, 'Keynote Address', at 96th Annual Meeting of the American Society of International Law (16 Mar 2002), in 96 *American Society of International Law Proceedings* 348, 350.

[32] Ginsburg, 'A Decent Respect to the Opinions of [Human]kind', ibid.

[33] S. Breyer, 'Keynote Address' (2003) 97 *American Society of International Law Proceedings* 265.

on elsewhere, taking what you learn for what it is worth, and using it as a point of comparison where doing so will prove helpful'.[34]

I have addressed this to some extent in the last couple of paragraphs of the previous section. I think it is an important argument, not just because we may learn about various bright ideas that have been tried in other countries, but because we may learn about new pathways of legal analysis. Consider for example the underlying issue in *Roper v Simmons*: the application of the death penalty to a young adult for a crime committed when he was a child. To try and figure this issue out, we have to take it apart, separating the application of various principles from one another, and laying out in some logical order a series of hard, interlocking, and quite abstract questions about the nature of culpability, the use of bright lines (such as an age of majority), the different functions of adult and juvenile courts, the *in terrorem* effects of being tried as an adult, the purposes of punishment, the rights of victims and their families, the impact of punishment on a young person (particularly in the way it relates individual action to outcomes over the course of a whole life), the connection between the mental element in culpability and the capacity to foresee the long-term impact of punishment, the purpose of having an array of penalties from the least to the most severe, and the nature and safeguards of whatever accompanying discretion might be vested in a court. There are many different ways to analyse and work through a tangled array of issues like this,[35] and I can imagine courts looking to how others have grappled with similar questions— just as New Zealand or South African courts look to American jurisprudence on (say) free speech or discrimination law to help them in figuring out orderly ways through the tangled webs of issues that present themselves in those areas.[36]

---

[34] Stephen Breyer, as quoted in N. Dorsen, 'The Relevance of Foreign Legal Materials in U.S. Constitutional Cases: A Conversation between Justice Antonin Scalia and Justice Stephen Breyer' (2005) 3 *International Journal of Constitutional Law* 519.

[35] Justice Laurie Ackermann, recently retired from the South African Constitutional Court, has observed that judges understand the importance of Karl Popper's and Albert Einstein's admonition that 'the formulation of a problem is often more essential than its solution, which may be merely a matter of mathematical or experimental skill'. A. Einstein and L. Infeld, *The Evolution of Physics* (Cambridge: Cambridge University Press, 1938), 95, cited by L. W. H. Ackermann, 'Constitutional Comparativism in South Africa: A Response to Sir Basil Markesinis and Jörg Fedtke' (2005) 80 *Tulane Law Review* 169. Ackerman continues: 'At some stage in a judge's reasoning process...the judge will come to a preliminary conclusion or hypothesis as to what the result should be and why. I suggest that the best way to test such preliminary conclusion is to attempt rigorously to falsify it. However, my experience—both of myself and other lawyers—has been that...one can easily become trapped into a sort of tunnel vision, from which it is difficult to escape, or to see other or lateral answers....One often ends up rehearsing the same line of reasoning or...trying to find additional authority for the provisional conclusions one has already reached. It is in this context that foreign law can play a particularly valuable role. It may be that, when one commences the enquiry into foreign law one is psychologically hoping to find confirmation for one's hypotheses, but if one remains alive to falsifying possibilities, the foreign law can be of particular value. In any event, foreign law may stimulate, in Einstein's words, "creative imagination" by "rais[ing] new questions, new possibilities...regard[ing] old problems from a new angle."' And Ackerman concludes: 'I should like to acknowledge my own great indebtedness to the American example and to American constitutional and human rights scholarship' (ibid 185).

[36] See eg *President of the Republic v Hugo* (1997) (6) BCLR 708 and *Police v Hopkinson* (2004) 3 NZLR 704.

When I read criticisms of the practice of citing to foreign legal materials by people like James Allan and Grant Huscroft, I get the impression that they believe there is nothing to be learned at this level of detail, or nothing important. There are just a few well-known options to choose from (which people disagree about), and the only interesting question is whether the choice is made by a democratic or an undemocratic will. I reject that crude voluntarist image of law utterly, and I bitterly regret that anything in *Law and Disagreement* encouraged the view that that is what legal decision-making is like.

Herbert Wechsler once said in his 'Neutral Principles' essay: 'Those who perceive in law only the element of fiat … will not join gladly in the search for standards of the kind I have in mind'.[37] I say the same. If you think that legal problems are ultimately solved in a simple Alexandrian fashion—just cutting through the Gordian knot with a determination to privilege *this* value or to promote *that* policy—then you will be uninterested in the exigencies of a jurisprudence that talks about patient analysis, the untangling of issues, the ascertaining of just resolutions, and the learning and cooperation that is characteristic of a scientific approach. Approaching law as a matter of fiat, you will not see any reason why expressions of will elsewhere in the world should affect our expressions of will in America. For you, the question is 'Whose will should prevail?' And you will see in the citation of foreign law nothing much more than Justice Scalia saw: 'the subjective views of five Members of this Court and like-minded foreigners'.[38]

I have tried to present law in a different light, as essentially a problem-solving enterprise. Even in the areas where law is governed entirely by democratic decision, I don't see it as a matter of will. I don't believe in a unitary 'will of the people', and I don't even think that voting should be construed as a mere expression of will. What I think is that in these areas, when there is reasonable disagreement about what the law should be, democratic legitimacy requires that each person has a right to have respect accorded to his or her reason and to have equal weight assigned to his or her reasoned conclusion.[39] But it's still reason that we are talking about in the context of democratic decision-making. (Even common people can reason, individually and together.) And reason will not refuse assistance, when it turns out that others have been wrestling with what we too are trying to figure out. And sometimes it is the obligation of courts—in the various ways I have described (eg strong judicial review, weak judicial review, minimal judicial review)—to see to it that this assistance is assembled, made available, and brought to bear on the issues that have to be faced in a democratic society.

But learning is not the only argument for the citation of foreign law. I mentioned earlier that, particularly when we think about individual rights, we should understand that various countries are engaged in what is more or less the same

[37] H. Wechsler, 'Toward Neutral Principles of Constitutional Law' (1959) 73 *Harvard Law Review* 1, 11.

[38] *Roper v Simmons*, 543 US 551 (2005) at 608.

[39] So I reject the view held by Roger Berkowitz, 'Democratic Legitimacy and the Scientific Foundation of Modern Law' (2007) 8 *Theoretical Inquiries in Law* 91, that a concern for democratic legitimacy is necessarily an embrace of legal voluntarism.

enterprise when they make decisions about individual rights. The language of their bills and charters of rights are boiler-plated from one country to another; and their enactment of rights standards in either constitutional or statutory form is often a common obligation that they have assumed under international human rights law. From the point of view of the human rights enterprise as a whole, it is important that a common set of rights standards be administered in the world—not just under the auspices of various international agencies, but also under the auspices of the positive law of the various countries that are responsible for the rights of the particular sectors of humanity committed to their care.

The argument for this is not a natural law argument.[40] It is not because the standards—at the international level and in the case of each country—purport to be universal (though they do). Some human rights advocates may believe that the universality of human rights is sufficient by itself to justify a requirement that various legal systems should try to harmonize their decisions about basic rights with one another. But harmonization does not guarantee that we have got the objectively right universal answer to a human rights issue; all it requires is that we have the same answer. Our common answer may be wrong, and there is no virtue in that from the point of view of universality. If our common answer is wrong, then it would be better from a God's-eye point of view if some of us moved away from the erroneous consensus and started looking for the right answer somewhere else.

Nor is the argument just a pragmatic one, though that is important. Harold Koh has argued, since 'concepts like "liberty," "equal protection," "due process of law," and privacy have never been exclusive U.S. property, . . . [t]o construe these terms in ignorance of these foreign and international precedents virtually ensures that our Supreme Court rulings will generate conflict and controversies with our closest global allies'.[41] (Think, for example, of the 1989 *Soering* case,[42] where it proved impossible for Virginia to extradite a young German man from the United Kingdom to be tried for the murder of the parents of his American girlfriend, since no credible assurance could be given that he wouldn't face the death penalty and hence suffer from 'death row syndrome', which in itself is regarded in European human rights law but not in American law as an inhuman form of punishment.)

The deep argument has to do with the value of consistency—the importance of *like cases being treated alike* on matters of rights. It is a matter of *fairness*—the unfairness of case B's being treated differently from the way case A has been treated, when the two cases are similar in all relevant respects, or the unfairness of denying one person a basic right when it has been accorded to another person who is similarly situated. Or it is a matter of *integrity*—the importance of law's speaking

---

[40] *Pace* Alford, 'In Search of a Theory for Constitutional Comparativism', above n 8, at 641 and 659 ff. See also E. Engle, 'European Law in American Courts: Foreign Law as Evidence of Domestic Law' (2007) 33 *Ohio Northern University Law Review* 99, at 103: 'The Court in its use of foreign law does not admit to invoking the idea of natural law, but that is what it is doing. It is looking for universal standards to be discovered in the law of foreign nations, "out there."'

[41] H. Hongju Koh, 'International Law as Part of our Law' (2004) 98 *American Journal of International Law* 43, at 47.

[42] *Soering v United Kingdom* 11 EHRR 439 (1989).

with one voice, coherently, on matters as important as this.[43] The argument is a difficult one—though its complexity does not detract from its importance—and I cannot do anything more than sketch it here. The point of this chapter is not to persuade readers of this argument, but to get you to see that *if* there is anything in it, its importance should continue to be felt notwithstanding one's opposition to strong judicial review.

Philosophers feel very pleased with themselves when they can respond to this argument as follows:

Ah! But treating like cases alike matters only when it is one and the same entity treating both or all of the relevant cases. And ex hypothesi that is not what is going on here, for we are talking about harmonizing the way in which legal system X treats case A and the way in which legal system Y treats case B.

One possible answer to this point is to question whether the various legal systems of the world are in fact operating utterly independently of one another, when they administer national basic-rights provisions under the auspices of the dual positivization of an international human rights document. That would be a 'top-down' answer, purporting to identify a single entity (albeit a complex, loosely federated entity: the system of states) responsible for the overall shape and consistency of law in this area. On this account the national courts of various countries are like Circuit Courts of Appeals in the United States. They are not rigidly bound to harmonize with each other's decisions. But they are in the end part of the same system, administering a common body of law in different regions of a continent-sized country, and they have some responsibility—based loosely in fairness, consistency, and integrity (as well as pragmatics)—to take each other's decisions into account. To the extent that we regard human rights as a common enterprise, pursued at multiple levels of positive law, it may be salutary to regard the high courts of the world in this light in their references to one another.

The more intriguing answer, however, is a bottom-up argument. It begins by denting the implication of the complacent philosopher's response—that like cases' being treated alike *does not matter at all* when it is not one and the same entity treating both or all of the relevant cases. That proposition is simply thoughtless. Sometimes when people are being treated in disparate and inconsistent ways, that is a reason for us to set up an entity which will take responsibility for the overall pattern of treatment.[44] But that couldn't be the case if inconsistency didn't matter when different cases were being treated by different entities.

---

[43] R. Dworkin, *Law's Empire* (Harvard: Harvard University Press, 1986), 176 ff.

[44] Here is an analogy. Imagine a large refugee camp after a famine or humanitarian emergency, where—as often happens—several different aid agencies, several different NGOs, are working side by side—working with the same large population, in the same camp. Suppose one of these organizations becomes aware that the provision that it is offering the refugees is radically different—say in quantity and quality—from the provision that the other aid agencies are offering to members of the same population. Oxfam is giving two meals a day to the people in the north part of the camp and other agencies are giving one meal a day to people in the southern sector; even though the people in the north are no more needy and no more deserving than the people in the south of the camp. And everyone can see what is going on. It seems to me that Oxfam, indeed all the organizations, would have to acknowledge that there is a problem here—a problem that doesn't evaporate when you say

In the area of human rights law, national courts are often called on to administer a general savings clause which looks something like this: '[T]he rights and freedoms contained in this Bill of Rights may be subject only to such reasonable limits prescribed by law as can be demonstrably justified in a free and democratic society'.[45] Many national bills and charters of rights have a clause like this,[46] and so does the International Covenant on Civil and Political Rights (though it is attached to various individual rights, rather than operating as a general savings clause).[47] 'Demonstrably justified in a free and democratic society' seems to mean justifiable *in any free and democratic society*, and it seems to me that cries out for us to take a look at what other free and democratic societies have regarded as justifiably consistent with their commitment to rights. I don't mean that the fact that a given restriction on rights has not been accepted in some or a few democracies is decisive; but it should be something to ponder. There is an obvious danger that clauses like these will be used opportunistically, as a sort of 'Get-out-of-jail-free' card for states and their publics, that it will be used whenever convenient as a way of avoiding political costs associated with particular rights demands in particular countries, to the detriment and demoralization of individuals or minorities that might have thought that there were rights here to rely on. I can imagine an individual complaining that the reasonable limitation clause was being administered inconsistently to his detriment, as between one legal system and another. For example, other flag-burning or hate-speech or press-embargo statutes are not given the benefit of this clause, but now in exactly similar circumstances the relevant statute of *his* country is being upheld. He might say, 'I have no quarrel with a reasonable limitation clause, but when it refers to a common idea, it is only fair that it be administered consistently. If no effort is made for consistency, then that gives the lie to any claim that we are all bound together in this common enterprise of securing one another's human rights in a sensible and moderate way.' On this account, then, courts should be anxious to apply such clauses in a way that is consistent with their application in other countries, so they are not and do not just appear as opportunities for unscrupulous governments to avoid inconvenient social and political costs associated with fundamental rights.

This is not an argument for any rigid deference to foreign sources. No one is interested in making such an argument. But it is an argument in favour of keeping an eye on the issue of consistency, just as the previous argument counts in favour of keeping an eye on foreign statutes and precedents to see what we can learn from

that no single institution is treating anyone inconsistently. The people in the south are likely to be distressed by this disparate treatment; they are likely to complain that their treatment is unfair; they may demand that like cases should be treated alike; and that demand does not *presuppose* a single agency responsible for all the treatment, although—and this is important—the complaint about unfairness may become the basis for a *demand* that the various agencies should start to behave as a unit. In other words, the demand for fairness could be a reason for the different entities to work as a system; their working as a system is not a precondition for the legitimacy of the demand.

[45] New Zealand Bill of Rights Act 1990, s 5.

[46] See Article 1 of the Canadian Charter of Rights and Freedoms, for example, or s 36 of the South African Constitution.

[47] See ICCPR, Articles 14(1), 21, and 22(2).

them. Also, since the issue of consistency is a matter of public concern and since it is a matter of public concern that courts publicly state their reasons for their decisions, these are also good arguments for citing foreign law officially and not just surreptitiously,[48] for it is important that the people of a country know what is going on in these various regards.

Arguments of this kind, then, together with the argument about what (in detail) can be learned from other jurisdictions, provide the basis of the case that has to be made to justify the practice of courts looking beyond the borders of their respective jurisdictions to see what else is being done in the world in regard to the types of issues that come before them. The point of this section has been to briefly outline these arguments and explain why there might be a reason to impel anyone—not just a supporter of judicial review—to countenance the citation of foreign law.

VII. Disagreement

If I am right, then in many cases reference to foreign law is indispensable to intelligent decision-making about basic rights in any given country. Whoever is charged in a polity with making decisions about basic rights, then, should be prepared and willing to cite to foreign law. The necessity of such citation does not evaporate when there is a problem about the legitimacy of strong judicial review in a country like the United States.

I have organized my career around an argument that people must be expected to disagree about rights, that their disagreements should be treated as good faith disagreements, and that they should respect one another's opinions sufficiently to accord one another an equal (and equally decisive) vote on matters of rights so that the issues on which they disagree can be settled democratically. In some countries, that argument prevails and the countries in question have not adopted strong judicial review: they settle important issues about rights through elective institutions. In other countries, the argument has not prevailed, though its premises are not denied as often as they used to be.

People's disagreements about rights are likely to include disagreements about the bearing of the sort of arguments I set out in Section VI. People will disagree about what there is to be learned from foreign law; they will disagree about the order in which to pose and untangle the various questions that a given rights-conundrum involves and accordingly they will disagree about whether we should try following the pathway through such a conundrum pioneered in some other country; they will disagree about the importance of consistency in a particular setting; they will disagree about how to understand the rights enterprise as a common enterprise

---

[48] Justice Stephen Breyer told an audience at NYU that he once said to a US congressman: 'If I have a difficult case and...a judge, though of a different country, has had to consider a similar problem, why should I not read what that judge has said? It will not bind me, but I may learn something.' Apparently the congressman replied, 'Fine. You are right. Read it. Just don't cite it in your opinion.' Stephen Breyer, as quoted in Dorsen, 'The Relevance of Foreign Legal Materials in U.S. Constitutional Cases', above n 34.

shared by various nations; they will disagree about the weight that should be given to the various reasons one country may have for remaining an outlier on some issue (because of its confidence that it is right, for example, or its desire to experiment, or because of some felt need to keep faith with its peculiar traditions); they will disagree about margins of appreciation; they will disagree about small differences in boiler-plate text and large differences in jurisprudential traditions. They will disagree as much about this as they do about any substantive issue about rights.

The fact that people disagree on substantive issues concerning rights is not a reason for their turning their backs on those issues. Also I have argued elsewhere that the fact that people disagree on procedural issues is also not a reason for them to abandon any concern for those issues. They should face up to the disagreements they have, debate them, and if action is necessary, adopt some respectful and effective decision-procedure. All this is true, too, of disagreements about the bearing that foreign law might have on particular rights issues. For each such issue, people should face up to this question of the bearing of foreign law, debate it, and factor that into the decision-procedure they have adopted for resolving the issue of rights.

I am certainly not suggesting that foreign law should trump reasonable disagreement at home. Sometimes when there is good faith disagreement among us at home about a contested issue, there will be good faith disagreement among foreign judges and foreign legal systems too. And an inquiry into foreign law will reveal that. In other cases, we will have to consider what impact information about foreign consensus should have on our own disagreements. We may or may not agree about what that impact should be; we may disagree in just the ways I have outlined. But that is no reason for flinching from the issue or banning consideration of this aspect of the matter.

Ultimately, as I have said, contested decisions about rights should be made through a respectful and effective decision-procedure. In my view, that requires that the ultimate decisions should be made by an elective institution such as a representative legislature. Others disagree, and the variety of constitutional arrangements in various countries reflects the existence and extent of this disagreement. In almost all advanced democracies, however, the courts play a role—though it is often not a decisive role—in the debate and decision-process on contested issues of rights. Even if they do not have powers of strong judicial review of legislation, they have an important role to play. I believe that, for any given rights issue that we face, the bearing of foreign legal arrangements is an important aspect of the issue that needs to be debated and decided. Courts—whatever their constitutional role—are in a good position to play a part (perhaps the most important part) in bringing this aspect of the issue into focus. So even though I believe that courts should not ultimately decide these issues, I cannot understand why there is such visceral opposition—among my fellow opponents of strong judicial review of legislation—to courts' consideration of foreign law.

21

Amateur Operatics: The Realization of Parliamentary Protection of Civil Liberties

Jonathan Morgan

I. Introduction

Human rights are the stuff of politics, not of law. They are inherently contestable, and contested. Debates over the proper extent of their legal protection should therefore take place in Parliament rather than being shut off in the cloistered world of the law courts. Society must give up 'the idea that certain basics of human interaction could, by the magic of metaphysics, be so solidly grounded as to put them beyond the cavil of political expediency'.[1]

While this pivotal assumption for what follows could be considerably expanded upon, it will henceforth be assumed that the contestability thesis is (incontestably?) true: Jeremy Waldron has observed that: 'No one in the trade now believes that the truth about rights is self-evident or that, if two people disagree about rights, one of them at least must be either corrupt or morally blind'; in thirty years of modern study of fundamental rights there has been a proliferation of theories, but no consensus.[2]

The present author has in the past called for outright repeal of the Human Rights Act 1998 (HRA),[3] and continues to believe that this would be the optimal course of action for British parliamentary democracy.[4] It is true that the early judicial approach to the HRA has been cautious,[5] and so the impact of the HRA has perhaps been 'significantly less, and significantly less negative, than some predictions made for it'.[6] But it would be rash to conclude from this placid infancy that constitutional crisis and judicial hegemony have ceased to be a significant possibility,

[1] K. Minogue, 'What is Wrong with Rights', in C. Harlow (ed), *Public Law and Politics* (London: Sweet and Maxwell, 1986), 2.09.

[2] J. Waldron, *Law and Disagreement* (Oxford: Oxford University Press, 1999), 225.

[3] J. Morgan, 'Law's British Empire' (2002) 22 *Oxford Journal of Legal Studies* 729.

[4] For good measure, I should have added repudiation of the European Convention on Human Rights and Fundamental Freedoms (ECHR).

[5] See eg A. King, *The British Constitution* (Oxford: Oxford University Press: Oxford, 2007), 135.

[6] Lord Falconer of Thoroton LC, 'Introduction', in Department for Constitutional Affairs, *Review of the Implementation of the Human Rights Act* (London, July 2006).

as the HRA matures. Sceptics must remain vigilant when juristocracy remains so dangerously close at hand. The Labour government's pantomime new Supreme Court might prove the catalyst for judicial supremacism.[7] Even if the early decisions under the HRA are thought progressive,[8] or at any rate seem personally congenial, this must be quite irrelevant for any rational discussion of institutional design. As Lord Devlin pointed out, typically a commentator's 'enthusiasm for an institution coincides with enthusiasm for what it is doing';[9] but such enthusiasms are dangerously misplaced since the same institution may later exercise the same powers in an unexpected way that merits serious disapproval, but will by then be difficult to halt.[10] For as Tom Campbell observes: 'History amply demonstrates that courts can thwart as well as facilitate progressive social, political, and economic changes'.[11] This is an important warning that recent left-leaning converts to the wonders of human rights would appear to have forgotten.[12]

This essay will also assume that, despite the author's continuing scepticism about the human rights project, outright repeal of the HRA is probably not a realistic political prospect at the current time.[13] Moreover, it is not clear whether the 'incorporation' of the ECHR would be fully reversible, even by such a repeal.[14] With reluctant realism, therefore, proposals are offered for the improvement rather than repeal of the HRA.

The focus will be upon the relationship between Parliament and the courts, and accordingly ss 3 and 4, HRA. These central provisions have often been praised for

---

[7] Although this is denied by Baroness Hale of Richmond: JCHR 29th Report, Session 2007–8, examination of witnesses (London, 4 Mar 2008), Q226. But cf Lord Neuberger MR, identifying a real risk of '[Supreme Court] judges arrogating to themselves greater power than they have at the moment' in 'Top Dogs: Britain's New Supreme Court' (London: BBC Radio 4, broadcast 8 Sept 2009).

[8] Cf K. D. Ewing, 'The Futility of the Human Rights Act' [2004] *Public Law* 829; A. Tomkins, 'The Rule of Law in Blair's Britain' (2007) 26 *University of Queensland Law Journal* 255.

[9] 'The Judge as Lawmaker', in P. Devlin, *The Judge* (Oxford: Oxford University Press, 1979), 7.

[10] Consider Ronald Dworkin, 'A Badly Flawed Election', *New York Review of Books*, 11 Jan 2001.

[11] T. Campbell, 'Human Rights: A Culture of Controversy' (1999) 26 *Journal of Law and Society* 6. See further, of course, J. A. G. Griffith, *The Politics of the Judiciary* (London: Fontana, 1977).

[12] Cf also Sir Stephen Sedley's comment on the judicial 'discovery' of human rights in constitutional orders: 'You can acclaim this as an enhancement of the rule of law, or denounce it as judicial supremacism, depending (if you are honest) on whether you agree or disagree with the substance of what the courts have done'. The *Guardian*, 20 Feb 2010 (reviewing *The Rule of Law* by Tom [Lord] Bingham).

[13] The position of the new Coalition government remains to be seen. The defining document ('The Coalition: Our Programme for Government' May 2010) promised only to establish 'a Commission to investigate the creation of a British Bill of Rights that incorporates and builds on all our obligations under the European Convention on Human Rights' (such a Bill of Rights had been a manifesto commitment of the Conservative Party, but sounds to this commentator no better (and quite possibly worse) than the HRA itself). For a 'Conservative Case for the Human Rights Act', cf the pamphlet by J. Norman and P. Oborne, *Churchill's Legacy* (London: Liberty, 2009).

[14] See eg Department for Constitutional Affairs, *Review of the Implementation of the Human Rights Act* (London, 2006), at 38: 'On the one hand, repeal could be expected to reduce and to some extent reverse the immediacy of the Convention's impact in UK law. But on the other hand, it is unlikely to restore fully the position immediately before the Act came into force, or to remove European Convention on Human Rights principles from UK law.' Campbell warns, similarly, that 'changes which entrench judicial power are harder to reverse than they are to implement', in Campbell, above n 11.

reconciling judicial protection of rights with parliamentary sovereignty. Particularly fashionable is the defence of this compromise as one promoting 'dialogue' between parliamentarians and judges.[15] It will be argued below that this alleged 'dialogue' resembles much more a one-way conversation,[16] in which Parliament tries to guess how the courts will react to its proposals (and if its prediction is misplaced, rapidly falls in with the judicial viewpoint). Conor Gearty has unforgettably described this 'legalisation of politics':

> Even if judicial interventions . . . were wholly benign, there would still be something wrong about a system which turned the elective process into a mere overture for the real thing, a few pleasant tunes before the legal opera gets properly underway, with a bevy of highly paid tenors (very few sopranos) bellowing out their arias in a language few can understand— and with not a surtitle in sight for the now forgotten legislators sitting in the gods straining to follow what is happening to their laws.[17]

This, unfortunately, captures exactly what happens in the HRA era.[18] The project here is to diminish the human rights opera in the courts, especially the judicial prima donnas,[19] and instead to promote communal singing from the massed ranks of legislators.[20] In brief, the judicial process should be silenced (or at any rate muted) by abolition of the power to declare statutes incompatible with the ECHR under s 4, HRA, and by replacing s 3 with an interpretive provision that does not permit judicial amendment of statutory wording. Parliament's voice might then be amplified by building on the existing Joint Committee of Human Rights (JCHR) as chorus-master.

II. Section 3 of the Human Rights Act

What are the limits of the 'possible' under this famous section?[21] We have been told that it does not extend to 'judicial vandalism' of the statutory language,[22]

---

[15] Interestingly, 'dialogue' was one of 200 jargon-words that the Local Government Association has stated that 'public bodies should not use if they want to communicate effectively with local people': Local Government Association, *Press Release* (18 Mar 2009).

[16] '[Such] "dialogue" has perhaps always been nothing more than "not quite monologue".' G. C. N. Webber, 'The Unfulfilled Potential of the Court and Legislature Dialogue' (2009) 42 *Canadian Journal of Political Science* 443, 444.

[17] C. Gearty, *Can Human Rights Survive?* (Cambridge: Cambridge University Press, 2006), 81–2.

[18] Cf the fury of one 'forgotten legislator', former Home Secretary Charles Clarke MP, deploring the 'human rights circus' in his evidence to the House of Lords Constitution Committee on 17 Jan 2007 (published in 6th Report of Session 2006–7, 'Relations between the Executive, the Judiciary and Parliament').

[19] Webber claims that in no Anglo-American legal system do judges display the 'disposition for intellectual and institutional humility' necessary for a meaningful 'dialogue' with legislatures. Webber, above n 16.

[20] As Tom Campbell points out: 'A human rights culture need not be a culture of litigation . . . A culture of rights may be political rather than legal in its nature, preferring debate to litigation and voting in representative assemblies to voting in the court room'. Campbell, above n 11.

[21] Cf A. Kavanagh, *Constitutional Review under the UK Human Rights Act* (Cambridge: Cambridge University Press, 2009), chs 2–4.

[22] *R (Anderson) v Secretary of State for the Home Department* [2003] 1 AC 837 at [30], per Lord Bingham. For the political reaction to this case, see D. Nicol, 'The HRA and the Politicians' [2004] *Legal Studies* 541.

but precisely what counts as 'vandalism' and how it differs from permissible judicial remodelling is more than a little obscure.[23] In the leading case, the majority of their Lordships showed an open impatience with arguments addressed to the wording of the statute—as if Parliament's choice of words were some optional extra, rather than the law itself.[24] This is quite mistaken, for as Waldron reminds us, the statutory text is *canonical*—the only intention that Parliament as a whole has, or can have, is to enact this precise text into law.[25] In a real sense, the very words of the text are the law.[26]

Hence why to give an 'abnormal construction' of statutory words pursuant to s. 3 might fairly be described as a 'quasi-legislative power, not a purely interpretative one; for the court is not constrained by the language of the statute in question, which it may modify (i.e. amend) in order to bring it into conformity with the constitution'.[27] It is true, indeed trite, that judges are the ultimate interpreters of all Parliament's words,[28] and thus that the judicial values inherent in the canons of interpretation play an important part in mediating the sovereignty of Parliament.[29] Dicey himself noted that the necessity of interpretation of a statute by the judges, 'influenced by...the general spirit of the common law', made it very difficult for Parliament to confer truly unlimited powers, thus reconciling parliamentary sovereignty and the rule of law.[30] But an 'interpretation' which no longer pays particular attention to the legislative text has become something quite different, as Lord Millett says.

---

[23] Lord Nicholls notes that 'Unfortunately...section 3 itself is not free from ambiguity'. *Ghaidan v Godin-Mendoza* [2004] UKHL 30 at [27].

[24] *Mendoza* at [31] per Lord Nicholls: 'once it is accepted that section 3 may require legislation to bear a meaning which departs from the unambiguous meaning the legislation would otherwise bear, it becomes impossible to suppose Parliament intended that the operation of section 3 should depend critically upon the particular form of words adopted by the parliamentary draftsman in the statutory provision under consideration. That would make the application of section 3 something of a semantic lottery.' According to Lord Steyn, 'misunderstanding' of the HRA stems in part from 'excessive concentration on linguistic features of the particular statute': [40]–[41]. Lord Rodger said at [123]: 'it cannot have been the intention of Parliament [in enacting s 3] to place a premium on the skill of those called on to think up a neat way round the draftsman's language. Parliament was not out to devise an entertaining parlour game for lawyers, but, so far as possible, to make legislation operate compatibly with Convention rights. This means concentrating on matters of substance, rather than on matters of *mere language*' (emphasis added).

[25] Waldron, above n 2, ch 4.

[26] Thus, s 3, along with the '*Marleasing* doctrine' in EU law (see *Marleasing SA v La Comercial Internacional de Alimentacion SA* [1991] 1 ECR 4135) threatens to subvert the entire enterprise of statutory interpretation, by relegating the text to (at best) secondary importance.

[27] *Mendoza* at [64], per Lord Millett (dissenting) (a speech revealing 'a scholarly mind driven to the end of its tether,' according to F. A. R. Bennion (2007) 171 *Justice of the Peace News*, at 381). Lord Millett was commenting on the broader judicial duty to construe laws in a way compatible with the Constitution commonly found in Commonwealth constitutions, such as Gibraltar's. But it does not take a leap of imagination to read this passage as a description, and condemnation, of what the majority did to the Rent Act 1977 in *Mendoza*.

[28] Bishop Hoadley famously claimed in his *Sermon before the King* (1717) that 'whoever hath an absolute authority to interpret any written or spoken laws, it is He who is truly the Law Giver'.

[29] See e.g. T. R. S. Allan, 'Parliament's Will and the Justice of Common Law: The Human Rights Act in Constitutional Perspective' (2006) 59 *Current Legal Problems* 27; Kavanagh, above n 21, 97–9.

[30] A. V. Dicey, *Introduction to the Study of the Law of the Constitution*, 8th edn (Indianapolis: reprinted by LibertyClassics, 1915), 273.

It is true that there are self-defined limits on the judges' use of this 'quasi-legislative power', but they have little if anything to do with the wording of the statute.[31] How can s 3 be reconciled with the sovereignty of Parliament? With great difficulty, it is submitted. Alison Young, a defender of ss 3 and 4 HRA as a promoter of 'dialogue', accepts that s 3 gives 'relatively greater authority' to the courts (vis-à-vis Parliament) to settle human rights controversies.[32] Hence, in Dr Young's view, the courts should use s 3 in cases where they are 'better placed to reach the answer' or have a 'more legitimate process' by which to decide it. (Conversely, when Parliament is thought 'better placed', the courts should issue a declaration of incompatibility under s 4: we return to these points below.) Dr Young maintains, however, that in either case the 'final say' is Parliament's. But Aileen Kavanagh concludes that the HRA only '*seem[s]*' to give Parliament the last word, whilst nonetheless giving the courts powers of constitutional review, not hugely dissimilar from those possessed by the US Supreme Court'.[33] As will be shown below, Dr Kavanagh is correct to argue that parliamentary sovereignty has been preserved only formally, while the HRA imposes serious limits of substance on what the legislature can do.[34]

Now it is true that Parliament might theoretically proof provisions against judicial rewriting under s 3 by making explicit its intention to legislate notwithstanding the HRA (whether in advance or *ex post facto* by re-enacting a provision that has been subject to 'reinterpretation'). It is unclear whether anything less explicit would suffice.[35] Thus, s 3 seems closer than is generally thought to s 33 of the Canadian Charter of Rights and Freedoms, whereby *express* 'notwithstanding clauses' can be enacted to protect statutes against judicial review; but otherwise the courts may strike them down. The English courts cannot invalidate legislation *per se* under the HRA of course, but rewriting statutes may be seen as an equally or even more potent power.[36] The real question becomes whether the legislature makes use of its power to legislate in defiance of the courts, and indeed whether it would be seen as proper for it to do so.

In Canada the answer seems to be a resounding 'no'. Janet Hiebert notes that despite the apparent provision for 'dialogue' in the Canadian constitution,[37] the Supreme Court is de facto the institution looked to by the public and indeed by the government for the authoritative protection of Charter Rights.[38] Outside Quebec, Canadian politicians have proved 'exceedingly timid' in their response to judicial invalidation of legislation, and shown 'extreme reluctance to use the

[31] See eg *Bellinger v Bellinger* [2003] 2 AC 467; *In re S (Minors) (Care Order: Implementation of Care Plan)* [2002] 2 AC 291. See generally A. Kavanagh, 'The Role of Parliamentary Intention in Adjudication under the Human Rights Act 1998' (2006) 26 *Oxford Journal of Legal Studies* 179.

[32] A. L. Young, *Parliamentary Sovereignty and the Human Rights Act* (Oxford: Hart, 2008), 131.

[33] Kavanagh, above n 21, 418.

[34] Ibid 336–7.

[35] Nicol, above n 22, 541.

[36] Kavanagh, above n 21, 319.

[37] The seminal article is by P. Hogg and A. Bushell, 'The Charter Dialogue between Courts and Legislatures' (1997) 35 *Osgoode Hall Law Journal* 75.

[38] J. L. Hiebert, 'Parliamentary Bills of Rights: An Alternative Model?' (2006) 69 *Modern Law Review* 7.

notwithstanding clause'.[39] Unsurprisingly, Hiebert concludes that Canada comes much closer to US-style judicial supremacism than to any meaningful 'dialogue' between judges and politicians.[40]

What of the United Kingdom? As noted already, Acts of Parliament may not be struck down under the HRA, but only 'declared incompatible' (while remaining valid) under s 4, should the 'interpretive' approach in s 3 be deemed untenable. But it has been argued that Canada and the United Kingdom are much closer together in practice than this difference might make it appear.[41] There is, as yet, no example of Parliament seeking to proof statutes against s 3 'reinterpretation' in advance, or to re-enact them in a suitably emphatic way 'notwithstanding' an s 3 defeat. However Danny Nicol suggests that we can view the radical changes to the substantive law of sexual offences (placing the burden of proving consent on the defendant) as a reaction to the House of Lords' radical rewriting of the rape evidence provisions in favour of defendants, in *Regina v A (No 2)*.[42]

Elsewhere, however, Professor Nicol has argued that Parliament has not been fully absorbed into the 'culture of compliance', in which a legislature becomes cast 'in the role of the adjunct of the courts'.[43] We may need to distinguish between the two Houses of Parliament for this purpose, Nicol suggests: while the Lords has been very keen on ECHR compliance and peers repeatedly urge such points during legislative debates, the Commons, by contrast, is a nucleus of 'controversy-culture'. The elected politicians 'were either hostile [to the HRA] from the start (in the case of the Conservatives) or swift converts to scepticism (in the case of Labour)'.[44] The Conservative Official Opposition (2000–10) consistently declined to adopt the strategy of opposition parties in Continental European countries, where attempts are made to defeat government proposals in the courts when parliamentary opposition to them has failed.

Professor Nicol is surely right to argue that continuing Tory scepticism invalidates claims that the values of the HRA are somehow 'above politics'. It is interesting to speculate whether the Labour Opposition may make more use of the judicial route for continuing the fight against the legislation of the Conservative-Liberal Coalition, since Labour still claims (fairly plausibly) to believe in the basic

[39] Ibid 19.

[40] See further eg G. Huscroft and P. Rishworth, ' "You Say You Want a Revolution": Bills of Rights in the Age of Human Rights', in D. Dyzenhaus, M. Hunt, and G. Huscroft (eds), *A Simple Common Lawyer: Essays in Honour of Michael Taggart* (Oxford: Hart, 2009) (and citations therein).

[41] Cf M. J. Perry, 'Protecting Human Rights in a Democracy: What Role for the Courts?' (2003) 38 *Wake Forest Law Review* 635, 672: judicial protection of rights in UK 'is at least as strong…as in Canada'.

[42] D. Nicol, 'Law and Politics after the Human Rights Act' [2006] *Public Law* 722. See *A* [2002] 1 AC 45; Sexual Offences Act 2003, s 75.

[43] Nicol, above n 22, adopting the framework of A. Stone Sweet, *Governing with Judges: Constitutional Politics in Europe* (Oxford: Oxford University Press, 2000).

[44] 574. Nicol notes the simplistic populism of Labour ministers in the debates on what became the Anti-Terrorism, Crime and Security Act 2001: what would the public expect Parliament to do, faced with the threat of terrorism after 11 September 2001? There was no hint of a belief that the courts would, or should, intervene to protect the human rights of those to be detained indefinitely under the legislation. Cf the subsequent 'Belmarsh Prison case', *A v Home Secretary* [2004] UKHL 56; [2005] 2 AC 68.

correctness of judicial protection of human rights. It would be politically risky for any government to seek explicitly to exclude the HRA when legislating, or to reverse judgments of the courts on human rights issues, without being accused of flouting the 'rule of law'. Here, of course, is the great difficulty with casting human rights as legal principles in the first place. This lends them their 'superior mystique'.[45] It implies that they are within the peculiar cognisance of the judges, and effectively off-limits for political debate, 'in some way an exception to the contestability of other normative choices'.[46]

It would therefore take a very brave government to face down an explicit judicial determination that its legislation had violated the ECHR. For this reason, describing the status quo as a meaningful 'dialogue' (or rather, duet) exceeds any reasonable limit of credulity. As will be set out in the next section, this is no less true of the s 4 remedy (declarations of incompatibility). It will be argued that removing these powerful weapons from the courts would allow a much more meaningful parliamentary discussion of human rights, one not in thrall to the legal-judicial viewpoint.

III. Section 4 of the Human Rights Act

The HRA makes provision for an exceedingly odd remedy, where a compatible 'interpretation' of a statutory provision is not 'possible' under s 3: 'If the court is satisfied that the provision is incompatible with a Convention right, it may make a declaration of that incompatibility';[47] however, such a declaration 'does not affect the validity, continuing operation or enforcement of the provision in respect of which it is given; and is not binding on the parties to the proceedings in which it is made'.[48] While declaratory judgments are not unknown in English public law,[49] the courts have insisted that their function is limited to 'declaring contested legal rights, subsisting or future, of the parties represented in the litigation before it and not those of anyone else'.[50] The oddity of the declaration of incompatibility, by its very definition and its effect (or lack of effect), is that the court is not declaring what the law is, but rather what the law isn't. In effect, the court is empowered to issue legal advice, without any binding legal effect,[51] to Parliament and the government.

---

[45] Campbell, above n 11.

[46] Ibid. A view apparently shared by former Prime Minister Gordon Brown, who opposed the inclusion of social and economic rights in any 'British Bill of Rights' on the ground that: 'I do not think [such rights] can ever be off-limits in a debate': evidence to House of Commons Liaison Committee, 13 Dec 2007.

[47] s 4(2).

[48] s 4(6).

[49] See eg *Gillick's* Case [1986] AC 112, described as an example at the 'extreme end of [the court's] supervisory jurisdiction' in Sir H. Woolf, J. Woolf, J. J. Clyde, and I. Zamir, *The Declaratory Judgment*, 2nd edn (London: Sweet & Maxwell, 1993), para 3.007.

[50] *Gouriet v Union of Post Office Workers* [1978] AC 435, 501, per Lord Diplock.

[51] NB that a declaration also triggers the 'Henry VIII' power for the government to amend the offending legislation by statutory instrument, under s 10, HRA. This undermines Parliament in a different way.

This is a striking constitutional innovation, and well outside the normal judicial function of applying the law as it stands.

In *Rusbridger*,[52] the House of Lords refused to use the power in s 4, HRA to declare that s 3 of the Treason Felony Act 1848 (making it a crime to advocate the peaceful abolition of the monarchy) was incompatible with Article 10, ECHR. While their Lordships unhesitatingly agreed that a prosecution under this provision would violate the Convention right to freedom of expression, they held that there was no prospect of the law being enforced (no prosecution had been brought since 1883), and that the question was effectively moot. The court made plain its view that this case, brought by the editor of the *Guardian* newspaper, was 'unnecessary litigation';[53] the courts 'have no concern with hypothetical, premature or academic questions... [and] are neither a debating club nor an advisory bureau'.[54] While it was no doubt undesirable for such legislation to remain on the statute book 'in a mummified state', it was not for the courts to 'chivvy Parliament into spring-cleaning the statute book, perhaps to the detriment of more important legislation'.[55]

All of this would in most legal contexts be wholly admirable,[56] but deploring 'hypothetical, premature or academic' litigation is a questionable reason for refusing a declaration under s 4, HRA (as opposed to refusing an ordinary declaration of legal rights), since the declaration of incompatibility is by its very nature both hypothetical and academic. It seems equally confused, in this unusual context, for the courts to protest that they are not 'advisory bureaux' when this is precisely the role that Parliament has allotted to them in enacting s 4, HRA. Also, while *Rusbridger* demonstrates the judicial concern to exclude 'pure' or abstract public-interest challenges from s 4, HRA, Tom Hickman has pointed out that, on the other hand, s 4 provides 'no incentive for [directly affected] individuals to litigate human rights cases because there is no opportunity of overturning the law in question. It is impossible to say how many claims have never been brought or defended or have fallen by the wayside'.[57] From this perspective, it is precisely in abstract challenges (like that in *Rusbridger*) that a declaration of incompatibility is most useful, as opposed to a claim seeking an actual binding remedy.

Leaving these puzzles aside, it is tolerably clear that s 4 is the key provision of the HRA, by which parliamentary sovereignty is supposedly preserved. The statute is left unscathed (cf s 3, discussed above), and it is for Parliament and the government to decide whether to take the necessary steps to amend the 'incompatible' provision, either through normal legislative procedures or the fast-track remedy under

[52] *Reg (Rusbridger) v Attorney-General* [2003] UKHL 38, [2004] AC 357.

[53] [47] Lord Scott.

[54] *Macnaughton v Macnaughton's Trustees* 1953 SC 387 at 392 (Lord Justice-Clerk Thomson), quoted by Lord Hutton at [35].

[55] [61] per Lord Walker of Gestingthorpe.

[56] See further *Oxfordshire County Council v Oxford City Council* [2006] UKHL 25 (not an HRA case).

[57] T. Hickman, Memorandum, para 24, published in JCHR, 29th Report, Session 2007–8, 'A Bill of Rights for the UK?'.

s 10, HRA. Here, then, is the supposed 'dialogue' between judges and politicians, in which the latter are left with the final say. Alison Young therefore argues that the courts should rely on s 4 in preference to s 3 when the issue is one that Parliament is better placed to address.[58]

It is submitted that, once again, such arguments are highly misleading, for they suggest that Parliament has considerably more freedom to ignore declarations of incompatibility than is actually the case in practice.[59] As Nevil Johnson observes, the claim that the HRA does not threaten Parliament's sovereignty because the courts cannot strike statutes down is 'disingenuous', since 'Parliament would really have no options but to amend the law in order to comply with the Convention'. The reason is not far to seek: if Parliament refused to amend the legislation, the losing party would proceed to the European Court of Human Rights (ECtHR) in Strasbourg, and almost certainly win. The government would then have little option but to pass remedial action, save for 'denunciation of the original agreements to accept the European Convention as well as repeal of the 1998 legislation'.[60] It is the threat of what amounts to an appeal to Strasbourg against post-declaration inaction (whether deliberate or inadvertent) that makes the HRA in effect just as potent as the Canadian Charter of Rights.[61] Therefore, it should not be surprising when the then Prime Minister Tony Blair complains about the courts 'striking down' anti-terrorism measures;[62] and to condemn his comments as 'misleading' itself misses the point.[63] Mr Blair was concerned with political reality rather than the (wholly theoretical) technical legal position. Moreover, 'anyone who has attempted to gain a proper understanding of the British Constitution will know that it is perilous to focus on the legal formalities alone, to the exclusion of the political practices and norms which surround them'.[64]

If it was not clear enough already, the de facto bindingness of declarations of incompatibility has recently been suggested by the European Court of Human Rights itself (and British reactions to it). In *Burden v UK*,[65] the Grand Chamber held once again that s 4, HRA does not provide an 'effective remedy' for violation of ECHR rights (cf Article 13) because a declaration of incompatibility formally 'places no legal obligation on the executive or the legislature to amend the law'.[66] But the Grand Chamber went beyond this trite recitation of the strict legal position,

---

[58] Young, above n 32.
[59] See generally Kavanagh, above n 21, 282–8.
[60] N. Johnson, *Reshaping the British Constitution* (Basingstoke: Palgrave Macmillan, 2004), 131.
[61] Perry, above n 41, 672.
[62] See Blair's exchange with Henry Porter, *The Observer*, 23 Apr 2006; also *Sunday Times*, 27 May 2007. Cf the Belmarsh case, above n 44 (where the House of Lords issued declarations of incompatibility).
[63] House of Lords Constitution Committee, 6th Report of Session 2006–7, 'Relations between the Executive, the Judiciary and Parliament' at para [94].
[64] Kavanagh, above n 21, 293.
[65] 29 Apr 2008.
[66] Para 40. It may be noted that after *A v Home Secretary* [2004] UKHL 56; [2005] 2 AC 68, a decision lauded as 'the finest assertion of civil liberties that has emerged from a British court since at least *Entick v. Carrington*' (C Gearty, 'Human Rights in an Age of Terrorism: Injurious, Irrelevant or Indispensable?'(2005) 38 *Current Legal Problems* 25, 37) the successful claimants were not immediately freed but remained immured in HMP Belmarsh for over three months; when finally released

declaring that 'it cannot be excluded that at some time in the future the practice of giving effect to the national courts' declarations of incompatibility by amendment of the legislation is so certain as to indicate that section 4 of the Human Rights Act is to be interpreted as imposing a binding obligation'.[67] Although this hadn't as yet occurred, the Grand Chamber noted 'with satisfaction that in all the cases where declarations of incompatibility have to date become final, steps have been taken to amend the offending legislative provision',[68] and also quoted Lord Irvine of Lairg LC's expectation 'that the government and Parliament will in all cases almost certainly be prompted to change the law following a declaration of incompatibility'.[69] The European Court of Human Rights makes it very clear that while Parliament might have the theoretical freedom to ignore a declaration of incompatibility, the UK's Convention obligation to provide an effective remedy for invasions of rights entirely negates that freedom.[70]

The JCHR argues that after *Burden*, 'through ensuring consistent, speedy, legislative responses to declarations', the United Kingdom may yet demonstrate to Strasbourg that s 4 is an effective remedy. The JCHR therefore calls on the government, *inter alia*, to 'provide clear guidance to individual Departments on the need for a prompt *and effective* response to every declaration of incompatibility'.[71] Calling for an 'effective response' here is somewhat question-begging, but it seems clear that the JCHR expects the government to amend the offending legislation in line with the court's 'declaration'. There is realistically no space here for the much-discussed ability of the British government to defy the (domestic) courts: if they do so, they will lose twice over in Strasbourg, both on the substantive challenge and also by revealing the inadequacy of s 4, HRA to provide an effective remedy for the ECHR violation.

Thus, in a recent debate on the JCHR report, Lord Goodhart declared that 'compliance with the decisions of the European Court of Human Rights, and indeed with the final decisions of domestic courts if the case does not go to Strasbourg, is absolutely necessary', arguing that since under the HRA 'the judiciary has power to declare primary legislation incompatible with the Act, but that does not invalidate that legislation', the 'duty of compliance therefore falls on the Government'.[72] Lord Bach, for the government, seemed to accept this (having made the usual recital that 'there is no legal obligation on the Government or Parliament to take remedial action' after a declaration of incompatibility), noting that the government was 'particularly pleased' with *Burden*. 'We know that we have a way to go to demonstrate the consistent practice that the court demands, but this is already a significant step forward in the court's jurisprudence.'[73]

on bail they were subject to the government's new system of 'control orders' (not wholly dissimilar to 'house arrest'). The *Guardian*, 12 Mar 2005. See Kavanagh, above n 21, 388.

[67] Para 43. [68] Para 41. [69] Para 23.
[70] Note that Art 13 is not one of the relevant Convention rights in the HRA: s 1(1).
[71] 31st Report, Session 2007–8, 'Monitoring the Government's Response to Human Rights Judgements: Annual Report 2008', paras 83–4 (emphasis added).
[72] *Lords Hansard*, 24 Nov 2008: col GC 132.
[73] 24 Nov 2008: col GC 136–7.

In the light of Strasbourg's view of s 4, we can conclude upon this remarkable provision as follows. The English courts are empowered to do something that is wholly futile in the legal sense: to declare what the law isn't. But the *political pressure* exerted by this 'advice' is extraordinarily potent (while unhelpful for the disappointed applicant). De facto the courts require the politicians to amend the statute,[74] with the looming threat of condemnation in the European Court of Human Rights as the sanction for recalcitrance. There is no room for any 'dialogue' here. This is, in Stone Sweet's terms, a 'culture of compliance' pure and simple, just as surely as when the courts use s 3 to rewrite the statute themselves.[75] When the judicial orchestra strikes up that curious modernist finale 'the declaration of incompatibility', the opera closes with the statute dying centre-stage, like Tosca or Violetta or Aida or Gilda or Mimi. What can the parliamentary spectators do, save applaud (and then bury the body)?[76]

IV. The Joint Committee on Human Rights

The parliamentary Joint[77] Committee on Human Rights is an organization with great potential for promoting political discussion of rights issues. But has been criticized for a tendency 'to restrict itself to making predictions as to whether legislative provisions breach the ECHR. It does not initiate a debate as to what the ECHR *ought* to mean'.[78] As Professor Feldman, the JCHR's first legal adviser claims, the committee has been instrumental in getting the government to take seriously its obligation to draft legislation compatibly with the ECHR.[79] The government's engagement with JCHR criticism (the Committee carefully reviews every government bill before Parliament) is surely more important than a bare recitation of whether a bill is ministerially believed to be compatible with the Convention, pursuant to s 19, HRA.

Yet while the JCHR has undoubtedly raised parliamentary awareness of human rights issues and provided valuable information for legislators,[80] it has nevertheless

[74] Kavanagh, above n 21, 287.

[75] Aileen Kavanagh similarly concludes that the dialogue metaphor is misleading, a metaphor 'radically divorced from constitutional practice'. Ibid 410.

[76] Or otherwise perform the last rites if, like poor Don Giovanni, the statute has been consigned to some *Juristischen Begriffshölle*. A provision once 'declared incompatible' is veritably in a state of limbo. In the Bad Old Days, Lord Lester of Herne Hill had declared it was 'time to bring down the curtain on this comic opera, in which governments use Parliamentary sovereignty to shield themselves against effective accountability to Parliament and to the rule of law', before concluding (accurately as it has turned out) *'La Commedia e finita'*; 'Taking Human Rights Seriously', in R. Gordon and R. Wilmot-Smith (eds), *Human Rights in the United Kingdom* (Oxford: Oxford University Press, 1996), 112.

[77] ie of both Houses.

[78] Nicol, above n 22, 475.

[79] D. Feldman, 'The Impact of Human Rights on the UK Legislative Process' (2004) 25 *Statute Law Review* 91. However, contrast Feldman's views of the importance of the JCHR (and ECHR) in the drafting and enactment of the Anti-Terrorism, Crime and Security Act 2001 with Nicol, above n 22.

[80] As Nicol notes, the House of Lords is the much more enthusiastic audience. See similarly Francesca Klug, Appendix to JCHR's 23rd Report of 2005–6 Session, 9.5–9.7.

seemed firmly a part of the 'Culture of Compliance' in which the legislature tries to predict and pre-empt adverse judicial decisions.[81] Indeed, it has been a main driver of it. As seen in the last section, the JCHR encourages prompt obedience to 'declarations of incompatibility' issued by English judges. Another revealing episode was the JCHR's reaction when the government unusually declined to certify that a bill was 'ECHR compatible', over what became the Communications Act 2003. A total ban on 'political advertising' looked to be of dubious legality under Article 10, ECHR,[82] but the government pressed ahead, considering that a respectable argument for the ban's compatibility could be advanced in any later legal challenge, although not one guaranteed of success.[83] The JCHR concluded that this stance did not 'evince a lack of respect for human rights' and was 'legitimate in the circumstances'.[84] But crucial for this conclusion was the government's 'expressed willingness' that (as Professor Feldman, then legal adviser to the JCHR puts it) it would 'legislate again to take account of any judicial decision, *in the UK or Strasbourg*, that the ban as operated under the Bill is incompatible with Article 10'.[85] As Janet Hiebert observes, this shows the 'prevailing political assumption' that any legislation judicially impugned would have to be amended to fit the 'legal' position.[86]

In an important and very interesting report commissioned by the JCHR itself in 2006,[87] Professor Francesca Klug OBE identified two very different visions of the work of the Committee. On the first view, the JCHR exists (primarily or even solely) to provide ' "quasi-judicial" legal advice to Parliament'.[88] This 'technical role'[89] for the JCHR seems to have been the dominant vision, for Professor Klug concludes that:

The current approach to scrutiny of published bills relies primarily on an estimation of the 'degree of risk' that a court will find legislation incompatible. The focus is on predicting how the domestic courts are likely to judge the legislation in question, based mainly on

[81] Hiebert, above n 38, notes that 'compatibility statements' under s 19 tend to be 'highly legalistic' rather than advancing political or policy arguments for a provision. The government's legal advisers, encouraged by the JCHR, presumably see mere policy as irrelevant to the 'compatibility' question.

[82] *VgT Verein gegen Tierfabriken v Switzerland* (2001) 34 EHRR 159.

[83] In the event, the government's arguments prevailed in both the Divisional Court and the House of Lords: *R (Animal Defenders International) v Secretary of State for Culture, Media and Sport* [2008] UKHL 15; [2008] 1 AC 1312.

[84] JCHR 4th Report, Session 2002-3, paras 40–1.

[85] Feldman, above n 79, 100 (emphasis added). The JCHR, above n 84, at para 40 was a little more circumspect/orthodox in noting that 'the Government would *feel obliged to amend the law if that particular provision were held by the European Court of Human Rights*, after argument, to be incompatible with Article 10, and would *consider its position if a court in the United Kingdom were to make a declaration of incompatibility* under section 4 of the Human Rights Act 1998' (emphasis added). It is suggested that David Feldman's revealing paraphrase of this, in a less formal setting, admits the truth of the matter.

[86] Hiebert, above n 38, 28.

[87] Published as an Appendix to JCHR's 23rd Report of 2005-6 Session, on 'The Committee's Future Working Practices' (hereafter 'Klug Report').

[88] Ibid 13.1(i). Cf 11.5.

[89] Ibid 4.9 (citing Robert Blackburn, 'A Human Rights Committee for the UK Parliament' [1998] EHRLR 534, 538).

the jurisprudence of the European Court of Human Rights or case law from the domestic courts interpreting the ECHR. The Committee only rarely makes judgements for itself on whether legislation is compatible or not.[90]

The Report describes the 'contortions' that such an approach of second-guessing the courts has required of the JCHR.[91]

However, Professor Klug identifies a second and broader role for the JCHR: less technical-legal,[92] engaging in the underlying debates about the proper role and scope of rights, particularly when balanced against each other and the public interest.[93] As she rightly observes, in human rights adjudication:

the issue at stake is often not wholly, or even mainly, a matter of 'technical compliance' as such. It is whether such limitations meet a 'pressing social need' in a democratic society and whether they have been proportionately applied, or whether a different policy could have been pursued with similar effects but with fewer incursions on fundamental rights. These are questions which members of parliament are, arguably, particularly well placed to consider, as the courts frequently suggest.[94]

A number of government ministers suggested to Klug that the JCHR's scrutiny was more effective when engaged with 'general arguments of policy . . . rather than in the purely legal field'.[95] The Human Rights Minister commented that the JCHR would speak with greater authority if it were open about the controversial, values-based nature of human rights assessments (of which both ministers and courts were well aware),[96] and the Solicitor-General similarly called for greater emphasis on the 'dilemmas' posed for government and Parliament by the HRA.[97] One member of the JCHR even complained that by importing Strasbourg judgments into the parliamentary process, the JCHR was illegitimately helping to bypass the democratic process.[98]

More significantly still, Murray Hunt, Professor Feldman's successor as the JCHR's legal adviser, also argued in favour of a broader remit for the Committee. Mr Hunt attacked the approach of 'predicting the degree of risk' for sending to Parliament the 'unfortunate message' that 'human rights questions [are] technical, legal questions to which only trained lawyers have access to the answers'.[99] This in turn 'discourages democratic debate and deliberation about human rights compatibility when one of the virtues of the HRA is that it is premised on the view that questions of compatibility should be subject to democratic debate'.[100] For good measure, Mr Hunt criticized the approach as 'slightly evasive of the issue at stake': the Committee should be forming its own view on compatibility rather than essaying predictions of the judicial view.[101]

---

[90] Ibid 13.14. See further 12.10–12.12.
[91] Ibid 12.7–12.8. But for the possible benefits of a detailed legal approach, cf 13.3.
[92] One former JCHR member called its *modus operandi* 'anally retentive', ibid 11.2. Cf also 11.6(ix): Committee's 'pompous, narrow way' of proceeding.
[93] Ibid 13.1(ii). Cf 11.6.   [94] Ibid 12.6.   [95] Ibid 8.6 (Harriet Harman MP).
[96] Ibid 8.8 (Baroness Ashton).   [97] Ibid 8.9 (Mike O'Brien MP).
[98] Ibid 11.6(vii).   [99] Ibid 12.9.   [100] Ibid.   [101] Ibid.

These views accord with those of the current author. But it is by no means clear that despite their eminent source, Mr Hunt's vision of the JCHR's remit will prevail. Professor Klug in her Report discerned 'sharp differences of view... over the focus and priorities of the Committee' amongst members of the JCHR appointed for the 2005–10 parliamentary session.[102] These correspond to the very different visions of the JCHR's role described above. While a majority of members favoured a *via media*,[103] there were nevertheless 'strongly held views by two or three members of the Committee that are probably irreconcilable with each other'.[104] In the light of these disagreements, it is perhaps unsurprising that in the JCHR's own Report founded on Professor Klug's research, there was no clear resolution of the dichotomy of 'visions' that she identified.[105] The thrust of the Report was to introduce a new 'sifting procedure' better to target the legislative scrutiny work of the JCHR, which would give it more time to engage in other activities such as pre- and post-legislative scrutiny, monitoring government compliance with UK and ECtHR judgments, and thematic inquiries into important human rights controversies so as to inform public debate. The closest that the JCHR came to addressing the key issue (for the concerns of this essay) was in its decision to make its legislative scrutiny reports 'shorter and more focused... [and] less expository of the relevant law', with a greater focus on 'proportionality' questions.[106] But, the JCHR concluded, rather disappointingly: 'We will give further consideration to Professor Klug's advice that we should more explicitly express our conclusions on compatibility questions in our own voice, rather than, as she puts it, "second-guessing" the view which courts might take in future cases'.[107]

It still remains to be seen whether the JCHR makes the decisive break from the 'Culture of Compliance' model criticized by Nicol, Hiebert, Klug, and Murray Hunt. The imminent appointment of a new JCHR[108] for the 2010–15 Parliament may, we hope, prove to be the watershed in this regard. Such a break with the past is greatly to be encouraged: the JCHR should be a locus of parliamentary *resistance* to the legal-monopoly-of-wisdom view of human rights. It will be argued below that the surest way to achieve this would be to diminish the role of the courts: there could then be little room for the second-guessing, risk-predictive approach which has been so unfortunately prominent in the first decade of the JCHR.

---

[102] Ibid 11.4.   [103] Ibid. Cf 11.8.   [104] Ibid 13.1.

[105] JCHR, 23rd Report of 2005–6 Session, 'The Committee's Future Working Practices'. Klug herself suggested that this was 'a primary question for the JCHR to consider in its examination of its working practices', Klug Report, above n 87, 13.5. However, the JCHR noted that 'we do not exhaustively reconsider all the issues covered so clearly by Professor Klug's report' ('The Committee's Future Working Practices', para 11).

[106] 'The Committee's Future Working Practices', para 47.

[107] Ibid.   [108] At time of writing: June 2010.

V. Proposals for Reform: Amendments to HRA

The objective of the proposals sketched here is to turn back the judicialization of politics. Primarily, this would be achieved by strictly limiting the courts' power to review the 'compatibility' of Acts of Parliament with the ECHR, whether under the guise of 'interpretation' of the statutes *contra legem*, or by 'declaring' them incompatible. It is hoped that these reforms by themselves would engender a renaissance of parliamentary human rights debate which is not colonized by narrow legalism. Predicting what the judges will do (and rushing to agree *ex post facto*, if one has guessed wrong) is simple obedience, not debate.

The suggested amendments of the HRA can be easily stated. Section 3 should be repealed, and replaced with a provision that makes clear that interpretation cannot distort the meaning of statutory language. Section 4 should be repealed and not replaced. This means that the 'fast track' procedure under s 10 would become redundant *pro tanto*, although it would still be triggered when 'it appears to a Minister of the Crown or Her Majesty in Council that, having regard to a finding of the European Court of Human Rights made after the coming into force of this section in proceedings against the United Kingdom, a provision of legislation is incompatible'.[109] It is suggested that as amending legislation by statutory instrument is essentially a way of avoiding full-dress legislative scrutiny and debate in Parliament, this procedure is itself incompatible with the promotion of a parliamentary culture of human rights. Thus s 10 should be repealed without replacement, along with s 4.

Conversely, s 19 in its way promotes parliamentary debate, and should be retained in some form; however, the duty to state whether 'the provisions of the Bill are compatible with the Convention rights' should be replaced by a wider and more useful obligation to provide a 'reasoned statement of the Bill's implications for civil liberties and human rights'.[110]

It should be made plain that ss 6–8 of the HRA are not considered here. As stated in the introduction above, *any* judicial protection of human rights is undesirable, for it promotes the myth that these rights are rare creatures surrounded by legal mystery, off limits for political discussion. Nevertheless, if anything substantial is to remain of the HRA (and the best guess of current political attitudes is that this is the general assumption), allowing judicial review of administrative action on human rights grounds is far less constitutionally damaging than allowing judicial review of Acts of Parliament. Section 6(2), of course, is the crucial provision dividing responsibility between ss 3, 4, and 6. There are many things that one could say about these provisions, especially concerning the definition of a public

---

[109] s 10(1)(b).

[110] It seems odd to have this in an Act of Parliament at all rather than Standing Orders on procedure in the two Houses of Parliament. It gives new life to the 'manner and form debate', on which see Young, above n 32. But this is more a theoretical than a practical problem, and I do not want to propose reforms to the HRA that are not strictly necessary when the ones I do put forward are more than contentious enough.

authority, and the still obscure effect of the HRA upon private parties. But as these are outside the present concern we pass over them. However this tactical withdrawal should not be taken as wholesale approbation, let alone enthusiasm, for the residuum of the HRA.

VI. Proposals for Reform: The JCHR

It is hoped that if the courts' role with regard to primary legislation was curbed in the way outlined in the last section, Parliament would perforce escape its role as second fiddle to the judicial virtuosi. The JCHR would continue to play an important role.[111] It is suggested that it should continue to scrutinize the human rights and civil liberties implications of bills before Parliament. Crucially, however, it should broaden its focus in the way recommended (*inter alios*) by Francesca Klug and Murray Hunt,[112] and no longer concentrate upon predicting what the judges might do when faced with the legislation in question. A political debate about the existence, and extent, of rights in the light of competing rights and interests is what is needed, not legalistic crystal-ball-gazing.

The position advocated here bears a striking resemblance to the somewhat neglected thesis of David Kinley, who in 1993 proposed 'compliance [with the ECHR] without incorporation', by the means of a parliamentary committee.[113] Kinley took the Australian Senate's Standing Committee for the Scrutiny of Bills as his model for a body within the legislature playing an influential role in the drafting of legislation by scrutinizing government proposals, and providing informative reports. We could say that, with the caveats entered above, the JCHR at Westminster has since 2000 successfully played an analogous role to the Australian committee. But as its title suggests, Kinley's proposal was intended as an *alternative* to full legal incorporation of the ECHR. He sought a way out of the 'stultifying intransigence' of the debate over incorporation.[114] As recently as 1993, as Kinley describes, both the Labour Party and the senior judiciary showed extreme antipathy to the wholesale transfer of power to the courts that incorporation of the ECHR would, inevitably, involve.[115]

Kinley made detailed proposals for how such a committee would fit into the legislative process, but did not consider that it should play any greater role than submitting reports to both Houses of Parliament, and thus aiding legislative scrutiny by the provision of information.[116] This, again, closely parallels the JCHR's role. But there might, perhaps, now be a case for strengthening the JCHR's formal

---

[111] We note but reject the argument that the JCHR would be emasculated without judicial review to back it up. Kavanagh, above n 21, 399–400.

[112] See pp 429–431 above.

[113] D. Kinley, *The ECHR: Compliance without Incorporation* (Dartmouth: Aldershot, 1993).

[114] Ibid at 11.

[115] It is for others to explain the astonishing, and rapid, *volte face* by both of these groups. Cf J. Young, 'The Politics of the Human Rights Act' (1999) 26 *Journal of Law and Society* 27.

[116] Ch 7.

procedural function under Standing Orders, given that while the House of Lords is an enthusiastic debater of JCHR reports and ECHR points, the Commons has remained fairly indifferent.[117] Each House could amend its Standing Orders to require that consideration of the JCHR's report before proceeding to the Committee Stage on any Bill.

Yet more radically, perhaps, the JCHR's proceedings could become in effect another 'stage' of the bill's passage through Parliament, with the JCHR being able to amend the text of the bill like a legislative Standing Committee. The whole House would, of course, as normal, be able to reject such amendments at the Report stage. Kinley is not alone in doubting whether such a formal enhancement of the JCHR's legislative role is desirable.[118] We would predict that the JCHR would become much more politically partisan, and the Whips would seek to control it much more tightly. Its current consensual approach would be impaired, and with it some of its authority and credibility. These would indeed be serious losses; on the other hand, such heightened political interest would accord with the central thesis here advanced that human rights are properly subjects for political debate. Hopefully, with backbench members from both Houses committed to the preservation of civil liberties, the JCHR could preserve some of its present bipartisan spirit while engaging in much more vigorous political debate, rather than the meek legalistic second-guessing of the past.

A final point to stress is the JCHR's potential for widening access and participation to human rights debates. One of the main justifications for having these issues decided in Parliament and not the courts is that this gives the public, and interest groups, more opportunity to express their views. It is true that the courts have shown a cautious increase in allowing interventions and even 'Brandeis briefs' in HRA litigation.[119] But this is still far from allowing an open public consultation, as the JCHR can and does. Similarly, parliamentary committees have much greater freedom in deciding from whom to take oral evidence than the standing rules in litigation. Finally, of course, it is possible for members of the public and others to lobby MPs and peers directly (whether in the JCHR or otherwise), in a way that is rightly seen as improper for the judiciary.[120] No doubt the JCHR could 'raise its profile' and so act as a more effective conduit for the public view into the parliamentary process. There are inevitably cost implications for proposing any additional role for a governmental institution; but in this case, it would hopefully be offset by a decrease in (horrifyingly expensive) ss 3 and 4, HRA litigation.[121]

[117] Nicol, above n 22.

[118] Kinley's limited proposals were welcomed by M. Ryle, 'Pre-legislative Scrutiny: A Prophylactic Approach to Protection of Human Rights' [1994] *Public Law* 192. Ryle rejected the argument that a parliamentary committee with no formal powers of disallowance or amendment would be 'toothless'. This, he said, underestimated the influence of publicity on a sensitive subject like human rights.

[119] See eg C. Harlow, 'Public Law and Popular Justice' (2002) 65 *Modern Law Review* 1; JCHR evidence, 26 Mar 2001 (Lords Woolf, Bingham, and Phillips), QQ 121, 124.

[120] Perhaps this will come as another undesirable (but predictable) effect of the HRA. For example, Blackmun J of the US Supreme Court received numerous death-threats (from pro-life campaigners, naturally) after writing the majority opinion in *Roe v Wade* (1973) 410 US 113.

[121] We do not pretend to have any empirical data about the cost of these proposals. The under-resourcing of parliamentary committees at Westminster, especially compared to those in the US Congress, is notorious and utterly deplorable.

VII. A More Radical Proposal: Parliamentary Resolution of Individual Disputes

This section tentatively outlines a proposal for a new parliamentary institution to provide remedies in individual cases when (consequent upon the reforms proposed above) the courts are unable to grant a remedy because primary legislation bars the way. Thus, we could square the circle of hearing individual-initiated claims for violation of their rights and liberties, but resolving them in the bosom of the parliamentary process rather than the courts.

A would-be radical should bear in mind Michael Ryle's warning that parliamentary reform is usually successful if it builds on existing procedures, with minimum constitutional and procedural innovation.[122] While what will be proposed is in some ways a new departure, there are venerable precedents for it. It is not as rash as to suggest we adopt (say) the French *Conseil Constitutionnel* as our model.[123]

The proposal in outline is this. Should any court find that an individual has a strong prima-facie claim for redress for restrictions of his human rights or civil liberties, but where the court is obliged as a matter of law to dismiss the claim because primary legislation is clear on the point against the individual, the court should have the power to stay the proceedings and make a reference to a new 'High Court of Parliament' (herein HCP), to consider the matter further.[124] Procedure in the HCP (a parliamentary body consisting of members from both Houses) would resemble litigation in some ways, with the parties to the referred case having automatic standing to appear. But like a parliamentary Select Committee, the HCP would have broad powers to investigate the matter, to gather evidence and consult the public, and to hear other parties' views in oral proceedings. The HCP could determine the case as it saw fit; this might include the introduction of a bill for enactment by expedited parliamentary process, to amend the legislation so as to provide a remedy in the petitioner's case and others like it.

The beauty of such an institution is that it would bring together the best of both worlds. As a parliamentary body, the HCP would have no concerns about accusations of usurping Parliament's sovereignty, for example by amending legislation under the aegis of 'interpreting' it. As Parliament can, of course, amend legislation, it would not need to pretend to be interpreting it—unlike the courts.[125] The closed and relatively ill-informed nature of judicial proceedings, inherent in litigation however generous the rules of *locus standi*,[126] could be avoided. The HCP could be furnished with all of the expert evidence, and public opinion, available to any other parliamentary body. Moreover, a parliamentary committee could make the moral

---

[122] Ryle, above n 118.

[123] For the unacceptability of the French approach, see Kinley, above n 113. But for a proposed Rights Council for Australia, modelled upon the French *Conseil*, see G. Winterton, in T. Campbell, J. Goldsworthy, and A. Stone (eds), *Protecting Rights without a Bill of Rights: Institutional Performance and Reform in Australia* (Aldershot: Ashgate, 2006).

[124] In terms of 'reference procedures', something basically comparable to Art 234 of the EC Treaty.

[125] See discussion of s 3, HRA, above.

[126] See eg L. L. Fuller, 'The Forms and Limits of Adjudication' (1978) 93 *Harvard Law Review* 353.

judgments inherent in human rights controversies just as well as the courts—and arguably rather better.[127]

The reason for proposing this curious institution is that it fills a lacuna that the earlier (less radical) proposals would otherwise create. Alison Young's consideration of the proper relationship between ss 3 and 4 of the HRA (in their current form) very sensibly uses comparative institutional competence as its guide.[128] When the courts are better placed to resolve a given dispute, Dr Young argues, s 3, which gives the upper hand to the judicial process, should be used; and conversely, when the issue is more suitable for Parliament, the court should issue a 'declaration of incompatibility' under s 4.[129] It is worth considering this assessment of institutional competence;[130] I will suggest that Dr Young convincingly identifies one category of disputes that are better resolved by judicial rather than traditionally legislative means. Hence my proposal for the HCP, which has some resemblance to judicial process despite being a parliamentary body.

Dr Young identifies basically three situations in which the courts are better placed to resolve human rights controversies.[131] First, courts are prima facie better placed to protect minority rights, because of the classic 'tyranny of the majority' problem. This, I suggest, is a falsifiable hypothesis rather than being incontestably true as an a priori matter.[132] One need only glance at the body of UK legislation protecting various minority groups in recent years to see that an elected body *need not* systematically discriminate against minorities. Conversely, courts cannot be trusted always to protect minority rights.[133] The record of British parliamentary democracy on the treatment of minorities, while not unmixed, is not wholly indefensible either. So the first argument seems questionable.[134]

Alison Young's second putative category for legislative deference to the judiciary is even less convincing. Courts, she opines, are better suited to resolving *issues of*

---

[127] Jeremy Waldron claims that those who defend the US Supreme Court's role in enforcing the Bill of Rights by praising the judges' ability to make moral judgments, insulated from the pressures of democratic election, are really arguing for an institution like the modern, appointed House of Lords in Britain. An appointed chamber of experts may be expected perform this 'moral' role far better than a cadre of senior lawyers (Eisgruber indeed deplores the technical legal reasoning in constitutional adjudication as a distraction from the real moral issues; so why advocate *court-based adjudication* at all?). J. Waldron, 'Eisgruber's House of Lords' (2002) 37 *University of San Francisco Law Review* 89 (commenting on C. L. Eisgruber, *Constitutional Self-Government* (Cambridge, Mass: Harvard University Press, 2001)).

[128] Young, above n 32.

[129] I have above argued that both sections in fact give the whip-hand to the courts, so this debate is of little relevance to the operation of the HRA as it stands.

[130] See more generally, J. King, 'Institutional Approaches to Legal Restraint' (2008) 28 *Oxford Journal of Legal Studies* 409.

[131] Young, above n 32, 130–40.

[132] Young, it is true, states her argument in the weaker 'prima facie' form, but it continues and adopts a persistent canard that needs firm rebuttal.

[133] Consider eg *Plessy v Ferguson* (1896) 163 US 537; *Korematsu v United States* (1944) 323 US 214. The 19th Century Supreme Court, far from being a 'palladium of liberty' (*pace* Black J) was in fact a 'bastion of racism': N Dorsen, 'The United States Supreme Court: Trends and Prospects', (1986) 21 *Harvard Civil Rights-Civil Liberties Law Review* 1, 3.

[134] Aileen Kavanagh also identifies 'the court's relative insulation from political pressure and short-term concerns' as the 'cornerstone' of her defence of constitutional review (and critique of parliamentary sovereignty). Kavanagh, above n 21, 365 (and see further 344–52).

moral principle, whereas Parliament is wont to give priority to short-term policy goals. Judges' principled reasoning gains the highest possible praise: the judiciary tackle problems 'in the same manner as a scholar'.[135] This is merely a (superficially attractive) variant of the rights-lawyer's unshakeable delusion that society should be run by unworldly philosopher kings sporting horsehair wigs.[136] This argument does not point to prima-facie priority for the judiciary in exceptional cases, but outright dismissal of the sordid democratic process in *all* cases. Jeremy Waldron's excellent defence of 'The Dignity of Legislation' provides the necessary dose of reality.[137] Moreover, the assertion that Parliament is unable to deliberate in a principled fashion while adjudication is intrinsically morally philosophical is, to say the least, questionable.[138] Professor Waldron points out that the quality of the debates in the House of Commons over the liberalization of the British abortion laws holds up very favourably on this (or no doubt on any other) score, in comparison with *Roe v Wade*—in which the US Supreme Court achieved the same result by (rather thinly reasoned) judicial fiat.[139]

But despite this familiar pair of dubious arguments, Alison Young cites a telling third reason for giving 'prima facie priority' to the judicial process. She correctly observes that legislatures are not capable of considering the possible impact on every individual who might be affected by the laws they are enacting. Conversely, courts are institutionally better suited to protecting specific applications of rights 'to the facts of the situation presented before the court by a particular applicant'.[140] This refers to a classic problem of the legislative process, that is, the inherent limit on a draftsman's prescience and thus the inevitability of unforeseen hard cases.[141] It may well be that legislation before 1998 was not drafted with human rights issues in mind (and legislation before 1950 logically cannot have taken the ECHR into account), so there is an added potential for the *casus omissus* here. But even with flourishing legislative scrutiny since the inauguration of the JCHR, it may be that the danger to liberty is not so much in the provisions of a bill but in how the powers that it confers on a minister ultimately come to be exercised.[142] Or more

---

[135] Young, above n 32, 136. Waldron points out that such a belief in the superiority of judicial reasoning is very common but has a 'flimsy basis': namely, that judges 'seem to reason as we [academics] do when we consider moral issues in our workshops and colloquia', in sharp contrast with 'the noisy, smelly, common and tumultuous majoritarian proceedings of our legislatures'. J. Waldron, 'Do Judges Reason Morally?' in G. Huscroft (ed), *Expounding the Constitution* (Cambridge: Cambridge University Press, 2008), 38–9.

[136] Or whatever the Well-Dressed Judge is Wearing this week.

[137] J. Waldron, *The Dignity of Legislation* (Cambridge: Cambridge University Press, 1999).

[138] Tom Campbell points out, *per contra*, that 'case law snares human rights in the tangled web of precedent and legal authority, thus threatening to devitalize its moral force'. Campbell, above n 11. Cf also Waldron at n 127 above.

[139] Waldron, above n 135, at 60-61, citing J. Waldron, 'The Core of the Case against Judicial Review' (2006) 155 *Yale Law Journal* 1346, 1383–5 and J. Waldron, 'Legislating with Integrity' (2003) 72 *Fordham Law Review* 373, 390–1.

[140] Young, above n 32, 137.

[141] We can foresee that such unforeseen situations will always arise. In Rumsfeldian terminology, these are known unknowns, the things that we know that we don't know.

[142] Cf House of Lords Constitution Committee, 6th Report, Session 2006–7, 'Relations between the Executive, the Judiciary and Parliament', at paras [91], [104]. The concession here to retain ss 6–8, HRA, might largely deal with such exercises of executive power.

broadly, the danger is that unforeseen effects on civil liberties will come to light only with the application of the law in individual cases.

These problems are a reason to have something like a judicial process, that is, a way of responding to individual complaints in factual situations that show that legislation is working in ways that might well not have been contemplated at the time of enactment. But the constitutional difficulties with allowing judges to re-write the statute (whether directly or under the guise of 'interpretation') are obvious enough. The suggestion here, for a parliamentary tribunal to hear references from courts, better resolves the third problem identified by Alison Young. The usual legal process would establish the facts of the case, and those findings of fact will reveal whether there was a possible *casus omissus*, or at any rate a human rights issue that Parliament should consider. The HCP could then consider the problem raised by the facts (if a judicial reference were made), but unlike the court would not be limited to the narrow question raised by the facts of the individual case. It is, of course, a commonplace of the common law that judges are 'Janus faced', deciding individual disputes with their eye on the development of law more generally (ie on future potential disputes). The HCP could play the latter role full-bloodedly, *fortissimo*, rather than incidentally and *sotto voce*, since it would not suffer from the constitutional and procedural constraints inherent in adjudication.[143] Thus, human rights in individual cases could receive due consideration, without judicial usurpation of debates properly belonging to Parliament.

I say little here about the detail of the proposed HCP, its procedures and crucially, its membership. Consistent with the assumptions underlying this chapter, membership should not be legally dominated. The point is to avoid a culture of compliance with law, and judicial supremacy.[144] However, it may be that having prominent legal members of the committee might render it *less* deferential to legal advice than the current situation in which it enjoys an official legal adviser, whose advice is no doubt extremely influential.[145] The procedure contemplated would, after all, see the HCP being addressed by counsel for the parties in the referred case, and so at least some legal experience amongst its membership would be advantageous. Best of all might be for the committee to contain several judicial members. They could issue opinions jointly or separately, to be published along with the HCP's report and recommendations. But the judicial members should always be in a minority and their opinion on the law ought not to determine the HCP's decision.

[143] See eg the discussion of the House of Lords' control orders decisions, in Kavanagh, above n 21, 391–3.
[144] Long ago, James Bradley Thayer lamented that in the United States, judicial review 'has had a tendency to drive out questions of justice and right, and to fill the mind[s] of legislators with thoughts of mere legality', in 'The Origin and Scope of the American Doctrine of Constitutional Law' (1893) 7 *Harvard Law Review* 129, 156.
[145] One JCHR member observes that the 'expectation was that the legal advice should be followed other than in exceptional situations leaving politicians wondering what their purpose was', Klug Report, above n 87, 11.6(viii). The 'culture of the "expert peer"' (sc *legally* expert) has dominated the JCHR to the disadvantage of MPs, ibid 11.6(ix). Cf also, 11.2 ('tension has arisen on the JCHR as a result of the differing perspectives of members with legal and non legal backgrounds'—Janet Hiebert).

Until recently the Law Lords would have been the obvious candidates for such a role. However, since the inauguration of the Supreme Court, the Constitutional Reform Act 2005 bars Supreme Court judges with peerages from sitting or voting in the House of Lords, or its committees, or any joint committees.[146] The 2005 Act is a monument to abstract constitutional theory over pragmatism and experience.[147] It is submitted that s 137 could be repealed without any damage whatever to the constitution, to allow Supreme Court judges to sit also in the proposed High Court of Parliament. It may be that this would too great a drain on the time of full-time judges, however, and so it might be preferable to give peerages to other persons with suitable judicial experience, allowing them to sit in the HCP while resigning from their other judicial duties.[148]

An alternative way of providing the HCP with judicial input would be to summon judges who were not themselves members of Parliament to hear the submissions of the parties, and to give advisory opinions on what they believe the ECHR to require, and thus how (if at all) the legislation in question might need amendment. There are of course precedents for this, although the House of Lords in its appellate capacity had not summoned the (other) judges for their opinions for over a century.[149] A more modern (although less British) example might be the Advocates General of the European Court of Justice, a quasi-judicial office providing very influential although non-binding opinions to assist the Court. A High Court judge might be seconded to the HCP to work as its standing judicial adviser, in like fashion.

VIII. Objections

Many objections might be raised to the proposal in the last section. First, that it is not yet worked out in the detail that would be necessary for its actual implementation. This is fair comment, although the proposal is consciously tentative. Secondly, it might be thought too much of a radical innovation to be constitutionally acceptable. Thirdly, it could be alleged 'unconstitutional' and, in particular, to violate the 'separation of powers'. These objections of precedent and principle will be briefly addressed.

---

[146] s 137.

[147] See eg N. Johnson, *Reshaping the British Constitution* (Basingstoke: Palgrave Macmillan, 2004), 256: 'no attention was paid to the possibility that the historically grounded arrangements evolved under the customary constitution might still be defensible, especially in the light of the absence of evidence that they are defective in operation'.

[148] A salary (and title, say 'Lord of Appeal in Ordinary'?) might be necessary to make this an attractive option.

[149] *Allen v Flood* [1898] AC 1. Sir Richard Buxton points out that under s 38 Constitutional Reform Act 2005, the President of the Supreme Court may invite any 'senior territorial judge' to form part of a panel, and observes that such a practice 'has not existed in the House of Lords in any form since the desuetude of the writ of assistance at the end of the 19th Century'. R. Buxton, 'Sitting en Banc in the new Supreme Court' (2009) 125 *Law Quarterly Review* 288, 291.

It is implicit in the discussion above that judicial membership of a body like the High Court of Parliament is hardly novel (until 2009 the judges of the final court of appeal in the UK were all members of the Upper House of Parliament, and might quite lawfully have taken part in its proceedings—although many did not).[150] Indeed, the name suggested obviously harks back to the medieval theory of Parliament as a grand tribunal redressing the grievances of the nation. It was from this historical role that the House of Lords' appellate jurisdiction ultimately derived.[151] It may be that this model has had its day with the brave new world of the Supreme Court; the Law Lords anyway formed a de facto distinct corps of professional judges within the Upper House for well over a century. So, the HCP would be turning the clock back to a much earlier form of parliamentary process.

Therefore, one should also consider the Private Bill procedure, still very much alive, even if it has become less important.[152] Where legislation is proposed by and for individuals, and stands to affect other individuals' interests, the latter may petition Parliament to be heard against the bill. They may lodge both written objections, and appear in person (or through counsel) in front of the Private Bill committee. The proposals here bear a strong resemblance to Private Bill procedure,[153] which as *Erskine May* notes derives (like the former appellate jurisdiction of the Lords) from the medieval conception of hearing and redressing individual petitions for relief, rather than the now-dominant conception of enacting general 'public' legislation.

Therefore, while it is true that the proposal is something of a hybrid between a Select Committee and an ordinary court, *neither* of those institutions is in any way novel within Parliament. Private Bill Committees provide a clear example of quasi-judicial procedures before members of Parliament who are in no way professional judges, or even legally qualified.

So there seem to be sufficient precedents in parliamentary history for a body like the proposed High Court of Parliament. But is it not a clear violation of the 'separation of powers'? It is submitted that this alleged principle has been elevated as an abstract dogma worshipped for its own sake, rather than for any actual constitutional value. Moreover, the current position under the HRA anyway results in a blurring rather than a separation between judicial and legislative functions. It would therefore be seriously confused to attack the current proposals for diminishing the separation of powers.

[150] Cf *Lords Hansard*, 12 March 2001: cols 626–9 for Lord Scott of Foscote's attack on the Hunting Bill as 'profoundly undemocratic'.
[151] See D. Lewis Jones, 'The Judicial Role of the House of Lords before 1870', in L. Blom-Cooper, B. Dickson, and G. Drewry (eds), *The Judicial House of Lords 1876–2009* (Oxford: Oxford University Press, 2009).
[152] See W McKay et al (eds), *Erskine May's Treatise on the Law, Privileges, Proceedings and Usage of Parliament*, 23rd edn (London: LexisNexis, 2004), chs 37–41.
[153] Note that membership of Private Bill committees is of 'ordinary' members of the legislature, and not professional judges like the Appellate Committee of the House of Lords.

It has been argued above that the HRA has brought about legalization of polit-ics and the simultaneous politicization of the legal process.[154] What the propos-als aim to do is to take human rights arguments away from the courts, and thus to shield Parliament from the hypnotic power of the judges when debating such issues. Paradoxically then, the effect of the hybrid High Court of Parliament would be to *reverse* the blurring brought about by the HRA. Judges would be spared from scrutiny of their moral impulses and political commitments, and could revert to their less exciting role of ordinary legal development.[155] Parliament, meanwhile, could revert to unhampered consideration of the polit-ics and the policy of human rights, rather than second-guessing what the judges might do. Thus, the proposal would actually ensure greater clarity in the division of labour than does the status quo.

The price for this, it is true, is that that new institution itself would be a flagrant violation of the Separation of Powers. It blends the judicial and legislative functions by design. But that is precisely because in a 'hard case' thrown up by fact situations that a legislator cannot have anticipated, the 'adjudicator' needs must become a legislator. There are simply no 'powers' (or functions) to separate in that situation. The point becomes more acute when the *casus omissus* concerns the inherently con-testable subject of human rights. Hence why the decision should be left ultimately to Parliament, even if legal submissions (and possibly judicial recommendations) on the law were factors to be considered in Parliament's decision.

In conclusion, the High Court of Parliament idea proposed here is a straight-forward way of making parliamentary protection of human rights work properly, by making use of some elements of legal procedure, but leaving the final decision in Parliament's hands. It might appear novel at first sight, but the proposal draws on a number of parliamentary procedures hallowed by centuries of practice. And in any event, constitutional reformers should not always be as timid as the dons of Cambridge who were said to abide by the precept that 'nothing should ever be done for the first time'.[156]

IX. Conclusion

The proposals contained in this chapter are of varying degrees of radicalism. While they will all, predictably, be attacked as novel and dangerous, it is sub-mitted that they are neither. By taking human rights away from the courts and

---

[154] On the latter, it is not just that judges have to use 'social, economic, political and philosophical values' more often in human rights adjudication, but that they are '*manifestly seen* to do so'. Kinley, above n 113, 9 (emphasis in original).

[155] Cf Lord Browne-Wilkinson, 'The Impact of Judicial Reasoning', in B. S. Markesinis (ed), *The Impact of the Human Rights Bill on English Law* (Oxford: Oxford University Press, 1998), 22: 'Moral attitudes which have previously been the actual but unarticulated reasoning lying behind judicial decisions will have become the very stuff of decisions on Convention points'.

[156] F. Cornford, *Microcosmographia Academia* (Cambridge: Bowes & Bowes, 1908), ch VII ('Argument').

452	Jonathan Morgan

placing them back at the centre of parliamentary debate and protection, where they belong, we would fulfil the European Convention on Human Rights and Fundamental Freedoms itself. It should not be forgotten that its preamble declares that 'an effective political democracy' is necessary for the protection of fundamental freedoms. The best interpretation of 'effective...democracy' elevates political debate over juristocratic fiat—however discordant politics might sound to an audience of human rights lawyers accustomed to the exquisitely modulated tones of Glyndebourne, Covent Garden, and the Royal Courts of Justice.

22

Parliamentary Review with a Democratic Charter of Rights

Tom Campbell

What is variously called the 'commonwealth',[1] the 'dialogue',[2] or the 'hybrid'[3] model of constitutional human rights implementation is in general characterized by a weak form of human rights-based judicial review of legislation,[4] a somewhat stronger form of judicial review of government administration, and a range of other mechanisms for protecting and promoting human rights, such as parliamentary scrutiny of proposed legislation. Many of the human rights advantages of the hybrid model stem from these scrutiny procedures backed up by a developing human rights focus within government departments, the work of human rights commissions, and the publicity and lobbying activities of human rights NGOs.[5] This raises interesting questions as to whether it would be possible and, if so, desirable, to retain the human rights advantages of the hybrid model which stem from these more political arrangements, while abandoning the controversial practices associated with human rights-based judicial review.

The quick, but largely unsubstantiated, response to such a proposal is to say that the political advantages of, for instance, the UK Human Rights Act 1998, would not eventuate if it were not for the shadow, and indeed the reality, of judicial

---

[1] S. Gardbaum, 'The New Commonwealth Model of Constitutionalism' (2001) 49 *American Journal of Comparative Law* 707, and P. Rishworth, 'The Inevitability of Judicial Review under "Interpretive" Bills of Rights: Canada's Legacy to New Zealand and Commonwealth Constitutionalism', in G. Huscroft and I. Brodie (eds), *Constitutionalism in the Charter Era* (Canada: LexisNexis, 2004), 236: 'That phrase has been used to denote the enactment of bills of rights that sit alongside a continuing commitment to parliamentary supremacy'.

[2] P. W. Hogg and A. A. Bushell, 'The Charter Dialogue between Courts and Legislatures (1997) 35 *Osgoode Hall Law Journal* 75.

[3] J. L. Hiebert, 'A Hybrid-Approach to Protecting Rights? An Argument in Favour of Supplementing Canadian Judicial Review with Australia's Model of Parliamentary Scrutiny' (1998) 26 *Federal Law Review* 115, and 'Parliamentary Bills of Rights: An Alternative Model?' (2006) 69 *The Modern Law Review* 7 at 9: 'an alternative or hybrid blend of political and juridical form of constitutionalism'.

[4] For a discussion of the variety of 'weak' forms of judicial review, see M. Tushnet, 'New Forms of Judicial Review and the Persistence of Rights- and Democracy-Based Worries' (2003) 38 *Wake Forest Law Review* 813.

[5] BIHR [British Institute of Human Rights], *The Human Rights Act—Changing Lives*, 2nd edn (2006).

review. An equally quick, if incomplete, reply to this response, which is to be found in other essays in this volume, is that the judicial review process distorts and undermines the more politically based, mechanisms by, for instance, embroiling moral and political human rights scrutiny in second-guessing the future outcomes of litigation in the light of case law which, it may be argued, carries no particular moral authority or political legitimacy.

With this debate in mind, this chapter explores how a bill or charter of rights might operate without the allegedly weak mechanisms of judicial review which characterize the hybrid model. This 'democratic charter of rights' model would seek to articulate and implement human rights through a number of political mechanisms and institutions untrammelled by the confines of human rights-based judicial review.[6] It is suggested that this human rights strategy would benefit from the development of a political philosophy of human rights which is political rather than legal in its focus.

I. Political Philosophies of Human Rights

Prior to the post-Second World War foundation of the United Nations and the promulgation of its Universal Declaration of Human Rights, human rights, or, in the terminology of the time, 'natural rights', were generally regarded as philosophically obsolete. 'Rights' as such were normally identified with a positivist conception of the entitlements recognized in the laws and customs of states and communities. The idea that there is a set of rights which exists in some moral or metaphysical realm, independently of actual social and political arrangements, was given little credence outside certain religious traditions. Rather, it was regarded as a matter for communities or nation-states to determine what rights should be ascribed to whom, within and beyond their domain, as they seek to embody values such as justice, liberty, equality, and welfare in concrete institutional arrangements.[7]

Then, in response to the brutal inhumanities of a Europe-centred world war, there emerged an international agreement to pursue the interlocking goals of justice, peace, and humanity through an international organization committed to certain fundamental values and associated institutional arrangements. This revived the civil and political affirmations of the Enlightenment, combined, to some extent, with the social and economic values and goals of the emerging welfare state. Scant philosophical basis was provided for this daring manifesto, which was put together on the basis of what we now call an 'overlapping consensus', that is an agreement on a common content derived from different cultures which does not

---

[6] T. Campbell, 'Human Rights Strategies: An Australian Alternative', in T. Campbell, J. Goldsworthy, and A. Stone (eds), *Protecting Rights without a Bill of Rights: Institutional Performance and Reform in Australia* (Aldershot: Ashgate 2006), 319.

[7] See J. Waldron (ed), *Nonsense upon Stilts: Bentham, Burke and Marx of the Rights of Man* (London: Methuen, 1987); M. M. MacDonald, 'Natural Rights', (1947) *Proceedings of the Aristotelian Society*.

make explicit the varied principles and beliefs, religious and philosophical, that are used to substantiate or justify that content.[8]

In one way and another the vision and values of the United Nations and its Universal Declaration of Human Rights have developed and flourished, so that they are now seen by many as the basis for the preservation of peace and the pursuit of justice. However, the intellectual and moral problems associated with natural rights remain to haunt the idea of human rights and hence the human rights project. There is little theoretical agreement as to their ontological and epistemological foundations, particularly outside the Western tradition, and increasing disagreement at the level of practical implementation.[9] In response, there has been an impressive revival of Enlightenment approaches, exemplified in the modernized Kantianism of John Rawls,[10] and hard-headed pragmatic utilitarianism, exemplified in the moral philosophy of Peter Singer,[11] associated with a vast literature seeking to identify the essence of a number of foundational normative concepts, such as respect, dignity, equal worth, well-being and human flourishing, in order to provide a general theoretical basis for the idea of human rights.

Nevertheless, there is no developing consensus, even within the confines of Western philosophy, as to the meaning, priority, and institutional arrangements which ought to be associated with such values. Moreover, as the Universal Declaration of Human Rights is progressively deployed in more specific treaties and agreements, the de facto plurality of values and their implications shows up more and more in disagreements that are of acute practical significance. In the process of turning affirmations of human rights into concrete social and political arrangements, underlying cultural disagreements are reasserted. As a result, 'human rights' are used to legitimate a wide range of diverse and often incompatible social and political arrangements, which weakens the moral compass and thus the widespread appeal of human rights discourse.

In this context there has emerged a renewed interest in what are sometimes called 'political philosophies of human rights', which attempt to overcome, or perhaps just bypass disagreement on human rights content through analysing the political functions rather than the content of human rights. Political philosophies of human rights focus not so much on what human rights are as on what they are for, that is on their political and social functions rather than their moral and theoretical foundations.[12]

An example of a political philosophy of human rights in the field of international relations, is the thesis that human rights are those rights the violation of which

---

[8] J. Rawls, *Political Liberalism* (New York: Columbia University Press, 1996), Lecture IV.

[9] R. Arneson, 'Against Rights' (2001) 11 *Philosophical Issues* 172; M. H. Kramer and H. Steiner, 'Theories of Rights. Is there a Third Way?' (2007) 27 *Oxford Journal of Legal Studies* 281; J. Griffin, *On Human Rights* (Oxford: Oxford University Press, 2008).

[10] *A Theory of Justice* (Oxford: Oxford University Press, 1971).

[11] *Practical Ethics* (Cambridge: Cambridge University Press, 1973).

[12] The approach was initiated but not developed in John Rawls. See J. Rawls, *Law of Peoples*, 2nd edn (Cambridge Mass: Harvard University Press, 1999). See C. R. Beitz, *The Idea of Human Rights* (Oxford: Oxford University Press, 2009).

either does or ought to prescribe or permit intervention in the internal affairs of another sovereign state. This analysis is adopted by some theorists working in the sphere of international politics and seems to have the endorsement of Joseph Raz.[13] A more historically based example is an interpretation of John Locke's natural rights along the lines that they are the basis for political obligation in that they are the interests which underpin the entitlement of sovereigns to rule and mark the limits of that sovereign right, limits which, if exceeded, entitle the oppressed citizen to withdraw their consent and dissolve their political bonds.[14] Another, usually implicit, political analysis of human rights is that they are those rights whose articulation and implementation either is or ought to be partially or wholly taken out of the normal (or democratic) political process to be protected or advanced through court-administered bills of rights involving powers to override or modify enacted legislation.[15]

Political philosophies of human rights are sceptical about attempts to define human rights or ascribe content to human rights in isolation from one or more specific political or social purposes. In their view, there can be no successful overarching theories, drawn from sources such as the discourse of rights or their foundational documents, which give us morally and politically neutral access to the content of authentic human rights discourse.[16] In these circumstances, the best that analytical philosophy can do is to help us to state clearly what political functions the speaker attributes to 'human rights' in certain contexts. There is no way of arriving at a moral theory of human rights which identifies those rights and correlative duties that are or ought to be human rights in the abstract, isolated from the political function or functions that such rights do or ought to fulfil in law or custom. On this view, we cannot, for instance, identify moral rights in general and then move on to specify which moral rights are human rights. No amount of moral reflection on what it is to be a human being, or what is essential to human dignity, or to moral agency, or in what sense human beings are of equal worth, can by itself provide an agreed and authoritative theory of human rights in the concrete detail that is required to generate clear normative implications relating to actual political disagreements.

This does not, of course, hinder the ascription of content and the development of institutions under the rubric of human rights, historical processes that are the objective of detailed empirical study and comment. In such studies human rights become identified with human rights law, and the discourse of human rights movements both domestic and international, and their associated institutions. Increasingly, human rights are thereby equated with particular constitutional

---

[13] J. Raz, 'Human Rights without Foundations' (2007), <http://www.ucl.ac.uk/laws/jurisprudence/docs/08_coll_raz.pdf>.

[14] J. Dunn, *The Political Thought of John Locke: A Historical Account of the Arguments of the 'Two Treatises'* (Cambridge: Cambridge University Press, 1983).

[15] Another example is the characterization of human rights in the business sphere as those rights which mark the limits of the business case in defining the boundaries of corporate responsibility. See T. Campbell, 'The Normative Grounding of Corporate Social Responsibility: A Human Rights Approach', in D. McBarnet, A. Voiculescu, and T. Campbell (eds), *The New Corporate Accountability: Corporate Social Responsibility and the Law* (Cambridge: Cambridge University Press, 2007), 529.

[16] For a recent attempt to provide such a theory of human rights, see Griffin, above n 9.

mechanisms.[17] It is then typically assumed that, when we discuss, for instance, the human rights implications of invading Iraq or allowing disgraced bankers to keep their pension entitlements, we are raising a particular sort of legal question, which requires answers drawn from the legal domain by legal experts, drawing on their knowledge of international treaties and the jurisprudence of human rights courts. This then provides a rich field of data for analysis within an empirically based and morally neutral political science of human rights which draws our attention to the variety of political functions, not all of which involve legal methods of articulation and implementation, served by human rights discourse.

These tendencies may be resisted by insisting on the essentially moral origins and continuing foundations of human rights. However, it is clear that this generalist approach does not effectively engage with the practical issues that arise in the various domains within which human rights discourse operates. One alternative is to develop further the sort of normative jurisprudence that concentrates on analysing evaluative issues that arise in the interpretation and application of human rights law as it operates within courts. Another is to concentrate on the roles which human rights do and could play within non-legal political processes that involve the articulation and implementation of human rights prior to such involvement as courts may have in the application of laws whose content is politically determined. A normative political philosophy of human rights, may, then, be expected to have at least two essential ingredients. First, it will assume that what counts as a human right should be decided only when we are clear as to the context, in particular the legal, political, or social purposes to which such rights are to be put and the mechanisms through which these purposes are to be effected. Secondly, it will assume that the nature of the choice leading to the adoption of a right as a human right involves essentially political questions requiring moral evaluation, empirical information, and pragmatic public reasoning. A third, but non-essential, characteristic of a political philosophy of human rights, which I adopt within the confines of this chapter, is that such a philosophy is primarily directed towards the making of human rights decisions within the legislative and executive branches of government, with court-based reasoning ideally coming into the picture only in relation to the application of specific legislation that clearly expresses the moral and political decisions arising from a democratic process.[18]

Evidently, normative political philosophies of human rights cannot be sceptical about the possibility of making better or worse moral judgments in general. Excising moral rights from the domain of law does not mean that we cannot successfully address the moral question as to what human rights laws and policies there ought to be in place. Nor do they exclude the utility of conceptual analysis in this process. To develop a political philosophy of human rights we need to be armed with a clear map of an extensive variety of human rights conceptions, such as correlative obligations (negative and positive), option rights, remedies, and so forth, in order to formulate the relevant moral recommendations. On the other

---

[17] This would appear to be Raz's position, above n 13.
[18] T. Campbell, *The Legal Theory of Ethical Positivism* (Aldershot: Dartmouth, 1996).

hand, these analytical ingredients do not hold out the prospect of arriving at a generalist theory of human rights with helpfully specific content. In particular, we should not seek to answer such questions as 'what are human rights?' and 'what human rights are there or should there be?' without knowing the use to which our answers will be put within the domains of social, political, and legal decision-making and institutional design.

II. A Democratic Charter of Rights

In the context of this book, the development of a normative political philosophy of human rights may be seen as part of a project that is designed to extricate human rights from overly legalistic and court-centred modes of articulation and implementation, and to commend and guide the potential of politicized versions of human rights principles and institutions, both for the revitalization of democratic politics, and as an expression of, and a more effective engine for, realizing human rights values generally.[19]

The particular genre is the critique of the 'juridification' of human rights and the promotion of democratizing human rights regimes.[20] Within the broader scope of legal philosophy it is also an exercise in prescriptive legal positivism, in opposition to natural law methods of legal adjudication.[21] Prescriptive legal positivism is the legal theory that formally good law is general, clear, intelligible, and relatively precise and hence does not require that controversial moral judgments have to be made in order to establish an applicable meaning for the law in question. The variety of arguments supporting this position include securing the prerequisites for the exercise of democratic control over the content of laws.

The project has particular relevance to constitutional modelling in Westminster-style democratic cultures that are founded on parliamentary sovereignty, legal positivist versions of the rule of law, and a moral commitment to the equal importance and intrinsic value of all people and the political implications of this moral stance. It also has some relevance to the determination of how so-called constitutional democracies, with judicially interpreted and/or created and/or enforced bills of rights, should approach the difficult problem of marrying substantive judicial review and democratic rights.[22]

---

[19] This is along the lines of the contrast drawn by Richard Bellamy between legal and political constitutionalism. See R. Bellamy, *Political Constitutionalism: A Republican Defence of the Constitutionality of Democracy* (Cambridge: Cambridge University Press, 2007). See also A. Tomkins, *Our Republican Constitution* (Oxford: Hart, 2005).

[20] R. Hirschl, *Towards Juristocracy: The Origins and Consequences of the New Constitutionalism* (Cambridge, Mass: Harvard University Press, 2004).

[21] F. Schauer, *Playing by the Rules: A Philosophical Examination of Rule-Based Decision-Making* (Oxford: Clarendon, 1991); L. Alexander and E. Sherwin, *The Rule of Rules* (Durham, NC: Duke University Press, 2001); T. Campbell, *Prescriptive Legal Positivism: Law, Rights and Democracy* (London: UCL Press, 2004).

[22] This debate may be traced back to J. B. Thayer, 'Origin and Scope of the American Doctrine of Constitutional Law' (1893) 7 *Harvard Law Review* 129–56. See M. Tushnet (ed), *Bills of Rights* (Aldershot: Ashgate, 2007).

More specifically, prescriptive legal positivism commends a particular sort of human rights regime—one centred on what may be called a 'democratic charter of rights'—as the preferred approach to protecting and promoting human rights.[23] The proposed human rights regime is one in which a statutory, perhaps even a constitutionally entrenched, bill or charter of rights, is used institutionally, not to service judicial review of legislation or executive discretion, but to provide the terms of reference for a variety of political mechanisms for agendizing, prioritizing, and developing a polity's human rights commitments within the mainstream of democratic process.

The model is designed to democratize the specification or articulation, and the implementation, of human rights through enhancing a number of instruments and institutions, some of which have been developed partly in the service of human rights, such as human rights commissions, parliamentary scrutiny committees, and human rights legislation, all of which are amenable to a degree of constitutionalization, to enable them better to correct the perceived human rights deficits of so-called 'majoritarian' decision-making. This would make for a politically stronger version of the UK Human Rights Act 1998, and its like.

This democratic model of human rights implementation in no way excludes judiciaries from their core role of implementing properly formed specific legislation, including human rights legislation (ie legislation which embodies positivist legal rules, as defined above, which are framed so as to produce human rights results and is identified or identifiable as such).[24] Indeed, most human rights are unrealizable without the impartial implementation of posited rules through the work of politically independent tribunals.

A democratic bill of rights does not, however, look to courts to have a significant role in fulfilling the complex and controversial political task of transforming abstract statements of fundamental moral values into the sort of specific requirements, policy formulations, and administrative arrangements that can be effectively instantiated within a polity. Participation in the translation of moral values into positivistically justiciable concrete rights and their correlative responsibilities is, in human rights terms, a democratic right that is, ideally, held equally by all those affected by the decisions in question. This is not to be seen as the often and confused idea of a compromise between human rights and democracy but as an embodiment of self-determination as a core political human right.[25]

To formulate this model, we require a conception of human rights that is not tied to or derived from human rights law, existing or projected, and which meshes with a working conception of democracy that can be used to service this concept of human rights, and yet takes into account the need to provide legal guarantees for the protection of specified human rights values in defined ways.

---

[23] See Campbell, above n 6, 319.
[24] T. Campbell, 'Legislating Human Rights', in L. Wintgens (ed), *The Theory and Practice of Legislation: Essays in Legisprudence* (Aldershot: Ashgate, 2005).
[25] J. Waldron, 'A Right-Based Critique of Constitutional Rights' (1993) 13 *Oxford Journal of Legal Studies* 18.

The starting point here is that 'human rights' is best understood as a moral concept with a certain social, economic, and political focus, which identifies the core values and supporting institutional arrangements to which special attention and weight should be given in a democratic polity that is committed to equality of human worth. While a developed political philosophy would be more precise than that, its full articulation ought to be (or perhaps, must be, if a human rights regime is to be internally consistent) democratic and hence the outcome of a complex process of debate and decision-making whose detailed outcome cannot be laid down in advance.

The reasons for commending this democratic dispensation of human rights are multiple.[26] They include the philosophical contention that the political salience of human rights is based on their moral, not their legal, pedigree, so that the only sound and effective source of human rights is moral conviction, not treaties, legislation, or legal precedent, all of which are morally derivative phenomena. Also, the affirmation that the authority of constitutions, including the constitutions that incorporate human rights, rests sociologically on political convergence, usually through shared history, and normatively on moral judgments relating to political legitimacy, and in neither case foundationally on legal sources. This means that the articulation of what particular human rights amount to in practice cannot be, for institutional purposes relating to the separation of powers, sharply distinguished from the remainder of moral/political discourse because the evaluative considerations that they represent, while distinctive in some ways, cannot be clearly disentangled from the factors that pervade other politically oriented moral debates whose provenance is accepted as being within the democratic domain. Human rights are not radically distinct from the other moral norms which raise issues requiring political determination.

This perspective enables a much wider compass of important human interests to be incorporated in a democratic charter of rights. Court-based human rights articulation is almost inevitably limited in its scope to civil and political rights and, within this, biased towards rights with which courts feel familiar and are perceived as having appropriate competence, particularly relating to legal process.

A major advantage of eliminating even weak forms of human rights-based judicial review is that it reduces the capacity of courts to give unwarranted legitimation to morally dubious legislation which is taken as being endorsed by the courts if they do not challenge through radical interpretation or declarations of incompatibility.[27] More generally, the identification of human rights as a court responsibility distracts from the responsibility of citizens, civil society, political parties, politicians, and governments from their human rights responsibilities. The moral hazard here is buck passing.[28]

Such is the eclipse of political approaches to human rights that those who are immersed in human rights law may be inclined to take these critiques and

[26] J. Waldron, 'The Core Case against Judicial Review' (2006) 115 *Yale Law Journal* 1346.
[27] See Tomkins, Chapter 2, this volume.
[28] See J. B. Thayer, 'The Origin and Scope of the American Doctrine of Constitutional Law' (1893) 7 *Harvard Law Review* 129.

reservations with respect to human rights-based judicial review as an outright attack on human rights. This is itself an example of the practical damage that is done by focusing too much human rights attention on a particular legal mechanism. Once the seemingly necessary association with judicial review is broken, it becomes possible to think of restoring human rights to their political origins and generating a culture of rights where it matters, in the moral commitments and prudential concerns that are firmly rooted in the broad culture of a population, together with the operation of a properly functioning legal system.

Faced with this transition to a political context, a prime issue becomes how to identify the non-legal sources of human rights to provide adequate guidance for determining the proper form and content of human rights. At this point it is tempting to adopt a simplistic political philosophy of human rights and move straight into identifying the political function that human rights do or ought to serve. This enables us to bypass the theoretical challenges involved in explaining human rights as a universal type of moral rights, but it opens up the problem of reaching agreement as to what these rights are and where they are to be found. One way forward at this point is to translate moral rights discourse into affirmations and debates about what (positivist) rights ought to exist or would be morally desirable to have in place.[29] This could involve, for instance, commending the utility of certain positive rights in solving social conflicts, enhancing social cooperation, and furthering the freedom and welfare of social beings in complex societies.

What, then, becomes of the discourse of non-positivist human rights, the rights that are routinely held to be the *justification* for having human rights laws, perhaps defined as the laws that are designed to protect equally the important interests of all human beings? One possibility is to regard human rights in this justificatory sense as important values, on the basis of which rights, in a positivist sense, ought to be enacted and enforced. Thus, declarations of human rights simply affirm the value of human life, the value of liberty, the value of speech, the value of movement, of health, of toleration, and so on. On this approach, it is on the high value of these things that we ought to found our political and social relationships.

As a matter of the logic of axiology, this may well be sound. Human rights, indeed rights in general, typically both express and presuppose values. However, values are not rights and rights are not just values, unless, that is, we drain all that is distinctive from the concept of a right.[30] At the very least, rights are claims that we make on each other, so that they are about social practices of inter-personal responsibility for securing what people value.[31] They are about demanded social relationships, requiring non-interference or actual assistance, one of the other. In their fully fledged positivist status rights are founded in the existence of accepted correlative duties, either negative or positive, on which rights-holders can rely for

[29] See Feinberg on 'manifesto rights': J. Feinberg, *Rights, Justice and the Bounds of Liberty: Essays in Social Philosophy* (Princeton: Princeton University Press, 1980).

[30] J. Waldron, 'A Right to do Wrong' (1981) 92 *Ethics* 21–39.

[31] D. Ivison, *Rights* (Stocksfield: Acumen, 2008), ch 2; D. Darby, *Rights, Race and Recognition*, (Cambridge: Cambridge University Press, 2009); L. W. Summers, *The Moral Foundation of Rights* (Oxford: Clarendon Press, 1987).

the protection and promotion of their interests. To have the right to life is not simply to have something, namely life, that is valuable, but to have an effective normative claim that others refrain from killing the right-holder or perhaps also assist her in staying alive. Hence the significance of law as one of the prime means whereby the right to life may be implemented. In other words, rights, in their distinctive meaning, have to do with institutional arrangements that are ultimately justifiable in terms of fundamental values but are not to be equated with those values.

Nevertheless, the partial insights of the value analysis of moral rights does provide a reasonable basis for being sceptical about human rights as a distinct form of moral discourse, in that general declarations of such rights as the right to life, which do not specify any correlative duties or other form of guaranteed protection or enhancement, are in many ways better categorized as statements of values rather than rights. De-institutionalized rights discourse can be cruelly deceptive in promising more than they deliver to those who are said to have the rights in question. Yet, calling these values 'rights' may have the unfortunate consequence of encouraging the idea that the identification as well as the administration of human rights is properly a matter for judicial organs of the state, 'rights' having a more legal and 'values' a more political connotation.

However, we need not conclude from this analysis that what we refer to as 'human rights' are not rights at all, or that the discourse of 'moral rights' has no utility apart from identifying the rights that we think ought to exist. For a start, some manifestations of human rights, such as the prohibition of capital punishment, may be sufficiently specific and clear as to the interests and correlative obligations involved to meet the positivist analysis of the concept of a right. Further, the distinctive status of more abstract human rights discourse can be defended, in so far as it goes beyond affirmations of fundamental values, by intimating not simply the desirability but the moral imperative of having in place a system of correlative duties or other institutional arrangements that serve to protect and further the important human interests identified through the value affirmations in question. Moreover, it is not always such a big step to turn value-based affirmations of inter-human responsibilities into conceptually fully fledged rights. Thus, the moral right to life, at its core, may be a shorthand for statements to the effect that we ought to create, accept, or acquiesce in an obligation on all other persons not to kill the right-holder.

The right to life also exemplifies a feature of all rights that is particularly pronounced with respect to human rights: the flavour of a categorical imperative that gives the normative edge to rights over other forms of evaluative discourse. On the dimension of overridingness, human rights are not simply universal rights, they are priority, sometimes absolute, rights and certainly more than simply one consideration to be lumped with others into the moral melting pot.

Of course, not all human rights are so simple, or so absolute, as the right to life. Indeed, it is evident that even the right to life, so construed, is neither so limited nor so overriding as my formulation above suggests. At its boundaries, this, like other affirmations of abstract rights, may readily be construed as simply identifying morally relevant factors that ought to be taken into account in determining rights in the sense that really matters, namely the implementation of specific correlative duties with respect to the interests identified.

Arguably, this is what has happened with human rights law. The enumerated rights, such as speech and liberty, are identified as activities or situations of the individual that ought to be protected, by law or other means, through the imposition of duties or other mechanisms, unless there are good countervailing reasons which are themselves to be expressed in law. Thus, the standard mode of analysis which is routinely undertaken in human rights adjudication takes the following form. First identify whether or not a human right is at stake by seeing whether that which the person is said to have a right to is limited by the suspect law or conduct in question. Then judge whether this limitation unavoidably or necessarily derives from the implementation of a legitimate purpose or goal. Finally assess whether the limitation of the 'right' is proportional to the benefits derived from the necessary consequences of the lawful purpose.[32]

While there is nothing inherently misguided about this process of reasoning, there is an unfortunate consequence of this way of presenting the normative situation, namely that it involves saying that the human right in question is qualified by other considerations (some of which may themselves be human rights) when it would be better for the conclusion to be expressed along the lines that the human right in question is as stated in the conclusion, after the qualifying factors have been taken into account, not in the prima-facie original affirmation. Thus the human right to freedom of speech is not the right to say whatever you like whenever you like, but the right to do that which remains after all the morally permitted limitations and qualifications are in place. However, this is not in fact the way in which contemporary human rights law is conceptualized. The form of words used is that human rights may be restricted if this is necessary to achieve a legitimate state purpose and the restriction is a proportionate response to a beneficial social outcome 'in a democratic society'. This can give rise to the impression that it is acceptable that human rights be routinely restricted, thus undermining their normative force.

Further, the standard mode of human rights judicial review interpretation creates a strong political presumption against a government exercising a power of human rights override, as with the 'notwithstanding' section 33 of the Canadian Charter of Rights and Freedoms, which enables the Parliament to pass legislation 'notwithstanding that it is in conflict with the Charter of Rights and Freedoms', thus appearing to legitimate the violation of human rights. Such legislative overrides would be better conceptualized as expressing disagreement as to what more precisely constitutes the concretization of the abstract right or human rights value, that is, what the right in question actually is.[33] The same can be said about the analysis of what is at stake when a UK court, pursuant of the Human Rights Act 1998, declares a piece of legislation to be incompatible with human rights, whereas

---

[32] C. Gearty, *Principles of Human Rights Adjudication* (Oxford: Oxford University Press, 2004).
[33] See J. Goldsworthy, 'Judicial Review, Legislative Override, and Democracy' (2003) 38 *Wake Forest Law Review* 452.

what is actually going on may be a disagreement about the content of the right in question.

The issue as to whether or not we should speak of human rights rather than human values until such time as we have decided on the form and content of the right as it is to be applied to concrete cases feeds into the issue of who should have the responsibility for human rights articulation. Arguably, accepting abstract moral norms into the domain of human rights discourse encourages the idea that such articulations are matters for courts, for what we are concerned with are rights, while the overt 'value' reading of human rights discourse points to a more political mode of articulation, suited to the resolution of value conflict.

In summary, there are three reasons for rejecting this solution to the conundrum. First, it deprives generalized human rights discourse of the priority weighting that serves to distinguish it from the rest of political discourse, since human rights become mere affirmations of values. Secondly, it effectively licenses allocating the care of human rights to legal process before they are in a form fit for this purpose. Finally, it neglects the distinctive utility of rights discourse as identifying entitlements, that is, things to which individuals and groups have a decisive normative claim that relieves them of the requirements to offer further justifications for its implementation.

Nevertheless, it is important for a normative political philosophy of human rights to identify what may be called the 'human rights values' for use in giving content and form to the specific human rights which are to be deployed in relation to the particular political functions of a democratic charter of human rights. In the next section this framework is developed in the concrete context of recent debates in the UK concerning the changing role of the parliamentary Joint Committee on Human Rights and the prospect of the amendment or replacement of the UK Human Rights Act 1998.

III. Parliamentary Human Rights Committees

The thesis of this chapter is that turning human rights values into human rights legislation ought to be within the domain of the democratic political process, but not submerged in the normality of ordinary democratic activities. The distinctiveness of human rights as setting forth the prime purposes of morally acceptable government, and identifying the prime hazards for individuals subjected to government power, needs to be recognized within the workings of a parliamentary democracy. The functions of a parliamentary human rights committee and hence the content of the charter that provides its terms of reference relate not only to the acceptable goals of government but, perhaps more so, to anticipating and preventing the characteristic failures of democratic systems.

The proposed democratic charter of rights is one model designed to promote these twin objectives, through the promotion of democratic ideology and democratic defences against the misuse of political power. This model requires the existence of a democratically endorsed charter of human rights, encompassing but

going beyond the existing human rights treaty commitments of the state and pref-
erably affirmed in a democratic plebiscite. This is required to recognize the universal or trans-border commitments associated with the idea of human rights and
to provide a basis for the development of a democratic civic culture. Utilizing this
charter there must be specific institutional arrangements designed to ensure that
the human rights considerations identified in the charter are directly addressed
within the democratic process. One example of this is fostering the implementation of a charter of rights through the operations of strong parliamentary human
rights committees whose duties are to propose new legislation as well as to scrutinize proposed and existing legislation, to comment on administrative practices from
a charter point of view, to conduct public enquiries on human rights matters, and
to take such other steps as they think fit to keep human rights at the forefront of
the political agenda.[34]

The feasibility of this model can be considered in the light of the operations of
the Joint Committee on Human Rights (JCHR) in the UK Parliament, and in
particular its recent decision to move, in crude terms, from second-guessing what
courts will make of proposed legislation once enacted, making its own views available to the executive and to parliament on a range of human rights concerns relating to proposed or neglected legislation.[35]

This development can lead us to consider what such a committee might achieve
in the absence of human rights-based judicial review of legislation from within a
particular jurisdiction.[36] What if the decision-making and normative reasoning of
the JCHR, or any parliamentary human rights committee, need not be a matter of
anticipating what courts, domestic or international, might determine with respect
to the 'constitutionality' of legislation? What if, instead, they concentrate on assisting the production of specific and effective human rights legislation, on the basis of
a moral conception of human rights as expressing fundamental moral values and
basic mechanisms for realizing those values that emerge from a political approach
to human rights? Given sufficient political support of a population that is to some
extent suspicious of government, could such committees become an effective focus
for improving the human rights performance of elected governments?

There are several hurdles to be cleared to make such an institutional arrangement powerful enough to be worthwhile. One problem in seeking to approach
human rights as a moral political discourse that can and ought to be viewed
discretely from its various legal implementations and expressions is that it then
becomes difficult to establish the distinctiveness of human rights discourse and
its boundaries with other discourses. This arises both in relation to arriving at a

---

[34] D. Kinley, 'Parliamentary Scrutiny of Human Rights: A Duty Neglected?' in P. Alston (ed),
Promoting Human Rights through Bills of Rights: Comparative Perspectives (Oxford: Oxford University
Press, 1999), ch 5; M. Tushnet, *Taking the Constitution Away from the Courts* (Princeton: Princeton
University Press, 2000).

[35] Joint Committee on Human Rights, *The Committee's Future Working Practices: Twenty-Third
Report of Session 2005–06* (London: Stationery Office Limited, 2006).

[36] Hiebert, above n 3; C. Evans and S. Evans, 'Legislative Scrutiny Committees and Parliamentary
Conceptions of Human Rights' [2006] *Public Law* 785.

conception of human rights, including their meaning and functions, and as a method of determining their proper content, scope, and weight.

At one extreme this model requires the articulation of a complete and comprehensive political philosophy. At another extreme it might involve no more than a collection of basic formal definitions of key terms and recommendations for the allocation of responsibilities in the articulation and implementation of this skeletal conception of human rights and human rights institutions by political process. The problem with the first, grandiose, approach is that, even if it can be accomplished to our own satisfaction, the chances of gaining widespread agreement are minimal, making it an unpromising basis for commending a constitutional arrangement. The problem with the second, more timorous, approach is that, while it might be achievable, it does not have much of substance to direct or guide the proposed process. This is not fatal to a deliberative process but it is hardly conducive to its effectiveness.

What is needed is a *via media* whereby broad agreement can be achieved over what, in general terms, human rights are in form, content, and function, which has sufficient substantive content to indicate what is at stake in allocating human rights discourse a specially important role in democratic political process, and gives some concrete content to recommendations as to how human rights ought to be determined and achieved. Within the framework of the adopted charter, such a political philosophy of human rights would offer some (but only some) guidance as to the correct form of moral political reasoning, the correct political method of determining the scope and content of human rights, and suggesting how these determinations are best implemented.

This strategy can usefully be explored in the context of the changing role of the UK parliamentary Joint Committee on Human Rights (JCHR), and the White Paper 'The Governance of Britain', with a view to considering how far the function of bills or charters of rights can be detached from the mechanisms of judicial review. The JCHR was set up by Parliament independently of the HRA 1998. The statement of the official role of the JCHR, the first permanent Committee of both houses, includes, in unusually broad terms, that it is 'to consider matters relating to human rights in the United Kingdom (but excluding consideration of individual cases)'. It then goes on to require the Committee to consider proposals for remedial orders that a government is empowered by the HRA to introduce when faced with 'Declarations of Incompatibility' by a court to the effect that a particular piece of legislation or part thereof is incompatible with the European Convention on Human Rights.[37]

The JCHR initially interpreted its role as being almost entirely a matter of scrutinizing bills that are before Parliament and doing so largely to determine the question of compatibility with the ECHR, a matter on which the minister responsible for the bill under consideration is also required to report when presenting a bill to Parliament. While the JCHR in its early stages did not confine its work to such

---

[37] House of Commons Standing Order No 152B; House of Lords Order of Appointment (19 July 2005).

scrutinizing and did not always take a purely technical and legalistic approach to this task, it is true to say that generally the JCHR saw its duty as being to draw the attention of Parliament to potentially adverse court decisions on the issue of compatibility.[38] The JCHT was not particularly successful in its attempts to second-guess what courts would make of the legislation in question once enacted, nevertheless this focus, undertaken with the assistance of its legal adviser, was the hallmark of its first few years of operation. It is probably fair to say that the outcomes of this process had very little impact on the legislative process.[39]

However, *Bringing Rights Home: Labour's Plan to Incorporate the ECHR into UK Law*[40] and the White Paper that preceded the HRA, in line with their general contention that Parliament has the prime responsibility for protecting human rights, clearly had a more expansive idea of what the JCHR should do by way of assisting Parliament with respect to human rights.[41] At that point the JCHR could have adopted a broader and more proactive role with respect to the furtherance of human rights in the United Kingdom, and could also have been more robust in coming to its own view as to how the abstract values of the European Convention on Human Rights (ECHR) should be brought to bear on the issue of the compatibility of UK legislation with the ECHR. Such an approach was advocated by some commentators who recommended a 'merits scrutiny' which would examine the balance of competing interests, considering issues of proportionality and involving itself in moral arguments as to the proper human rights outcome. This was in contrast to the 'technical scrutiny' commended by Professor Blackburn of King's College, London, which is a matter of 'comparing and predicting the compatibility of the law proposed with the prospect of litigation under the ECHR'.[42]

'The Committee's Future Working Practices' can be seen as the JCHR's statement of intention to adopt the merits scrutiny that was, perhaps, originally intended. Drawing on a report it had commissioned from Professor Francesca Klug,[43] the JCHR determined to be more selective in its choice of bills to scrutinize, to be more inclined to develop its 'own voice' in conducting that scrutiny, and to spend a greater proportion of its time on more proactive activities, such as conducting enquiries and critiquing government policies from a human rights point of view.

This development suggests that the JCHR could have a role which is largely independent of Parliament's interface with the courts over matters of legal interpretation and legislative compatibility with the ECHR and be more concerned with enabling and encouraging Parliament and the executive to play

---

[38] D. Feldman, 'Parliamentary Scrutiny of Legislation and Human Rights' [2002] *Public Law* 323.

[39] M. C. Tolley, 'Parliamentary Scrutiny of Rights in the United Kingdom: Assessing the Work of the Joint Committee on Human Rights' (2009) 44 *Australian Journal of Political Science* 41.

[40] J. Straw and P. Boateng, *Bringing Rights Home, Labour's Plan to Incorporate the ECHR into UK Law* (United Kingdom: Labour Party, 1996).

[41] 'Rights Brought Home', para 3.6.

[42] R. Blackburn, 'A Human Rights Committee for the UK Parliament' (1998) *European Human Rights Law Review* 534.

[43] *Report on the Working Practices of the JCHR*, Appendix 1, Joint Committee on Human Rights, above n 35.

an independent part in achieving human rights outcomes. The JCHR has now determined to undertake human rights scrutiny by making its own assessment of incompatibility in its own 'less technical' voice, in particular when 'proportionality considerations apply'. This coincides neatly with the purported aim of the Green Paper, 'The Governance of Britain', which seeks to give Parliament more power by increasing its capacity to hold the executive to account, and the suggestion that the JCHR should have a greater impact on policy and legislative debates.[44] It coincides also with the recent 'British Bill of Rights' movement, which seeks to make the UK political system more involved in the specification of human rights in Britain.[45]

Some of the arguments presented in favour of this more adventurous role for the JCHR are of considerable relevance to the issues of human rights development in a democracy. One relates to the reasons given for the JCHR's failure to accurately predict how courts would react to legislation that might be thought to impinge on human rights. The first reason is the tendency of courts to defer to Parliament when they believe that the matter is not within their competence.[46] Thus most radical interpretations or effective rewriting of legislation under the rubric of the HRA have had more to do with issues of personal liberty and property, matters with which the courts are accustomed to deal. And even in their traditional competences, courts have, although not consistently, been cautious about questioning the legislative outcomes of democratic process, and therefore very deferential. The other explanation given for the failure to predict judicial outcomes is the insight that decisions about how vaguely worded affirmations of fundamental values and institutions, which cannot be put to work in particular cases without engaging in moral assessment of the weight that is to be given to these and other often conflicting values in actual circumstances, are in themselves unpredictable due to the indeterminacy of the interests at risk, the frequent intangibility of the countervailing objectives of the legislation, and the morally controversial nature of the significance that should be given to such competing considerations within a democratic society. Such matters are not amenable to technical legal determination and cannot therefore be predicted through a process of standard legal reasoning.

There would certainly appear to be sound human rights reasons why the JCHR should not persist with the legal prediction model.[47] Courts are restrained in their human rights judgments by considerations such as the controversial legitimacy of their interventions with enacted legislation, their awareness of the lack of competence in many areas of policy, and their reluctance to take in morally controversial decisions that will prompt unfavourable media comment. The shadow of unconstitutionality hangs over their operations and restrains their interventions. Such considerations have much less relevance to parliamentary committees, for these do not have to show such deference to a body of which it is a part (except in relation to

---

[44] <http://governance.justice.gov.uk>.
[45] See Ministry of Justice, 'Rights and Responsibilities: Developing our Constitutional Framework' (Mar 2009), Cm 7577.
[46] See Chapter 2, this volume .
[47] Evans and Evans, above n 36.

the fact that it is only a part), and is only advisory (although it may come to have procedural powers). Therefore the parliamentary committee mechanism can have more positive and broader roles than judicial scrutiny since its function is not so much to control as to enhance parliamentary outputs. Further the JCHR does not have to confine itself to those rights that concern matters within legal cognizance, so it can range over the broad field of human rights, both within and beyond the ECHR. As part of a democratic forum, the JCHR can serve as the conduit for submission of those representing potential human rights victims beyond the parties to legal cases, and can in other ways draw on evidence beyond that available to courts, and is aiming at improving debate, not drawing lines and making 'decisions'. It can and ought to be open to a greater diversity of sources.

On the other hand it could be argued that what the Committee is suggesting in the way of scrutiny of bills could be read as in some ways actually adopting the methods now used by courts to determine compatibility. This means encouraging the JCHR not to guess what the courts will decide but to play the same game as the courts by first deciding if a convention right is at issue, then deciding if there are legitimate reasons for that perceived restriction of such a right, and then asking if the restriction is necessary and proportional to the restricting reason. Indeed it could be argued that, in the existing arrangements, this would make the JCHR better at predicting what courts will decide. By mimicking the courts' methods, they may better anticipate their conclusions. This is rather unlikely given the subjective elements in the judgment process as outlined above, and the generally open-ended nature of the reasoning involved.

However, the flavour of the Committee's proposal is more that their own voice will be different and have a different focus: on guiding the Parliament not standing in judgment over it, particularly with respect to demanding evidence from ministers and government departments that is required, in their view, to justify the human rights-endangering aspects of purported legislation. And in any case we should note the intention to perform less scrutiny of bills and more actively engage in human rights promotion and investigation, alongside the new Equality and Human Rights Commission.

Yet, within these activities, once the JCHR has cut itself somewhat adrift from a legal approach to determining if proposed legislation is human rights compatible, on what criteria can it draw to identify what it calls the 'major human rights significance' on the basis of which it intends to select what to scrutinize and how to scrutinize and when to make its views known to Parliament, and the nation? In this, of course, the JCHR has a freedom that is, or at least ought to be, denied to courts. They are part of a law-making not a law-application body. Nevertheless, there is little credibility in the committee acting in a manner which is arbitrary in its identification of matters which are of human rights significance and therefore within their ambit.

One rather distant prospect is that the JCHR interpret its terms of reference in the light of the envisaged 'Bill of Rights and Responsibilities' that is contemplated in the Green Paper, a bill that is intended to clarify and render precise 'British values', which would appear to range from the National Health Service to parliamentary democracy. This is an optimistic scenario which is in any case obscured by the uncertainty as to whether the Bill of Rights and Responsibilities is to be rendered justiciable. If the idea is to add the British Bill of Rights and Responsibilities to existing grounds for judicial review of legislation, then its content will inevitably be too narrow in scope to serve the new political purposes of the JCHR.

IV. Conclusion

The recent and foreshadowed adaptation in the methodology of the UK JCHR helps to establish a context for developing a political philosophy of human rights to underpin a democratic charter of rights in which there are no special procedures for judicial review. Such a philosophy of human rights might be of service to such bodies as the JCHR in going about the business of identifying, investigating, and, perhaps with constitutional authority, requiring that such matters be considered by government, some it by way of legislative and pre-legislative scrutiny.

The task can be seen as parallel to that Connor Gearty sets himself in *Principles of Human Rights Adjudication*,[48] where he seeks to guide British courts as to when and how they should be judicially active with respect to their duties under the HRA. As he notes, this piece of legislation is one which courts could use very extensively to produce radical interpretations and frequent declarations of incompatibility. Such behaviour would, of course, create a constitutional crisis that would likely lead to the amendment or repeal of the Act. So, when should the courts 'intervene'?

Gearty crafts three principles from his overview of the emerging HRA jurisprudence. Courts, he contends, usually do (and always should) confine their activism to (1) civil and political rights, (2) the protection of vulnerable minorities, and (3) cases where human dignity is at stake. Otherwise, they should show 'judicial restraint' (over what the court is not equipped to do) and 'judicial deference' (over what the court should not do because what is proposed trespasses on the legislative role.[49]

Difficult questions can be raised concerning Gearty's principles. They appear to be selectively drawn from existing ECHR case law, and, especially with respect to the third principle, are alarmingly open-ended in the potential power thereby granted to courts. However, whatever we think of Gearty's particular principles, his objectives are clearly important and need to be replicated in relation to parliamentary human rights committees operating in the context of broadly expressed charter of rights.

This chapter has not discussed in sufficient detail what should be the content of a democratic charter of rights or how that should be decided. This derives in part from the expectation that the content of a democratic charter should clearly be determined by a democratic process. Given the important role of international human rights in international relations, such charters would have to incorporate

[48] C. Gearty, *Principles of Human Rights Adjudication* (Oxford: Oxford University Press, 2004).
[49] Ibid 120 f.

the substance of existing human rights treaties and conventions ratified by the state in question. However, a democratic charter opens the possibility of going beyond existing international agreements both in scope and in detail. In the absence of judicial review, a democratic charter could be expected to permit a wide range of human rights, perhaps with a certain regional flavour, and certainly including the social and economic rights normally excluded from court-centred models.

An important task for a political philosophy of human rights is to suggest how this extension of domestic charters can be achieved without undue expansion of the content of human rights to the point where they lose their distinctive moral salience. Given the political role of the charter, crucial criteria for inclusion in the charter of rights are likely to include: (1) the identification of fundamental interests that in general terms are relatively (i) uncontroversial, (ii) potentially universal, and (iii) either very important for human well-being in themselves (intrinsically valuable) or necessary for the attainment of intrinsic goods (instrumentally valuable) or both, but only, (2) in so far as these interests give grounds for recognizing correlative obligations (negative or positive) to respect, protect, or promote these interests in an institutionalized manner, and only if (3) there is a reasonable prospect that the necessary material resources are available to achieve the human rights objectives in question.

Whatever their content, parliamentary human rights committees dealing with a democratic charter of rights would have difficult practical choices to make, which would generate lively disagreement, increased demand for evidence-based justifications for controversial legislation, and wide-ranging enquiries into the human rights issues that are pressed upon them. This is not, in itself, a matter for concern. Indeed it illustrates just some of the ways that a democratic charter of rights could raise the profile of human rights within the political process and lead to human rights outcomes that are more extensive, more radical, and more securely based than is currently the case.

23

Beyond the Human Rights Act

Conor Gearty

As it leaves childhood and prepares for what promises to be a turbulent (perhaps even fatal) adolescence, it is surely right now to acknowledge just how neglected in its early years, cruelly treated even, the Human Rights Act has been. This is not to say that the Act has not had its friends, particularly among lawyers of course,[1] but also in the NGO sector where the Convention rights in schedule 1 have grown into useful pegs upon which to hang activism of many shapes and sizes.[2] The parliamentary Joint Committee on Human Rights has done its best to promote an enthusiastic understanding of the measure,[3] and the Equality and Human Rights Commission threatens to make a real contribution in its support just as soon as it irons out or otherwise resolves the personnel difficulties that appear to have dogged it since its inception.[4] Despite this support, however, the Human Rights Act has distinctly failed to build up any intellectual or political head of steam. The universities remain largely uninterested in constructing any kind of serious foundations for human rights in general, much less for a Human Rights Act that is largely seen as the preserve of lawyers and even then—when viewed from within that discipline—as little more than a branch of public law (and certainly not an ethical field in its own right).[5] The old left is still largely sceptical about the deployment of the language of general rights within law, continuing to see it as the ally

[1] We need look no further than R. Clayton and H. Tomlinson, *The Law of Human Rights*, 2nd edn (Oxford: Oxford University Press, 2009) for evidence of the vast amount of case-law generated by the Act. See also for two other substantial treatments: A. Lester, D. Pannick, and J. Herberg, *Human Rights Law and Practice*, 3rd edn (London: Lexis Nexis, 2009) and J. Beatson, S. Grosz, T. Hickman, R. Singh, with S. Palmer, *Human Rights: Judicial Protection in the United Kingdom* (London: Sweet & Maxwell, 2008).

[2] See eg A. Donald and E. Mottershaw, *Poverty, Inequality and Human Rights: Do Human Rights Make a Difference?* (York: Joseph Rowntree Trust, 2009).

[3] Much of the Committee's activity could be regarded as engaged with this kind of work, but see especially *The Work of the Committee in 2007 and the State of Human Rights in the UK* (6th Report of Session 2007–8, HL 38, HC 270 (2008)).

[4] See Joint Committee on Human Rights, *Equality and Human Rights Commission* (13th Report of Session 2009–10, HL 72, HC 183 (2010). For an indication of the Commission's current work in the field, see *Ours to Own: Understanding Human Rights* (2008) and its *Human Rights Inquiry* (2009).

[5] There are few counterparts to T. Campbell, K. Ewing, and A. Tomkins, *Sceptical Essays on Human Rights* (Oxford: Oxford University Press, 2001). But see for two good (and very recent) treatments, A. Kavanagh, *Constitutional Review under the UK Human Rights Act* (Cambridge: Cambridge

of regressive rather than progressive forces,[6] and such doubters are unpersuaded by the argument that the respect accorded parliamentary sovereignty by Britain's Act makes any difference in practice to what is seen as its reactionary thrust.[7] The modernizing left, or New Labour as it was once known, might be the closest thing to a parent the Human Rights Act will ever have, but if so, it is a parent that has never bothered to inform itself of the responsibilities entailed in nurturing its off-spring through its early years. From the moment of its birth, successive Labour administrations have been hostile, first almost not bringing it into force, and from then on giving the impression that the Party had never had anything to do with this anti-populist piece of foreign/European law.[8] Only in the last years of what had already been a long stint in office did even the department primarily respon-sible for the measure awaken from its torpor sufficiently to issue occasional papers in its defence.[9]

In the gap left by the quiescence of its promoters, critics of the Human Rights Act have had a field day. This has not usually included the old left—the social-ism of New Labour has been so diluted in office that there have been hardly any egalitarian or strongly progressive measures for the courts to prove their supposed reactionary qualities by destroying.[10] In fact, and bizarrely from any kind of historical or political perspective, the judges have been a fairly progres-sive force in a culture that has lurched so far to the right that old Labour cen-trists who refuse to disavow their long-held positions now seem left-wing.[11] The mass circulation media has led the charge against the Act, gleefully taking the modifications to libel law that it has inspired,[12] while focusing their wrath on the

---

University Press, 2009) and A. Young, *Parliamentary Sovereignty and the Human Rights Act* (Oxford: Hart Publishing, 2009).

[6] Campbell et al, n 5 above.

[7] K. D. Ewing, 'The Futility of the Human Rights Act' [2004] *Public Law* 829.

[8] See eg David Blunkett, 'Freedom from Terrorist Attack is also a Human Right', *Independent* (12 Aug 2004), and the speech of John Reid when he was Home Secretary at a European summit in Venice on 12 May 2007 in which he called for the Act to be watered down in order to assist in the bat-tle against terrorism: *Sunday Times* (13 May 2007). The prime minister responsible for the Act also engaged in attacks on it from time to time: see eg 'Revealed: Blair Attack on Human Rights Law', *Observer* (14 May 2006).

[9] Starting with Department for Constitutional Affairs, *Review of the Implementation of the Human Rights Act* (July 2006). See also Ministry of Justice, *Making Sense of Human Rights* (Oct 2006).

[10] An indicator of this is how unusual it has been for the executive to register (under s 19 of the Act) its judgment that measures it has desired to introduce have been incompatible with the Convention. A rare example was the Communications Bill 2003 which sought to regulate political advertising against the background of a potentially difficult Strasbourg judgment, *VgT Verein Gegen Tierfabriken v Switzerland* (2001) 34 EHRR 159: in the event, in *R (Animal Defenders International) v Secretary of State for Culture Media and Sports* [2008] UKHL 15, [2008] 2 WLR 781, the Strasbourg decision was distinguished and no violation of the Convention found on the facts as they were before their lordships.

[11] Roy Hattersley being the best example of such a figure, interesting also for the fact that he was a consistent opponent of enactment of a human rights law: see his newspaper article 'A Fatally Flawed Approach to Protecting Fundamental Liberties', *Independent* (4 May 1989).

[12] *Reynolds v Times Newspapers Ltd* [2001] 2 AC 127, decided before the coming into force of the Human Rights Act but much influenced by its terms: see *McCartan Turkington Breen v Times Newspapers* [2001] 2 AC 277.

'political correctness' which the measure is said to have underpinned and on the right to privacy which the courts have hewn out of its raw materials. So far as the first of these is concerned, the Act has been a very easy target once it is decided to make no distinction between launching a case under its terms and actually winning one. Anyone can do the former, and many do, seeking (unsuccessfully, but who cares?) pornography in prison, immediate liberty from justified incarceration, or whatever else happens to be the litigant in person's latest passing desire. As regards the second, the development of a right to privacy might be thought to be one of the more beneficial effects of the Human Rights Act, not least because it has sent the editor of the *Daily Mail* into paroxysms of rage.[13] It is hardly the fault of the judges that none of their many lawyers told the newspaper editors and proprietors that were so keen on enactment of the European Convention in the mid to late 1990s that it contained a right to respect for privacy as well as its more celebrated guarantee of free speech.[14] It has surely been at least partly concerns about profits lost that have given the right-wing assault on the Human Rights Act such a venomous flavour.

The Conservative Party under the leadership of David Cameron has climbed aboard the anti-Human Rights Act bandwagon. The Party made a firm promise to repeal the measure on entry to government, and it has only been its failure to secure a majority that appears to have given the Act a stay of execution. In place of the anticipated repeal there is to be a review by a commission of the field, though exactly what this entails remains to be seen: the Coalition Programme for Government does not explicitly commit to the Act's survival, and the Home Secretary Theresa May has already suggested that possible repeal is one of the matters that is being discussed between her Party and the Liberal Democrats.[15] In the minds of members of the Conservative Party, the Act has been conflated with health and safety laws and other forms of legislative control on 'freedom' as further evidence of a Britain where liberty has been sacrificed at the altar of bureaucracy and in which the officialdom of the nanny state has been allowed to get completely out of control.[16] This criticism of the Human Rights Act does not spill over into harsh words for the idea of human rights itself, however: in the minds of modern Conservatives there is a clear difference between the two. It was at the launch of the Party's annual report on human rights in 2008 that David Cameron made what was one of his most direct attacks on the

[13] See Paul Dacre's speech to the Society of Editors on 9 Nov 2008, set out in full at <http://www.pressgazette.co.uk/story.asp?storycode=42394> (last visited 7 Dec 2009).

[14] See J. Fiddick, *The Human Rights Bill: Privacy and the Press*, Research Paper 98/25 (London: House of Commons Library, Feb 1998). The late discovery of the threat to free speech posed by article 8 eventually produced s 12 of the Human Rights Act, purportedly guaranteeing freedom of expression but in fact easing in the horizontal application of the privacy right as between private parties: *Douglas v Hello! Ltd* [2001] QB 967.

[15] *The Coalition: Our Programme for Government* (HM Government, 2010), p 11. For a report of the comments of Theresa May, see the *Guardian*, 19 May 2010: <http://www.guardian.co.uk/politics/2010/may/19/theresa-may-coalition-human-rights-act-scrap> (last visited 22 May 2010).

[16] This broader background is well developed in David Cameron's Hugo Young lecture in late 2009: see <http://www.conservatives.com/News/Speeches/2009/11/David_Cameron_The_Big_Society.aspx> (last visited 7 Dec 2009).

Human Rights Act.[17] While the term is usually used only i.
eign affairs among Tory thinkers and activists, were the Tories
the plan within Britain would be not solely a matter of repealing
Rights Act, thereby ending what would have proved to have been a su.
of enforceable generalized rights within British domestic law. Rather it wou.
be also to replace the Act with a supposedly better version of a similar kind
of quasi-constitutional instrument, a new Bill of Rights and Responsibilities
for Britain which (it is said) would be more carefully honed to the needs of
UK citizens, protecting their interests better than the universalist-inclined but
above all markedly European charter which has insinuated itself into British
law under cover of the Human Rights Act.[18] The Liberal Democrats appear to
have agreed a remit along these lines for the Commission which is to review the
whole area. From the Conservative point of view, it would seem that the objection, therefore, is to the Act rather than to the idea of individual rights which
lies behind it. Towards the end of its tenure in office, Labour had also begun to
develop similar ideas for what it also called a new 'bill of rights and responsibilities', albeit in Labour's case the plan was for such a document not to supersede
but rather to complement the Human Rights Act.[19] However, it was surely not
impossible that were such a Bill to have been brought before parliament by a re-
elected Labour administration, government ministers would have yielded to the
temptation to include the occasional amending provision, quietly diluting one
or two of the aspects of the Human Rights Act that have proved from its governmental perspective to be somewhat problematic. The energy of the Party's
commitment to the Human Rights Act was throughout its time in office in
inverse proportion to its expectation of electoral victory.

This chapter considers the paradoxical plight of a Human Rights Act which
has proved so unpopular to the two largest mainstream political parties that the
commitment to rights of which it is the epitome was likely to be greatly expanded
whichever party (or indeed parties) emerged victorious from the electioneering
of 2010.[20] Of course this is a rather glib way of making the point, but the fact
remains that each of the two major parties has shown a distaste for the Human
Rights Act, either committing itself to repeal (the Tories) or flirting with the idea

[17] For further details and the full speech see the website of the Conservative Human Rights
Commission at <http://www.conservativehumanrights.com/events/annualreport2008.html> (last
visited 7 Dec 2009).

[18] See the speech of the then Shadow Minister for Justice Nick Herbert at the British Library
on 24 Nov 2008, 'Rights without Responsibilities—A Decade of the Human Rights Act' (British
Institution of Human Rights Lecture).

[19] Ministry of Justice, *Rights and Responsibilities: Developing our Constitutional Framework*, Cm
7577 (Mar 2009).

[20] The Liberal Democratic Party have, in contrast, been strong supporters of the Human Rights
Act when in opposition, as well as of still stronger rights' protection in the form of a new bill of rights:
see <http://www.libdems.org.uk/siteFiles/resources/Word%20Docs/Policy%20Briefing%20-%20
%20Constitutional%20Affairs%20Oct%2009.doc> (last visited 9 Dec 2009). But now that the
Party has entered government it remains to be seen how strong this commitment will prove to be,
especially if the commission to review these matters suggests a full bill of rights as a potential replacement for (rather than complement to) the Act.

of truncation (Labour), while enthusiastically embracing the rights language that lies at its core. We are concerned in what follows primarily with thinking through what would be entailed in the repeal of, or the making of debilitating amendments to, the Human Rights Act. It will be suggested that two questions need to be carefully addressed before such a legislative process is embarked upon, lest the changes produce consequences of an unexpected, perhaps even chaotic, nature. These 'European' and 'British' questions will be considered in the next two sections, after which the chapter will conclude with some reflections on the contemporary durability of rights-talk in a political environment as ambiguously hostile as that of the United Kingdom. Noting the strength of this discourse, certain ideas will be briefly floated in that final section as to how the language of human rights can best be rescued from the lawyers and returned to those for whom in the first place it was mainly designed, the poor and disadvantaged and unlucky—all those for whom the idea of being treated as an equal and with respect accorded to their dignity would be likely radically to affect for the better the quality of their lives.

I. The European Question

The first of our two issues has always been implicit within the Human Rights Act and as a result of recent case-law from Strasbourg it has gradually bubbled to the surface. In *Burden and Burden v United Kingdom*,[21] the straightforward question arose as to whether a declaration of incompatibility under section 4 of the Human Rights Act could be regarded as 'an effective remedy' for European Convention purposes. The point matters because there is a right to the latter in the European Convention on Human Rights, albeit not in the Act (where the relevant provision, article 13, does not appear), and also because (of course) the essence of the declaration of incompatibility is that it is just that, an avowal or announcement or affirmation of a breach of the Convention—anything and everything, in other words, *except* an order to the same effect carrying legally enforceable duties of compliance. The unenforceability of such declarations is critical to the whole structure of the Human Rights Act; it is what makes the measure acceptable to those on the left (and some in the centre and even on the right) who regard parliamentary sovereignty as a democratic fundamental and who have therefore long been suspicious of the overweening potential of rights-talk. From the perspective of such potential critics, the solution offered by the Strasbourg judges in *Burden* is hardly reassuring—declarations of incompatibility are not in themselves effective remedies for Convention purposes, but they may become so if practice confirms that they are always implemented by the other branches of government; in other words (using traditional British constitutional language), if a strong convention emerges that such declarations are always to be acted upon, then (but only then) will they be deemed 'effective' for Convention purposes. However, if this is to be routinely the case, then while Strasbourg may well be happy, it would seem that little will be

[21] European Court of Human Rights, 29 Apr 2008, (2008) 47 EHRR 857 (Grand Chamber).

left of the sovereignty of parliament—are those of parliament's provisions which are enacted in the knowledge that they are inimical to human rights to enjoy no more than a kind of legislative half-life while all await the declaration of incompatibility by the Supreme Court that is bound to lead to their dismantling? But if this is not to be the case, and parliament does continue to assert its sovereign right to pick and choose which declarations it will follow and which it will ignore, then a serious incompatibility with Strasbourg's version of human rights will have been laid bare and it will have been found to exist not in some draconian law but within the Human Rights Act itself. The point was avoided in *Burden* only because no breach of the Convention was found in the laws under scrutiny.

The European question which is the subject of this section is suggested by this discussion of an imminent conflict between parliament and Strasbourg, although it goes beyond the immediate issue we have just discussed: What is the British government (and indeed parliament) to do when their version of rights-protection is contradicted by the Strasbourg court, under whose jurisdiction (through continued commitment to the Council of Europe) that same government (and parliament) continue voluntarily to place themselves? We are not just now concerned with situations, as with regard to DNA data retention for example, where the domestic courts view that there is no Convention breach is overturned by the Strasbourg court.[22] Such judicial wrangling on detail does not have the same constitutional implications as does a dispute between the elected domestic authorities on the one hand and the supranational judicial rights-invigilators on the other. As *Burden* makes clear, this question can already arise under the current arrangements. Suppose the Conservative/Lib Dem or a future Conservative government were to persevere with the Human Rights Act but to indicate an explicit (perhaps even an enthusiastic) willingness to regard section 4 declarations as no more than purely advisory, picking and choosing which to ignore and which to follow up. This might be because ministers disagreed with a court's interpretation of the human rights law, or it could arise because the national interest was thought to dictate rejection of a rights approach. If Strasbourg were later regularly to back the human rights interpretation of the British judges in cases where inaction had been the deliberate governmental response, then it is clear that this would provoke a series of crises, with the United Kingdom regularly finding itself before the enforcement machinery of the Council of Europe, facing accusations of ongoing and deliberate breaches of article 13.[23]

---

[22] *S and Marper v United Kingdom* European Court of Human Rights, 4 Dec 2008. And see, for a further possible conflict of a similar nature, *R v Horncastle* [2009] UKSC 14, [2010] 2 WLR 47.

[23] Committee on Legal Affairs and Human Rights of the Parliamentary Assembly of the Council of Europe, *Implementation of Judgments of the European Court of Human Rights* AS/Jur (2008) 24; Committee of Ministers, *Supervision of the Execution of Judgments of the European Court of Human Rights*, 1st Annual Report 2007 (Council of Europe 2008). The rules governing the process are at annex 6 of the second of these documents. And see now the procedural changes brought about by Protocol No 14 to the Convention for the Protection of Human Rights and Fundamental Freedoms, amending the control system of the Convention, agreed at Strasbourg on 13 May 2004 and which finally came into force on 1 June 2010.

Such showdowns would be even more likely and also more frequent if such an administration were also to make changes to the substance of the Human Rights Act itself so as to make it harder for the judges to come to decisions which were in accord with how the Strasbourg judges might determine matters were the same issues to come before them. Three examples of how this could be done come to mind. First, section 3's directive to the courts to do all that is possible to achieve Convention-compatible outcomes in the cases before them could be watered down so that the courts would have to issue declarations of incompatibility under section 4 much more often than at present because they would have reached the end of the section 3 road much earlier than is now the case. Or secondly, a new caveat could be added to section 3, demanding of the judges a rebalancing in favour of the public interest (and against individual human rights) where national security is asserted by the state to be in issue in any given case. Once again the effect of this would be to widen the number and range of section 4 declarations and consequentially (given that the declarations in both of these examples would most likely be ignored by government), adverse article 13 judgments in Strasbourg. If the executive was being really aggressive it might make findings of breaches of the rights set out in schedule 1 of the Act more difficult by inserting a general saving clause for national security within the definition of the rights themselves (or some of them). This would lead the courts not towards a finding of incompatibility (and therefore a section 4 declaration as in each of our first two examples) but towards a discovery that the rights set out in the schedule had not been breached at all. To make this work it would probably also be necessary to add a directive that the courts not have regard to the Strasbourg case-law, thereby turning on its head the requirement to take such material into account which is set out in detail in section 2 of the Act as currently drafted. Clearly this third approach goes well beyond the DNA-type case where views of what the Convention entails differ as between the two sets of judges since in this scenario the British judges would not be applying the Convention *simpliciter* but rather an amended version of the instrument to be found in the amended schedule to the Act. If this third approach were taken, a large number of cases would potentially find themselves generating a conflict between the insulated and human-rights-lite approach of the British courts (mandated by Parliament of course) and the Strasbourg judges, whose role as the ultimate guardians of an unemasculated Convention would necessarily have continued unabated.

The word 'necessarily' in the last sentence may be thought to be tendentious. Why should Britain be assumed to want to remain within a European system with which it would clearly be (on the series of hypotheses rehearsed above) manifestly so out of sympathy? However that may be, it is clear that there is no mainstream political party in the United Kingdom with any kind of appetite to push its hostility to the Human Rights Act in this direction, however logical it might appear to be. In particular there is no current political inclination on the part of the Conservative Party to withdraw from the Strasbourg mechanism altogether, with the departure from the Council of Europe (and even the EU) that that might be thought to entail, or at least to bring within the frame of reasonable discussion.[24] Against the background of these political realities, the effect of the making of any of the changes to the Human Rights Act identified above—by the Conservative/Lib Dem coalition or the Tories—would be a likely return to the situation that pertained in the mid 1980s and 1990s under the successive prime ministerships of Margaret Thatcher and John Major. A close examination of the record during this time is revealing.[25] It is clear that each of the successive Tory administrations under both leaders was often impatient with the Strasbourg rulings adverse to them. Ministers were sometimes overtly critical, particularly when a case impinged on—or was perceived to impinge on—national security, the Gibraltar killings ruling in 1995 for example,[26] or the condemnation of seven-day detention without charge as a breach of article 5 in 1988.[27] The attempted suppression of Peter Wright's *Spycatcher* book, so dear to Mrs Thatcher in her last years in power, also involved high-profile trips to Strasbourg, just as it had done to so many other judicial venues around the world.[28] Even John Major raised the stakes in advance of certain Strasbourg decisions that he thought might play badly in the home media if they were to go against his government.[29] But in contrast to all the bluster, the actual record of implementation of Strasbourg decisions under both prime ministers was generally very good. No fewer than fifteen decisions led directly to legislative change. In five others, subordinate legislation or relevant standing orders were altered to achieve compliance. The seven-day detention case produced a derogation that was carefully crafted to be understood to be legitimate within its framework, an assessment that was afterwards confirmed by the Strasbourg court itself.[30] Even in the Gibraltar case, the legal costs of the applicants' lawyers were paid as required by the court, and the right of individual application to Strasbourg (not then the mandatory part of the system that it has since become) was quietly renewed for a further five years shortly afterwards.[31]

In summary, it may well be that if the United Kingdom system drifts far from its Convention moorings but without jettisoning Strasbourg oversight, we will be

[24] See articles 3 and 8 of the Statute of the Council of Europe (European Treaty Series No 1) and articles 2, 6, and 7 of the consolidated version of the Treaty of European Union, OJ C115, 9 May 2008 <http://eur-lex.europa.eu/JOHtml.do?uri=OJ:C:2008:115:SOM:EN:HTML> (last visited 7 Dec 2009).

[25] The details of what follows are drawn from C. A. Gearty, 'The United Kingdom', in C. A. Gearty (ed), *European Civil Liberties and the European Convention on Human Rights: A Comparative Study* (The Hague: Martinus Nijhoff, 1997), ch 2.

[26] *McCann v United Kingdom* (1995) 21 EHRR 97.

[27] *Brogan v United Kingdom* (1988) 11 EHRR 117.

[28] *Observer and Guardian v United Kingdom* (1991) 14 EHRR 153; *The Sunday Times v United Kingdom (No 2)* (1991) 14 EHRR 229.

[29] See reports of the then Lord Chancellor's visit to Strasbourg in 1996—'Mackay Steps Up Court Reform Bid', *Independent* (26 Nov 1996) (see <http://www.independent.co.uk/news/mackay-steps-up-court-reform-bid-1354268.html> (last visited 8 Dec 2009)). The decision the same day upholding the law of blasphemy in the context of a challenge mounted by the makers of an erotic video *Visions of Ecstasy* no doubt made the visit less difficult than it might otherwise have been: *Wingrove v United Kingdom* (1996) 24 EHRR 1.

[30] In *Brannigan and McBride v United Kingdom* (1993) 17 EHRR 539.

[31] House of Lords Parliamentary Debates, vol 567, col 117 (written answer) (Baroness Chalker) (14 Dec 1995).

likely to get two narratives operating in tandem. The first (particularly emphasized if the Tories find themselves ruling alone) will be conducted for the benefit of the media and the public and will be overtly hostile to Europe and all that it stands for, the risks that the Strasbourg judges are taking with security, the threat they pose to Britain's values, and so on. The second will be quieter, operating under the radar and on a longer time frame, and will be engaged in the process of covert implementation of Strasbourg judgments under Council of Europe oversight. The two story lines may only occasionally intersect and, when they do, officials and thoughtful ministers will gamble on the attention span of the public being as short as it usually is. The one high risk area lies in the field of interim measures. Under rule 39 of the European Court's rules, the Strasbourg judges may 'indicate to the parties any interim measure which it considers should be adopted in the interests of the parties or of the proper conduct of the proceedings before it'. This will make it difficult to remove a person to face likely ill-treatment abroad if his or her lawyers are able to get to the European Court before the expulsion occurs.[32] But even here the issue can be presented as one of delay before expulsion rather than non-removal, thereby putting off the eventual jurisdictional conflict in the hope that it might never arise or that, if it does, the public will have forgotten (and not be reminded of) its earlier indignation, thereby allowing a Strasbourg final ruling ordering non-removal to be quietly followed.

Suppose, however, that parliament were to go the whole hog and repeal the Human Rights Act in its entirety; as we have seen, a by no means impossible event even with the coalition government and as likely as not if the Conservatives manage to become the sole governing party once again. Perhaps counter-intuitively, Strasbourg would be reasonably relaxed about this. As the court made clear as recently as February 2009,[33] the Convention does not require that a signatory state allow challenges to primary legislation on Convention grounds as a matter of course. What matters is the substance not the form of rights-protection. In pre-Human Rights Act days, the Strasbourg court had resisted the temptation offered to it on a number of occasions to require incorporation[34] and it can be expected that such case-law would be kicked back into place to cover this unexpected return to the past. Of course there might be more cases, more conflict, and therefore more discussion of all those 1990s issues that drove the New Labour logic that it was time to 'bring rights home', but these would not be a concern to the Strasbourg judges (exasperated though they might be by a likely increase in their UK case-load through the ease with which applicants would now once again be able to demonstrate exhaustion of local remedies). But if there is no European question in such circumstances, there might well be a 'British question' that will need to be resolved and it is to this that we now turn.

---

[32] As in eg the recent French case of *Daoudi v France*, 3 Dec 2009.
[33] In *A and Others v United Kingdom*, 19 Feb 2009 (Grand Chamber).
[34] eg *James v United Kingdom* (1986) 8 EHRR 123.

II. The British Question

This can be posed as follows: 'If the Human Rights Act were to be repealed, what effect would there be on the judicial protection of Convention rights within the United Kingdom?' There are a number of complicated dimensions to this apparently simple query with which any new legislation of this sort would need to deal. First, there are the inevitable (and surely obvious) consequential issues raised for the devolved arrangements in Scotland, Wales, and Northern Ireland, all of which places have specific controls on their local governmental bodies which are rooted in requirements of respect for human rights.[35] The issue has an international dimension so far as Northern Ireland is concerned, with the Good Friday Agreement having committed Her Majesty's Government to the incorporation of the Convention into Northern Ireland law.[36] Secondly, there are the multiplicity of public authorities whose decision-making and training have been rooted in the assumption that they are bound by section 6 to act in a way that is compatible with Convention rights. The temptation will be to persevere with this approach, particularly given the continuing binding nature of the Convention both as a matter of international law and in light of the ongoing possibility of being taken to Strasbourg by a victim of a decision-making process that—shed of all sensitivity to human rights—will be certain to be at much greater risk of being found in breach of the Convention. Thirdly, there are the many cases which have interpreted statute law in Convention-compatible ways which have now bedded down in the case-law and become routinely applied without specific dependence on—or with only a passing reference to—the requirements of the Convention: would this learning now need to be unlearnt? If so, would it matter whether the legislation had been re-enacted since the judicial decisions on the point? If this were to be judged relevant, would specific reference to the Convention change that had been wrought be necessary and, if necessary, would it be sufficient to preserve the Convention meaning intact despite repeal of the very Act without which the interpretation would never have occurred?[37] Fourthly, there is the question of what would be done with regard to those pieces of legislation which have contained within them 'get-out' clauses through which human rights have been able to do modifying work—provisos based on exceptionality as in *Offen*, for example,[38] or specifically safeguarding human rights as in *Limbuela*.[39] Will these interpretations be permitted to continue even though the Act which provided

---

[35] Scotland Act 1998; Government of Wales Act 1998; Northern Ireland Act 1998.

[36] 'The British Government will complete incorporation into Northern Ireland law of the European Convention on Human Rights (ECHR), with direct access to the courts, and remedies for breach of the Convention, including power for the courts to overrule Assembly legislation on grounds of inconsistency.' See <http://www.nio.gov.uk/agreement.pdf> (last visited 8 Dec 2009).

[37] An outstanding example is *R (Middleton) v Her Majesty's Coroner for the Western District of Somerset* [2004] UKHL 10, with their lordships' interpretation of the coroners' law being explicitly carried forward into the Coroners and Justice Act 2009: see s 5(2).

[38] [2001] 1 WLR 253.

[39] *R (Limbuela) v Secretary of State for the Home Department* [2005] UKHL 66, [2006] 1 AC 396.

their rationale has disappeared? Fifthly, will the judges regard the common law changes brought about by the partial application of the Convention within that non-statutory realm to be sufficiently independent of the statute to survive the Act's disappearance?[40]

As if these were not complexities enough to be getting on with, there are also the larger jurisprudential issues. With section 3(1) gone, there would be no legislative requirement to stretch language to render words and phrases compatible with the Convention rights. But how far away from human rights would this in fact lead the courts? Long before incorporation via the 1998 Act, the judges had become familiar with the idea that the Convention, like all international treaties and agreements, provided a guide map through legislation whose meaning appeared uncertain on its face.[41] The Convention had also been acknowledged as influential in the development of the common law well before enactment of the Human Rights Act.[42] In a succession of cases in the early 1970s, two senior members of the judiciary, Lord Denning MR and Lord Justice Scarman (as he then was) sought to stake out a further, and more ambitious, space for the Convention. In *R (Bhajan Singh) v Secretary of State for Home Affairs*,[43] for example, the former asserted that the courts 'should take the Convention into account...whenever interpreting a statute which affects the rights and liberties of the individual',[44] and the latter, long an advocate for a stronger role for international law within the British system, suggested in one judgment in 1975 that it was 'the duty of the courts, so long as they do not defy or disregard clear and unequivocal provision, to construe statutes in a manner which promotes, not endangers' the basic rights to be found in the ECHR.[45] It is acknowledged that these judges did not carry their arguments for incorporation further into the case law in the course of their long judicial careers, and nor were their dicta on these matters taken up enthusiastically by their contemporaries on the bench. Nor did the common law shift to any kind of Convention template before section 6(3)(a) of the Human Rights Act provided the legislative scaffolding for such a move. Nevertheless the language is there if judges anxious about the impact of repeal of the Human Rights Act want to find it. And it is worth recalling that the climate for engaging in this way with international (and regional) human rights law in domestic judgments is much more receptive than it was when Lords Denning and Scarman were on the Bench. In the post-*Pinochet*

---

[40] Principally the emerging law on privacy (eg *Douglas v Hello! Ltd*, n 14 above), but also many other areas including defamation (see cases at n 12 above), breach of the peace (*R (Laporte) v Chief Constable of Gloucestershire* [2006] UKHL 55), and nuisance law (see *Dennis v Ministry of Defence* [2003] EWHC 793 (QB), [2003] *Env LR* 34).

[41] See *Salomon v Commissioners of Customs and Excise* [1967] 2 QB 116. The best example from a Convention point of view is *Waddington v Miah* [1974] 1 WLR 683.

[42] As in *Attorney General v BBC* [1981] AC 303, for example, in which the House of Lords held that a local valuation court was not subject to the law of contempt, with two of their lordships (Lords Fraser and Scarman) making explicit references to the Convention.

[43] [1975] 3 WLR 225.

[44] Ibid 231.

[45] *R (Phansopkar) v Secretary of State for Home Affairs; R (Begum) v Secretary of State for Home Affairs* [1975] 3 All ER 497, 511.

judicial world, much more can be achieved than could ever have been envisaged in the 1970s.[46]

There is also the question of the remit of judicial review. The world of *Wednesbury* unreasonableness is a judge-made one, capable of being filled with a content which is not pre-determined by the legislature, or at least not unless it decides to speak in a very particular and specific way via statute (which with regard to administrative law it has yet to do). As with the cases on statutory construction, the pre-Human Rights Act record contains plenty of references to the need for administrative decision-making to be especially vigilant where fundamental rights are engaged.[47] As Sedley J (as he then was) noted as early as 1995, '[o]nce it is accepted that the standards articulated in the [European] convention are standards which march with those of the common law and inform the jurisprudence of the European Union, it becomes unreal and potentially unjust to continue to develop English public law without reference to it'.[48] It is not improbable that in any period following repeal of the Human Rights Act, remarks along these lines will be revived and applied in a way that may well thicken the common law heads of review of administrative action to the point where it will be prudent for all public authorities to act as though the repealed section 6 of the Human Rights Act was still in force. Does *Daly* still need the crutch of section 6 to be able to operate?[49] And if it does not, how will anyone be able to tell that the Human Rights Act has disappeared? Will this be another example, analogous to the situation that will by then also pertain with regard to Europe, where there will be two realities in operation, one aimed at the general public and one dealing with the realities of litigation?

Of course in one important particular there will have been a change if the Act is repealed—the declaration of incompatibility will disappear. But proponents of parliamentary sovereignty need to be careful over their advocacy of such a course of action, since the incompatibility procedure serves to buttress rather than to undermine parliamentary sovereignty. Without it, the courts might be emboldened to act in defence of what they would see as constitutional principle in a way that subjugates not just administrative action but the very legislative output of parliament itself to the dictates of a common law rooted in respect for the rule of law, separation of powers, and fundamental rights. The point is not just an obscure, theoretical one. There has long been a sub-theme in the academic literature which has argued that the courts are constitutionally entitled to refuse to recognize legislation which violates fundamental rights.[50] Lord Denning briefly toyed with such an idea in the 1970s,[51] since when advances in EU law have made the non-enforcement of an Act of Parliament less heretical than had long been supposed.[52] In *R (Jackson) v*

---

[46] See *R (Simms) v Secretary of State for the Home Department* [2000] 2 AC 115.

[47] eg *Bugdaycay v Secretary of State for the Home Department* [1987] AC 514.

[48] *R (McQuillan) v Secretary of State for the Home Department* [1995] 4 All ER 400, 422.

[49] *R (Daly) v Secretary of State for the Home Department* [2001] UKHL 26, [2001] 2 AC 532.

[50] eg T. R. S. Allan, *Constitutional Justice: A Liberal Theory of the Rule of Law* (Oxford: Oxford University Press, 2001). And see also the extra-judicial thoughts of Sir John Laws, 'Is the High Court the Guardian of Fundamental Constitutional Rights?' [1993] *Public Law* 59.

[51] *Birdi v Secretary of State for Home Affairs* (1975) 119 *Solicitors Journal* 322.

[52] *R (Factortame) v Secretary of State for Transport (No 2)* [1991] 1 AC 603.

Attorney General,[53] the idea was given further traction. This was the case in which the Hunting Act 2004 was challenged as beyond the powers of Parliament to enact—it will be remembered that the legislation, which banned hunting with dogs, had been achieved only in the face of the opposition of the House of Lords and had therefore only got to the Queen for signature through invocation of the procedures for bypassing the Lords set out in the Parliament Acts 1911–49. *Jackson* commanded the attention of nine law lords and provoked a series of dicta on what exactly constituted an Act of Parliament, suggestive of the idea that the final say lay not with parliament but with the courts. It is not a large step from this to say that a piece of (purported) legislation containing an egregious breach of fundamental rights is not in fact a law at all. The removal of the specific respect accorded Acts of Parliament in the scheme of the Human Rights Act (and in particular sections 3(2) and 6(2)) makes this noticeably easier to achieve. It would be ironic indeed if the repeal of the Human Rights Act, motivated in large part by a desire to rein in the judges, in fact led to their further unleashing and to greater rather than less judicial power over the elected branches of government.

III. Conclusion: A New Bill of Rights for Britain?

Where should the energies of true advocates of human rights be deployed? It is suggested that it is a waste of resources to devote too much time to arguing for repeal of the Human Rights Act. The measure is not the kind of American (or even Canadian) style charter that was being pushed so hard by so many in the mid 1990s. The judges have a place within rather than above the system of rights' protection that it sets out, with its civil and political rights acknowledging (unusually for a rights' document to be sure) that their logic requires that primacy be ultimately accorded to the elected forum which flows out of the system of government in the creation and maintenance of which these rights play such an important part. It is true that the Strasbourg conflation of 'effective' with 'judicial' for article 13 purposes is outside the British solution, yet capable, via cases like *Burden*, of being imposed upon it, riding roughshod over the shrewd compromise between representative government and human rights which is the Human Rights Act's greatest achievement. Future governments of a more social democratic bent than in the recent past (or it goes without saying the present) may need to be willing to suffer defeat first in the United Kingdom on the substance and then in Strasbourg on both the issue and article 13, arguing the case both on the occasional need to override individual rights in the interests of underlying human rights values (such as equality or fairness for example), while seeking to demonstrate that the scheme of the Human Rights Act, with its legal duties to respond to such declarations, its parliamentary accountability, and much else, is far from ineffective, at least when effectiveness is viewed within the broad scheme of politics rather than being solely embedded within the narrower frame of law. If defeat follows despite these

[53] [2005] UKHL 56, [2006] 1 AC 262.

arguments, then a confident government—sure of itself and of the importance of the underlying values behind the rights it promotes—may simply have to take it on the chin, implement only if it can and then as best it can, but in as non-disruptive way as it is possible to be. There will be no uncontrollable constitutional crisis because it will be recognized (not least because such a government will have developed the terms of discussion) that the British authorities might be failing to follow some narrow reading of the Strasbourg judiciary, but that in doing so they will have been going *with* rather than *against* the grain of human rights protection. It is not an argument that is impossible to win, nor is it one that it is a disgrace to lose.

Should human rights protection go further than this? The natural instinct of the democratic socialist is to say no, that there are concepts broader than human rights which can better capture the drive towards a fairer and more egalitarian society than a phrase such as this one, replete as it is with a history that can appear narrow and a political engagement that has been as often reactionary as it has been progressive. In a perfect world, the language of socialism, and in particular of democratic socialism and of social justice, would function more effectively than that of human rights as the intellectual basis for underpinning the kinds of movements towards change which a true commitment to justice must inevitably call for. It can be readily acknowledged that these phrases work better than human rights to legitimize a key facet of the work of social justice campaigners, the struggle against the powerful and the many beneficiaries of vested interests who oppose change and many of whom are not above deploying the rhetoric of libertarianism in defence of their privilege. But, and perhaps sadly, we do not live in such a perfect world. Socialism would seem to have some years of penance to make yet for its early 20th century error in believing that the road to justice could be separated from the democratic path. Even Sweden, that paragon of a social democratic society, has (after some initial hesitations to be sure) found itself compelled to embrace the language of human rights.[54] In the relatively barren landscape of post-Cold War globalized capitalism, we must all be human rights advocates or we are nothing at all. The key is to broaden the meaning of the term to incorporate the field previously occupied by ideas of socialism and of social justice.

The European Convention on Human Rights clearly does not fit this bill, with its emphasis being on civil and political rights and with only the very occasional nod towards a richer vision of society.[55] Nor do any likely Coalition proposals for a bill of rights (and responsibilities?). In so far as there were any details of the Conservatives' earlier thoughts available, the plan seems to be for a charter which is civil libertarian in content and backward looking in its identification of key freedoms, as well as emphatic on the need for duties and responsibilities of all

[54] The constitutional and political (as well as legal) background to Sweden's move towards acceptance of the European Convention on Human Rights is well-laid out in I. Cameron, 'Sweden', in Gearty (ed), n 25 above, ch 6.

[55] eg the reference to a right to education in article 2 of the first protocol, which has (unsurprisingly it might be thought) attracted very little creative judicial interpretation, as though the judges were unsure what to do with a right that sits so uneasily with the rest of the document.

sorts.[56] The now departed Labour government's *Rights and Responsibilities* Green Paper was much more promising in this regard, and it is a document that might well be fruitfully built upon in opposition.[57] First, it accepted and indeed declared an intention to defend the Human Rights Act—whatever might be the case in the future, the Party seems for now to have eschewed the temptation to bowdlerise the measure in the name of counter-terrorism.[58] Secondly, the document extends the language of rights to cover the kinds of issues with which the traditional Labour Party has always been identified: there are separate sections on 'equality', 'social justice and the welfare state', 'healthcare', 'children', and 'living within environmental limits'. Thirdly, the Green Paper displays a healthy scepticism about the ability of the courts to deliver these valuable, life-enhancing rights. There is a degree of diffidence about entrusting all this to the courts and a keenness instead to locate the search for rights within the political system, an inclination that fits very well with the traditional, social democratic emphasis on democratic engagement. Of course there are disconcerting elements to the proposals, a concentration on responsibilities for example and a reluctance to think through the universalistic dynamic of rights-talk—but perhaps these can be put down to governmental pressures that will in all likelihood not be felt over the course of the next few years. If the idea of 'human rights' is to be rescued in Britain, then such work could usefully begin with a robust campaign to transform these tentative Labour Party beginnings into a blueprint for a powerful kind of human rights-based universalism, rooted in the equality and dignity of all and unbeholden to power and money. Indeed, it may even be that in today's political and economic climate this is (for now anyway) the best and most effective way of doing socialism.

[56] J. Fisher QC, *A British Bill of Rights and Obligations* (Conservative Liberty Forum, 2008). David Cameron fleshed out the Party's plans for a bill of rights along these lines in the course of a contribution to the Convention on Modern Britain: see 'Cameron pledges Bill to Restore British Freedoms' *Guardian* (28 Feb 2009) (see <http://www.guardian.co.uk/politics/2009/feb/28/conservatives-human-rights> (last visited 9 Dec 2009)). See further D. Blackburn, 'What should be in the British Bill of Rights?' on the *Spectator* website (22 Nov 2009): <http://www.spectator.co.uk/coffeehouse/5561873/what-should-be-in-the-british-bill-of-rights.thtml> (last visited 9 Dec 2009). For startling evidence of quite how vague Tory plans were see J. Rosenberg, 'Retaining Rights', *Standpoint* (Nov 2009), accessible at <http://standpointmag.co.uk/node/2320/full> (last visited 9 Dec 2009). Contrast the interesting if heretical Tory perspective of J. Norman and P. Oborne, *Churchill's Legacy: The Conservative Case for the Human Rights Act* (London: Liberty, 2009).

[57] n 19 above.

[58] See n 8 above. Of course, as observed above, it does not follow that a change would not be made to the Human Rights Act along these lines in the context of a new bill of rights for Britain (or indeed quite separately) if the political climate of the moment were to seem to require it, as was the case to some extent during the mid 2000s.

Index

absolute versus relative values 355–6
abuse of rights language 333
access to legal advice, terrorism and 196
access to public documents 7, 393, 394–5,
    402, 406–7
accountability 4, 9, 43, 60–5, 275
adjudication, politicization of 373, 375–7, 382
advertising ban on tobacco 439
advocacy networks 362
Advocates-General of European Court of
    Justice 449
AFSJ *see* area of freedom, security and justice
    (AFSJ)
airfields, demonstrations at 153–68, 173–4
alternative forms of protection 1–2, 5–6
Amnesty International 183–5, 202–3
Amsterdam Treaty 269, 291
Anti-Terrorism, Crime and Security
    Act 2001 19–21
area of freedom, security and justice (AFSJ) 3,
    269–93
    accountability 275
    Amsterdam Treaty 269, 291
    availability principle 275
    biometrics 271–2
    blacklists, legality of terrorist 285–8, 289
    Carpenter case 289–90
    Charter of Fundamental Rights of the
        EU 269, 276
    constitutional law 270
    criminal justice 269–82, 285–8, 291–2
    Customs Information System 270
    data collection 270–2, 274, 282–5
    democracy 269–70, 291
    democratic deficit 269–70
    dignity, right to 290
    direct effect 287, 288–9
    Directorates-General 282
    emergency, times of 272, 291–2
    Eurojust Information System 270
    European Convention on Human
        Rights 293
    European Court of Justice 269–93
    European Evidence Warrant 282
    European Parliament, increased
        role of 276, 292
    Europol Information System 270
    free movement of goods and
        services 289–90
    freezing of assets 285, 288
    future of AFSJ and human rights 291–3
    G6 274–5

general principles of law, human rights
    as 276
Hague Programme 272, 282
immigration 289
industrial action, freedom to provide
    services and 290
information
    availability principle 275
    collection of 270–2, 274, 282–5
intelligence gathering by national
    agencies 270–1
international law, compliance
    with 287–9
judicial review 276–7, 285, 288–90, 292
justice, concept of 292
lawmaking, undemocratic 272–6
legal certainty 273–4
liberty and security, right to 287
Lisbon Treaty 272–3, 276, 292
Maastricht Treaty 276, 288–9
normalization of AFSJ 291–3
Omega case 289–90
passenger names records (PNR) agreement
    with United States 282–5, 289
passports, biometric information in 271
police and judicial cooperation in
    criminal matters (Third Pillar) 272–6,
    288–9, 291
pre-charge detention of terrorist
    suspects 293
proportionality 290
Prüm, Treaty of 274
public authorities, individuals and 270
repatriation of AFSJ 291–3
rule of law 273, 275, 286, 291–3
Schengen area 274
Schengen Information System 270–1
Schmidberger case 289–90
security 269, 271–2, 292–3
Security Council (UN) resolutions,
    compliance with 285–7
sensitive personal information, misuse
    of 271–2
September 11, 2001 terrorist attacks on the
    United States 272
supremacy of EU law 286–9
surveillance 271–2
state of exception as the norm 272–3
terrorism
    blacklists, legality of terrorist 285–8
    broad definition 269
    data collection 270

area of freedom, security and justice
    (AFSJ) (*cont.*)
  legislation 272–3, 291–2
  Schengen Information System 270–1
  torture, evidence obtained by 293
  transparency 273–4
  United States 271, 282–5
  violation of rights 272–6
armed forces
  airfields, demonstrations at 153–68, 173–4
  Bloody Sunday 187–93
  Iraqi civilians, murder of 205
  lethal force, use of 187–93
  Northern Ireland 179–80, 187–93
  removal from armed forces list 136
  terrorism 179–80, 187–93
arrest
  Committee of 100 peace campaigners, civil
    liberties and 151–2, 157–61, 167, 169,
    170, 173, 175
  European Arrest Warrant 269, 277–82
  extension of powers 1
  interrogation 195–6
  Northern Ireland and terrorism 178, 181,
    195–6, 197
  reasons, right to be informed of 197
Attorney Generals
  bills of rights 51–2, 55–6, 89–90, 95–100,
    103–4
  Committee of 100 peace
    campaigners 154–6, 158–9, 164–6
  New Zealand Bill of Rights 89–90, 95–100,
    103–4
  United Kingdom 55–6, 59, 63
Australia *see also* Australian party politics,
    human rights and
  abuse of rights language 333
  balancing rights 335
  bicameralism 123
  bills of rights 330–1, 343
  blocking legislation 6
  capacity of parliament and parliamentarians
    to protect rights 337–42
  civil and political rights 334, 343
  committees 331, 337–9, 341, 344, 346
  complexity of legislation 344–5
  compromise 340–1
  conscience votes 340–1
  constituents, importance of rights to 335–7
  debates on legislation 339
  declarations of incompatibility 87
  discipline 340–1
  dominance of executive 341–2
  economic and social rights 334, 343
  electronic technologies, participation by 6
  entrenchment, problems of 343
  examples of rights 333
  executive 330–1, 341–2
  expert, independent advice, importance
    of 338–9

  expertise, lack of 344–6
  Federal Government issue, rights as a 334–5
  Henry VIII clauses 344, 345
  identification of rights issues 337–9, 345
  importance of rights for working life of
    parliamentarians 334–5, 343
  incremental change, vigilance against 336–7
  information, sources of 339
  inherence possession of human rights 333
  international human rights
    instruments 332–3
  interviews with parliamentarians 330–46
  judicial review 344–5
  legislation
    complexity and volume 344–5
    confidentiality of bills 341
    debates 339
    expertise, lack of 344–6
    identification of human rights issues 338
    judicial review 344–5
    scrutiny 332, 342, 343, 344, 346
    terrorism 341–2, 345
    time issues 344
  libraries 339
  lowest common denominator 344
  media 337, 345
  national security 342
  nature of rights 332–7, 343
  origin of rights 332–3
  parliamentarians, rights protection
    and 329–46
  party discipline 340–1
  political compromise 340–1
  political parties 332, 340–1, 343
  pre-charge detention of terrorist
    suspects 121
  public interest 337
  public opinion 336–7
  public participation 6
  raising rights issues, methods of 339–40
  reform 342–3
  religion as origin of rights 333
  resources 342
  rights impact statements 343
  scepticism about rights 333, 336
  scope of rights 333–4, 343
  scrutiny of legislation 6, 332, 342, 343,
    344, 346
  shadow portfolios, creation of 340
  statements of incompatibility 343
  terrorism 121, 341–2, 345
  time 342, 344
  transparency 340
  volume of legislation 344–5
Australian party politics, human rights
    and 312–28
  Australian Labour Party 312–13, 318–20,
    322, 324, 326–8
  bills of rights 312–17
  branches of government 315–16

citizenry, relationship of parties with 317
collective bargaining 314–15, 324
competition for power 325–6
compulsory voting 326
conscience votes 324–5
courts as forum for principles 312
deliberative aspects of parties 322
dialogue theories of bills 315–16
discipline 320–5
elections 325–6
entrenched minorities 327–8
faction 320, 325–8
Fair Work Act 2009 (Cth) 312–15, 318–20,
    322, 324
Forward with Fairness policy 312–13,
    314, 319
franchise, extension of 326
functional agencies, parties as 325
generous contention for power 325–6
governance function 317, 318
ILO conventions 315
intermediary organizations 317–18
judgments, elected representatives' duty to
    use own 321–3
legislators as trustees or delegates 320–1
Liberal-National Coalition 312–15, 319,
    324, 326
majoritarianism 326–8
media as intermediary 317–18
minority rights 326–8
normative status of US political parties 318
parliamentary sovereignty 320
participation 320
policy 313–14
political representation, simplistic view
    of 317–20
power/questions of policy 313
pressure groups 325
principles/questions of rights 313
proportional representation 326
responsible government 318
responsive functions of parties 317–18
Rights at Work campaign 319
separation of power 316
statutory individual contracts 314–15
transformative effect of political parties 317
tyranny of the majority 326–8
United States 318
Victorian Charter of Human Rights and
    Responsibilities 315–16
Work Choices policy 312–15, 319, 324
Austria 369

'B' specials 178–9
backbenchers 302, 305–6
Baha Mousa Inquiry 186–7, 205
bail 24
Baker Report 196
balancing rights 335, 374–5
bank bailouts 232

basic rights 378–9, 385–91
Battle of Trafalgar Square 152–4
Belfast Agreement 79, 481
below, globalization from 3–4, 349, 359
bicameralism 123
bills of rights *see also* New Zealand bill of
    rights
accountability 43, 60–3
Attorney Generals 51–2, 55–6
Australia 312–17, 330–1, 343
Bill of Rights 1689 418
Bill of Rights and Responsibilities Green Paper
    (United Kingdom) 460–70, 475
Canada 40, 42, 45–50, 53–62, 315, 379
capacity to hold government accountable,
    increase in parliament's 43, 60–4
changes, insulation of legislation
    from 49–50
committees 464–71
Commonwealth model 87
compatibility of legislation 40–65
constitutional review 372
constitutionalism 41–2, 127, 146–7
constitutions 460
criteria for inclusion 471
declarations of incompatibility 460, 463
democratic charter of rights model 458–71
dialogue theory 315–16
economic and social rights 8
entrenchment 109, 343
executive 42, 43–8
Finland 370, 384
foreign law, citation of 418–19, 425
Human Rights Act 1998 46–7, 50–2,
    67–72, 79–84, 109–16, 126,
    460–70, 475
hybrid bills 87
identification of sources of human
    rights 461
instability of weak forms of bills 43, 52–60
institutional scepticism 5
international relations 470–1
Joint Committee on Human Rights 464–70
judicial appointments 123–4
judicial influence on legislation, extent
    of 43, 48–54, 64
judicial review 5, 40–65, 372, 460–4
judiciary, power of 116–20
juridification of human rights 458
legal positivism 458–9, 461–2
legislation
    compatibility 42, 43–8
    development and evaluation 5
    non-compliance, costs to government
        of 42, 43–8
legislature
    capacity to hold government accountable,
        increase in 43, 60–4
    democratic charter of rights
        model 458–71

bills of rights *see also* New Zealand bill of
         rights (*cont.*)
    legitimacy 45
    review 458–71
    legitimacy 45
    life, right to 462–3
    living document or living tree
         metaphor 113–15
    majoritarianism 120–1
    moral rights 461–2
    non-compliance, costs to government of 42,
         43–8, 49, 54–5, 56, 59, 61
    parliamentary sovereignty 120
    policy 44, 56, 59–61, 64
    political approaches to human
         rights 460–1, 471
    political behaviour, altering 52, 65
    political parties 56, 343
    political philosophies of human rights 456
    political systems, influence on 42–3
    pre-charge detention of terrorist
         suspects 121–2
    referendums 121
    responsibility for compatibility 55
    risk aversion 49
    savings clauses 425
    Scotland 67, 68–72, 79–84
    separation of powers 460
    South Africa 218
    statutory interpretation 109–16
    strong form or entrenched bills 120, 126
    terrorism 121–2
    United Kingdom 40, 42, 46–56, 58–63,
         67–72, 79–84, 109–16, 418, 475
    United States 53–4, 127, 146–7, 418–19
    values 461–2
    Victorian Charter of Human Rights and
         Responsibilities 315–16
    weak or statutory forms of bills 5, 43,
         52–60, 116–22, 126
    Westminster-type parliamentary
         systems 40, 42–60, 458
binding over 151–2
biometrics 271–2
blacklists, legality of terrorist 285–8, 289
Bloody Sunday
    armed forces, use of lethal force of 187–93
    demonstrations, bans on 187–8
    evidence 188–93
    internment 187
    IRA 187–8
    Magilligan incident 187
    Saville Inquiry 187–9, 203
    Widgery Inquiry 188, 191–3, 196
    withholding of evidence 192
Brandeis briefs 444
Brazil 213–14, 362
Brize Norton, demonstration at RAF 154
bugging of suspects' homes 405–6
business rights as human rights 3, 229–43

bank bail-outs 232
    Canada, tobacco advertising in 229
    compensation 242
    competition 231, 232, 233–4, 239–42
    constitutionalism 231, 243
    constitutionalization 232–3
    corporate free movement as a fundamental
         right 234–9
    corporations 229, 234–9, 242–3
    definition of human rights 229
    economic and social rights 215
    enforcement 230, 233
    EU law
         breach of EU law, legislation in 233–4
         competition 231, 232, 233–4, 239–42
         enforcement 230, 233
         entrenchment 234
         free movement 230, 233, 234–9, 241
         free trade 230–2, 234
         fundamental rights 234
         market liberalism 234
         nationalization 230–1
         preliminary references 234
         supremacy of EU law 233–4
         treaties 229
    European Convention on Human
         Rights 230, 242
    free movement 230, 233, 234–9, 241–2
    free trade 230–2, 234, 242–3
    fundamental rights 234–42
    Human Rights Act 1998 229–30, 233–4
    ideological scepticism 2–3
    international economic law 231
    judicial supremacy 230, 233, 243
    judicialization 233
    labelling 233
    market liberalism 234
    NAFTA 229, 232
    nationalization 230–1
    neoliberalism 232, 242, 243
    parliamentary sovereignty 243
    peaceful enjoyment of possessions 242
    private sector domination 230–1
    property as fundamental right,
         corporate 242–3
    statutory interpretation 229–30
    supranational agreements 229, 243
    supranational economic law 233
    tobacco advertising 229
    United Kingdom 229–43
    WTO agreements 229, 230, 231–2,
         242–3

Calman Commission 69–71, 75, 85
Campaign for the Limitation of Secret Police
         Powers 140–2
Canada
    bicameralism 123
    Bill of Rights 40, 42, 45, 47, 48–9, 87, 106,
         379, 418

capacity to hold government accountable,
    increase in parliament's 60, 61–2
Charter of Rights 45, 47, 49–50, 55–7, 61–2
    constitutionalism 127
    dialogue 315
    economic and social rights 209,
        211–13, 221
    Human Rights Act 1998 432–3, 436
    New Zealand Bill of Rights 89
    notwithstanding clause 57–8, 106, 209,
        432–3, 436, 463–4
    statutory interpretation 113–15
constitutionalism 127
changes, insulation of legislation
    from 49–50
compatibility assessments 48–9, 50, 60,
    61–2
constitutional review 379
cruel or inhuman treatment 418
Department of Justice, role of 50
dialogue 315, 432–3
economic and social rights 209, 211–13, 221
English Bill of Rights 1689 418
federalism 66
Finland 380–1
Gouzenko defection 128–9
health care 211–12
instability of weak forms of bills 53–8
judicial influence on legislation, extent
    of 48–50, 53–4
judicial review 40, 42, 45, 47–9, 56, 61–2,
    209, 379
legislative process, incorporation of case law
    in the 45
limitation clause in Charter of
    Rights 57–8, 209
living document or living tree metaphor 113
Minister of Justice 55–6, 57
New Zealand Bill of Rights 87, 89, 106
non-compliance, costs to government of 42,
    45, 47, 49, 54–5, 56–7, 61
notwithstanding clause 57–8, 106, 209,
    432–3, 436, 463–4
policy 56, 209, 211–12
provincial governments 50
purposive approach to interpretation 113–14
responsibility for compatibility 55
risk assessment 50, 54, 61
risk management 56–7
rule of law 127
same sex marriages 62
statutory interpretation 113–15, 213
subsistence rights 211–12
tobacco advertising 229
weak form of judicial review 209
weak or statutory form of bills of
    rights 53–4
welfare benefits 212
capital punishment 410–12, 413, 415–23
CCTV, increase in use of 1

Central and Eastern Europe 369, 376–7, 383
charges, threshold test for 23–4, 30–1
Charter of Fundamental Rights of the EU
    binding effect 269
    collective bargaining 252
    constitutional review 366
    European Arrest Warrant 278
    freedom, security and justice, area
        of 269, 276
    labour rights in Europe,
        constitutionalization of 246,
        249–52, 255
    passenger names records (PNR) agreement
        between EU and United States
        on 284–5
    strike, right to 252
charters of rights *see* bills of rights
Chilcot Review 24, 31–4
children, execution of 410–12, 413, 415–22
China 214
citation of foreign law *see* foreign law,
    citation of
citizens, rights of 2
civil and political rights
    Australian parliamentarians, rights
        protection and 334, 343
    citizen, rights of 2
    economic and social rights 2
    European Convention on Human
        Rights 2, 485–6
    global South 349, 352–3
    ideological scepticism 2
    International Covenant on Civil and
        Political Rights 418, 425
    labour rights in Europe,
        constitutionalization of 245
civil disobedience 149–50, 152, 169, 182
civil law systems
    constitutional courts 369–70
    constitutional review 365–70, 377–88
    constitutionalization 368
    EU law 365–6
    European Arrest Warrant 279
civil rights in Northern Ireland 178–80
civil servants, vetting
    Campaign for the Limitation of Secret Police
        Powers 140–2
    Communists 128–43, 145–7
    constitutionalism 128–43, 145–7
    Fascists 137, 138, 139–40
    Gouzenko defection in Canada 128–9
    industrial workers, purging of 133–5
    national security 128–43, 145–7
    negative vetting 128–38, 145
    positive vetting 138–43
    private firms, dismissal of employees
        of 134–5, 141–3
    purging procedure 129–43
    Radcliffe Report 142
    representation 131–3, 142

civil servants, vetting (*cont.*)
rule of law 128–43, 145–7
safeguards, proposals for 132–4, 141–2, 145–6
statistics 142–3, 146
Three Advisers, hearings before the 132–4, 142, 145–6
trade unions, reaction of 131–4, 141, 144, 146
United Kingdom 128–43, 145–7
United States 143–6
coalitions 302
coercive methods of control 177
Cold War 148–76, 351
collective action 235–8
collective bargaining
Australian party politics 314–15, 324
Charter of Fundamental Rights of the EU 252
labour rights in Europe, constitutionalization of 244–6, 249, 251–60
collective good 388–9
collusion 202–3
Colombia, land rights of U'wa indigenous people of 360–1
colonialism 4, 348, 350–2
Committee of 100 peace campaigners, civil liberties and 148–76
airfields, demonstrations at 153–68, 173–4
arrest 151–2, 157–61, 167, 169, 170, 173, 175
Attorney General 154–6, 158–9, 164–6
bans, restraints by use of 149–53, 169
Battle of Trafalgar Square 152–4
binding over orders 151–2
Brize Norton, demonstration at RAF 154
Cabinet consideration of Committee of 100 156–7
Chandler v DPP 149, 172–3, 175, 176
civil disobedience 149–50, 152, 169
Clark, George, imprisonment and release of 170–2
CND 149–50
Cold War 148–76
Committee of 100 149–61
Communist party, banning of 148–9
constitutionalism 148–9, 166, 175–6
criminal proceedings 151–2, 154–66, 170–3
Defence Minister, intervention by the 154–6
demonstrations 149–74
espionage 163–4, 175
evidence 148–9, 150–2, 155, 159–61, 163, 170–1, 175
exclusion of Communists from sensitive government positions 148–9
executive 149
freedom of assembly and association 150, 173–4

Greece, state visit by King or Queen of 169–70
House of Lords, appeals to 161–6
imprisonment and release 170–3
judiciary and executive 149
jury challenges 173
jury trials 160–1, 165, 172–3
Magna Carta 159
Marham, demonstration at RAF 167–8
national security 148–76
obstruction 167, 170–3
official secrets 156–67
Official Secrets Act 1911, prosecutions under 158–67
Parliament Square, demonstrations in 149–51
perjury by police 170
planting of evidence 170
police 149–53, 156–61, 167, 169–75
political trials 151–2
prejudicial to safety or interests of the state 160–1, 163–6
prosecutions 151–2, 154–66, 170–3
public nuisance, obstruction causing 170–3
RAF Brize Norton, demonstration at RAF 154
RAF Marham, demonstration at 167–8
RAF Ruislip, demonstration at RAF 154
RAF Wethersfield, demonstration at 153–8
Ruislip, demonstration at RAF 154
rule of law 175
search warrants 155
secret bunkers, revealing of location of 168
spies for peace 168
surveillance 148–9, 150–2, 159–60, 175
taxation for financing nuclear weapons, legality of 173–4
Trafalgar Square, demonstrations in 149–54, 169–74
United States, involvement of 156, 158
use of force by state 152–8, 175
Vassall spy inquiry 175
Wethersfield, demonstration at RAF 153–67, 174
committees *see also* Joint Committee on Human Rights
Anti-Terrorism, Crime and Security Act 2001 19–20
Australian parliamentarians, rights protection and 331, 337–9, 341, 344, 346
democratic charter of rights model 464–71
Finland 6–7, 380–3
House of Commons Home Affairs Committee 22, 25–6
House of Lords Select Committee on the Constitution, report of 22
Human Rights Act 1998 443, 445–6, 449, 450
New Zealand 63, 99–100, 106

pre-charge detention of terrorist
    suspects 25–6
Sweden, pre-legislative review in 7, 393–4,
    396–8, 404–5
United Kingdom 22, 62
common market 268
Communist party 127–49
    bans 148–9
    civil servants, vetting 128–43, 145–7
    Cold War 127, 146, 148–9
    Committee of 100 peace campaigners, civil
        liberties and 148–9
    constitutionalism 127, 146
    defection 139–40
    rule of law 127, 146
    vetting 128–43, 145–7
companies *see* **corporations**
compatibility *see also* **declarations of**
    incompatibility
    bills of rights 48–9, 50, 60, 61–2
    compatibility assessments 48–9, 50–2,
        58–63, 89–98
    judicial influence on legislation, extent
        of 48–9
    New Zealand 42, 47–9, 51–2, 59, 60–1, 63,
        89–98
    statements of compatibility 51, 59, 72,
        119–20, 343
    United Kingdom 48–9, 51, 58–9, 60, 62–3
compensation 202, 242 *see also* **damages**
competition
    EU law 231, 232, 233–4, 239–42
    fundamental right, as 239–42
    labelling 233
    liberalization 241
    public monopolies, legitimacy of 240–1
    public sector 239–40
    secondary legislation 241–2
    transnational corporations 241
    United Kingdom 231, 232, 233–4, 239–42
    WTO law 242
complexity of legislation 344–5
compliance, culture of 7–8
Compton Commission 183–5, 196–7
compulsory voting 326
confession evidence 195–6, 198–9
conscience votes 324–5, 340–1
constitutional courts 369–70, 376–9, 389–90
constitutional law/rights
    Denmark 213
    economic and social rights 207–28
    Finland 367
    freedom, security and justice, area of 270
    Norway 213
    Scotland, Human Rights Act 1998
        in 69–71, 75, 85
    Sweden 213
Constitutional Treaty of EU 366
constitutionalism
    armed forces list, removal from 136

Attorney General's list 144, 145
bills of rights 41–2, 127, 146–7
business rights as human rights 231, 243
Campaign for the Limitation of Secret Police
    Powers 140–2
Canadian Charter of Rights 127
checks and balances 146
civil servants, vetting 128–43, 145–7
    Campaign for the Limitation of Secret
        Police Powers 140–2
    Communists 128–43, 145–7
    Fascists 137, 138, 139–40
    Gouzenko defection in Canada 128–9
    industrial workers, purging of 133–5
    national security 128–43, 145–7
    negative vetting 128–38, 145
    positive vetting 138–43
    private firms, dismissal of employees
        of 134–5, 141–3
    purging procedure 129–43
    Radcliffe Report 142
    representation 131–3, 142
    safeguards, proposals for 132–4, 141–2,
        145–6
    statistics 142–3, 146
    Three Advisers, hearings before
        the 132–4, 142, 145–6
    trade unions, reaction of 131–4, 141, 146
    United States 143–6
Cold War 127–47
Committee of 100 peace campaigners, civil
    liberties and 148–9, 166, 175–6
Communists, vetting of 128–43, 145–7
constitutional review 369–70, 379
defection of Communist spies 139–40
definition of constitutionalism 127
definition of rule of law 127–8
dual process 246–50
due process 127, 144, 145–6
European Convention on Human
    Rights 127
executive 143–7
Fascists, vetting of 137, 138, 139–40, 143–4
Finland 370
France 369–70
Germany 379
global South 348, 352, 359, 364
Gouzenko defection in Canada 128–9
House Committee on Un-American Activities
    (HUAC) (Dies Committee) 143
industrial workers, purging of 133–4
interception of communications, executive
    power and 146
juridical form 41–2
labour rights in Europe,
    constitutionalization of 244–50, 266
legal or political global South 348, 352,
    359, 364
loyalty investigations 143–5
McCarthy period 128, 141, 143, 145–6

constitutionalism (*cont.*)
  membership of subversive organizations 144
  national security 127, 128–47
  natural rights 127–8
  negative vetting 128–38, 145, 146
  new constitutionalism 244–5, 369–70, 379
  official secrets 127, 129–43, 145–7
  politics 348, 352, 359, 364
  positive vetting 138–43
  private firms, dismissal of employees
    of 134–5, 141–3
  purging of the civil service 129–43, 145–7
  Radcliffe Report 142
  rule of law 127–47
  separation of powers 146
  Smith Act 143
  statutory interpretation 147
  structure of government 128
  trade unions 131–4, 141, 144, 146
  United Kingdom 127–47
  United States 127–8, 141–7
  vetting 128–43, 145, 146
constitutionalization
  business rights as human rights 232–3
  constitutional review 365–70, 373,
    377–8, 388
  Continental Europe legal systems 368
  Europeanization 365–70
  labour rights in Europe, of 244–67
  legal order 368–9
  neoliberalism 232
  new constitutionalism 369–70
  new constitutionalization 246–7
  over-constitutionalization 373, 377–8, 388
constitutions
  democratic charter of rights model 460
  Finland 370, 381–2, 384–5, 387, 388, 391
  Germany 387
  India 212
  South Africa 217–18
  Sweden 391
construction *see* statutory interpretation
contents of human rights 466
Continental Europe legal systems *see* civil law
  systems
control orders
  Belmarsh case 46
  closed material 37–8
  Chilcot Review 34
  Counter-Terrorism Act 2008 23, 30, 34–9
  curfews, length of 35
  declarations of incompatibility 36
  fair hearing, right to a 36–7
  Human Rights Act 1998 35–6
  information, disclosure of 38
  intercept evidence, scrutiny of 34
  internment 204
  Joint Committee on Human Rights 23, 30,
    34–9
  liberty and security, right to 35, 204
  national security 23, 30, 34–9
  non-derogating control orders 20, 35
  Northern Ireland 204
  Prevention of Terrorism Act 2005 20
  reasons 37
  reform 23, 30, 34–9
  special advocates, role of 36–8, 204
  standard of proof 37
  witnesses, ability to call 37–8
corporations
  business rights as human rights 229, 234–9,
    242–3
  free movement 234–9
  property as a fundamental right 242
  transnational corporations 341
Cory Commission 203
Council of Europe 8
counterhegemonic human rights 359–64
Counter-Terrorism Act 2008 (United
  Kingdom)
  28-day limit for detention, extension
    of 21–2, 23–4
  42-day limit for detention, extension of 21,
    23–4
  bail 24
  charging, threshold test for 23–4, 30–1
  Chilcot Review 24, 31
  control orders 23, 30, 34–9
  House of Commons Home Affairs
    Committee, report of 22
  House of Lords Select Committee on the
    Constitution, report of 22
  inquests without juries 23
  intercept evidence in criminal trials, use
    of 23–4, 28–33
  Joint Committee on Human Rights, reports
    of 18–39
  national security, parliamentary scrutiny
    and 18–20
  parliamentary scrutiny 18–19, 21–39
  post-charge questioning 23, 30–1
  pre-charge detention of terrorist
    suspects 21–2, 23–8, 30
  safeguards 30–1
  scrutiny 18–20
  special advocates, role of 36–7
  Terrorism Act 2006 21
crime *see also* police; terrorism
  bugging of suspects' homes 405–6
  Committee of 100 peace campaigners,
    civil liberties and 151–2, 154–66,
    170–3
  death penalty 410–12, 413, 415–23
  delay 73, 86
  executive 74
  extradition 277–8, 279, 281, 423
  freedom, security and justice, area
    of 269–82, 285–8, 291–2
  intercept evidence, scrutiny of 23–4,
    28–33

Northern Ireland, removal of distinction
between criminal and political
behaviour in 194–5
organized crime 284
passenger names records (PNR) agreement
between EU and United States on 284
proscribed organizations 177
Scotland, Human Rights Act 1998 in 73–5,
83–4, 86
statute of limitations, abolition of 403–4
Sweden, pre-legislative review in 403–4
cruel or unusual treatment 410–13, 415–20
culture
global South 350, 354–5, 357, 360–1
identity 360
judges 306
multiculturalism 355, 360
political nature 360–1
relativism 350, 354–5, 357
curfews 35, 180
Customs Information Service (CIS) 270
Czechoslovakia 369

damages 76–7, 197, 198 *see also* compensation
data collection 270–2, 274, 282–5
data protection 282–5
databases 271–2
deadly force, use of 177, 187–93, 200–4
death penalty 410–12, 413, 415–23
death row phenomenon 423
debates on legislation 339
declarations of incompatibility *see also*
declarations of incompatibility in
United Kingdom
Australia 87
democratic charter of rights model 460
freedom of expression 435
New Zealand Bill of Rights 87–8,
103–4, 107
declarations of incompatibility in United
Kingdom 87, 416, 432–40
abolition, proposal for 430, 434–8
amendment of legislation 434–8
bills of rights 46
control orders 36
democratic charter of rights model 463
dialogue 436
economic and social rights 209
effect 434–5
effective remedy, right to an 437, 476–7
European Court of Human Rights 436–7,
477–8
High Court of Parliament, proposal for
references to 449
Joint Committee on Human Rights 437,
439, 466
judiciary, power of 116–19
parliamentary sovereignty 116–19, 435–6,
476–7, 483
reading down 110, 120

repeal of HRA, effect of 483
statutory interpretation 118–19, 432–3, 442
Defence of the Realm Acts 16–17
definition of human rights 229, 456
delay 73, 86
democracy
charter of rights model 458–71
constitutional review 371–3, 375–6, 383,
387–8
deliberative democracy 374
democratic deficit 269–70, 329–30
foreign law, citation of 412–15, 417, 422, 426
freedom, security and justice, area
of 269–70, 291
Human Rights Act 1998 428, 440, 447
judicial appointments 123, 124–5
lawmaking 272–6
legitimacy 123, 124–5
social democracy 309–11
Sweden, pre-legislative review in 402–3, 407
democratic charter of rights model 458–71
Canadian Charter of Rights and Freedoms,
notwithstanding clause in 463–4
committees 464–71
constitutions 460
criteria for inclusion 471
declarations of incompatibility 460, 463
identification of sources of human
rights 461
international relations 470–1
Joint Committee on Human Rights 464–70
judicial review 460–4
juridification of human rights 458
legal positivism 458–9, 461–2
life, right to 462–3
moral rights 461–2
parliamentary review 458–71
political approaches to human
rights 460–1, 471
separation of powers 460
values 461–4
Westminster-style democracies 458
demonstrations
airfields, at 153–68, 173–4
Bloody Sunday 187–8
Committee of 100 peace campaigners, civil
liberties and 149–74
detention by police 205
internment 187
Northern Ireland and terrorism 179, 187–8
Parliament Square, demonstrations in 149–51
police 149–57, 205
prosecutions 151–2, 154–66, 170–3
Trafalgar Square, demonstrations
in 149–54, 169–74
Denmark 213
deportation 13
detention without trial *see* pre-charge
detention of terrorist suspects in
United Kingdom

developed countries of the North, power
     of 3–4
developing countries *see* global South
development movements 362
devolution 66–86, 481–4
dialogue
     Canadian Charter of Rights 432–3
     declarations of incompatibility 436
     global South 354, 355, 357
     Human Rights Act 1998 430, 432–4, 436–8
     institutions 87–107
     judicial review 4, 5
     New Zealand Bill of Rights 5, 87–107
     Scotland 5
dignity 290, 354
Diplock Commission 182, 193–5, 196–7
Diplock courts 194–6, 198–200
direct effect
     constitutional review 370, 386–7
     EU law 370
     freedom, security and justice, area of 287,
          288–9
     horizontal direct effect 235–6, 256, 368,
          384–6, 388–91
     indirect effect 387
     labour rights in Europe,
          constitutionalization of 256–7
     trade unions 256
     vertical effect 379
Directorates-General 282
discipline in political parties 320–5, 340–1
discrimination *see* inequalities and
          discrimination
DNA database increase in use of 1
documents, access to public 7, 393, 394–5,
          402, 406–7
double criminality principle 277–8, 280
double jeopardy (ne bis in idem) 279
drugs, campaign for anti-retroviral 362
due process 127, 144, 145–6, 286

EC law *see* Charter of Fundamental Rights of
     the EU; EU law
economic and social rights
     Australian parliamentarians, rights
          protection and 334, 343
     bills and charters of rights 8
     Brazil 213–14
     business interests 215
     Canadian Charter of Rights and
          Freedoms 209, 211–13, 221
     China 214
     civil and political rights 2
     comparative rights 211–23
     competing rights and long-term
          sustainability 217
     constitutional protection 207–28
     Denmark 213
     distribution and redistribution 215–16, 221

     economics 208
     education 226–7
     enforcement 223–5
     EU law 250–1, 253
     European Social Charter 2
     global South 349, 352
     globalization 3
     health care 211–12
     housing, right to adequate 214
     Human Development Index (HDI) 222–3
     Human Rights Act 1998 209
     Hungary 225
     ideological scepticism 2–3
     India 212, 214
     inequalities 216, 219–22, 225–8
     institutional conditions 210–11
     Israel 221, 226–8
     judges
          activism 209, 225
          appointments 224
          political pressure 224
          public opinion 223–5
          strategic behaviour 223–8
     judicial review 208–10, 213, 224–5
     labour rights in Europe,
          constitutionalization of 245, 250–1,
          253
     left-oriented countries 214–15
     long-term sustainability 217
     negative freedoms 216
     neo-corporatism 215
     neoliberalism 227
     New Zealand Bill of Rights 221
     Nordic countries 213–15
     Norway 213
     parliamentary sovereignty 209
     politics 208–9, 224–5
     post-communist bloc countries 214
     precedent 223
     prison, privatization of 227–8
     public opinion 223–5
     public policy 208, 209, 211–12, 217, 223
     realpolitik 208, 211, 225
     resources of governments 217
     social welfare provision 3
     South Africa 3, 217–18, 220–1
     Spain 214
     strategic judicial behaviour 223–8
     strong form of judicial review 209–10
     subsistence rights 210–12, 226
     Sweden 213
     trade unions 215
     transformative potential of rights 216
     United States 210–11, 214
     weak form of judicial review 209–10
     weak rights 217
     welfare benefits 212–14
     welfare state 214–16
     Westminster style systems 209

education 226–7
effective remedy, right to an 284, 437, 476–7
elections
   Australian party politics 325–6
   candidate selection 303–4
   compulsory voting 325
   disenfranchisement 307–8
   first past the post systems 303
   franchise 326
   institutions 303, 306–8
   proportional representation 303, 326
electronic participation, public participation
   by 6
emancipatory politics 348, 353, 354, 356
emergencies
   Anti-Terrorism, Crime and Security Act
    2001 19, 21
   emergency powers regulations 16–17
   freedom, security and justice, area of 272,
    291–2
   internment 16–17
   national security, parliamentary scrutiny
    and 16–17, 19
   New Zealand Bill of Rights 107
   pre-charge detention of terrorist
    suspects 14, 26
   Prevention of Terrorism Act 2005 21
   scrutiny 16–17, 19
   Second World War 16–17
employment *see* employment, right to;
   International Labour Organization
   (ILO); labour rights in Europe,
   constitutionalization of
employment, right to 353
encouragement of terrorism 21
enforcement
   business rights as human
    rights 230, 233
   economic and social rights 223–5
   EU law 230, 233
   European Convention on Human
    Rights 230, 264
   labour rights in Europe,
    constitutionalization of 264
   WTO law 230
Enlightenment 454–5
entrenchment
   Australia 327–8, 343
   bills of rights 109, 343
   EU law 234
   free movement 236
   free trade 3
   Human Rights Act 1998 109
   minorities 327–8
   South Africa 220–1
enumerated rights 7
environmental movements 360–1
equality *see* inequalities and discrimination
espionage

Committee of 100 peace campaigners, civil
   liberties and 163–4, 175
   defection 139–40
   Official Secrets Act 1911 163–4
   spies for peace 168
   Vassall spy inquiry 175
establishment, freedom of 235–6, 241,
   254, 259
EU law *see also* **Charter of Fundamental Rights
   of the EU; European Court of Justice**
   accountability 275
   Advocates-General of European Court of
    Justice 449
   Amsterdam Treaty 269, 291
   Anglo-American law 365–6
   arrest 3
   availability principle 275
   biometrics 271–2
   blacklists, legality of terrorist 285–8, 289
   breach of EU law, legislation in 233–4
   business rights as human rights 3, 230–42
   Charter of Fundamental Rights of the
    EU 268–9, 276, 366
   civil law systems 365–6
   collective action 253–60, 263–5
   common law 365–6
   common market 268
   competition 231, 232, 233–4, 239–42
   constitutional review 365–8, 370, 383
   Constitutional Treaty 366
   criminal justice 269–82, 285–8, 291–2
   Customs Information System 270
   data collection 270–2, 274, 282–5
   democracy 269–70, 291
   democratic deficit 269–70
   dignity, right to 290
   direct effect 287, 288–9, 370
   Directorates-General 282
   double movement 250–3
   economic and social rights 250–1, 253
   emergency, times of 272, 291–2
   enforcement 230, 233
   entrenchment 234
   Eurojust Information System 270
   European Arrest Warrant 3
   European Convention on Human
    Rights 293, 263–4
   European Evidence Warrant 282
   European Parliament, increased
    role of 276, 292
   European Social Charter 2, 246, 255
   Europol Information System 270
   free movement 230, 233–41, 254, 259,
    289–90
   free trade 230–2, 234
   freedom of establishment 254, 259
   freedom of services 254, 259
   freedom, security and justice, area of 3,
    269–93

EU law *see also* **Charter of Fundamental Rights of the EU; European Court of Justice** *(cont.)*
  freezing of assets 285, 288
  fundamental rights 234–45, 268–9
  G6 274–5
  general principles of law 268, 276, 366
  Hague Programme 272, 282
  harmonization 250–1
  Human Rights Act 1998 233
  ideological scepticism 3
  immigration 289
  industrial action 253–60, 290
  information
    availability principle 275
    collection of 270–2, 274, 282–5
  intelligence gathering by national
    agencies 270–1
  international law, compliance with 287–9
  judicial activism 3
  judicial review 3, 276–7, 285, 288–90, 292
  justice, concept of 292
  labour rights in Europe,
    constitutionalization of 250–60,
    263–6
  Laval case 254–7, 259–60, 292
  lawmaking, undemocratic 272–6
  legal certainty 273–4
  legislature, independence of courts from
    the 367
  liberty and security, right to 287
  Lisbon Treaty 251, 267, 272–3, 276, 292
  Maastricht Treaty 241, 268, 276, 288–9
  market liberalism 234
  nationalization 230–1
  neoliberalism 3
  passenger names records (PNR) agreement
    with United States 282–5, 289
  passports, biometric information in 271
  police and judicial cooperation in
    criminal matters (Third Pillar) 272–6,
    288–9, 291
  Posted Workers Directive 256–7
  pre-charge detention of terrorist
    suspects 293
  preliminary references 234, 370
  proportionality 256–8, 265, 290
  Prüm, Treaty of 274
  public authorities, individuals and 270
  repatriation of AFSJ 291–3
  rule of law 273, 275, 286, 291–3
  Schengen area 274
  Schengen Information System 270–1
  Schmidberger case 289–90
  security 269, 271–2, 292–3
  Security Council (UN) resolutions,
    compliance with 285–7
  sensitive personal information, misuse
    of 271–2

  September 11, 2001 terrorist attacks on the
    United States 272
  Services Directive 253
  Single European Act 251
  state of exception as the norm 272–3
  supremacy of EU law 233–4, 268–9, 286–9,
    366–8, 370
  surveillance 271–2
  terrorism
    blacklists, legality of terrorist 285–8
    broad definition 269
    data collection 270
    legislation 272–3, 291–2
    Schengen Information System 270–1
  torture, evidence obtained by 293
  trade unions 253–60, 263–7
  transparency 273–4
  travaux préparatoires 366–7
  treaties 229, 250–2, 255–6
  United Kingdom 230–42
  United States 271, 282–5
  Viking case 254–6, 258–60, 292
Eurojust Information System 270
Europe *see* **EU law; European Convention
  on Human Rights; individual
  countries; labour rights in Europe,
  constitutionalization of**
European Arrest Warrant (EAW) 3, 269,
  277–82
  Advocaten voor de Wereld case 278–80, 289
  challenges 277–9
  Charter of Fundamental Rights of the EU 278
  civil law systems 279
  common law systems 279
  discrimination 280–1
  double criminality principle 277–8, 280
  double jeopardy *(ne bis in idem)* 279
  European Convention on Human
    Rights 281–2
  extradition 277–8, 279, 281
  Hague Programme 282
  harmonization 279
  holocaust denial 280–1
  implementation 277
  legal certainty 280–1
  legality, principle of 277, 280
  minimum standards 281–2
  mutual trust, lack of 277, 279–81
  preliminary references 278–9
  proportionality 280
  racism or xenophobia 280–1
European Convention on Human Rights
  see also **European Court of Human
  Rights**
  Anti-Terrorism, Crime and Security Act
    2001 20
  business rights as human rights 230, 242
  civil and political rights 2, 485–6
  Cold War 127

common law, development of 482–3
compensation 242
constitutional review 365–6, 367, 370, 379, 388, 390–1
constitutionalism 127
corporate property as fundamental right 242
derogations 13–14, 20
enforcement 230
European Arrest Warrant 281–2
Finland 367, 370, 388
freedom, security and justice, area of 293
Human Rights Act 1998 66, 72, 83–4, 438–9, 443–4, 447, 452
incorporation 379, 482–3
Joint Committee on Human Rights 467–9
judicial interpretation 230
legislature, independence of courts from 367
liberty and security, right to 388
limitation clause 390–1
margin of appreciation 383
national security, parliamentary scrutiny and 20
Northern Ireland 481
peaceful enjoyment of possessions 242
policy 390
precedent 367
pre-charge detention of terrorist suspects 13–14, 121–2, 195, 293
private and family life, right to respect for 390–1
rule of law 127
Scotland, Human Rights Act 1998 in 66, 72, 83–4
scrutiny 20
September 11, 2001 terrorist attacks on the United States 20
Sweden, pre-legislative review in 404–5
United Kingdom 47, 51, 58, 66, 72, 83–4, 438–9, 443–4, 447, 452
European Court of Human Rights
appeals 47
collective rights 260–5
constitutional review 367–8, 383
declarations of incompatibility 436–7, 477–8
discrimination on grounds of trade union membership 262
enforcement 264
freedom of assembly 264–5
freedom of association 245–6, 250, 260–2, 264–5
Gibraltar, shooting of terrorists in 479
Human Rights Act 1998 436–7, 440–2, 477–81
interim measures 480
International Labour Organization 263
jurisprudence, obligation to respect 51, 58

labour rights in Europe, constitutionalization of 245–6, 260–7
interpretation 264
trade unions 260–5
European Court of Justice 268–93
Advocates-General of European Court of Justice 449
constitutional review 365–6, 370, 383
free movement 236–7
labour rights in Europe, constitutionalization of 252–60, 263–6
passenger names records (PNR) agreement between EU and United States on 282–5
preliminary rulings 234, 278–9, 370
terrorists, legality of blacklists of 286–7
European Evidence Warrant 282
European Parliament, increased role of 276, 292
European Social Charter 2, 246, 255
Europol Information System 270
evidence
Bloody Sunday 188–93
Chilcot Review 24
Committee of 100 peace campaigners 148–52, 155, 159–61, 163, 170–1, 175
confessions 195–6, 198–9
inquests 202–3
intercept evidence in criminal trials, use of 23–4, 28–34
lethal force, use of 204
Northern Ireland and terrorism 188–96, 198–200, 202–6
planting of evidence 170
police perjury 170
special advocates, ability to call witnesses of 37–8
torture 195–6, 204–5, 293
exceptionalism 146
executive
Australian parliamentarians, rights protection and 330–1, 341–2
bills of rights 42, 43–8
chief executives 301, 305
coalitions 302
Cold War 132–7
Committee of 100 peace campaigners, civil liberties and 149
constitutionalism 132–7
criminal trials 74
dominance 341–2
Human Rights Act 1998 74
institutions 297, 300–2, 305
Joint Committee on Human Rights 465
judicial review 4
judiciary
appointments 123–4

executive (*cont.*)
   Committee of 100 peace
     campaigners 149
   legislature
     dependence on the 301
     parliamentary systems 300–2
   New Zealand Bill of Rights 88–9, 92–3,
     97–8, 106–7
   non-compliance costs of 42, 43–8
   political parties, control by different 301
   political philosophies of human rights 457
   rule of law 132–7
   Scotland, Human Rights Act 1998 in 74
   scrutiny 5–6
   terrorism 30
   United Kingdom 30, 74, 123–4, 149, 465
   United States 123–4, 132–7
exclusion 351
experts 338–9, 344–6, 393–4, 397–409
extradition 277–8, 279, 281, 423

factions 302, 305, 320, 325–8
fair hearing, right to a 14–15, 36–7, 73
Fascists, vetting 137, 138, 139–40, 143–4
fast track procedure 209, 442
financial restrictions proceedings 31–2
Finland
   basic rights 387
   Bill of Rights 370, 384
   Canadian Charter of Rights and Freedoms,
     notwithstanding clause in 380–1
   collective good 388–9
   Constitution 370, 381–2, 384–5, 387,
     388, 391
   constitutional law 367
   Constitutional Law Committee of
     Parliament 6–7, 380–3
   constitutional review 365, 366, 367, 370,
     377–85, 387–91
   European Convention on Human
     Rights 367, 370, 388
   ex post judicial review 7, 370, 381–3, 391
   external constitutional review 6–7
   horizontal effect 388–9
   judicial activism/restraint 383, 391
   judicial review 6–7, 365, 366, 367, 370,
     377–85, 387–91
   life, personal liberty, integrity and security,
     right to 388–9
   new constitutionalism 370
   parliament, prominence of 379–80
   politics, juridification of 382
   precedent 367, 379–80
   pre-legislative review 6–7, 377–85
   principle orientation 368
   privatization 384–5
   rule orientation 368
   security 388
   statutes of exception 380–1

strong judicial review 381
supremacy of EU law 366
travaux préparatoires 379–80, 382–4
weak judicial review 381
first past the post systems 303
foreign law, citation of *see also* foreign law in
    United States, citation of
   bills of rights, savings clauses in 425
   Commonwealth 411–12
   consistency 423–7
   democracy 417, 422, 426
   fairness 423–4
   harmonization 8
   integrity 423–4
   International Covenant on Civil and
     Political Rights 425
   judicial review 8, 410–27
   natural law 423
   New Zealand Bill of Rights 411–12, 416–17
   precedent 8–9, 425–6
   savings clauses 425
   South Africa 413, 421
   standards, common set of 423
   universality of human rights 423
foreign law in United States, citation of 8,
    410–27
   Bill of Rights, interpretation of 418–19
   cruel or inhuman treatment 410–12, 413,
     415–20
   death penalty 410–12, 413, 415–23
   death row phenomenon 423
   democracy 412–15
   English Bill of Rights 1689 418
   extradition 423
   judicial activism 412–13
   judicial review 412–15, 419, 426
   minors, execution of 410–12, 413, 415–22
   precedent 418–19
   reasons for citing foreign law 420–6
   Roper v Simmons 410–12, 414–15, 419–22
   sources of law 418–19
   strong judicial review 412–20
   Supreme Court 410–13
franchise 326
France 369–70, 387, 392, 399
'Free Derry' 179, 182
free movement
   business rights as human rights 230, 233,
     234–9, 241
   Cassis de Dijon 234–5
   collective action 235–8
   entrenchment 236
   establishment, freedom of 235–6, 241, 254,
     259
   EU law 230, 233, 234–9, 254, 259, 341
   freedom, security and justice, area
     of 289–90
   goods 234–5, 289–90
   horizontal direct effect 235–6

industrial action 235–8
interpretation by European Court of
   Justice 236–7
labelling 233
labour rights in Europe,
   constitutionalization of 245–6, 250,
   252, 250, 254, 262–5, 282
proportionality 235, 237
services 235–6, 241, 289–90, 254, 259
trade unions, industrial action and 235–8
WTO law 238–9, 242
free trade 2–3, 230–2, 234, 242–3
freedom of assembly and association 150,
   173–4, 245–6, 250, 260–5
freedom of expression 308, 435, 439
freedom, security and justice, area of *see* **area of
   freedom, security and justice (AFSJ)**
freezing of assets 285, 288
fundamental rights *see also* **Charter of
   Fundamental Rights of the EU**
business rights as human rights 234–42
competition 239–42
corporate free movement 234–9
EU law 234, 268–9
labour rights in Europe,
   constitutionalization of 244–5

G6 274–5
Gardiner Report 198–9
general principles of law 268, 276, 366, 385–8
Geneva Conventions 186
Germany
Basic Law 378
basic rights norms as general legal
   principles 378–9, 385–9
collective action and individual rights,
   balancing 389–90
Constitution 387
constitutional complaints 377
Constitutional Court 377–9, 389–90
constitutional review 369, 373, 377–9, 382,
   384–91
ex ante control 377–8
Finland 377–8
horizontal effect 384–5
judicial activism/restraint 384
judicial supremacy 379, 382
kompetenz-kompetenz 378
legitimacy 378
new constitutionalism 379
over-constitutionalization 373, 377–8, 388
preliminary rulings 377–8
proportionality 378–9
separation of powers 378
gerrymandering 178–9
Gibraltar, shooting in 201, 479
global South 347–64
absolute versus relative values 355–6
activism, institutionalisation of 358

advocacy networks 362
below, globalization from 349, 359
Brazil, land reform in 362
civil and political rights 349, 352–3
Cold War 351
colonialism 348, 350–2
constitutionalism, legal or political 348,
   352, 359, 364
counterhegemonic human rights 359–64
culture
   identity 360
   multiculturalism 355, 360
   political nature 360–1
   relativism 350, 354–5, 357
development movements 362
dialogue 354, 355, 357
dignity 354
drugs, campaign for anti-retroviral 362
economic and social rights 349, 352
emancipatory politics 348, 353, 354, 356
employment, right to 353
environmental movements 360–1
equality 255
exclusion 351
globalization 349, 359, 360–1
governance 352
health movements 362
hegemony 360, 363
Hindu perspective on human rights 354
identity politics 360
India, Working Women's Forum in 362–3
indigenous movements 360–1
institutions 356–9, 363–4
Islamic perspective on human rights 354
knowledge of human rights 354–8,
   360, 364
lifestyles 360
lowest common denominator 355
minority rights 361–2
misogynist movements 361–2
multiculturalism 355, 360
neoliberalism 350, 360–1
oppression 361–2, 363
politics
   constitutionalism 348, 352, 359, 364
   culture 360–1
   emancipatory politics 348, 353, 354, 356
   engagement 363–4
   progressive politics 348, 351, 355,
      356, 362
   reactionary politics 355, 361–2
   transformation 362–3
poverty 355–6
progressive politics 348, 351, 355, 356, 362
reactionary politics 355, 361–2
regressive movements 361–2
resistance 352
resources 360
scarcity 352

global South (*cont.*)
  self-determination 351–2
  social movements 359–64
  social transformations 351, 362
  South Africa, campaign for drugs
    anti-retroviral in 362
  strategies 360
  subaltern law 363–4
  suffering, alleviation of human 356–7, 361
  universal rights 348–55
  U'wa indigenous people of Colombia, land
    rights of 360–1
  values 360
  war on terror 355
  West 349–56, 359, 361, 362–3
  women's rights 361–2
  World Social Forum 359, 361, 362
  xenophobic movements 361–2
globalization
  below, globalization from 3–4,
    349, 359
  colonialism, human rights as justification
    for 4
  constitutional review 369
  economic and social rights 3
  global South 349, 359, 360–1
  ideological scepticism 3–4
  labour rights in Europe,
    constitutionalization of 246–7
  non-governmental organisations 3–4
  social movements 3–4
  third wave of legal globalization 369
  umbrella groupings 3–4
  World Social Forum 3
Good Friday Agreement 79, 481
goods, free movement of 234–5
Gouzenko defection 128–9
governance 317, 318, 352
government *see* executive

Hague Programme 272, 282
health care 211–12
health movements 362
hegemony 359–64
Henry VIII clauses 344, 345
High Court of Parliament, proposal for
  references to UK 8, 449
Hindu perspective on human rights 354
holocaust denial 280–1
horizontal direct effect 235–6, 368, 384–6,
  388–91
House Committee on Un-American Activities
  (HUAC) (Dies Committee) 143
House of Commons Home Affairs
  Committee, report of 22
House of Lords Select Committee on the
  Constitution, report of 22
housing, right to adequate 214
Human Development Index (HDI) 222–3

Human Rights Act 1998 (United
  Kingdom) 428–52, 472–86 *see also*
    declarations of incompatibility in
    United Kingdom
  Advocates-General of European Court of
    Justice 449
  amendment of HRA 8
  amendment of legislation 434–8, 442
  appeals, Supreme Court and 71–2
  Bill of Rights and Responsibilities Green
    Paper 460–70, 475
  bills of rights 46–7, 50–2, 67–72, 79–84,
    109–16, 126, 460–70, 475
  Brandeis briefs 444
  British question 481–4
  business rights as human rights 229–30,
    233–4
  Calman Commission 69–71, 75, 85
  Canadian Charter of Rights,
    notwithstanding clauses in 432–3, 436
  Canadian federalism 66
  civil and political rights 485–6
  Coalition Government 67, 84–5, 433–4,
    474–5, 477, 479–80
  committees 443, 445–6, 449, 450
  common law 482–3
  Conservative Party 474–80
  constitutional issues 69–71, 80, 84–5
  Constitutional Reform Act 2006 71–2
  constitutionalized bills of rights 109–16
  control orders 35–6
  Council of Europe, relations with 8
  criminal trials 73–5, 83–4, 86
  culture of compliance 438, 439, 441
  delay 73, 86
  democracy 428, 440, 447
  detention without trial of terrorist
    suspects 121–2
  devolution 66–86, 481–4
  dialogue 430, 432–4, 436–8
  economic and social rights 209
  effective remedy, right to an 437, 476–7
  entrenchment 109
  EU law 233
  European Convention on Human
    Rights 438–9, 443–4, 447, 452, 481–6
  European Court of Human Rights 436–7,
    440–2, 477–81
  European question 476–80
  European Union, relations with 8
  executive 74
  fair hearing, right to a 73
  fast track procedure 209, 442
  freedom of expression 435, 439
  Gibraltar, shooting in 479
  Health and Social Care Bill 77–8
  High Court of Parliament, proposal for
    references to 8, 445–52
  Hunting Act 2004, Parliament Acts and 484

inhuman or degrading treatment 417–18
instability of weak bills 46–7, 50–2
interim measures 480
Joint Committee on Human Rights 69,
    79–81, 430, 437, 438–41, 443–4,
    447–8, 465, 472
judicial appointments 124–5
judicial review 5, 85, 118, 126, 442,
    453–4, 483
judicial supremacy 230, 233, 429
judicialization 233
judiciary, power of 108–20, 429–52
Labour Party 67–9, 433–4, 473, 475–6,
    480, 486
legitimacy 67–8
living document or living tree
    metaphor 113–16
majoritarianism 126
media 473–4, 479
minority rights 446
national security 478
Northern Ireland
    devolution 481
    European Convention on Human Rights,
        incorporation of 481
    Good Friday Agreement 481
    terrorism 177–8, 202, 481
originalism 114
Parliament Acts 484
Parliament and courts, relationship
    between 429–52
parliamentary committees 443, 445–6,
    449, 450
parliamentary resolution of individual
    disputes 445–52
parliamentary sovereignty 69, 84, 109–10,
    115–19, 430–2, 445, 473
political advertising, ban on 439
political correctness 474
political parties 8
politics, judicialization of 442
precedent 445, 449–50
private and family life, right to respect
    for 474
Private Bill procedure 450
Privy Council 71, 73–5
public authorities 77, 442–3, 481
public interest 478
purposive approach 113–14
quasi-legislative power of judges 432
reading down 108–16, 430–4, 442
reform proposals 8, 84–5, 428, 442–52,
    474–86
repeal, proposals for 8, 428, 474–86
reserved matters 72
rule of law 112–13, 431, 434
Scotland 5, 66–86
Scottish Commission for Human Rights 81
scrutiny 443

segregation of prisoners 76
separation of powers 449–51
Sewel motion 72, 78
slopping out cases, damages in 76–7
social policy 80–1
statements of incompatibility 119–20
statutory interpretation 8, 76, 108–19,
    122–3, 209, 229–30, 431–4, 442
strong form or entrenched bills of
    rights 109–10, 113–14, 126
Supreme Court 71–2, 86, 449, 450
terrorism 177–8, 202
weak form of judicial review 209
weak or statutory form of bill of rights,
    as 46–7, 50–2, 109–10, 113–20, 126
Wednesbury unreasonableness 483
West Lothian Question 70
Hungary 225, 376
hunger strikes 194–5
Hunting Act 2004, Parliament Acts and 484

identification of rights 337–9, 345, 461
identity in public places, concealment of 404
identity politics 360
ideological scepticism 1, 2–4
    business rights 2–3
    citizen, rights of the 2
    civil and political rights 2
    developed countries of North,
        power of 3–4
    economic and social rights 2–3
    economic power 2
    European Union 3
    free trade 2–3
    globalization from below 3–4
    neoliberalism 3
    rights of man 2
    social welfare provision 3
immigration 289
India
    Constitution 212
    welfare benefits 214
    Working Women's Forum 362–3
indigenous movements 360–1
indirect effect 387
industrial action 235–8, 244, 249, 252–62,
    267, 290
inequalities and discrimination
    economic and social rights 216, 219–22,
        225–8
    European Arrest Warrant 280–1
    Gini coefficient 219–20
    global South 255
    holocaust denial 280–1
    Israel 226–8
    measuring inequality 219
    racial profiling 205
    racism or xenophobia 280–1
    South Africa 217–18, 220–2

inequalities and discrimination (*cont.*)
   Standardized World Income Inequality
      Database (SWIID) 219
   trade union membership 262
information
   Australian parliamentarians, rights
      protection and 332–3
   availability principle 275
   collection 270–2, 274, 282–5
   control orders 38
   Customs Information System 270
   data collection 270–2, 274, 282–5
   Eurojust 270
   freedom, security and justice, area of 270–2,
      274–5, 282–5
   intelligence gathering 270–1
   libraries 339
   Schengen Information System 270–1
   sensitive personal information, misuse
      of 271–2
informers 199–200
inhuman or degrading treatment 186, 195–9,
   206, 417–18
inquests
   collusion 202–3
   evidence 202–3
   Inquests Act 2005 203–4
   juries, without 23
   lethal force, use of 201–4
   Northern Ireland and terrorism 201–4
institutions *see also* political institutions of
      rights-protection
   alternative forms of protection 1–2
   bills of rights 5
   constitutional review 369, 376–8
   definition 4
   dialogue 87–107
   economic and social rights 210–11
   global South 356–9, 363–4
   judicial review 4–5
   legitimacy 4
   New Zealand 5, 87–107
   means of protection 4
   political control 4
   scepticism 1, 4–5
   Scotland, Human Rights Act 1998 in 5
   terrorism, UK legislation on 4–5
integrity 423–4
intelligence gathering 270–1
intercept evidence, parliamentary
      scrutiny and
   Chilcot Review 24, 31–4
   control orders 34
   criminal investigations 32, 34
   criminal trials 23–4, 28–33
   evidential standards 33–4
   financial restrictions proceedings 31–2
   Joint Committee on Human Rights 23–4,
      28–34
   national security 28–34

PII Plus 33–4
Privy Council, review by 31
Proscribed Organisation Appeal
   Commission 28
public inquiries 31–2
Public Interest Immunity 33–4
safeguards 31, 32–3
security and intelligence services 33
Serious Organised Crime Agency 32
special advocates 33
Special Immigration Appeals
   Commission 28
terrorism 23–4, 28–33
interception of communications *see* intercept
      evidence, parliamentary scrutiny and;
      surveillance
interest groups 304–5, 325
interim measures 480
International Covenant on Civil and Political
      Rights 418, 425
international economic law 231
International Labour Organization (ILO)
   conventions 245–6, 262–3, 265, 315
   European Court of Human Rights 263
   labour rights in Europe,
      constitutionalization of 245–6,
      262–3, 265
   Social Declaration 249
   standards 261–2
international law 231, 287–9
international relations 455–6, 470–1
internment
   Bloody Sunday 187
   control orders, replacement with 204
   damages 197, 198
   demonstrations, bans on 187
   Diplock Commission 182, 193–4
   emergency powers legislation 16–17
   judiciary, record of 197
   legal basis 194–5, 197
   national security, parliamentary scrutiny
      and 16–17
   Northern Ireland and terrorism 177, 178,
      180–7, 193–200, 204
   release without charge 196
   statistics 183
   supergrass system 199–200
   suspicion as legal basis 182, 194, 195, 197
   statutory basis 194–5
   terrorism 13, 16–17, 177, 178, 180–7,
      193–200, 204
   torture 183–7
   wartime, deportation and internment in 13
interpretation *see* statutory interpretation
interrogation of terrorist suspects in Northern
      Ireland
   access to legal advice 196
   arrest 195–6
   centres 195–6
   confessions 195–6, 198–9

damages for assault 198
inhuman or degrading treatment 195–6, 198
torture 177, 183–7, 195–6
investigative duty, right to life and 201–3, 205–6
IRA 179–82, 187–8
Iraq
  judicial review 15
  judiciary, record of the 178, 205
  military detention 15
  Mousa, Baha, inquiry into death of 186–7, 205
  war, enquiry into 15
Irish Republic Army (IRA) 179–82, 187–8
Islamic perspective on human rights 354
Israel
  Basic Law: Human Dignity and Liberty 226–8
  Basic Laws 221, 226–8
  economic and social rights 221, 226–8
  education 226–7
  inequalities 226–8
  judges 226–7
  neoliberalism 227
  prison, privatization of 227–8
  subsistence rights 226
Italy 377

JCHR *see* **Joint Committee on Human Rights (United Kingdom)**
Joint Committee on Human Rights (United Kingdom)
  Anti-Terrorism, Crime and Security Act 2001 19–20
  Belfast Agreement 79
  Bill of Rights and Responsibilities Green Paper 460–70
  bills of rights 62–3
  British values 469–70
  charging, threshold test for 31
  compliance, culture of 7–8
  constitutional review 379
  content of human rights 466
  control orders 23, 30, 34–9
  Counter Terrorism Act 2008 18–29
  declarations of incompatibility 437, 439, 466
  democratic charter of rights model 464–70
  enumerated rights 7
  Equality and Human Rights Commission 469
  European Convention on Human Rights 467–9
  executive 465
  High Court of Parliament, proposal for 8
  Human Rights Act 1998 69, 79–81, 430, 437–44, 447–8, 464–70, 472
  intercept evidence, scrutiny of 23–4, 28–34
  judicial review 465
  misuse of political power 464–5
  Northern Ireland 79

parliament 465–70
political approach to human rights 465–8
post-charge questioning 36–7
pre-charge detention of terrorist suspects 21–2
proportionality 467
reform 443–4
remedial orders 466
reports 18–19, 21–9
scope of human rights 466
scrutiny of legislation 443, 466–9
sifting procedure 441
statutory interpretation 8
terrorism 18–19, 21–9
judicial activism/restraint
  Canada 379
  constitutional review 374, 379, 383–4, 391
  Finland 383, 391
  foreign law, citation of 412–13
  Germany 384
  United States 383
judicial appointments in UK 122–5
  bicameralism 123
  bills of rights 123–4
  democratic legitimacy 123, 124–5
  executive 123–4
  Human Rights Act 1998 124–5
  Judicial Appointments Commission 124–5
  Lord Chancellor 124
  self-selection or memes 125
  United States Supreme Court 123–4
judicial constitutional review
  adjudication, politicization of 373, 375–7, 382
  Austria 369
  balancing rights 374–5
  basic rights norms as general legal principles 378–9, 385–91
  bills of rights 372
  Canada 379
  case against constitutional review 370–7
  Central and Eastern Europe 369, 376–7, 383
  Charter of Fundamental Rights of the EU 366
  collective good 388–9
  common law systems 365–6
  Commonwealth 379
  constitutional courts 369–70, 389–90
  Constitutional Treaty 366
  constitutionalization 365–70, 373, 377–8, 388
  Continental Europe legal systems 365–70, 377–88
  Czechoslovakia 369
  deliberative democracy 374
  democracy 371–3, 375–6, 383, 387–8
  direct effect 370, 386–7
  EU law 365–70, 383

judicial constitutional review (*cont.*)
   European Convention on Human
      Rights 365–6, 367, 370, 383,
      388, 390–1
   Europeanization 365–70
   ex ante judicial review 377
   ex post judicial review 369–70, 391
   Finland 6–7, 365, 366, 367, 370, 377–85,
      387–91
   foreign law, citation of 8, 410–27
   France 369–70, 386
   general principles of law 385–8
   Germany 369, 373, 377–8, 384–91
   globalization, third wave of legal 369
   horizontal effect 368, 384–6, 388–91
   Hungary 376
   indirect legal effect 387
   institutions 379, 376–8
   Italy 377
   judicial activism 379, 383
   judicial restraint 374, 383–4, 391
   judicial supremacy 371–2, 376–7, 382
   judicialization 366
   juridification of politics 373, 375–6, 382
   last resort, as a 365–91
   lawmaking, legal principles and 368
   legislature, independence of courts from
      the 366, 367
   liberty and security, right to 388
   liberty rights, extension of 384–5
   life, personal liberty, integrity and security,
      right to 388
   majoritarianism 373
   margin of appreciation 383
   negative legislator, courts as 369
   new constitutionalism 369–70, 379
   New Zealand Bill of Rights 379
   Nordic countries 366–8
   over-constitutionalization 373, 377–8, 388
   parliamentary supremacy 369–70, 376–7,
      379, 382–3
   policy 372, 390–1
   politics, juridification of 373, 375–7
   positive legislator, courts as 369
   precedent 367, 368
   preliminary rulings 370
   principles 368, 385–91
   private and family life, right to respect
      for 390–1
   privatization 384–5
   proportionality 373, 378–9, 390
   rule orientation 368
   security, right to 388–9
   separation of powers 372, 378, 387
   Spain 377, 386
   statutory interpretation 386
   strong and weak judicial review, borderline
      between 379
   Supreme Court 392
   supremacy of EU law 366–7, 370

   Sweden 383, 391
   travaux préparatoires 366–7
   United Kingdom 366, 377, 379, 382
   United States 4, 53–4, 369, 371, 375, 377,
      379, 383–4, 410–27
   vertical effect 368, 388–91
   weak judicial review 379
judicial influence on legislation
   bills of rights 43, 48–54, 64
   Canada 48
   judicial review 43, 48–52
   New Zealand 48–9, 51–2
   reporting on compatibility of
      legislation 48–9
   United Kingdom 48–9, 50–1, 54
judicial preview 392
judicial review *see also* **judicial constitutional
     review; Sweden, pre-legislative
     review in**
   accountability 4
   administrative action 442
   Australian parliamentarians, rights
      protection and 344–5
   bills of rights 5, 40–65
   Canada 40, 42, 45, 47–9, 56, 61–2, 209
   control orders 14
   cruel or inhuman treatment 420
   democratic charter of rights model 460–4
   Denmark 213
   deportation based on evidence obtained by
      torture 15
   dialogue model 4, 5
   economic and social rights 208–10, 213,
      224–5
   educating judiciaries 8–9
   EU law 3
   European systems 43–4
   executive 4, 42, 43–8
   foreign law, citation of 412–15, 419, 426
   freedom, security and justice, area of 276–7,
      285, 288–90, 292
   Human Rights Act 1998 5, 85, 453–4, 483
   hybrid model 453
   improvements 8–9
   infringements, prevention of 41
   institutional scepticism 4–5
   institutions 4–5, 300, 308, 310
   Iraq War, enquiry into 15
   judicial influence on legislation, extent
      of 43, 48–52
   labour rights in Europe,
      constitutionalization of 244
   legislation 40, 42–52
   legislatures 4, 13–18
   legitimacy 4
   limiting judicial review 8
   national security 13–18
   New Zealand 5, 40, 42, 47–52, 87–98, 420
   Norway 213
   precedents from foreign jurisdictions 8–9

Saudi Arabia, abandonment of Serious Fraud
    Office inquiry into arms deal with 15
Scotland, Human Rights Act 1998 in 5, 85
scrutiny 453
sources of law, extending range of 8–9
special advocates, use of 14–15
stop and search 14
strong forms of judicial review 52, 91,
    209–10
Sweden 213, 392–409
terrorism 13–18, 285
United Kingdom 13–18, 40, 42, 46–53,
    62–3
United States 53
weak judicial review 52–60, 91, 118, 126,
    209–10, 453
weak or statutory form of bills of rights 43,
    52–60
judicial supremacy
    business rights as human rights 230,
        233, 243
    constitutional review 371–2, 376–7, 382
    EU law 230, 233
    Germany 379, 382
    Human Rights Act 1998 230, 233, 429
    Supreme Court 429
    United States 371, 379
judicialization 233, 366, 442
judiciary *see also* **judicial constitutional
    review; judicial review; statutory
    interpretation**
    activism/restraint 374, 379, 383–4, 391,
        412–13
    appointments 122–5, 224
    bicameralism 123
    bills of rights 43, 48–54, 64, 116–20, 123–4
    Committee of 100 peace campaigners, civil
        liberties and 149
    confession evidence 198–9
    constitutionalized bills of rights 109–16
    culture 306
    declarations of incompatibility 116–20
    democratic legitimacy 123, 124–5
    detention of protestors by police 205
    economic and social rights 209, 223–8
    educating judiciaries 8–9
    enumerated rights 7
    executive 123–4, 149
    Human Rights Act 1998 108–20, 124–5,
        429–52
    institutions 297–9, 305–6, 310–11
    internment 197
    Iraq 178, 205
    Iraqi civilians by British troops, murder
        of 205
    Israel 226–7
    Judicial Appointments Commission 124–5
    judicial preview 392
    judicialization 233, 366, 442
    juridification of politics 373, 375–7, 382

legislation, influence on 43, 48–54, 64
legislature 87, 110–11
Lord Chancellor 124
New Zealand Bill of Rights 87
Northern Ireland and terrorism 178,
    196–200, 204–6
police and judicial cooperation in criminal
    matters (Third Pillar) 272–6, 284,
    288–9, 291
political pressure 224
public opinion 223–4
quasi-legislative power 432
racial profiling 205
self-selection or memes 125
statutory interpretation 108–9, 111–16
strategic behaviour 223–8
torture, evidence obtained by 204–5
United States 109, 123–5
statements of compatibility 119
statutory interpretation 118
supremacy 230, 233, 243, 371–2, 376–9,
    382, 429
weak or statutory form of bills of
    rights 116–20
juridification of politics 373, 375–7, 382
juries
    challenges 173
    Committee of 100 peace campaigners, civil
        liberties and 160–1, 165, 172–3
    inquests without juries 23
    Official Secrets Act 1911 160–1, 165
justice, concept of 292

knowledge of human rights 354–8,
    360, 364
kompetenz-kompetenz 378

**labour rights in Europe, constitutionalization
    of** 244–67
    Charter of Fundamental Rights of the
        EU 246, 249–52, 255
    civil and political rights 245
    collective bargaining 244–6, 249, 251–60
    collective rights 245–6, 252–65
    constitutionalism 266
    direct effect 256–7
    discrimination on grounds of trade union
        membership 262
    double movement 247–8, 250–3, 266
    dual process of constitutionalism 246–50
    economic rights 250–1, 253
    enforcement 264
    EU law 250–60, 263–6
    European Court of Human Rights 245–6,
        260–7
    European double movement 250–3
    European Social Charter 246, 255
    free movement 245–6, 250, 252, 250, 254,
        262–5, 282
    free trade 244

labour rights in Europe, constitutionalization of (*cont.*)
freedom of assembly 264–5
freedom of association 245–6, 250, 260–2, 264–5
freedom of establishment 254
freedom of services 254
fundamental rights 244–5
globalization 246–7
harmonization 250–1
human rights, labour rights as 248–50
industrial action 253–62, 267
International Labour Organization (ILO)
Conventions 245–6, 262–3, 265
European Court of Human Rights 263
Social Declaration 249
standards 261–2
interpretation 264
judicial review 244
Laval case 254–7, 259–60, 292
Lisbon Treaty 251, 267
Maastricht Treaty 241
neoliberalism 244–8, 266
new constitutionalism 244–5
new constitutionalization 246–7
Posted Works Directive 256–7
proportionality 256–8, 265
Services Directive 253
Single European Act 251
social rights 245, 253
strike, right to 244, 249, 252, 255, 267
trade unions 253–67
Viking case 254–6, 258–60, 292
land rights 360–1
legal advice, access to 196
legal certainty 273–4, 280–1, 399–400
legal positivism 458–9, 461–2
legality, principle of 102, 277, 280
legislation *see also* **bills of rights; compatibility; Counter-Terrorism Act 2008; legislatures; Sweden, pre-legislative review in; scrutiny of legislation; statutory interpretation**
Australian parliamentarians, rights protection and 332, 338–9, 341–2, 344–6
changes, insulation of legislation from 49–50
complexity and volume 344–5
confidentiality of bills 341
debates 339
enumerated rights 7
EU law, breach of 233–4
expertise, lack of 344–6
identification of human rights issues 338
institutions 304–5
judicial influence 43, 48–54, 64
judicial review 8, 344–5
non-compliance, costs to government of 42, 43–8

scrutiny 332, 342, 343, 344, 346
terrorism 4–5, 272–3, 291–2, 341–2, 345
time issues 344
legislatures *see also* **parliamentary sovereignty**
Australia
bicameralism 123
parliamentarians, rights protection and 329–46
party politics 320–1
scrutiny of legislation 5–6
backbenchers 302, 305–6
bicameralism 123
bills of rights 40, 42–64, 87–107
Canada 123
capacity to hold government accountable, increase in parliament's 43, 60–4
chief executives 301
conscience votes 324–5, 340–1
constitutional review 366, 367
debates on legislation 339
democratic charter of rights model 458–71
democratic deficit 329–30
elections 306
EU law 367
European Convention on Human Rights 367
executive 5–6, 300–1
Finland 379–80
Human Rights Act 1998 429–52
ideal legislature 329–30
independence of courts 366, 367
institutions 297–8, 300–2, 306–11
intercept evidence, scrutiny of 23–4, 28–34
Joint Committee on Human Rights 465–70
judicial review 4
judiciary 87, 110–11
legitimacy 45
minority groups 306–7
moral constraints 92
New Zealand Bill of Rights 87–107
political constraints 92
political parties
Australia 320–1
control by different parties 301
political philosophies of human rights 457
Scotland 80–2
scrutiny of legislation 5–6, 16–39
separation of powers 300–1
terrorism 6, 13–39
trustees or delegates, legislators as 320–1
United Kingdom 13–39, 110–11, 123
Westminster-type parliamentary systems 40, 42–60
legitimacy
bills of rights 45
democracy 123, 124–5
Germany 378
institutional scepticism 4
judicial appointments 123, 124–5
judicial review 4

public monopolies 240–1
Scotland, Human Rights Act 1998 in 67–8
lethal force, use of 177, 187–93, 200–4
liberalism 234, 309–11 *see also* neoliberalism
liberalization 241
liberty and security, right to
    constitutional review 388
    control orders 35, 204
    Finland 388–9
    freedom, security and justice, area of 287
    Iraq, military detention in 15
    judicial review 15, 388
    Northern Ireland and terrorism 186, 204
    pre-charge detention of terrorist
        suspects 13–14, 46
    terrorists
        blacklists, legality of 287
        Northern Ireland 186, 204
        pre-charge detention of terrorist
            suspects 13–14
    torture 186
liberty rights, extension of 384–5
libraries 339
life, right to 201–3, 205–6, 388–9, 462–3
Lisbon Treaty 251, 267, 272–3, 276, 292
living document or living tree
    metaphor 113–16
Lord Chancellor, judicial appointments
    and 124
lowest common denominator 344, 355

Maastricht Treaty 241, 268, 276, 288–9
Magilligan incident 187
Magna Carta 159
majoritarianism
    Australian party politics 326–8
    constitutional review 373
    Human Rights Act 1998 126
    institutions 297, 300–1
    living document or living tree
        metaphor 114–15
    minority rights 347
    weak or statutory form of bills of
        rights 120–1
margin of appreciation 383
Marham, demonstration at RAF 167–8
market liberalism 234
McCarthyism 128, 141, 143, 145–6
media
    Australia
        parliamentarians, rights protection
            and 337, 345
        political parties 317–18
    Human Rights Act 1998 473–4, 479
    intermediary, as 317–18
    political parties 317–18
    private and family life, right to respect
        for 474
    responsive function 318
    Sweden, pre-legislative review in 398, 405–7

membership of subversive organizations 144
minority rights
    Australian party politics 326–8
    entrenched minorities 327–8
    global South 361–2
    Human Rights Act 1998 446
    institutions 306–9
    legislatures 306–7
    majoritarianism 347
minors, execution of 410–12, 413, 415–22
misogynist movements 361–2
monopolies, legitimacy of public 240–1
moral rights 456–8, 461–2
Mousa, Baha, inquiry into death of 186–7,
    205
multiculturalism 355, 360

NAFTA 229, 232
National Conversation about Scotland 70–1
National Council for Civil Liberties
    (NCCL) 131–9, 143, 153, 173
national security *see also* official secrets
    access to public documents 406–7
    Anti-Terrorism, Crime and Security Act
        2001 19–21
    Australian parliamentarians, rights
        protection and 342
    Campaign for the Limitation of Secret Police
        Powers 140–2
    Chagos Islanders, right of abode of 16
    civil servants, vetting 128–43, 145–7
    Cold War 127, 128–47
    Committee of 100 peace campaigners, civil
        liberties and 148–76
    constitutionalism 127, 128–47
    control orders 23, 30, 34–9
    Counter-Terrorism Act 2008 18–19, 20
    Defence of the Realm Acts 16–17
    emergency legislation, 16–17, 19
    emergency powers regulations 16–17
    encouragement of terrorism 21
    European Convention on Human
        Rights 20
    Human Rights Act 1998 478
    intercept evidence, scrutiny of 28–34
    internment 16–17
    judicial review 13–18
    Northern Ireland and terrorism 177
    Prevention of Terrorism Act 2005 18, 20, 21
    Prevention of Terrorism (Temporary
        Provisions) Act 1974 17–18
    rule of law 127, 128–47
    scrutiny 16–39
    security and intelligence services 26–7, 33
    September 11, 2001 terrorist attacks on the
        United States 20, 21
    Sweden, pre-legislative review in 406–7
    terrorism 13–39
    Terrorism Act 2006 18, 20–1
    United Kingdom 16–39

nationalization 230–1
natural law 435
natural rights 127–8, 454–6
negative freedom 216
neo-corporatism 215
neoliberalism
    bank bailouts 232
    business rights as human rights 232,
        242, 243
    constitutionalization 232
    EU law 3
    global South 350, 360–1
    ideological scepticism 3
    Israel 227
    labour rights in Europe,
        constitutionalization of 244–8, 266
new constitiutionalism
    constitutional review 369–70, 379
    France 369–70
    Germany 379
    labour rights in Europe,
        constitutionalization of 244–5
    transnational aspects 370
New Zealand bill of rights
    Attorney General 51–2, 56, 89–90, 95–100,
        103–4
    Bill of Rights Act 1990, inter-institutional
        rights dialogue under 87–107
    Canadian Bill of Rights 87, 106
    Canadian Charter of Rights and
        Freedoms 89
    Attorney General 51–2, 56
    capacity to hold government accountable,
        increase in parliament's 63
    changes, insulation of legislation from 49
    collaboration between judiciary and
        legislature 87
    committee system 63
    compatibility assessments 48–9, 51–2, 59,
        60–1, 63, 89–98
    constitutional review 379
    culture of justification 88
    declarations of inconsistency 87–8,
        103–4, 107
    dialogue 5
    economic and social rights 221
    ex-ante compatibility assessments 91
    executive 88–9, 92–3, 106–7
    ex-post compatibility assessments 91–2
    foreign law, citation of 411–12, 416–17
    government bills 97–8
    influence of bill of rights over
        legislature 89–91, 104–7
    instability of weak forms of bills 59–60
    inter-institutional rights dialogue 87–107
    judicial influence on legislation, extent
        of 48–9, 51–2
    judicial review 5, 40, 42, 47–9, 51–2,
        87–98, 379

legal advice 93–6, 103–4
legality, principle of 102
Legislation Advisory Committee 51, 93–4
legislature 87–107
local or member's bills 98–9
Ministry of Justice 95–6
non-compliance, costs to government of 42,
        45, 47–8, 49, 59
notwithstanding clause in Canadian Bill of
        Rights 106
parliamentary sovereignty 90–1,
        97–100, 105
policy 59–60
political moral constraints on legislature 92
reform 106
reporting duty of Attorney General 89–90,
        95–100, 103–4
responsibility for compatibility 56
rights friendly statutory
        interpretation 101–3
safeguards 106–7
scrutiny of legislation 92–100
select committee stage, submissions
        during 99–100
standing committee, proposal for 106
statements of compatibility 59
statutory interpretation 5, 47–8, 101–3
strong-form judicial review 91
structure of relationship between parliament
        and courts 91–4
UN Human Rights Committee, individual
        communications with 105
urgency motions 107
vetting 93–6
weak-form judicial review 91, 420
non-compliance, costs to government of
    bills of rights 42, 43–9, 51, 54–5, 56, 59,
        61, 63
    Canada 42, 45, 47, 49, 54–5, 56–7, 61
    executive 42, 42–8
    legislative process, influence on 42, 43–8
    New Zealand 42, 47–8, 49, 59
    United Kingdom 45, 46–7, 49, 51, 54–5,
        59, 63
non-governmental organisations (NGOs) 3–4
Nordic countries 213–15, 366–8
North American Free Trade Agreement
        (NAFTA) 229, 232
North, power of developed countries of
        the 3–4
Northern Ireland *see also* Northern Ireland and
        terrorism
    devolution 481
    European Convention on Human Rights,
        incorporation of 481
    Human Rights Act 1998 481
    Joint Committee on Human Rights 79
Northern Ireland and terrorism 177–206
    access to legal advice 196

armed forces
    arrival of British soldiers 179–80
    lethal force, use of 180, 182, 187–93,
        200–4
arrest 178, 181, 195–6, 197
B specials 178–9
background 178–80
Baker Report 196
bans 178–9, 197
Bloody Sunday 187–93, 196, 203
burden of proof, reversal of 194
Catholics,
    arrival of British soldiers, attitude
        to 179–80
    civil rights, demand for 178–80
    discrimination 178–9, 182
    internment 181–3
civil disobedience 182
civil rights
    demand for 178–80
    marches 179
coercive methods of control, use by police
    of 177
collusion 202–3
compensation 202
Compton Commission 183–5, 196–7
confession evidence 195–6, 198–9
control orders 204
Cory Commission 203
curfews 180
damages 197, 198
deadly force by police, use of 177
demonstrations 179, 187–8
Diplock Commission 182, 193–5, 196–7
Diplock courts 194–6, 198–200
direct rule 178, 181, 193–4
discrimination against Catholics 178–9
documents, Special Powers Act powers
    relating to 180
evidence 194–6, 198–200, 202–6
expression, criminalization of forms of 177
'Free Derry' 179, 182
Gardiner Report 198–9
Geneva Conventions 186
gerrymandering 178–9
Gibraltar, shootings in 201
Good Friday Agreement 79, 481
Human Rights Act 1998 177–8, 202
hunger strikes 194–5
informers 199–200
inhuman or degrading treatment 186,
    195–6, 198–9, 206
inquests 201–4
internment 177, 178, 180–7, 193–200, 204
    control orders, replacement with 204
    damages 197, 198
    demonstrations 187
    Diplock Commission 182, 193–4
    judiciary, record of 197

legal basis 194–5, 197
    release without charge 196
    statistics 183
    supergrass system 199–200
    suspicion as legal basis 182, 194, 195, 197
    statutory basis 194–5
    torture 183–7
interrogation
    access to legal advice 196
    arrest 195–6
    centres 195–6
    confessions 195–6, 198–9
    damages for assault 198
    guidelines 185–6
    inhuman or degrading
        treatment 195–6, 198
    torture 177, 183–7, 195–6
investigative duty, right to life and 201–3,
    205–6
IRA 179–82, 187–8
judiciary, record of 178, 196–200, 204–6
jury intimidation 194
lethal force, use of 180, 182, 187–93, 200–4
    Bloody Sunday 187–93
    compensation 202
    disclosure of evidence 204
    Gibraltar, shootings in 201
    inquests 201–4
    investigative duty, right to life and 201–3
    life, right to 201–3
    Northern Ireland police
        ombudsman 204
    public interest immunity (PII)
        certificates 202
    Stalker/Sampson investigation 201–2
    United States 203
liberty and security, right to 186, 204
life, right to 201–3, 205–6
Magilligan incident 187
marches 179
membership of organizations
    bans 178, 194
    burden of proof, reversal of 194
    criminalisation of 177
    republic clubs 179, 197
national security 177
Northern Ireland Civil Rights Association
    (NICRA) 179
Northern Ireland police ombudsman 204
Official IRA 180
ombudsman 204
Operation Demetrius 181–2
Parker Committee 185–6, 196
police 178–9, 204
political motive and criminal behaviour,
    removal of distinction between 194–5
pre-charge detention 177, 178, 180–7,
    193–200, 204
Prevention of Terrorism Act 1984 197–8

Northern Ireland and terrorism (*cont.*)
  Prevention of Terrorism (Temporary
      Provisions) Act 1974 194–5
  Protestants, internment of 183
  Provisional IRA 180, 182
  public interest immunity (PII)
      certificates 202, 205
  reasonable suspicion 197–8
  reasons for arrest, right to be informed
      of 197
  rent and rates strikes 182
  republic clubs, bans on 179, 197
  riots 179–80
  RUC 178–9
  Saville Inquiry 187–9
  shoot to kill 180, 200–4
  silence, abolition of right to 200
  special advocates 204
  Special Powers Acts and Regulations 181,
      194, 197
  Stalker/Sampson investigation 201–2
  statistics 180, 182–3, 194–5
  supergrasses, use of 199–200
  suspicion 182, 194, 195, 197
  torture 177, 183–7,195–7, 204–5
  Troubles, start of the 179
  United States 203
  use of force
      Bloody Sunday 187–93
      IRA 177
      lethal force, use of 180, 182, 187–93,
          200–4
      police 177, 182
      terrorists 177
  violent incidents, statistics on 182–3
  Widgery Inquiry 188, 191–3, 196
  withholding of evidence 192
Norway 213
**notwithstanding clause in Canadian Charter
    of Rights** 57–8, 106, 209, 432–3, 436,
    463–4
**nuclear weapons, legality of taxation for
    financing** 173–4
nuisance 170–3

obstruction 167, 170–3
official secrets
  Cold War 127, 129–43, 145–7
  Committee of 100 peace campaigners, civil
      liberties and 156–67
  constitutionalism 127, 129–43, 145–7
  espionage 163–4
  House of Lords, appeals to 161–6
  jury trials 160–1, 165
  Official Secrets Act 1911, prosecutions
      under 158–67
  prejudicial to safety or interests of the
      state 160–1
  rule of law 127, 129–43, 145–7

  statutory interpretation 163–4
ombudsmen 204, 408–9
Operation Demetrius 181–2
oppression 361–2, 363
organized crime 284
originalism 114
over-constitutionalization 373, 377–8, 388

Parker Committee 185–6, 196
Parliament Acts, Hunting Act 2004 and 484
Parliament Square, demonstrations in 149–51
parliamentary sovereignty *see also*
          **parliamentary sovereignty in the
          United Kingdom**
  Australian party politics 320
  constitutional review 369–70, 376–7, 379,
      382–3
  economic and social rights 209
  France 369–70
  living document or living tree
      metaphor 115–16
  New Zealand Bill of Rights 90–1,
      97–100, 105
  weak or statutory form of bills of rights 120
**parliamentary sovereignty in the United
          Kingdom**
  business rights as human rights 243
  constitutional review 377, 379, 382
  declarations of incompatibility 116–19,
      435–6, 476–7, 483
  Human Rights Act 1998 69, 84, 109–10,
      115–19, 430–2, 435–6, 445, 473
  New Zealand Bill of Rights 91
  reading down 109–10, 115–16, 432
  Scotland, Human Rights Act 1998
      in 69, 84
  statutory interpretation 115–16
  weak or statutory form of bills of rights 109
parliaments *see* legislatures; parliamentary
          sovereignty
party politics *see* political parties
**passenger names records (PNR) agreement
          between EU and United States
          on** 282–5
  Charter of Fundamental Rights of the
      EU 284–5
  Data Protection Directive 282–5
  effective remedy, right to an 284
  European Court of Justice 282–5
  Framework Decision on retention of PNR
      data 284–5
  freedom, security and justice, area
      of 282–5, 289
  organized crime 284
  police and judicial cooperation in criminal
      matters (third pillar) 284
  private and family life, right to respect for 284
  profiling 285
  terrorism 284

passports, biometric information in 271
peaceful enjoyment of possessions 242
PII Plus 33–4
PNR *see* passenger names records (PNR)
    agreement between EU and United
    States on
police
    arrest 1, 151–2, 157–61, 267, 170
    'B' specials 178–9
    brutality 152–3
    Campaign for the Limitation of Secret Police
        Powers 140–2
    Committee of 100 peace campaigners, civil
        liberties and 149–53, 156–61, 167,
        169–75
    demonstrations 149–57, 205
    detention of protestors 205
    freedom, security and justice, area of 272–6,
        288–9, 291
    militarization 1
    Northern Ireland and terrorism 178–9, 204
    ombudsman 204
    perjury 170
    planting of evidence 170
    police and judicial cooperation in criminal
        matters (Third Pillar) 272–6, 284,
        288–9, 291
    post-charge questioning 23, 30–1
    RUC (Royal Ulster Constabulary) 178–9
    use of force 152–3, 177, 182
policy
    Australian party politics 313–14
    bills of rights 44, 56, 59–61, 64
    Canada 56, 209, 211–12
    constitutional review 372, 380–1
    economic and social rights 208, 209,
        211–12, 217, 223
    European Convention on Human
        Rights 390
    New Zealand 59–60
    orientation 372
    power 313
    principles 390–1
political correctness 474
political institutions of rights-
        protection 297–311
    alternative means of protection 5–6
    backbenchers 302, 305–6
    candidate selection 303–4
    chief executives 301, 305
    choice of institution 297–305, 309–11
    coalitions 302
    competition over rights protection 301
    courts 297–9, 305–6, 310–11
    disenfranchisement 307–8
    elections 303, 306–8
    executive 297, 300–2, 305
    factions 302, 305
    finance 304

first past the post systems 303
freedom of expression 308
groups 299–300, 306–9
incentives on institutional performance,
    differing 305–9
interest groups 304–5
judges 297–9, 305–6, 310–11
judicial review 300, 308, 310
leaders of parties 303–4, 306
legislation, significance and character
    of 304–5
legislatures 297–8, 301–2, 306–11
liberalism 309–11
majoritarianism 297, 300–1
minority groups 306–9
parliamentary systems 300–1
philosophies of human rights 456–7
political parties 6, 301–7
political system, nature of 6
proportional representation 303
scepticism 5–7
separation of powers 300–2, 309
social democracy 309–11
specification, role of 297–300, 307
United States 303–4
veto points 309
political parties
    agents of and forums for political
        deliberation and activism, as 6
    Australia 312–28, 332, 340–1, 343
    backbenchers 302, 305–6
    bills of rights 56, 343
    candidate selection 303–4
    cartels 6
    coalitions 302
    Communist party 127–49
    competition for power 325–6
    conscience votes 324–5, 340–1
    deliberative aspects of parties 32
    discipline 320–5, 340–1
    donors 304
    entrenchment 343
    executive and legislature controlled by
        different parties 301
    factions 302, 305, 320, 325–8
    finance 304
    functional agencies, parties as 325
    generous contention for power 325–6
    Human Rights Act 1998 433–4, 473–80,
        486
    institutions 6, 301–6
    interest groups 304–5
    intermediary organizations 317–18
    judgment, elected representatives' duty to use
        own 321–3
    leaders 303–4, 306
    legislatures 301
    minority parties 306–7
    non-governmental organisations 304

political parties (*cont.*)
normative status of US political parties 318
pressure groups 325
repeal or amendment of Human Rights Act
    1998 8, 428, 442–52, 474–86
transformative effect of political parties 317
United States 303–5, 318
political philosophies of human rights 545–8
bills of rights 456
context 457
definition of human rights 456
Enlightenment 454–5
executive 457
institutions 456–7
international relations 455–6
legislature 457
moral rights 456–8
natural rights 127–8, 454–6
overlapping consensus 454–5
political questions 457
Universal Declaration of Human
    Rights 454–5
utilitarianism 455–6
West 454–5
politics *see also* **civil and political rights;
    political parties**
accountability 9
adjudication, politicization of 373,
    375–7, 382
advertising, ban on 439
behaviour, altering political 52, 65
bills of rights, influence on political systems
    of 42–3
Committee of 100 peace campaigners, civil
    liberties and 151–2
constitutional review 373, 375–7
constitutionalism 348, 352, 359, 364
culture 360–1
democratic charter of rights
    model 460–1, 471
devolution 70
economic and social rights 208–9, 224–5
emancipatory politics 348, 353, 354, 356
engagement 363–4
Finland 382
global South 348, 352–6, 359–64
Human Rights Act 1998 70, 442
identity politics 360
institutional scepticism 4
judges, political pressure on 224
judicialization of politics 442
juridification of politics 373, 375–7, 382
legislature, constraints on 92
misuse of political power 464–5
Northern Ireland, removal of distinction
    between criminal and political
    behaviour in 194–5
political philosophies of human
    rights 545–8

political correctness 474
progressive politics 348, 351, 355, 356, 362
reactionary politics 355, 361–2
Scotland, Human Rights Act 1998 in 70
transformation 362–3
trials 151–2
post-charge questioning 23, 30–1
Posted Works Directive 256–7
poverty 213–14, 355–6
power
Australian party politics 313
counterhegenomic human rights 359–64
economic power 3
misuse of political power 464–5
North, power of developed countries of
    the 3–4
policy 313
precedent
constitutional review 367, 368
economic and social rights 223
European Convention on Human
    Rights 367
Finland 367, 379–80
foreign law, citation of 8–9, 418–19, 425–6
Nordic countries 367
WTO law 239
**pre-charge detention of terrorist suspects in
    United Kingdom** *see also* **internment**
5 days 25
28-day limit, extension of 21–2, 23–8
42-day limit for detention, extension to 21,
    23–8
90-day limit 24
24-hour limit 24–5
36-hour limit 24–5
96-hour limit 25
Anti-Terrorism, Crime and Security Act
    2001 19
Australia 121
Belmarsh case 4, 13–14, 19, 46
bills of rights 121–2
control orders 23, 30, 34–9, 46
Counter-Terrorism Act 2008 21–2, 23–8, 30
derogations from ECHR 13–14, 195
European Convention on Human
    Rights 121–2, 293
freedom, security and justice, area of 293
House of Commons Home Affairs
    Committee 25–6
Human Rights Act 1998 121–2
Joint Committee on Human Rights 21–7
legislature 4, 13–14
liberty and security, right to 13–14, 46
normalization of long periods of
    detention 177
Northern Ireland 177, 195
public emergency threatening the life of the
    nation 14, 26
safeguards 27–8

scrutiny 21–8
security services 26–7
Terrorism Act 2006 21
weak or statutory form of bills of
    rights 121–2
preliminary rulings 234, 278–9, 370
pressure groups/interest groups 304–5, 325
Prevention of Terrorism Act 1984 (United
    Kingdom) 197–8
Prevention of Terrorism Act 2005 (United
    Kingdom) 18, 20, 21
Prevention of Terrorism (Temporary
    Provisions) Act 1974 (United
    Kingdom) 17–18, 194–5
principles
    constitutional review 368, 385–8, 390–1
    Finland 368
    general principles of law 385–8
    lawmaking 368
    policies 390–1
    rule orientation 368
prisons and prisoners
    privatization 227–8
    segregation 76
    slopping out cases, damages in 76–7
private and family life, right to respect for
    constitutional review 390–1
    Human Rights Act 1998 474
    media 474
    passenger names records (PNR)
        agreement between EU and United
        States on 284
Private Bill procedure 450
private sector domination of EU 230–1 cd
privatization
    constitutional review 394–5
    Finland 384–5
    prisons 227–8
Privy Council, Judicial Committee of the 31,
    71, 73–5
profiling 205, 285
progressive politics 348, 351, 355, 356, 362
property as a fundamental right 242–3
proportional representation 303, 326
proportionality
    constitutional review 373, 378–9, 390
    EU law 256–8, 265, 280, 290
    European Arrest Warrant 280
    free movement 235, 237
    freedom, security and justice, area of 290
    Germany 378–9
    Joint Committee on Human Rights 467
    labour rights in Europe,
        constitutionalization of 256–8, 265
    trade unions 256–8
proscribed organizations
    burden of proof, reversal of 194
    Northern Ireland and terrorism 177–9,
        184, 197

Proscribed Organisation Appeal
    Commission (POAC) 28
republic clubs in Northern Ireland, ban
    on 179, 197
protests *see* demonstrations
Prüm, Treaty of 274
public authorities
    care homes, functions of a public nature
        and 46
    competition 239–41
    definition 46, 77, 442–3
    freedom, security and justice, area of 270
    Human Rights Act 1998 46, 77, 442–3, 481
    individuals 270
    monopolies 240–1
    Scotland, Human Rights Act 1998 in 77
    United Kingdom 46
public documents, access to 7, 393, 394–5,
    402, 406–7
public inquiries 31–2
public interest
    Australian parliamentarians, rights
        protection and 340–1
    Human Rights Act 1998 478
    Northern Ireland, public interest immunity
        and 202, 205
    PII Plus 33–4
    public interest immunity 33–4, 202, 205
public nuisance 150–3
public opinion 223–5, 336–7
public participation 6, 320
purposive approach to interpretation 113–14
racism or xenophobia 280–1

Radcliffe Report 142
RAF airbases, demonstrations at 153–8, 167–8
reactionary politics 355, 361–2
reading down provision in Human Rights
    Act 1998 (UK) 108–16, 430–4, 442
    constitutionalized bills of rights 109–16
    declarations of incompatibility 110, 120
    entrenched bills of rights 109
    judiciary, powers of 108–16, 120
    living document or living tree
        metaphor 113–16
    originalism 114
    parliamentary sovereignty 109–10,
        115–16, 432
    purposive approach 113–14
    rule of law 112–13
    statutory interpretation 108–9, 111–16
    strong form or entrenched bills of
        rights 109–10, 113–14
    weak or statutory form of bills of
        rights 109–11
reform
    Australian parliamentarians, rights
        protection and 342–3
    control orders 23, 30, 34–9

reform (*cont.*)
  Human Rights Act 1998 78–9, 84–5, 428,
    442–52, 474–86
  Joint Committee on Human Rights 443–4
  New Zealand Bill of Rights 106
  Scotland, Human Rights Act 1998 in 78–9,
    84–5
regressive movements 361–2
relative versus absolute values 355–6
religion
  Hindu perspective on human rights 354
  Islamic perspective on human rights 354
  origin of rights, as 342
remedial orders 466
remedy, right to an effective 284, 437, 476–7
resistance 352
right to liberty and security *see* **liberty and**
    security, right to
right to life 201–3, 205–6, 388–9, 462–3
right to silence 200
rights impact statements 343
rights of man, definition of 2
riots 179–80
risk assessment/management 49–59
RUC (Royal Ulster Constabulary) 178–9
rule of law
  Committee of 100 peace campaigners, civil
    liberties and 175
  definition 127–8
  freedom, security and justice, area of 273,
    275, 286, 291–3
  Human Rights Act 1998 112–13, 431, 434
  Saudi Arabia, abandonment of Serious Fraud
    Office inquiry into arms deal with 15
  terrorism 13–14, 286
rules orientation 368

same sex marriages 62
Saudi Arabia, abandonment of Serious Fraud
    Office inquiry into arms deal with 15
Saville Inquiry 187–9
savings clauses in bills of rights 425
scarcity 352
scepticism *see* **ideological scepticism;**
    institutional scepticism
Schengen area 274
Schengen Information System 270–1
Scotland, Human Rights Act 1998 in 5,
    66–86
  appeals, Supreme Court and 71–2
  bill of rights debates 67, 68–72, 79–84
  Britishness theme 68–9
  Calman Commission 69–71, 75, 85
  Canadian federalism 66
  Coalition government 67, 84–5
  constitutional issues 69–71, 80, 84–5
  Constitutional Reform Act 2006 71–2
  criminal trials 73–5, 83–4, 86
  delay 73, 86

  devolution 66–86
  dialogue 5
  European Convention on Human
    Rights 66, 72, 83–4
  European Union, membership of 83
  executive 74
  fair hearing, right to a 73
  final appeals 71
  Health and Social Care Bill 77–8
  institutional scepticism 5
  Joint Committee on Human Rights 69,
    79–81
  judicial review 5, 85
  Labour government 67, 68–9
  legitimacy 67–8
  Lord Advocate 74
  modification of Human Rights Act
    1998 78–9, 84–5
  National Conversation about Scotland
    (SNP) 70–1
  parliamentary supremacy 69, 84
  politics of devolution 70
  Privy Council, Judicial Committee
    of 71, 73–5
  public authority, definition of 77
  Referendum Bill 85
  reform of Human Rights Act 1998, proposal
    for 78–9, 84–5
  reserved matters 72
  Scotland Act 1998 5, 66–8, 71–82, 85–6
  Scottish Commission for Human
    Rights 81
  Scottish Parliament 80–2
  segregation of prisoners 76
  Sewel motion 72, 78
  slopping out cases, damages in 76–7
  social policy 80–1
  Social Work (Scotland) Act 1968 78
  Somerville 68, 75–7
  statements of incompatibility 72
  statutory interpretation 76
  Supreme Court, establishment of 71–2, 86
  West Lothian Question 70
  Westminster Parliament 66, 69, 81
scrutiny of legislation
  Anti-Terrorism, Crime and Security
    Act 2001 19–21
  Australia 6, 332, 342, 343, 344, 346
  Counter-Terrorism Act 2008 18–19,
    20–39
  Defence of the Realm Acts 16–17
  emergency legislation, 16–17, 19
  emergency powers regulations 16–17
  encouragement of terrorism 21
  European Convention on Human Rights
  France 499
  Human Rights Act 1998 443
  intercept evidence 23–4, 28–34
  internment 16–17

Joint Committee on Human Rights 443, 466–9
national security16–39
New Zealand Bill of Rights 92–100
pre-charge detention of terrorist suspects 21–8
Prevention of Terrorism Act 2005 18, 20, 21
Prevention of Terrorism (Temporary Provisions) Act 1974 17–18
September 11, 2001 terrorist attacks on the United States 20, 21
Sweden, pre-legislative review in 392–3, 396–401
terrorism 15–39
searches 1, 155
secrecy *see* official secrets
security *see also* liberty and security, right to; national security
constitutional review 388–9
Finland 388
freedom, security and justice, area of 269, 271–2, 292–3
security and intelligence services 26–7, 33
Security Council (UN) resolutions, compliance with 285–7
segregation of prisoners 76
self-determination 351–2
sensitive personal information, misuse of 271–2
separation of powers
Australian party politics 316
Cold War 146
constitutional review 372, 378, 387
constitutionalism 146
democratic charter of rights model 460
executive 302
Germany 378
Human Rights Act 1998 449–51
institutions 300–2, 309
parliamentary systems 300–1
rule of law 146
United States 54, 146
veto powers 309
September 11, 2001 terrorist attacks on the United States
European Convention on Human Rights 20
freedom, security and justice, area of 272
national security, parliamentary scrutiny and 19–20, 21
Serious Fraud Office inquiry into arms deal with Saudi Arabia 15
Serious Organised Crime Agency (SOCA) 32
services
free movement of services 235–6, 241, 254, 259
Services Directive 253
Sewel motion 72, 78
shoot to kill 180, 200–4
silence, right to 200

Single European Act 251
slopping out 76
SOCA (Serious Organised Crime Agency) 32
social democracy 309–11
social movements 3–4, 359–64
social policy 80–1
social rights *see* economic and social rights 8
social transformations 351, 362
social welfare provision 3, 212–16
Social Work (Scotland) Act 1968 78
socio-economic rights *see* economic and social rights
sources of law, extending range of 8–9
South *see* global South
South Africa
Bill of Rights 218
Constitution 217–18
drugs anti-retroviral, campaign for 362
economic and social rights 3, 217–18, 220–1
entrenchment of Constitution 220–1
foreign law, citation of 413, 421
Gini coefficient 220–1
housing, right to adequate 217–18
inequalities 217–18, 220–2
weak rights 217
sovereignty *see* parliamentary sovereignty; supremacy of EU law
Spain 214, 377, 386
special advocates
closed material 36–7
control orders 36–8, 204
Counter-Terrorism Act 2008 36–7
fair hearing, right to a 36–7
Northern Ireland 204
intercept evidence, scrutiny of 33
witnesses, ability to call 37–8
Special Immigration Appeals Commission (SIAC) 28
Special Powers Acts and Regulations 181, 194, 197
spying *see* espionage
Stalker/Sampson investigation 201–2
Standardized World Income Inequality Database (SWIID) 219
state action doctrine 384
state security *see* national security; official secrets
statements of compatibility
Australian parliamentarians, rights protection and 343
bills of rights 51, 59
Human Rights Act 1998 72, 119–20
judiciary, power of 119
New Zealand 59
Scotland, Human Rights Act 1998 in 72
statutory interpretation
after the fact creation or construction of meaning 113
basic rights 386

statutory interpretation (*cont.*)
  business rights as human rights 229–30
  Canadian Charter of Rights 113–15, 213
  constitutional review 386
  constitutionalized bills of rights 109–16
  declarations of incompatibility 118–19,
      432–3, 442
  European Convention on Human
      Rights 230
  executive 147
  Human Rights Act 1998 8, 76, 108–19,
      122–3, 209, 229–30, 431–4, 442
  Joint Committee on Human Rights 8
  judicial, powers of the 108–9, 111–16, 118
  living document or living tree
      metaphor 113–16
  new approach 111–13
  New Zealand 5, 47–8, 101–3
  Official Secrets Act 1911 163–4
  originalism 114
  parliamentary sovereignty 115–16
  purposive approach 113
  rewriting legislation 115–16
  Scotland, Human Rights Act 1998 in 76
  strong form or entrenched bills of
      rights 113–14
  United States 114, 147
strike, right to 244, 249, 252, 255, 267
strong form of judicial review
  constitutional review 379
  definition 209
  economic and social rights 209–10
  foreign law, citation of 412–20
  New Zealand Bill of Rights 91
  statutory interpretation 113–14
  weak judicial review, borderline with 379
strong form or entrenched bills of
      rights 109–10, 113–14, 120, 126
subsistence rights 210–12, 226
supergrasses, use of 199–200
supremacy *see* parliamentary sovereignty;
      supremacy of EU law
supremacy of EU law
  business rights as EU rights 233–4
  constitutional review 366–7, 370
  Finland 366
  freedom, security and justice, area of 286–9
  Nordic countries 366–8
  terrorists, legality of blacklists of 286–7
supreme courts
  appeals from Scotland 71–2
  Human Rights Act 1998 71–2, 86, 449, 450
  judicial appointments 123–4
  Scotland 71–2, 86
  United States 123–4, 392
state of exception 272–3
subaltern law 363–4
suffering, alleviation of human 356–7, 361
supergrass system 199–200

surveillance
  bugging of suspects' homes 405–6
  CCTV 1
  Cold War 146
  Committee of 100 peace campaigners,
      civil liberties and 148–9, 150–2,
      159–60, 175
  constitutionalism 146
  databases 271–2
  freedom, security and justice, area of 271–2
  intercept evidence in criminal trials, use
      of 23–4, 28–33
  rule of law 146
  United States 146
Sweden
  access to public documents 7, 393, 394–5,
      402, 406–7
  bugging of suspects' homes 405–6
  committees 7, 393–4, 396–8, 404–5
  complaints 396–7
  Constitution 391
  Constitutional Committee of Parliament,
      scrutiny by 7, 393–8, 404–5
  constitutional review 383, 391
  constitutional rights 213
  criminal law, abolition of statute of
      limitations in 403–4
  democracy 402–3, 407
  economic and social rights 213
  European Convention on Human
      Rights 404–5
  evidence-conflict criterion 391
  experts 393–4, 397–409
  identity in public places, concealment
      of 404
  Instrument of Government 392–4,
      398–9, 403
  investigations 396
  judicial review 213, 392–409
  Law Council 398–409
    critical comments, unminuted 402
    expert opinions of 7, 393, 397–409
    hearings 399
    major critique 404–7
    minor critique 402–4
    nothing to say 402
    practice, work in 401–7
  legal certainty 399–400
  legislative committees, system of 7, 393–4
  manifest conflicts 392
  media 398, 405–7
  national security 406–7
  Parliamentary Ombudsman 408–9
  pre-legislative review 392–409
  public reports 393–4
  publish public documents, right to 7,
      393, 395
  scrutiny of legislation 392–3, 396–401
  written statements 394

taxation for financing nuclear weapons,
  legality of 173–4
tobacco advertising 229
terrorism *see also* **Counter-Terrorism Act 2008**
  (United Kingdom)
  Anti-Terrorism, Crime and Security
    Act 2001 19–21
  Australian parliamentarians, rights
    protection and 341–2, 345
  Belmarsh case 4, 13–14, 19, 46
  bills of rights 121–2
  blacklists, legality of terrorist 285–8
  control orders 14, 23, 30, 34–9, 46
  data collection 270
  Defence of the Realm Acts 16–17
  definition 3, 269
  deportation 13, 15
  derogations from ECHR 13–14, 195
  emergency legislation 16–17, 19, 21
  encouragement of terrorism 21
  EU law 3, 284
  European Convention on Human
    Rights 13–14, 20, 195
  executive powers 30
  freedom, security and justice, area
    of 269–73, 285–8, 291–3
  Gibraltar, shooting of terrorists in 479
  House of Commons Home Affairs
    Committee 25–6
  Human Rights Act 1998 121–2
  intercept evidence, scrutiny of 23–4, 28–33
  internment 13, 16–17 ff
  Joint Committee on Human Rights 21–7
  judicial review 4–5, 13–18
  legislation
    Australian parliamentarians, rights
      protection and 341–2, 345
    freedom, security and justice, area
      of 272–3, 291–2
    United Kingdom 4–6, 54–5
  lethal force, use of 479
  liberty and security, right to 13–14, 46
  national security constitution 13–18
  normalization of long periods of
    detention 177
  parliament 13–39
  passenger names records (PNR) agreement
    between EU and United States on 284
  pre-charge detention of terrorist suspects 4,
    13–14, 21
  Prevention of Terrorism Act 2005 18, 20, 21
  Prevention of Terrorism (Temporary
    Provisions) Act 1974 17–18
  public emergency threatening the life of the
    nation 14, 26
  rule of law 13–14
  Schengen Information System 270–1
  scrutiny 15–18, 21–8
  security services 26–7
September 11, 2001 terrorist attacks on the
    United States 19–20, 21, 272
  shoot to kill 479
  special advocates 14–15
  stop and search 14
  Terrorism Act 2006 18, 20–1
  torture, deportation based on evidence
    obtained by 15
  United Kingdom 13–39
  United States, passenger names records
    (PNR) agreement between EU
    and 284
  use of force 479
  war on terror 1, 355
  wartime, deportation and internment in 13
  weak or statutory form of bills of
    rights 121–2
tobacco advertising 229
torture
  Amnesty International 183–5
  Baha Mousa Inquiry 186–7, 205
  Bennett Inquiry 195–6
  Compton Commission 183–5, 196–7
  confessions 195–6
  evidence obtained by torture 195–6, 204–5,
    293
  freedom, security and justice, area of 293
  Geneva Conventions 186
  inhuman or degrading treatment 186
  internment 183–7
  interrogation 177, 183–7, 195–6
  Iraqi citizens, murder by British troops
    of 186–7, 205
  liberty and security, right to 186
  Northern Ireland and terrorism 177,
    183–7,195–7, 204–5
  Parker Committee 185–6, 196
trade unions
  civil servants, vetting 131–4, 141, 144, 146
  Cold War 131–4, 141, 144, 146
  constitutionalism 131–4, 141, 144, 146
  direct horizontal effect 256
  discrimination 262
  economic and social rights 215
  EU law 253–60, 263–7
  European Court of Human Rights 260–5
  free movement 235–8
  industrial action 235–8
  labour rights in Europe,
    constitutionalization of 253–67
  Posted Workers Directive 256–7
  proportionality 256–8
  rule of law 131–4, 141, 144, 146
  Services Directive 253
  United States 144
Trafalgar Square, demonstrations in 149–54,
    169–74
transnational corporations 341
transparency 273–4, 340

travaux préparatoires 366–7, 379–80, 383–4
Treaty of Lisbon 251, 267, 272–3, 276, 292
Treaty of Prüm 274
Treaty on European Union (Maastricht) 241,
 268, 276, 288–9
tyranny of the majority 326–8

United Kingdom *see also* Committee of 100
 peace campaigners, civil liberties
 and; Counter-Terrorism Act 2008
 (United Kingdom); Human Rights
 Act 1998 (United Kingdom); Joint
 Committee on Human Rights (United
 Kingdom); Northern Ireland and
 terrorism; parliamentary sovereignty
 in the United Kingdom; pre-charge
 detention of terrorist suspects in
 United Kingdom
 Anti-Terrorism, Crime and Security Act
  2001 19–21
 appeals to European Court of Human
  Rights 47
 Attorney General 55–6, 59, 63
 bank bailouts 232
 Belmarsh case 46
  control orders 46
  liberty and security, right to 46
 bicameralism 123
 Bill of Rights 1689 418
 bills of rights 40, 42, 46–63, 418
 business rights as human rights 229–43
 capacity to hold government accountability,
  increase in parliament's 60, 62–3
 changes, insulation of legislation from 49
 committee system 62
 compatibility assessments 48–9, 51, 58–9,
  60, 62–3
 compensation 242
 competition 231, 232, 233–4, 239–42
 constitutional review 366, 379, 382
 constitutionalism 231, 243
 constitutionalization 232–3
 control orders 23, 30, 34–9
 corporate free movement as a fundamental
  right 234–9
 corporations 229, 234–9, 242–3
 declarations of incompatibility 46, 87
 Defence of the Realm Acts 16–17
 definition of human rights 229
 emergency legislation, 16–17, 19
 emergency powers regulations 16–17
 encouragement of terrorism 21
 enforcement 230, 233
 EU law 230–42, 365–6
 European Convention on Human
  Rights 20, 230, 242
 European Court of Human Rights 47,
  51, 58
 executive 30

free movement 230, 233, 234–9, 241
free trade 230–2, 234, 242–3
instability of weak forms of bills 52–5, 58–9
international economic law 231
internment 13, 16–17
judicial activism 379
judicial influence on legislation, extent
 of 48–9, 50–1, 54
judicial review 13–18, 40, 42, 46–53, 62–3
judicial supremacy 230, 233, 243
judicialization 233
labelling 233
legal advice 58
Legislation Committee 51
legislature
 bicameralism 123
 terrorism 13–39
market liberalism 234
NAFTA 229, 232
national security 13–18
nationalization 230–1
neo-liberalism 232, 242, 243
non-compliance, costs to government of 42,
 45–7, 49, 51, 54–5, 59, 63
peaceful enjoyment of possessions 242
political behaviour, altering 52
Prevention of Terrorism Act 2005 18, 20, 21
Prevention of Terrorism (Temporary
 Provisions) Act 1974 17–18
private sector domination 230–1
property as fundamental right,
 corporate 242–3
public authority, definition of 46
responsibility for compatibility 55–6, 58
risk assessment 51, 54–5, 59
rule of law 13–14
scrutiny 15–18
September 11, 2001 terrorist attacks on the
 United States 20, 21
statements of compatibility 51, 59
statutory interpretation 229–30
supranational agreements 229, 243
supranational economic law 233
terrorism 13–39
tobacco advertising 229
terrorist legislation 17–39, 54–5
wartime, deportation and internment in 13
weak or statutory form of bills of
 rights 52–4
WTO agreements 229, 230, 231–2
United Nations (UN)
 Human Rights Committee, individual
  communications with 105
 New Zealand Bill of Rights 105
 Security Council resolutions, compliance
  with 285–7
United States
 Australian party politics 418
 bill of rights 53–4, 127, 146–7, 418–19

biometrics 271
candidate selection 303–4
checks and balances 146
civil rights 371
civil servants, vetting 143–6
Cold War 127–8, 141–7, 156, 158
Committee of 100 peace campaigners, civil
    liberties and 156, 158
Communists 128, 141, 143–7
Congress 53–4
Constitution 127, 146
constitutional review 8, 53–4, 369, 371,
    375, 377, 383–4, 392, 410–27
constitutionalism 127–8, 141–7
cruel or inhuman treatment 410–12, 413,
    415–20
death penalty 410–12, 413, 415–23
death row phenomenon 423
democracy 412–15
diffused judicial review 377
due process 127, 144, 145–6
economic and social rights 210–11, 214
English Bill of Rights 1689 418
EU law 365–6
exceptionalism146
executive
    executive orders 144–5
    judicial appointments 123–4
    loyalty of employees 143–6
    statutory interpretation 147
extradition 423
Fascists, purge of 143–4
financing of political parties 303–4
foreign law, citation of 8, 410–27
freedom, security and justice, area of 271,
    283–5
House Committee on Un-American
    Activities (HUAC) (Dies
    Committee) 143
institutions 303–4
interception of communications, executive
    power and 146
investigations 143–5
judicial activism/relativism 388, 412–13
judicial appointments 123–4
judicial review 53
judicial supremacy 371, 379
judiciary, power of 109
lethal force, use of 203
loyalty investigations 143–5
McCarthy period 128, 141, 143, 145–6
membership of subversive organizations 144
minors, execution of 410–12, 413, 415–22
national security 143–7
Northern Ireland and terrorism 203
originalism 114
passenger names records (PNR) agreement
    with European Union 282–5, 289
political parties

institutions 303–5
    normative status 318
    precedent 418–19
    Roper v Simmons 410–12, 414–15, 419–22
    rule of law 127–8, 141–7
    separation of powers 54, 146
    September 11, 2001 terrorist attacks on the
        United States 19–20, 21, 272
    Smith Act 143
    sources of law 418–19
    state action doctrine 384
    statutory interpretation 114, 147
    strong judicial review 412–20
    structure of government 128
    subsistence rights 210
    Supreme Court 123–4, 392, 410–13
    terrorism in Northern Ireland 203
    trade unions 144
    United Kingdom, comparison with 145–6
Universal Declaration of Human Rights 454–5
universality of human rights 348–55, 423
urgent situations *see* **emergencies**
use of force
    Bloody Sunday 187–93
    Committee of 100 peace campaigners, civil
        liberties and 152–8, 175
    compensation 202
    evidence, disclosure of 204
    inquests 201–4
    investigative duty, right to life and 201–3
    lethal force, use of 177, 187–93, 200–4
    life, right to 201–3
    Northern Ireland and terrorism 177, 182–3,
        187–93, 204
    police 152–3, 177, 182
    public interest immunity certificates 202
    Stalker/Sampson investigation 201–2
    state forces 152–8, 175, 187–93
    United States 203
utilitarianism 455–6
**U'wa indigenous people of Colombia, land
        rights of** 360–1

Vassall spy inquiry 175
vertical effect 368, 388–91
veto powers 309
vetting 93–6, 128–43, 145–7
**Victorian Charter of Human Rights and
        Responsibilities** 315–16
voting *see also* **elections**
    Australian 324–6, 340–1
    compulsory voting 326
    conscience votes by parliamentarians 324–5,
        340–1

war on terror 1, 355
wartime, deportation and internment in 13
weak judicial review
    Canada 209

Index

weak judicial review (*cont.*)
  constitutional review 379
  cruel or inhuman treatment 420
  economic and social rights 209–10
  Finland 381
  Human Rights Act 1998 118, 126, 209
  New Zealand 91, 420
  strong judicial review, borderline with 379
weak or statutory form of bills of rights
  Canada 53–8
  economic and social rights 217
  Human Rights Act 1998 109–11,
      116–20, 126
  instability 43, 52–60
  institutional scepticism 5
  judicial review 43, 52–60
  judiciary, power of 116–20
  majoritarianism 120–1
  New Zealand 59–60
  parliamentary sovereignty 109, 120
  pre-charge detention of terrorist
      suspects 121–2
  referendums 121
  strong form or entrenched bills of
      rights 120, 126
  terrorism legislation 121–2
  United Kingdom 52–5, 58–9
Wednesbury unreasonableness 483
welfare provision 3, 212–16
West

Enlightenment 454–7
global South 349–56, 359, 361, 362–3
political philosophies of human
    rights 454–5
West Lothian Question 70
Westminster-type systems 40, 42–60, 458,
    209, 458
Wethersfield, demonstration at
    RAF 153–67, 174
Widgery Inquiry 188, 191–3, 196
witnesses, special advocates and 37–8
women
  global South 371–2
  India, Working Women's Forum
      in 362–3
  misogynist movements 361–2
World Social Forum (WSF) 3, 359, 361, 362
World Trade Organization *see* WTO law
WTO law
  business rights as human rights 229, 230,
      231–2
  competition 242
  dispute settlement 239
  enforcement 242
  free movement 238–9, 242
  free trade as a human right 242–3
  precedent 239
  United Kingdom 229, 230, 231–2, 242

xenophobic movements 361–2